The Colour Library Book of
GARDENING

COLOUR LIBRARY BOOKS

CONTENTS

CLB 1896

This edition published 1987 by Colour Library Books Ltd,
86 Epsom Road, Guildford, Surrey.

Original material © 1985 Marshall Cavendish Ltd
This arrangement © 1987 Marshall Cavendish Ltd
Prepared by Marshall Cavendish Books Ltd
58 Old Compton St, London W1V 5PA

Printed in England.

ISBN 0 86283 518 6

CHAPTER ONE
PLANNING AND DESIGN

PLANNING AND DESIGN

In the past, gardens were planned either for show and pleasure or for vegetable, fruit and flower production. Today, although there are small gardens designed solely for pleasure and others used for food, most are planned to provide crops and enjoyment combined.

The particular form of a garden you want to make depends primarily on its function but another consideration will be the current use of the site and the plants already growing there (unless, of course, it is a fresh plot). Soil type, local climate, and the money you have available must be considered, too.

You must also realize that the garden needs of a family or a single person change greatly over the years and, therefore, the garden must be easily adaptable. A young couple may be quite happy with a mainly grassed and partly shaded area, where lazing in deckchairs is the main activity, enlivened by the occasional barbecue. Babies require a quiet, shaded area for a pram or play-pen in summer, young children a place for tricycles or a sand-pit or swing, and older children a place for ball games. The state of family finances when the children are around could mean that a supply of home-grown fruit and vegetables would be very welcome.

When the children have left home, there will be about twenty years of active gardening ahead of the average gardener, with time, energy and money at their optimum balance. However, retirement usually brings with it a decreased income and a greater intolerance of the extremes of weather. The routine chores of weekly gardening maintenance and the large seasonal tasks can become a burden. A free-standing greenhouse or a lean-to conservatory could then provide pleasure throughout the year, irrespective of the weather, as well as small quantities of fruit and vegetables.

Consider, too, what you want your garden to look like. What is the effect you are trying to achieve? A garden should always be thought of in the context of your own home and the nearby buildings – its style should be in sympathy with its location. Contrasting styles of house and garden can be very successful but it is often better to avoid this.

If you have a thatched country cottage, the 'cottage garden' style is the obvious choice; likewise a 'modern' house of the 1930s suggests bold plants arranged geometrically, and a terraced town-house with a minute backyard is ideal for a paved patio with container-grown shrubs. However, modern estate homes are built in such a diversity of architectural styles and with such a wide range of construction materials that it is often difficult to decide on a style for the oddly-shaped patches of builders' rubble that is often provided as a garden.

Fortunately, there are many other factors which can help to decide style, in particular the idea that the garden is an extension of the home. The internal layout of a house and its interior decor can influence a garden layout and the type of plants to be used.

To most people, however, the immediately relevant factor is the cost of creating a garden. Remember that money is needed not only for the initial construction, but also for the continuing maintenance. In the long term, it is cheaper to spend more on building and stocking a relatively expensive but labour-saving garden now, than to build it too cheaply with low quality materials that require expensive maintenance or replacement after a few years.

In order to reduce costs, many plants can be obtained free from neighbours and usually these plants are better adapted to local conditions than commercial nursery stock. In addition, many of the more expensive, rarer trees and shrubs are now available as seed from specialist seed merchants. These seeds may be more difficult to germinate than well-known garden annuals or vegetables but, once transplanted, are much more likely to become established. In any case, they can be planted closely together and then thinned to allow the best specimens to grow.

Materials for paving, walls, fences and such garden features as seats, greenhouses, sheds, ponds and arches must be of good quality and can be particularly expensive. However, some of the most suitable material is sold secondhand and at low cost.

Probably the greatest satisfaction can be gained by designing and building a garden for your own specific needs from scratch. For some people, however, the ultimate achievement is to enhance and develop an already exisiting garden, particularly if it is overgrown and long untended.

Opposite *A rose garden of traditional design combines simple but effective elements: geometrically arranged beds, rustic trelliswork and neatly trimmed lawns. Even on a much smaller scale, such a design would retain all of its classic elegance.*

ASSESSING YOUR SITE

Before planning your garden in detail, you should assess the site as carefully as possible. Look at its shape and size, find out about its soil and climatic conditions and decide what your main requirements will be for the immediate future.

When you have more or less decided on the kind of garden you would like to have, you should then think about the advantages and disadvantages of the site. If you have the time and money, it is possible to clear the site and create your ideal garden from scratch. Unfortunately, few of us have the patience to do this and, in any case, there may be certain features already existing that really should be saved. Even if they are not wonderful, they could be refurbished to give shelter or screening until more suitable structures can be built and any new plants have established themselves. So, all features of the site should be investigated before constructing or planting anything. Size, shape, soil, climate, access and circulation should be assessed as well as the type and condition of the trees and shrubs already planted.

Shapes and sizes of garden
Gardening books and magazines usually assume that small gardens are either rectangular or square but the truth is often quite different. The size of 'small gardens' can vary from a paved patio 36 sq m (100 sq ft) to a 0.2 hectare (½ acre) plot. Even greater variation is found in the shapes of small gardens. Many are rectangular or square, others are almost linear, and some taper away in various directions. Newer houses, particularly in high-density housing estates, may have very irregularly-shaped plots. They are quite literally the spaces left over after the houses have been built. In some extreme cases, the garden may not even adjoin the home to which it belongs! Nevertheless, do not be disheartened by an oddly-shaped plot, as every space, no matter how unpromising it might seem, has the potential to become your ideal garden.

Aspect
In all gardens, the exposure and general aspects are very important in determining the type of plants to grow and their position. The site may be exposed to all weathers, to the gaze of all the neighbours and to the pedestrians in the adjoining streets. On the other hand, it could be surrounded by the blank wall of office blocks and street walls which, although protecting it from view, also seriously reduces the sunlight and the rainfall.

You should always remember that just as you can look out of your garden, others can look in and you must decide whether you want privacy at all costs or if you wish strangers to admire your handiwork. The distant view, too, may influence your final design. Is it of the open countryside or, say, the local gas works? Another very relevant factor is the view from indoors: most people spend much more time looking at the garden from the kitchen window than from the sitting room and the view from any upstairs rooms will add yet another dimension that you might want to consider.

Climate and microclimates
If the area is generally cold and wet, the vegetable patch should be close to the house to enable you to harvest crops in the wettest weather without getting too soaked and cold. In warmer areas, a shady patio through which cool breezes can flow is a useful feature. These are only two examples of the importance of climate in garden design. Although the overall climate of the area in which you live controls the plants that can and cannot be grown, the success of individual varieties and the flowering and fruiting times of particular specimens depends on the microclimate of the garden itself and of its different parts. Every garden has its own microclimate and, each time a plant is grown or removed, or a wall or other feature is built or demolished, the microclimate is altered.

In any garden both the local and the specific climate must be considered. Temperature, rainfall, duration of direct sunlight, the date of the last spring frost and the first autumn frost, the general direction of the prevailing winds and their speed all determine the form and content of a garden. Late frosts in spring can vary very much from one garden to another and are very important in controlling the time when you can transplant half-hardy or tender

Opposite *The climate, soil and general location of a garden are all important factors in its design. Very few sites are perfectly level, for example, and most have awkward shapes or shady corners that will need careful planning.*

plants. Late frosts can be a crucial factor affecting the pollination of fruit trees. Gardens in a hollow are particularly vulnerable to frost because cold air sinks and accumulates in low-lying pockets. Such gardens can be up to three weeks 'late' compared with those in adjoining areas.

Town gardens and pollution

The presence of cities, large towns and industrial areas can affect gardens in several ways. The large amount of heat generated by machines and office blocks alters the local climate by raising the average temperatures by up to 3°C (5°F) and can even make a garden virtually frost-free. The tallest buildings can intercept rain-bearing clouds and create a rain- Of particular concern is the atmospheric pollution given off by some factories. It has been thought that very dilute pollution can actually be beneficial to some plants by controlling pests and diseases but, in other cases, the pollution is so concentrated that even when crops will grow they should not be eaten and many flowers never come into full bloom. Even if the pollution has no visible effect on the plants themselves, the soil micro-organisms can be affected and

Below *The city environment has influenced the design of this garden and the kind of plants that are growing in it. Shrubs and climbers help to screen off the surrounding buildings, while an old fig tree (Ficus carica) flourishes in the sheltered conditions.*

Below right *In this basement garden, the main consideration is privacy and almost every available space around the sitting-out area has been crowded with lush foliage and colourful pot plants.*

Left *The texture of a soil is determined by the size of the particles in it and is critical because it affects the amount of air and water that reaches the plant roots. Clay soils are mostly made up of very fine particles which swell when they are wet and quickly block air from the roots. By adding plenty of organic material, clay can be made into a fertile and easily worked medium. Sandy soil, by contrast, comprises large, gritty particles through which water drains quickly and carries away essential nutrients. The addition of organic material and regular watering will greatly improve it.*
1 Loamy sand
2 Clay
3 A well-balanced loam
4 A sandy clay loam

Below *A little effort and some imagination could transform this lacklustre site into a colourful and well-designed garden.*

this can reduce the fertility of the soil.

Dust and soot, although not poisonous, can clog the breathing pores of plants and stunt their growth. Salt is quite commonly found in the air up to 8 km (5 miles) from the coast and can damage many plants. It is much better to go and see what grows well in parks and gardens along the coast and use the same sort of plants than to try to grow your favourites only to have them die or become increasingly stunted. Many of the seaside plants grow even better inland!

Your garden's soil

A well-known broadcaster on gardening topics used to reply to a great number of questions that the answer lay in the soil. Soils are very important in the life of plants. Apart from a few, true rock-dwellers and floating water-plants, all plants require soil to provide most of their food and water and to give them anchorage. The most important aspects of a soil are its depth, physical nature and chemical composition. Before a successful garden can be created it is essential to find out as much as possible about the soil. Not only does this tell you which plants to grow, it also indicates the treatment that may be necessary to improve or even to alter conditions so that you can grow a greater variety of plants.

A soil is not a uniform covering of small stones, sand and clay spread evenly over the earth's surface. It varies from place to place and, even in a small garden, can be different in every part of the plot. All soils contain sand and clay and are classified according to which is dominant. By adding organic

matter (humus), clay or sand soils can be greatly improved. The best soil has a near-perfect combination of these three basic ingredients and is known as loam. Soils develop very slowly from the weathered base rock acted upon by the climate, the vegetation cover and man's activities over hundreds of years. Being arranged in layers, soils also vary from top to bottom The vital layer for plants is the topsoil. This can be as shallow as 7.5cm (3in) or as deep as 6m (20ft) but most gardens have about 30cm (1ft) overlying the subsoil. In turn, there

A derelict garden before and after renovation. By following the original layout fairly closely, the feeling of old-fashioned charm has been retained although the immediate impression is very different.

can be a varying depth of subsoil on top of the base rock. Some gardens on new sites have no topsoil at all or have a covering of builders' rubble. In other gardens the subsoil may have been brought to the surface. In these cases it is probably easier to buy a load of good topsoil from a nurseryman or alternatively from a landscape contractor.

Digging by hand is still the best way to improve a soil. It aerates the soil, improves the drainage, kills the smaller weeds, allows you to remove the larger weeds and incorporates manure and other organic material into the soil structure. In neglected or new garden sites, a major problem can be severely compacted soil devoid of many of the micro-organisms essential for fertility. A mechanical cultivator can be used in these cases but the final stages before planting should be done by hand, using a spade or fork. There can never be too much organic matter dug into a soil and although rotted stable manure and straw are the best, almost any waste household or plant material can be used. There are many proprietary brands of soil conditioner which can be successful but they are very expensive when compared with free waste materials.

Many plants are very sensitive to the degree of acidity or alkalinity of the soil. Rhododendrons, for example, are best grown on acid soils while scabious (*Scabiosa* spp.) prefer alkaline soils. The soil acidity or alkalinity is usually quoted as a pH number, with pH 7 being neutral (above 7 is alkaline and below 7 is acid). The pH of any soil can be easily measured, using simple kits obtainable from garden centres and nurserymen. Most of these kits are very useful for giving not only the pH figure but also details of what should be done to the soil to alter its acidity or alkalinity.

The speed at which water drains through the soil and the amount which is retained in it has a great effect on plant growth. By and large, sandy soils are very well-drained and retain very little water whereas clay soils drain slowly and can easily become very heavy and waterlogged. Fortunately, most garden soils contain both sand and clay and, therefore drainage or water retention is not a major problem. However, nearly all soils require some watering in a dry season, particularly when plant growth is at its peak in the warmest months.

Water drainage and 'run-off' on the surface are also controlled by the slope of the garden. These gradients in a garden are not always obvious but a survey of the levels can be carried out quite easily and is usually very worthwhile.

Existing plants

Most garden plots have some existing vegetation even if it is only a few weeds or neglected trees and shrubs. It is important to note all the plants before deciding to remove any. Some may be mature and, healthy and could well remain where they are growing in the new plan. Some may be younger specimens that would transplant easily to a more useful spot and others, although not wanted in the long term, could still be useful to give protection to new plants you want to add. It is better to retain a cover of weeds to stabilize the soil on a slope than to remove it before you are really ready to plant. A knowledge of the plants on a garden site, useful or not, gives an indication of the type of plant that does well there and certainly will show up those that are not really at home.

Even old shrubs and trees can often be rejuvenated by cutting them down to encourage new growth from the base. Apart from 'weed' trees such as many elms and sycamores, all trees should be checked to see if they are healthy. Those that have many dead or weak branches may have to be removed but, by careful pruning and, perhaps, bracing of the larger limbs, many fine old specimens can be saved. It is usually better and certainly safer to employ a professional tree surgeon to undertake this sort of work, than to attempt to undertake it yourself.

When a tree has to be cut down there often remains an old tree trunk in the ground. It can be rotted away slowly by chemicals but it is quicker to have it removed by a contractor or tree surgeon. However, considerable expense can be spared by keeping it as a base for a garden seat or table or letting clematis, ivies or other climbers cover it.

If you decide to move some plants to another spot, it is better to do this in late autumn, late winter or early spring. Conifers and other evergreens should always be transplanted in the spring. It is possible to move plants at other times, but the losses can be great and, in the hotter days of summer, it is essential that all transplants are copiously watered for several weeks afterwards.

Access and circulation

Many garden plans seem ideal until the time comes to mow the grass, show an elderly or disabled person around, or take delivery of a do-it-yourself greenhouse or garden shed. You could then discover that it is very difficult to manhandle a heavy lawnmower over a flower-bed or across a rock garden, that the wheelchair carrying an invalid will not fit the paths, or that the garden gate is not big enough to pass the pieces of garden shed through.

Access to a garden and circulation within it must always be given top priority. Garden plans should begin with an indication of the routes to, from and in the garden. The paths to everyday features such as the dustbin, the compost heap and the bicycle shed or greenhouse should be direct and as short as possible. They should also be wide enough to take a wheel-barrow, a pram or a wheelchair and, ideally, two people should be able to walk side by side.

Curving paths may seem ideal on a plan but they can lead to 'unofficial' tracks being made across the edge of a lawn or flower-bed in order to reach somewhere quicker.

Garden steps and terraces should always be accompanied by a gently sloping ramp both for wheeled vehicles and for the elderly, the very young and the infirm, all of whom may find steps difficult.

There must always be at least one entrance to a garden that is wide enough to accommodate large plants, pieces of garden furniture and awkwardly-shaped machinery. This is important even if the only entrance is through the house.

Above *A problem like the stump of a dead tree can be turned to advantage by letting fast-growing climbers, such as ivy, transform it into a decorative feature.*

Left *Bricks are easy to lay for making curved paths in an informal garden. Here, they skirt a bed at the foot of a tree and, to soften the lines still further, self-seeded plants and tufts of grass have been allowed to grow between the bricks.*

DESIGNING & DRAWING UP YOUR PLAN

Once you have measured your site and noted the position of any permanent features such as good or bad views, you can begin to sketch in the elements of its overall design and decide how much space to allocate to each one.

Before any measuring or drawing-up of a detailed garden plan is to be done, you should sit down and design the garden in your mind's eye. A very rough plan of the site can be useful at this stage, just to remind you of the site's limitations (caused perhaps by neighbouring houses and the street outside), and of the opportunities offered by good existing plants and, perhaps, views to the distant countryside. It is always useful to discuss your plans with your family, your neighbours and your friends but in the end only you can really decide what you want and what can reasonably be achieved.

Sit down in various parts of the garden, stand by the garden gate or the kitchen, lounge or bedroom window and visualize what you would like to see. Do not limit your imagination to what you would like in midsummer when all the flowers are in full bloom, or to mid-autumn when the trees and shrubs are just shedding their red, yellow and brown leaves, or to spring when the earliest daffodils, crocuses and snowdrops are just peeping through. Think about your garden at less attractive times of the year. It is easy to imagine it in midwinter, when snow has covered all its imperfections, but what about late autumn when the first really heavy frosts have blackened the leaves of high-summer plants, or late summer when the grass has turned brown? Try to imagine it as a place to be enjoyed at all times: do you really want unwieldy large trees, masses of tender summer plants or big patches of easily scorched lawns?

Take a stroll into the street outside or even ask your neighbours if you can look at your property from the vantage points in their gardens, so that you can see your ideal garden as others will eventually see it.

The purpose of a garden

Day-dreaming at this stage should be counteracted, or at least balanced, by practicalities. Keep in your mind that a garden has four main uses. Firstly, it must set off your house to its best advantage, camouflaging the ugly bits and emphasizing the best aspects. Ideally, you should consider the house and garden as equal partners occupying your site.

Secondly, a garden is for flowers and ornamental plants to be enjoyed at all seasons and from all angles. Thirdly, it is a place in which to relax, entertain or play and, finally, it can be a source of food. These last three uses need not be of the same importance nor occupy equal spaces, but can be catered for according to your priorities.

The vegetable and fruit garden

Small gardens may only have enough space for growing a few plants of thyme, chives and parsley in a window box. It may be practicable in slightly larger plots to grow some vegetables among the flowers. Sweet corn, runner beans and red cabbages can be grown among the decorative plants in a mixed border. There are now many edible beets and cabbages with multi-coloured leaves grown purely for display as well as the attractive tree onion (*Allium cepa* 'Prolifera') or the globe artichoke.

The growing of vegetables in any case should not be thought of as a means of saving a lot of money. The vegetables in shops, stalls and supermarkets are usually grown on specialized farms and market gardens in which large scale operations mean that they can be produced at less cost than in your garden. Paradoxically, the centralized marketing system for commercially grown crops means that they are usually cheaper in cities than in the countryside. Vegetables and fruit should be included in the plans for a small garden for the convenience of having really fresh food easily available, particularly salad crops, which deteriorate quickly.

Some idea of the space needed for

Opposite *Once your ideas have taken shape and you have a clear picture of the kind of garden you think you would like, try drawing up a detailed plan of the design.*

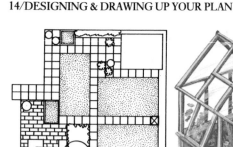

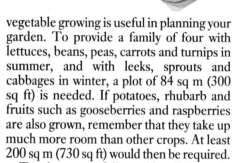

Even on a small site, careful planning will make it possible to be relatively self-sufficient. Most of this garden is taken up by three vegetable plots, measuring about 2.5 × 4m (7 × 12ft), to allow for the correct rotation of crops. Every spare corner is used, with strawberries in pots, fruit trees against the fencing and a bee hive at the end of the path. Next to the house is a small terrace with a herb bed beyond, while the other corner makes a utility area for the compost and rubbish bins.

vegetable growing is useful in planning your garden. To provide a family of four with lettuces, beans, peas, carrots and turnips in summer, and with leeks, sprouts and cabbages in winter, a plot of 84 sq m (300 sq ft) is needed. If potatoes, rhubarb and fruits such as gooseberries and raspberries are also grown, remember that they take up much more room than other crops. At least 200 sq m (730 sq ft) would then be required.

To become fully self-sufficient in vegetables and fruit at least 400 sq m (1500 sq ft) would be needed.

If space is limited, concentrate on 'perpetual' or 'cut-and-come-again' strains of green vegetables, such as broccoli and spinach, or high-yielding plants, such as marrows and dwarf beans, and salad crops such as radishes, lettuces, spring onions and tomatoes.

The sitting-out area

Consider the sitting-out and play area carefully, as it will be the major centre of activity. Ideally, this area should be paved and just outside the kitchen door so that food can easily be passed in and out, vegetables prepared on a warm day and muddy boots removed there in winter. However, if the garden side of the house faces north, you will have to consider a south- or west-facing site further away from the house. This will also need to have a well-drained and mud-free path joining it to the house door.

Depending on where you live and on your own preferences, the sitting-out area can be used to watch the people walking by in the street or nearby park, or the neighbours working in their gardens. Always remember, however, that if you can see out, other people can also see in!

The ornamental garden

The ornamental part of the garden has to be thought of for its total effect, often linking together all the other parts and features. To many gardeners, it will also be a place where favourite plants can be grown as specimens as well as contributing to the overall pattern of plants.

A common mistake is to assume that all gardens must have a mown lawn. Certainly, a well-kept lawn sets off colourful flower-beds and can be used as an extension of the sitting and play areas. But a lawn requires constant attention if it is to continue looking good. There is nothing more distracting in a small garden than an overgrown, weedy lawn, particularly when it is dead-looking at the end of the summer. Ground-cover plants like ivies (*Hedera* species), heathers (*Calluna vulgaris* and *Erica* spp.) and creeping comfrey *(Symphytum grandiflorum)* are less demanding and will thrive in places too uneven or too steep for lawns, although they cannot withstand wear and tear. Stepping stones can be used in these places.

At this stage there is no need to note exactly which varieties of decorative plants are to be used but their places should be roughly decided. Keep in mind their approximate height, spread and rate of growth, and the purpose – or purposes – you want them to fulfill. These could include screening and privacy, shelter from wind, sun and rain, summer flowers, autumn leaf colours or winter fruits and attractive bark colour.

Many ornamental plants, especially larger trees and shrubs, will be grown as specimens by themselves, but the smaller plants will almost certainly be grouped in borders. The width of flower beds and shrub borders needs particular attention: if you make them much over 2m (6ft) wide it could be difficult to handweed or hoe without trampling. If they are too narrow, there will be little room for effective arrangement of plants. Aim for year-round interest: as one plant finishes its display there should be another kind close by to take its place.

Structures in the garden

The siting of individual structures, particularly the less attractive ones, such as dustbins and oil-tanks, can be difficult. It is easier to look after them and hide them from view if they can be grouped. Unfortunately this will often conflict with access: the coal-shed should be close to a good path to the house, the oil-tank needs a clear run for the delivery-man's feed pipe, the dustbin must be close to the garden gate but not too far from the kitchen door. The greenhouse should be in a sunny spot but with some screening in midsummer. If it is a 'lean-to' or conservatory type the house-wall will protect it from frosts but can reflect too much heat in summer. A free-standing, east-to-west greenhouse is probably better.

The front garden

At this early planning stage, hard standing and good access for a boat, caravan or visitors' cars must be considered. This will probably have to be in the front garden, which is very small with most houses. Unfortunately, the front garden is what visitors first see! Ideally, the front garden

should be welcoming to guests and provide safe, well-lit and easy access for young and old, fit and disabled, to the front door. It is very much a challenge to combine these with a space for a boat, caravan or car and at the same time not obscure the view from the front room's windows. Privet (*Ligustrum ovalifolium*) and Leyland cypress (×

Above *This storage space for dustbins and fuel is accessible to the street but, because of its covering of ivy and honeysuckle, manages to preserve a garden atmosphere.*

Below *This design for a family with young children includes a grassy play area and sandpit with cycle track around. The pergola hides the front of a garage and provides a shady space for a pram or other toys.*

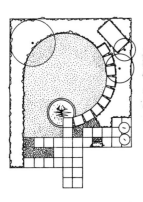

As children get older, a large terraced area will give them room for different activities, while a shed can be used for bicycles, a workshop or playroom. The soft, grassed area can be reduced in size by including a shallow garden pool which will add less functional interest.

Cupressocyparis leylandii) hedges are ideal as thick screens preventing strangers from looking in but they are visually dull and few plants can grow with them because they dry up the soil in summer and cast a deep shade. Other hedging plants you can use are barberries (*Berberis* spp.) roses (*Rosa* spp. and hybrids) and hardy fuchsias (*Fuchsia magellanica* and its varieties) but they are not so easily trimmed and can quickly overhang the paths, especially when dripping wet after a storm. The front part of a garden often needs much more thought than the back, although it is usually smaller.

The practical garden

Whatever pattern of garden finally forms in your mind, remember that your ideal garden must be translated into reality. Not all building materials or plants are readily available in all areas. Paving stones can be prohibitively expensive if they have to be transported a long distance and plants bought from a nursery in one area do not always transplant well in another. Bricks are a very satisfying material for paths as well as walls but, unless they are laid properly, they can be damaged by wear and tear. Professional help may be too expensive and you may not have the expertise or time or even confidence to do it yourself.

You may have decided that a garden pool is essential for your garden. With water plants in summer flower, fish in the clear water and the constantly changing reflection of the sky, a pool is a very attractive proposition. Pools require a lot of attention, though, and during the hottest days of summer you may have to top-up the water level every day. Plants grow quickly in water and you have to keep them under control or they will take over and leave no room for the fish.

Drawing up a plan

The very rough plan you have been using to help your ideas take shape must now be drawn out more accurately so that you can work out precisely the number and kinds of plants and the correct amounts of building materials.

Fortunately, if you live in one of the many newer houses, there is probably a plan of your house plot attached to your title deeds. If not, the local library or council planning department may let you trace your site boundaries from their large-scale maps. Even if this is not possible, it is very easy to draw your own site plan.

First of all you should measure the edges of your site, including the house, whether it occupies just a corner or the whole width. Using squared graph paper and working at a scale of about 1 to 50 (i.e. 2cm on paper equals 1 metre on the ground or ¼in equals 1ft) draw these measurements as lines. With some adjustment the four or more corners will meet! The size and shape of the house should then be added and you should also plot all the existing features that cannot be moved. These include manhole covers, water stop-taps and garden entrances to the house and road. Remember that all the space not occupied by your house is available for your garden. Even if house and garden are very small, they should always be treated together in just the same way as the early landscape architects such as 'Capability' Brown treated country mansions and palaces as part of the surrounding landscape.

Plants that cannot be moved should be plotted, as well as those that you want to move elsewhere or get rid of altogether. As you develop your plan on paper you may well have to rethink some of your earlier decisions. Some favourite plants may have to be abandoned and not-so-good specimens may have to be kept for a while until others have grown up.

Next on your plan you should draw the circulation within the garden and the routes to and from each feature. Straight lines between two points are usually preferred by people in a hurry but are not always pleasing to look at. A gently curving path is usually best but remember that when turned into reality from the plan, the foreshortening of it by the eye can make it almost too winding. A symmetrical and formal plan built around a straight central path with the dustbins at the far end, the sitting-out area next to the house and a flower-garden one side of the path and the vegetable garden on the other may look very neat on paper but is very dull in real life. An informal layout with an off-centre path giving access to all parts is just as easy to build and often much easier to maintain. If it changes slightly from year to year it does not matter but a symmetrical layout will look very odd if only one feature is out of place.

It is useful now to mark out the design on the site itself using sticks, string and stones and ignoring the present garden. You should walk up and down where the paths will be, sit where the play and relaxation area is planned and pretend to work where the vegetables will be grown. It is surprising how many minor re-adjustments or even major rethinking may be required when you have actually seen the plan roughly transferred to the ground.

Eventually, however, you will decide exactly what is possible and desirable and you should then draw up the final design. The paths should now be drawn to scale and the varieties of plants inserted on the plan. Finally you should ink in all the main lines you have drawn as well as the dots marking the positions of plants. Rub out the pencil lines and then have a few copies made on a photocopier. It is very easy for your only plan to blow away and be lost or to perhaps get trodden on by a very muddy boot!

Now you are ready to start to create your garden, remember that it will be many seasons before it is exactly as you visualized. Trees and shrubs take a long time to reach a satisfactory size. However, before planting you can start to build the necessary surrounds, the walls, paths and other structures.

Right *The first step in drawing up an accurate plan of your garden is to mark in the house and any other large buildings such as a garage or greenhouse. Include all ground floor windows and doors so that you can think about access and view points. With this done, mark in the site boundaries: if your site is reasonably regular in shape, you should be able to plot them by extending lines at 90 degrees from the house.*

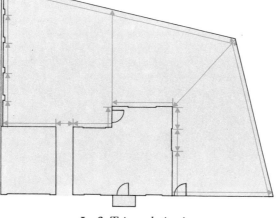

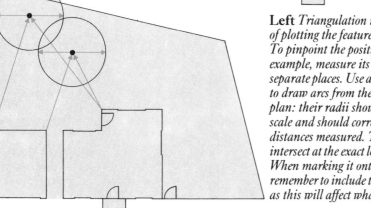

Left *Triangulation is an accurate way of plotting the features in your garden. To pinpoint the position of a tree, for example, measure its distance from two separate places. Use a pair of compasses to draw arcs from these points on your plan: their radii should be reduced to scale and should correspond to the distances measured. The arcs will intersect at the exact location of the tree. When marking it onto your plan, remember to include the overhang area, as this will affect what you can grow.*

GARDEN BUILDING MATERIALS

The variety of building materials available will provide you with a host of design possibilities involving colour, texture and overall shape so take a look at as many examples as you can before making your final choice.

The kind of building materials you can use for making garden features are determined by four main factors: cost, availability, ease of use, and, most important of all, suitability for the job.

Natural materials such as stones, gravel, wood and manufactured types like concrete, bricks and tiles, have now been joined by entirely man-made products such as rigid and flexible plastics. A recent innovation is the use of special materials added to provide great strength and increased durability, an example being glass-reinforced concrete.

Do not overlook the possibilities offered by second-hand materials. These can help the garden to take on a matured and more natural look soon after construction. Old bricks from a demolished house (provided they are suitable for garden use), or disused wooden railway sleepers or telegraph poles, sawn into shorter lengths, are sometimes obtainable from garden centres and builders' merchants. If you do buy any materials, check them carefully for any flaws.

When choosing any materials you must always remember that the cheapest is not necessarily the bargain it may seem. It may be less costly to buy some but the 'special offer' maintenance costs may be much higher, and parts may need replacing more often. In any case, whatever the price, the materials you buy must be suitable for your garden.

Bricks and tiles

One of the most pleasing and useful materials is brick, but it requires considerable care in choice and installation.

Bricks blend well with most plants, and with other building materials, and they are equally appropriate in town, suburban and country gardens, for formal or informal layouts. You can use bricks as a background to plants for the very practical reason that they soak up the sun's heat and release it slowly over a long period. This provides a favourable microclimate for ripening fruit. The more tender trees such as apricots and peaches grow particularly well against brick walls. There is another great advantage with bricks and that is their wide availability in a great choice of colours, textures, sizes and shapes. Yellow, blue, grey, brown, black as well as many shades of traditional red; rough, smooth; dimpled, flaked and ribbed bricks are usually on sale at builders' merchants or, sometimes, at large garden centres. Each part of the country generally has one predominant brick type due to the local clay from which they are made. It is often cheaper to buy these and, of course, they are usually much more in keeping with the character and building style of the area than 'foreign' ones.

You can also use bricks that have already been used once. These can be obtained from demolition contractors and are much cheaper than new ones. Having weathered over a number of years, re-used bricks quickly create a mellow, well-established look in a new garden. Bear in mind, however, that not all bricks used for buildings are equally suitable for paths and garden walls – the more exposed use may cause some of them to flake or crumble.

The cost of bricks is about twice that of concrete blocks but not usually as much as that of natural stones. Bricks, as well as being used for paths, terraces, sitting-out areas, small walls, and as a base for garden buildings, can be used for high walls, though a brick wall over 60cm (24in) high will need to be 'full brick' (double thickness), or have strengthening piers. A wall that is long, or over 1.8m (6ft) high will need ties and considerable re-inforcing even though it is built to double thickness. In such cases, the higher cost of bricks is very noticeable. Moreover, unless you are already a good bricklayer, any brick wall over 1.8m (6ft) should be built under close professional guidance and this again can greatly increase the cost of the wall.

Opposite Bricks can be particularly useful for building projects in the garden. They are hard wearing and can be laid in many unusual patterns to create different effects.

Top *Walls can be built in a variety of different patterns, according to the way the bricks are laid. The most common pattern, in which the bricks all have their long faces visible, is needed for single thickness walls. In double thickness walls, more complex and less monotonous patterns can be created by using other types of bonding. You can experiment with these patterns by laying a few courses of dry bricks.*

Above *While the same material for walls, paving and seating will create a unified effect different bonding patterns and the natural differences in brick colour will combine to make a more interesting finish.*

However, lower brick walls can be laid quite easily by any reasonably good do-it-yourself gardener providing it is remembered that a single-thickness wall requires a double thickness re-inforcing pillar about every 3m (10ft). At these points the underlying foundations must be correspondingly stronger.

Bricks are laid in a number of different patterns called 'bonds'. Which one you choose may be influenced partly by its strength or use, and partly on its decorative effect. When you are building a long wall it is a good idea to vary the bond every so often to avoid it looking very monotonous. If the wall has to bear any weight, either on top, as with a shed or greenhouse, or at the side as with a terrace support, the bond must be very strong, but if the wall is not load-bearing you can experiment with different patterns. It may even be un-bonded such as a basket-weave effect, but horizontal reinforcing rods or steel-mesh

laid along the mortar joints of such designs is essential.

Double brick walls can be built with a wide space between the two layers that can be packed with soil and plants grown along the top of the walls. However, so that the soil does not become water-logged you should leave a few un-mortared spaces ('weep holes') for drainage. Although not as strong or as private as a solid wall, 'honeycomb' brick walls can be attractive, especially in older gardens. They are very easy to lay, give support for plants and, despite the holes, provide a pleasant and effective windbreak.

Manufactured by a similar process as that for bricks, quarry tiles give an elegant and durable paving surface that is virtually maintenance-free. They can be bought in many colours, sizes and shapes, including the interlocking tiles; these give added strength to well-used areas.

Stone and gravel

Natural materials like stone and gravel can be used in any garden but are usually expensive. It is best to use those that are in common usage in your area; if stones from another area are used they can look very much out of place. In some areas it may even be an offence under the planning regulations to build a boundary wall out of the wrong material. Your local council planning office should be asked for advice before you buy any natural stones for a high boundary wall. If you have just moved to a new area, have a walk around the neighbourhood to see what and how local materials have been used successfully.

It is also very important with natural materials to build with them in the locally acceptable manner. A dry-stone wall may bring back memories of the countryside in your schooldays but in the suburbs of a large city, or in the garden of a terraced house, it may look very much out of place. In the same way, a solid concrete wall in the countryside looks equally odd. Fortunately, locally used stones are generally much cheaper than those from elsewhere.

Natural walls may be of 'hard' or 'soft' stones. Commonly used hard stones include granite and flint, the soft ones are limestones and sandstones. Soft stones are ideal for walls as they are fairly easy to trim and lay as well as forming a sympathetic background to the plants to be grown on and in front of them. Where there will be most wear and tear, granite and other hard stones are more suitable. You can buy hard and soft stones as rough-cut rubble, more or less as it was quarried, as squared rubble which is fairly evenly cut, or ashlar, which is square-shaped with a smooth finish.

Quarry-finished stones are available with a variety of textures and surface patterns.

Rough-cut rubble is always laid in a random fashion but regular blocks and ashlar are laid in 'courses' in the same way as bricks and concrete blocks. Patterns such as the herring-bone 'Cornish Hedge' can be made but stones lose much of their strength if not laid along their natural grain. Not all blocks of stone are the same size and shape unless you are prepared to pay very much more for them.

When you build a wall of mixed blocks considerable care is needed to make sure the finished result is really as strong as it will look. Mortar is generally used between the blocks but in some parts of the country experts build dry walls, which are almost as strong as mortared ones. All stone walls should be built on a good concrete foundation at least 30cm (1ft) deep and always at least twice as wide as the wall. If you have plenty of stone available you can use stone 'footings' instead of concrete foundations. However, with any stone wall over 1m (3ft) high you should take professional advice; in any case, you should always get help when building a stone wall, especially if you are not used to handling and carrying such heavy objects for long periods. Many 'bad backs' and 'slipped discs' are caused by unusual gardening operations!

Natural stone walls can weather quite rapidly if not properly protected by a continuous waterproof coping course laid along the top. It need not be of the same stone as the wall itself. Other natural materials like slates are often used, but bricks, roof-tiles and cast concrete are usually quite acceptable. When concrete is used upright stones can be inserted into it to give a castle-like appearance. Never use broken glass to top a wall.

Gravel is widely used in the building industry and is of two main types, natural

1 *The joints in a dry course wall will gradually fill with soil and stone chips and be ideal for creeping plants.*
2 *Each block in this dry wall has been separately shaped and the gaps between filled in with small chippings.*
3 *Reconstituted stone blocks have variable colours, shapes and textures.*
4 *A dry stone wall of round boulders and flat slabs needs skilfull work.*
5 *A more formal mortared wall has been carefully brushed to give it the appearance of a dry stone construction.*
6 *Mounted on a mortared rubble core, cut and uncut flints look striking.*
7 *This wall is known as a 'Cornish hedge'. Slabs are laid in flat courses and a herringbone pattern.*
8 *If used apart from natural stone, reconstituted types can look convincing and effective.*
9 *A heavily mortared rubble wall is softened by a rambling clematis.*

Borders alongside a gravel path soften its formal lines. Verbascum, fatsia and white-flowering hydrangeas make a composition of cool greens, while an isolated clump of Alchemilla mollis *adds a natural, 'self-seeded' look.*

and processed. Both are quite acceptable for garden uses such as paths, scree beds and other open areas. Traditionally gravel was obtained as small water-worn pebbles from river beds and much of the gravel sold today is of this type dug up from local gravel pits. In many parts of the country truly natural gravel is not available or is very expensive and, therefore, a substitute has to be used. This is generally crushed limestone or granite 'chippings'. It is not rounded, being angular, but it is very cheap to buy and readily available in various sizes or mixed.

Gravels can be used for all paved areas except where there is very heavy use or where the soil of adjoining beds is very wet and sticky. There is one great advantage in using gravel on a path – small plants will grow in it and soften the otherwise hard edges. You should always prevent the gravel from spreading on to the soil by using

kerbing blocks or narrow planks of well-preserved wood secured by small pegs of wood driven into the ground. For a more natural look, unbarked poles can be used for this and are very cheap to install. However, they may need replacing after three or four years.

If you have an awkward corner in your garden, possibly a patch of subsoil clay or builders' rubbish, you could cover it with gravel to give a very attractive feature in which many kinds of plant can be grown. You will need about 5cm (2in) of medium-sized gravel to cover it. This will partly smooth out any irregular mounds and smother most weeds already there. Rock garden plants should be planted in little pockets of soil and then the gravel scattered around their roots. The gravel will also act as a moisture-retaining mulch during the summer. Before long all you will have to do is trim the plants before they start

competing with each other for space.

Quarried granite shaped into cubes or rectangular blocks called 'setts', and large, rounded pebbles called 'cobbles' were once the most widely used road-surface materials in cities and towns. Nowadays asphalt and concrete have taken over but cobbles and setts are increasingly being used in pedestrian shopping areas and are very useful and exceptionally hard-wearing for garden use. Cobbles and setts can be expensive but small quantities are sometimes available from a local council's roads department. You must remember, however, that it is usually illegal to remove cobbles from beaches, even in small quantities.

Wood

Wood was once a very cheap building material for garden use but, as over 90 per cent of the timber used in this country is now imported, it can be very expensive. However, it is often obtainable second-hand, when it can be very cheap. Even new, it is generally much cheaper than bricks, concrete or stones.

Wood is used for building garden structures like sheds, summerhouses, pergolas, seats and tables, as a screening and fencing material and, occasionally, for paths and steps. Before being used in the garden, all timber should be treated to prolong its life by reducing insect and fungal attack.

You can buy most new timber already treated. It is usually much cheaper to brush

or soak it with preservatives yourself, although professional pressure or vacuum impregnation is better. The traditional chemical to use is creosote, but you must be careful not to splash it on to plants or into your eyes as it can be dangerous. Even its fumes can kill nearby plants when newly applied.

There are now proprietary brands of wood preservative available from shops and garden centres that are easier to apply than creosote and more pleasant to work with. Even so, most are based on poisonous copper chemicals and care must still be taken when using them. The great advantage most of them have over creosote is that they come in a variety of colours including cedar, green and even transparent to retain the appearance of the wood underneath.

Old sawn-off telegraph poles or disused railway sleepers are very useful for paths, stepping 'stones' or supports for terraces and banks because they would have been pressure-treated with preservatives when they were used the first time. Railway sleepers can be expensive if bought from a garden centre but they are also available from contractors appointed by British Rail.

Top left *Concrete slabs, cobbles and brick make an interesting contrast of colour, form and texture.*

Bottom left *Set around a tree a radiating pattern of cobbles has been fringed with a double row of bricks.*

Below left *Built along the same lines as a wooden fence, this pergola has added an attractive and shady nook to the garden.*

Below *Simple notched joints* **(1)** *can be strengthened with a T-shaped brace* **(2)** *which will help to reduce side sway on the posts. A double beam and spacer block bolted through the posts* **(3)** *will give more interest to a framework that is viewed from above.*
Bottom *Support posts can be fixed in a poured concrete foundation set into the ground.*

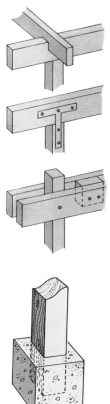

Above *An informal touch has been given to this patio by the inclusion of sawn-off sections of timber that serve as steps, play features and decoration all in one.*

Right *Timber discs can be used as individual stepping stones or, as here, to form a continuous paved surface.*

You cannot, however, buy sleepers direct from British Rail.

It does not matter if the wood you use has already been treated or you have done it yourself, you must always apply a fresh coat of preservative at least once every five years to prevent rot. One of the more expensive timbers is red cedar but it has the exceptional property of being virtually rot-proof. It has a disadvantage in that it is not so strong as timbers like oak and, therefore, cannot be used for wide unsupported spans such as in larger greenhouses, but for smaller structures and as a cladding it is unbeatable. When you consider that it does not need preservatives and rarely needs replacing, it is much cheaper in the long run.

Very thin pieces of wood such as small branches and twigs have been used for centuries as supports for crops like peas and beans and in herbaceous borders. They may not last as long as metal supports and plastic netting but are much cheaper and quickly become covered with plants to give a natural look.

Bamboo canes last longer than twigs, especially if you remember to soak the end in a wood preservative before use. Ideally, you should use a brand of preservative that does not harm plants; if you do use creosote make sure it dries well first. An advantage of canes is that, even when the ends have rotted away, you can still use the middles as shorter canes or split them to make supports for house plants.

Large pieces of timber such as old tree trunks can be used as the base for garden benches and tables. If the trunk is still in the ground, where you have cut down an old tree for example, there is always the chance that it will start to grow again. In this case you must continually prune away all shoots that sprout even if they are several yards away. Incidentally, willow branches nearly always take root when pushed into the ground and many fine willows in suburban gardens today started off as makeshift posts during the Second World War!

Concrete and reconstructed stone

Many people shudder at the thought of using concrete in the garden, except perhaps for foundations or a garage. Do not dismiss concrete so readily; if treated with care and used with imagination, it is a very versatile and strong material equally at home in both modern and traditional gardens.

Concrete is available in almost any colour and even the most stark types quickly weather to give a mellow look, especially when mosses, algae and lichens start covering the surface.

One of the most important qualities of concrete is that its surface finish can be varied to suit your requirements. Have a look at any modern city or shopping centre and you will see that many surface textures are available. By carefully selecting the gravel and sand from which it is made, quite different looks can result. The pebbles in it can be emphasized in the surface, or a smooth, almost polished look can be achieved. The surface can also vary according to the texture of the mould in which the concrete was cast. If wooden planks with a well-marked grain are used, this grain will be transferred to the concrete to give it a wood-like appearance. Even the knot-holes become impressed on the surface.

Concrete can be used either as large cast pieces or as smaller building blocks. Concrete blocks are used in the same way as bricks, being laid in regular courses held together by mortar. They must never be laid dry in the way that some natural stones are, and with any wall over 1.5m (5ft) high some reinforcing is necessary.

As well as simple concrete blocks, generally rectangular in shape, many more interesting shapes and finishes are obtainable. They are not usually much more expensive.

Besides the many solid walling blocks that are available, pierced blocks (often called screen blocks, although they offer little privacy) are another option. These are particularly useful for patio walls or even as dividers between properties where the barrier does not have to be peep-proof.

Pierced blocks are generally light in

colour and, with the strong geometric design formed by the pattern within each block, they make a powerful design element in the garden.

Pierced blocks can be used very effectively in combination with bricks or walling blocks, but as block dimensions vary from one manufacturer to another, check that the units are compatible before you order.

One specialized form of concrete block is a reconstructed stone where the main ingredient is the dust and chippings from natural stone. Such stones are no substitute for the real thing, but are often stronger, much easier to lay, and usually cheaper. It is better to consider them as an alternative material and not a poor imitation. It is best to avoid the type where the surface of a single block has been moulded to look like several different sized stones with mortar between, although even these can be attractive if laid carefully. They are most useful for dwarf walls which will soon be covered with trailing plants.

If concrete is used for large or irregularly shaped structures, it is usually cheaper to buy it already cast. With items such as statues, urns and vases, the concrete is generally cast in one piece. For sheds and coal-stores, each side is cast as a large slab or series of slabs and the whole structure bolted together in your garden. These

concrete slabs can be used for fences, for compost bins and for supporting walls on terraces. Larger plant containers are sometimes made from concrete slabs bolted together.

You can easily cast smaller pieces of concrete yourself but larger items need considerable expertise.

Metals, glass and plastics

Iron railings, path-edges, arches, seats and tables as well as steel wire and expanded metal mesh fencing are all well-established in gardens. Unfortunately, metal can be expensive and, unless there is time to look after it properly, it can corrode and rust away quite quickly.

A recent innovation is plastic-covered metal, usually in green, white or black. It can be used for mesh fencing and even for tables and chairs.

Plastics alone are used where their weather resistance or waterproof qualities are required rather than a permanent and heavy-duty structure. Plastics are sometimes used in fences to give a wind-proof viewing panel which is more durable than glass.

Glass, a much older material, is used in most gardens for cloches, garden frames, greenhouses and summerhouses. It is easily broken but is usually longer lasting than most modern plastics.

Above left *Blocks of pierced concrete make an attractive yet sturdy screen for partitioning off different parts of the garden. Sections of the screen are supported by piers (or pilasters) and reinforcing mesh runs through the mortar joints.*

Above *Where a garden overlooks an especially pleasing view, glass or plastic can be inserted into the fence to make an unobtrusive viewing panel.*

MAKING A GARDEN FRAMEWORK

When the contours and layout of your site have been plotted on a flat plan, you can begin to translate the pencilled outlines into proper walls, steps and paved areas which will form the basic skeleton of the garden.

Having planned your garden on paper, the time comes when theory has to be put into practice.

Before you start excavating or ordering materials, transfer the plan from paper to garden, marking out the various beds and features with pegs and string. Proportions, path dimensions and bed sizes can look very different on the ground from on paper. This is your chance to modify the plan if necessary.

Leave the markers in position for several days, looking at the layout from different angles and observing how shadows fall.

This cannot be hurried and whatever you use as markers must be robust enough not to be easily disturbed or blown away. Resist the temptation to further change your plans unless you find · it is really necessary to improve the layout.

Where your markers meet an existing feature, a plant or a structure that is to be retained, it is a good idea to mark it specially to prevent accidental removal later. If necessary, protect it with a small fence made of pots or pieces of old wood. Chestnut fencing is very good for this as it is cheap and can be used again elsewhere.

If the plant, particularly a tree or large shrub, requires attention, this is generally a good time to see to it. But do not carry out any pruning at the wrong time otherwise future flowering could be affected, or the tree made vulnerable to certain diseases. If you do decide to prune away dead branches, you can treat the cut surfaces with a wound paint, although there is evidence that this is not always effective.

Remember that really large scale pruning and perhaps bracing of old, large branches requires professional advice from a tree surgeon. However, you should wait until you have noted all trees needing treatment as it will be cheaper to call out the professionals for one big job rather than for several short visits.

Small trees and shrubs that you wish to keep in the garden but not in their present place should be removed, provided it is the right time of year and that you have already prepared a place for them. You should attempt to make ready their final position but if this is not possible because something else is already there, you could try moving them to a temporary position first, although this is best avoided.

Most plants can be moved during the dormant season, from late autumn until spring, unless the ground is frozen. Evergreens are best moved in the separate seasons of autumn or spring.

Plants can be moved at other times, but a general principle is the larger the plant, the less likely it is to survive.

Always move plants in the late afternoon or evening, and always give them plenty of water. for several weeks afterwards unless the ground is already very wet.

Do not be tempted at this stage to buy the plants you want. They are much safer in the nursery than on your construction site.

Structures that you wish to keep should be treated just like the plants. They should be protected from subsequent damage, and the opportunity taken to make any repairs that are necessary. It is not wise, however, to apply the final coat of paint at this stage, as it may easily get damaged during construction work, but you should certainly treat all exposed timber and replace any rotten pieces as you come across them.

Structures such as coal stores, dwarf walls or paths that are damaged or well worn should now be re-mortared. Broken bricks, tiles and slabs are best replaced. With badly cracked paving, it is worth considering re-laying all or most of the area. It is much easier to take it up now and start again than to replace individual tiles, setts, cobbles, bricks or blocks.

Any structures that have to be moved or demolished are best taken down. This can be a long and difficult task, as it will be necessary to remove the foundations too.

Opposite *When you are ready to begin preparatory work on your garden site, take care to protect any established areas you do not wish to change. Permanent features will need protecting from the risk of damage, especially if major building tasks are to be undertaken.*

Above *Before its alteration, this town garden was dominated by the curving flower beds and a flight of steps that carried the eye directly towards an unsightly backdrop of neighbouring houses.*

Right *Within five months, the beds had been reshaped into rectangles that reflected the geometric outline of the garden, the lower steps had been widened for greater visual effect and the crazy paving had given way to a covering of washed gravel through which plants could grow. A wooden screen across the back had hidden the view and helped add a sense of privacy.*

However, it is worth remembering that, even if you are not going to re-build elsewhere, the waste materials will almost certainly come in useful later. Small, broken-up pieces of concrete foundation can help to form the foundation for a new path or paved area, and old bricks can be used as curbs or as the base for a barbecue pit, for example. If you intend to re-erect the structure, store the pieces where they are protected from damage. However, it is not usually worth spending a very long time in chipping off every piece of mortar from a brick as new ones are not that expensive.

The stage will be reached when your ideal garden looks like a builder's yard with just a few isolated plants and features standing in their final places. Now is the time to start building the new structures.

Start with the walls, fences, pergolas, arches and other uprights and only then tackle the pavings. If the soil is very muddy or very uneven, it may be useful to lay the path foundations at an early stage to provide easy access to most parts of the garden, but do not lay the final surface until most of the heavy work is finished.

Changing level

The next thing to do is to deal with the inevitable changes of level in your garden. In your original plan you may have decided that the changes could be dealt with by a gentle slope rather than by a series of steps, terraces and retaining walls. Even if your site is perfectly flat, you will probably

their techniques of ground shaping. A low mound in the foreground can obscure an ugly tall building in the distance. Japanese gardeners emphasize the mounds they build by surrounding them with an arrangement of stones or setting them in an evenly raked sand or gravel-scattered surface.

Mounds are also a very useful way of hiding piles of rubbish left by builders or by the demolition of an old wall.

A word of warning – the steeper the mound of soil, the more vulnerable it will be to damage by children, who always seem to be attracted by a slope. To reduce the risk of damage, the slope should be no steeper than 30 degrees. Once the grassed surface is damaged, rain will quickly wash away the soil covering and the carefully shaped mound will become an eyesore. If the mound is steeper than this for any reason, use plants to protect it from wear and tear.

If it is necessary to go up and over a piece of steeply rising and falling ground, a well-built ramp, possibly paved or made of gravel, which can be easily raked back, should be used. When the path is to be used by a pram, wheelchair, tricycle or wheelbarrow, it may be better to re-route it around the base.

If your garden is on a sloping site, such as a hillside, the changes in level may have to be dealt with by terracing. It could even be necessary to have a terrace with its retaining wall right across the plot, but as this is not usually very attractive it may be better to think about a series of overlapping and alternating terraces with steps or ramps in between. By skilful use of winding steps and small walls, quite steep slopes can be concealed and made safer, at the same time providing a range of smaller gardens within the overall design. The side edges of steps can be made less severe if plants can tumble over them, but for safety reasons the front edge should never be hidden.

Terraces with retaining walls and wide flights of steps may be subject to control by your local authority if over 1.2m (4ft) high. If in doubt, it is always sensible to ask your local council or seek professional advice. The council may insist that such structures are built to a statutory specification to prevent accidents. Even lower walls, if their purpose is to retain a considerable weight of soil, especially when it is very heavy because of waterlogging in the winter, should be built with expert advice.

A cheap, easily constructed, long-lasting, readily maintained, very safe and attractive type of retaining wall can be made from old railway sleepers. These can be laid either upright or horizontally and can withstand considerable sideways pressure.

For a simple yet dramatic effect, Japanese gardeners have perfected the art of asymmetric deisgns. The raked sand and small mossy mounds above are a feature of the Tofukuji Temple gardens at Kyoto.

decide that some artificial change of level could add interest and variety to an otherwise monotonous scene.

The eighteenth-century landscape architects reshaped the land into gentle hills and shallow valleys so that it looked like a natural lowland landscape. Often a lake was built, streams diverted and trees planted or re-planted to provide an idealized and romantic pastoral scene from a legendary past. These projects usually involved large scale civil engineering and required many labourers working over a long time. In some cases, whole villages and large farms were re-sited to create a landscape to hide ugly views. In your garden, despite the vast differences in scale, you can achieve similar results by

Sawn-off lengths of telegraph poles sunk into the ground for at least half their length are also very strong and attractive.

Fences

You have probably decided to build a fence around your garden for three good reasons. The most obvious one is that it marks the boundary of your property. Secondly, it serves to keep out unwanted animals such as stray dogs, prevents trespassers entering, and deters 'peeping-toms'. Finally, but most important if you have a young family, it will prevent your children as well as your own pets, from straying on to the road or into your neighbours' gardens. Fences also help to hide ugly views and act as very effective wind-breaks protecting not only delicate plants but making it much more pleasant to sit out in the summer. Even a simple, wide wire mesh fence will reduce wind speeds. If you live in a very windy area, such a fence is less likely to get damaged or blown down than a solid one which must be strong enough to deflect the worst gales.

By shading adjacent parts of the garden from the sun and wind, fences will help to increase the range of microclimates in your garden. In this way you may be able to grow a wider range of plants.

Although a fence may be built of attractive material, such as well-grained timber planks or woven wood strips, and is therefore a decorative feature in its own right, most are generally dull. A long fence may be used to guide your eyes to an attractive feature, such as a tree, at its end but this is not always possible. The only thing to do with such a fence is to grow plants against it, on it, and over it. Climbing, twining and some rambling plants are suitable but you should not just let them grow all over the fence without some additional support. A mature climber can be heavy enough to topple over an old fence, and a mass of branches and leaves against a fence may retain so much moisture, and attract so many insects and fungi, that it finally rots. By using vine-eyes and galvanized nails with wire stretched between them, or preferably with a light framework just in front of the fence itself, the plants will not rely solely on the fence for their support. However, there is no good excuse for not building a very strong fence in the first place.

Ensure that the uprights, whatever you are going to hang on them, prefabricated panels, planks, or wire-mesh, are firmly and deeply embedded in the ground. As a rule of thumb, all wooden fences over 1m (3ft) high require concrete foundations for the uprights; with a 1.8m (6ft) high fence the foundations should be 75cm (30in) deep at least, and higher ones should be proportionately deeper.

Remember that in most areas any boundary fence over 1.8m (6ft) high may require planning permission if it is likely to obscure the view for drivers. There may also be restrictions to the height of any fencing laid down in covenants in the deeds for the property.

With the post-hole borer, which you can hire from garden centres if you do not own or cannot borrow one, you should first

Below *Horizontal, roughly-hewn boards make up a heavy and strong overlap-type fence.*

Below right *Wide-spaced horizontal timbers make a less weighty looking fence.*

Bottom *An attractive 'triple' combination of low wall, rustic fencing and a hedge.*

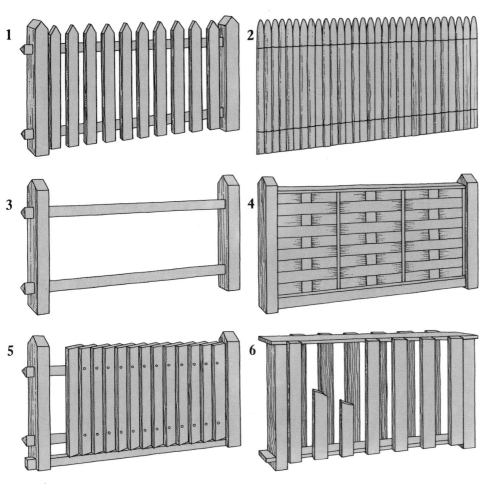

Although the basic design of wooden fences is the same, the final appearance can be very different:
1 *Picket fence*
2 *Palisade*
3 *Post-and-rail*
4 *Woven panels*
5 *Feather-boarded*
6 *Close-boarded*

make a hole about 30cm (12in) square, and 10cm (4in) deeper than the foundation depth. In the bottom 10cm (4in) add gravel or small stones to help drainage and then hold the post in place while somebody else pours in the concrete. A suitable mix would be 3 parts coarse aggregate, 2 parts sharp sand and 1 part Portland cement.

Support the post with smaller struts of wood or blocks at its base. Leave them in position for about five days, then remove them and, if it has not been done already,

affix the panels, mesh or wire to the posts.

Even if properly treated with pre-servative, the uprights will probably rot in time and need to be replaced. However, you can avoid this if you use concrete posts into which the panels can be slotted. If the wooden posts are rotten only at the bottom, they can be replaced by short concrete posts, to which the sound wood is bolted. You can also get square-shaped metal supports, into which the uprights are placed and secured.

Walls

Garden walls may serve exactly the same purposes as fences, which are to act as boundaries and screens and to keep people and animals in or out. However, walls are also used much more than fences within gardens to denote changes of use, and to act as visual screens and wind-breaks enclosing sitting-out and play areas.

Walls can be made from natural or reconstructed stone, bricks, or concrete blocks or poured concrete slabs. Usually only one type of material is used for each wall except for the coping on the top and the foundations. All walls over 1.8m (6ft) high are susceptible to damage by gales and, as with fences, may require planning permission from the local council.

One way to reduce costs and still provide

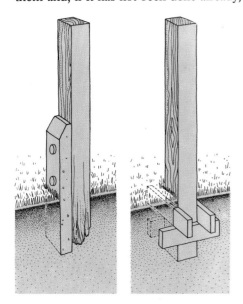

Far left *All wooden posts rot in time, but instead of replacing them completely, you can bolt them to short concrete posts.*

Left *Where damp is not a problem, the posts can be anchored with wooden cleats nailed across the base.*

Above *Dry stone retaining walls are often built at quite an angle to the earth behind so that they seem to lean slightly into it rather than act as supports. The angle should be about 50mm in 300mm of height (2in in 1ft), with each stone leaning downwards into the bank of earth to lodge it firmly in place.*

Above right *Large paved areas and patios are generally most successful when only a few different materials are used. Here, soft, brick red and slate grey combine well with the surrounding foliage and simple furniture.*

a strong garden wall is to use an inner core of concrete blocks faced on one or both sides by bricks or natural stones. As already mentioned, decorative concrete blocks can be used by themselves as a substitute for bricks or natural materials.

Although most walls, whatever they are made of, have the spaces between the blocks filled with mortar or cement, it is becoming increasingly popular to build a dry stone wall. Dwarf walls of this kind are very good for growing small rock plants along the top and in the sides. Unfortunately, they often look out of place and require much more skill in building if they are to be stable. To help overcome the stability problem, you could use mortar but wipe the joints out very deeply. The result will closely resemble a dry stone wall.

When laying a rubble wall with the stones laid randomly to give a 'country' look, you must always use plenty of mortar and lay each stone carefully, making sure that all cavities are filled in. The technique is quite different from the almost mechanical and repetitive process of building a brick wall. For the bigger holes you can use smaller stones, such as flints, to help fill the spaces. To improve stability, a pillar of regularly shaped stones or bricks should be built

every 1.8m (6ft). With rubble walls laid in courses rather than randomly, it is necessary to add a short course of even-sized stones every 2-3m (6-10ft).

Brick walls and those made from smoothly finished and regularly shaped ashlar must always be mortared, and great care always taken to ensure that they are upright (retaining walls may need a slight backwards slope). A bricklayer's spirit-level or plumb-bob is a must for this. If you intend to make a really strong and long-lasting wall you must also be sure to use the appropriate mortar.

You can make mortar from ordinary cement, soft sand and lime, but it is much more convenient to buy masonry cement (which already contains a plasticizer to keep the mortar workable for longer) and soft sand. For laying blocks or bricks use 1 part masonry cement to 4 parts sand (3 parts sand for dense masonry blocks or more substantial retaining walls).

The colour of the mortar depends largely on the colour of the sand but you can buy dyes to add to the cement. You must be very consistent with quantities and mixing to avoid varying shades. Try a small area first, and wait until the mortar is completely dry before assessing the colour. Always mix any

dye with completely clean water.

Until you really feel competent at building walls, you should only make a small amount of mortar at a time as it becomes too stiff to use after about an hour. Remember, however, that even if you are very careful, some mortar will be wasted by dropping it on to the ground. Never be tempted to pick it up and use it again as it will be contaminated with soil or dust.

Paths and patios

After building the walls and erecting the fences, tackle the large areas of paving, followed by the paths. The large areas will probably be adjoining the house, where they will be used for sitting out, or at the back or side for play areas, say, and at the front, for a car, caravan or boat. You may also need another fairly large area for standing dustbins and other storage space. If it is a really small garden surrounded by tall trees and buildings, it could be necessary to have more than one paved area so that you can use different ones for shelter or sun depending on the time of day and season of the year.

Large paved areas, commonly called patios, should generally be linked by the path network, but whether they should both be made of the same materials, is a matter of personal preference. Patios can be made from many materials, each having its own features of resistance to wear and tear, ease or difficulty of laying, initial costs, routine maintenance cost, and colours or textures.

Unless you are skilled in garden design and construction, it is usually safer to use as few materials as possible. Combinations of wood and brick, or paving slabs and granite setts, or concrete blocks and cobbles can be very effective if chosen with care and laid well. If poorly chosen and inadequately laid, they can very quickly look incongruous as well as being unsafe.

Whatever the type of paving or path, you must always pay attention to drainage. There is nothing more annoying or unsightly than a large pool of water in the middle of the area. Puddles can also be dangerous, particularly when they turn to ice in winter or get full of slippery, half-rotten leaves in autumn. Paving should always be laid so that it slopes very gently away from the house. If it is a small patio of about 10sq m (12sq yd) there is no need to provide any special drainage channel at the garden edge. Areas larger than this should have a gully leading the water away to the main surface drainage system or into a soakaway. If this is not done, the soil of the surrounding grass or flower beds can easily become waterlogged and the plants will either die or grow very rank and coarse.

Above *Echoing the natural contours of the ground, this curved brick retaining wall is surprisingly graceful.*

Below left *The choice of brick for this patio complements the shape and edging of the pool beyond and makes a formal but stylish sitting out area.*

If the patio adjoins your house, make sure the surface of the paving is at least 15cm (6in) below the level of the house damp-proof course. When the patio is immediately outside a door or a sliding window, you may need to provide a step or even a steep ramp.

All paths and patios must be laid on firm and even foundations. The more wear and tear they are likely to receive and the heavier the loads, the greater the need for firm foundations.

Paving slabs, whether of concrete or natural stone, should be bedded in mortar although, if they are only going to be used lightly, they could be laid on sand. If this is the case, it is essential that the underlying earth is consolidated with a garden roller or by tamping.

If bedding on mortar, prepare a base of hardcore at least 7.5cm (3in) deep, well tamped down until it is quite firm and does not 'give' when you walk on it. You can use broken pieces of brick, concrete and stones, provided they are small enough, bond with ashes, gravel, or small pebbles.

Over the hardcore base spread a 'lean' concrete mix (1 part cement, 3 parts sand) or other fine material such as ash if this is available. Roll or tamp it to bind the materials together.

Trowel the bedding mortar on to the base and carefully lay the paving slabs. You can put mortar between adjacent slabs but a more pleasing result can be had by filling the gaps with sand. To make sure even gaps are left, whether filling with mortar or sand, insert small wooden wedges between each slab, removing them once the underlying mortar has set. Dry sand can then be brushed into the gaps and will serve to drain away surface water. If the path is not going to receive heavy use, you could brush fine soil between the slabs so that small plants can be grown among the paving – but remember that this is also an open invitation to weeds to join them!

Crazy-paving is quite popular, but it is usually uneven. This makes it difficult to keep clean and can spoil the visual effect; most important of all, it can be quite dangerous to walk on. If properly laid, however, crazy-paving can be a satisfactory as well as inexpensive surface. Broken slabs or stones of uneven size are usually much less expensive than whole pieces.

Try to arrange the stones in a random fashion with no continuous joint lines. As edge stones are the most liable to damage, make sure that you use the largest pieces for this; it will also help to keep the outside edges fairly even.

Ordinary red, yellow, or grey wall bricks are traditional materials for paths but in damp areas they quickly become covered with slippery mosses and slimy algae. Unsuitable bricks can also suffer from the effects of frosts, which cause them to flake or crumble. Heavy engineering bricks could be used in their place but they are much too expensive for all but the hardest wear areas, and are not necessary as 'special

Though more time-consuming to lay, paths made of different materials can add a powerful design element to a garden:
1 Stone slabs and bricks of a similar colour have weathered to give a path of attractive yet uniform tones.
2 A brick area has been broken up by strong, straight lines of wood and slate laid on edge.
3 For a wider setting, stone-faced concrete slabs have been both softened and framed by rows of bricks.
4 Granite setts and concrete slabs have produced a simple pattern of contrasting scale and texture.

quality' bricks will be perfectly satisfactory.

Even better than bricks for paving are brick pavers (sometimes called flexible pavers because of the method of laying). These are thinner than ordinary bricks and have a slightly different surface area which means they can be laid without the gaps that occur with bricks (because of the space left for mortar joints).

Finishing touches

With the backbone of the garden complete, the remaining structural work can be tackled. Garden buildings (a shed or summerhouse, for example) a pergola, or perhaps a pond and garden lighting, can be erected or installed (if you plan carefully, cables can be laid before the paving).

Ideally you should complete all of these fixtures before you start planting, but as plants take some time to become established, once most of the essential and extensive building work is over, do not hesitate to start planting.

Above *The corner of this garden has been converted into a purpose-built dining area with benches, barbecue pit and storage unit. The basic use of only one type of brick reinforces the clean, simple lines of the design and the white, wooden framework of the pergola matches the wooden bench tops and cupboard doors for a functional yet attractive finish.*

Left *The choice of crazy paving for this winding, and informal 'wooded' path matches the mood of the garden perfectly. Laying crazy paving requires much more precision than the name implies: the large, irregular pieces should fit together snugly with as few continuous joint lines as possible.*

DESIGNING WITH PLANTS

Though selecting plants is one of the final stages in planning a garden it is, in many ways, the most important. The right choice will complement the layout, soften the hard lines of the framework and add that vital, personal touch.

Although you will probably have included the names of the plants when you drew up your plan, it is not too late to reconsider your choices. Often the planting list consists of many individual plants included for a variety of reasons, and they may not necessarily provide a good balance. Plants may have been included because you like the fragrance of the flowers, the colour of the fruits, or, perhaps, the autumn leaf colour. Maybe the plant was seen in a garden or at a flower show, and it appealed. Pictures in seed or plant catalogues, or their glowing descriptions, are also a strong temptation.

For impact, however, the borders should be more than a collection of individually desirable plants. It is important to consider how they look together, and to take into account habit, leaf form, and overall impact, as well as the more specific qualities that appeal to you.

More than anything else it will be the plants that give the garden its three-dimensional look, enabling your flat, two-dimensional plan to become a reality. Treat your garden as a block of space with the walls of buildings and fences as its edges, and its lower surface made from the paths, soil and other permanent features. It is the plants that mould this space into attractive shapes, creating special places which you will feel compelled to enter.

The plants that you choose must be those that appeal to you, but they should also be able to reinforce your garden plan. Consider each plant in relation to its neighbours in terms of shapes, sizes, colours, textures and patterns of seasonal growth, so that it becomes integrated into the overall design. This is how a garden can become more of an art form, and can also to some such extent reflect your own particular personality.

There are obviously many approaches to planting design, but generally a planting scheme either tries to control nature by confining bulk planting to beds and borders which have a definite shape, size and position, or it attempts to reflect nature. To achieve a more natural appearance you could even use native plants to try to re-create a woodland, meadow, or heathland scene. Neither approach is wrong and both have many good and bad points. There are good and bad examples of both!

There is another approach, one that allows you to plant a selection of plants which you then view at different seasons to decide whether or not they are suited to a particular position. If they are suitable you keep them, if they are not you can either get rid of them altogether or move them to a better position, replacing them with more suitable plants. This trial and error method can be expensive and takes a long time, but the final result will be plants that really are required both in their own right and as part of the overall scene – as long as you have the resolution to discard failures.

In the confined space of a small garden the 'natural' and the 'controlled' design approaches are not really that different. Even the most formal and precise designs must still succeed naturally and in a re-creation of nature you still have to control the tendency of certain plants to take over and smother the less vigorous species. Self-seeding happens with all sorts of plants and you must try to balance the conflict between removing all the seedlings on one hand, because they upset your plan and, on the other hand, keeping them all because they give a well-established mellow look.

Your design may be fairly formal if the space available will not allow anything else, but there should always be room for one wild patch. This will soon become a focal point in its own right as seasonal changes take place as well as a slow development over the years. Almost certainly the wild patch will attract a selection of insects such as butterflies and moths and also, as would be expected, birds of many kinds. However, if you wish to make a realistic wild garden you must visit a piece of truly wild countryside to see which plants grow in different places and which grow with each other most successfully.

Wild plants grow in natural groupings depending on the climate, soil and history of the area. Over the years, in a wild

Opposite *With the basic framework of your garden established, you can move on to the challenge of choosing plants that will harmonize perfectly with the design and bring your two-dimensional flat plan to life.*

The two plans illustrated here show how to build up a planting design in careful stages. The owners of this small, enclosed garden wanted a 'jungle' effect that could be achieved as quickly as possible. The first plan gives details of the plants they chose for the basic framework, while the second shows the decorative elements they then added.

Framework planting (right)

1. *Hebe anomala*
2. *Pyracantha rogersiana* 'Flava'
3. *Romneya coulteri* (Californian tree poppy)
4. *Hedera helix* 'Goldheart'
5. *Yucca flaccida*
6. *Euphorbia wulfenii*
7. *Choisya ternata* (Mexican orange blossom)
8. *Lonicera japonica* 'Halliana'
9. *Daphne odora* 'Aureomarginata'
10. *Fatsia japonica*
11. *Catalpa bignonioides* 'Aurea' (golden Indian bean tree)
12. *Pittosporum tenuifolium* 'Silver Queen'
13. *Hedera canariensis* 'Varegata'
14. *Taxus baccata* 'Fastigiata' (Irish yew)
15. *Camellia japonica* 'White Swan'
16. *Rhus typhina* (stag's horn sumach)
17. *Viburnum davidii*
18. *Betula papyrifera* (paper birch)

Decorative planting (far right)

19. *Alchemilla mollis* (lady's mantle)
20. *Hydrangea macrophylla*
21. *Caryopteris × clandonensis*
22. *Potentilla fruticosa*
23. *Acanthus mollis*
24. *Rosa* 'Mermaid' (climber)
25. *Nicotiana* (tobacco plant) in summer; tulips in winter
26. *Jasminum nudiflorum* (winter jasmine)
27. *Salvia officinalis* 'Purpurascens' (purple sage)
28. *Rosa* 'Iceberg' (floribunda)
30. *Cortaderia selloana* (pampas grass)
31. *Clematis* 'Madame le Coultre'
32. Herbs

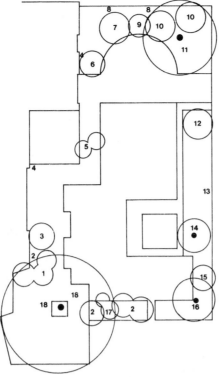

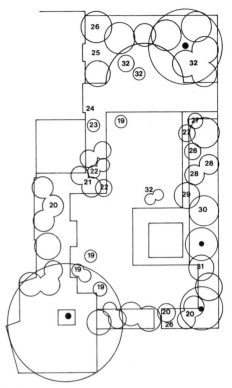

situation, the first colonizing plants eventually become overtaken by later introductions so that, eventually, the most complex vegetation that can be supported remains. In this so-called 'climax' vegetation, there are usually one or two species that dominate the rest of the plants (thus we have oak wood, or heath moor for example), and some of the wild plants appear in large numbers, whereas others are only found as scattered individuals. Bluebells usually cover the ground but only for about three months before the leaves dry up and disappear. As a contrast the gorse bushes scattered on a heathland nearly always have some of their bright yellow flowers on show.

If you intend to make a wild garden always plant the larger plants first. For a woodland effect, plant the dominant trees, then the underlying shrubs and finally the plants of the woodland floor. The lowest layer, the mosses, will follow naturally.

There are three stages or elements of planting in the implementation of all garden designs. The first stage is to establish the garden's basic plant framework of trees and larger shrubs. Next you should provide the bulk of the garden planting against which the third element, the decorative plants, are set. Do not give priority to the decorative plants and then add just a few 'sculptural' larger specimens. Always start with the largest plants to give the general setting for the rest of the garden. Remember, too, that a clump of medium-sized plants grouped together can achieve the same effect as a single large one.

Using trees

Trees always dominate the areas in which they grow, particularly if they have large or unusual leaves or especially bright and abundant flowers and fruits. Weeping willows, ornamental cherries, cedars or perhaps the handkerchief tree (*Davidia involucrata*) all have a very distinctive appearance but can be overpowering when used in a very small garden.

Tree shapes and their leaf textures can create quite distinctive moods. A group of upright trees like Lombardy poplars (*Populus nigra* 'Italica') and the fastigiate beech (*Fagus sylvatica* 'Fastigiata) give a feeling of vigour whereas a weeping willow such as *Salix × chrysocoma* or a birch such as *Betula pendula* 'Youngii' produce a calmer, almost sad, atmosphere. Many trees have associations that reinforce these moods, such as the familiar yew (*Taxus baccata*) which is commonly found in graveyards.

When choosing trees, you must consider their rates of growth and the size they will reach after, say, 30 years. Do not be tempted to choose a vigorous grower that will have to be unnaturally restrained by the continual pruning needed to stop it overshadowing everything else. Some of the so-called 'dwarf' conifers can be useful plants because they are not really miniature forms but very slow growing, although there are some real pygmies!

The rate of growth of all plants depends partly on their nature and partly on the soil and climate in which they are growing. As a general rule, plants grow more quickly in

damp areas than in dry ones.

Another decision to make with trees is whether to grow deciduous ones (these lose their leaves in autumn), or to concentrate on evergreens. Both have their good points as well as their disadvantages. The best policy is to grow some of each, preferably intermingled. Evergreens tend to be monotonous as they change little from season to season, apart from their flowers and fruits, but they do provide a year-round visual screen as well as an effective windbreak. Deciduous trees are generally more attractive during the warmer months, but are not so good for a shelter or a screen.

Leaf size and shape is important too. Large-leaved trees such as the Indian bean tree (*Catalpa bignonioides*) can be used to reduce the scale of adjoining properties and high walls, whereas plants with relatively small leaves like birches and willows can sometimes give the illusion of making a garden bigger. Round-leaved trees like

limes (*Tilia × europaea* for example) give quite a different effect from those with long narrow leaves like many of the willows.

The feathery leaves of the false acacia (*Robinia pseudoacacia*) and the tropical appearance of fairly hardy palms such as *Trachycarpus fortunei* create their own special atmospheres.

Downy-leaved trees such as the whitebeam (*Sorbus aria*) and those with shiny red leaves like the scarlet oak *(Quercus coccinea)* have their uses.

In the autumn, even the dullest green-leaved trees can turn into torches of red, yellow and orange before their leaves finally fall.

In winter, deciduous trees can be fairly monotonous but there are several varieties that have very attractive barks on trunks and larger branches. Nearly all of the birches have thin, peeling, light-coloured barks, the best being the paper birch (*Betula papyrifera*), but the red-barked ornamental

In this low-maintenance garden, islands of lush foliage are scattered across the basic rectangle of quarry tiles and stone paving. Wild flowers and weeds have been allowed to grow unchecked and the various groups of plants spill haphazardly across the courtyard. In the foreground, a Japanese pagoda tree (Sophora japonica) *is underplanted with thyme, lavender and* Gypsophila repens *while a tamarix dominates the section beyond.*

Above *One of the best-known and most popular of the barberries is the South American* Berberis darwinii. *The holly-like leaves and rich orange-yellow flowers make a superb spring-time display.*

Right *Hornbeam* (Carpinus betulus) *can grow into a sizeable tree but also responds well to clipping into a dense hedge. Although deciduous, its dead leaves remain through the winter while decorative, yellow catkins appear in the spring.*

cherry (*Prunus serrula*) is also very attractive. However, if you really wish to brighten up your garden in winter try the autumn cherry (*Prunus subhirtella* 'Autumnalis Rosea'), which flowers on the bare branches from mid-autumn to mid-spring on all but the coldest days.

Other aspects of trees include the movements they make in the wind. Whole branches of beeches sway like waves in the sea, and the leaves of the aspen (*Populus tremula*) are never still. These movements are often accompanied by gentle, rustling sounds that make these trees even more delightful.

Using shrubs

There may only be room for two or three trees in your garden but no garden is too small for shrubs. These are many-stemmed woody plants that can be deciduous or evergreen, and slow or fast growing.

Many have the virtue of tolerance to pruning to achieve a desired shape. In most cases pruning increases their vigour, though you should take professional advice if you are in any doubt as to where, when and how often to prune. They may not need annual pruning.

Shrubs have as great a range of flower, fruit and leaf colours as do the trees. Their barks include almost the whole range of colours and textures. The red-barked dogwood (*Cornus alba*) has several varieties of garden merit, particularly the brilliant, red-stemmed 'Sibirica' and the shiny, black-purple barked 'Kesselringii'. Several of the willows that can grow equally well as trees or shrubs have brilliant orange, green,

and rubble. Flower colours include purest whites, deep purple-reds, magentas, blues and pale lilacs. Although deciduous and occasionally cut right down to the ground by heavy frosts, it keeps its leaves throughout the winter in sheltered areas.

Shrubs are frequently grown as hedges, which can be clipped to give a formal and symmetrical shape or pruned only occasionally to give a more natural and informal look. Hedge shrubs can be quick-growing such as the hawthorn (*Crataegus monogyna*) Leyland cypress (× *Cupressocyparis leylandii*), both of which soon produce an impenetrable screen. Others are much slower, such as the Box (*Buxus sempervirens*), cotton lavender (*Santolina chamaecyparissus*) and lavender (*Lavandula* spp.).

Hedges can be used instead of walls and fences to mark the outer boundaries of your garden, but they are also used for subdividing the garden itself. As a background to a colourful border, hedges could be used much more within a garden than they are. Although technically trees, both hornbeam (*Carpinus betulus*) and beech (*Fagus sylvatica*) can be trimmed to form hedges and are excellent as a foil to a border because they retain most of their dead brown leaves throughout the autumn into late spring. Even the dull privet (*Ligustrum ovalifolium*) particularly if interspersed with the golden privet (variety 'Aurea') has its uses as it generally keeps its leaves throughout the year and will tolerate poor, dry soils. The golden form is an especially attractive plant.

Using climbers and wall plants

Climbing and scrambling plants have two quite different uses in a garden. You may have the problem of an ugly structure that you want to hide rather than spend a lot of time and money on demolishing – a climber scrambling all over it is the solution. The Russian vine (*Polygonum baldschuanicum*) and the ornamental or edible grapes (*Vitis coignetiae, V. Labrusca* and *V. vinifera*) are very useful for this purpose as they are such quick-growers once established. Also very good are the scarlet, autumn-leaved Virginia creepers (*Parthnenocissus quinquefolia* and its relatives) and the hop (*Humulus lupulus*).

The other use of climbers is as decorative plants in their own right. The place in the garden where there is no space for a tree or shrub to grow may be ideal for a climbing plant. A light, wooden trellis or arch can be quickly covered with such well-known climbers as clematis. The first to flower in late spring on walls, over sheds and garages and among the branches of the still bare fruit trees is *Clematis montana*

Left *Clematis is one of the most useful and diverse groups of climbing plants. All of them need support of some kind and are ideal for growing on trellis work, pergolas or other wall shrubs.*

or yellow stems. Generally, these colours develop better on new growth and this should be encouraged by cutting away the older stems.

One of the most useful groups of shrubs are the barberries (*Berberis* spp.). Many are armed with prickles that deter dogs, cats and small children, and most thrive in any soil. They either have attractively coloured leaves such as the purple *Berberis thunbergii* 'Atropurpurea' or brightly-coloured flowers and equally attractive fruits such as the orange-flowered, purple-fruited *Berberis darwinii.*

All gardens should include at least one butterfly bush (*Buddleia davidii*) as it is so attractive to butterflies and other flying insects when it is in flower. All varieties will grow in almost any situation, including very shallow and dry soils or among old stones

Above Clematis × jackmanii *'Superba', with fine purple blooms up to 15cm (6in) across, flowers in midsummer.*

Above right *Most of the honeysuckles (*Lonicera *spp.) are vigorous and sweet-scented climbers that will fill the evening air with their fragrance.*

(particularly attractive in its pink form 'Rubens'). It is soon followed by the larger flowered, deep blue or pink Jackmanii hybrids and the delicate-looking species such as *Clematis viticella* and the yellow asiatic types (*Clematis tangutica* and *C. orientalis*). Even the native old man's beard (*Clematis vitalba*) can be grown because, although its flowers are not very spectacular, the feathery-headed fruits are very attractive in the autumn.

For winter interest you could try growing *Rubus cockburnianus* which has purple stems covered with a white waxy bloom (the overall appearance is of white stems). For winter flowers, the winter jasmine (*Jasminum nudiflorum*) is very useful and, in the summer, its close relative *J. officinale* is a must because it is so sweetly scented.

Many gardeners do not approve of variegated or non-green plants as they consider them to be unnatural, but they have many merits. For brightening up a dark corner one of the variegated ivies (*Hedera helix*) such as 'Goldheart', 'Discolor', 'Glacier' and 'Tricolor', or the less hardy but more vigorous and larger-leaved *Hedera canariensis* 'Variegata' (also known as 'Gloire de Marengo') can look particularly good. Golden-leaved forms like *H. Helix* 'Buttercup', and the Japanese honeysuckle (*Lonicera japonica* 'Aure-oreticulata') with its delicate yellow-veined leaves and long-lasting fragrant flowers, are also very useful plants.

Pride of place among garden climbers must be given to the roses. There are hundreds of varieties available today and many more are being introduced into cultivation each year (it is always worth consulting a specialist rose nursery if you can). Most of them produce illustrated catalogues and with roses the camera does not lie – the flowers are usually just as bright and colourful as in their photographs.

Although roses are generally grown only for their flowers, some of them also produce large, bright vermillion hips in the autumn. Roses are deciduous but the extremely vigorous and large flowered 'Mermaid' keeps its shiny green leaves throughout most of the winter. Perhaps the most beautiful of all climbing roses is 'Mme Grégoire Staechelin', which thrives on a north-facing wall and bears heavily-scented, coral-pink flowers shaded with crimson.

An old-established rose of particular use for arches and pergolas is 'Albertine', with its coppery-pink flowers turning brown on the stem quite a time before being shed. Although it requires more support than most climbers, 'Zéphirine Drouhin' is very useful, flowering over a very long period.

You will see from rose growers' catalogues that many favourite hybrid tea roses are also available as climbers. Examples include 'Crimson Glory', 'Gloire de Dijon', 'Mme Butterfly' and 'Shot Silk'.

Rambling roses are better grown over arches and other frameworks as they are liable to become mildewed if there is not much air circulating around them. Their flowers are usually smaller than those of climbers, but there are generally many more of them. Probably the best known is the blush pink 'Dorothy Perkins', which is also available with a deep crimson flower (variety 'Excelsa'). The most vigorous rose of all is the rambling 'Wedding Day' with very fragrant, creamy-yellow flowers soon becoming white as they open. It will grow up to 5m (16ft) in a single season. *Rosa filipes* 'Kiftsgate' is similar and, in some gardens, even more vigorous.

Using herbaceous plants and bulbs

Non-woody herbaceous plants that usually die down in winter after flowering, form the bulk of the planting in most gardens. They can be perennials which means they will grow again next spring, biennials which need two years to complete their life cycle, or annuals that carry out all their functions from seed through germination, growth and flowering, to ripening and shedding their seeds in about nine months.

Bulbs, corms, and tubers are a special type of perennial. Many vegetables are biennials and are harvested in their first year, before they flower. Decorative biennials such as wallflowers (*Cheiranthus cheiri*) and sweet williams (*Dianthus barbatus*) are usually kept in the nursery border and planted out late in their first season to a position where they will flower the following year.

In different climates these differences between annuals, biennials, and perennials may not be so clear-cut. But for garden purposes they should be grown as listed in most books and catalogues.

It is very difficult to give an account of herbaceous plants and their specific uses without producing long lists, but it is reassuring to know that there is always one or more available for any specific purpose in any soil type or microclimate.

Above *'Goldheart' is a distinctive, variegated ivy* (Hedera helix) *with elegantly pointed leaves and attractive colouring.*

Left *Two richly-scented roses, 'Albertine' (a rambler) and 'Zéphirine Drouhin' (a climber) enhance the old-world atmosphere of this cottage garden.*

Even in one group of herbaceous plants, for example the chrysanthemums, daffodils, or dianthus, there are many separate species each with its own preferences and garden uses. As well as increasing the range of flower colours, plant breeders also aim to change the behaviour of herbaceous plants. You can now buy chrysanthemums that can be grown as house plants, as greenhouse specimens for the cut flower market, and as outdoor border plants. Chrysanthemums of one type or another are now available to produce flowers throughout the year.

Early-flowering daffodils such as 'February Gold' and 'Peeping Tom' extend the daffodil season from late winter to late spring.

Another example of the plant breeders' work is the sweet pea (*Lathyrus odoratus*) which is now available in any flower colour other than true yellow, either as a tall, vigorous, herbaceous climber or as a dwarf border plant.

It is a good idea to write down the names and features of plants you see in a garden or read about in a catalogue but, before you finally decide to buy any, check again in a reference book to make sure they are suitable for your soil and site. This checking is important because if one plant was, say, a half hardy annual, it would not be suitable for planting out until all danger of frost was over.

Your list of plants should be divided into groups based on their features. You could list them according to flower colour, scent, height, or cost. But it is probably better to list them under their possible garden uses.

Make a special note of plants that have a well-defined shape such as the giant rhubarb (*Gunnera manicata*) and some of the spurges (for example *Euphorbia wulfenii*). Plants of this type are called 'architectural' or 'sculptural' plants.

A very useful list can be made of plants that can be depended on to succeed in almost any garden. They may be common plants or much rarer ones, but the quality they have in common is that they are guaranteed to flower each year whatever the weather. The garden cranesbills (*Geranium* spp. – not to be confused with the indoor, scarlet geraniums, correctly called pelargoniums) are very dependable and available in a range of colours. Russell lupins (*Lupinus polyphyllus*), day lilies (*Hemerocallis*), Japanese anemones, plantain lilies (*Hosta* spp.), and red hot pokers (*Kniphofia* spp.) are also reliable.

Decorative vegetables can form an unusual group. Asparagus, ornamental beetroot, globe artichoke, maize and red and variegated cabbages, are all distinctive.

All of these can be eaten as vegetables but are equally at home in the flower border. Culinary herbs form another group of plants equally at home in the flower garden or vegetable patch. Marjoram (*Origanum vulgare*), sage (*Salvia officinalis*), tarragon (*Artemisia dracunculus*), and any of the mints could be put into the list.

Another useful category is plants for special conditions, such as damp sites. This list should include the double buttercup (*Ranunculus acris* 'Flore Pleno'), globe flower (*Trollius* spp.) and monkey flower (*Mimulus luteus*). Other lists could be for pollution-resistant plants or those suitable for cold and exposed sites or the salt-laden air of the seaside.

Ground cover plants

A trend in gardens today is not to have patches of bare earth between plants but to use low-growing scramblers or mat-forming plants as a ground cover. The advantages of these are that weeds are suppressed once the ground cover is established, therefore reducing the tiring tasks of hoeing and hand weeding. The taller plants may benefit from a permanent, moisture-retaining 'mulch' around their roots. Ground cover plants are also attractive in their own right, often bearing colourful flowers or decorative leaves.

Lawns are a form of ground cover using a wide variety of grasses, many of them especially bred for this purpose. However, in the Middle Ages lawns were often made with other plants such as thyme (*Thymus serpyllum*) and chamomile (*Chamaemelum nobile*, syn. *Anthemis nobile*). These are not as hard-wearing as grass, and are difficult to weed and maintain but, when they are walked on, the crushed leaves release a very pleasant perfume.

In rose borders and between small shrubs, the Russian comfrey (*Symphytum grandiflorum*), St John's wort (*Hypericum*), epimediums, and periwinkles (*Vinca major* and *V. minor*) establish themselves very well. If the taller plants are close together and cast deep shade, you should consider a ground cover plant that naturally grows on the floor of woodlands. *Pachysandra terminalis* and the yellow deadnettle (*Galeobdolon luteum*) can be used. Damp soils can be covered well with creeping jenny (*Lysimachia nummularia*), or with any of the many forms of bugle (*Ajuga* spp.) that are available.

You should experiment to see what will grow as ground cover in your garden. Even those plants that you normally consider to be weeds may become acceptable if they are not too vigorous or do not spread to other parts of your plot.

By choosing plants that fit together in a unified colour scheme – blue with white and pink with grey for example – or those that have strong leaf shapes and textures, a herbaceous border can be turned into a striking design feature.

GARDEN FEATURES

Your choice of furniture and decoration will create a very individual atmosphere in your garden and, according to your lifestyle, you can turn it into a calm retreat, an outdoor dining room or a children's play area.

Walls, fences, plants, and paving will give a garden its basic shape and character, but the finishing touches like garden furniture, lighting, or perhaps a fountain or a pergola will make it look complete.

Tables and chairs for sitting out, a pool where you can enjoy the pleasures that water brings, a greenhouse, a garden-shed, interesting plant containers, and garden lights are all possibilities. Obviously any project that involves mains electricity in the garden calls for professional help but you can install low-voltage lights and pumps yourself (the transformer is kept indoors and only a low-voltage cable is used outside). All the other projects should be within the scope of a keen do-it-yourselfer.

Whatever the garden feature you tackle, there are two important principles: plan exactly what you require before you start, and try not to compromise on the quality of materials you use. Buy the best materials within your budget. This does not necessarily mean that you have to buy new materials, as old ones may often be as good. However, you must always be wary of 'special offers' at ridiculously low prices. The initial result may appear satisfactory but the feature may only have a short life. A good example would be a very cheap greenhouse which might last only a few years. Also remember that, if you do not have the money now, many of the garden features can be added from one year to the next over quite a period of time.

Pergolas

A pergola is essentially a series of arches linked together, generally over a paved area but frequently along a walkway of any type. The upright supports and the overhead beams can be all of the same size and material, but usually it is the 'roof' which is emphasized. An overhead framework gives the illusion of more floor space than there really is and, therefore, a pergola is a very useful feature for a small garden.

A pergola can be free-standing within the garden, or it can adjoin the home like a patio-overhead, to form a half-way point between an indoor sun-lounge and the outdoor garden itself. It will provide some shelter and shade as well as being a place on which plants may grow. A pergola could also be considered as a very cheap type of house extension.

Of course, a pergola is not much help in really bad weather, but a well-made one with a good covering of plants will let you sit and even eat out-of-doors from mid-spring to mid-autumn. If the pergola is south facing and enclosed on two or three sides by the house walls or boundary fences, it could even be quite pleasant to sit there on bright winter day.

Pergolas are very useful design features to include if a house has a monotonous outside wall or has a very irregular outline. Built along a straight wall, the inclusion of a pergola makes an easy way to disguise the dullness, particularly once it is covered with climbing plants. In the same way, odd spaces between walls and a shed or garage can be brought into use.

Where a pergola is built alongside the house, the adjoining indoor room can be floored with a material similar in colour and texture to that used under the pergola itself, so that a sense of 'unified space' is achieved. In the summer, the difference in being 'indoors' or 'outdoors' would seem to disappear, again giving the illusion of more space. However, you should remember that the outdoor paved area will be subject to very bad conditions in the depths of the coldest and wettest winters: it should be frost resistant, non-slippery, and laid with a slight fall to shed water so that a pool does not form on it.

If the pergola is to be built next to your house, it will look better if it is designed to reflect the materials of the building. If the house is made of brick, for example, the pergola supports should be brick also, though metal is quite acceptable with many materials. You should also make sure that the pergola bears some relationship to the lines of the adjoining window and doors. As a general rule, the top of the pergola should be just above the lintel of the ground-floor window or door frame.

If you are having a new house built, it

Opposite *A delightful corner has been created in this garden by using two simple features: an arbour of roses and a decorative stone vase.*

Above *A pergola can be built as an extension to the house or to make a shady retreat in the larger garden.*

Above right *A paved yard can be brightened up by a display of shrubs and summer bedding annuals planted in suitable containers.*

might be worth trying to persuade the builder to extend outside the upstairs floor beams to form the overhead timbers of the pergola.

If you have small children make sure that the pergola does not become an easy route from an upstairs bedroom! Nevertheless, it should always be a strong structure and not just a set of poles or planks loosely nailed together. Ideally, it should be able to support a child's swing or an adult hammock.

The pergola itself generally looks better when it is a fairly plain structure without too much ornamental brickwork; it is the plants that grow on it that give its particular qualities. Occasionally, it may be difficult to design a plain pergola to look right – say, alongside a house which is old and highly ornate. In this case a trellis can be used to considerable effect.

Using containers and ornaments

Although most of your plants will be in the garden itself and planted in the soil, there is always room for plants in containers. Most greenhouse plants and indoor pot-plants will benefit from some time out-of-doors in a sheltered space during the summer. These can be arranged and re-arranged at will to suit the mood of the garden and to make the most of what is available.

There are also plants that grow better outdoors, if kept in pots or larger containers (sometimes referred to as 'planters'). Some plants only flower and fruit well when their roots are restricted. The best known example of this is the edible fig (*Ficus carica*) which fruits very well when grown in a sawn-off wooden barrel or large urn.

When grown in the garden, the position of a plant is fixed but displays in a planter can be moved to the most appropriate spot for each season. Planters are also very useful for growing plants in parts of the garden where there is no soil or where it would be difficult to have an open flower bed of any size.

It is possible to buy a wide range of pots and planters, but you can have fun making them yourself. An old coal-scuttle, chimney-pot or wheelbarrow can be used as long as there is some outlet hole for surplus water to drain away. If you are lucky enough to have an old stone sink or even a newer type glazed earthenware one, you could create a miniature landscape by making a sink garden of dwarf plants.

Plant containers need not always have plants in them to be attractive in a garden. They can be treated as 'sculptures' and in many ways are more appropriate than many of the modern glass-fibre or concrete replicas of classical statues. Modern abstract sculpture or carefully placed boulders and unusually shaped driftwood can be used, but brightly-painted garden gnomes or decorative features need more thought before they are introduced.

Water in the garden

Water features have been used in gardens for well over two thousand years. Sometimes you may be lucky enough to have a natural pool or even a small stream running through your plot. If you are particularly fortunate you may even have a river or canal at the bottom of your garden, though this is unlikely.

In such cases however, remember that you must not divert the water flow or enlarge a river bed or bank without permission from the local water authority. It is not only illegal but could have an effect on the river's ability to cope with flood water. Also, you should not pump water out of a river or canal to irrigate your garden or to fill your pond unless you have obtained permission beforehand. In most areas, too, you will require a special licence to use a hose-pipe or garden sprinkler with mains water, even if only a couple of times a year.

As well as being decorative, a garden water feature can serve the useful purpose of lowering the air temperature around it on a hot day. A pool placed in your overall garden design serves not only as a focal point but as a line between other features. Water can create a variety of moods both in your garden and in the users of the garden. An upright, spouting fountain gives a sense of vigour and continuing energy whereas a very still pool, with a glass-like surface reflecting the water-side plants, suggests something very tranquil and contemplative.

A gently bubbling flow, even though powered by an electrical circulating pump, may recall a range of early childhood memories. Today the sound of a gurgling water feature can camouflage the noise of the traffic and industry outside and may even drown the sound of neighbours.

The combination of plants and design features such as containers or figurines can be used to add a decorative touch on the small or grand scale and can be simple or highly ornate.

Elegance is the keynote in this classically designed patio which combines a unified planting scheme with the coolness of a small water garden and white-painted furniture.

There are certain rules to remember when siting a garden pool. Water should always have some direct sunlight on most of its surface for at least an hour each day, preferably for much longer. Water plants require good light to enable them to grow and flower.

Ideally, pools should not be too near trees that drop large numbers of leaves in the autumn. Grass-clippings, dead leaves or any other organic matter must not be allowed to accumulate in a pool because they quickly foul the water and make it unsuitable for plants and fish. Never use a pool to clean or rinse garden tools and never shake out a fertilizer bag over it in the hope that this will help the plants.

When a pool is first made and stocked, you will find that for some time it will look quite unnatural being either very clear or very cloudy. However, sooner or later it will settle down and the clear water become slightly cloudy or the very cloudy water become clearer. In hot weather it may suddenly become murky almost overnight only to become very much clearer just as suddenly a few days later. This is because minute single-celled plants called algae multiply very rapidly when the conditions are right but die off quickly when they have used up their food supply. However, you need not worry as these natural processes gradually lead to a 'balanced' environment in your pool where the plants, snails and fishes are all living in harmony.

To encourage the natural balancing of a pool you should first of all plant plenty of submerged oxygenating plants, preferably in the plastic mesh baskets sold for this purpose (clay flower pots can be just as good but tend to topple over more easily). Also try to introduce plants with floating leaves, such as water-lilies, as soon as possible, as the reduced light reaching the water below will also help to inhibit the algae that cause green water. At this stage you can add water snails and water insects. But there is no need to go to much trouble; before long various types of water beetle will have found their way into your pool.

It is best to wait for about a month after planting before introducing any fish. Although large specimens of Japanese Koi carp are very expensive, small ones are much cheaper and they grow quickly. Goldfish, too, are bright and interesting even though they lack the spectacular colouring and size of Koi carp, and they are much cheaper.

Do not be tempted to overfeed any type of fish: in a well-balanced pool with adequate and variable planting there will be enough insects and other pool life to make it unnecessary to feed them at all for most of the year (except, perhaps, early autumn).

Try not to overstock the pool. As a rough guide, one medium-sized fish for every square metre of water surface is about right. If there are more than this they will suffer in the summer when high water temperature will reduce the dissolved oxygen content just at the time when the fish are at their most active and, therefore, require most oxygen.

Pools can be formal or natural-looking. A formal pool with a square or rectangular shape, for example, is useful in some gardens as it lends itself to being sited in almost any position, whereas a natural pond is more limited in this respect. A formal pool can be raised above the general garden level and its surrounds can be used as a seat. This is a useful feature as it reduces the chance of small children falling in.

Never leave very young children or very old and infirm grown-ups near any pool unless they are under supervision.

An informal pool is probably the cheaper

to make as you can readily buy pre-formed plastic shapes to place in a pit dug out beforehand and lined with damp sand. Alternatively you can use a flexible pool liner; these easily adapt to the contours of an informal shape, though it is wise to avoid tight or unnecessary curves. To finish it off the top edges are best covered with paving slabs.

Garden buildings

Unless they are very large, permanently fixed to the walls of your house, or that of a neighbour, or sited in the front garden, you do not need planning permission from your local council for any garden building. Nevertheless it is always worth enquiring from the local planning officer to make sure you are not breaking any regulations. Some buildings are covered by building regulations, but those provided by a reputable company should meet the specifications.

Greenhouses, conservatories, summerhouses and garden sheds can all be bought ready-made, generally in kit-form – all you have to do is to bolt them together, although you may have to provide the foundations.

Before deciding which to buy, send for as many different manufacturers' catalogues as possible. List the features you would

A generously sized, but informal, pool fits naturally into its lush surroundings while the small pool-side statue makes a delightful focal point right at the water's edge.

Above *Storage can be a problem in a garden and the addition of a small shed may prove a great asset. There are many different styles to choose from but most will need fitting out with some shelves, hanging racks and a work surface or table.*

like, including size, shape, ease of erection and special facilities as well as cost and the annual maintenance required. Then consult all the catalogues and see as many as possible of the buildings erected at the manufacturer's showground or garden centres. Do not always buy the cheapest model; it may not last long and may be very difficult to adapt to your own special requirements.

The most important building must be the shed in which you store your garden equipment, perhaps your seeds and, if it is frost-proof (very few are!) some of your crops like apples and potatoes. If you have garden tools of reasonable quality, they deserve adequate protection.

Shelves, racks, a work-top and storage bins should be found in all toolsheds, though these are features that you will probably have to add yourself. As some tools like powered mowers will be heavy, you should avoid having steps by the door. Otherwise, it is helpful to keep a wide plank of wood handy so that you can push the mower in easily.

After a shed, the most useful garden building is a greenhouse. It can be used solely to bring-on seedlings for summer bedding, followed by tomatoes and cucumbers until early autumn, However, most greenhouses also attract many other 'occupants' and are used for all sorts of other purposes, not all connected with growing plants! A deck-chair in a heated greenhouse in winter is an ideal retreat

from a busy house! Greenhouses are used as a hospital for sick house-plants, a place to keep a collection of cacti and succulents, to produce extra-early pickings of daffodils and other spring flowers, and to house tender summer crops such as aubergines, peppers, and melons.

Greenhouses can be free-standing or 'lean-to'. A free-standing greenhouse might be easier to fit into the overall garden design. Traditional greenhouse shapes are not particularly attractive, but this will not matter if you can find an inconspicuous position (avoid tucking it away at the end of the garden – providing a power supply and water will be more of a problem).

Some less traditional designs, such as dome-shaped and octagonal greenhouses can be made into a feature, even on a patio.

A lean-to may provide less favourable growing conditions for some plants, but because it is likely to be against the house it is likely to be used more. Some modern lean-to greenhouses are almost like conservatories.

If you can afford one, a conservatory or sunroom is a very valuable addition to any house. Although they are meant mainly for people, conservatories are ideal places to grow plants. You can create a tropical-looking scene in which you are cut off from the outside world. Or you can stock it with palms, ferns, and aspidistras and pretend you are back at the turn of the century!

If space or money are the limiting factors, you can always make a 'picture-

Right *Modern metal-framed greenhouses can be put up quite easily. If possible, the greenhouse should be placed on open ground, away from the main part of the garden but within reach of both power and water.*

Above left *At one time conservatories were the height of fashion and even town houses were graced with the addition of tiny, attractive sun rooms of distinctive style.*

Above *If a conservatory can be built against a brick wall which faces the sun, it will make an ideal place for growing tender plants and exotic trees.*

window' or 'plant-window' in which plants are grown either inside or outside the house window in a miniature greenhouse attached to the frame.

For a sheltered sitting-out space, a summerhouse can be surprisingly cheap and extremely versatile. You can treat a summerhouse as a building half-way between a greenhouse and a shed and, if it is large enough, it can be used for growing a selection of plants as well as storing garden equipment and providing a place to sit almost throughout the year. Do not expect plants to do very well, however. A summerhouse can be very hot or very cold in comparison with the home, and the light cannot compare with that in a greenhouse.

A summerhouse may be placed anywhere in a garden, but ideally it should receive sunlight for most of the day. Some shelter from the hottest mid-day summer sun is useful and it should not be in a very windy space. In order to make the most of the sunlight in smaller gardens, summer-houses can be built on a base which can be rotated to face the sun at different seasons of the year. This, however, is a very complex job and needs professional advice.

Garden lighting

Garden lighting is usually installed for the very practical reason of illuminating a garden path, gate, porch, or patio. It is always useful to have lighting in a garden shed or greenhouse. However, outdoor lights can be pretty as well as practical. And they can enable you to enjoy your garden when it is dark, and not just during the day.

As well as being very friendly and welcoming, it is helpful to have good lighting for garden paths, particularly where there is little or no street lighting. There is no need to install a full-sized, lamp-post – you can get a range of short-pillared lighting fitments. They usually have a reflecting shade which throws the light on to the ground in a wide circle so that you can see where you are walking without everything else being illuminated. To avoid excessive glare, they can also be fitted with frosted-glass shades.

If the main aim is to light an outside sitting area, there are many waterproof light fittings obtainable from larger garden centres and some electrical goods shops. Individual plants can be illuminated to emphasize their colour, leaf-shapes or textures. A single rotating spot-light is useful for this and its use is not confined to plants – a soft light playing on a frosty winter scene can be very effective.

Do not be tempted to bathe your garden with festoons of multi-coloured lights strung permanently across the trees. They rarely do more than bleach out the natural colours of the plants around them.

The secret of many of the really successful garden lighting schemes is to

Above *The dramatic effects of garden lighting can be used in a variety of ways. Bright colours will make decorative features in their own right, while plain fittings can be concealed among tall shrubs and trees to cast patterns through the foliage or provide stronger illumination below.*

ensure that the light source is hidden. A single beam of light shining on a statue or boulder, or on the surface of a pool can create an impressive as well as mysterious atmosphere.

It cannot be stressed too highly that all electrical light fittings used out of doors must be suitable for the job. Ordinary domestic fittings must not be used. All outdoor fittings must be waterproof and strong enough to withstand many more knocks than indoor types.

All electric wiring should be installed professionally, unless you are using a low-voltage system. Even if you feel sufficiently experienced to wire the lamps yourself, you

should get the whole system approved by a qualified electrician before you use it.

For a temporary effect or occasional use, it is not necessary to use electricity to light your garden. A range of bottled gas light fittings are available and, although they are not so decorative, they are very powerful and friendly for illuminating a barbecue or outside sitting area.

To create a romantic atmosphere, oil-lamps, flares and candles can be used. If you have a pool, try floating lit candles on pieces of wood. Always remember, however, that great care must be exercised if children or pets are around where there are hot surfaces or unguarded flames. Caution is

weather resistance. You can always take the furniture in and out of doors as you require it, but this is not practicable with items that are very heavy or require a lot of storage space.

The folding, traditional, brightly-striped canvas wooden deck-chair is always acceptable and easily stored. An alternative arrangement is to have the basic furniture outdoors all the time and just bring cushions and table coverings indoors when they are not needed.

Before finally deciding on the type of chair you want, you should think about how you will use it. If eating outdoors is likely to be the main use, upright chairs will be best. Deeply reclining loungers are most unsuitable for this, but they are ideal for sunbathing.

If you have robust trees in your garden, the old-fashioned hammock can make a very simple all-purpose seat, although you need to be fairly nimble to get in and out of it!

Most garden centres and departmental stores offer a range of different swinging seats and settees, usually with protective awnings to match.

Wood is a popular material for outside furniture and will last many years provided you remember to treat it with an annual coat of linseed oil, wood-preservative, or paint, depending on what was used on the original surface.

A really big wooden table is useful in any garden. A brightly-coloured tablecloth will quickly turn it into a picnic table, but for the rest of the time it can be used as a work-top or play surface.

The most durable of all garden furniture is that made from stone, brick, or concrete. It is not so comfortable as wood, being hard and cold in cool weather and hard and hot in the summer. However, it has the advantage of needing little or no maintenance and is easy to clean. If you have a barbecue area, brick or stone are the most suitable materials as they are least affected by the oil and fat that accompanies much outside eating.

Finally, do not assume that good garden furniture is only really for sophisticated gardens or wealthy gardeners. Many very serviceable, tough and attractive items can be made by the average do-it-yourself enthusiast. Make sure you use good timber and rust-proof nails, and always treat the wood with an appropriate preservative followed by a coat of linseed oil, (or if painted, a primer plus two undercoats before applying the top gloss). If you are not that good at carpentry, many items of garden furniture can be bought as easy-to-assemble kits at prices lower than ready-made pieces.

Left An informal garden setting is best matched by simple furniture and, if this can be built around existing features, it will make the placing look more natural. Furniture that will be constantly exposed to the elements should be made of sturdy materials (slatted surfaces are also practical as they allow rain water to drain off) while more delicate fittings should be brought indoors during bad weather.

also needed if such lighting is used during the summer months, when hot spells may have left nearby plants tinder-dry or, of course, if it is a windy evening!

Garden furniture

As 'outdoor living' has increased so has the range of outdoor furniture available to enable you to enjoy it. The choice of furniture should be influenced by the style of your garden. Tubular metal or moulded plastic is suitable for the ultra-modern garden but wickerwork is better for the more traditional retreat. Price and availability are important too, of course, but also take into account durability and

SAMPLE PLANS

All gardens are different in the problems they pose and the way they are planned and planted. From rooftops and balconies to a fully productive vegetable plot, the following pages illustrate the scope of design possibilities for almost any site.

Good design ideas often spring more readily to mind if they are developed from existing examples. Someone else's solution to a problem may suggest a modification that would help to solve a similar problem in your own garden.

A plan for someone else's garden can never be taken as a whole for your own; size, aspect, and soil are all likely to be different. But they can serve as a source of inspiration.

This final chapter shows you how other people have created their own successful gardens on a range of sites. Most of these sites presented some difficulties, and most of the owners had their own special requirements. Most of them also had a good idea of the sort of garden they wished to make and the atmosphere they wished to establish.

The sites covered by these plans range from a very steep slope to a flat penthouse roof, while individual requirements range from a herb garden to a jungle-like retreat in the middle of a city.

There is usually one central feature or focal point in each plan. Sometimes it is a plant or group of plants, but it is often a structure such as a pool.

You will get plenty of ideas from looking at these plans, but bear in mind that not only are no two sites identical, and that each individual will have different requirements, but also that no two garden designers, professional or amateur, will have the same solutions to the problems. Each garden shown is unique, in the same way that your garden is unique to you.

Hopefully each garden here has one feature you could adopt, but you must always make sure that your garden is designed as a complete entity and is not just a motley collection of other people's ideas.

Besides these illustrated gardens, it is always worth visiting any site 'in the flesh': it does not matter if it is large or small, private or public, good or bad (you will know what you want to avoid!). Visit places not only in late spring and during the summer months but also in the autumn and winter to see how they rate as all-year-round designs.

Remember that you will have to look out on your garden almost every day of the year and it should have something attractive and interesting in it at all seasons. Whenever possible, speak to the owners of the gardens you see to find out what the plots were like beforehand. Do not be afraid to inquire if their gardens are really what they wanted to achieve when they started out.

Let them tell you of the problems they have faced and how they have tried to solve them. There are booklets published that list all the major gardens of interest but you should not confine yourself to these. If you see an interesting or unusual garden anywhere, the owner may be pleased to show you around and talk about it.

Nowadays many of the big flower shows, such as that held in London, at Chelsea (in May), feature small gardens designed for particular clients or inspired by a particular theme. Some of these gardens are really no more than a good excuse to exhibit a large number of flowering plants often at unusual times, while others are filled with so many features that they could never be lived with. However, most of them are very good samples of the work of current garden designers and show what can be achieved in a short time provided you know clearly beforehand what you want to do. Unfortunately most of them require much more labour than you could provide to give their 'instant' effect, but they could be built by one person over a couple of years.

Old meets new

The great problem the owners, a young couple with a small child, faced with their garden was that it was only part of the original garden. The original eighteenth-century mansion was split up some time ago to form smaller dwellings and, so that each household had a plot of its own, the large garden was subdivided as well. Their piece was partly enclosed by a very high, south-facing wall covered with an old trellis and a well-established ivy. The working parents wanted a garden that required very little routine maintenance but would be suitable for their child to use at all times.

Opposite *Before settling on a design for your garden, it's always worth looking at the way other people have tackled the problem. Many useful ideas can be gleaned this way and, even if you do not want to follow a particular scheme exactly, you can pick out the themes that appeal to you or adjust the various features to suit your needs.*

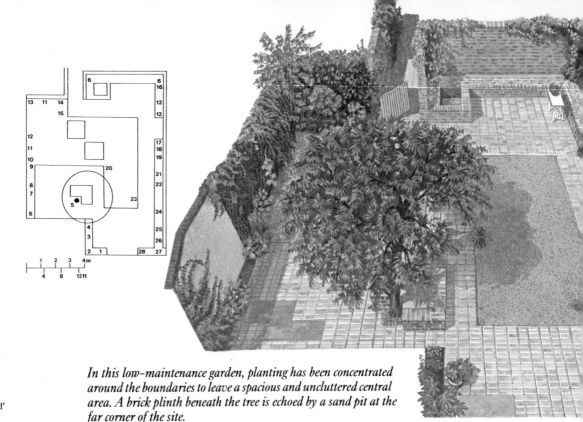

In this low-maintenance garden, planting has been concentrated around the boundaries to leave a spacious and uncluttered central area. A brick plinth beneath the tree is echoed by a sand pit at the far corner of the site.

There was a very small, stone-paved area already and this has been extended by using bricks similar in colour and texture to those making the south-facing wall. The large central area was covered by local gravel. At the edge, against a wall, were added a few plants of bamboo (*Arundinaria murielae*) and self-seeding, single-flowered hollyhocks (*Althaea rosea*) to provide seasonal colour and movement. Across the gravel, 'stepping stones' were made of small brick-paved squares.

The only significant plant in the garden when the owners arrived was a tall box elder (*Acer negundo*). This was retained and became the focal point, enhanced by building a brick plinth around part of the base of the trunk. This plinth is now used for sitting out and as a ledge for potted plants in the summer. The tree had very few low branches as the previous owners had lopped them away in the past. The result is a very useful 'umbrella' which is only penetrated by the heaviest showers in summer.

An unfortunate feature of the garden is that, for most of the year, it is far too shaded for many plants to develop their full potential. The decision was therefore made to concentrate on plants with distinctive forms and evergreen leaves in a variety of shapes and textures. One advantage of this is that the garden has colour and interest around the year and provides an attractive outlook from the house. For the odd splash of spring and summer colour, containers have been arranged around the terrace and these can be planted up with spring bulbs and annuals as required.

Above left *Planted in the gravel bed along a sunless wall is the graceful bamboo,* Arundinaria murielae. *Bright splashes of colour are provided by self-seeded hollyhocks* (Althaea).

Above *Interest is maintained throughout the year because of lush, evergreen planting. Here, the dark green foliage of* Choisya ternata *and* Euonymus radicans *contrast well with the variegated ivy.*

Left *The garden is linked to the path beyond by neat brick stepping stones across an area of gravel broken by the occasional plant.*

Some summer colour was possible at the end of the garden furthest from the house but, because this was the sunniest corner, it was decided to use the area for sitting, outdoor eating and sunbathing. A wide brick-bench seat with a raised sandpit was also built. When the child grows up, the pit can be used for barbecues or, perhaps planted with some summer annuals.

In all parts of the garden different types of climber have been encouraged to scramble over the walls. The result is that, after only three years, vigorous growers like ivy, clematis and jasmine already look as if they had been there for much longer.

Above *The miniature elegance of a window box contrasts with the rampant growth of a Virginia creeper which both covers the dull brick wall and provides a showy autumn display.*

Right and far right *Set against plain, white timber, strong foliage plants dominate this paved garden. Contrasting leaf shapes and colours provide a wealth of interest, especially in the shaded corner leading up to the house.*

A city jungle

There is always noise in the city and it is not possible to block it out completely. However, if all movement can be disguised and a tropical-look achieved it becomes quite easy to forget where you are once you relax in this sort of garden.

Like a true tropical jungle, the emphasis is not on flower colour but on a wide variety of plant and leaf sizes, shapes and textures.

The plants were also chosen for their different shades of green foliage. Access to the garden is from the house through a high level door and down a few steps. White timber steps and rails blend with the house cladding and emphasize the greens of the 'jungle' plants. There is also another entrance from the street along a narrow passage. To add interest to this route an old

cannon has been partly restored and is used as a piece of sculpture. Whichever way you enter the garden, you find yourself in a tropical, green room.

The garden is furnished very simply with white painted chairs, which again echo the house cladding and the steps.

The centre of the garden is paved with concrete slabs of several, very pale colours. The planting around it is not really as unplanned as the word 'jungle' would suggest. The position of each plant was drawn on the plan beforehand. A focal point is the bamboo (*Arundinaria japonica*) and the small pond next to it.

Cordyline australis, a spiky plant, and the palm *Trachycarpus fortunei* add to the jungle look. The raised bed in the centre has a very vigorous juniper and a couple of the

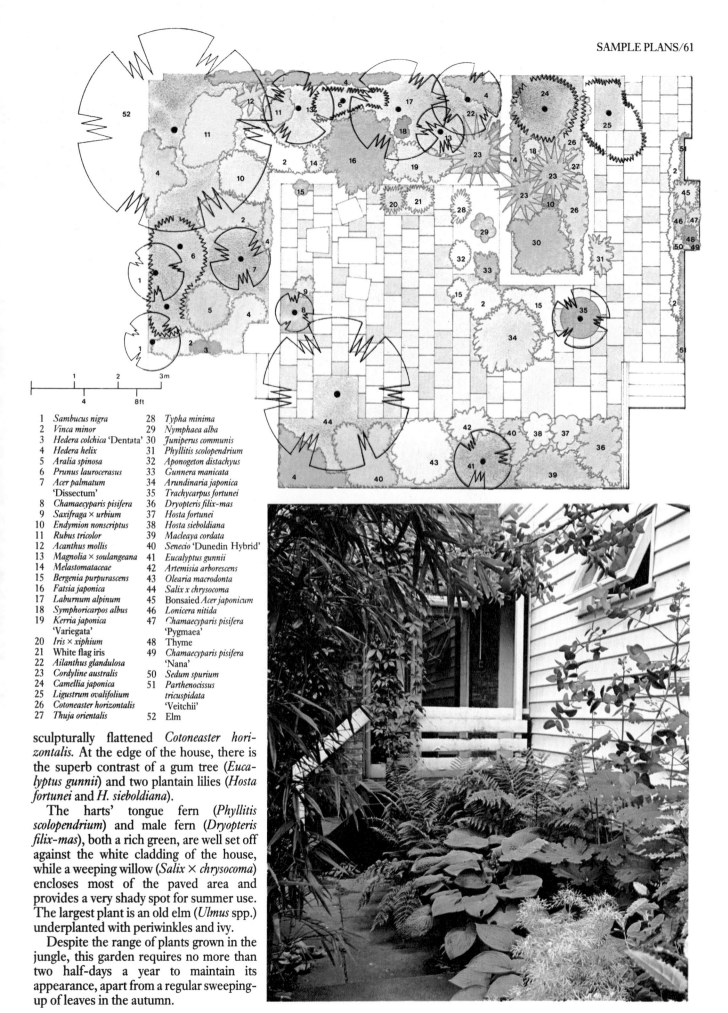

1 Sambucus nigra
2 Vinca minor
3 Hedera colchica 'Dentata'
4 Hedera helix
5 Aralia spinosa
6 Prunus laurocerasus
7 Acer palmatum
   'Dissectum'
8 Chamaecyparis pisifera
9 Saxifraga × urbium
10 Endymion nonscriptus
11 Rubus tricolor
12 Acanthus mollis
13 Magnolia × soulangeana
14 Melastomataceae
15 Bergenia purpurascens
16 Fatsia japonica
17 Laburnum alpinum
18 Symphoricarpos albus
19 Kerria japonica
   'Variegata'
20 Iris × xiphium
21 White flag iris
22 Ailanthus glandulosa
23 Cordyline australis
24 Camellia japonica
25 Ligustrum ovalifolium
26 Cotoneaster horizontalis
27 Thuja orientalis

28 Typha minima
29 Nymphaea alba
30 Juniperus communis
31 Phyllitis scolopendrium
32 Aponogeton distachyus
33 Gunnera manicata
34 Arundinaria japonica
35 Trachycarpus fortunei
36 Dryopteris filix-mas
37 Hosta fortunei
38 Hosta sieboldiana
39 Macleaya cordata
40 Senecio 'Dunedin Hybrid'
41 Eucalyptus gunnii
42 Artemisia arborescens
43 Olearia macrodonta
44 Salix x chrysocoma
45 Bonsaied Acer japonicum
46 Lonicera nitida
47 Chamaecyparis pisifera
   'Pygmaea'
48 Thyme
49 Chamaecyparis pisifera
   'Nana'
50 Sedum spurium
51 Parthenocissus
   tricuspidata
   'Veitchii'
52 Elm

sculpturally flattened *Cotoneaster horizontalis*. At the edge of the house, there is the superb contrast of a gum tree (*Eucalyptus gunnii*) and two plantain lilies (*Hosta fortunei* and *H. sieboldiana*).

The harts' tongue fern (*Phyllitis scolopendrium*) and male fern (*Dryopteris filix-mas*), both a rich green, are well set off against the white cladding of the house, while a weeping willow (*Salix × chrysocoma*) encloses most of the paved area and provides a very shady spot for summer use. The largest plant is an old elm (*Ulmus* spp.) underplanted with periwinkles and ivy.

Despite the range of plants grown in the jungle, this garden requires no more than two half-days a year to maintain its appearance, apart from a regular sweeping-up of leaves in the autumn.

1	Tomatoes	35	Camphor
2	Quince	36	Borage
3	Potatoes	37	Comfrey
4	Sweet corn	38	*Lavandula angustifolia*
5	Cucumber	39	*Lippoia citriodora*
6	Gourds	40	*Aster novi-belgii*
7	Courgettes	41	Beans
8	Marrows	42	Globe artichokes
9	Herbs, including: basil	43	Aubergines
	dill, sorrel, cayenne,	44	*Buddleia crispa*
	marjoram, parsley,	45	Loganberries
	chamomile, caraway,	46	Gooseberries
	lovage, fennel, sage,	47	Redcurrants
	rosemary, thyme, chervil,	48	*Vitis vinifera*
	bay, garlic, juniper,	49	*Clematis* × 'Vyvian Pennell'
	chives, bergamot, winter		
	savory, Russian		
	tarragon, French		
	tarragon, sweet cicely,		
	Artemisia arbrotanum		
	and *Artemisia absinthium*		
10	Chicory		
11	*Rhododendron* 'Elizabeth'		
12	*Lonicera japonica*		
13	Mint		
14	*Ficus carica*		
15	Rhubarb		
16	Parsnips		
17	Carrots		
18	*Tropaeolum majus*		
19	*Camellia* × *williamsii*		
20	*Rosa* 'Mme Alfred		
	Carrière' (climber)		
21	*Hedera helix* 'Goldheart'		
22	Lettuces		
23	Peppers		
24	*Fuchsia* 'Brilliant'		
25	*Olearia gunniana*		
26	Sprouts		
27	Strawberries		
28	Radishes		
29	Beetroot	50	Peach
30	Leeks	51	*Ailanthus glandulosa*
31	Broccoli	52	Apricot
32	Horseradish	53	*Wisteria sinensis*
33	Lemon balm	54	*Heliotropium* × *hybridum*
34	Angelica	55	Blackberry

Above *The dainty fronds of a 'tree of heaven' (Ailanthus glandulosa) are well set off by the white-washed wall at one end of this vegetable plot, while a large blackberry has been allowed to ramble across the adjoining section.*

Far right *The uniformity of the raised brick beds has been offset by contrasting foliage and occasional pot plants. Here, the spiky leaves of young globe artichokes grow next to aubergines and outdoor tomatoes and clumps of nasturtiums spill right across the concrete paving.*

The beauty of a kitchen garden

A kitchen garden supplying you and your family with fresh vegetables, fruit and herbs need not be just a rectangular plot with straight rows of plants. It can be designed to be ornamental as well as functional, and still produce just the same amount of crops. A well-designed kitchen garden could rival a flower bed in attractiveness at various times of the year.

The owners of this garden took it over when it had been derelict for some time. The original greenhouse had been vandalized and glass and debris were scattered all over the place. The garden was originally part of a much larger walled garden but, fortunately, the owners had the sunniest south-facing corner.

The first year was spent in clearing a small area of unwanted weeds and removing the broken glass. This area had once been a small herb patch and a few herb plants still survived. To their surprise these herbs started to flourish again and this encouraged the owners to clear up the whole area to grow fruit and vegetables. The old garden walls were whitewashed and the greenhouse repaired and re-glazed. It was decided not to restore the

rows of brick-based garden frames but to use the bases for raised vegetable-beds.

The owners were also very fortunate in that a river bordered one side of the garden. Among the rubbish that had been tipped into the river were several old wooden barrels and a park bench. These were rescued and restored for use in the garden.

The plants include a few partly ornamental ones like Chinese asters (*Callistephus sinensis*), nasturtiums (*Tropaeolum majus*) and fuchsias which are grown along the edges of the vegetable-beds and in large flower pots. On the walls, decorative climbers such as ivies, clematis and wisteria provide colour and interest. The grape vine and blackberries provide plenty of edible fruit.

In front of the wall tomatoes thrive, as do fruit trees such as apricots and peaches. Soft fruit which grows well include loganberries, red currants and gooseberries. A 'Brown Turkey' fig (*Ficus carica*), planted in a large barrel to restrict its roots and encourage fruiting, grows in the shelter of the south wall.

The vegetables in the raised bed provide crops at all times of the year. As the garden gets direct sun for most of the day and is

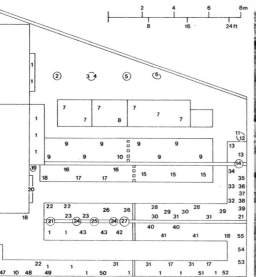

well sheltered, productivity is high. Some of the more exotic vegetables cultivated successfully are courgettes, sweet corn, peppers and aubergines.

Perhaps the most striking thing about this garden is the enormous variety of herbs that are grown – over 30 at the last count. Many of these are characteristically scented, such as camphor, lemon balm, and absinthe, which makes sitting out in this garden such a pleasure.

The overall effect of the garden is predominantly a green haven but the annuals in summer and fruits from late summer onwards provide splashes of colour over a long period.

The garden is built as a series of shallow terraces retained by dark-painted timber walls. The regularity of hedgerows of box and rosemary is softened by colourful groups of pansies, primulas and other annuals.

Terracing a steep site

Very few gardens are on an absolutely flat site, most having a slight slope in one direction or a few hummocks and hollows scattered around the plot. All of these give you great scope to plan your ideal garden. However, there are some sites with such steep slopes that you are quite restricted in what you can do. This garden rises very sharply from the house which is at the very bottom of the slope.

The first priority here was to counteract the feeling that the garden is just about to topple over or slide down into the house. The owners of the site illustrated here decided to overcome this problem by making the main entrance to the garden from the first floor of the house rather than from the ground floor. They built a timber bridge spanning the red-brick, sitting-out area at basement level. From the bridge,

you enter the garden at the second terrace level and go down to the paved area. The terraces stretch across the whole width of the garden making it appear much wider and less steep than it really is. Green-stained timber walls retain the terraces and the width of the garden is emphasized by plantings of clipped box to make horizontal lines of dwarf hedge.

It is basically a fairly rigid layout, as it must be on such an awkward site. No attempt was made to hide the rigidity and in fact this feature has been enhanced by growing sculptural plants such as New Zealand flax (*Phormium tenax*) and African lilies (*Agapanthus* 'Headbourne Hybrids') in bold clumps. To give additional colour several perennials and annuals flower from late spring to early autumn and, nestling in among the various enclosures there are many little corners for sitting or sunbathing.

Bottom *Looking down towards the brick-paved area by the house highlights the enclosed garden atmosphere.*

Below *In this multi-level garden the main emphasis is horizontal, though trees like the flowering cherry in the foreground create interest.*

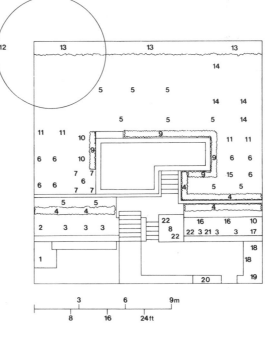

1 *Citrus sinensis*
2 *Phormium tenax*
3 Succulents
4 *Buxus sempervirens*
5 *Fragaria chiloensis*
6 *Raphiolepis* 'Coates Crimson'
7 *Agapanthus campanulatus*
8 *Prunus* 'Shirotae'
9 *Erica × darleyensis*
10 *Viburnum × burkwoodii*
11 *Chaenomeles speciosa*
12 *Quercus ilex*
13 *Ligustrum japonicum*
14 *Arbutus unedo*
15 *Fagus sylvatica purpurea*
16 *Rosmarinus officinalis*
17 *Laurus nobilis*
18 *Primula malacoides*
19 *Betula papyrifera*
20 *Camellia japonica*
21 Parsley
22 *Viola × wittrockiana*

1 *Rosa* 'Dagmar Hastrup'
2 *Rosa eglanteria*
3 *Hosta sieboldiana*
4 Common marjoram
5 Mint
6 Balm
7 Horseradish
8 Burnet
9 Basil
10 Parsley
11 Chives
12 Gooseberry
13 *Rubus trilobus*
14 *Paeonia officinalis*
15 Dill
16 Strawberries
17 *Rubus phoenicolasius*
18 Sweet cicely
19 *Chamaecyparis obtusa* 'Nana Gracilis'
20 *Ilex* 'Veitchii'
21 Summer savory
22 Hyssop
23 Chervil
24 Thyme
25 Sage
26 *Lilium longiflorum*
27 Rhubarb
28 *Petasites japonicus* 'Giganteum'
29 *Lavandula angustifolia*
30 *Buxus sempervirens*
31 *Rosa* 'Peace'
32 *Ruta graveolens*
33 Lovage
34 Sorrel
35 *Asperula odorata*
36 Fennel
37 *Vaccinium corymbosum*
38 *Juniperus squamata* 'Meyeri'

The geometric centrepiece of box hedge.

A pattern of herbs

You probably will not wish to grow only herbs in your garden but, if you have a larger than average plot, a garden-within-a-garden devoted entirely to these plants is very rewarding. The small herb garden shown here is based on a medieval plan with formal herb beds arranged more or less evenly over the site. A few flowers provide colour in the summer months but the herbs provide pleasant scents throughout the year. The two halves of the garden are not exactly the same but they are well balanced.

The garden is entered through an archway cut into an old cypress (*Chamaecyparis obtusa* 'Nana Gracilis') hedge. The central feature is the clipped dwarf box hedge with a solitary rose ('Peace') in the middle. On one side of the garden are two large beds containing dill (*Peucedanum graveolens)* and peonies (*Paeonia officinalis*), and on the other side two narrower, but formal, beds with lavender, lilies, rue (*Ruta graveolens),* rhubarb, and lovage (*Ligusticum scoticum*). Most of the herbs are grown in eight smaller beds offset by a single large rectangular bed planted with blueberry (*Vaccinium corymbosum*), fennel (*Foeniculum vulgare*) and woodruff (*Asperula odorata*).

The circulating and sitting-out area is mainly red-brick paved with gravel in the space around the central box hedge. The western boundary is emphasized by a 16m (50ft) border of the giant butterbur (*Petasites japonicus* 'Giganteum').

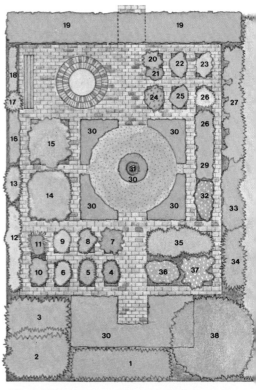

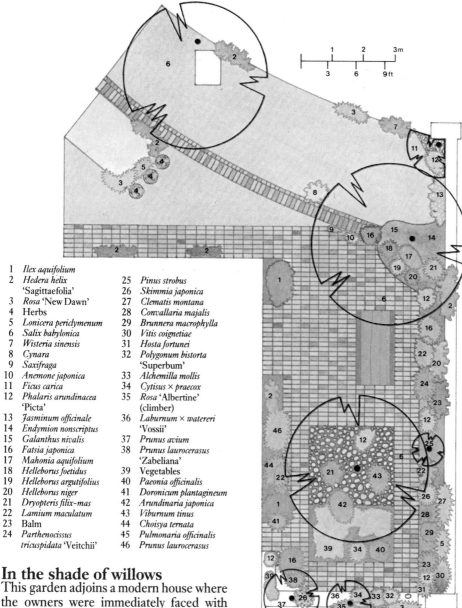

Scale: 1 2 3m / 3 6 9ft

1 Ilex aquifolium
2 Hedera helix
   'Sagittaefolia'
3 Rosa 'New Dawn'
4 Herbs
5 Lonicera periclymenum
6 Salix babylonica
7 Wisteria sinensis
8 Cynara
9 Saxifraga
10 Anemone japonica
11 Ficus carica
12 Phalaris arundinacea
   'Picta'
13 Jasminum officinale
14 Endymion nonscriptus
15 Galanthus nivalis
16 Fatsia japonica
17 Mahonia aquifolium
18 Helleborus foetidus
19 Helleborus argutifolius
20 Helleborus niger
21 Dryopteris filix-mas
22 Lamium maculatum
23 Balm
24 Parthenocissus
   tricuspidata 'Veitchii'
25 Pinus strobus
26 Skimmia japonica
27 Clematis montana
28 Convallaria majalis
29 Brunnera macrophylla
30 Vitis coignetiae
31 Hosta fortunei
32 Polygonum bistorta
   'Superbum'
33 Alchemilla mollis
34 Cytisus × praecox
35 Rosa 'Albertine'
   (climber)
36 Laburnum × watereri
   'Vossii'
37 Prunus avium
38 Prunus laurocerasus
   'Zabeliana'
39 Vegetables
40 Paeonia officinalis
41 Doronicum plantagineum
42 Arundinaria japonica
43 Viburnum tinus
44 Choisya ternata
45 Pulmonaria officinalis
46 Prunus laurocerasus

In the shade of willows

This garden adjoins a modern house where the owners were immediately faced with the common problem of ensuring that the house and garden spaces quickly blended with each other and with the neighbourhood. This was made more difficult than usual when they discovered that one edge of their garden bordered an ancient cemetery. The wall along this side was over 150 years old but their house was newly built. The first thing they did was to plant weeping willows (Salix babylonica) to relive the stark angular lines of the house and to give shade to the brick paved area they had laid over the builders' rubble. This particular kind of weeping willow is useful as it is a very vigorous grower and bears its leaves from mid-spring to early winter.

It was soon realized that the fact that there was a burial ground next door could never be competely disguised. It was decided instead to take advantage of its overgrown mystery and use it as a theme for the garden. Mainly shade-loving shrubs have been used, with ground cover over most of the soil surface. To increase the range of plant forms and textures, several ferns and bamboos have also been introduced. The

bulk planting is mainly contrasting greens with the occasional blue or white flowered plants. Climbing on the walls are ivies, clematis and honeysuckles (Lonicera spp.) and there is a minute vegetable plot set in the courtyard.

This garden is not yet complete and it is planned to add a pool with tall reeds and dwarf mosses, as well as some attractive, carefully placed pieces of statuary.

Above *Delicate fronds of weeping willow* (Salix babylonica) *overhang the brick-paved court yard and shelter the bamboos and ferns planted in their shade.*

Right *A small plot in the corner of the courtyard has been planted with vegetables and herbs (cabbage, lettuce and fennel, for example) which are grown as much for their decorative foliage as for eating.*

Top *In this rooftop garden, planting is concentrated along the side walls so that the main weight is distributed at the strongest part of the structure.*

Above *One side has been left unscreened to take advantage of the view over a local park. Wisterias twine up the central supports while among the many container shrubs are* Aucuba japonica, Fatsia japonica *and yuccas.*

Rooftop garden

For some people living in cities, a rooftop may be the only place they have for a garden. The owners of this roof garden live in the adjoining penthouse flat and, over almost 20 years, have created a very successful garden planned as a green and peaceful contrast to the busy streets below.

When they moved in, the flat roof was coverd with asbestos tiles and there were a few built-in planters containing no more than a few pebbles.

The first step was to improve their privacy by screening off the sides, leaving only the narrow side to give them a long south-facing view over the rooftops. Soil was put into the planters and a small pool with a gurgling fountain was made in the space between them. Any water that might overflow is easily led away by the already-installed storm drain.

Climbers such as honeysuckle, wisteria, clematis and the rose 'Albertine' soon covered the bare walls at the back of the planters and, over the years, more climbers have been added so that the stark walls are now almost completely hidden.

Much of the rest of the planting had to be carried out on a trial-and-error basis as some plants did not like the unusual site. Surprisingly, it was often the tender plants that survived and the normally dependable ones that suddenly died. An area like this can be very windy and, in summer, very hot and dry. Plants normally found in Mediterranean regions seem to do particularly well: oleander (*Nerium oleander*) and oranges (*Citrus sinensis*) not only grow in summer but have survived outside in a sheltered spot throughout the coldest

Left *An attractive group of pot plants stands near the apartment wall. They contain white* Alyssum maritimum, *some red pelargoniums, the daisy-like* Anthemis *and several different herbs.*

Below *Small plants in a strawberry pot provide year-round interest: grey foliage of yellow alyssum contrasts the green sea pink (*Armeria maritima*) and* Iberis sempervirens.

months of the winter.

Over the years more large plant containers have been built and planted with a great range of shrubs such as yucca, and the false castor oil plant (*Fatsia japonica*). Pot geraniums (*Pelargonium zonale* and *P. regale*), alyssum and herbs like thyme and mint are grown in small pots grouped together. A white daisy-flowered chamomile (*Anthemis* spp.) has been allowed to establish itself by self-seeding and gives continuity to the many different shapes and sizes of plant pots.

The garden is ideal for sunbathing and out-of-doors eating as it faces south. Lamps have been fixed to the walls so that entertainment can continue into the long summer evenings. In fact, after so many years of effort, this is a very successful garden in a most unusual way.

1	*Prunus laurocerasus*
2	*Cotoneaster franchetii*
3	*Helianthemum nummularium* and *Wisteria sinensis*
4	*Aucuba japonica*
5	*Mahonia japonica*
6	*Yucca flaccida*
7	*Armeria maritima, Alyssum argenteum, Iberis sempervirens* and *Wisteria sinensis*
8	*Fatsia japonica*
9	*Hosta fortunei*
10	Mixed border of *Rosa* 'Halliana' (climber), *Wisteria sinensis, Lonicera japonica* 'Halliana', *Agapanthus caulescens* and *Senecio* 'Dunedin Hybrid'
11	*Hydrangea macrophylla*
12	Mixed border of *Clematis montana, Lonicera japonica halliana, Forsythia ovata, Hedera,* various roses
13	*Nerium oleander*
14	*Laurus nobilis*
15	*Citrus sinensis*
16	*Pelargonium, Alyssum maritimum* and herbs

1   *Chamaecyparis lawsoniana*
    'Ellwoodii'
2   *Cotoneaster*
    melanocarpus laxiflorus
3   *Dianthus deltoides*
4   *Aubrieta deltoidea*
5   *Lavatera olbia*
6   *Gypsophila paniculata*
7   *Iris germanica* 'Joanna'
8   *Phlox subulata*
9   *Geranium psilostemon*
10 *Juniperus communis*
    'Hornibrookii'
11 *Gentiana lagodechiana*
12 *Salvia turkestanica*
13 *Typha latifolia*
14 *Bergenia* 'Silberlicht'
15 *Anemone vitifolia*
16 *Helianthemum nummularium*
17 *Campanula portenschlagiana*
18 *Festuca glauca*
19 *Sedum spectabile*
20 *Centranthus ruber*
21 *Stokesia laevis* 'Blue Star'
22 *Rosa* 'Baroness Rothschild'
23 *Physostegia virginiana*
24 *Yucca flaccida*
25 *Saponaria ocymoides*
26 *Delphinium*
27 *Chelone obliqua*
28 *Buddleia farreri*
29 *Epimedium pinnatum*
30 *Iberis sempervirens*
31 *Geranium pratense*
    'Johnson's Blue'
32 *Spiraea japonica* 'Alpina'
33 *Echinops banaticus*
34 *Taxus baccata*
35 *Vaccinium corymbosum*
36 *Mahonia pinnata*
37 *Picea abies* 'Echiniformis'
38 *Rosa* 'White Wings'
39 *Bergenia* × 'Morgenröte'
40 *Aconitum arendsii*
41 *Alchemilla mollis*
42 *Primula pulverulenta*
43 *Astilbe* × *arendsii* 'Red
    Sentinel'
44 *Tradescantia virginiana*
45 *Iris laevigata* 'Monstrosa'
46 *Hemerocallis* 'Black Prince'
47 *Primula florindae*
48 *Pennisetum compressum*
49 *Cornus kousa chinensis*
50 *Jeffersonia diphylla*
51 *Aruncus dioicus*
52 *Rhododendron forrestii repens*
53 *Nymphaea indiana*
54 *Iris kaempferi*
55 *Hemerocallis* 'Bonanza'
56 *Astilbe* × *arendsii*
57 *Rodgersia pinnata*
58 *Primula rosea*
59 *Hosta sieboldiana* 'Elegans'
60 *Betula pendula* 'Youngii'
61 *Lysichiton camtschatcense*
62 *Astilbe* × *arendsii* 'Fanal'
63 *Astilbe* × *arendsii* 'Erica'
64 *Petasites japonicus* 'Giganteum'
65 *Petasites hybridus*

'Professor van der Wielen'

A water garden

This garden is dominated by the high enclosing cypress hedges and by the pools. However, there is still plenty of room for land plants as well as a wide variety of aquatic specimens. The main area of water is L-shaped but there is also a smaller pool separated from the long edge of the 'L' by a narrow path. The straight edges of the pools are softened in places by bold plantings of the giant reedmace (*Typha latifolia*) and a vigorous water-lily *Nymphaea indiana* in the water, and grasses such as *Pennisetum compressum* on the pool edge.

A series of long flower beds stretching almost the whole length of the site are planted with a range of flowering shrubs and herbaceous plants stepped-up against the background hedge. The idea behind the major planting is contrasting plant forms and leaf textures and shapes. However, there is plenty of summer colour from plants such as *Geranium* 'Johnsons Blue', wall valerian (*Centranthus ruber*) and the rock roses (*Helianthemum nummularia* and its many varieties).

Sitting out is possible anywhere on the stone-paved area but a favourite spot is under the large yew tree opposite the main flower beds.

The overall effect of the garden is one of contrasting areas linked together by a sense of completeness and by the pools. Despite the formal appearance of the plan, however, the garden is also both rambling and full of interest – a difficult blend to achieve.

Right *Dense foliage in the main pool stands out against the long flower bed behind. Plants include the giant reedmace,* Typha latifolia, *with a clump of* Pennisetum compressum *to the right and water lilies to the left.*

A heather garden

Acid sandy soils are not generally as fertile as clay or chalky soils, and the choice of plants that will thrive tends to be limited. However, nearly all the very attractive heathers (*Erica* spp.) prefer an acid soil, so a heather garden is an obvious choice for these conditions. This particular plot was awkward because it sloped steeply away from the house towards the drive and access road.

It was planned in a way that would get rid of the difficult slopes by making a series of low terraces retained by dwarf walls cut into the slope. These were built as dry-stone walls so that water would not collect behind them and waterlog the soil. The curved pattern of the levels was emphasized by hedges of dark-green yews contrasting greatly with the paler and blue-green leaved heathers. In addition, some of the yellow-leaved and red-leaved heathers were grown.

Heathers are available with a good range of flower colours from purest white to deep pinks, and many of these varieties have been planted in this garden.

As well as the heathers, other acid-loving and acid-tolerant species have been included in this design. Rhododendrons, brooms and dwarf conifers are planted along the edges to give height. Bulbs are used to grow through the heathers for colour when the heathers are still dormant.

As an added bonus, this garden is virtually weed-free and requires little maintenance.

Below *Mixed planting of heathers has created soft mounds of rich colour on the front terraces. Variation in the height and foliage comes from the broom (Genista lydia) in the foreground and Juniperus chinensis in the middle. The pampas grass at the back is planted in the neighbouring garden; there is no formal boundary, so that the adjoining lawns run together.*

1 *Pyracantha coccinea*
2 *Rosa* 'Anna Wheatcroft'
3 *Chamaecyparis lawsoniana* 'Stewartii'
4 *Rhododendron japonicum*
5 *Erica cinerea* 'Lavender Lady'
6 *Erica carnea* 'King George'
7 *Erica carnea* 'Springwood White'
8 *Erica cinerea* 'Rosea'
9 *Calluna vulgaris* 'Gold Haze'
10 *Erica cinerea* 'C.D.Eason'
11 *Calluna vulgaris* 'Alilportii'
12 *Juniperus sabina* 'Tamariscifolia'
13 *Calluna vulgaris* 'H. E. Beale'
14 *Rosa* 'Evelyn Fison'
15 *Potentilla fruticosa*
16 *Cytisus scoparius*
17 *Viburnum carlesii*
18 *Cytisus scoparius*
19 *Hebe* 'Pagei'
20 *Rhododendron fastigiatum*
21 *Fritillaria imperialis*
22 *Erica x darleyensis*
23 *Rhododendron* 'Blue Diamond'
24 *Rhododendron* 'Praecox'
25 *Hebe* 'Autumn Glory'
26 *Cytisus praecox*
27 *Cotinus coggygria*
28 *Iris germanica*
29 *Senecio* 'Dunedin Hybrids'
30 *Rhododendron* 'Vanessa'
31 *Betula papyrifera*
32 *Crataegus oxyacanthoides*
33 *Polyanthus*
34 *Prunus cerasifera* 'Nigra'
35 *Cotoneaster horizontalis*
36 *Rhus typhina*
37 *Pinus mugo pumilio*
38 *Taxus baccata* 'Fastigiata'
39 *Genista hispanica*
40 *Geranium subcaulescens*
41 *Calluna vulgaris* 'Mrs Ronald Gray'
42 *Juniperus* × *media* 'Pfitzerana Aurea'
43 *Calluna vulgaris* 'Alba Plena'
44 *Iris pumila*
45 *Genista lydia*
46 *Chamaecyparis pisifera*
47 *Chamaecyparis lawsoniana* 'Fletcheri'
48 *Lithospermum diffusum* 'Grace Ward'
49 *Calluna vulgaris* 'Foxii Nana'
50 *Rhododendron impeditum*
51 *Chamaecyparis obtusa*
52 *Daphne collina*
53 *Rhododendron* 'Elizabeth'
54 *Chamaecyparis lawsoniana* 'Columnaris'
55 *Dryas octopetala*
56 *Picea glauca*
57 *Saponaria ocymoides*
58 *Lonicera nitida*
59 *Skimmia japonica*
60 *Primula juliae* 'Wanda'
61 *Corylopsis pauciflora*

CHAPTER TWO
SHRUBS AND SMALL TREES

Left: *A bed of dwarf rhododendrons, heathers and conifers will provide colour and interest all year round.*

SHRUBS AND SMALL TREES

If you've just taken on a new garden, or want to change the one you have, you're in a fortunate position. Whatever size it is, whether an acre in the country, or a tiny and shaded courtyard in the inner city, you can accommodate lovely trees and shrubs. You can have somewhere nice to sit in summer, serene and leafy if you want that, or a blaze of colour if you prefer, somewhere to potter about in spring and autumn, and to watch or work in during the winter.

However small your garden, however overlooked, however difficult the shape or the soil, with a bit of thought, and the help of your plants you can have a space that will delight both you and others. There are a few basic points, though.

Don't be in too much of a hurry. The more 'difficult' your garden, the more consideration it needs, both as to what you actually want from it, what it can give, and what trees and shrubs will grow. Most new gardeners want, understandably, 'instant' gardens, and so plant fast growing subjects, or anything which is in flower at the garden centre. This can lead both to lost opportunities, and expensive mistakes. So stop and consider.

Every gardener and every garden is unique. The garden is there to do what you want it to do – so think about what you want. It's easy to accept conventional ideas about what makes a 'good' garden – but do you actually want a rockery? Do you really want a blaze of colour all the year round? Isn't an infinite series of greens just as good? Is a heather garden really a good idea? Do you actually like heathers? Is 'low maintenance' important, when gardening can be immense fun and very satisfying?

Once you've decided, there are one or two easy-to-remember things that will help the final results look good. Most people are quite greedy, and gardeners are no different. However, try to keep things simple. If you don't like dwarf conifers, but you do like yellow roses, fill the whole garden with different sorts of yellow rose (try planting them with ferns, variegated hostas, periwinkles, and have a few pots of carmine pink petunias for contrast). If you like flowering cherries, plant a dozen of the same type – there are many plants you could grow underneath – and if you have window boxes, plant them all the same way.

Brilliant colours can look wonderful set against plenty of gentle greenery to cool them down. If you really do want sheets of colour (and plenty of plants will give you just that), you'll find that the softer the colours, the more easily and elegantly they combine. Use brilliant colours for occasional 'accents'.

Garden maintenance is always a problem. Lots of gardeners opt for low maintenance plants not because they're so enormously busy, but because they're not sure about pruning, training, pests, and so on. Absolutely none of these is a real difficulty – almost no-one would garden if they were. Even worse, almost every low maintenance solution to planting gardens eventually becomes boring – partly because it really is never changing, partly because it demands no involvement on the gardener's part. There isn't any reason why even a tiny garden should bore you. The following chapters describe only a tiny portion of the trees and shrubs you could grow, and yet they still include plants to give you flowers and perfume in deepest winter (or even attractive winter stems) – and all sorts of good things to look at in the other seasons.

Of course, gardening isn't all plants, though there are often 'garden' solutions to other garden problems. If you want to eat outdoors and in shade, rather than buy an umbrella, why not build a small pergola against a wall, where you can dine in the shade of vines, roses and jasmine? Rather than expensive seating, at least consider a turf bank – a medieval idea, wonderfully comfortable and damp only after heavy rains. If parts of your garden are too shady for grass, why not try some of the many lovely ivies available, as a cheaper substitute for concrete slabs?

You'll find that garden accessories often look 'right' if they're made of natural materials. Folding chairs of wood and canvas often look better than alloy and floral nylon ones; a simple earthenware pot soon looks better than a curly white plastic urn. Wooden benches, even if white painted, often look better than fancy white-coated aluminium ones. Unfortunately, natural materials are often more expensive than modern ones, but they do age and mature – developing an atmosphere of their own. And in a pretty garden, atmosphere is all.

Opposite Skimmia japonica *is an excellent ground-cover shrub for shade and moist soil and will berry freely if planted in groups of male and female plants. Generally, birds leave the berries alone, so they can be enjoyed for a long period.*

BUYING AND CARING FOR SHRUBS

To get the most benefit and long-term pleasure from shrubs and trees, it is important to start off with healthy plants and exactly the right selection of plants for your particular garden.

Before you buy plants for your garden, it's always worth deciding in advance where your new purchase is going to go. A good motto is 'Know your garden': that way, you'll know which parts are always in shade, which parts get baked by the sun, which parts are wind tunnels, which are damp or dry, and which have good or bad soil.

There are always quite a few plants which will grow in almost any combination of these conditions, but only very few that will grow happily in all of them. If you're going to get the best value from the plants you buy, you'll need to match the plants' requirements with the sorts of environment you can offer.

Most of the plants described in the following chapters have strong constitutions, but even they will only give of their best if you can give them their favourite conditions. However, there are thousands and thousands of garden plants, and some of these can be finicky indeed. Garden centre plants often have informative labels, so always have a quick look at those before you buy. If you're buying from a nursery, always ask the sales assistant what the plant likes or dislikes.

If you're in the fortunate position of planning and planting a new garden, it's always tempting to write out a list of all the shrubs, trees and flowers that you like, then rush off and buy them. You'll probably find that, once you get them home, they all need to planted in perfect soil and in full sun.

Try to work from what you can offer your plants, and not put plants into places where they won't grow. That way, you'll soon have a lovely and luxuriant garden, full of colour and perfume, and one that will repay in full the little bit of extra research you've had to do at the start.

Where and when to buy

Plants are available from all sorts of sources – from the little nursery down the road, from chain stores, garden centres, right up to the glossy and famous nurseries that could stock a botanic garden. Good plants can be bought from all of these sources.

Don't, on the whole, buy mixed collections of shrubs advertised in newspapers. Some can be excellent, but others are simply surplus or unsaleable stock, put together with no thought of what will grow or look good in your own garden.

If you buy through mail-order firms, and you're not after anything rare, choose a large and reputable nursery. Almost all are exceptionally helpful if you run into any problems, and the material they send out is of good quality.

The only difficulty with mail order is that your plants will arrive during the winter, and will probably be 'bare rooted'. They need to be planted at once, and it's sometimes difficult to judge how they will look together.

If you're keen to buy containerized plants, you'll find a good range at most garden centres and more unusual plants at most nurseries.

Let mail-order nurseries know what you want as early as you can in autumn – that way, you ought to get everything you've asked for. Mail-order buying means winter work in the garden.

You can plant containerized plants as soon as you've got them home, but there's no rush. It's worth moving the new plants around a bit to see where they make the most impact, then plant them. Don't do this job, though, just before you go on holiday – they often need careful attention for the first month or two after planting.

What to look for when buying

Plant shape, leaves, flowers and even the weeds growing in the containers are all worth looking at – so the best time to visit garden centres is between late spring and late summer.

Shape If you're buying a tree, whether a full standard, or a half standard, look for a good, straight trunk, with undamaged bark, secured loosely but well to its support. The plant should have a good, open crown with

Opposite An old apple tree makes an excellent support for one of the ornamental ivies, which revels in the dappled shade and cool moist soil. The underplanting is formed with other shade-lovers: ferns and spurges.

If bare-rooted shrubs and trees cannot be planted immediately on arrival, perhaps due to frozen or very wet soil, they can be temporarily heeled-in, in a sheltered, well-drained corner of the garden, until conditions improve. The plants are set in a trench and the roots covered with soil.

a symmetrical arrangement of branches. Don't buy anything lopsided or tangled – both will cause problems later on.

Shrubs should generally have several stems, evenly spaced. Again, avoid damaged plants, or lopsided or untidy ones (unless that's the way the plant grows). If there's not an alternative plant, ask for a reduction in price. The manager will probably be only too keen for you to buy it.

Leaves Unless it's very late in the season, avoid any plant with yellowed or shrivelled leaves. The plant's been badly looked after, and may take a long time to recuperate. It is also worth checking the leaves for signs of unwelcome pests such as greenfly.

Flowers Don't worry if your plant isn't in flower – even if it's the right season. Some shrubs and most trees will need several more years' growth before they flower. Labelling can sometimes be inaccurate, so if the flowers turn out to be not what you expected – complain. Ask for the correct plant, or a refund (remember to keep the label).

Pots or bags? Plants grow equally well in either. Bags are much cheaper, and so should be the plant.

Weeds These are a useful indication of the plant's past, so have a look at them. If there are none, your plant has possibly been newly potted or bagged, and may deeply resent being replanted yet again. If the soil surface is tightly packed with dwarfed weeds, the plant will have been a year or two in its container. It will be root-bound and the soil will be exhausted. The roots will be difficult to disentangle when you're planting it. The ideal container plant should be sharing its container with a few healthy green weeds.

Soil preparation and planting

Your shrubs and trees will be the most permanent part of your planting, and are usually the most expensive to buy. If they are to do well, it is essential to supply the roots with the best conditions for growth.

Bare-rooted plants are all best planted in autumn, but if they don't arrive until early spring, don't worry. As long as they're not trying to open buds, they'll be all right. If your garden is on moderate to heavy soil, carry out as much advance soil preparation as you can in mid-autumn. By the time your plants arrive, the soil's nutrients, aeration, and drainage should be at their best. Leave preparing light, sandy soil until nearer the planting date.

Soil preparation for containerized plants is exactly similar, and is best carried out a month or two before planting. However, many garden centre plants are bought on impulse, so simply do as much as you can when actually planting.

Almost all soils are improved by the addition of rotted organic material, whether farm or stable manure, garden compost, spent hops or mushroom compost, or even peat mixed with bonemeal (a bucketful of the first to a handful of the second). Heavy soils need about a medium sized bucketful for each square metre (square yard). Light soils need 2–3 bucketfuls for each square metre (square yard).

Dig in the organic matter, at least two spits deep if possible, excavating the topsoil first, and forking half the organic material into the exposed, deeper layer, then adding the rest as you replace the topsoil. Planting holes should be at least 60 × 60cm (2 × 2ft) square, and should be 90 × 90cm (3 × 3ft) or more for all trees.

If you are planting in late autumn, bonemeal is a useful addition. Add about two good handfuls for each square metre (square yard), mixing it into the topsoil with a fork. Bonemeal contains plenty of slowly released phosphorus which will be needed by the developing roots.

When digging the area, large stones and weeds should be carefully removed; roots of bindweed, ground elder, couch grass, perennial thistle and horsetail are quite awful things to get amongst the roots of your plants. Most are easily sifted out of the soil as you dig.

If you have a limy or alkaline soil, and you want to grow rhododendrons, azaleas, some ericas and some camellias (some sorts of each of these are lime tolerant), it is possible to make pockets of acid soil by adding 3–4 bucketfuls of peat for each square metre (square yard). However, the desired effect of the peat eventually wears out, so you'll have to keep adding more. You might well find it simpler to grow them in big pots, or tubs. Better still, leave such plants for friends whose gardens have the right sort of soil, and concentrate on lime-tolerant plants: clematis, cotoneaster, buddleia, box, ceanothus, cistus, forsythia, fuchsia, laburnum, lilac (some with perfumes far more exciting than most azaleas, the best of all being the ancient Persian lilac), philadelphus, viburnum (with some wonderful winter-flowering sorts), and dozens of others.

Planting bare-rooted shrubs and trees

Though planting bare-rooted shrubs and trees is best done in late autumn when the soil is still relatively warm from the summer and the plants are not yet fully dormant, you may not always have that option. If your plants arrive in the depths of winter, have a look at your soil. If it's frozen or water-logged, wrap the plants' roots in damp sacking, straw, peat or compost. Do not let

them dry out. Don't store them in plastic sacks – rot easily sets in. Certainly don't drown them in a bucket of water. Store in a garage or shed until the soil is workable. Alternatively, if you're too busy to plant or store properly, plants can be heeled in, in a specially dug shallow trench in a sheltered part of the garden.

Remember that there is a quite major rule about planting: always make sure that the roots are spread out to their fullest extent. The planting hole must be large enough. Never plant a bush or tree with the roots all tangled up – the plants won't establish properly, won't ever anchor themselves well, and as the roots grow in thickness, they will begin to strangle each other.

Dig out a hole which is more than big enough. Make a shallow mound in the base and set the plant on the mound so that the roots spread naturally. If there are broken or damaged roots, trim them off with sharp secateurs. Crumble good topsoil, or a soil and compost mixture, in over the roots, shaking the plant gently during the process, so that the gaps between the roots fill pro-

perly. Firm the soil as you go, starting at the ends of the roots and working inwards.

Try to ensure that the planting level remains the same. On tree stems, it's usually easy to see the soil mark. If you can't, check to see if the plant is grafted (many trees are). If grafted you should be able to see a swollen oblique ring where the scion joins the stock and this should be left 5–7.5cm (2–3in) above ground level.

All trees (whether bare rooted or containerized), some large shrubs and all standard roses, will need the support of a stake. Hammer a suitable post into the bottom of the planting hole before you put the plant into position. This way, you'll avoid damaging the roots, as well as giving extra stability. The top of the post must reach only to just below the lowest branch. If it projects into the crown, nearby branches will get badly damaged in the first gale.

Planting containerized trees and shrubs
Always remove the plant from whatever container it's in – even whalehide pots. Have a look at the base of the root ball. If

1 *Planting holes for shrubs should be at least 60cm (2ft) square and plenty of organic matter, such as peat, worked into the lower soil.*
2 *With containerized shrubs, the top of the root ball should be slightly below soil level. Do not disturb the ball of roots when planting.*
3 *Return fine soil round the root ball, firming it with your heels as you proceed.*
4 *Finally, tidy up the surface of the soil to remove footprints.*

Left: *The eight shrubs are:* **1** *juniper (*Juniperus × media *'Pfitzerana Aurea'),* **2** *firethorn (*Pyracantha *'Orange Glow'),* **3** *lavender (*Lavandula angustifolia *'Munstead'),* **4** *veronica (*Hebe *'Autumn Glory'),* **5** *stag's-horn sumach (*Rhus typhina *'Laciniata'),* **6** *viburnum (*Viburnum × burkwoodii*),* **7** *broom (*Cytisus × kewensis*),* **8** *barberry (*Berberis thunbergii *'Atropurpurea'). One square = 1 metre.*

With careful choice of shrubs, even a small shrub border can be interesting and colourful throughout the four seasons. Here, only eight kinds of shrubs have been used, yet there is marvellous contrast in shape, colour and texture.

there's a thick coil of roots at the base, try to uncoil them as much as you can without doing major damage. When planting, spread out the uncoiled roots as if you were planting a bare-rooted plant. Try not to break up the rest of the root ball too much.

Once planted, water generously. Thereafter, check every day or so, especially in hot weather, and water at the least sign of drooping leaves.

Spacing and interplanting

When deciding where to plant, remember that the spacing of plants is very important. You will need to know the spread of a plant as well as its eventual height. These measurements are quite as important for shrubs as well as trees – climbers need

checking, too, for there's no point in planting, say, a *Clematis montana* against a bungalow wall, where it will be up over the roof and around the chimneys in a season.

Thinking ahead will pay dividends and, before settling on where to plant anything, it is also worth considering how new additions will fit in colour-wise. Bright colours can look wonderful but, as a general rule, simplicity is best: try to avoid setting dozens of different plants, each with a contrastingly bright colour, too closely together.

Getting a garden to look 'right' isn't difficult, but you do need to look at your trees and shrubs, examine how they grow, how they look with their neighbours, or work out how they are likely to look with any new additions you make.

Shrubs and trees are often planted too closely, for an instant effect. In a season or two, plants are cramped, growing and flowering far less well than they should, and becoming more prone to pests and diseases. Proper spacing means, sadly, an empty-looking garden for a year or two, but patience really does have its rewards.

It's always tempting to do something with the empty ground – planting annuals or herbaceous perennials. While this will give you a quick dash of colour, if you've prepared the soil properly, the vigorous vegetation will absorb all the nutrients that you've carefully dug in, as well as possibly shading out your chosen, long-term plants.

If you can possibly do so, avoid any inter-planting. If you must have colour, choose low-growing annuals (candytuft, French marigold, annual pinks, night-scented stock and antirrhinum are all useful). Tall-growing annuals, and most herbaceous plants, will soon swamp the chosen plants and make them grow even more slowly.

An alternative idea (more expensive, too), is to include in the shrub and tree planting some fast growing and showy sorts, to discard once the choicer ones need the space. Tree lupin, rock rose, and various sorts of broom are useful for this; lupin and broom improve the soil as well. However, it takes almost as much self-discipline to remove the 'flashy' shrubs when you ought to (they're usually at gorgeous maturity by then), as it does not to plant them in the first place.

If you're replacing a shrub, or want to insert one in an already mature border, make sure that not only do you prepare its site properly, but that you also clear enough surrounding vegetation to give it a chance to grow. Nothing is more frustrating than seeing a tiny twig get elderly but no bigger because your other plants won't let it grow. If possible, feed it with liquid manure once a fortnight for its first year.

Avoiding rose sickness

If your garden has got an old rose bed that you want to replant with yet more roses, beware. Your new plants may not flourish if they have been budded onto the same sort of rootstock that supported the ones you've thrown out. If at all possible, use a new site, or excavate the old one to a depth of 75cm–1m (30–36in) and replace with soil from another part of the garden. Remember to keep the top spit (one spade's depth) of soil separate when excavating, so that you can replace it on the top. Species roses, or roses grown on their own roots are often not affected by rose sickness so such preparations will not be necessary.

Aftercare

Once your newly purchased trees and shrubs are planted, certain routine aftercare procedures will help ensure that your plants get off to a good start.

Protection

Some plants, particularly evergreens and conifers, need a certain amount of help and protection from wind and hot sunshine when newly planted. If possible, set up some sort of screening from both. Either use a proper windbreak netting (always useful elsewhere in the garden, especially among vegetables and salad crops), or use split polythene sacks. Remember that it's a shelter, not a greenhouse, so don't enclose the plants too tightly.

Watering

Bare-rooted plants should begin new root formation in early spring, and soon become reasonably self-supporting. However, keep checking the leaves through late spring and summer, and water when necessary. Summer planted container plants of all sorts, but trees especially, take time to establish a root system beyond the original confines of the old container. If you don't pay them sufficient attention, they can collapse very quickly. They should, though, be self-supporting by their second summer.

Feeding

Unless your shrubs and trees find themselves in highly uncongenial situations, they'll grow. Except for the few that *need* poor soil, to get the very best out of your plants keep them well fed, particularly for the first couple of years. There's no point in feeding a bush 3m (10ft) across, or a tree that's as high as the house; although you will probably have to feed plants growing beside or beneath them.

Give plants an annual dressing of bone-meal in winter or early spring, or of chemical fertilizers in mid-spring. Much better, if you can manage it, is to give an annual mulch of compost or rotted manure – lightly forking it into the ground, as long as there are no nearby bulbs. In general, the plants' roots occupy an area more or less equal to the spread of the branches – so the plant itself gives you some idea of the most useful area to feed.

Deadheading

If you've all the time in the world, or a tiny garden, deadheading is worth doing for most of your plants. If you can't do it, don't worry, though it does help prolong the season of flowering of some varieties of rose. It does also help subsequent flowering in rhododendrons.

The planting scheme season by season
1. *Spring, with viburnum and broom in flower.*
2. *Summer, with flowers on firethorn, barberry, lavender and veronica.*
3. *Autumn, with berries on firethorn and barberry, and coloured foliage of stag's-horn sumach.*
4. *Winter, the juniper foliage comes into its own, and the firethorn is still in berry.*

TRAINING AND PRUNING

To keep shrubs and trees within bounds, looking good and flowering well, some training and pruning may be necessary. It is not at all difficult if you understand the reasoning behind it.

In nature, shrubs and trees only get pruned in the most random way – by bad weather or grazing animals. In the garden, pruning is essential for quite a number of plants, to keep them within the space you can provide, to keep them flowering properly, or producing decorative foliage or stems. Pruning can also keep the plants well-shaped, though this depends rather on your 'eye' for such things.

Pruning also contributes to your plants' health by removing dead or dying branches. By avoiding the build up of dense tangles of twigs, it will also reduce the likelihood of fungal infection or insect attack.

Most new gardeners view the need to prune with some alarm. The actual act of pruning isn't at all difficult – the most important thing is to use a properly sharpened tool. Secateurs are the most useful, and as you'll need them for much of the year, buy the best ones that you can. Never use secateurs to cut through a branch that is too thick for them. Twisting the secateurs round in a tearing motion to complete the cut tears both wood and bark, and leaves a very untidy wound – a future site for infection. Make sure that the cutting blade remains sharp – it's not difficult to ensure.

For branches over 20mm (¾in) thick, use a pair of long-handled pruners (also useful for rose suckers). These have much more powerful cutting heads, and with the extra leverage of the handles, will cut nearly anything that you can get between the jaws.

Alternatively, use a pruning saw. Most of these have fine teeth on one edge and coarse ones on the other. Use the first set on hard woods, the other on soft. The main disadvantage of such saws is that the edge not in use can damage nearby branches. Some gardeners prefer saws with a curved and single-edge blade; these are much more useful when working in confined spaces.

The cleanest cut

Good secateurs or pruners give good cuts. If using a saw, try to support the end of the branch you're cutting, otherwise its weight will tear apart the wood below the cut. If there are torn and ragged parts, tidy them up with a sharp knife and the plant will soon heal itself.

If at all possible, small cuts should be slightly sloping from the horizontal. It's best to make large ones fairly vertical – that way, water won't collect on bare wood and start it rotting. Commercial wood wound sealers may be useful.

If buds are visible, cut just above an outwards facing one. This will ensure that new growth will be in a useful direction. If you cut too far above a bud, you'll eventually be left with a spur of dead wood, which will become unsightly, and an entry point for infection.

On thicker wood, buds can be difficult to see. You'll just have to cut where it's most convenient, and hope that there's a bud nearby. If several develop, remove the ones you don't want.

To prune or not to prune?

Few small shrubs (see page 106) need anything beyond removing dead or diseased wood, and shaping, if branches grow in awkward directions or at awkward angles. Larger ones that need little work include Mexican orange blossom, *(Choisya ternata)*, *Corylopsis*, all the cotoneasters and daphnes, euonymus, genistas, witch hazels (though you'll be cutting sprigs to take indoors) hibiscus, some hydrangeas, most mahonias, olearias, skimmias, viburnums, and some of the gorgeous 'old' shrub roses.

There are five main groups of shrubs that do need pruning, plus climbers, each requiring a separate treatment. It's usually easy to decide which group your various shrubs fall into, and then you can prune them accordingly.

Early-flowering deciduous shrubs

In this group are some of the most popular and colourful sorts, including forsythia, the flowering currants *(Ribes)*, weigelas, deutzias and the closely related mock oranges *(Philadelphus)*, and the spring-flowering spiraeas. Climbers in this group include *Clematis montana* and *C. alpina* and winter-flowering jasmine (see page 86).

In all of these, the flowers are carried on shoots that grew in the previous summer.

Opposite *Dogwoods can be pruned almost down to ground level, leaving the bases of shoots with one or two buds.*
Below *Shrubs grown for coloured stems, like the shrubby dogwoods* (Cornus), *can be pruned each year in early spring to encourage plenty of new shoots, which have the best colour.*

Top left *Hardy fuchsias are pruned virtually to ground level in early spring each year, just before they come into growth. They will produce flowers on the new shoots.*
Above left *Sometimes, coloured-leaved shrubs can produce odd shoots with green leaves, as with this spiraea. Such shoots should be cut out as soon as they are noticed.*
Above right *Mock orange* (Philadelphus) *is pruned immediately after flowering, by cutting out completely, or back to new shoots lower down, all stems which have carried flowers.*

You should wait until they have finished flowering before you prune, otherwise flower-bearing shoots will be cut off.

There's no need to prune young plants until they have filled their allotted space. Later, when they're the size you need, try to prune at least every two to three years, cutting out tangled branches, or ones that cross and rub against one another, and anything dead or diseased.

Prune immediately after flowering has finished, so that there's plenty of time for the plant to put on new growth to give you yet more flowers next spring.

Summer flowering deciduous shrubs

These include all the buddleias, the fuchsias, many hydrangeas, caryopteris, and the late-flowering spiraeas. All these flower on branches that have grown in the current season; pruning has to be done in early spring just before they start into growth. All should be pruned annually once they are big enough for your garden.

You can, if need be, cut the previous season's growth right back, either to ground level for some fuchsias, or to fairly short stumps, as in buddleias. It depends on how big you want the shrubs to be. Un-pruned buddleias can be vast, and dramatic looking, too. However, heavy pruning often improves their flowering.

The hortensia and lacecap hydrangeas need rather less severe treatment, simply cutting off each faded flower head back to a healthy-looking bud, and removing any very weak growth at the same time is all that is necessary.

Shrubs grown for leaves or stems

These can be left unpruned if you like, but quite a number can be treated almost like herbaceous perennials, or cut back to ground level in early spring. The fast-growing shoots produced in the following summer are lush and large-leaved, and can make a dramatic contrast to your other plants.

The coloured stemmed dogwoods (*Cornus*), willows (*Salix*) and brambles (*Rubus*) are treated like this, as are the lovely smoke tree (*Cotinus coggygria*), the huge-leaved foxglove tree (*Paulownia*), some of the variegated sorts of the common elder (*Sambucus*), and some aralias. If you are a flower arranger, try using this technique on eucalyptus, and you'll get plenty of juvenile, round blue foliage ideal for cutting.

Evergreens

Early-flowering rhododendrons, azaleas, camellias, and the lovely, perfumed *Osmanthus* do not need pruning. If you need to cut them back do so immediately after flowering has finished. If you have the time to deadhead the rhododendrons, be careful of the young growth buds growing at the base of the flower stalks.

How summer-flowering evergreens are pruned depends on the flowers. In most cases, clip the shrubs over once flowering has finished. For lavenders, use hedge shears. For hebes, just nip out old flower spikes, and do a little shaping.

If the flowers are unimportant, as in cotton lavender *(Santolina),* the senecios, and other grey-foliaged plants, prune them back in late spring. Shears will do for cotton lavenders, secateurs for the rest.

Foliage evergreens, such as laurel, the various splendid hollies, aucubas and elaeagnus, need as little pruning as possible consistent with a good shape. Variegated forms sometimes grow all-green shoots. Cut these out when they appear. Always use secateurs, not hedge trimmers or shears. For heathers, trimmers or shears are excellent. All need cutting back as soon as the flowers have faded.

Wall shrubs

This diverse group consists in general of slightly tender plants that are grown against walls to give them some shelter from cold and wind. Common examples include pyra-canthas, ceanothus, winter jasmine, and *Garrya elliptica.* There are, though, some splendid, less common plants, such as *Cytisus battandieri, Berberidopsis,* and others.

For most wall shrubs, initial pruning sets up the structure of the young plant. Later pruning takes out vigorous shoots growing away from the wall, and those not needed for tying in and training. Mature plants are pruned as for their free-standing counter-parts. Evergreen ceanothus are pruned immediately after flowering. The later flowering sorts (all deciduous) are pruned in early spring. Shorten any over-vigorous growth and remove weak shoots.

Climbers

Self-clinging climbers, such as, ivy, Virginia creeper, and climbing hydrangea, need no regular pruning. Growth liable to block gutters, or obscure the windows, can be removed at almost any time, though winter is best. Climbers always look best when luxuriant, so just keep them within bounds.

Twiners, such as clematis, honeysuckle, jasmine and wisteria need some care. Early-flowering clematis, such as *C. montana* and *C. alpina* are pruned, if need

Wisterias need regular pruning to prevent a tangled mass of growth. The new side shoots from the main framework of branches should be shortened in late summer and again in winter.

be, as soon as they have flowered. Summer flowering ones are often cut back to 75cm (30in) in late winter. Thin honeysuckles of all sorts after flowering. Wisterias have their long, whip-like shoots cut back to within 15cm (6in) of their base in late summer. The flower buds form along the spurs that remain. If possible, the spurs themselves are again pruned, in the depths of winter, to just ahead of flower buds, which are fatter-looking than leaf buds.

Renovation

If you've taken over an old garden, you may find some immense and tangled shrubs that don't actually add anything to the charms of your garden. If you don't feel like grubbing them out and starting again, it's usually possible to prune right back to a few basic branches, or even trunks. Do this in winter, sealing major wounds with a sealant. Don't worry if you can't see any buds – there will be plenty hidden in the bark. Mulch the plants with manure, or peat mixed with bonemeal.

Most deciduous shrubs will produce masses of new growth. With this you will have to be ruthless, allowing only a few new shoots from each old branch. Not all evergreens will respond to drastic cutting back and may even die. It's worth trying to take a

few cuttings just in case this does happen (see 'Making More').

Suckers

Some shrubs 'run' underground, producing new plants some distance away. The new ones are generally easily pulled up – they can make useful presents for gardening friends. The worst sort of suckers are produced by plants which have been grafted onto vigorous stock. Lilacs, roses and witch hazels are typical examples. As the sucker is produced by the rootstock, it won't look at all like the plant above. Worse, if allowed to grow, it will absorb nutrients that ought to be going to the plant you actually want. Young suckers are often difficult to see when the main plant is in leaf, so always have a careful look in autumn. If you find any, scrape the soil away from the base, then cut them out as far down as you can get. Pruners are often more use for this job than secateurs.

Pruning trees

Pruning mature trees is a job best left to professionals. It's an arduous and dangerous task for an amateur. However, if you've planted some young trees, there are several jobs you do need to do. Small-growing trees are often happy to turn themselves in to big bushes, so if you want

Wall-trained roses which have been neglected can be hard pruned in winter.
1 *This tangled mass of growth is in need of drastic thinning.*
2 *Start by cutting out any dead and diseased wood, and then remove the oldest.*
3 *Try to leave young stems, which will flower the following summer, and tie them in with soft garden string.*
4 *Space out the stems as evenly as possible.*

to keep them as standards, keep pruning off shoots that start to develop from the main stem. You might also find that the crown starts too low down so, as the crown starts to develop, you can remove the lower branches. Prune in midwinter.

Pruning hedges

The time to clip or trim a hedge depends on what type of hedge it is, especially whether it's evergreen or deciduous, whether it's supposed to flower (as in informal hedges), and whether it's newly planted or getting mature. Newly planted deciduous hedges are best cut back hard to within 23–30cm (9–12in) of ground level in early spring. Evergreens, such as privet or *Lonicera nitida* may be similarly pruned. Yew, holly, and the popular Lawson cypress are best not trimmed in any major way – just pinch out the tips of the more vigorous shoots. Beech and hornbeam should not be pruned at all for the first two years of growth.

Later, as the plants develop, encourage good, bushy growth by clipping the hedge into a wedge shape, wider at the base then at the top. Don't let the plants take over, otherwise you'll soon have a hedge full of growth at the top, with bare and leafless stems beneath.

Large-leaved evergreens like holly and laurel are better trimmed using secateurs, rather than shears or trimmers. Unfortunately, it's a time-consuming job, needing doing once or twice a year. However, a well-grown holly hedge looks quite marvellous, and worth all the trouble. Shears or trimmers damage more leaves than they cut, resulting in a messy finish.

Allow hedges to nearly reach the height you want, before you 'stop' them by cutting out the leaders. Overgrown hedges of blackthorn, hornbeam, and thorn can usually be rejuvenated by hard cutting during the winter months. Yew, box, laurel and privet can all be drastically cut back, preferably in early spring, when the new growth that the cutting stimulates won't be hurt by frost. You'll have to get used to the mutilated trunks for a year or two, but after that, you'll have a nice, fresh hedge.

Topiary

Really a specialized sort of hedging, topiary has been in and out of fashion since at least Roman times. The Romans tried most of the possibilities too, carving out of their box bushes, full-scale hunts and heraldic animals, as well as more formal pyramids, obelisks and urns. 'Topiarius' was the Roman word for gardener.

Nowadays, formal topiary is mostly found in grand gardens that can carry the heavy expense of endless clipping, but other sorts of topiary can look lovely in small gardens – especially of country cottages – and it can be great fun to experiment.

Simplest of all, and often visually the most effective, are globes, cubes and, perhaps, obelisks. These look good making ends or entrances in hedges, or for making the corners or centres of formal beds (an obelisk of yew, surrounded by ferns, low annuals, or even bush roses, can look very attractive).

Peacocks, chess pieces, or tiered 'cake stands' need to be on a large scale to be effective, and small gardens can only usually support one or two. If you've got the right sort of house, the traditional place to put them is in the front garden, especially beside the gate.

However, topiary can form almost any shape you like, from sentry boxes (the most splendid ones large enough to hold seats and a table), elephants, whole sitting-rooms, four-poster beds or battleships.

Holly isn't actually very much use as a

Below *Shears can be used to trim small-leaved hedging plants; larger-leaved kinds are best pruned with a pair of secateurs.*

Bottom *Examples of formal hedges (from left to right):*
Chinese honeysuckle
Common yew
Common holly
Laurel
Hornbeam
Common beech
Golden privet
Leyland cypress

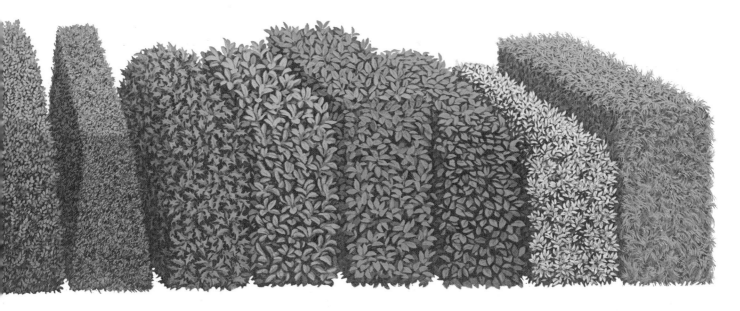

Above *Animals of various kinds are favourite subjects for topiary, a specialized sort of hedging which has been in and out of fashion at least since Roman times.*
Above right *Today, formal topiary is mostly found in grand gardens, a notable example being this 'chess set' at Haseley Court in Oxfordshire.*

topiary plant, though yew and box are excellent. *Lonicera nitida* and privet are rather less good.

Topiary is fairly easily made. Some complex examples are made up along a wirework frame, the young branches trained as they grow. These form the 'bones', the eventual side branches forming the 'flesh'. Start topiary from young plants, it isn't generally possible to cut down an old bush and turn it into a satisfactory piece.

Quick topiary

Real topiary takes time, patience and energy. It is possible to make quite acceptable garden features, using simple shapes and quick-growing climbers. One of the best ways is to make up the shape you want, using wire netting on some sort of rigid frame – bamboo poles for obelisks. Then train up several plants of a climber, pinching out as regularly as you can, until the netting is covered. The most effective covering is of ivy, using perhaps one of the decorative forms (*Hedera helix* 'Caenwoodiana' is excellent).

If you're really in a hurry, and have an ivy plant somewhere that you can raid for cuttings, pack the wire frame with damp moss, and push in ivy cuttings over the whole surface. Keep damp – a spray is a good device to use for watering. Soon, the ivy should root into the moss, and eventally into the ground. Clip annually in winter.

Care

If you decide to go for the grandest sort of topiary, and plant young yew bushes, make sure that the soil is fertile and well drained. Allow new plants a year before starting to shape them. Prune in early winter, and in the following summer, pinch back side shoots to encourage bushy growth. Keep

the plants growing fast by mulching with compost or lawn clippings, and keep well watered in dry weather.

Topiary in pots

A pleasant fashion is returning to favour, and it's now possible to buy standard bay trees with a ball-shaped crown, as well as obelisks and spheres of box. They're quite expensive to buy, but perfectly easy to grow at home. If you want to make some, remember that the pots need fairly constant attention, but also that you can use a much wider range of species. Making 'standard' plants is described below, but to make simple, low-growing shapes, try using cotton lavender for silvery ones, gold-variegated box, and most of the shrubby herbs (hyssop is especially good).

Formal training

While many gardeners like their gardens to look as natural as possible, a little formality can make an exciting contrast. Formal hedges, of course, are entirely artificial, and so is topiary, but shrubs, trees and climbers can be used in other formal ways. 'Standard' bushes, whether in the open ground or in pots, can look splendid. Tunnels, pergolas and arches are all lovely garden features which require a little skill in training, and even straightforward wall shrubs will need a little work.

Standard trained plants looks especially good in patios or courtyards, by doorways or entrances. Standard roses look wonderful by paths or in formal gardens. Roses are the most difficult to make (see page 93), but the others are easy, especially if you can start with a young, single stemmed, plant – perhaps a cutting you've rooted.

Even if they're intended for the open ground, it's usually best to start them off in

a 9cm (3½in) pot. Add a pea cane for support, tying the young stem to the cane at 5cm (2in) intervals; the sort of wire ties used for freezer bags are useful for this. Feed regularly, and rub off any buds that develop from the main stem. The idea is to get maximum growth from the only growth point, and a nice, straight stem. Re-pot, regularly, as soon as the roots have filled the available soil. If the plants try to flower (and if you let them get pot bound, they certainly will), don't be greedy; remove all flower buds straight away.

As you re-pot, remove the old cane, and

Climbing roses trained over arches or pergolas make lovely garden features and require very little skill in pruning and training.

Opposite *A system of galvanized wires is often used to support climbing plants on a wall. Here, a fan shape has been formed, but wires can also be horizontal, spaced about 30cm (1ft) apart. Stems are tied in with soft garden string.*

substitute a taller one. Once the main stem is tall enough, let the leading shoot produce four pairs of (or four single) leaves beyond the top of the support, then pinch out the growing point. When new shoots form from the top four growing points – or nodes – pinch out their growing tips when they're 10cm (4in) long. Pinch out subsequent shoots that grow from those when they are also 10cm (4in) long.

If you're using a flowering plant, perhaps a fuchsia, a lantana, a geranium, or even an orange or a grapefruit seedling, or most grandly of all, a wisteria, allow it to flower. If you're training a foliage plant, such as bay, box or laurel, or something tender – like one of the *Helichrysum* species – you'll need to keep pinching out the growing shoots.

Supporting plants

Many wall shrubs and a number of climbers need some sort of support. Most look best when grown informally, though some make handsome espaliers or fans (these two sorts of training are essential for most major fruit, but can also look excellent using pyracanthas or cotoneasters).

Excellent wall shrubs that don't need support include various sorts of ceanothus, *Garrya elliptica*, pyracantha and the less tough sorts of escallonia.

For those that need support (and that includes all the 'climbing' and 'rambler' roses) as well as the twining sorts of climber, you'll need to set up some sort of framework. This can consist of an arrangement of wires stretched through vine eyes, or trellis work or even wire netting attached to the wall.

A system of wires is generally the best support in the long run. Although you'll have to tie in the soft stems of plants that won't support themselves, it's easy to untie them in the future, should you need to carry out pruning, or to paint or point the wall behind. It's important to remember that large climbers can weigh a great deal, so ensure that the wires are anchored properly, and can be tightened if they stretch.

Trellis work can look very pretty on suitable houses, and can look particularly nice if it's of unpainted wood. White plastic, while long lasting, can sometimes look so bright and shiny that no plant can compete. Once a plant, particularly a vigorous climber like *Clematis montana* or jasmine, has become thoroughly attached to the trellis, it can be impossible to detach it. This is especially annoying if you need to prune.

Wire netting is cheap and easily attached, and it's easy to thread through the stems as they grow. However, it makes any subsequent thinning virtually impossible. If you eventually want to remove the plant, the netting

has to come off, too. Roses are particularly bad, for you are then left with an unmanageable sheet of fiercely armoured vegetation, reinforced with steel mesh.

Pergolas and arches

Pergolas and arches can be constructed of anything from unbarked poles (nice in cottage gardens), to grand affairs of stone columns and dressed wood. As with wall plants, remember that the weight of vegetation can become quite large, and that gales can be a major problem – build the supports as securely as you can.

When planting them up, include a few foliage climbers, such as *Vitis vinifera* 'Brandt' or the purple leafed vines, or the Dutchman's Pipe *(Aristolochia)*. This will ensure that even when nothing is in flower, the overall appearance will still be attractive. It's always tempting to add something fast growing, like a Russian vine or a rampant clematis. If you do want to use these plants, it's best to give them a structure all to themselves (they're quite nice enough), or they'll quickly swamp slower-growing subjects. The Russian vine in particular, is an excellent choice for covering unwanted sheds and the like.

In the early stages of growth, tie in young shoots. It's often neater to tie them to suitable placed nails, rather than tie them directly to part of the structure.

Laburnum, hornbeam or fruit tunnels look wonderful when mature, but are expensive things to build and maintain. The basic structure needs to be of metal, with regularly spaced wires stretched between them. Apples are espaliered along the wires, but laburnum stems, being pliable, can be threaded in between them.

Tripods

If you have a new and empty garden, tripods planted with climbers can be a useful means of getting some fast bulk and height. In their simplest form, they can be built with three 3m (10ft) poles (unbarked if possible), sunk 45cm (18in) into the ground, and tied at the top to make a rough wigwam. Carry the string on down between the poles to make a framework to help the climbers get a hold. Tripods like these will support rambler roses, or plant them up with clematis (especially ones that are easily propagated – most often the early-flowering species), or anything else you like. Honeysuckles are good.

They can either be left as a permanent feature of the garden, or can be removed when the permanent shrubs in the garden have grown sufficiently to give you enough visual height. It's worth taking cuttings, if you dismantle a tripod.

MAKING MORE

Propagating your own shrubs and trees is pleasurable as well as economic. It is an easy way to fill out a new garden, or change the look of an old one, virtually for free. Any extra plants can be shared among friends or neighbours, so you can never have too many.

Some shrubs and trees can be propagated as easily as herbaceous plants – by division. Many have underground stems which grow through the soil, producing roots as they go, then turning upwards into the light to make a new plant. Some plants produce underground stems so energetically that they become almost a nuisance – in which case the new plants are called 'suckers'. However, if you have a new garden, such plants are remarkably useful, for you'll soon have plenty of material – and the garden will rapidly appear mature. Examples of suckering shrubs are all the japonicas *(Chaenomeles)*, some of the low-growing hypericums and artemisias, the pernettyas, the decorative sorts of raspberry and blackberry *(Rubus)*, the exotic, perfumed clerodendrons, and the equally exotic but more commonly planted sumach *(Rhus typhina)*, as well as lilacs and roses.

Lilacs and roses are often grafted, so the suckers are part of the rootstock, and aren't worth keeping. However, if you've found lilacs or roses that have been propagated from cuttings – and so are on their own roots – then the suckers will be the same as the flowering part of the plant and are worth keeping.

The best time to remove suckers for propagation purposes is in autumn or early spring. There often isn't all that much in the way of root, so cut the leafy part back to about 10cm (4in).

Other shrubs and trees produce what are in effect suckers, but with almost non-existent underground 'stolons', so that the centre of the plant becomes a mass of upright stems, each one with some roots of its own. These can often be separated from the main plant, either by digging the whole thing up and hacking them apart with a spade, or by forcing a trowel down into the clump and levering a few of the outer stems away from the centre.

Again, this is best done in autumn or early spring, cutting the shoot back so that the young roots will be able to support it. Plants that can be treated like this include hazels *(Corylus)*, fuchsias, some mock oranges *(Philadelphus)*, amelanchiers, winter-flowering viburnums, the eating quince *(Cydonia)*, some mahonias, most barberries *(Berberis)*, kerrias and spiraeas, The snowberries *(Symphoricarpos)*, will produce so many shoots as to positively menace your garden.

Layering

Division is easy because at no time is your young plant without roots in the way that a cutting is. However, there's a very useful garden technique intermediate between division and taking cuttings: layering.

The basic sort of layering is useful for most climbers, and shrubs with branches near enough the ground, or flexible enough, to peg them to the soil. For most suitable plants, start the job in mid-spring, choosing a healthy shoot that grew last year. Using a sharp knife, make a longish cut on the underside, if possible slicing along beneath the point from which a leaf grows.

Carefully bend the whole stem to the ground (take care that it doesn't snap at the cut – or you'll have a cutting), and peg the cut shoot to the ground – or even just weight it down with a stone. The cut must be in contact with the soil, or even slightly buried. Some gardeners like to keep the cut open, using a matchstick as a wedge. The cut should be several centimetres (inches) from the branch's tip – up to 45cm (18in) from it. You'll get a better shaped young plant if you can tie the free length to a short, upright cane, though this needs great care if you aren't to snap the stem.

The layers should have rooted by late autumn. To check that rooting has taken place, give a gentle tug. If it has, simply cut the young plant away from the parent, and replant elsewhere.

Good plants for layering include all rambling and climbing roses, many rhododendrons, viburnums, magnolias, laurels, aucubas and other evergreens. Layering is an especially good way to propagate wisterias. Start layering clematis in autumn, using one-year-old or two-year-old stems. Climbing honeysuckles are also best started off in the autumn.

Long stems can be layered in several

Opposite *One of the easiest and most successful ways of propagating a wide range of shrubs, including viburnum shown here, is by layering young stems in spring. The stems root where they are pegged down into the soil. Some will be rooted by the autumn of the same year, while other plants take at least a year to form a root system.*

Air layering is an easy way of propagating trees and shrubs, particularly camellias, cherry and plum, and rhododendrons.
1 Prepare a young stem by cutting a tongue about 5cm (2in) long.
2 Dust the cut surfaces with a hormone rooting powder to encourage rooting.
3 Keep the tongue open by packing it with moist sphagnum moss.
4 A polythene sleeve is partially secured to the stem, and then filled with moist sphagnum moss, into which the stem will root.
5 Finally, the sleeve is completely sealed, using waterproof tape.

places, a process called serpentine layering. Honeysuckle will root at every node if you weight it down along the length of the stem.

Stooling

Of course, not all your shrubs will have branches flexible enough to make them suitable for layering. Some of these, such as dogwood *(Cornus)* and ceanothus, can be stooled. Pile soil into the centre of the bush you want to propagate so that the bases of the branches are covered. During the course of the summer, these put out roots. In autumn and early winter, the piled-up soil is carefully removed and the rooted shoots detached.

There are various refinements, but most of them are of more interest to commercial nurseries. Stooling is particularly good for heathers *(Erica)* once they've grown leggy and you need some young plants.

Air layering

This is another easy method, especially useful if the tree or shrub has no low-level branches. There is none of the risk involved in taking cuttings, and you don't need a frame or propagator.

Air layering is similar to ordinary layering, except that the soil is replaced with damp moss and, to stop the moss drying out, it is wrapped in polythene. When air layering older plants, cut a tongue in the bark but do not sever the stem. Lift up the tongue of bark to leave the wood exposed. That way, the stem above your hoped-for layer won't break off if there's a gale. A handful of damp moss is wrapped around the sliced area, which is then wrapped in polythene. Tie off each end to make a sort of sausage. Use black polythene if you can – a cut-up rubbish bag is ideal. Though clear polythene does let you see when roots begin to form, it also lets weeds and algae grow.

Try to use healthy young shoots, about the thickness of a pencil, and of last summer's growth – do not use old and hard wood. Not all plants will layer in this way, but it is especially useful for camellias, various sorts of cherry and plum, and, most importantly, rhododendrons.

There are two disadvantages, though. Black polythene parcels look fairly awful, clustering in your bushes. Secondly, the young plants have very fragile roots, and need to be potted up with the very greatest care to avoid damaging them.

Cuttings

Taking cuttings of shrubs and trees is often easy, always good fun, and surprisingly productive. While some species can be tricky, hundreds upon hundreds of sorts will root easily. Sometimes you will need to know the right time of year to do it, and perhaps even a few 'tricks of the trade', but you will find that lots of your plants will grow from almost any twig stuck in the ground.

The most common cutting is taken from the top 10–15cm (4–6in) of stem, usually of what is called 'semi-mature' growth, with bark that is begining to turn brown. Carefully remove the lower leaves before inserting it in the soil.

A cutting made from the same sort of shoot, but still soft and sappy, is a 'soft' cutting, while fully ripe wood is called a 'hardwood' cutting. Cuttings can be made of sections of stem of almost any age, and even of single leaves with a fragment of stem attached (as in camellias, figs and vines for instance).

The simplest shrubs to take cuttings from are those which can tolerate fairly dry conditions. Sage, lavender, rosemary, rock rose *(Helianthemum)*, cistus, hebe, santolina and even hydrangea are suitable subjects. Take cuttings in summer, and insert them to about half their length in a pot of moist, sandy soil or soil-based seed compost. The latter is much better for the beginner than any of the peat-based composts. If you don't want to fuss with watering the pots, just plant the cuttings in a cool, shady part of the garden. Give the cuttings a light daily spray with water to keep them from wilting. Don't use the watering-can for this, or you will saturate the soil and the stems will rot.

For less tough shrubs and trees, including fuchsias, spiraeas, mock oranges *(Philadelphus)*, caryopteris, shrubby verbenas and most ceanothus, it's easy to stop the cuttings drying out by inserting them in a pot, then tying a clear polythene bag over the top. Stop the bag collapsing by using a few wire hoops to form a framework over the cuttings.

As conditions inside the bag will be extremely humid, it is worth spraying your cuttings with a general garden fungicide – though don't use too much, for some fungicides actually inhibit root formation as well as disease.

Early autumn is also an excellent time to take yet more cuttings, of trees as well as shrubs, hedging plants, and especially of roses. Many will 'do' in the open ground, and that's certainly the simplest way of starting up new hedges or edging. Remove the lower leaves and insert sprigs of privet, *Lonicera nitida*, box, holly, deutzia, or lavender, every 15–30cm (6–12in) along the centre line of where you want the hedge. Firm the soil around each cutting, then leave well alone.

A shady part of the garden can be used to root rambler, climbing and shrub roses – just line the cuttings out as if you were planting a hedge. You will find that some really need two seasons in the row before they're sufficiently established to move.

For slightly trickier material, it's worth having a cold frame. The still air inside it stops the unrooted material drying out, and the slightly less cold soil stops the cuttings going completely dormant. It's worth taking cuttings of whatever you need. You will certainly have some failures, but plenty of successes, too.

Conifers, such as cypresses, junipers, cedars and larches, will all root from 'heel' cuttings. These are small side branches pulled off larger ones, with a small strip of older wood at their bases. Some conifers ooze resin over the tear. The resin hardens and can prevent rooting, so try dipping the ends of spruce and fir cuttings in hot water for a few moments to stop this happening.

Propagation aids
Most garden centres sell powders or liquids containing the plant hormones essential for root formation. However, not all plants are interested in hormones from the outside world, and others need very particular concentrations – so the effects of using them, even under ideal circumstances, are variable.

However, the formulae usually also contain a fungicide, so even if the hormones don't help, the fungicide might result in more cuttings surviving to form roots.

Buy a new container annually, for the hormones gradually lose effectiveness. All things considered, they are worth using – but don't expect magically improved results. The thing that will drastically improve your results is gardening experience – so do not give up if your first few cuttings fail.

Many sorts of propagator are marketed, but only the largest ones are really useful. Small ones are difficult to keep at even temperatures – and anything that you can get to root in them you can probably root in the garden under a jam jar just as easily. A good quality cold frame, a soil-warming cable, and a good quality hand-spray will give you much better results.

Mist propagation is much talked about and there are even small kits available for the amateur gardener. The kits provide a

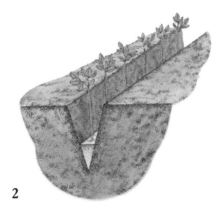

1

2

Many kinds of roses can be rooted from well-ripened cuttings in early autumn.
1 *Cuttings should be approximately 25cm (9in) in length, with the soft tip removed.*
2 *Set them out to about two-thirds of their depth in a slit trench lined with sharp sand for good drainage.*
It is important to choose a sheltered, shady part of the garden for rooting rose cuttings.

closed environment with a high degree of humidity control, and can provide short bursts of mist every few minutes. There are lots of problems with it, so unless you really want to propagate in a big way, don't bother with this method.

Being able to supply bottom heat to your cuttings is quite useful for anyone with a moderately large garden – and it is easily achieved by putting a soil-warming cable into one of your frames. It's as useful for raising seeds as it is for rooting some of the more difficult cuttings.

Seeds

All trees and shrubs produce seeds, so seeds seem initially a perfect way of getting new plants. However, many garden plants are, in fact, special, named varieties (a variety is a small sub-unit of a proper species), or hybrids (resulting from cross-breeding), and very few of them will come true from seed. Seedlings are sometimes quite different from the parent plant. The new plants might be more beautiful – or less. Indeed, that's one of the excitements of growing from seed.

Unfortunately, it's an excitement that is available to rather few gardeners, because growing large numbers of young plants, and waiting to see which are worth keeping, needs considerable space and time. Even so, seeds are a useful means of increasing shrubs that are not named varieties, or that will not increase easily from cuttings, such as daphnes. Hedging plants such as yew and hawthorn, are also suitable.

Almost without exception, all tree and shrub seeds should be sown in autumn, preferably in pots, and left outside all winter. The seed needs to be frozen, sometimes frozen and thawed several times, before it will consent to germinate. This process can be carried out in the fridge, but you will find that the natural process is generally more effective.

If the seed is very small, to stop it being splashed out of the soil, cover the pot or pan with a sheet of glass. You can stretch polythene over, but make sure that it's tightly done, or rain water will soon weigh the sheeting down onto the soil. Some seed, roses in particular, may need two full winters to break their dormancy. So, if nothing comes up the first spring, not all is lost.

If seeds you have ordered arrive late, then you will have to use your refrigerator. There's no special virtue in using the freezer compartment – the open shelves will do. If someone in the household objects to having pots of earth in the refrigerator, wrap the seeds in damp blotting paper or a coffee filter, put in a freezer bag, then chill. Dry seeds are often impervious to cold.

Budding and grafting

These techniques are scarcely used by amateurs, though budding is both easy and useful. It's by far the easiest way of increasing the hybrid sorts of rose (cuttings of these can be difficult to root). It is also useful if you want to increase tree fruits, or to make family trees, which have several varieties of a fruit growing from a single trunk. It's also useful if you want to make your own standard roses, standard or weeping trees, or even standard wisterias.

Budding is almost risk free. It uses only a few buds of the 'scion' (the plant you are wanting for its flowers or fruit), and hardly damages the 'stock' (the plant that provides the roots and the lowest part of the stem).

Once you have decided which plant you want to increase, you will have to get a supply of one or more stock plants. For roses, some lilacs and fruit trees, this can be easy. When suckers appear, simply dig them up carefully so that they have a few roots still attached, then replant elsewhere. Most stocks are of plants that reproduce easily – often from cuttings. Should you need a quantity, take cuttings in mid-summer, or in early autumn, to see which of them do best.

Budding works best during the summer. Unless you have both stock and scion potted up in a greenhouse, wait for moist, showery weather when the plants will be well filled with water. Avoid hot, dry days, if at all possible, or the buds you insert may dry out and die.

Look for plump buds in an 'axil' (the joint between stem and leaf stalk) on the current year's growth, and carefully cut it out using a very sharp knife. Special budding knives are available, though a sharp stainless steel kitchen parer will do. Start

Hybrid roses are best propagated by budding the varieties onto rootstocks during the summer.

1 *A dormant bud, situated in a leaf axil, is removed as a shield-shaped piece of bark with a sliver of wood behind it. This sliver may be carefully removed.*

2 *At the bottom of the rootstock make a T-shaped cut in the bark and lift the two flaps.*

3 *Slide the bud down underneath the bark and trim off the top of the shield if it projects above the T-cut.*

4 *Bind in tightly with raffia or insulating tape, but leave the actual bud exposed.*

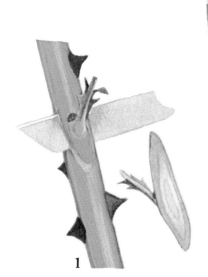

1

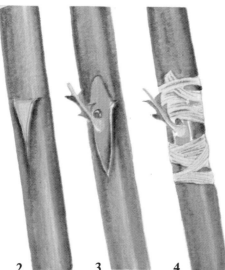

2   3   4

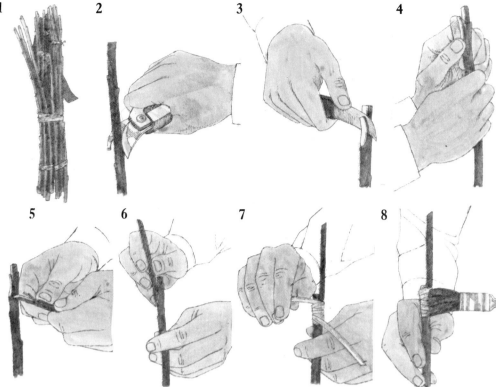

1   **2**   **3**   **4**

5   **6**   **7**   **8**

If you are feeling adventurous, you could try propagating trees by whip and tongue grafting, including fruit trees. As with budding, the variety to be propagated is put on to a suitable rootstock. Whip and tongue grafting is carried out in late winter/early spring.
1 Scions of the variety can be gathered in winter, bundled up and heeled in a spare piece of ground.
2 Scions should be prepared to about three or four buds in length.
3 The rootstock is prepared by first cutting off the top; a 2in (5cm) long rut is then made at the top, followed by a short downward cut to form a tongue.
4 The tongue must be of even thickness but not too thick.
5 Matching cuts are then made at the base of the scion.
6 The scion is fixed to the stock, with the tongues interlocking.
7 The union should be tightly bound with raffia or grafting tape.
8 It is then sealed with a suitable product such as tree-pruning paint.

the cut 20–25mm (¾–1in) above the bud, and gently curve it down to about the same distance below. The bud, complete with the oval sliver of wood beneath it, can then be lifted off. Trim away the leaf, but leave enough of its stalk to act as a handle for transporting the bud.

Some gardeners leave the oval of wood in position, but it's sometimes better to gently lever it away from the green bark. Go carefully, otherwise it may pull the all-important centre of the bud away as well, and you will have to start again. If the wood is unwilling to come away leave it in position.

Next, make a T-shaped incision into the bark of the stock, with the upright of the T running down its stem. Cut through the bark, but as little as possible into the wood below. Gently lever the bark away – budding knives are specially adapted to doing this, but a potato peeler will start you off quite well at the angles of the T. Enough has to be levered back to enable the bud and its shield to be slipped right down underneath the stock's bark.

Once the shield is in position – the inside of the base of the bud *must* be in contact with the wood of the stock – trim off the little handle and firmly bind the base and top of the T with insulating tape (easy to peel away afterwards), leaving the scion bud exposed. If there's too much of the top of the shield projecting above the T, trim it off with a very sharp blade.

In about three weeks the bud should have 'taken', in which case it will still be a nice

fresh green. If it hasn't, it will have gone brown. If all's well, leave the tape in position, but as soon as the bud begins to sprout, cut back the stock to just above the new bud.

How high up the stem of the stock you carry out budding depends on what you want. For bush roses, most bushes and trees, work as near ground level as you can. For standard roses, or weeping decorative trees, insert the bud where you want the clear stem to branch out. The stock may attempt to produce its own branches and these must be rubbed off.

If the bud fails, remove the tape, the failed bud, then retape. The wound should soon heal. It's possible to try several buds on the stock – as an insurance. If several 'take', prune to the lowest, or the stock will keep trying to take over.

Whip and tongue grafting, an alternative but equally effective way to increase trees and shrubs, is illustrated above.

Below *Grape vines can be propagated from eye cuttings. A portion of young stem, complete with bud, is taken in winter. The bark on the opposite side to the bud can be removed to encourage rooting. Press the cutting down into sandy compost and place in heat to encourage rooting.*

PLANT PROBLEMS

Fortunately, ornamental trees and shrubs are much less vulnerable to pests and diseases than fruit, vegetables and herbaceous plants. Still, problems do occur from time to time, and it pays to be prepared, so you can solve them as quickly, effectively and economically as possible.

Pests come in many forms:
1 Cutworms and leatherjackets chew the roots of many plants.
2 Birds are notorious for stripping berries and damaging buds.
3 Caterpillars of various moths and butterflies eat holes in leaves.
4 Leaf miners are grubs which tunnel inside leaves.
5 Slugs and snails will eat almost any soft young growth.

1

2

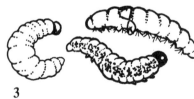

3

4

5

There are innumerable things that can go wrong with your garden plants, but very few things that actually do. The most important single thing that you can do, right from the very beginning, is to garden with your garden, not against it. Check the soil – dozens of sorts of soil test kits are available from garden centres and shops, most of which are inexpensive and easy to use – and take any corrective measures that are necessary, preferably before planting.

If your soil is especially acid, grow suitable, acid-loving plants, such as rhododendrons and heathers. If your garden has acid inner-city soil, the acidity probably isn't natural and can be corrected by adding lime and well-rotted manure or compost.

If your garden is on limestone, chalk or shell sand, it will be dry and alkaline. Again, you have a vast range of lime-loving plants from which to choose, and you will be able to create a lovely garden using the right plants. Some may very occasionally suffer from nutrient deficiencies, but this can be corrected by digging in plenty of organic matter and by feeding, as above. Sometimes iron and magnesium are held in by the alkaline soil itself and so are not available to your plants. (The main symptom is that the leaves will look yellow when they shouldn't). Either add peat, or buy 'sequestered' nutrient compounds (ones which the soil can't catch) and water these in.

On light soils, or in dry areas, drought can be a problem. Simplest is to plant only drought-resistant plants. If you have to keep watering endlessly, not only will you waste time you could probably spend doing something else, you'll probably also be washing precious nutrients out of the soil, and making even more work for yourself.

If your garden is wet or boggy, it is very much cheaper to buy plants that grow well with damp root conditions than it is to drain it.

However, by far the majority of gardens have fairly neutral soil, are reasonably well drained, and in reasonable 'heart'. With good basic maintenance, most garden plants should grow for you.

Chemical fertilizers

Apply all these with care, following the manufacturers' instructions to the letter. Oversupply of nutrients can damage plants' roots, or even alter the overall balance of other elements in the soil, causing problems.

If things do go wrong, there's most often a simple reason, and it's usually better to suspect disease, insect attack, seasonal factors, or a gardening 'mistake' than a deficiency in the soil.

However, if no plants will grow properly, there may be something radically wrong with your soil. It's possible to get your local agricultural college or horticultural advisory service to help (they'll charge a small fee), with a full soil analysis.

Garden pests

How much damage any pests do will vary from year to year. Almost every garden pest has its own enemies, and the balance between a pest and its predators changes. Remember that most pesticides also kill beneficial insect predators, and once the predators have gone, there's nothing to stop a subsequent build up (and triumph) of the pest. So, if possible, trap slugs and snails, then kill them by sprinkling salt over them. Rub greenfly off leaves and buds with your thumb and forefinger, or cut off infected shoots and burn them. Most importantly, make sure that your plants are growing well so that both you and they can tolerate slight amounts of damage.

Insecticides should really be a last resort for most insect pests, though they're a first resort for whitefly, scale insects and mealy bugs. These foreigners have no native predators, all are most common under glass.

Types of insecticide

These are now almost as various as the insects themselves. When choosing, check first that they will kill the pest you want to eradicate, then check that they won't damage the plant you want to save. If there are several that will do the job, check how long lasting they are. Persistent insecticides now available can remain lethal for up to two weeks, which will protect your plants, but will kill all sorts of other insects as well as the pest you want to control. If you need such a chemical, good ones to use are HCH and fenitrothion. Non-persistent sorts, such as derris, pyrethrum or resmethrin are lethal only for one day.

Many garden insecticides are contact poisons. Droplets of spray have to actually touch the pest concerned to be effective, hence the need for a good sprayer, and a good, thorough soaking of the plant, including the leaf undersides.

Systemic insecticides are actually absorbed by the plant, and any insect eating it, or sucking its juices, is poisoned. The chemicals are circulated throughout the plant, so insects feeding some distance from the parts you've actually sprayed are also killed. Systemic insecticides are consequently useful for plants with dense foliage which is difficult to spray.

If using a contact spray, try to avoid spraying open flowers, and try to spray in the evening. That way, you will avoid killing bees and butterflies. If using a systemic insecticide, remember that you will be killing anything that visits the flowers.

Spray left over in the sprayer needs treating with care, so try not to make up more than you need for the immediate job. Most sprays are lethal to aquatic life, so don't let them get into ponds, streams, or even the sewage system. Many are also poisonous to mammals, so don't let the spray drift onto you, your children or your pets.

What to look out for
Aphids, including greenfly, blackfly and the reddish, rose aphids, but not whitefly, do not move around much, so they're often easily seen. Other mobile pests often feed at night, so most gardeners don't see them. Visible symptoms of such pests are curled-up leaves (caused by aphids or caterpillars), a peppering of tiny holes in the leaves (caused by capsids or earwigs), rusty-looking leaves, sometimes with a covering of fine webbing (caused by red spider), oblong sections chewed from the leaf margins (caused by weevils), rounded sections removed from the margins of rose leaves (caused by the leaf-cutting bee) and leaves with pale tracks excavated between upper and lower surface (caused by leaf miners, especially in holly). Lastly, disappearing fruits or berries are caused by various birds and small mammals.

Diseases
Plant diseases are caused by fungi, bacteria or viruses. Though bacterial and viral diseases are of great importance in the kitchen garden, they are hardly ever problems in the ornamental garden – and then mostly affect herbaceous plants.

Fungal diseases are slightly more of a problem. These are more commonly found in ornamental forms of kitchen garden plants, such as flowering almonds, plums and apricots, or in some of the highly bred shrubs and climbers, especially some roses and clematis. In general, the closer a plant is to its wild form, the less prone it is to attack, and the more capable it is of withstanding one.

Many sorts of fungal infection get to work inside the plant's tissues, so by the time you see the effects, the disease may be difficult to cure. Many fungi, such as peach leaf curl and rose blackspot, overwinter in fallen fruit, leaves or twigs, so garden hygiene can play an important role in preventing infection. Some fungi have spores so light that they're virtually always present in the atmosphere, so there's nothing you can do to keep them out of your garden. However, the spores can't penetrate the surface of many plants, and can penetrate others only when the plants are weak, because they are growing in shade and moist situations when they need sun, or in dry conditions when they need moisture. Some plants are susceptible at any time to the fungi that like them.

There are three possible solutions to the problems caused by disease. You can select and grow totally resistant sorts of plant, which is the easiest, and in many ways the most sensible solution. You can also grow the susceptible plants so well that they are resistant to disease and, lastly, you can spray. Ideally, it is best to spray before the infection occurs, though this can be expensive and is always a bother. It's perfectly acceptable though, to spray roses once you've noticed blackspot, for the spraying will stop the fungus spreading, and once the infected leaves have dropped, your plants will look fine. Mildew on roses is tougher to get rid of, or on some varieties, even prevent.

Peach leaf curl is fairly easily controlled, but if it's prevalent in your area, spray in spring as the leaves expand.

Perhaps the most difficult disease to control is honey fungus, a soil-borne infection which attacks the roots of woody plants. It is sometimes called bootlace fungus, because of the black threads, or bootlaces, by which it spreads under the soil. There are special fungicides for treating the problem, but it is difficult to eradicate completely. Badly infected trees and shrubs are best burnt, and the site not replanted.

Always burn any infected wood, leaves, flowers or fruit. Left lying around, they will eventually produce more spores, and you will have more trouble.

Many shrubs and trees are affected very little by pests and diseases, but unfortunately one of our favourites, the rose, has more than its fair share and generally requires regular spraying during the growing season to keep it clean and healthy.

Pests

1 Birds *Various species do various sorts of damage – flower buds, particularly of forsythia, can be attacked, as can all sorts of ornamental fruit. You can protect vulnerable shrubs and trees, to a certain extent, with black thread strung over the branches, or use netting for wall bushes, scarecrows or cats.*

2 Blackfly *Some seasons these can ruin flowering cherries and much else. At the first sign of infestation, spray with malathion or derris, or simply pick off affected shoots and burn. Spraying is better if shoots are important for the plant's shape.*

3 Chafer beetle *This is a double pest, the grubs eating plant roots, and the adults feeding nocturnally – often on your rose buds in late spring and summer. Use a soil pest killer against grubs, if the infestation is bad. Spray roses with HCH (BHC) against the adults.*

4 Greenfly *These attack a wide range of plants, including roses. Most standard insecticides will kill them. Avoid using systemic insecticides on roses, especially single-flowered ones, which are popular with bees and hoverflies. Derris is best for these.*

1

5

2

3

4

5 Holly leaf-miners *These can, occasionally, ruin holly bushes and hedges. The leaves develop unsightly blisters in the centre. At the first sign of infestation, pick off and burn the affected leaves. In bad attacks, spray the holly with dimethoate.*

6 Leaf-rolling sawfly *This pest is a particular danger to your roses, and it can strip the bush of leaves and buds. Look closely at any plant apparently late in leaf. Unroll any suspect leaves and inspect them; the sawfly grubs are pale green. Pick off rolled leaves and burn them.*

7 Slugworms *are the grubs of sawflies and feed on the upper surface of leaves. The best known are the rose slugworm, and the pear and cherry slugworm which is shown here. These pests are controlled by spraying with an insecticide such as malathion at the first signs of attack.*

8 Vine weevils *A dual nuisance, the adults eat oblong sections out of the leaf margins of many plants, rhododendrons, roses and vines. The grubs, which curl up if disturbed, eat the roots. Vine weevils can kill plants grown in tubs, especially hydrangeas. Dust the soil with HCH (BHC), or fork in a dressing of soil insecticide, to kill the grubs.*

9 Snails *These are not often a major problem for trees or shrubs, though they like hiding in bushes, especially box. Wall plants and climbers, such as clematis, can be attacked. Poison snails with proprietary slug pellets scattered round the base of the plant. Alternatively, an old-fashioned method is to catch snails at night (you'll need a torch) and sprinkle well with salt to kill.*

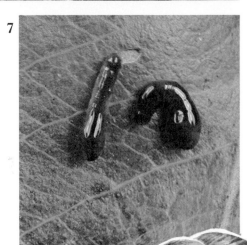

Diseases

1 Bacterial canker *This is occasionally seen on ornamental cherries, peaches and plums. Shoots or branches with prematurely yellowing leaves, later dying, are one symptom, and small, circular 'shot holes' on leaves in late spring are another. Remove and burn unhealthy wood. Spray the plant with Bordeaux mixture in autumn and spring.*

2 Blackspot *This fungal infection appears as dark, rounded marks on rose leaves from late spring onwards. Infected leaves soon drop. Remove and burn infected leaves. Spray plants, where feasible, with benomyl or captan.*

3 Honey fungus *Honey-coloured toadstools appearing at the base of tree trunks or shrub stems are a sign of honey fungus. If you peel away the bark, there will be whitish fungus, and black strands in the surrounding soil, which gives the disease its other common name, boot lace fungus. Try one of the commercial remedies, but it is difficult to cure and badly infected plants should be dug up and burned.*

4 Mildew *This first appears as whitish patches on leaves and flower buds, especially on some sorts of rose. The disease spreads rapidly, so spray with benomyl, dinocap or sulphur-based spray. Some plants attacked in damp conditions, others in dry.*

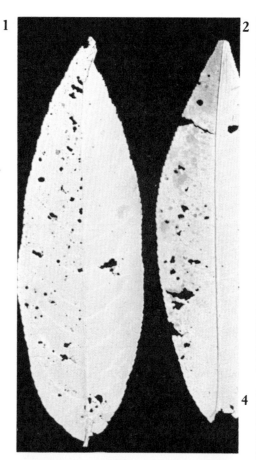

5 Peach leaf curl *On ornamental almonds, apricots and peaches, infected leaves become swollen and reddish. The disease can be fatal. Spray as the buds unfurl in spring with copper or sulphur-based fungicide, then again in a fortnight. Spray also in autumn just before leaf fall.*

6 Rust *Types of this fungus attack many plants feeding inside the leaves, later showing in summer as rust-brown pustules. Remove and burn infected leaves. If serious, prevent further infection by spraying with thiram or zineb at fortnightly intervals.*

7 Rhododendron bud blast *Infected buds die, and sprout black hairs the following spring. These contain spores. Remove and burn infected buds. The disease is spread by leaf-hoppers so, if practical, spray the plant with derris or malathion.*

8 Fire blight *A bacterial disease most likely to attack pear trees, but may also occur on ornamental shrubs such as cotoneaster and pyracanthus. In spring and summer, blossoms turn black and discoloration spreads to young shoots and along branches. Leaves hang down, blackened as if by fire. This is a serious disease and, if an outbreak is suspected, it should be reported to the Ministry of Agriculture.*

SMALL SHRUBS

For sheer versatility, small shrubs are hard to beat and a selection of them will readily transform even the tiniest garden. Choose those that are suitable for the soil and the site – then sit back and enjoy the display.

These smallest of shrubs include some of the garden's most popular plants, and many of the most adaptable. All of them can play an important role in your garden, whether you have a 'pocket size' one, or something much grander. They can be used at the front of borders, to soften the edges of path or patio, or even to make exclusive but miniature gardens.

Some of the most charming small shrubs have the same habits and shapes as their larger relatives, so dwarf rhododendrons, dwarf conifers, and the low growing sorts of heather can be used to make tiny landscapes, in large tubs, earthenware troughs or old sinks. Old-fashioned white-glazed sinks are easily found in builders' yards. You can give them a stone-like appearance by coating the surface with a suitable glue and pressing a mixture of coarse sand and peat onto the glue. Most of your plants will like a free-draining, peaty soil, so make sure that the container has good drainage holes.

Mini-landscapes don't have to be in containers. They can look equally pretty in raised beds (useful, because all the plants are worth looking at closely), beside steps, at the edge of your patio, or as a rockery. Rockeries are difficult to do well, but if you do want one, try to make the stones look like a natural outcrop of rock, and tuck the plants in between in an equally natural way. Don't just scatter plants and stones at random over a pile of soil – it will never look attractive, and you will have wasted your money.

When planning mini-landscapes, it's often a good idea to have a larger shrub to provide a backdrop. If you are planting a raised bed, plant a shrub that will sprawl over the edge to give a less raw appearance. Many of the small brooms *(Genista* and *Cytisus)* can be useful in these situations.

Small shrubs are essential, too, at the front of shrub borders to give masses of low-growing colour. All the rock roses (the name covers plants of both *Helianthemum* and *Cistus)* are good for this, though they do need full sun. If your shrub border is in partial shade, try a shrubby *Potentilla* – they have flowers in creamy-white, yellow, apricot,

orange or red, according to cultivar. *Caryopteris* × *clandonensis* is another alternative. It's a plant that should be in every garden, and right at the front so that you can touch its fragrant leaves, as well as admire the clusters of soft blue flowers.

Small shrubs make wonderful 'softeners' for the edges of borders, especially when there's a path along the front. Masses of the silvery leafed cotton lavender *(Santolina)* look good spilling over brick or stone, as does the even more brilliant white curry plant *(Helichrysum italicum)*. Its leaves have an exciting spicy smell, though it's worth trimming off the flowers – they aren't especially interesting, and smell very much stronger. The various sorts of rock rose look equally effective, though some of the helianthemums have such brilliantly intense flowers that they need using with discretion. Try using different shades of the same colour rather than the strongest possible contrasts.

If you have a paved terrace or patio, and you find that the large expanse of stone or concrete looks a little 'hard', it's often worth removing a few sections of the surface (away, that is, from where you sit or walk), and planting up the space with some small shrubs. Good shrubs to plant in hard-paved areas include daphne (the glossy leaved *D. retusa* makes a low and attractive bush, filled with heavily perfumed flowers in late spring, and later hung with garnet berries) and the pretty 'herring bone' cotoneaster *(C. horizontalis)*. The berries of daphne are poisonous, so if young children use your garden, it is best not to grow them. If your patio is shady, plant a few of the evergreen and crimson-berried skimmias.

Elsewhere in the garden, it is always an attractive idea to have the paths actually hedged on either side. Cottage garden paths have always looked inviting when edged with lavenders (there are pink and white sorts as well as the softly coloured 'Munstead' or the intensely violet 'Hidcote') or variegated thyme. Cuttings of all of these root easily, so you only have to buy a plant or two to start with. If you like standard roses, try underplanting them in the same way –

Opposite *The rock roses or cistus, like* C. crispus *'Sunset', are excellent front-of-the border shrubs for a sunny, well-drained position and will flower over many months in the summer.*

Opposite 1 *The low-growing barberry (Berberis thunbergii 'Atropurpurea Nana') is ideal for edging or for forming a low hedge.*
2 *Ideal for the deepest shade is the butcher's broom (Ruscus aculeatus). It will also tolerate very dry soil.*
3 *The low-growing Caryopteris × clandonensis is a front-of-the-border shrub for full sun.*
4 Cotoneaster horizontalis *produces masses of flowers in early summer, much loved by bees, followed by red berries.*
5 *There are many dwarf conifers available; thujas especially make neat globular bushes.*
6 *There are also dwarf varieties of spruce or picea, which make suitable specimen conifers for a rock garden.*

an Elizabethan idea well worth copying. If you want something more modern, many of the small sorts of berberry also make good low hedges, especially in front gardens, but it's also worth trying Irish heath (*Daboecia cantabrica*) or some of the smaller sorts of spiraea.

If you like herbs, there are quite a number of small shrubby ones. There are lovely silver or gold variegated thymes, many sorts of marjoram, six or seven interesting types of sage, winter savory, hyssops with various flower colours, the lavenders, lad's love (*Artemisia abrotanum*) with its grey-green foliage, the small-growing sorts of rosemary, and plenty of others as well.

Most of them do excellently in window boxes or pots (don't grow thymes, though, in windy or exposed situations). However, if you've space, it is better still to have a herb garden. Although quite a few of the herbs you need for the kitchen are annual or herbaceous plants, the shrubby ones will provide the basis for the garden design, as well as giving you something to look at in winter. Edge the paths with hyssop (there are ones with pink or white flowers, as well as the usual – and lovely – blue sort), winter savory, or the various thymes.

If you do not have space for a full-scale garden, try a herb 'wheel'. These are sometimes made from an old cartwheel, placed flat on the ground and with a different herb planted in each of the sections between the spokes. If you don't want to use an old wheel (they rot after a year or two), it is just as easy to use bricks set on edge to make a similar design. The end result is often better looking, too.

Some of the most popular of all small shrubs include the vast numbers of heaths and heathers (from the two genera – *Erica* and *Calluna*). It's easy to have varieties in your garden that flower every month of the year, and as the varieties also have different growth habits and leaf colours, it's possible to have an interesting garden made from them alone. Most gardeners like to add a few dwarf conifers to get an extra bit of visual contrast. The only problem with heather gardens is that as all the flowers are pretty much the same shape and size, you might eventually feel like having something more exciting. Add some pernettyas or sarcococcas – the first for berries, the second for perfumed flowers. Heather gardens are often planted for 'low-maintenance', but even if that is what you want, it's important to watch out for the various perennial weeds, couch grass and convulvulus especially, that can establish themselves almost without your noticing and rapidly take over.

Recommended Shrubs

Barberry (*Berberis thunbergii* 'Atropurpurea Nana')
This lovely foliage and berry shrub does well in sun or shade, and on most soils. The leaves are a deep, coppery purple, the flowers orange, and the berries that follow, bright red. It makes a colourful 'accent' plant, especially in association with heathers. It's also a good 'edger'.

Broom (*Cytisus × kewensis*)
This marvellous hybrid has elegantly sprawling branches that vanish beneath sheets of creamy flowers. The spectacular display lasts for a few weeks in spring, but makes the plant essential to have. Broom needs full sun, but will do in most soils. It makes a wonderful edging to a path or a raised bed.

Broom (*Genista lydia*)
Another sort of broom, *G. lydia* is one of the best dwarf forms, with graceful, arching branches covered in intense yellow flowers in late spring and early summer. It is perfect for rock gardens and heather beds. It does well in almost any soil, though it flowers best in full sun.

Butcher's broom (*Ruscus aculeatus*)
An odd member of the lily family, this evergreen grows well in the deepest shade, and even in very dry soil. What look like leaves are flattened stems, and the tiny flowers produced on their surface later form long-lasting crimson berries. It is a tolerant shrub, good where little else will do.

Caryopteris (*C. × clandonensis*)
A tough shrub for almost any soil, caryopteris likes plenty of sun. The leaves are pleasantly aromatic. It can be cut back in late winter or early spring if you need to keep it small. The soft-blue flowers open in late summer and last into mid-autumn. It is good for a low hedge.

Cotoneaster (*C. horizontalis*)
Sometimes called the 'herring-bone' cotoneaster because of the regular arrangement of its side branches, it is a most attractive bush for rockeries, against low walls or even the house wall. The plant adapts itself to the shape of whatever it grows over. The leaves are small and glossy and the tiny flowers are followed by masses of berries.

Conifers
There are vast numbers of dwarf kinds. The dwarf cedar develops a short trunk, but its weeping branches are perfect for the rock garden. The thuja, a dwarf form of the

Opposite 1 *Heathers, like varieties of* Calluna vulgaris, *make excellent ground cover and flower over many months.*
2 *Lavender has many uses: plant it with old shrub roses, use it for edging a path, or plant it in a group by the front door.*
3 *There are few shrubs which have such a long flowering period as the potentillas. Most are dwarf compact shrubs, ideal for small gardens.*
4 *Rock roses (or cistus) are good companions for potentillas, needing the same sunny conditions and well-drained soil.*
5 *Rock roses (or helianthemums) are low spreading shrubs, ideal for rock gardens or dry sunny banks.*
6 *To obtain the showy berries on skimmia, plant groups of male and female plants together. Skimmia is also attractive when in flower.*

Chinese arbor-vitae, makes a small, globular bush, while the picea, or white spruce, will make a bright-green cone 2m (6ft) high in thirty years' time. Dwarf juniper will eventually give sheets of grey-blue leaves.

Cotton lavender *(Santolina neapolitana)*
There is another popular white leaved species *(S. chamaecyparissus)*, but this one, with its longer, more feathery leaves, is the prettier. It makes an excellent shrub to sprawl over paths or paving. Cotton lavender is happy in poor soil, prefers full sun, and is exceptionally tough.

Curry plant *(Helichrysum angustifolium)*
This is an easy and attractive bush for sun or light shade. The narrow white leaves give off a pleasing curry smell when touched. The plant is happy in any free-draining soil. It is a good sprawler for patio or paths, or as an 'accent' plant among shrubs.

Daphne *(D. retusa)*
A gorgeous evergreen daphne, it eventually makes a dense, rounded bush. The leaves are oval and glossy, and the pale-lilac pink flowers, carried in mid-spring, will perfume the whole garden. They're followed by large, translucent, garnet berries.

Euonymus *(E. fortunei* 'Emerald 'n' Gold')
This popular shrublet, looks good planted with conifers and heathers, or as ground cover. Planted in the rockery, or against walls, the stems will climb and clamber. It's extremely tough, and does well in sun or shade. In this form the leaves are green, yellow and pink. Named forms like 'Silver Queen', and 'Colorata' which has purple tinged leaves in winter, are equally pretty.

Heaths and heathers *(Erica* and *Calluna* varieties)
Vast numbers of sorts can be found at most garden centres. All do well in moderately peaty soil and full sun. Use them in rockeries, or in a small bed. Gentians do well in similar conditions, and the wonderful blue flowers will give added interest.

Irish heath *(Daboecia cantabrica)*
A plant for loamy or peaty soils, it soon makes a handsome clump of glossy leaves and spikes of large, long-lasting, amethyst, purple, pink or white flowers. Clip over when finished. Useful to give height to heather beds, or to plant below rhododendrons and azaleas.

Lavender *(Lavandula* varieties)
These well known and much loved shrubs have fragrant leaves and fragrant flower spikes, often in various colours. 'Hidcote' is deep purple, but others are paler, even pink or white. Lavender is lovely with 'old' shrub roses, or edging a path, or as bushes by doorways. Replace every few years with cuttings, as it tends to get leggy.

Potentilla *(P. fruticosa)*
There are many lovely, shrubby potentillas with arching branches and silvery, grey or green leaflets. For much of the summer, single flowers are produced, in white, cream and yellow, or even red, according to cultivar. Grow them in sun or partial shade, in rockeries, or as edgings.

Rhododendrons
While some species are tree sized, there are dozens of tiny sorts, all good in peaty pockets in the rockery, as part of the heather bed, or with azaleas (which are also part of the *Rhododendron* family). 'Pink Drift' is ideal for rockeries, with lavender-pink flowers. 'Yellow Hammer' is early and bright yellow. 'Moonstone' has fine reddish buds which open to palest yellow flowers. *R. sargentianum* is good for a cool shady place in the rock garden, with soft yellow to whitish flowers.

Rock rose *(Cistus* species and varieties)
These plants love hot, dry positions, so they're excellent in rockeries, or dry banks, or even in pots. No single flower lasts long, but they're produced in such abundance for much of the summer that it doesn't matter. They are good, also, for window boxes.

Rock rose *(Helianthemum nummularium* 'Fireball')
Fine for dry, sunny positions, even on poor soil, rock roses are fast growing. They are excellent for a rockery, pots on the patio, or at the front of the shrub border. 'Fireball' has exceptional double flowers, brilliant red, and in profusion for most of the summer. Look for other cultivars, too, with white, yellow, scarlet or pink.

Skimmia *(S. japonica)*
These compact evergreens have fine, glossy leaves and panicles of white flowers, often attractively fragrant. The form 'Wisley' is the easiest to grow, but you must buy male and female plants to get the splendid red berries that will last most of the winter. Shade and moist soil suit it.

Spiraea *(S. × bumalda* 'Anthony Waterer')
This is a good plant for almost any garden with plenty of sun. Prune hard in spring if you need a tidy-looking plant. As well as the flat bunches of crimson flowers in mid and late summer, the plant occasionally produces charming variegated shoots.

MEDIUM-SIZED SHRUBS

The many medium-sized shrubs now available can provide autumn and winter colour, choice specimen plants or attractive fillers for borders and beds that will suit all conditions and will grace any garden, large or small.

Even if you have a tiny garden, it's important to include at least a few larger plants to give visual emphasis and a sense of scale. You have an immense range of lovely plants to choose from. Even if your garden is a bit larger, then you'll need medium-sized shrubs for the shrubbery, for 'specimens' to add interest to your lawn or patio, to make informal hedges, to use as large scale ground cover, or even to plant in tubs.

If you can only allow yourself one medium-sized shrub, look for one with several good points. *Mahonia aquifolium*, for example, has dramatic evergreen leaves, as well as sprays of wonderfully scented flowers in spring, and black berries in summer. Equally good are all the azaleas related to the popular *Rhododendron luteum*, most of which have heavily perfumed flowers and good autumn colours.

If you do have enough room for a shrub border, medium-sized plants are essential for their own sake, as well as making a good backing for all of the smaller sorts. Evergreen shrubs are especially important for giving 'body' to the shrubbery in winter, and stop the bare branches of the others looking too glum.

If you have room for some informal hedges, these can be used to screen off the compost heaps, the vegetable garden, or even the sand pit or swimming pool. Many sorts of barberry make wonderful hedging, offering attractive leaves, fine flowers (though sometimes with a nasty smell), often very colourful berries, and thorns too. Many other shrubs are quite as good, especially the upright sorts of rosemary. Fuchsias can be used for gorgeous hedges in warmer gardens, where they can become almost too large for this chapter. Also good value is the charming hypericum called 'Hidcote', smothered in shiny golden flowers from early summer into late autumn.

If you have room, it's fun to use some of the shrubs that have only one short flush of beauty before returning to the usual, and rather duller, state. A low hedge of the slow-growing and pineapple-scented mock orange, *Philadelphus microphyllus*, is a delight for the weeks that it is in flower. Try underplanting with the creeping plumbago *Ceratostigma willmottianum*, whose intense blue flowers will soon take over once the mock orange is finished, and will give you colour into the last days of autumn.

A wonderful hedge, too, can be made of the common daphne *(D. mezereum)*. To buy a hedgeful would be expensive, but once you've got a plant, it is easily increased from seed. The white-flowered form is the loveliest, though the smell of both, in early spring, is quite magnificent. The flowers are followed by good berries, amber after white flowers, scarlet after purple. Underplant with *Anemone blanda* if you want a spring display, or *Crocus speciosus* for wonderful flowers in autumn.

Many gardeners like to have some sort of specimen plant set in a lawn to offer a contrast to the flat green of the grass. If you have a small, grassed front garden, and really don't want a small tree or a really large shrub, there are plenty of grand medium-sized ones that will look good. Many sorts of *Pieris* look splendid, with their crimson or pink young leaves held in tufts at the end of each branch, soon followed by sprays of white or soft pink flowers. 'Firecrest' is a lovely form.

Abelia chinensis is another splendid specimen, not especially common and best in a rather sheltered site, but with soft-pink flowers in early summer, and a quite wonderful smell. The growth habit is fairly open, so you could easily plant bulbs beneath it – perhaps the intensely blue *Scilla sibirica* or one of the dwarf sorts of daffodil (*Narcissus asturiensis* is lovely).

Evergreens can make wonderful accents for a lawn, especially some of the narrowly pyramidal sorts. *Chamaecyparis pisifera* 'Boulevard' is good. They look better if you can group two or three, all of different sizes.

It's always difficult to decide exactly where a specimen plant (or plants) should go. If you buy containerized ones, shift them around to see where they look best. Alternatively, use some bamboo canes as dummy bushes. In general, the worst possible place for a specimen (except in the most formal of gardens) is in the centre of your lawn so try to avoid this.

Opposite *The hardy fuchsias are ideal medium-sized shrubs for gardens in milder areas, where they can be grown as specimens in a shrub or mixed border and the stronger-growing varieties as hedges, or as tub plants.*

Opposite 1 *The barberry* (Berberis darwinii) *flowers in spring, the blooms being followed by purple berries. It makes a particularly good informal hedge.*
2 *In full flower in late winter,* Daphne mezereum *likes moist soil and partial shade.*
3 *There are few better shrubs for autumn leaf colour than* Euonymus alata *and it grows particularly well on chalky soils.*
4 *An indispensable shrub for spring,* Forsythia intermedia *'Spectabilis'. It will grow virtually anywhere.*
5 *The lace-cap hydrangeas, like 'Blue Wave', make a welcome change from the usual mop-headed kinds but also like light shade and moist conditions.*
6 *Japonica* (Chaemomeles *'Rowallane') flowers in early spring and makes a good wall specimen.*

Another way of using shrubs as a 'feature' is to plant them in tubs, or very large pots. Good places to stand them are by doorways (not necessarily on either side), by flights of steps, in courtyards and patios, or to emphasize changes in direction of a path. The tubs must be big enough to let the plants grow properly, and will be too heavy to move around once planted, so move the empty tub from place to place until you've found exactly the right spot for it.

Tubs enable you to grow plants that wouldn't otherwise 'do' in your garden, and so you can try the lime-hating rhododendrons, azaleas and camellias (all three doing well with only the most basic care) however alkaline your soil. Another sort of shrub that does splendidly in tubs is the hydrangea, both the big showy 'hortensia' types and the subtler 'lacecap' ones. Almost any of the fuchsias look fine too, whether hardy or half hardy. An exceptional hardy sort with pinkish and variegated leaves is *Fuchsia magellanica* 'Versicolor'. If you have time, this can be cut to within a few centimetres (inches) of the soil in autumn, giving plenty of space to whatever bulbs you plant – some of the species tulips look wonderful. As the bulbs finish, the fuchsia begins to grow, and soon its lovely leaves and flowers tumble over the container.

Some medium-sized shrubs can even be used as large-scale ground cover – often useful in under-used parts of your garden. The laurel, *Prunus laurocerasus* 'Otto Lukyen' is particularly good, with glowing, deep-green leaves, and spikes of scented flowers in spring. A planting of this can look very good, and if you need some variegated foliage to make a particularly telling contrast, plant *Hebe × franciscana* 'Variegata'. Otherwise, use *Euonymus alata*, with its extraordinary autumn colour.

Another shrub which makes excellent large-scale ground cover is the mahonia (*M. aquifolium*), which is also known as the Oregon grape. It forms dense, suckering thickets of growth, effectively supressing most weeds. What is more, it is very adaptable, growing in sun or in shade, and in all kinds of soils, whether moist or dry. Often it is used for ground cover under trees. To keep it fairly low growing, it can be pruned back after flowering, but in this instance you will lose the purple berries, which are quite an attractive feature.

Some medium-sized shrubs are suitable for planting on very hot, dry banks, which can prove difficult for many plants. One of the best for this purpose is the rosemary (*Rosmarinus officinalis*), which has aromatic foliage, particularly noticeable in hot conditions. *Senecio greyi* would also be a suitable choice.

Recommended shrubs

Abelia *(A. chinensis)*
One of the less common shrubs, abelia is a relative of the honeysuckle. Good soil, full sun and a bit of shelter suit it. It produces clusters of small flowers, pale pink, much deeper in the bud, with an extraordinary perfume. It also does well in pots and tubs.

Azalea *(Rhododendron luteum)*
This lovely, loose-growing shrub, grows best in partial shade and peaty soil, but tolerates most other soils if you mulch. Wonderfully scented, luscious yellow flowers are produced in early summer. The leaves turn yellow and scarlet in autumn. Plant by your door, in a tub, or among other shrubs.

Barberry *(Berberis darwinii)*
Often voted one of the best of all shrubs, *B. darwinii* is good as a specimen shrub, in the shrubbery, or even clipped as a hedge. Evergreen, with handsome, prickly leaves, its sprays of soft-orange flowers are followed by purple fruits with a heavy 'bloom'. It tolerates any soil, preferably not dry, and in sun or shade.

Daphne *(D. mezereum)*
This easily grown daphne does well in most sites and soils. Flowers appear on leafless branches in late winter or earliest spring. They're in white or shades of purple, with a powerful fragrance. Attractive berries follow.

Euonymus *(E. alata)*
Not too common, but worth looking out for, one of the most splendid of all shrubs for autumn colour. Tolerant of almost any soil, it grows especially well on chalk.

False Cypress *(Chamaecyparis pisifera 'Boulevard')*
The species offers a good range of shrubs and small trees, this one a conical and neat-growing plant with silvery blue foliage. It makes an excellent specimen, though feed and water well. Lightly clip it if you need a particularly formal shape.

Forsythia *(F. × intermedia* 'Spectabilis')
'Spectabilis' is one of the best medium-sized forsythias, and deservedly popular. Branches disappear in a mass of yellow flowers in late spring. Any soil, full sun or partial shade suit it. If you'd like to try another colour, use 'Primulina', a lovely, pale yellow.

Fuchsia *(F. magellanica* 'Versicolor')
Often thought of as a foliage shrub, the

Opposite 1 *The dwarf laurel (Prunus 'Otto Luyken') is excellent for ground cover in shady areas.*
2 Mahonia aquifolium *looks good all the year round: purple berries follow the flowers.*
3 *One of the smallest of the mock oranges is* Philadelphus microphyllus, *with deliciously fragrant flowers.*
4 Pieris formosa forrestii *must have an acid or lime-free soil and a reasonably sheltered position.*
5 *Rosemary* (Rosmarinus officinalis) *is a culinary herb as well as a most attractive ornamental shrub for dry, sunny places.*
6 *St John's wort (*Hypericum *'Hidcote') flowers throughout summer and into autumn.*

leaves are pink when young, grey green with cream variegations when mature. However, the flowers, crimson, add a touch of gaiety from midsummer onwards. It is excellent for tubs and pots, by steps or at the front of the border in sun. Any soil suits it.

Hebe (*H. × franciscana* 'Variegata')
An excellent foliage shrub, this hebe has leaves broadly margined in creamy white. Spikes of white flowers appear in summer. It grows in any well-drained soil, and is good for city or seaside gardens. It makes attractive informal hedges, and looks well combined with other evergreens.

Hydrangea (*H. macrophylla* 'Blue Wave')
'Blue Wave' is considered by many to be the finest of the lace-caps, which have a ring of large-petalled, sterile flowers surrounding a lacy mass of smaller fertile ones. It has strong, handsome leaves, and a graceful, low-growing habit. Feed and water well, and provide light shade. It is good for tubs or shaded courtyards.

Japonica (*Chaenomeles* 'Rowallane')
'Rowallane' is one of the best forms of this familiar plant, growing easily in most soils and sites. It is good as a specimen bush, can be clipped, or most splendidly of all, trained up a wall. The blood-red flowers are followed by speckled amber fruits.

Juniper (*Juniperus communis* 'Sentinel')
A pencil-thin variant of the common juniper, 'Sentinel' makes an excellent contrast to other plants in the rockery or heather garden, and makes a fine specimen plant, too. It does well in poor soil.

Laurel (*Prunus laurocerasus* 'Otto Lukyen')
A lovely, smaller form of the common laurel 'Otto Lukyen' has narrow, shiny leaves, held slightly upright. The spikes of white, heavily perfumed flowers are held well above the foliage, and appear in early spring. An excellent plant for shady courtyards or corners, it is very hardy, and not fussy about soil.

Mahonia (*M. aquifolium*)
Spiky leaves, purple or reddish all winter, long sprays of beautifully perfumed, pale-yellow flowers in late winter and early spring (worth bringing indoors), then rosettes of dark green new leaves, with strings of purple berries, makes this plant worthy of a space in any garden. It is happy in any soil, sun or shade.

Mock orange (*Philadelphus microphyllus*)
This twiggy bush with small greyish green leaves is fairly slow growing. It provides masses of delicate, white flowers with a magnificently rich scent that will fill the garden and grows to about 1.2m (4ft) high. It grows well even on poor soils.

Osmanthus (*O. heterophyllus*, syns. *O. ilicifolius, O. aquifolius*)
This is a slow-growing shrub of compact, rounded habit. It can be grown for hedging, in which case it will bear fewer flowers. Ideal for a scented shrub or flower bed, its clusters of white, fragrant flowers are borne from late summer through to autumn. The leaves are variable, some being similar to holly, while others on the same shrub may be spiny only at the tip. Though hardy, osmanthus needs shelter from cold winds.

Pieris (*P. formosa forrestii*)
A showy relative of the heather and rhododendrons, pieris likes the same sort of conditions, and looks splendid when planted with any of them. The young foliage is pretty, and masses of large, waxy, pale-pink flowers are produced in mid-spring.

Rosemary (*Rosmarinus officinalis*)
A lovely shrubby herb, rosemary is as essential in the kitchen as in the garden. Upright growing sorts make fine low hedges. Rosemary flowers prodigiously in late spring to summer, in shades of blue, pinkish, or white. Plant somewhere sunny, where you can touch it as you pass by.

St John's wort (*Hypericum* 'Hidcote')
An easily grown and exceptionally hardy bush, St John's wort is covered with bright-yellow flowers for much of the summer and well into autumn. The leaves, deep green, are more or less evergreen. It makes a good hedge. Site it carefully, because the flower colour sometimes clashes with other shrubs.

Senecio (*S. greyi*)
A popular, tough and easily grown silver-leafed shrub, senecio is rather sprawling but easily pruned. Any well-drained soil is suitable, but the shrub will grow best in full sun. Sprays of egg-yolk yellow flowers can be removed if they don't suit your colour scheme. Senecio is good in tubs, and at the seaside. Also listed as *S. × Dunedin* Hybrids or *S. paxifolius*.

Woolly willow (*Salix lanata*)
This attractive, spreading shrub has silvery-grey leaves after the yellow catkins have faded. It is particularly useful where you need to see something flowering in early spring – in a rock garden near the house, or by the edge of the patio, for example.

LARGE SHRUBS

Deservedly a popular choice for the bigger garden, large shrubs also have a worthy place in quite small plans. Depending on the space you have available, you can opt for a wide-ranging display or a single, special show piece.

Among the large shrubs are some very aristocratic plants indeed, but ones which can look quite as 'at home' in tiny gardens as they do in vast ones. If you do have a small area, it's easy to reject them all as being far too big, but that would be a mistake. A single well-grown plant of, say, *Magnolia stellata* or the witch hazel *(Hamamelis)* or even *Choisya ternata* can absolutely make a garden, even if you have to restrict the other planting to accommodate it. Certainly, if your front or back garden is larger than 4 sq m (12 sq ft), it is essential to have something in this category.

In a very small space, use one of the wall shrubs. *Garrya elliptica* does well in shade, producing long silvery grey catkins in late winter, which last right through until the following summer. It's also possible to use *Choisya*, though it will try to sprawl forwards and you may need to fasten it up. It's certainly one of the top ten evergreens, with perfectly polished leaves of three leaflets, and clusters of white, perfumed flowers in spring and early summer. It looks very much at home in small paved courtyards, planted among ferns and periwinkles.

Against sunny walls, the possibilities are enormous. If you want something that perfumes the air in deepest winter, try the winter sweet *(Chimonanthus praecox)* with its waxy yellow flowers. Slightly showier are the so-called winter flowering viburnums. In fact, they flower from autumn through spring, but only during mild spells. Nevertheless, once your plants are big enough, you can cut a few sprigs with their groups of white or pink tubular flowers to perfume a whole room.

For summer flowers, there are so many lovely plants that will enjoy growing on a moderately sunny wall, that you will find choosing difficult. Many sorts of ceanothus are good – 'Gloire de Versailles' isn't too big, and its powder-blue flowers suit the skies of late summer. There are also large numbers of escallonias – all with a scattering of short tubular flowers, either white, every possible shade of pink or some fine, soft reds. Many of the also have attractive glossy leaves.

If you want berries for autumn, plant some of the pyracanthas – some of the yellow berried sorts are exceptional. Birds will often strip your crop before winter really sets in, so you may need to net the plants. Black nylon netting is less obtrusive than the bright green sort.

In larger gardens, large shrubs will play an important role – forming the most dramatic elements in the shrubbery. Use some for a burst of early summer flowers. All the lilacs are marvellous, from the simple elegance of the Persian sort to the gorgeous range of double-flowered ones. Dramatic foliage plants can be found too, including the dozens of sorts of the common elder *(Sambucus nigra)*, some with frilled or jagged leaves, others variegated with silver or gold, and perhaps the most splendid of all – the golden elder. This has red berries, so you will need another sort if you want to make properly coloured jelly or wine. Even the common privet has variegated forms, and these can make splendid fillers for the shrubbery if allowed to grow unchecked.

Of course, many large shrubs make good hedges too. Even sorts that don't take kindly to trimming can be used to make fine informal hedges. Almost any of the mock oranges *(Philadelphus)* are wonderful, and if you plant several varieties, you will be able to have flowers for most of early and mid-summer.

Several other shrubs included in this chapter also make very fine hedges. Escallonias, for example, make fine flowering informal hedges, and they are particularly recommended for gardens near the sea, although they will also grow inland.

If you want a berrying hedge, then choose one of the firethorns or pyracanthas. These are spiny, so will form an impenetrable boundary hedge. Usually the firethorn is grown as a semi-formal hedge, for if it is pruned too hard it will produce very few berries. The best time for light trimming is after flowering as then it is easy to see whether or not berries are being removed.

The golden privet *(Ligustrum ovalifolium* 'Aureum') also makes a very bright and

Opposite *The smallest of the magnolias is* M. stellata, *which flowers in mid-spring. Sun or dappled shade, shelter from cold winds, a good soil and plenty of feeding will ensure masses of gorgeous flowers each year.*

Opposite 1 *There are many varieties of butterfly bush* (Buddleia davidii), *a popular one being 'Royal Red'.*
2 *'Donation' is one of the best of the* Camellia × williamsii *varieties and flowers in early spring.*
3 *Suitable for seaside gardens, the deciduous* Ceanothus *'Gloire de Versailles'.*
4 *The peach-pink flowers of Escallonia 'Peach Blossom' appear in summer. It is an evergreen shrub, reaching about 2m (6ft) in height.*
5 *One of many good firethorns,* Pyracantha *'Orange Glow' is evergreen and attains about 4m (12ft).*
6 Garrya elliptica *makes a good wall shrub and the male catkins appear in mid and late winter.*

colourful hedge and should be trimmed regularly to produce a formal shape. It is a particularly good subject for town gardens. The problem with privet, though, is that it needs trimming several times during the growing season if it is to look neat at all times.

The place for the grandest shrubs of all, though, is somewhere that they can lord it over all your other plants – either as a specimen on the lawn, or rising above a bed planted with evergreen carpeters, bulbs or dwarf shrubs.

Earliest to flower is the witch hazel (*Hamamelis mollis*). The other species and varieties of witch hazel differ in flower colour and size – some being a showy, pink-stained orange. Alas, the showier sorts lack fragrance, and have thus lost the principal pleasure that the plant can give. The sort called 'Pallida' has pale lemon flowers and the strongest perfume – half almond, half rose. Later in the season comes the smallest of the magnolias, *Magnolia stellata*. The flowers (narrow petalled, bowl shaped, in white or palest rose) are borne in huge quantities, and a large bush in full flower is genuinely breathtaking.

Good for neutral or acid soils are the wonderful camellias. For some reason these are often thought of as difficult, though few really are. Not all have flowers that resist bad weather well, and others refuse to drop them when they're over, but some are amongst the grandest of all garden plants. The single sorts, the anemone-flowered ones, the semi-doubles and sumptuous full doubles come in all shades of pink and scarlet, and most elegant of all, white. Many are veined, splashed or streaked in different shades. Some even have an elusive and delicious scent, though you really need to grow the plants in a cold greenhouse to fully enjoy it. One of the easiest of camellias, with wonderful drifts of orchid-pink flowers, is the lovely 'Donation'. It's a plant that every gardener should have.

The only disadvantage of large shrubs for modern gardens is that most of them take quite a few years to reach full size, and so to make their full effect. There are, though, some quick growing sorts. It's worth planting these in a new shrubbery, or wherever you need size quickly. Most of the large buddleias are excellent for this. Often called the butterfly bush, *Buddleia davidii* comes in various colours, from lovely white forms, to ones of the very deepest reddish-purple. Another good, quick and colourful plant is the broom *(Cytisus scoparius)*. Some have cascades of velvety scarlet flowers; others are pink and yellow or even rusty red. Perhaps the most spectacular of all is 'Cornish Cream' in just that colour.

Recommended Shrubs

Broom (*Cytisus scoparius* 'Cornish Cream')
This handsome shrub has closely packed, upright, whippy stems. From early to late summer, they are weighed down by masses of creamy white flowers. A quick-growing plant that likes full sun, and almost any dryish soil, it is particularly suitable for seaside planting.

Butterfly bush (*Buddleia davidii* 'Royal Red')
The graceful, arching branches in this cultivar are terminated by long trusses of unusual, red-purple flowers, which make an attractive background for the butterflies that will congregate in late summer. Prune the shrub hard in early spring to keep it compact and flowering well. Full sun and any soil are suitable.

Camellia (*C.* × *williamsii* 'Donation')
All camellias are wonderful shrubs for neutral or acid soils, either in open ground or in tubs. They have elegant, glossy leaves, a rather pendulous habit of growth and, in this sort, immaculate, semi-double pale-cerise flowers. Camellias do best against a sheltered wall, and are happy in sun or shade.

Ceanothus (*C.* 'Gloire de Versailles')
This handsome, rounded bush has bronzy green, strongly veined leaves. It flowers in late summer, producing spikes of a fine and delicate blue – though the framework stays behind and needs trimming back in late winter. Full sun and good soil are necessary, and it is a suitable plant for seaside gardens.

Escallonia (*E.* 'Peach Blossom')
A fine group of plants, escallonias are not fussy about soil or site, though some prefer shelter in winter. All are fine near the sea. Use them as hedges, windbreaks, wall shrubs, or single specimens. 'Peach Blossom' has bright pink flowers and particularly shiny leaves.

Firethorn (*Pyracantha* 'Orange Glow')
A splendid hedge or wall shrub, firethorn is very tough and vigorous. The white flower clusters are quickly followed by bunches of fine, orange–scarlet berries. The orange colour of this cultivar doesn't seem to attract the birds, so the berries are often safe until deepest winter. Any soil or site suits.

Garrya (*G. elliptica*)
Good against east or north facing walls, garrya is evergreen. The leaves can get

Opposite 1 *Plenty of space is needed for* Hydrangea paniculata *'Grandiflora', although it can be pruned hard to keep it more compact.*
2 Kerria japonica *'Pleniflora' flowers in spring, after which it is pruned hard.*
3 *The lilac called 'Sensation' has unusual flowers: purple-edged white.*
4 *The Mexican orange blossom (*Choisya ternata*) is pleasing all the year round with its evergreen foliage. It is hardly ever without flowers in spring and summer.*
5 *Most people think of privet only in terms of hedging, but the golden privet (*Ligustrum ovalifolium *'Aureum') makes a striking specimen in a shrub border.*
6 *A rather choice but easy winter-flowering shrub, ideal for wall training, is the wintersweet (*Chimonanthus praecox*).*

scorched by winter gales, though, so plant in shelter. Garrya is not fussy about soil or moisture levels, and is grown for its handsome male catkins, produced in mid and late winter. Female plants have long strings of berries in late summer.

Golden privet (*Ligustrum ovalifolium* 'Aureum')
The privets have a reputation for being boring, but when well grown make handsome shrubs. Golden privet can be hedged, but makes a spectacular specimen shrub, with brilliantly variegated, evergreen leaves. The flowers are perfumed. Very tough, golden privet prefers sun but will tolerate shade.

Hydrangea (*H. paniculata* 'Grandiflora')
If you want something really showy, this is it. The white flowers, carried in late summer, are immense 'mop heads', fading to dramatic tones of pale pink. Hydrangeas like a little shade and very rich feeding.

Kerria (*K. japonica* 'Pleniflora')
A useful and exceptionally tough shrub, kerria suckers so vigorously that it makes useful hedges and screens. The attractive, pom-pom flowers are orange-yellow. It is suitable for slightly wild gardens, under trees and to shelter more tender plants.

Lilac (*Syringa vulgaris* varieties)
These handsome, tree-like shrubs are best in full sun, but happy in most soils. Their perfume is a characteristic of early summer, and their trusses of spectacular flowers come in a multitude of shades of lilac, or in white. They can be single or double.

Magnolia (*M. stellata*)
An aristocratic plant, this magnolia likes a rich living – good soil, plenty of feeding, some shelter, and sun or dappled shade. It will reward you, once it's had a chance to grow, with a wonderful display of white or pale-pink flowers in mid-spring. Good plants to grow with it are ferns, ivy and white autumn crocuses.

Mexican orange blossom (*Choisya ternata*)
Happy in sun or shade, Mexican orange blossom likes a certain amount of shelter – the leaves can be damaged by icy wind. It appreciates feeding and moisture, but will do without. It has a splendid shape, aromatic evergreen leaves, and a thick scattering of scented, white flowers in spring and summer.

Mock orange (*Philadelphus* 'Avalanche')
Mock oranges do well even on poor soils, but do need sun. Out of flower, the form

'Avalanche' is upright and twiggy, clothed with neat leaves. In midsummer, the flowers are so abundant that the branches are weighed down in a very spectacular way. The flowers are single, white, and very heavily perfumed.

Red-barked dogwood (*Cornus alba* 'Elegantissima')
This dogwood is good in winter, when the thin, upright branches glow red among the other drab, brown shrubs. It is even better in summer, when clothed with narrow leaves, brilliantly variegated white and green. A good shrubbery plant and happy in most sites and soils.

Smoke bush (*Cotinus coggygria* 'Atropurpureus')
A splendid bush, its Latin name refers to the smoky purple plumes of tiny flowers and stems. It is pretty in the shrubbery or as an informal hedge. Try planting one behind small Japanese maples. The leaves have subtle autumn colouring, though for a more striking effect, try one of the purple-leafed forms, such as 'Royal Purple'.

Viburnum (*V. × carlecephalum*)
A 'high value' shrub, this viburnum is easily grown in sun on almost any soil. Its rounded clusters of white flowers appear in late spring, pink in bud, with a powerful and marvellous scent. The leaves are light green and attractively veined, often giving spectacular autumn colours.

Winter-flowering viburnum (*V. farreri*)
This will keep you out in the garden in midwinter, when its pink-budded, white flowers can perfume a sunny afternoon. The leaves are attractive, too, bronzy green and very nicely veined. Winter-flowering viburnum forms a picturesquely shaped bush, thriving in sun, or light shade. It tolerates most soils.

Wintersweet (*Chimonanthus praecox*)
This pretty and undemanding wall shrub is ideal if you've plenty of space on a sunny site, and don't mind waiting a few years before your shrub flowers. When it does, the small, yellow flowers will enliven winter with their very special scent.

Witch hazel (*Hamamelis mollis* 'Pallida')
This is a 'high value' shrub, though it lacks spectacular flowers. They are pale yellow, a bit spidery, but produced in midwinter and wonderfully scented. The leaves turn amber and yellow in autumn. A good 'specimen' shrub, witch hazel is happy in most soils, and will tolerate partial shade, if necessary.

SMALL GARDEN TREES

For most people, no garden is complete without at least one tree somewhere in sight and, whether for decoration, for fruiting, or for foliage and bark effects, small garden trees seem to add an extra dimension to even the most grandiose layout.

It is possible to garden without trees, though trees are often what gives a garden its atmosphere. Even if your garden is tiny, look at it carefully to see where you could possibly fit a tree in – remember that all sorts of lovely plants will happily grow in the light shade of its leaves.

Trees can give your garden a sense of scale and serenity, can screen you from neighbouring properties, provide you with flowers in spring, shade in summer, and often good leaf colour in autumn. In winter, they can stop your garden looking too bleak and empty – some even have wonderfull bark to add interest to the winter scene.

Once you are convinced that you need a tree or two, it's tempting to be greedy and plant something fast growing – while promising yourself that you will cut it down when it's too big. However, by the time you notice that it's too big, it will probably be vast, and you won't feel able to tackle it. It is much better to plant something slower growing, which will remain reasonably in scale with your garden without too much work. Alternatively, use something moderately quick growing, but also easily pruned. The eating quince *(Cydonia oblonga)* is just such a plant, making a marvellous garden tree, its arching branches of silvery leaves covered with large flowers in spring. In autumn, the leaves turn clear yellow, and the branches are hung with amber quinces until you harvest them in early winter (they'll make the whole kitchen smell delicious).

If you like the idea of fruit trees in the garden, but don't want to encourage raiding parties of children, the quince is good but, if anything, the medlar is even better. It's quite slow growing (so you won't have to prune at all), but it eventually produces a very picturesque tree, ideal as a specimen tree on a small lawn. The flowers are large, creamy white, and held at the tip of every twig. The fruits are russet apple shaped – you should harvest them before the first hard frosts and store them indoors until they soften a few weeks later. Eat them fresh or turn them into delicious jelly. The leaves turn purple, bronze and red before

they fall, making it one of autumn's best sights. Its official name is *Mespilus germanica*.

The medlar has been almost forgotten as a fruit tree, but many gardeners still plant crab apples (*Malus* varieties). There are vast numbers of these, with fruit in all sorts of shapes and colours, though one of the best for both decoration and cooking is the popular 'John Downie'. The flowers are more heavily scented than most other apples, and they're followed by immense crops of oblong yellow fruits with a rosy flush. Jelly made from them is lovely.

The rowan *(Sorbus aucuparia)* has berries that are edible too, though if you want something more unusual than the wild plant's red fruits, look for some of the sorts with orange or yellow ones. *S.* 'Joseph Rock' has yellow fruit, *S. sargentiana,* scarlet. Birds, often being rather conventional, leave them alone until they're really hungry.

However, if you'd like a flowering tree (as opposed to one that fruits as well), there are hundreds to choose from. Laburnums are widely planted, but that doesn't stop them being wonderful to own in early summer, when they are decked out in yellow. Once your tree's big, plant a clambering rose beside it to grow up through the branches – laburnums are a bit dull when the flowers are finished. Never dull are the false acacias (*Robinia* species and varieties), and the drooping racemes of scented flowers are almost a bonus. The increasingly popular *R. pseudoacacia* 'Frisia' is grown for its golden foliage. It's worth growing by itself, or perhaps against something with dark-green leaves – an ivy-covered wall perhaps. Keep it well away from any other tree with coloured leaves, especially any of the purple ornamental apples or plums.

Some of these can look splendid elsewhere, though look for ones that have white flowers, or which flower before the leaves open. Two shades of pink on one tree can sometimes clash.

Amongst the flowering cherries (*Prunus* varieties) there are so many wonderful trees that you will wish you had enough room to plant them all. *P. sargentii* is perfect for a small front garden, but the winter-

Opposite There is a very wide range of crab apples available and most are of a suitable size for small or medium-sized gardens. The spring flowers are followed by fruits, which in most varieties are highly decorative. The variety shown here, Malus × eleyi, is considered to be one of the most beautiful of all the crab apples.

flowering *P. subhirtella* 'Autumnalis' is more easily found. In spite of its name, it flowers mostly during mild spells, and more abundantly near spring.

Sometimes it's useful to have a very narrow tree to give an 'accent' to a garden, perhaps by a path, or to make the corner of a boundary. Some of the evergreens do this exceptionally well. Not many gardens are warm enough to support the lovely Italian cypress *(Cupressus sempervirens)*, but there are several sorts of juniper that fulfill the same function. All are fairly slow growing, but can eventually reach 8m (25ft). To keep them in shape, it's worth putting a few twists of black twine around them in autumn, so that the snow doesn't build up on the branches and begin to bend them dangerously outwards.

Narrow forms of the flowering cherry have been very popular, though they almost always look tight and unnatural. They also get quite big. Try using instead one of the multitude of Japanese maples (mostly varieties of *Acer palmatum)*. These are ideal small garden trees, often growing well even in very shaded gardens. New leaves are beautiful in youth and middle age, but all put on an extraordinary display of colour in autumn – though check the variety you're buying to see what colour it goes.

Many people, when they want a weeping tree, choose the weeping willow. This is generally a great mistake, for it eventually makes a gigantic tree, invariably swamping the entire garden. It is only, therefore, suitable for really large gardens.

Instead choose one of the small weeping trees, an excellent one being the willow-leafed pear (*Pyrus salicifolia* 'Pendula'). This is suitable even for small town gardens, and in spring and summer is most attractive with its narrow, silvery-grey leaves.

Trees are expensive to buy, and once they're established, are difficult to move, so place them carefully and plant well. Few small trees are particularly dangerous to house or wall foundations, but to be on the safe side, try to keep them 1.8m (6ft) away from danger areas. It's always pleasing to be able to walk underneath something, so plant one or two beside a path, beside the front gate or car entrance, or where they can shade a seat. Remember, too, that all trees help improve the 'townscape' if you live in a city, or the landscape in the country. Try to visualize how the tree will fit in with the location outside your own particular garden. In towns, the showiest and most colourful of trees can look excellent, though the same tree can look out of place in the country. In general, the best trees there are ones closely related to native species, or to kitchen garden fruits.

Recommended Trees

Bonfire tree (*Malus tschonoskii*)

This is a 'high value' small tree. It produces flower clusters in white or apple pink, followed by yellow–green fruits with a red flush. Most glorious of all in autumn, its leaves glow in flame colours. The bonfire tree is a good choice for a small, paved courtyard or patio, or as a lawn specimen. It will grow in most fertile soils.

Crab apple (*Malus* 'John Downie')

A handsome crab apple, 'John Downie' is slightly graceless in its winter shape, but is covered with heavily perfumed flowers in spring, followed by small oblong apples, rich golden yellow with a red blush on one side in autumn. They're delicious, but the birds clear them by early winter.

False acacia (*Robinia pseudoacacia* 'Frisia')

A very graceful plant with attractive furrowed bark in winter, this form has bright-yellow foliage in summer, as if in permanent sunshine. When it flowers, it does it tastefully, in white and yellow, and the flowers are fragrant. It is good in town gardens, and in most soils. It will also tolerate shade.

Golden Indian bean tree (*Catalpa bignonioides* 'Aurea')

The most dramatic of all the gold-leafed trees, this one has huge leaves, so plant it in a sheltered spot. Otherwise it is easy to grow, though it won't flower in colder areas. If you treat the plant as a shrub and cut it back annually, the leaves produced will be even bigger.

Golden sycamore (*Acer pseudoplatanus* 'Brilliantissimum')

This is a smaller, and special, form of the common sycamore. There are other yellow-leafed forms available, but this has very decorative young leaves, bright pink at first, turning yellow-green, then, for a short while, dark green. It needs sun and good soil, and regular feeding for best results.

Irish juniper (*Juniperus communis* 'Hibernica')

This lovely juniper is a very narrow-growing variant of the common juniper. It is very hardy and easily grown, even in poor soils. It is an excellent 'accent' in wild gardens, and essential in all formal ones.

Japanese maple (*Acer palmatum* 'Osakazuki')

A charming plant, the Japanese maple is interesting to look at even when leafless. The reddish buds produce jade-green,

Opposite 1 *The best of the laburnums is the form 'Vossii' as it has the longest flower trails of all. Laburnums grow particularly well on chalky soils.*
2 Magnolia × soulangiana *'Alba Superba' can be trained against a wall if space is at a premium.*
3 *Not often thought of as an ornamental tree, the medlar* (Mespilus germanica) *makes a good lawn specimen and the leaves colour well in autumn.*
4 *The snowy mespilus* (Amelanchier canadensis) *is attractive in spring when it is covered in white flowers, and in autumn when the leaves change to brilliant hues.*
5 *The thorn* (Crataegus prunifolia) *has superb autumn leaves and berries and will grow in exposed and windy situations.*
6 *A far better choice for most gardens than the huge weeping willow is the willow-leaved pear* (Pyrus salicifolia *'Pendula'). It makes a very shapely weeping specimen and is particularly suitable for urban gardens.*

lobed leaves. The colour lasts until autumn, when they turn almost laquer scarlet, and stay that way, for several weeks. It is happy in shade and good for courtyards.

Laburnum *(Laburnum × watereri 'Vossii')*
One of the grandest of the laburnums the form 'Vossii' is slow growing though eventually it makes a good-sized tree. In late spring, it is covered with immense trails of yellow, perfumed flowers. Being a sterile hybrid, it won't produce the poisonous seeds that are normally associated with laburnums.

Magnolia *(Magnolia × soulangiana 'Alba Superba')*
This magnolia is immensely popular, and justifiably so. It is best planted in rich, deep soil, never on chalk, and it does well in towns. It is a first class specimen tree, particularly if planted against a plain background. Large, perfumed flowers, perfectly white, appear in late spring.

Medlar *(Mespilus germanica)*
Medlar is a lovely and ancient fruit tree, of gnarled and picturesque appearance even when quite young. It carries showy, pale-cream flowers in early summer, and bronzed green foliage. In autumn, small russet fruits are produced, and the leaves turn purple, yellow and scarlet. Medlar is easily grown, and makes a good specimen tree.

Paper-bark maple *(Acer griseum)*
This is a 'high value' small tree, but in unusual seasons: autumn and winter. The leaves are orange, scarlet and red in autumn, and then in winter, the old bark peels away in sheets, revealing smooth, chestnut-brown bark beneath. It is very picturesque, easily grown, and is good as a specimen tree. Plant ivy or periwinkle beneath it.

Purple-leafed plum *(Prunus cerasifera 'Pissardii')*
This is probably one of the most popular purple-leafed trees with deep-red young leaves, turning purple as the season progresses. The flowers are white, though pink in bud. It is good in town gardens, or for a hedge, and easily grown.

Quince *(Cydonia oblonga 'Portugal')*
The quince is an ancient inhabitant of gardens. Its graceful growth habit is interesting when leafless; the young leaves are silvery, later dark green. Its handsome flowers are held above the foliage, like candles, and are white with a pink flush. The large, oval fruit is freckled in amber, brown and green, and is heavily scented. The leaves turn yellow in autumn.

Rowan *(Sorbus cashmiriana)*
A lovely small rowan tree, with many jagged leaflets to each leaf, it is very pretty even when not in flower or fruit. The flowers are whitish pink in clusters, and the fruits that follow are very large and white, like beads. They remain on the tree long after the leaves fall, and look very dramatic. It is easily grown.

Snowy mespilus *(Amelanchier canadensis)*
This pretty, twiggy plant makes a large bush or small tree, depending on pruning. A mass of tiny white flowers are produced in spring, before the leaves appear, and these are followed by edible berries. The leaves often colour wonderfully in mild autumns, and can be spectacular. It is very hardy and wind tolerant, and grows particularly well in damp soil.

Thorn *(Crataegus × prunifolia)*
This hybrid tree has purple twigs, handsome, glossy leaves, and the prominent cluster of flowers are followed by long-lasting, orange berries. These are wonderfully set off by the contrasting, scarlet autumn leaf colour. It is easily grown on most soils, and is excellent near the sea, or in similarly harsh environments.

Variegated holly *(Ilex aquifolium 'Aureo-marginata')*
This holly is often grown as a bush, but it is easily grown as a handsome tree. 'Aureo-marginata' has shiny green leaves in the familiar shape, but with an edge of cream. Excellent in town gardens, and easily shaped as you need, it can be allowed to grow to its full size in country locations. It is also good near the sea. The berries are a familiar red.

Willow-leafed pear *(Pyrus salicifolia 'Pendula')*
The willow-leafed pear is good for urban gardens and, as a specimen tree, it's often seen in 'white' gardens. A graceful, silver-leafed, weeping tree, it makes all sorts of colour schemes possible. Surround it with old roses, and lavenders, or twine clematis up through it. It is happy in most soils and prefers sun.

Winter-flowering cherry *(Prunus subhirtella 'Autumnalis')*
This cherry has rather small flowers compared to some other flowering cherries, but it is valuable because of its flowering season. In spite of the name, there is most flower in early spring. The leaves can colour well in long slow autumns. It is easily grown in most fertile soils but prefers a sunny location.

CLIMBERS

In every garden, use can be made of vertical space by growing a few climbing plants. A combination of flowering and foliage kinds will enhance the walls of a house, but climbers can also be grown up pergolas and arches or through old trees.

All the climbers are immensely useful plants, and there can be no garden that isn't improved by having at least one or two of them. There's no reason why any gardener should have to look at an ugly wall, when it can be a source of great pleasure if covered with Virginia creeper *(Parthenocissus quinquefolia)*, one of the hundreds of sorts of ivy (mostly *Hedera helix*), or even the climbing hydrangea *(Hydrangea petiolaris)*. Climbers are perfect for small, city gardens which are surrounded by high walls, and where there isn't really room to plant some of the larger wall shrubs. Few climbers are ever thicker than 15cm (6in), so the wall can be entirely green while hardly reducing the ground area of the garden.

It's always worthwhile using several sorts of climber, if there is room. A large wall of one plant can get dull, but if there are several shapes and colours of foliage, you will find that they make a much better background for your other plants. Even if you can't provide some sort of support, there's still an exciting range of self-clinging climbers to choose from. All the ivies are good, whether you plant the spiky 'birds foot' ivy (*H. h.* 'Caenwoodiana'), or some of the handsome variegated sorts. Even that doesn't exhaust the ivy's range, for some types have leaves almost as frilled as parsley, others have elaborately jagged ones. When buying, make sure that the ivy is suitable for climbing – some are better for ground cover, or even small bushes.

Ivies are evergreen, but some of the deciduous self-clinging climbers are valuable for handsome summer foliage and dramatic autumn colours. The well-known Virginia creeper is deservedly popular, but try combining it with its pretty relative *Parthenocissus henryana*, or Boston ivy *(P. tricuspidata)*.

If at all possible, add the climbing hydrangea to the other creepers. This gets off to a slow start, but grows fast once it gets started – and is worth waiting for. The autumn leaf colour is a lovely clear yellow which combines well with the scarlet and bronzes of the *Parthenocissus* species.

If you can provide wire supports or a trellis for your climbers, your range expands enormously, though on the whole most of the new possibilities need more sun than the self-supporting types.

Russian vine *(Polygonum baldschuanicum)* and *Clematis montana* are only suitable for the largest walls, and both can quickly swamp a small house. Even some of the honeysuckles can be quite rampant – though their luxuriance is a good part of their charm, the trumpet-shaped flowers the rest. If you choose your plants carefully, you can have them flowering from early summer well into early winter.

It's fun to have something a little bit grand against your house walls. All the summer-flowering clematis are lovely, though there are some extremely attractive, spring-flowering species. Sadly, the two sorts need to be pruned in different ways, so it isn't possible to plant them together, though the spring sorts can be combined with the summer-flowering solanums or with jasmine.

Some clematis are scented but common jasmine *(Jasminum officinale)* pours out its scent. Try growing it around doors or windows – cottages often have a wirework or wrought iron porch wreathed in masses of it. In slightly grander gardens, try making an 'arbour' – a spacious framework large enough to take a few chairs and a table – and covering it with jasmine. It will soon become a perfect place to spend a warm summer evening.

For south-facing house walls, at least in the warmer parts of the country, it's possible to get good crops of grapes. White sorts are usually easier than black ones, and check that you have an early variety. The leaves of most dessert types generally go amber-yellow in autumn, but the wonderful 'Brandt' goes scarlet (the fruit is black, small and very sweet), and *Vitis vinifera* 'Purpurea' has wine-purple leaves in summer, turning bronze and crimson in autumn. Both are very much worth growing, though in colder areas they won't actually produce a crop.

Even more than with other garden plants, with climbers it's important to think about

Opposite *The hybrid clematis, such as 'Hagley Hybrid', are summer-flowering climbers which can be trained to walls, fences and even through trees and large shrubs. All clematis appreciate cool roots and these should be shaded, with their top growth exposed to the sun.*

Opposite 1 Akebia quinata *is not one of the hardiest climbers and needs a warm sheltered wall.*
2 *The vigorous Chilean potato tree (*Solanum crispum *'Glasnevin') can be pruned fairly hard if it outgrows its allotted space.*
3 *The Chinese Virginia creeper (*Parthenocissus henryana) *will succeed on a north-facing wall, and although vigorous can be trimmed to keep it within bounds.*
4 *Producing small flowers, but plenty of them, is* Clematis montana *'Elizabeth'.*
5 *Large-flowered clematis include the well-known 'Mrs Cholmondeley', vigorous and easy.*
6 Clematis *'Ville de Lyon' produces large blooms from midsummer to early autumn.*

the flower colours. Against old stonework or old brick, or against weatherboard or wooden shingles, almost any colour will look good. However, it can be difficult to choose good colours to set against new red or orange brick, or even Victorian red brick. Colour-washed rendering can also be difficult. Against red brick, only the palest colours, or white, look at all right. One of the most floriferous of the white-flowered climbers is the lovely *Solanum jasminoides* 'Album', which stays in flower for most of the summer. It is actually related to the humble potato of the vegetable garden. Hard winters can cut it back, so protect the lowest parts of the stem with straw or sacking. White wisteria can look good but, on the whole, it's safer to go for foliage climbers. Try some of the *Vitis* or *Parthenocissus* species. Avoid anything variegated.

Pink rendered wall are only slightly less difficult, though flowers in other shades of pink can look nice. Pale, bleached-out colours that you might not consider for the rest of the garden can also work very well.

There's no problem at all with climbers in the garden itself, where almost everything looks perfect. Apart from climbers over arches, pergolas or fences, it's a good idea to use climbers over other plants – and if you choose species with different flowering times, you can have a long season of colour from a small area of ground. Some clematis look lovely scrambling through shrubs, particularly through some of the larger bush roses, or through old fruit trees. Ivies grow up trees in nature, and the garden forms can look really fine on the trunks of garden trees. The climbing hydrangea can look better still, though it needs a fairly substantial tree. If you don't mind a picturesque tangle (some gardeners are dreadfully tidy), the vines look splendid when allowed to twine upwards through a wall trained rose, and the autumn colours take over from the last of the flowers.

Sometimes, when gardeners cut down a large tree, which may have died, they are unable to remove the stump of the lower part of the trunk. In this instance, it is worth growing a suitable climber over it as camouflage. Several are suitable, especially the evergreen ivies or any of the honeysuckles.

Some climbers can even be grown without supports, being used as ground cover to clothe banks as an attractive alternative to grass. Clematis can be used in this way, particularly the small-flowered kinds such as *C. montana* varieties. Most of the ivies can also be used in this way and are ideal for shady banks. When buying ivies for such use, make sure you buy those sold as ground cover, and not those trained to canes.

Recommended Climbers

Akebia (*A. quinata*)
This lovely, almost evergreen climber can reach 9m (30ft) in height. The leaves, like a hand, are made up of five leaflets, oval and dark green. Against a south-facing wall, it will also have purplish, fragrant flowers in spring, and in a hot year, exotic looking fruit.

Chilean potato tree (*Solanum crispum* 'Glasnevin')
A fairly tough and hardy climbing potato, it is good for walls, low fences, even sheds and garages. Clusters of nightshade-like flowers in soft purple with a yellow centre bloom all summer and early autumn. It does best in full sun, but tolerates any soil.

Chinese gooseberry (*Actinidia chinensis* 'Aureovariegata')
This climber has stems covered with red bristles, producing dramatic and quite large variegated leaves, often of three colours. It likes sun and rich soil, and will produce both whitish yellow, fragrant flowers and fruit (the familiar 'kiwi' – though if you plant seeds from bought fruit you won't get variegated leaves).

Chinese Virginia creeper (*Parthenocissus henryana*)
This climber produces clusters of sticky discs to help itself up your walls. The leaves are very handsome, composed of several leaflets. In shade, the leaf veins are distinguished and pale. In all situations, the leaves turn wonderful reds in autumn. Fruits, if you're lucky, are blue. It is an extremely vigorous plant.

Clematis (*C. montana* 'Elizabeth')
'Elizabeth' is an attractive, pink-flowered variant of the species. It is slightly less vigorous, which makes it more useful, and slightly more fragrant. Good in most situations, but in a sunny one it will produce a sheet of flowers in spring and early summer. It can be pruned after flowering.

Clematis (*C.* 'Mrs Cholmondeley')
This is an excellent plant, vigorous (they aren't all) and easy. It produces hosts of elegant, pale-blue flowers, its petals quite narrow, giving a more delicate effect than some other large-flowered clematis. It is excellent for training along fences or around windows.

Clematis (*C.* 'Ville de Lyon')
This flowers best against a south facing wall, but grow among other plants, so that the lower stem and roots are shaded. Cut back, if you want, in late winter. Otherwise

Opposite 1 *One of the earliest honeysuckles to flower is the early Dutch (*Lonicera periclymenum *'Belgica').*
2 *Many varieties of ivy (*Hedera helix*) have variegated foliage, like the popular 'Goldheart'.*
3 *The summer jasmine (*Jasminum officinale*) will rapidly cover a wall or fence.*
4 *Although the vine (*Vitis vinifera *'Brandt') produces fruit in a good summer, it is grown primarily for autumn leaf colour.*
5 *The Virginia creeper (*Parthenocissus quinquefolia*) will rapidly cover a house wall and is self-clinging. Brilliant autumn leaf colour is its main attraction.*
6 *Regular pruning is necessary for wisteria (*Wisteria sinensis*) or it will produce a tangled mass of growth.*

allow it its head, and get earlier, and higher, flowers. It looks lovely scrambling among big roses or up old fruit trees.

Climbing hydrangea *(H. anomala petiolaris)*
The lovely chestnut-brown stems make nice patterns when leafless, the leaves are fresh green and glossy. Heads of creamy white flowers stand out from the main vegetation. It is perfect for north-facing walls, or up bare and boring tree trunks. It is an easy plant to grow, but slow at the start.

Early Dutch honeysuckle *(Lonicera periclymenum 'Belgica')*
This is a selected form of the lovely native woodbine, familiar in hedgerows and cottage gardens. 'Belgica' begins flowering in late spring and early summer, then flowers a little more in early autumn. Its flowers are reddish on the outside, fading to deep cream. It is a vigorous and very fragrant plant, suitable for sun or shade.

Ivy *(Hedera varieties)*
All the ivies are excellent and versatile garden plants, happy in sun or shade. All the sorts listed here are good for walls, tree trunks, over rockeries, or even over bare ground if you need ground cover. Ivies do well on most soils, and thrive in the best and worst corners of a garden.
H. helix 'Caenwoodiana' has rather small leaves, divided into three to five, narrow spiked lobes. It takes a while to cover fully, but is exceptionally graceful.
H. helix 'Gold Heart' has attractive leaves, each a glossy, dark green with three pointed lobes and a prominent spash of gold at its centre.
H. colchica 'Dentata Variegata' A most spectacular ivy, it has large, variably shaped leaves, green and greyish green, with a dramatic cream margin. It can be difficult to get started, but soon grows away fast.

Japanese honeysuckle *(Lonicera japonica 'Halliana')*
This very vigorous climber has evergreen leaves in shelter or warmth, but it loses its leaves in severe winters or exposed gardens. The flowers start in early summer and finish in midwinter. They are white, becoming creamy orange. Although the flowers are a little sparse, they are deliciously scented. Good for cutting.

Jasmine *(Jasminum officinale)*
The immense popularity of this climber is due to its pure-white flowers, overwhelmingly scented, in mid to late summer. It needs full sun, a little shelter, and rich soil. Easy and very vigorous, it is also good for growing in pots.

Jasmine nightshade *(Solanum jasminoides 'Album')*
A slightly tender climber of great beauty, it grows best against sheltered, south-facing walls. Give protection to the base of the stems in winter. It is covered with graceful, white, bell-shaped flowers all summer and until the first frosts. Vigorous, it happily grows up to 7–8m (20–25ft). Take summer cuttings as an insurance.

Russian vine *(Polygonum baldschuanicum)*
A quick growing and wildly rampant climber, it has coarse and undistinguished foliage. Russian vine is quite pretty in summer, when covered with sprays of small cream flowers. The plant will swamp sheds, garages, even small houses and trees. Good for quick cover, it creates problems when big.

Vine *(Vitis vinifera)* 'Brandt'
This popular, hardy vine is vigorous, growing up to 10m (30ft). It can fruit against a south-facing wall in a good summer. The blue-black fruit is both interesting and delicious, but the vine is primarily grown for the leaves – handsome in summer, dramatic as they change to scarlet and purple (the veins stay green) in autumn.

Vine *(Vitis vinifera)* 'Purpurea'
This is another dramatic vine, worth growing near 'Brandt', or mixing with a clematis or training up a silver-leafed tree. The leaves are red, then deep purple, finishing bronze and scarlet. The fruit, if you get it, is black and sweet. It thrives in good soil and plenty of sun.

Virginia creeper *(Parthenocissus quinquefolia)*
This familiar climber is still often seen covering Victorian houses. It is a vigorous climber, doing well in most soils and on most walls. Keep it trimmed if it endangers your gutters or windows. Virginia creeper provides wonderful autumn colours.

Winter jasmine *(Jasminum nudiflorum)*
This wall shrub should be in every garden, for it is very hardy, will grow almost anywhere and is happy even against a sunless north-facing wall. Growing to about 3m (10ft), its bright yellow flowers are produced from autumn to spring.

Wisteria *(Wisteria sinensis)*
One of the most aristocratic of the climbers, vigorous but not swamping, wisteria needs full sun, good soil, and some pruning to be at its best. In flower, it's worth all the work. Try it on walls, or if you've nothing suitable, on pergolas, up trees, or even as a standard.

ROSES

Roses are so diverse in habit that there is one to meet almost every garden need: they can combine with other shrubs, fit formal bedding schemes or even make good hedges.

History

Gardeners seem to have loved roses almost since gardening began, and some sorts have been in cultivation for at least five thousand years. In Europe, by Greek and Roman times, though there were only a few rose varieties, they were already the epitome of beauty and luxury. Their flowering season was still very short, so roses were actually forced – to give rich Romans their pleasures a few weeks earlier. One Roman emperor of unusual tastes drowned his guests in rose petals at the end of a particularly good orgy. It's difficult to know what varieties he used, but several still grown are sufficiently old – including the so-called Jacobite rose *(Rosa alba maxima)* and the equally fine centifolia rose – to have been possibilities.

By Elizabethan times, British gardeners had quite a number of fully double roses, from the ancient and striped 'Rosa Mundi' to the absoutely lovely 'Empress Josephine' also known as 'Francofurtana'. Elizabethan gardeners also had rather more of what they called 'musk' roses, but they also liked briars, including the scented-leaf eglantine *(Rosa rubiginosa)*, and the double field rose. All had medicinal uses.

The passion for roses developed at the same time as more and more sorts of rose were brought in from the Middle East, India and China, and though no-one knew anything about sophisticated breeding mechanisms in plants, exciting new sorts began to appear. By the end of the 18th century, lovely new varieties appeared every season, mostly fully double, in white or in subtle shades of pink. All were marvellously scented but had (with one exception), a short flowering season of three to four weeks in midsummer.

The 19th century, with the gardening world now fully aware of the possibilities of plant breeding, was poised to make use of the China rose. This ancient Chinese garden plant (still worth growing in its own right) flowers throughout the growing season, and new, long-season roses soon appeared, still in the 'old' colour range. Though the yellow flowered Austrian briar, *(R. foetida)* had been in gardens here for centuries, in the latter part of the 19th century it was crossed with some of the new 'perpetual' roses to give a completely new series of shrill reds, oranges and, most exciting of all, fully double yellows. The Austrian briar also allowed an obscure fungus – black spot – that attacked it to attack all its progeny.

With more and more species still arriving, and more breeding taking place, nursery catalogues listed thousands of roses. The tea scented rose *(R. × odorata)* arrived in 1810, but took fifty years before it, too, was crossed with the new sorts of rose. It produced the hybrid tea roses, which soon became so popular that all the other sorts or rose, however lovely, were almost instantly dropped. It's gone on to become almost the rose of the 20th century.

Classification

Nothing in the rose world stands still. Most sorts of rose cross with most other sorts, so no sooner does one classification become established than the groups of roses it defines dissolve or vanish as breeders get to work. None of this stops roses, old and new, being any less beautiful – but the present classification is more or less as follows:

Wild roses This group includes all the basic species (though remember that some of these are not true species, found in the wild, but simply ancient garden plants that have been given names like *R. damascena, R. alba* etc.). It also includes the varieties of wild and garden species, as well as some of the simplest crosses between them. Thus the lovely 18th century Alba shrub rose 'Céleste' finds itself here, as does the modern 'Nevada', derived from *R. moyesii.* There are dozens of wonderful garden plants, from immense climbers that will produce shoots 8m (25ft) long in a season, right down to dwarf forms of *R. chinensis.*

Old garden roses These comprise the many roses, mostly fully double and with short flowering seasons, that were in gardens before 1860, the date that marks the advent of the hybrid teas. Over the last thirty or forty years they have become newly fashionable as some gardeners have turned away from the strong colours and sometimes poor perfume of hybrid teas and polyanthas.

Opposite One of the most popular groups of roses are the cluster-flowered or floribunda roses, which are ideal for mass planting in beds. The variety shown here is 'Dearest'.

They've rediscovered some wonderful plants – and as old garden roses rarely need pruning, they rather suit gardeners who are busy and don't insist on colour all summer. Ironically, some breeders have started crossing the best of the old types with modern ones – in the hope of getting perpetual flowering roses with the old shape, colour and scent. Some of the results are very pretty and do have a long season, but have (so far) lost a little of the finesse of the old sorts.

Modern garden roses The Victorian passion for bedding schemes needed plants that flowered all summer. The hybrid tea, easily pruned and kept as a small bush, fitted their ideas perfectly. The colours, once the Austrian briar had been mixed in, were strong, rich, or at least cheerful (none of those anaemic pinks of the previous generation). Many gardeners still like rose beds, and the hybrid teas are still ideal. They're now assigned to a sub-group called large-flowered bush roses, and have elegant buds, opening into flamboyantly large flowers.

Plants with small leaflets and bunches of small, rosette-shaped flowers comprise the polyantha group, and also contain many roses especially suitable for bedding.

Tall-growing roses, classed as ramblers or climbers, recruit roses from all classes. Some are simply climbing 'sports' (a sort of minor mutation) of hybrid tea varieties, others are hybrids between rampant species (like the musk rose) and various sorts of bush rose, and others are closely related to, or exactly the same as, wild species. Some can be used on house walls, on pergolas and arches, or even to climb up trees. If you have a large-scale wall, try covering it with *R. brunonii* 'La Mortola' or *R. filipes* 'Kiftsgate'.

The miniature roses are largely developed from the dwarf form of the China rose. They're exceptionally pretty, though they are difficult to integrate into the general garden – their refinements are rather lost if planted with other small shrubs. They do well in large pots, and that's probably the best way of actually *seeing* them.

However, don't worry about rose groups too much. It is some help in knowing how to prune – though that's most important for the bedding roses – but if you begin to explore some of the tens of thousands of marvellous roses now available, you'll be too excited to care.

Growing roses
Buying
If you want a few colourful bushes for a rose bed, have a look at what your local garden centre sells. Wait until flowering starts; that way, you can see exactly what the flowers are like, and also check that the plant is properly established in its container. It is best to choose plants with a few strong-growing shoots, with good bark and leaves, rather than one with a greater number of scrawny stems.

However, no garden centre can hope to carry anything like a representative selection of this vast group, so you're unlikely to find anything much outside the three or four dozen most popular plants. If you need something unusual, you'll almost certainly have to buy from a specialist nursery. If at all possible, visit it during the season – you might see roses even more beautiful than the ones you initially wanted. If you can't visit in person, get your order in as quickly as possible once you've read the catalogue.

Your roses will arrive bare rooted. It's almost always worthwhile giving the roots a soak in a bucket of water for a few hours as soon as they arrive. In the unlikely event of your plants arriving badly shrivelled, bury the plants in a trench in the garden for a week or so.

Planning
If you want proper rose beds, remember that maintenance is much easier, the simpler the design. It's best to have the rose beds in an open part of the garden, rather than against a wall or fence. Beds should be about 1.5m (5ft) wide, which will allow you to plant bushes three deep, and still give yourself 30cm (12in) between the outermost rose and the edge of the bed. That's enough to avoid too much overhang, which can make mowing, weeding and even walking past difficult. The paths between the beds need to be at least 1m (3ft) wide. If your design needs height to make it look exciting, plant standards in the centres of the beds, or plant ramblers up a tripod of poles.

Colours can be problematical. Unless you are keen to look at lots of different varieties of bloom, plant simply. A bed with every rose a different variety often ends up looking a mess. One famous rose garden is planted up in white and different shades of yellow – and looks wonderful.

Don't forget that you don't *have* to prune rose bushes. Quite a number of hybrid teas or cluster flowered sorts make perfectly respectable shrubs, and can simply be added to the rest of the garden. 'Iceberg' and 'Allgold' are particularly good.

All the proper shrub roses do well in the general garden. Watch colours, though. Don't try to combine 'old' roses with modern sorts, because they'll clash badly. Do plant old roses with silvery leafed shrubs and herbaceous plants, all sorts of herbs, especially sages, lavenders and

Below *Roses may be supplied bare-rooted, in which case planting should be carried out between autumn and the end of early spring.*

Bottom *Many garden centres sell roses in containers, in which case planting can take place at any time, provided the ground is not frozen or waterlogged.*

thymes, and always where you can easily reach them. A garden seat with a bush of 'Ispahan' or 'Fantin Latour' on one side, and an eglantine rose on the other, will be the favourite one in the garden. Alternatively, plant shrub roses by doorways, under windows, along paths, or surrounding the edge of a patio.

Climbers and ramblers look good on tripods, house walls, pergolas, arches or screens. In small gardens, choose perpetual-flowering sorts, unless you're perfectly happy with one burst of splendour or are prepared to plant other climbers as well.

Planting
Autumn is the best time if you can manage it – order early. The end of early spring is about the latest for bare-rooted plants. Roses give you back what you give them. Prepare their quarters well, and when planting, add a bucketful of peat mixed with a handful or two of bonemeal for each plant. Check for any developing suckers, dead and damaged roots and shoots. Most of your roses will be budded, and the union of stock and scion should be just below the final soil level.

If you are planting bedding roses, the average distance between plants is 45cm (18in), but some vigorous types such as 'Peace' need 60cm (2ft). Standard roses need to be staked at planting, so make sure that you have suitable posts to hand.

If you have spare rotted manure or compost, give the new plants a good mulch. It's helpful if you can get them to do well in the first season.

Pruning
New plants may have been pruned before they were sent out. Otherwise, once you have got them planted, clear out weak twiggy growth and prune bush roses hard, then leave well alone. In subsequent seasons, if pruning is needed, try to prune between midwinter and early spring.

How you prune hybrid teas depends mainly on your garden soil. On rich heavy loam, prune hard. Remove all but three of the main stems, shortening those to about 15cm (6in), and to an outwards-facing bud. On light, sandy soils, give only a light pruning. Do this by removing weak growth, and shortening the remaining stems by a third. Gardeners gardening on light soil who like their hybrid teas grown low, will find they need to keep their plants well fed and watered.

Floribundas need more work; new shoots that grew from the base of the plant last summer are clipped back to any bud just below the old flower truss. It will go on to produce flowering side shoots – these are shortened by half in the subsequent winter. The shoots later produced by those trimmed side shoots are cut back hard in the third winter, leaving just two or three buds. Meanwhile the plant has produced second and first season shoots for you to prune.

You can leave most of the shrub roses ('old' ones included) almost entirely alone. Some occasionally produce a few very fast-growing shoots and these can look ungainly. Simply shorten them. Others have rather pendulous growth, and if the stems get long the bush falls apart. Either shorten or, better still, build low supports of lath to hold the flowers up where you can see them.

Some 'wichuraiana' hybrids need treating like raspberries, in that canes produced one year flower in the second, and are then cut out. Most other ramblers and climbers can be left to their own devices, except to remove dead or inconvenient stems. In others, all new growth may go to the tips of old stems, and the plant become leggy and bald lower down. Stems of these can be induced to bud and flower along their length by training them horizontally or fan-wise. In general, though, most ramblers and climbers will give you plenty of flowers if you feed them well, watch out for pests and diseases, and sit back and simply admire the product.

Climbers and ramblers
'Albertine' A glorious and popular rose for walls, tall hedges or screens. Its red-tinged foliage and stems make a good foil to the large, coppery-pink flowers with a lovely, cool, perfume. The long flowering season can be marred by bad weather.

R. brunonii **'La Mortola'** A vigorous climber with grey–green leaves, pink early on and masses of white or creamy flowers with a heavy fragrance that will fill the garden. 'La Mortola' is wonderful on big pergolas, screens, or large walls. It is not for cold or exposed gardens.

'Cécile Brunner' The climbing form of 'Cécile Brunner' is vigorous and good for walls or pergolas. It has exquisite, pink, 'hybrid tea' shaped blooms, heavily perfumed. It flowers abundantly until late summer, then occasionally into autumn.

'Danse du Feu' A vigorous climber, good on north-facing walls. The flowers are fiery orange red, fading to a darker bluish red. Not for the faint hearted, it flowers all season, and is good on tall tripods or a pergola. Cool down with other paler colours.

'Félicité et Perpétue' A splendid rose for screens, walls or tall poles. It is strong growing but won't engulf you. For a long season, it is covered with very double, pale-pink flowers, exquisite in bud.

R. filipes **'Kiftsgate'** A grand large-scale

Top *Plant roses in well-prepared soil, to which has been added peat enriched with bonemeal. Budded roses should be planted so that the union between rootstock and scion is just below the final soil level.*

Above *Newly planted bush roses, such as hybrid teas, should be pruned back hard as indicated by the 'pruning marks'. Always cut to an outward-facing bud.*

Opposite 1 *An old but still favourite climbing rose is 'Albertine' which is noted for its long flowering season.*
2 *A strong-growing climber, 'Félicité et Perpétue' also has a long season and is excellent for quickly forming a screen.*
3 *'Golden Showers' flowers throughout most of the summer and is one of the most popular of the yellow climbers.*
4 *There are not many roses suitable for north-facing walls, but 'Mermaid' can certainly be recommended.*
5 *The perpetual-flowering climber 'New Dawn' makes a good background for other roses or shrubs.*
6 *'Constance Spry' is a modern hybrid shrub rose, ideal for associating with other shrubs.*

plant for gable walls, 'Kiftsgate' will turn a ramshackle garage into a romantic pavilion. A single but astonishing season of vast clusters of single, cream, scented flowers is followed by small red hips.

'Gloire de Dijon' A vigorous and handsome climber, this flowers well on north walls, but even better in sun. Its large, very double flowers, in buff apricot, are heavily scented. It has a fairly long season. If the plant gets scrawny below, plant low-growing ground cover in front.

'Golden Showers' This fairly perpetual flowering rose is a good yellow for tripods, poles or walls. Elegant buds, open to semi-double flowers, nicely scented.

'Madame Alfred Carrière' A vigorous climber that does well in shade; even more flowers are produced in sun. It is almost perpetual flowering, very double, with a wonderful perfume, the very palest possible pink. It cuts well and is very grand.

'Mermaid' This is another fast climber good on north walls, but even better in the sun. Immense, rather floppy, single, soft-yellow flowers. It looks good against old stone walls or weatherboarding but swamps bungalows.

'New Dawn' Fully perpetual flowering, the first flush leaves a snowfall of silvery-pink petals. The flowers are well shaped. Wonderful for walls or fences, it makes a good background for other roses or shrubs.

'Paul's Scarlet Climber' This vigorous climber is good on walls or pergolas and bears clusters of dog-rose flowers in intense red, paler in the centre and scarcely perfumed. It is unfortunately vulnerable to mildew.

'Souvenir de la Malmaison' A moderately strong climber, 'Souvenir de la Malmaison' is excellent on pillars or walls and produces a midsummer and early autumn flush of flowers. An 'old' flower shape, fully double, soft, fleshy pink, paler after opening, with a luscious scent.

'Wedding Day' This is vigorous, but not overpowering, with good, glossy leaves, and thornless stems. Vast flower clusters, deep-creamy yellow in bud are much paler when open. Good for screens, it can also be threaded along wires to make a hedge.

'Zéphirine Drouhin' A wonderful, thornless climber, this is easily pruned. It is heavily perfumed, with fully double flowers of a gorgeous, rich pink. Flowers are produced almost all summer and into early autumn. It is good for pillars.

Shrub roses

'Ballerina' A good dense shrub, this sometimes grows quite low. It makes an excellent hedge. Its big clusters of small, single flowers are light pink, shading dramatically

to a white centre with yellow stamens.

'Blanc Double de Coubert' This eventually makes a large shrub. It has good foliage and a long season of substantial double, white flowers with a powerful fruity fragrance. It is excellent for the shrub border, or for hedging.

'Buff Beauty' Makes a good medium-sized shrub, or is splendid against a wall. It has a succession of flower clusters, each flower double, marvellously fragrant and an attractive colour in between apricot and beige.

'Canary Bird' Looks like a species rose and is lovely in flower with arching branches of delicate leaflets, supporting handsome single flowers of bright yellow. Excellent for the wild garden, or big shrub border.

'Céleste' This is a strong and eventually large Alba shrub with grey–green leaves and abundant, single pink flowers, of perfect form and perfect scent. Plant as a specimen, or by a path or back door. It has been popular since the 18th century.

'Complicata' An odd name, for a rose bearing enormous and perfect single roses, in a perfectly simple pink, shading to paler at the centre. It has a short season, but nothing is more spectacular.

'Comte de Chambord' A vigorous but fairly small shrub with yellowy green leaves, sumptuous and heavily perfumed flowers, a tight mass of rich pink petals. It has a longer season than most old roses, so should suit everyone.

'Constance Spry' A modern hybrid, using one 'old' parent making a good, slightly floppy bush. Fine dark leaves, set off the splendid, fully double, strongly fragrant, flowers with rich, slightly sharp, pink petals. Good on low walls, or amongst shrubs.

'Empress Josephine' Familiar since Tudor times, this weak shrub (also known as 'Francofurtana') bears the most wonderful, very double, very heavily scented, flowers of a sumptuous bluish pink, shading to an intense centre.

'Felicia' A superb rose for any garden, either in the shrubbery, or as a dense hedge. It covers itself with flowers in midsummer, and with lots more later. They are buff-pink in bud, silvery pink after opening.

'Ispahan' One of *the* old roses and still used for making 'attar of roses'. The flowers are very double, of perfect form, gorgeously scented, intense pink, and appear over quite a long season. They cut well. Plant it by walls, steps, or against a dark background of foliage.

'Little White Pet' If you read the description of 'Félicité et Perpétue', but thought it might be too big for your garden,

grow this charming bush form of the climber. It looks lovely by doorways, or flopping over a low wall.

'Lord Penzance' An attractive, slightly gawky briar, with tiny jagged leaflets, which smell of apple pie, especially after rain. The briar-like flowers are abundant, rosy buff with yellow centres. Good in semi-wild gardens, or by paths in glossier, more formal ones.

'Madame Hardy' Makes a good strong bush, quite big if happy, with pale green leaves. The perfect white flowers have an intriguing green 'eye' and a wonderful cool, clear, smell. Very sophisticated – perfect with pale delphiniums, ferns, 'Bowles Mauve' wallflowers or pulmonarias.

R. moyesii **'Geranium'** A lanky shrub, tall if happy. Single flowers appear on each side shoot, in an astonishing red. Large vase-shaped hips of a different, but equally exciting shade follow. The hips last until winter. Plant near to a path.

'Nevada' Eventually makes a large shrub, so plant at the back of the border. Spectacular when the first flowering covers every branch with large single cream (sometimes with a pink flush) flowers with slight fragrance. Scattered flowers appear until autumn.

'Rosa Mundi' A medieval, if not older rose. Its pale green leaves are smothered for a few weeks with heavily perfumed, double flowers, striped in palest and deeper cerise pink. It makes a stunning hedge but clip over after flowering. Petals may be dried for pot-pourri.

'Roseraie de l'Hay' A stout, medium sized shrub, with handsome leaves and very handsome double flowers, rich velvety crimson-purple, with a heady perfume to match. A long season, though few hips follow. Excellent for hedging and splendid planted by a seat.

R. rubrifolia A splendid, moderately sized shrub with fine greyish-red foliage making a wonderful background to other plants. Small dog-rose flowers are followed by black hips. Not a showy plant, but beautiful.

Bush roses
Large flowered
'Alec's Red' A popular hybrid tea, with all of that group's attractive fragrance. An abundance of flowers, a good bright cherry red, with a good shape. Vigorous and a rose with few problems.

'Fragrant Cloud' Deservedly a most popular variety, the perfume living up to the name, and produced by fine coral scarlet flowers of excellent shape. They grow either singly, or in clusters. A vigorous plant, though watch for blackspot.

'Grandpa Dickson' These medium sized plants, have enormous, rather open flowers of lemon yellow, fading rather paler and often with pink edges to the petals. All too luscious for some, but other gardeners love them despite their poor fragrance.

'Just Joey' Good strong bushes, supporting coppery orange flowers, the slightly frilled petals dramatically threaded with red veins.

'Silver Jubilee' A strong growing, disease resistant bush with attractive glossy foliage. The flowers are large and handsome, lusciously coloured in pink, but shaded with oranges and cream.

'Whisky Mac' This nice bush is fairly compact and vigorous. The flowers are attractively shaped and full of petals, fragrant but not intoxicating. Their shade of amber is close to some sorts of the drink.

Cluster flowered
'Allgold' A good bush, or a shrub if you leave it alone when it will flower early, too. The handsome flowers of a good deep yellow are not in the least harsh. They cut well and are of moderate fragrance.

'Café' The dark foliage (watch out for mildew) makes a fine setting for the fully double flowers, flattish when finally open, in a pretty series of coffee shades.

'Elizabeth of Glamis' An attractive, vigorous and popular plant. The fine and full flowers are of a slightly orange pink, smell good and cut well.

'Glenfiddich' A vigorous and healthy bush. The flowers are of quite good shape, and a nice peaty yellow that works well with all the other yellows in the group.

'Iceberg' A bedding rose, or a bush if you don't prune, with nice glossy leaves and loose sprays of the hybrid tea shaped flowers of perfect white. The flowers cut beautifully, and look good by candlelight.

'Korresia' A floribunda with dusky golden yellow flowers of perfect shape, it is a strong grower, and generally quite healthy.

'Lavender Lassie' Makes a tall graceful shrub if left unpruned with clusters of double, rather flattened flowers in a pale pinkish lilac. An excellent rose.

'Margaret Merrill' An attractive bush, the flowers open to a warmer white than 'Iceberg', and so are preferred by many; (the buds are pink). It has a good fragrance and blends well with pink and red roses.

Miniatures
'Cinderella' This is a real miniature less than 30cm (12in) high, with the tiniest of white roses, rosette shaped, with a slightly pinkish centre. It is very graceful.

'Perle de Montserrat' A tiny pink rose, with petals that are darker on the reverse and so have an interesting effect. Best planted where it's easily seen.

CHAPTER THREE
ROCK GARDENS & ALPINE PLANTS

Left: *A well-planned rock garden with a balanced selection of flowering and evergreen plants can be a joy all year round.*

ROCK GARDENS AND ALPINE PLANTS

There can be few with a genuine love of plants who have not been tempted to create in their own garden a home for alpines and rock plants. Despite the harshness of mountainous and rocky landscapes, these are the natural environments of some of the loveliest wild plants. The inhospitable conditions they have to survive include thin soils, sharp drainage, searing winds, frequent low temperatures and, in the alpine zone, snow cover during part of the year. At first, therefore, it is surprising to find that some of these natural landscapes convey the impression of a managed garden.

The plants have had to make many adaptations to cope with these hostile conditions but the most characteristic is a compact or ground-hugging habit of growth. It is this characteristic that gives alpine and rock plants their managed appearance in the wild and can be exploited so easily and to such good effect in cultivation.

One of the great advantages of these small-growing plants is that there is room for them in almost any garden. Perhaps it is the vast and elaborate rockeries of botanic gardens that, paradoxically, has led people to feel that they are not gardening on a scale grand enough to embark on growing these miniature and dwarf plants. In fact, almost any open space has room to grow a selection of rock plants combined with a few large stones arranged in such a way as to suggest their natural environment.

Working on a very small scale, a stone or imitation stone sink can be planted with an appropriate selection of really miniature alpines and rock plants and placed to form a focal point in a paved yard. Even without a special area being devoted to them, alpines and rock plants can be fitted in to many gardens, improving features that might otherwise be bare or weedy.

Perhaps more than anything else, gardeners are discouraged from planting alpines and rock plants in the mistaken belief that they are difficult to grow. Not surprisingly, there are some, among the high alpine plants in particular, that justify their reputation for being pernickety. To the enthusiast, they are probably the most exciting plants to grow, giving enormous satisfaction when cultivated to perfection. The ordinary gardener, however, wants adaptable, attractive plants that do not require specialist experience and close attention in order to be grown well.

The range of beautiful and easy plants suitable for rock gardens is truly vast, showing a great variety of foliage and flowers and with representatives from around the world. For many of the most desirable, the basic requirements are no more than free-draining soil, a sunny position and an adequate supply of water. The most common rock garden plants are much less troublesome than, for instance, the majority of popular border plants.

Coping with Latin names

One of the consequences of having such a wide range of plants to chose from is that you will encounter more Latin names than with most groups of garden plants, because many of them do not have familiar common names.

The scientific name, which is recognized internationally, normally consists of two parts and is printed in italics. The first is the name of the plant's genus – the group of closely related plants to which it belongs. It is rather like a surname and is always written with a capital letter. The second part, which does not have a capital, is the name of the species – the group of plants that, in all important respects, are the same. To take an example, the scientific name of the common snowdrop is *Galanthus nivalis*: *Galanthus* is the generic name of all snowdrops; *nivalis* is the specific name applied to all snowdrops having the botanical characteristic of the common snowdrop.

Sometimes naturally occurring varieties of a species are given an additional name. For instance, *G. n. reginae-olgae* is a naturally occurring, autumn-flowering variety of *Galanthus nivalis*. Cultivated forms of species are also given additional names, which are not italicized and are placed within quote marks. *G. n.* 'Atkinsii', for example, is a vigorous cultivated form of the common snowdrop. Note that, where there is no possibility of confusion, the generic and specific names are abbreviated to initials.

One further convention of the scientific naming of plants is that the symbol '×' is used to indicate that a plant is a hybrid (a cross between two or more species or, more rarely, genera).

Opposite *On the banks of Loch Ewe, numerous plants thrive at the water's edge and provide a sheltered, but natural, setting for the display of many different rock plants.*

CONSTRUCTING A ROCK GARDEN

Planning your rock garden can be great fun, but careful thought needs to be given to how big it's going to be, the site and what stones and soil are going to be used.

To build a rock garden from scratch may strike you at first as a truly ambitious undertaking. It is certainly not something to be embarked on at a whim, without considering fully the budget you can work to, the suitability of a site, the availability of materials, and the kind of help you can reasonably expect from family or friends. However, it is not a job of construction that requires vast financial resources, an unusual site, materials that are difficult to obtain, or advanced building techniques. In fact, there are many other tasks about the garden or the home that require much more sophisticated do-it-yourself skills.

Provided you are reasonably fit, or have the assistance of someone who is, and you are patient enough to set about the job methodically, there is no reason why you cannot build, at modest expense, the sort of small rock garden that will fit happily in many small to medium-sized gardens.

Choosing a site
It is not likely that the average suburban garden is going to have the absolutely ideal site for a rock garden but there are a few basic requirements on which there is limited room for compromise.

Many alpines and rock garden plants are sun-lovers, doing best in positions where they have full sun for at least half the day. While it would be perfectly possible to assemble an interesting collection of dwarf plants that flourish in shade or part shade, it would hardly be worth building a rock garden to accommodate them. They would probably look very much better in a raised bed, preferably one made of peat blocks.

For a rock garden, it is always best to provide a south-facing, sunny position. This will almost certainly mean an open area not overhung by trees, which also overcomes the problems of shade and drips from overhead branches and a heavy fall of dead leaves in autumn. If dead leaves are left on the rock garden they encourage

pests and disease, and small plants completely covered by them may be lost. Some shelter is desirable but this is best provided by a background of shrubs giving protection from the prevailing wind.

Although a sloping site has advantages, a level site is perfectly satisfactory, for a slight southward inclination can be created in the construction. What is much more important than the slope of the site is that it is one with adequate drainage.

You should aim to convey an impression of plants growing in their natural environment. The impression of naturalness will be diminished if the rock garden is closely associated with formal elements of the garden. However, if your space is limited, the best position may be against a wall or at the corner of two walls. Do not, though, build against the outside wall of a house because the dampproof course will almost certainly be bridged, and the scale of the building will be out of proportion to that of your miniature landscape.

One further and not negligible consideration to bear in mind when selecting a site is its accessibility. The basic materials of which a rock garden is constructed are heavy and can be awkward to manoeuvre. Firm and reasonably level access will make the job that much easier.

Designing a small rock garden
Before deciding on the layout of your rock garden, it is worth looking at the ways other gardeners have achieved a natural effect. Even a much larger rock garden than the one you have in mind can be a useful source of ideas but any scheme inspired by a large garden must be tailored to the space you have available.

A serious mistake you may sometimes find in suburban gardens is a rock structure of many tiers built on a relatively small base. It is as though someone has tried to miniaturize a mountain rather than suggest a rocky outcrop. Inevitably, such a structure

Opposite *When building a rockery, the choice of stones will make the difference between success and failure. A few large boulders will look much more natural than many smaller ones.*

Above *Choice of rock will partly depend on where you live: locally quarried stone is generally the cheapest available and will fit in with the surroundings.*

looks totally unnatural. Furthermore, it requires an unnecessary amount of the most expensive component, rock, and it places emphasis on the wrong element of the garden, the stones of which it is made, rather than the plants growing in it. If you are building on a small scale, an arrangement of two tiers of large rock gives as much height as is necessary and allows for treatment of the stone as natural layers.

Another error that gardeners sometimes make is to devise a layout that is too regular or geometrical. If the surroundings impose a regular form, it would almost certainly be better to build a raised bed of the appropriate shape rather than a rock garden. For the latter, a useful outline to work to is an irregular, blunt wedge shape, the mound having a jagged profile sloping to the south.

Before beginning any construction work, mark out the outline using rope or string and pegs, fixing in your mind's eye the volume that your rock garden will occupy.

Rock to build with

There are few gardeners fortunate enough to have available on their own site sufficient rock of adequate size to make a worthwhile rock garden. For one reason or another you may have a large stock of old bricks or dressed stone. Do not be tempted to use these as a substitute for undressed stone in the construction of a rock garden that is intended to look like a small, natural landscape. They will be perfectly satisfactory as materials for constructing a raised bed in which rock plants can be grown most successfully, but they will never combine with plants to create an impression of a rocky outcrop as found in nature.

Buying the rock

Rock, regrettably, is an expensive material to purchase, largely because the cost of transporting it is so high. The more local the source of the rock you buy the less expensive it is likely to be. You may find in your own area quarries or stone merchants

Right *A newly-built rock garden made of relatively small stones. In a year or two it will be flourishing with a fine display of plants.*

that will sell to you direct; the larger garden centres are an alternative source of supply.

Most of the rock available falls into one of two broad categories: the sandstones and the limestones. If you want to include lime-haters, such as dwarf rhododendrons, heathers and soldanellas, you should choose a porous but not soft sandstone, preferably of a kind that is local (a consideration based not only on cost but also on the desirability of using stone that looks as though it belongs to a particular location).

If the soil of your garden is limy, the case for choosing a local limestone is very strong. You will not be able to grow acid-loving plants but you will have a rock garden that is in keeping with the rest of your garden.

Tufa, an unusual type of limestone that is porous and very light, is remarkable in that many acid-loving plants can be grown in it very successfully. Because it is so soft it is easily drilled; small alpines that are plugged into drilled holes root readily and flourish.

Marble and granite are the least satisfactory types of rock to build with. Their hard surfaces and non-porous textures are unsympathetic to plants.

Once you have chosen the type of rock you are going to use, do not mix it with rocks of another type. To do so will destroy the effect of naturalness you want to create. Although you need some variation in rock size, the larger individual pieces are (provided that they are not so heavy that they cannot be manoeuvred) the better the effect they will create. In any event, no rock should be smaller than half the size of the largest piece.

A minimum quantity of rock for a small garden of about 4 sq m (15 sq ft) is in the order of 1 cu m (3 cu ft). A reputable supplier will be able to give sound advice on quantities needed for large gardens.

When ordering rock, also get a supply of chippings or pea shingle, to dress the surface of the rock garden and help conserve moisture and discourage weeds. Use limestone chippings if you are building with limestone, but do not mix with other kinds of rock.

Improving the soil

Provided it is reasonably fertile and weed-free, ordinary garden soil to which is added sharp sand and leaf-mould or fine grade moss peat can be used to provide the earth core of the rock garden. The soil you excavate when establishing a foundation for the rock garden may be of good enough quality to form the loamy constituent but the quantity may be insufficient.

If you have to add compost, a good mixture consists of two parts of good loam to one part of well-rotted leaf-mould or fine grade moss peat and one part of sharp sand (all parts by volume, not by weight). It is important that the sand is really gritty so that it gives the mixture the open, free-draining texture that most rock plants require. The soft sand used by builders should never be used in the mixture. The components need to be mixed together thoroughly. In the process, add a general, slow-acting fertilizer (bone-meal is very suitable).

Preparing the site

Before excavating a base for the rock garden, ensure that both the site you have marked out, and the surrounding area, are free of perennial weeds, such as bindweed and couch grass. If these are not eliminated before construction begins they will become firmly established among rocks and will be almost impossible to eradicate without dismantling the structure (although there is now a selective weedkiller that will kill grasses among rock plants).

Once the site is free of such weeds, excavate the marked area to a depth of about 15cm (6in), taking off the turf first, if you are building on the site of a lawn. The

Top left *When buying your garden rock you will have to decide on sandstone or limestone and choose your plants accordingly.*

Top *Peat can be incorporated as a soil conditioner and will greatly improve clay soils.*

Above *Organic material such as farmyard manure will supply essential nutrients as well as improving the texture of the soil.*

Left *Preparation for the rock garden is extremely important. All weeds should be removed before construction begins.*

1. *The rockery should be built to a roughly wedge-shaped pattern. Try to choose a well-drained site, preferably on a slight gradient.*

2. *Once you have marked out the position of the rockery, dig out the foundations to a depth of 15cm (6in). Compact the soil firmly in the hole.*

3. *Prepare the bedding material near the edge of the hole. Mix one part grit to five parts topsoil and refill to 5cm (2in) below ground level.*

4. *Move the largest 'key' stone into position first. Pack the soil firmly underneath to hold it securely in the right place.*

5. *Complete the L-shaped outcrop with two lines of closely packed stones that are all tilting slightly backwards and pack soil around them.*

6. *Once the lower outcrop is complete, fill the inside with bedding mix. Rake the mix out and tread it flat – do not disturb the positioned stones.*

turves will be useful if you are intending to build a sump to give your garden extra drainage. Keep them, in any event, as they can be used for repairs to other parts of the lawn.

If the excavated soil is of good quality, it can be used as the loamy constituent of your rock garden mixture. Poor quality soil will have to be disposed of completely.

Under normal circumstances, when you have excavated to the necessary depth, compact the soil in the floor of the hole by trampling it down. This will give the rock garden a stable bed and there will be little likelihood of it sinking later on.

If there is any danger of the natural drainage on your site being inadequate, before compacting the foundation provide additional drainage in the form of a sump. For a small to medium-sized rock garden the sump should consist of a centrally placed hole about 30cm (12in) square by 45cm (18in) deep filled with well-firmed hardcore. The hardcore can then be covered with turves that have been turned grass-side down, or a thick layer of gravel to prevent the soil mixture working its way down into the sump and clogging it up. This layer of turves or gravel needs to be firmed down, as does the rest of the floor of the hole.

Putting rock and soil together
Before moving any stone, make sure that you have the necessary equipment. You will probably possess basic garden tools, such as spade, shovel, fork and, perhaps, pickaxe. You may also find it useful to hire two crowbars (with these you will need blocks of wood to use as fulcrums and wedges) and the sort of two-wheeled trolley that is used in warehouses to move sacks about. If you are using such a trolley, it will pay to lay down planking over any soft ground between your pile of rock and the rock garden site.

If you are building on a medium-to-large scale and using a lot of really heavy stones, an arrangement of planks and rollers may provide the easiest method of moving rocks about. Rocks are levered one at a time onto a plank that is sitting, temporarily wedged,

5

6

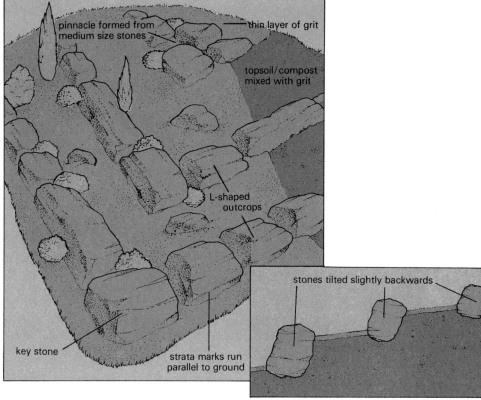

pinnacle formed from
medium size stones

thin layer of grit

topsoil/compost
mixed with grit

L-shaped
outcrops

key stone

strata marks run
parallel to ground

stones tilted slightly backwards

on five or six rollers, which are themselves sitting evenly spaced and parallel to each other on firm planks. Once the rock is securely on the top plank the wedges can be removed and the whole top plank with rock on board can be pushed along on the rollers, each roller being moved to the front as it is exposed by the plank moving forward.

Whatever method you adopt for moving rock, remember to work steadily and patiently. Accidents can happen but almost always because commonsense has been defeated by impatience. As an added precaution, wear really stout boots and a pair of working gloves.

Positioning the stones

The first stone to be positioned, the key stone, will determine the way the rest of the rock garden is built up. It should be the largest rock that you have available and, therefore, you must decide before laying it where the high point of your first tier ought to be. In most pieces of rock you can see quite clearly the layered pattern of the strata lines. To create a natural effect in the

rock garden, the strata lines should all run more or less horizontally and the weathered side of the rock should face out. If rock is not laid with the strata running horizontally, quite apart from creating an unnatural appearance, there is the risk of water and frost penetration, which may result in the rock breaking up.

Place the key rock, bearing in mind the direction of the strata, in such a way that it tilts slightly backwards. The tilt will cause rainwater to run back into the earth behind it. The rock must be really firmly bedded in so that it is absolutely stable, even when someone stands on it. Take time to get this first stone properly positioned, packing soil around the base to get it sitting right.

Once the key stone is in place, choose a smaller stone to butt against it. To create a rock garden that is really sound structurally, it is important that one stone is pushed hard against another to form a close joint. Sometimes, of course, the irregular shape of a rock will make gaps unavoidable. Such gaps can be plugged with smaller pieces of stone wedged from behind so that soil is not washed out. However, small gaps between rocks can often be just the position to suit the kind of plant that, in its natural environment, would be found lodged in a crevice. While most planting in the rock garden is better left until after the soil mixture has settled down, it may be much easier to put in some of the crevice-loving plants during construction; at this stage it is much easier to ensure that their roots are

Above *The rockery is built on a shallow foundation filled with a carefully graded mix of grit and topsoil/compost. Stones are then placed on top and formed into a number of L-shaped rocky outcrops one above the other with planting terraces in between. To aid drainage (inset) each stone should be positioned so that it tilts slightly backwards at an angle of about 15 degrees.*

7. *Construct the second outcrop in the same way as the first.*

8. *The final outcrop should consist of a few medium-sized stones formed into a small pinnacle.*

9. *Finally, cover all the exposed soil with a 25mm layer of clean grit to keep down weeds.*

10. *After a few weeks when the rockery has settled down you can start putting in the plants. When planting, turn the pot upside down grasp the stem and pull gently out.*

11. *Firm in the soil around the plant, cover with grit, and then water adequately.*

7

8

9

10

not simply packed into a hole but are 11 worked through into soil that can sustain the plant.

As you continue to lay the stones of the first layer, step back after positioning each one to make sure you are happy with the impression you are creating. Adjustments will be so much more difficult to make at a later stage. Aim for an unforced irregularity, with some stones jutting out in front of others and, perhaps, some slight variation in the progression towards smaller stones.

Adding the soil

Once you have completed laying the stones of the first layer, shovel in the soil mixture to within 5cm (2in) of the top of the rocks. Make sure that soil is well worked in at the back of the stones. For the second tier begin, as before, with the largest rock and create the impression of an outcrop with a loosely L-shaped grouping. Follow the same approach as with the first tier, repeating the angled position of the rocks and ensuring that they are firmly bedded into the mixture and fitting tightly against one another. When all the rocks are in place, add the soil mixture to the second

level, so that it comes to within 5cm (2in) of the top of the rocks.

The temptation will now be very strong to set about planting immediately but you should allow a good two or three weeks for the soil to settle. Only after planting should the layer of chippings be added, when it should be spread over the surface to a depth of 2.5cm (1in). Work the small stones right round the neck of plants.

A sloping site

The scheme as outlined here for combining rocks and soil to make an attractive, natural-looking home for dwarf plants can be modified in many ways to suit the size and position of your own site. If you are lucky enough to have a gently sloping site, you will probably have much greater room for flexibility than if you only have a flat area. For instance, it may then be perfectly appropriate to extend to three or even more tiers of rock, which can be arranged in roughly semi-circular outcrops. Bed the rocks, always with a backward tilt, well in and keep the pockets of soil nearly level. If soil slopes too steeply, there is the danger of erosion and the whole rock garden being put at risk.

The larger garden

Where you have space for a rock garden on a larger scale, it is even more important to use stones of good size. The impression created by a few well-placed rocks will be very much more natural than clusters of insignificant stones.

In the medium or large-scale rock garden it is well worth considering a pool. The availability of flexible synthetic pool liners and glass-fibre shapes has greatly simplified the addition of this feature to the garden. What is important is that, if a pool is to be incorporated in a rock garden, it adds to the impression of a natural landscape and that it does not appear as a foreign and jarring element. Planning its position and excavating for it should be done at an early stage.

The rock garden surrounds

Relating the rock garden to its surroundings can present problems for there must not be an abrupt transition from informal to formal. There are, furthermore, disadvantages in having a lawn running right up to the rock garden. It makes for difficult mowing and there is a tendency for grasses to work themselves up between the rocks. One of the most satisfactory solutions is to surround the rock garden with a girdle of stone chippings or gravel and paving. The ideal would be paving of the same stone as has been used in the construction of the rock garden. In any event, the paving stones should be laid in such a way as to form an edge with the lawn and allow for easy mowing of the grass.

One way of softening the base of the rock garden is to position a few tufted or clump-forming plants so that they grow against the bottom tier of rocks. Planting the paved and gravelled girdle will further enhance the impression of naturalness.

Left *An ideal way of setting a rock garden into its surrounds is to edge it with paving stones of a similar material. They also go well around pools or ponds.*

ALPINES WITHOUT A ROCK GARDEN

Building a traditional rock garden may not always be practicable. Filling a raised or scree bed or possibly a miniature garden with colourful dwarf plants might well be the answer.

Although there is a particular pleasure in growing alpines and rock plants in a manner that suggests a wild, rocky landscape, there are many dwarf plants that can be a great asset in a garden where no attempt has been, or perhaps, can be made, to simulate a natural environment. In fact there are many circumstances in which the construction of a rock garden would be an unwarranted labour.

Raised beds

In a small garden the raised bed offers the most attractive alternative to the rock garden as a way of growing alpines and other small plants. Indeed, many gardeners would claim that the raised bed has many advantages over the rock garden itself. One of its principal advantages is that, while it needs to be sited, as the rock garden does, in an open but sheltered and reasonably sunny position, it can be co-ordinated very readily with formal or informal settings. Furthermore, the range of materials that can be used satisfactorily in its construction is very wide. This may mean that if you have available, say, a supply of old bricks, the materials for construction need not be an expensive item. One very attractive advantage that the raised bed has for anyone who is partially disabled is that, once constructed, it makes a particularly easy garden to maintain. Even from a wheelchair, it is possible to do most or all of the work that will keep a raised bed in good condition.

Constructing a raised bed

In essence, a raised bed consists of suitable free-draining soil raised to a height of anything between 15cm (6in) and 75cm (30in) by low walls of any stable material. In practice, most raised beds are built to a height of about 60cm (24in) and to a width, rarely more than 1.5m (5ft), that allows the whole surface to be reached from one side or the other. A raised bed can be of almost any shape, including circular, curved, rectangular or L-shaped. What is important is that it fits comfortably into the space that you have available for it.

Among the materials most commonly used in construction are stone and artificial stone, bricks and railway sleepers. Whatever the material, a fundamental requirement is that the walls are absolutely firm and stable. Constructing with bricks and mortar, for instance, may require greater building skills of you than are called for in the erection of a small rock garden, but there are other materials that pose few problems. One of the most satisfactory results is achieved with dry stone walls, which allow many possibilities for rock plants to be grown so that they hang down the rock face.

Although each of the materials requires a different treatment in construction, you must always start with a firm, weed-free base that has good drainage. Make sure that, in addition to good drainage at the base, there are drainage holes in the retaining walls near ground level.

Once the walls have been constructed, put in a bottom layer up to 15cm (6in) deep of rubble and firm it down. It is a good idea to cover this with gravel to a depth of 5cm (2in) before putting in the soil mixture. As for the rock garden, the compost should consist of a well-blended mixture two parts loam, one part well-rotted leaf-mould or fine grade peat moss, and one part of sharp sand (all parts by volume) to which has been added a slow-acting general fertilizer. Fill the bed to within 5cm (2in) of its top with the mixture and then allow to settle over a period of several weeks before planting.

Break up the surface of a raised bed with one or two medium-sized stones jutting out in a natural-looking way. They will help to give substance to the bed in the quieter months of the year and, more importantly, they will provide the cool root run from which so many alpine plants benefit.

Opposite *Raised beds can be constructed in most garden locations and have the great advantage of being extremely easy to maintain.*

Choosing plants

The plants that are grown in raised beds are much the same as those grown in rock gardens. Particularly where the construction is of dry stone, there is plenty of accommodation for those plants that do best wedged in the crevice of a near-vertical face. Once planting is completed, cover the whole surface of the bed with a 5cm (2in) layer of stone chippings, of limestone if your soil is limy, otherwise of a neutral or acid type of rock.

Peat beds

An interesting variant of the raised bed, the peat bed, while not strictly speaking a rock garden, provides an ideal way of growing a number of dwarf, lime-hating plants, especially if your garden is on chalk. The bed raises the plants sufficiently so that their roots do not reach the chalky soil beneath. A peat bed can also be a happy solution to the problems posed by a shady garden as many acid-loving alpines tolerate shade, but a site directly under trees is not suitable. Wherever the bed is situated, the foundation should be reasonably free-draining and clear of any perennial weeds.

Constructing a peat bed

The peat blocks that are used to construct the walls of a peat bed are available at good garden centres and from some nurseries. The blocks, which measure about 30 × 10 × 10cm (12 × 4 × 4in), are rather like fibrous bricks and they, too, should be laid with one course overlapping another.

Before beginning construction, soak the bricks thoroughly for a day. Excavate a course for the first layer of blocks so that they will be half-bedded in the ground. The peat walls can then be built to a height of about 60cm (24in). As each course is completed, fill the bed to the height of the course with a mixture of peat and lime-free soil in equal quantities by volume.

Below *Once constructed, a peat bed can be cultivated with as wide a variety of plants as an ordinary rock garden.*

Below right *Raised beds are ideal for growing rock plants in a confined area and the harsh edges will soon be softened by a tumbling, colourful display of flowers.*

Choosing plants

Among the lime-hating plants that flourish in the moist and acid conditions of a peat bed are the magnificent dwarf rhododendrons and numerous small herbacous plants and ferns. Growing some of the smaller plants in the peat walls will help to knit the blocks firmly together.

A peat bed is easy to maintain but it should never be allowed to dry out; once thoroughly dry, peat blocks are very difficult to wet again. Give the bed an annual top-dressing of fresh peat and a general fertilizer in early spring.

A scree garden

In a garden with a gentle slope (preferably facing south) that links two levels, it may be preferable to construct a scree bed rather than a rock garden. The gardener's scree bed is a miniature and modified version of a feature that is sometimes very extensive in mountains, where wind, rain and frost are endlessly breaking down the rock mass. In alpine screes, many plants have adapted to the growing conditions of these sometimes rather unstable accumulations of weathered, rocky debris. The requirements of these and similar plants can be satisfied without too much difficulty by the creation of this uncomplicated and extremely charming feature in the garden.

Constructing a scree bed

To construct a scree bed you need to excavate your sloping site to a depth of about 60cm (24in) and to ensure that at the base of the slope there is very free drainage. It may be necessary to lay drainage tiles that will carry water away to a lower level, but a trench some 45cm (18in) wide and deep filled with hardcore will be an adequate sump in most conditions.

Use a fork to loosen the floor of the excavated area and then fill to between half and two-thirds of the excavated depth with a mixture consisting of equal parts by volume of good loam, well-rotted leaf-mould or peat, and sharp sand. The remainder should be filled with stone chippings. If your soil is naturally limy, do not fight against it but reconcile yourself to the exquisite, dwarf, lime-loving and lime-tolerant plants and provide for them a covering of limestone chippings.

Choosing plants

On a sloping site where the soil is naturally neutral or acidic it is perfectly possible to provide neutral or acidic conditions at the top of the slope and limy conditions at the bottom, so that plants of widely varying soil preferences can be grown.

The surface of the scree bed needs to be broken up with several rocks or groups of rocks. Many small plants seem to grow more happily when they are snuggled against a stone and certainly there are many alpines that need the kind of cool root run that a few well-placed rocks will provide.

Although the plants suitable for a scree bed demand free-draining conditions, they also require plenty of moisture in spring and summer. At these times of the year, especially in hot spells, some watering will almost certainly be necessary. A sprinkler or a hose fixed at the top of the scree will make long, thorough soaking easy; a light sprinkling of water will be of very little use.

The scree bed is not the place for boisterous tumbling plants, for these would soon swamp the little cushion plants, neat trailers and compact mat-formers that do best in these conditions. When planting in the scree bed try to get the roots down as deeply as you can so that they can quickly

Top left *A scree garden can be constructed to provide the very sharp drainage needed for some alpines.*

Above *A slightly raised bed can be made into a scree garden and provides a labour-saving feature along the path. It is colourful in the early spring and, by careful selection, can be interesting all year round.*

Above *An ideal container for a miniature garden is a stone sink or trough where small alpines can be assembled permanently.*

Above right *A simple indoor miniature garden can be made in a clay seedpan, using small perennial plants from pots. The garden will be a delightful and fascinating source of interest for a long time.*

penetrate to the soil mixture beneath the chippings. Especially in the early stages after planting, you will need to maintain an adequate moisture level in the stones to support the plants until they are well established. Make sure, too, that your planting includes one or two small shrubs and dwarf conifers as well as suitable herbaceous perennials.

The construction of a scree bed is a very simple matter that requires no special equipment and little heavy work. Furthermore, weeding is not a serious problem, for the deep mulch of chippings discourages the growth of undesirable plants. It has to be admitted, though, that unlike the rock garden or raised bed, all work on the scree bed is at ground level so that it is not an attractive proposition for the less mobile gardener.

Miniature gardens in troughs and sinks

A really miniature alpine garden can be created very effectively in a trough or sink of quite modest dimensions. There are, in fact, any number of tiny plants of exceptional beauty that, when planted in a large setting, can easily go unobserved.

Real stone troughs have become difficult to obtain and when they are available they are generally very expensive. There is no doubt that there is something about them when planted up with alpines and dwarf rock plants that is not matched by their substitutes. A stone trough well-positioned in an open sunny part of a paved yard makes a really distinguished feature.

Making an imitation stone sink

However, an old glazed sink, preferably a deep one, can be treated to look very like stone and is far from being a poor alternative. The treatment consists of applying a rough, stone-like coating comprising one part sand, one part cement and two parts peat. Clean the sink thoroughly and remove any piping still attached. Coat the sink on the outside and to about 7.5cm (3in) inside the lip with a PVA adhesive (for this operation it will be easier if you mount the sink on blocks). When the adhesive is tacky, combine the mixture with water to get a stiff consistency and apply it to the sink. The easiest way to get a rough natural effect is to apply by hand, but wear rubber gloves. Protect the sink from weather for a few days and then leave exposed for several weeks before filling and planting.

Before adding the soil mixture or plants, place the sink or stone trough in its permanent position, an open sunny site, raised on bricks so that water can escape without difficulty from the drainage hole or holes. Take care when moving a coated sink about for, although the covering will stand up well to weathering, it is easily chipped. Except in the case of shallow sinks, fill the base with a 5cm (2in) layer of broken crocks, and in all cases make sure that the drainage hole is clear but covered so that soil will not be washed through.

The soil to use in a sink will depend on the plants you want to grow, but a standard mixture consists of two parts loam, one part leaf-mould or peat and one part of sharp

Left *A sink, or trough, garden is the perfect location for hardy, cushion-forming alpines, evergreens and also small succulents.*

sand, all by volume. Fill to within 5cm (2in) of the top and then cover the surface with a layer of stone chippings. One or two pieces of rock protruding from the surface will give a natural effect. Tufa goes particularly well in trough or sink gardens and allows the flexibility for plants to be grown at more than one level.

Choosing plants

Among the many plants suitable for these delightful miniature gardens are the truly dwarf species of dianthus and campanulas as well as a great range of saxifrages and sempervivums. The dwarfest available forms of conifers can also look very much at home.

Maintaining a sink or trough garden requires very little work and, because there is little bending involved, can be a source of very great pleasure to the semi-invalid or to the fully able gardener. Watering is the one job you will need to be attentive to, as these small gardens can dry out very quickly in hot weather.

There is no room in such a tiny garden for plants that grow too big or too fast. If you find that by mistake you have introduced something that is too vigorous, make sure you are ruthless in replacing it.

Rock plants in paving and dry stone walls

Even without a purpose-built location, such as a rock garden or raised bed, there are positions in many gardens where dwarf rock plants and alpines can be grown to very good effect. The bright flowers or soft foliage of a few well-chosen plants can really transform areas of the garden that might otherwise be nondescript and appear rather boring.

Planting dry stone walls

In many gardens there are dry stone retaining walls which sadly are often left bare or are allowed to be colonized by weeds. They offer enormous scope for growing some vigorous and free-flowering rock plants.

It is very much easier to plant in a dry stone wall during the process of construction rather than later; but even in an established wall it is possible to get plants to take. Some can be put in as seeds, mixing them with damp soil to make little pellets that you can work into the crevices.

The best way to introduce most plants, however, is to insert small rooted cuttings into cracks and crevices, pushing damp soil in around them. Inevitably, there will be failures but it only requires a few of the vigorous plants to become established and in a very short time you will have a wall that is a highly ornamental feature of the garden.

It is particularly worthwhile persevering with some of the rosette-forming plants that resent water collecting at the base of

Below left and right *A garden wall can often be an ideal place to grow some colourful dwarf rock plants and alpines.*

their leaves and are, therefore, often difficult to grow on level sites. Lewisias, for instance, are excellent plants when grown lodged in a crevice whereas in a level garden it can be difficult to give them the drainage they need. Many of the larger saxifrages also do very well grown vertically so that their handsome sprays of flowers arch out from the wall.

Planting paved areas

The softening effect of plants can seem even more important in paving than on walls. So often it is desirable to blur the edge where one part of the garden meets another and to introduce variations of colour and texture to relieve a monotonous expanse of paving.

Unless there is a more general need to renovate existing paving, lifting it with the intention of improving the growing conditions for rock plants should not be undertaken lightly. Look instead for some other way of softening the surroundings. It is surprising, however, the way some plants, the thrifts, for instance, will establish themselves in the poor quality soil that lies between and underneath most existing paving. The best chance you have of establishing plants is to take out what sand and grit you can where there is a sizeable gap between paving stones and then work in a loamy

Below *A single specimen can be grown in a small pot where space is limited. Featured is* Dionysia curviflora.

mixture into which a small rooted cutting can be planted. Water frequently in the weeks immediately after planting until it is well established.

If you are laying new paving, there is much greater opportunity to allow for spaces in which rock plants can be grown. At the outset it is important to decide which paved areas are going to take a lot of traffic. These should be left without planting and with the paving materials closely fitted. Elsewhere, however, gaps can be left and soil of good quality incorporated. Among the plants suitable for growing in these little pockets are the smaller bulbs, cushion and mat-forming perennials and dwarf conifers.

It must be said, however, that the planned accommodation of rock plants in paving rarely achieves the natural effect that results from the apparently casual colonization of old paving.

An alpine lawn

For those who have the scope to garden on a more generous scale, a lawn planted with dwarf bulbs is one of the loveliest ways of recreating an alpine meadow. What must be borne in mind at the start is that such a lawn will not be cut for much of the year because the leaves of bulbs must be allowed to die down naturally. If they are cut off too soon the bulbs become progressively weaker, and flowering suffers. You must decide at the beginning that you can live with uncut grass through spring and early summer.

There will be few gardeners who have a rock garden large enough to take an alpine lawn. Almost certainly, it is better to make it a feature of its own or one that blends into a more extensive lawn. An ideal site is a sunny gently sloping piece of ground with good drainage.

Before planting, make sure that the area is free of perennial weeds. Provided that it is applied according to the manufacturer's instructions, a hormonal weedkiller used in mid-summer will leave grass undamaged but deal with broad-leaved weeds.

Bulbs should be planted at their normal times and, for most, this is late summer or early autumn. Remember, however, that snowdrops do best transplanted immediately after flowering. To achieve a natural effect, plant bulbs in clumps, avoiding a rigidly symmetrical arrangement. Individual bulbs can be planted by lifting out a plug of turf and soil, adding a little bit of fresh soil and the bulbs and then replacing the plug. With the really small bulbs it is enough to ease open a hole by working a trowel back and forwards in the soil but be sure that when the bulb is planted it is firmly bedded in earth and that there is no air pocket underneath it. To plant ten or twelve bulbs

in a clump, lift a square of turf, loosen the exposed soil, and plant the group well-spaced before replacing the turf.

Crocuses, miniature daffodils, and snow-drops are obvious choices for the alpine lawn but others that do well are anemones, chionodoxas, hardy cyclamen, erythroniums and scillas. Most bulbs need to be planted at a depth of 5–7.5cm (2–3in) but *Cyclamen hederifolium* (syn. *C. neapolitanum*) and *C. coum* should have their corms only just covered by soil.

Growing in pots

The emphasis of this book rightly falls on ways of growing alpines and rock plants in ways that suggest their setting in the wild. However, many of these plants can be grown to good effect in pots and some of the choice, but difficult, dwarf alpines are best grown in this way.

Pans of sempervivums and miniature bulbs require little special attention and can be moved about in the garden to give them prominence at the most appropriate time of the year. The alpines that are more delicate in cultivation are fully hardy but suffer in relatively mild, wet winters. In their natural habitat, snow cover in winter provides insulation and keeps them comparatively dry. At lower altitudes, if exposed to wet weather, these plants are likely to rot.

Alpine houses

The principal purpose of an alpine house, in which these plants are commonly and most successfully grown, is to provide an environment in which it is possible to control the amount of moisture these plants receive. It is also possible in the alpine house to cater for the individual requirements of more difficult plants, by adjusting the soil mixture, drainage, or exposure to light; for a few difficult plants these adjustments may tip the scales for success.

While it has to be admitted that the alpine house is for the real enthusiast, there is no doubt that it can be made into an exceptionally interesting garden feature, giving a changing display of miniature plants – dwarf bulbs, cushion-forming saxifrages, primulas, campanulas and small-growing conifers, to mention a few – that sustains interest throughout the year and is especially fine in winter and the very early spring.

Above *Many plants grown in pans and pots in an alpine house provide a riot of bloom during the coldest months of the year.*

CHOOSING, PLANTING & CARING FOR ALPINES

Once the construction of your rock garden is complete, you can then have the fun of choosing all the different varieties of rock plants and alpines that you want to include.

Building a rock garden or whatever similar feature you have decided on is the hard work. The selection, planting and care of alpines and rock plants is almost all pleasure. Of course, it is not a matter of grabbing armfuls of plants in the garden centre willy-nilly and thrusting them in with reckless abandon. That kind of gardening may work very satisfactorily with annual bedding plants but it is certainly not worth taking the trouble to construct a rock garden or raised bed if that is how you want to set about planting it. With alpines and rock plants your choice should be a matter of discrimination in which several factors are taken into account, among them the soil requirements of plants, their ultimate size and the way that they will fit into an overall scheme that has year-round interest.

Where to get your plants

You are most likely to start looking for alpines and rock garden plants at your local garden centre, where there will probably be a special section devoted to them. However, the choice a garden centre offers is generally limited to a relatively small range of the commonest plants, which frequently means those that are easiest to propagate. Simply because these plants are common does not make them any less desirable, particularly as a starting point, but once you have started with a few alpines and rock plants you may want to try the less familiar.

Specialist nurseries

There are, fortunately, a number of first-class nurseries specializing in plants suitable for the rock garden. For most of the nurserymen involved, their business is as much a labour of love as it is a commercial enterprise. Their catalogues are a source of valuable information on the requirements of particular plants and the staff at the nursery are generous with advice when it is requested. To find the names and addresses of nurseries begin by consulting gardening magazines.

Some nurseries do not have the staff or the facilities to welcome visitors; they take orders and despatch by mail. But there are others with retail outlets at the nursery site and these are worth visiting for the ideas you can glean on the way plants are grown and for the pleasure of seeing a wide range of unusual plants in cultivation.

Gardening clubs

Do not overlook the advantages of joining a club. An encounter with a rock gardening enthusiast may lead to suggestions of ways to grow this or that, and a gift of a few rooted cuttings. Making personal contact with others who share an interest in rock garden plants is a very pleasurable way of expanding one's own knowledge of them.

By joining a society that caters for the specialized interest of the rock gardener you will be able to draw on the accumulated wisdom and experience of amateur and professional growers through casual contacts and an organized programme of lectures and visits to gardens. Quite apart from the opportunities that you will have for exchanging plants, there is generally an annual distribution of members' surplus seeds organized by specialist societies. Seeds from such distributions can provide an interesting way of building up a collection of some of the less usual plants.

Testing the soil

How is one to set about choosing from the many plants that are suitable for growing on the rock garden? A first consideration must be the nature of your soil, specifically its acidity or alkalinity. The standard measure of acidity/alkalinity is the pH scale. On this, a reading of 7 is neutral, below 7 indicates acidity and above 7 alkalinity. There are simple soil-testing kits available using a liquid chemical indicator that, when mixed with a soil sample, changes colour according to the acid or alkaline content. The colour

Opposite *Successful rock gardens take a lot of careful thought. The plants need to be chosen for their suitability rather than at random.*

of the liquid is measured against a colour chart to give an approximate pH reading. Green indicates that the soil is neutral, red that it is acid and blue that it is alkaline.

Many plants that do well on limy, (that is, alkaline), soils can also be grown quite satisfactorily on neutral or slightly acid soils. Acid-loving plants, however, can be more precise in their requirements. Although most will tolerate a neutral soil, they will fail to thrive if put into a more alkaline soil.

Whatever limitations your soil imposes on your choice, the range of really desirable plants will still be vast and there will always be something else to try!

Remember, too, that the raised bed can be a means of providing soil conditions that are different from those at ground level. If you have more than one raised bed or trough garden it will not be difficult to have different soil conditions in each, so that you can grow plants ranging from those that flourish in acid soils to those that love lime.

Sun or shade?

The degree to which the rock garden is exposed to the sun will be another factor influencing the plants you choose and where you position them. While it is true that very many alpines and rock plants require, or at least prefer, full sun, and most rock gardens are built in an open position, there is usually room on the shady sides of rocks and walls for those dwarf plants that prefer cool, moist conditions.

The choice of plants

It is sometimes said of rock gardens that, although they are wonderfully colourful in spring and early summer, for the rest of the year they have little of interest to show. It would be remarkable if any part of the garden could sustain throughout the year the sort of performance that the rock garden puts on in spring. Nonetheless, as with other parts of the garden, there is no reason for the rock garden to be dull at any time of the year. If a garden falls short in this respect it is because the gardener has failed to exploit the full range of species and cultivated forms of dwarf plants. But the rock gardeners who achieve the most appealing results are the true plantsmen, people with a passionate love of plants in all their forms, who choose their plants with an overall scheme always in mind.

Dwarf conifers

Although the core plants of the rock garden are the dwarf herbaceous perennials, there are other categories that should be allowed to play an important role. There is sometimes a rather imprecise line dividing the herbaceous perennials and the dwarf flowering shrubs, while the dwarf conifers make a quite distinct group. These miniature versions of sometimes giant cone-bearing trees are slow-growing evergreens that look completely at home among rocks and with alpines. True, if planted to excess, they risk creating a grotesque impression, but when

Below *A rock garden constructed in an enclosed situation with a seemingly natural scree but with dwarf conifers and shrubs to break up the level effect.*

Below right *Many ferns will thrive in the conditions provided by a rock garden and are well suited to the shady areas around large outcrops.*

Left *The elegant drooping fronds of a well-placed fern contrast with the texture of the rock behind.*

Above *Miniature bulbs provide a welcome burst of colour and* Iris histroides *'Lady Strawley's Form' flowers early in the year.*

planted judiciously they are enormously valuable for giving a green backbone to the rock garden or raised bed.

The word 'green' is far from adequate to describe the considerable variations of colour among conifers – there are shades of silver, blue-grey, reddish-brown, and gold. Their scale and rate of growth are also far from uniform. While some will reach a height of 1m (3ft) in about 12 years, there are others that are so tiny and slow-growing they can be planted in a sink garden. Another characteristic to take advantage of is the wide variation in habit. Many forms are pyramidal or conical in shape, while others are prostrate or columnar; some have very upright growth, while others have a weeping habit. It is not difficult to make a selection of dwarf conifers that, far from being a desperate arrangement to ensure that the rock garden is clothed at all times of the year, brings into it a group of plants that are very desirable in their own right.

Miniature bulbs

While dwarf conifers are the evergreen mainstay of the rock garden, it is the miniature bulbs that provide the most colourful element in autumn, late winter and early spring. They are not plants to be dotted about, for then their effect is lost. They make their greatest impact when planted as groups according to kind. Then it is as if the garden is lit by a series of minute, timed explosions beginning in the shortest days of the year. It is hard to praise too highly the virtues of the early spring bulbs, which, for all the appearance of fragile beauty, are astonishingly robust and capable of standing up to the worst weather of the year. However, they are plants whose merits are widely recognized.

The hardy dwarf cyclamen, on the other hand, although greatly appreciated by many keen gardeners, are still not as widely grown as their qualities deserve. Between them, the species give a very long flowering season, extending well into the grim winter months. Their pretty shuttlecock flowers stand up well to rough weather and the leaves, which are marvellously patterned in silvery green, are a long-lasting bonus in the winter months. To complete their list of virtues, some are sweetly scented and most are very easy to grow. No rock garden should be without them.

Ferns and grasses

Two other groups of plants that are often unnecessarily neglected are the ferns and grasses. In the rock garden, as in the large-scale garden, variations of texture and form can be as important in giving interest as brightly coloured flowers. Foliage plants with linear or bold, deeply divided leaves can make striking contrasts set against rock or other leaves. Ferns are far from being plants exclusively of dank and dark places, but they are particularly useful for planting on the shaded walls of raised beds.

Replacing plants

The choice of plants should not be thought of as something that, once done, has been done for good. There will be outright failures and plants that fail to thrive in one position but flourish when moved somewhere else. Many rock plants and alpines are long-lived and those that are not tend to self-seed freely. However, from time to time you will need to replace old plantings with freshly propagated material or with completely new stock. Experimenting with the range of plants available to the rock gardener is an inexhaustible source of pleasure.

Planting

The main planting period for the herbaceous perennial and shrubby alpines and rock plants is between autumn and mid-spring. However, because stock is available from nurseries and garden centres pot-grown, the gardener has great freedom in choosing the time to plant. What must be avoided in the autumn-spring period is planting when the ground is frosted or snow-covered. At other times of the year, the problem is to ensure that the plant has adequate moisture. It is easy to lose specimens if you are unable to keep them watered when there is a dry spell.

When choosing where to position individual plants, you must try to bear in mind your overall scheme while at the same time meeting their special requirements. Sequences of flowering and contrast of form and colour are important considerations but in allowing for them do not forget to leave plenty of room for vigorous, spreading plants. Keep them well away from your choice miniatures, which might otherwise be swamped.

If your garden is an established one with a layer of chippings on the surface, brush these back before digging a hole with a small trowel (one with a narrow blade is particularly useful in the rock garden). The hole must be large enough to take the rootball but not so large that the plant, once in the ground, will sit any deeper than it does in the pot. There is a risk of plants succumbing to rot if they are put in too deeply. At this stage, you have the chance to make slight modifications to the soil to suit more precisely the requirements of individual plants: peat can be incorporated for those preferring a moisture-retentive soil and additional grit can be worked in for those types of plants needing particularly sharp drainage.

To remove a plant from its pot, place two fingers on the surface of the soil, one either

Right *Autumn and mid-spring is the best time for planting alpines, but you must make sure that the ground is not frosted. The saxifrages featured can be planted when they are in flower.*

side of the plant, then turn the pot upside down and tap it to free the soil ball; the pot can then be pulled away. If the plant has started to become pot-bound, loosen the roots slightly before dropping the plant into its hole. However, it is much better to avoid buying pot-bound stock; when you are buying, inspect the underside of the pot and do not take plants with roots that can be seen to be growing noticeably through the drainage holes.

Once the plant is in the ground, check that it is at the right depth, adding or taking away soil in the bottom of the hole if necessary and then fill round it before firming in. If the plant is not well firmed in, there will be moisture loss, the roots will not spread readily into the soil of the rock garden, and there is the danger that wind will further loosen the plant. Finish by spreading chippings over the surface of the soil, working them well up to the base of all the plants.

Planting in crevices

Planting in crevices, as has been suggested, is most successfully done at appropriate stages in the construction of the rock garden. In the established rock garden or dry stone wall the problem is to ensure that the roots have enough moisture-retentive

soil about them to connect with the body of soil behind the rocks. Planting between stones is most successfully done in the autumn to mid-spring period using small, rooted cuttings. Work in as much soil underneath and above the plant as you can and, in the case of a vertical crevice, trickle in some chippings so that you completely cover the soil.

Transplanting

If mature plants need transplanting, this, too, should be done in the autumn to mid-spring period. Pay particular attention to firming the soil around the plant; the easiest way may be to tread it in with the feet.

Bulbs

Unlike the herbaceous and shrubby plants, bulbs have a limited planting season. Dry bulbs should be planted in late summer or early autumn, the sooner the better, except for tulips, which, to reduce the risk of a disease called tulip fire, are planted in late autumn. Snowdrops become established more readily when planted 'in the green', in the period just after flowering, than as dry bulbs. Some specialist nurseries offer them at this time and it is certainly the moment to choose if you are transplanting your own stock.

As everywhere in the garden, bulbs look best planted in groups. The miniatures, in particular, lose their effect if dotted about. Bulbs can be dropped into individual holes but it is generally easier to dig out a hole to a depth of 5–7.5cm (2–3in), large enough to take a clump of five or six bulbs. If the species or variety requires particularly sharp drainage, the bulbs can be bedded in a layer of coarse sand.

Planting in pots

For pan cultivation of perennials and shrubs as well as bulbs, ensure that there is good drainage by placing a layer of crocks in the bottom of the pot. Make sure that the drainage holes are not blocked but suf-

Below *Bulbs are most effective when planted in groups – here a cluster of miniature tulips add a blaze of colour.*

Bottom and bottom left *Many rock plants look good and grow well in the crevices between stones. Dianthus (bottom) contrasts well with the soft sandstone of the rock work.*

Above *Lack of rainfall in a rock garden can be made up by watering or by using artificial sprayers that provide a gentle supply of water over a long period.*

Right *A well-cared for rock garden will require little attention through the year, though wooded locations will need tending in the autumn months. Fallen leaves should be gathered up regularly.*

ficiently covered so that the compost is not washed out. The soil mixture can be very finely adjusted to suit the requirements of the plants you are growing but, for many, it will not be necessary to vary a standard mix of two parts loam to one part coarse sand and one part peat or leaf-mould (all parts by volume). The surface of the compost should be covered with a layer of fine chippings or gravel.

With bulbs, it is possible to get a really striking display by planting two layers to a pan. The bulbs of the first layer are covered to their necks with the compost and the bulbs of the second layer are then set above them.

Caring for rock garden and alpine plants

A rock garden with a well-balanced soil covered with a mulch of stone chippings is unlikely to need much attention apart from routine maintenance, throughout the year.

Watering

In periods of prolonged drought, a thorough soaking will be necessary every two or three days. If possible, apply as a fine spray with a sprinkler. Small raised beds, including those made of peat blocks, scree gardens and sink gardens, will probably need watering more frequently during warm dry weather than does a simple rock garden. Do not delay watering until plants show signs of flagging, for by then the damage may have been done. You will quickly get a feel for the water needs of whatever feature you have.

In an alpine house, some form of automatic watering will save a lot of work. A common practice is to bed the pans of plants in trays of gravel into which there is a controlled flow of water.

In winter, excess water will be a problem with some of the rock garden plants with most interesting foliage. Those with woolly, felted and hairy leaves are prone to rot in long spells of wet weather during the dormant season. The solution is to provide a shelter that will keep off excess rain but will allow light to reach the plant and a free circulation of air. This is easily done with small panes of glass held above the plants by wire supports. These will probably need to be in place from late autumn to early spring; and it must be admitted that they then detract from the overall impression of the rock garden as a small piece of natural landscape.

Collecting leaves

Many rock garden plants are liable to rotting if buried under accumulations of dead leaves. From winter through to early spring, collect and dispose of any leaves that gather. As well as encouraging the development of destructive moulds, piles of dead leaves provide lurking places for slugs, the most destructive pest in the rock garden. It is, therefore, worth clearing all debris away as a frequent routine job.

Weeding

Weeding, too, should be treated as a routine activity. The mulch of stone chippings on the surface of the rock garden will do much to discourage the growth of weeds but inevitably there will be some that will take root. Annual weeds, such as chickweed and groundsel, develop quickly and, as a rule, are prodigious seeders. They must be uprooted long before their seed has had a chance to set and been dispersed about the garden. Perennial weeds including bindweed and ground elder, are so vigorous and tenacious that they can pose a threat to the viability of a rock garden once firmly established. All weeds compete with cultivated plants for nutriments and moisture.

The use of a hoe is not advisable in the rock garden as you are likely to cause damage to the roots of plants. Instead use a small hand fork to loosen weeds before pulling them out and disposing of them.

Chemical weedkillers are rather difficult to control in the rock garden but it may be necessary to use an appropriate proprietary brand if perennial weeds are difficult to remove physically. With some it may even be necessary to paint the weedkiller onto the leaves.

Weeds are easily introduced to the garden lodged among the roots of new plants that have been bought or received from friends. Always check new stock to make sure that you are not introducing an unwelcome or serious nuisance.

Top-dressing

The plants in the rock garden do not need a rich soil but will benefit from an annual top-dressing. A suitable mixture consists of two parts loam to equal parts coarse sand and peat or leaf-mould to which has been added a slow-acting fertilizer such as bone-meal. Do one section of the rock garden at a time, sweeping the rock chippings to one side before applying the top-dressing. Then return the stone chippings to the surface, topping up with new chippings if necessary. The top-dressing should be worked in among the leaves and branches of dense mat-forming plants.

Pruning

Most rock garden plants do not need to be pruned or trimmed but the exceptions include some of the most popular and easily

Below *All the plants in the rock garden will benefit from an annual top-dressing of fertilizer. The rock chippings should be removed before the dressing is added and replaced afterwards.*

grown. Alyssum, aubrietas and saponarias, for instance, benefit from being cut back as soon as flowering is over. If left untrimmed they become loose and untidy. Cutting them back will keep the growth compact and in some cases may encourage a later flowering the same year. Some vigorous sprawlers may need trimming, too, simply to prevent them engulfing other less robust plants. Plants that become untidy and loose at the centre will benefit from being lifted and divided every two or three years, the worn-out core being discarded. Divide plants in the dormant period, between autumn and early spring.

Propagation

For the beginner and the experienced gardener alike there are few greater pleasures in gardening than that derived from managing the processes by which plants increase themselves. There is a very special pleasure in looking on a collection of plants that you have raised from seed or from cuttings and brought to maturity. It is a satisfaction that in some ways is out of proportion to the role the gardener plays – with so many plants there is little that needs to be done to encourage the reproductive process. For the gardener with a new rock garden or raised bed, it would require pointlessly stoic patience to raise all plants from seed or cuttings and it would mean a rather bare rock garden for at least a season. Once the first planting has been done, however, it is well worth trying your hand at a fascinating and economic way of increasing your stock.

Raising plants from seed

The most straightforward way of increasing stocks is to raise plants from seed. However, many cultivated varieties of plants will not come true when raised from seed and, where closely related plants are grown near to one another, there is the likelihood of hybridization.

The seeds of plants vary considerably in size and in the length of time that they take to germinate. In the case of many alpines, seed only germinates freely after being subjected to a period of sharp cold. Generally, it is not until early spring that seed becomes available for sowing but it is often better to sow fresh seed at the end of summer or in early autumn.

Many sorts of containers are now used for raising plants from seed but, for alpines, clay pots are still preferred by most gardeners. Before using them for new sowings, clean them thoroughly and then place a crock over the drainage hole or holes so that the compost is not easily washed out. The compost should be soil-based rather than peat-based; the most satisfactory mix for most plants will be the John Innes seed compost to which has been added about half as much again by volume of coarse sand or grit. Remember that the compost for lime-hating plants must be neutral or acidic. When the compost has been firmed down it should come within 18mm (¾in) of the pot's rim.

Sow the seeds thinly and evenly on the firmed surface. It is easier to distribute very fine seeds evenly if they are mixed with a little dry sand and shaken onto the surface from a folded piece of paper. The seeds need to be pressed lightly into the compost before a thin layer of compost is sprinkled on top. At this stage, stand the pot in a basin of water until the surface darkens to show that water has been taken up.

Complete the job by adding a thin layer of grit over the surface, then label. The gritty layer reduces the risk of seeds being washed out in heavy rain and prevents the surface becoming compacted. Make sure that the labelling is durable for the seeds can take more than a year to germinate.

The pots need to be placed in a cool, lightly shaded position until the seeds germinate. The ideal is an open frame with a bed of coarse sand into which the pots can be sunk, for this will help maintain an even level of moisture.

Keep an eye on the pots; as soon as the first true pair of leaves show, the seedlings should be pricked out and potted up, either individually or with several to a larger container (with enough space for the roots to develop without being cramped). A suitable mixture for this consists of two parts by volume of John Innes No. 1 potting compost to one part peat and one part grit. Before the roots have filled the container, sturdy specimens should be planted in their permanent positions.

Division

The simplest method of vegetative propagation is by division. Perennial rock plants with fibrous roots can be lifted between autumn and early spring and divided into several pieces. Only vigorous, well-rooted pieces should be kept; old woody and straggly material should be discarded. The vigorous portions, which should be put in immediately, give instant new plants. Division of herbaceous perennials is an important part of the cycle of renewal in the garden.

With bulbous plants, division consists of lifting established clumps in the dormant summer months and separating the offsets from the main bulbs. The offsets can then be planted up individually and brought on until they are of flowering size.

Below *All newly propagated plants should be carefully labelled to avoid confusion when the time comes to set them in a permanent position.*

Cuttings

Propagation from cuttings is another vegetative method of increasing stock. It is the commonest way of reproducing the cultivated forms that would not come true if grown from seed. There are two major types of cutting that are relevant to rock garden and alpine plants. The first are soft, fresh stems taken early in the summer. Healthy, non-flowering stems about 2.5cm (1in) long should be cut just below a leaf or a pair of leaves. The lower leaves are then removed.

The second main type is again of young growth but firmer. The cutting is taken with a heel; of older wood by tearing the stem sharply downwards.

Hormonal powders and liquids, generally containing fungicides to inhibit the growth of moulds, are commonly used now to promote rooting but they are far from being indispensable. Whether you use them or not, insert the cuttings up to their leaves round the edge of pots containing an equal mixture of peat and coarse sand. The cuttings need to be kept in a warm, humid environment but out of direct sunlight. As with seedlings, a useful way of maintaining an even humidity and temperature is to plunge the pots in a bed of sand or grit inside a frame.

Cuttings need to be watched closely; any that show signs of wilting or mould should be removed immediately. When they have taken, they should be potted up individually using a mixture consisting of two parts by volume of John Innes No. 1 potting compost to one part peat and one part grit.

Layering

This technique of vegetative propagation calls for patience but it is useful as a means of increasing woody plants that are difficult to propagate from cuttings.

The technique consists of choosing a flexible, young branch that can be bent down to the ground. Here, it is pegged down in soil to which peat and sharp sand have been added. Before fixing the branch in position, make a cut on the underside of the stem about 2.5–5cm (1–2in) long so that it passes through a joint. This is the part that must be kept in the soil with the cut kept open, for instance by lodging a small pebble in it. An application of hormonal rooting powder or liquid at the cut may speed up the process of root formation. The stem must be held securely in position with a rock or brick and the end of the stem should be staked in as near an upright position as possible.

It may take a year or 18 months for a layer to develop an adequate root system that will allow it to be severed completely from the parent shrub.

Left *When you are housing small cuttings of rock plants in cold frames, some ventilation must be given during the day in the winter months. Condensation and a stagnant atmosphere encourage damping off.*

Below *Growing cuttings inside a frame can be very successful as they get the humidity and temperature necessary to develop.*

WHAT CAN GO WRONG

Rock plants and alpines are naturally quite hardy plants but from time to time they can be troubled by pests and diseases. Easy preventative measures can be taken to reduce these risks.

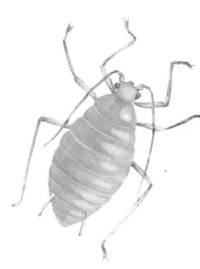

Greenfly

Caterpillar

The point has already been made that rock garden plants are remarkably trouble-free, provided that their basic growing requirements are satisfied. From time to time, however, there will be problems with pests and diseases, but the damage can be limited by taking preventative measures and dealing promptly with attacks when they occur.

Pests
Like almost all garden plants, alpines can be attacked by various pests and, unless action is taken to safeguard them, some much-loved favourites may be lost.

Slugs and snails
The most troublesome pests in the rock garden are the slugs and snails. They have a particular passion for some of the choice alpines, including the dwarf campanulas, and can make devastating raids on mild, humid evenings.

The use of a stone mulch on the rock garden will go some way to discouraging the movement of slugs and snails, and the removal of all debris, particularly dead leaves, will reduce the number of areas that could harbour these pests. A reasonably effective protection can be achieved by laying proprietary slug baits. For instance, particularly vulnerable plants can be surrounded by a ring of slug pellets. These will need to be renewed at reasonably frequent intervals in the critical period of spring and early summer. It is difficult to devise a method of keeping rain off pellets that is not unsightly but it may be feasible to prop up a piece of slate relatively inconspicuously and place the pellets underneath this.

Birds and animals
After slugs, birds are probably the greatest cause of damage to rock garden and alpine plants. They can be a great test of one's good-natured acceptance of wildlife in the garden; at some times of the year, late winter and early spring especially, their activities are little short of vandalism. The plants that suffer most are the rosette and cushion-forming alpines, which can be set upon and torn about until there is very little left to salvage. Sparrows may also vandalize early spring bulbs, energetically pulling apart yellow crocuses particularly.

Sparrows

Mice

Again, the problem is to find a way of discouraging their activities that is not unsightly and, frankly, it is a problem not easily resolved. Cones of mesh can be put over highly valued plants but this is certainly not an inconspicuous solution. Perhaps the best approach is to use a crisscross web of black thread supported on sticks just above the flowering plants.

Mice can also be a problem, especially with young rock plants. Rodent repellent, however, can be sprayed on the plants.

Aphids
In the main, garden aphids are among the most troublesome pests, sapping plants of their strength and transmitting often serious viral diseases. These pests reproduce at a phenomenal rate so that they form quaking black, pink or greenish clusters on any sappy growth. Although many rock garden and alpine plants are too thrifty to be appetizing to aphids, new growth will sometimes be attacked. Infestations should be dealt with promptly. The most convenient treatment is to spray with a systemic insecticide.

Caterpillars
Some other pests will occasionally cause minor problems. For example, caterpillars

may eat leaves or flowers. If there is leaf damage and there are no silvery trails as slugs or snails would leave, then caterpillars are likely to be the culprits. Proprietary sprays can be used to deal with them but the best solution is to search among the leaves, particularly in the centre of plants, and remove the pests by hand. If you go out with a torch at night you will probably find them fully active.

Ants
If ants build nests around the roots of plants this can cause water loss. With cushion plants, for example, the appearance of brown patches may be a clue to this problem. Proprietary ant killers are available and these should be used around the plant according to the manufacturer's instructions.

Diseases
While there are numerous diseases that can attack the various plants that are grown in the rock garden, there are very few that affect a large range of plants, and surprisingly few that, in the ordinary course of events, the gardener has to worry about.

Grey mould
Grey mould (botrytis) is a fungal disease that can cause serious damage in damp weather. It is a fungal infection that shows as grey woolly patches on parts of leaves and stems that have darkened. Plants with hairy or felted foliage are especially vulnerable in the winter months and it is for this reason that they are protected from excess moisture with panes of glass.

In the alpine house an outbreak of grey mould suggests that ventilation is inadequate. One has to remember that the purpose of an alpine house is not to provide an environment that is warmer and snugger than outdoors, but one where it is possible to control the amount of moisture that reaches plants, with a free movement of air.

Grey mould can be treated by spraying with fungicides, the systemic kinds are probably the best to use, but in the case of a seriously debilitated plant the best course is to take it out and burn it. It is sometimes tempting to persist but a plant that has been seriously attacked can be a source of infection for the rest of your collection.

Viruses
The same ruthless approach is advisable when plants are suffering from viral attacks. These are not common in the rock garden but occasionally plants show distorted growth and abnormal streaking and mottling of foliage. There is no way of treating viral infections, so plants suffering from them should be dug up and burned.

Other disorders
If you have tested your soil properly and chosen your plants well, it is unlikely that you will have planted a lime-hating plant, such as a rhododendron, in soil that is alkaline. However, if leaves on an acid-loving plant turn yellow between the veins, it is likely that the soil is too alkaline. The best course may be to lift the plant and grow it in a pot with an appropriately acidic soil. An alternative to try first is to incorporate peat, which is normally strongly acidic, around the plant and to apply a proprietary chemical compound (chelated iron) that will help to correct the chlorosis caused by the lime.

There are other mineral deficiencies that may cause yellowing leaves and, for instance, the symptoms of manganese, magnesium and nitrogen deficiencies may be difficult to distinguish. Treatment for these problems involves spraying or feeding with appropriate chemicals – manganese sulphate for manganese deficiency, magnesium sulphate for magnesium deficiency, and for lack of nitrogen a nitrogenous fertilizer. If you are not sure what the problem is, try spraying with a foliar feed containing trace elements as well as major nutrients.

One other problem that is sometimes encountered in the rock garden is damage to buds when they thaw too rapidly, after a frost. This can mar the beauty of early-flowering rhododendrons planted in open positions where early-morning sun reaches them. If it is a problem, it is worth repositioning plants so the sun touches them later in the day and frost, therefore, has a chance to thaw slowly.

Slug

Below *Soil can easily be tested with a kit and any acidity that is found can be quickly corrected.*

ROCK GARDEN CALENDAR

Planning the plants of your rock garden should always be done on a seasonal basis to keep the right balance of flowering and evergreen plants throughout the year.

Early spring

The flowers of the first weeks of spring are probably more eagerly anticipated than those of any other season of the year. It is the moment above all others for the dwarf bulbs to bring life to the rock garden, but there are strong splashes of colour from easy perennials, such as the aubrietas.

Jobs to do

Clear away dead leaves and other debris that might harbour pests and diseases. The dead leaves attached to herbaceous perennials can now be cut down.

Weed and, if not yet done, loosen the soil with a small hand fork, taking care not to damage roots.

Apply a top-dressing, which, for the majority of plants, should consist of two parts of loam and equal parts of coarse sand and peat (all by bulk) to which has been added a dusting of bone-meal. After top-dressing renew the mulch of stone chippings.

Firm plants and labels that have been lifted by frost, and make a check of plants that have been lost over the winter.

Plant out own-raised stock grown on from the previous year or new stock as soon as it becomes available. Label at planting time.

Propagation by division of deciduous

Crocus tomasinianus.

and evergreen perennials should be completed promptly. If snowdrops need lifting and dividing, this should be done as soon as flowers die. Continue sowing seeds and prick out all the seedlings when they develop.

Clean and put away glass panes that have been used to keep excess moisture off hairy and felted plants throughout the winter months.

Plants to enjoy

Alyssum, Androsace, Chionodoxa, Crocus, Daphne, Erythronium, Galanthus, Iris, Muscari, Narcissus, Primula, Saxifraga.

Mid-spring

The small bulbs continue to play an important role during this season but at last the rock garden begins to look more clothed with green. From now until early summer the dwarf rhododendrons are among the most conspicuous of the flowering shrubs.

Spring-flowering gentians.

Jobs to do

Continue weeding and complete forking the surface and top-dressing.

Planting should be finished as soon as possible to allow plants to become fully established before the warmer, drier weather of summer puts them to the test. It is the best time of the year to plant dwarf conifers, which are beautiful plants in

A rock garden in the spring.

their own right and useful as major components in the design of a rock garden. Water in all new stock thoroughly and label clearly.

Sow seeds of rock plants and prick out seedlings as they germinate. As the weather becomes warmer, the seed pans will dry out more quickly. Do not water from overhead but stand the pan in a basin of water and let it take up moisture until the surface darkens.

Cut back trailing stems of early-flowering perennials, such as aubrieta and alyssum, as they finish flowering. This keeps the plants compact and shapely.

Plants to enjoy

Alyssum, Androsace, Arabis, Aubrieta, Cytisus, Erythronium, Gentiana, Leucojum, Muscari, Narcissus, Primula.

Late spring

Late spring is without doubt one of the loveliest periods of the year in the rock garden for it is a time when the last of the spring bulbs combine with a number of free-flowering perennial and shrubby rock plants to give a really full display.

Alyssum saxatile *and Aubrieta.*

Jobs to do

Pests, encouraged by the milder weather and new growth, will multiply rapidly. The most troublesome are likely to be aphids; the best method of control is to spray with a systemic insecticide, repeating regularly about every ten days. Ants, too, can sometimes be a nuisance, tunnelling among the roots of plants. Use a proprietary powder sprinkled around the nest holes if there is serious damage. Although more isolated, devastating pest damage in the rock garden can be caused by slugs, which are active in warm and

Ants can be a problem.

moist weather. To protect vulnerable plants, lay slug pellets in their vicinity.

Weeds will be encouraged by warm moist weather. Check them before they have a chance to seed.

Check seeds. Continue to watch seed pans closely, and prick out seedlings as soon as they have developed two true leaves.

Propagation. At this time of the year many plants can be propagated from cuttings of new, soft growth. Insert in pans of sandy compost, cover with a pane of glass or clear plastic, and keep moist.

Plants to enjoy

Aethionema, Achillea, Aquilegia, Armeria, Aubrieta, Campanula, Cytisus, Dryas, Genista, Gentiana, Geum, Gypsophila, Iberis, Phlox, Potentilla, Pulsatilla, Rhododendron, Scilla, Tulipa, Veronica, Viola.

Early summer

The fullness of late spring continues into early summer, with the alpine pinks and the campanulas among the most conspicuous plants.

Jobs to do

Watering may be necessary if there are long spells of dry weather. Do it in the cool of the evening, applying in a fine spray.

Pest control is still important. Continue

to use a systemic insecticide regularly against aphids and similar sucking pests. From time to time change the insecticide used so that pests do not build up a resistance to a particular chemical.

Collect seedheads of the less common alpines and rock plants, throughout the summer and the autumn. Sowing seed as soon as it is ripe is likely to produce good results. In this way you will be able to maintain and increase your own stocks of a desirable plant and have material to exchange with other gardeners for uncommon plants you do not yet have. Germination of some species can be very slow, so mark pans of seed carefully.

Continue to take soft cuttings and start taking cuttings of older wood with a heel.

Cut back trailing plants that have finished flowering, to encourage compact growth. In some cases this may induce a second crop of flowers in late summer.

Dwarf rhododendrons should have dead heads removed to encourage a good crop of flowers next year.

Plants to enjoy

Achillea, Alchemilla, Allium, Androsace, Aquilegia, Aster, Aubrieta, Dianthus, Genista, Geranium, Geum, Helianthemum, Gypsophila, Hebe, Hypericum, Iberis, Leontopodium, Papaver, Phlox, Sedum, Rhododendron, Veronica, Viola.

Remove dead flowerheads from rhododendrons to help future flowering.

Mid-summer

Throughout this season there are still many plants in flower in the rock garden but the flush of late spring and early summer is over.

Jobs to do

Continue weeding. It is particularly important to get rid of weeds before they seed.

Aphids may still be a problem so maintain a programme of spraying against them.

Clip back trailing plants as they go over.

Water if prolonged dry weather persists. Give a thorough soaking every two or three days rather than a light watering more frequently. Pay particular attention to sink gardens, which are very prone to drying out in hot, rainless weather.

Continue to collect seed of choice plants, clean it and sow as soon as ripe.

Propagate suitable plants from soft and heel cuttings.

When lifted bulbs can be kept in a box.

Bulbs that need to be lifted should be taken up as their leaves die down. Most can be replanted immediately but store tulip bulbs in the warm until autumn.

Plants to enjoy

Alyssum, Dianthus, Campanula, Gentiana, Geranium, Hebe, Helianthemum, Hypericum, Phlox, Penstemon, Potentilla, Sedum, Sempervivum, Viola.

Late summer

At the end of summer the rock garden can seem rather short of flowering plants. This is a good moment to review your whole planting scheme and to consider what should be added by way of late-flowering and long-flowering plants, and those with interesting foliage and shape throughout the year. Take the opportunity of looking at other gardens to see what late-season plants there are and consult the catalogues of specialist firms. Get orders in early for autumn delivery.

Jobs to do

Plant bulbs as they become available; purchases should be made without delay. Except for tulips, the sooner bulbs are planted the better. Avoid dotting single bulbs here and there but plant in clusters.

Top *A rock garden in the late summer.*

Above *Take azaelea cuttings in August.*

Lift and divide bulbs if necessary. Small offsets can be potted up to be brought on to flowering size.

Continue to take cuttings, ensuring in particular that you strike replacement stock for short-lived plants and those that have become tired and straggly. It is a good time to take heel cuttings of the dwarf rhododendrons. Rooting is often easier if some soil from where the plants grow is added to the compost.

Plants to enjoy

Alyssum, Cyclamen, Gentiana, Oenothera, Papaver, Potentilla, Viola.

Left *Saxifraga oppositifolia latina.*

Early autumn

As elsewhere in the garden, the range of plants now in flower is very much reduced. There are, however, some plants of real quality that give the garden a lift at this time. They include dwarf cyclamen, autumn-flowering crocuses and some of the Asiatic gentians.

Jobs to do

Tidy up the rock garden, clearing away leaves and debris. Keep an eye out for attacks of mould, which can be dealt with using a fungicidal spray.

Sow freshly gathered seed. Many alpines will germinate freely provided the sown seed is exposed to frost during winter.

Take dwarf conifer cuttings.

Finish planting bulbs other than tulips.

Plant shrubby and herbaceous rock plants. New stock should be well watered in and clearly labelled. As mid-autumn approaches plants can be lifted and divided. Some evergreen shrubs can be satisfactorily transplanted at this time of the year.

Begin construction of a new rock garden or raised bed. Ensure that basic preparation, including the elimination of perennial weeds, is thorough.

Plants to enjoy

Acer, conifers, Crocus, Cyclamen, Gentiana.

Below *Dwarf conifer cuttings.*

Below right *Protect plants in the winter with sheets of glass.*

Mid-autumn

This is generally a stormy period, with a lot of rain and spells of cold weather.

Take what opportunities you can to tidy up the rock garden so that it is well in order before winter.

Jobs to do

Clear away dead leaves; if they are left lying damp on rock garden plants they may cause rotting. In addition, they provide a cover for slugs, which can be active at this time of the year.

Protect plants with woolly or hairy leaves grown in the open. They may need protection from excess water in the winter

Left *Tidy up the rock garden in mid-autumn.*

months, and this can be done by fixing small panes of glass on wire frames over individual plants.

Continue planting herbaceous and shrubby perennials if it is not too frosty.

Divide established plants.

Continue with the construction of new rock gardens and raised beds if the weather is dry. Some planting, particularly in rock crevices, is more easily done during construction than later. In

A two-pronged fork is good for planting.

general, however, it is advisable to allow a period of settling before planting, which can be carried out in the spring.

A stone or imitation stone sink can now be planted up.

Plants to enjoy

Acer, conifers, Cyclamen, Gentiana.

Late autumn

There is still a little flower colour in the autumn rock garden, particularly from the hardy dwarf cyclamen. However, from now until winter, the principal interest will be in the foliage of evergreens such as the dwarf conifers. Some of these take on new interest at this time of year, turning bronze or deeper shades of blue-grey. Examine your rock garden in the winter months to see if the look of it might be improved by the addition of dwarf evergreens.

Jobs to do

Check for weeds and self-sown seedlings. Some plants self-seed so prodigally that fairly drastic thinning is desirable.
Remove dead leaves from the rock garden. Check over the plants at least once a week.
Plant tulips. Other dwarf bulbs should have been planted by early autumn but now is the time to put in tulips.
Plant deciduous shrubs in mild weather. Many established deciduous shrubs can now be transplanted safely.
Herbaceous perennials can still be planted in good weather.

Plants to enjoy

Conifers, Cyclamen, Erica, Galanthus, Gentiana.

Early winter

There is probably no period of the year when there is less happening in the garden. Yet the rock garden need not be without interest. The enormously varied ericas, for instance, which flower right through until the early spring, are colourful and attractive little plants that are well worth using in moderation to brighten the rock garden during the winter months.

Jobs to do

Remove dead leaves promptly during regular checks on the rock garden.
Birds can be a considerable nuisance during the next few months. In cold spells they will attack small plants, particularly choice rosette and cushion-forming kinds, and pull them to pieces. The vandalism can be devastating. There is no simple solution that is entirely satisfactory, but one method of discouraging attacks is to tie black thread on sticks to form a criss-cross net a few centimetres (about an inch) above vulnerable plants. Another good method is to cover single plants or groups with small cones of chicken wire.

Plants to enjoy

Conifers, Cyclamen, Erica,

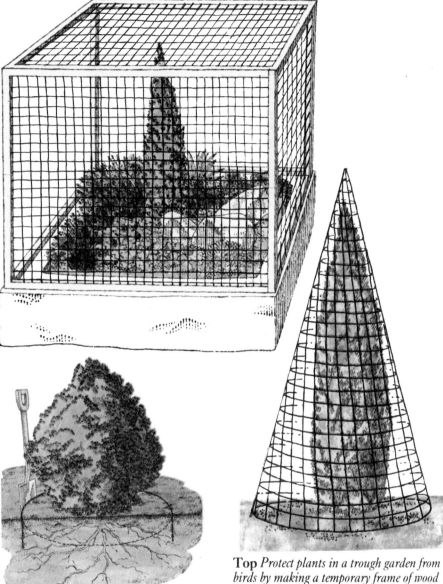

Mid-winter

Although mid- and late winter are the coldest periods of the year, and many plants are still dormant, there is already a sense of growth getting under way. The shoots of dwarf bulbs are starting to show and some of the most precocious begin to flower even while snow is on the ground.

Jobs to do

Slugs can still be a problem during mild spells. Ensure that dead leaves are cleared away and continue to lay slug pellets.
Dislodge heavy falls of snow that have accumulated on the branches of shrubs.
Continue with the planting of herbaceous perennials and deciduous shrubs in fair weather.
Seeds are often sent out by specialist gardening societies at this time of the year. Sow alpines as soon as received.
Take root cuttings of plants that can be

Top *Protect plants in a trough garden from birds by making a temporary frame of wood covered with chicken netting.*

Above *Protect plants in the rock garden with cones or wigwams of chicken netting.*

Left *Evergreen shrubs can be transplanted in late autumn.*

propagated in this way.
Avoid construction work in wet weather. If, however, the surface of the ground is very frozen, this is a good opportunity to move rock or some compost about.

Plants to enjoy

Conifers, Crocus, Cyclamen, Erica, Galanthus, Iris, Saxifraga.

Late winter

Nowhere in the garden is there a more dramatic foretaste of the advent of spring than in the rock garden. The flowering rhythm of dwarf bulbs begins to pick up speed despite unpleasant spells of cold bleak weather, and the aubrietas are already beginning to break into flower.

Jobs to do

Clear away debris accumulated over winter and set about weeding the rock garden in a methodical way, clearing a small section at a time. The sooner weeds are dealt with the less work they will make. Start going over the rock garden with a small hand fork loosening the soil but avoiding any damage to the roots of cultivated plants.

Apply a top-dressing consisting of two parts of loam and equal parts of coarse sand and peat (all by bulk) in which a dusting of bonemeal has been incorporated.

Remove the dead rosettes of plants such as saxifrages, and work stone chippings into the gaps.

Dress the rock garden with chippings. Use limestone for lime-tolerant plants, granite for lime-haters. This will help conserve moisture and suppress weeds. **Sow** alpines and rock garden plants as soon as the seeds become available.

Plants to enjoy

Aubrieta, Chinodoxa, Crocus, Daphne, Erythronium, Galanthus, Iris, Muscari.

Left and below *The typical winter rock garden.*

Bottom Galanthus nivalis flore plena, *the double form of the snowdrop.*

PLANT GUIDE

There are numerous varieties of plants available for your rock garden. This guide contains a comprehensive selection to add interest and colour to all types of garden.

This chapter contains an alphabetical list of plants that you might want to grow. It is not exhaustive and you may well find other species and varieties, especially in specialist nurseries, but the plants included here will provide plenty of interest throughout the year . . . and there are plants to suit every situation in the rock garden.

In some cases, the nomenclature is confused because on the one hand botanists are prone to change names as new research comes to light and, on the other, the plants distributed through the trade may not be botanically correct. Where this is likely to lead to particular confusion this has been pointed out, but generally the plants are listed under the names used commercially.

Most of the plants are available from garden centres or from specialist alpine plant nurseries, but you will find some are difficult to obtain even from specialists. They may, however, be available from seed, or even through seed exchanges among members of specialist societies – a good way to obtain some of the rarer kinds.

Abies *see* Conifers.

Acer
The slow-growing maples are among the best-suited deciduous small trees to introduce to the larger rock garden or raised bed. Mature plants will reach over 3m (10ft), with matching spread, but it is worth growing them even if they have to be discarded when they become too large. They are plants of exceptionally beautiful foliage, as lovely in spring and summer as they are in autumn, when the leaves take on vivid colouring.

A. japonicum 'Aureum', 1m (3ft), has lime-yellow leaves throughout summer, turning bright red in autumn.

A. palmatum 'Dissectum', 1m (3ft), forms an elegant mound of finely divided, light green foliage.

A. palmatum 'Dissectum Atropurpureum', 1m (3ft), is like the former except that the leaves are a deep purplish-red, making a particularly good foil for lighter colours.

Cultivation: Plant acers in sheltered positions (the leaves can be damaged by cold winds or frosts) in moisture-retentive soil that is neutral or acid. Reputable nurseries will supply named forms grafted onto appropriate root-stocks. Propagation of maples from seed is possible but germination can be erratic and named forms will not come true.

Achillea
The achilleas, popularly known as yarrows or milfoils, were named after the Greek hero Achilles, who is said to have used the leaves as a dressing for his wounds. The dwarf achilleas are admirable and easy rock garden plants. The fern-like leaves form attractive silvery mats above which the flat flower heads are borne over a long period throughout the summer. The fragrance can be rather pungent.

A. clavennae, 15cm (6in), has finely cut, bright, silvery foliage and pure white flowers.

A. × 'King Edward', 15cm (6in), is an excellent hybrid, forming tufts of grey-green foliage and producing sulphur-yellow flower heads.

A. tomentosa, 15cm (6in), a plant with downy, grey-green leaves, makes dense heads of deep yellow flowers.

Cultivation: Grow in any ordinary, well-drained soil in full sun. Plants can be grown from seed sown in spring or early summer. Division is an easy method of propagation and is advisable every two or three years, if plants are to be kept neat.

Adiantum
The maidenhair ferns are commonly grown as indoor plants but one species that is reasonably available is fully hardy and suitable for planting in a wall.

A. venustum, 25cm (10in), is a deciduous species with triangular fronds and a rhizomatous root. In winter the dead fronds are attractively coloured.

Cultivation: Plant in well-drained (but not too dry) soil in the light shade. The easiest dried method of propagation for this plant is by division.

Opposite There are many hundreds of rock plants and alpines to choose from, with a wide selection for all locations. Most rhododendrons, for example, are excellent for acid soil.

Aethionema

The stonecresses are evergreen trailing plants which, in their native Mediterranean region, are found in sunny, dry conditions. They are useful in the rock garden for the long season, from late spring well into summer, during which they produce a profusion of candytuft-like flowers.

A. grandiflorum, 30cm (12in), makes a spreading plant with grey-green leaves and a lasting display of delicate, pink flowers.

A. pulchellum, 15cm (6in), is similar to *A. grandiflorum* but on a smaller scale. The pink of the flowers is more intense.

A. 'Warley Rose', 15cm (6in), has wiry stems and blue-grey leaves that make an attractive background for the pink flowers.

Cultivation: Aethionemas prefer an alkaline soil but in this respect are not unduly fussy provided they have good drainage and full sun. The hybrid *A.* × 'Warley Rose' can only be increased from cuttings but the species can be raised from seed.

Right Androsace lanuginosa *is one of the easiest rock jasmines to grow and its delicate pink blooms make a fine summer display.*

Below Aethionema *'Warley Rose' is a hardy evergreen popular for its long flowering season.*

Allium

The dwarf ornamental members of the onion family include a number of attractive bulbs suitable for planting among herbaceous and shrubby rock garden plants. Few of them are showy flowers but they are useful for carrying the bulb season on into summer.

A. amabile, 15cm (6in), a plant with a rhizomatous root, is neat and small enough to be grown in a sink garden. In late summer there are loose heads of two to six purplish flowers.

A. beesianum, 25cm (10in), is a rhizomatous species, which in mid-summer produces heads of pendant white and blue flowers.

A. cyaneum, 15cm (6in), rhizomatous, is a tufty plant of narrow leaves that in mid-summer bears erect, deep blue flowers.

A. narcissiflorum, 20cm (8in), rhizomatous, is one of the loveliest of the dwarf alliums. The hanging bell-like flowers, which can vary in colour from pink to plum, appear in mid-summer.

A. oreophilum (syn. *A. ostrowskianum*), 15cm (6in), a bulbous species with narrow leaves. In summer it produces heads up to 5cm (2in) across and consisting of numerous purple-pink flowers.

Cultivation: Plant in any well-drained soil in a sunny position. The bulbous species benefit from drying out after flowering. Alliums can be propagated from seed, which sets readily, and by splitting bulb clumps or division of rhizomes.

Alyssum

The alyssums, as their common name madwort suggests, were once thought to cure madness. They include a number of dwarf species that are easy and showy plants for the rock garden.

A. montanum, 15cm (6in), makes a loosely spreading plant with grey-green leaves. The yellow flowers are borne in late spring and early summer.

A. saxatile, 15–30cm (6–12in), the commonest rock garden alyssum, may spread up to 45cm (18in). The dense heads of bright yellow flowers make a fine display from mid-spring to early summer. Among named forms 'Citrinum', with pale yellow flowers, and 'Plenum', a rich yellow double form, are particularly desirable.

Cultivation: Alyssums tolerate a wide range of soils but should be planted in a dry position in full sun. They can be grown very successfully on walls and banks. After flowering, trim plants to prevent them becoming straggly. Plants are easily raised from seed. They can also be propagated by division or from cuttings which have been taken early in the summer.

Androsace

The androsaces, or rock jasmines, are essentially alpines. Some are among the choicest plants for the alpine enthusiast but their cultivation can be difficult. However, there are some species that are not too demanding and these can be grown satisfactorily in the scree bed or rock garden provided there is very good drainage.

A. carnea, 2.5–7.5cm (1–3in), makes a tight cushion of small leaves, that in early to mid-summer, is covered with pink primula-like flowers.

A. lanuginosa, 7.5cm (3in), has a trailing habit and is a useful plant for planting in a crevice. The silvery leaves make a pretty foil for the pink flowers, which are borne in the late summer months.

A. primuloides (syn. *A. sarmentosa*), 10cm (4in), is probably the easiest to grow of the androsaces and makes small, dense rosettes from which the pink flowers emerge in late spring. A number of different named forms are available.

Cultivation: Plant androsaces in full sun in soil that is freely draining and preferably containing limestone grit. Some overhead protection from excess moisture may be advisable in winter. Plants can be propagated from seed, from cuttings, or by division in spring.

Anemone

Among the anemones, or windflowers, are a number of dwarf species that are easy and attractive plants for the rock garden. When planted in numbers and allowed to naturalize, they make vivid splashes of colour in spring. Those listed are all plants with rhizomes or tubers.

A. apennina, 15cm (6in), has fern-like leaves and flowers similar to those of *A. blanda* in pink, blue, and white that come out in early to mid-spring.

A. blanda, 15cm (6in), one of the loveliest and best known of the spring-flowering anemones. The flowers are normally blue but there are also other excellent named forms that are deep blue, pink and white in colour.

A. coronaria, 15–30cm (6–12in), is one of the parents of the De Caen and St Brigid anemones. Though these large-flowered hybrids generally look out of place in the rock garden, the true species, which has white, red, or blue flowers, is a plant well worth growing.

Cultivation: These spring-flowering anemones do well in most well-drained soils in full sun or light shade. Plant the tubers or rhizomes in autumn. Stock can be increased from offsets or by division of the rhizomes when the top growth has died down in summer.

Antennaria

Among the antennarias only one species and its forms is commonly cultivated as a rock garden plant.

A. dioica, 10cm (4in), is a mat-forming plant of silvery foliage spreading as much as 45cm (18in). The small heads of white flowers tinged pink are borne in late spring and early summer. The form 'Minima' is more compact, while 'Rosea' has deep pink flowers.

Cultivation: These plants are easily pleased if given a sunny position in well-drained soil. They do well planted in paving and, in the rock garden, make an effective planting associated with vigorous small bulbs.

Aquilegia

The dwarf columbines are flowers of late spring and early summer, as lovely for their foliage as they are for the distinctive spurred flowers.

A. alpina, 30cm (12in), has grey-green leaves and has large blue or blue and white flowers.

A. bertolonii, 10cm (4in), is a lovely plant for the rock garden, rich blue flowers being borne over a tuft of very attractive blue-green leaves.

Cultivation: The columbines listed are not difficult plants and will do well in sunny or lightly shaded positions. Individual plants are not long-lived but stocks are more than maintained by self-seeding. *A. alpina* is, in fact, too generous a seeder to plant among choice plants. Where different species of columbine are grown together they will hybridize freely and pure stock will be difficult to maintain.

Top *One of the best-known alyssums is* A. saxatile *'Citrinum', its showy lemon-yellow blossom has earned it the popular name of Gold Dust.*

Above Anemone blanda *is an excellent spring-flowering anemone available in many different colours.*

Arabis

The common snow-in-summer (*A. albida*, syn *A. caucasica*) grows too vigorously for it to have a place in the rock garden but there are related plants that are more amenable.

A. ferdinandi-coburgii, 'Variegata', 7.5cm (3in), forms mats of variegated foliage that are of more interest than the white flowers. *Cultivation:* The plants listed need well-drained, gritty soil and positions in full sun.

Arenaria

The arenarias are not showy plants but they are useful mat-forming creepers.

A. balearica, 3cm (1in), forms mats of bright green leaves spreading as much as 45cm (18in) and starred with white flowers in late spring and early summer.

A. montana, 7.5cm (3in), makes a mat of deep green leaves with a spread up to 45cm (18in). In early summer it produces a profusion of glistening white flowers.

A. purpurascens, 5cm (2in), a prostrate plant making a mat some 30cm (12in) across, and bearing purplish flowers in the summer months.

Cultivation: Arenarias should be planted in well-drained soil. *A. balearica* needs a shady position. *A. montana* tolerates part shade but it and *A. purpurascens* do well in full sun. Plants can be propagated by division and, in the case of *A. montana*, from cuttings taken in summer.

Armeria

The common thrift (*A. maritima*) is one of the conspicuous wild plants of rugged ground by the seashore. It and its relations are thoroughly at home in the rock garden and they are among the plants that can be introduced very effectively between slabs of paving.

A. caespitosa, (syn *A. juniperifolia*), 7.5cm (3in), is a really miniature alpine that is suitable for a small sink garden. The flowers are normally pink. The selected form 'Bevan's Variety' has deep colouring.

A. maritima, 20cm (8in), despite being such a familiar plant (the common thrift) is well worth a place in the garden. Selected forms are very desirable. These include: 'Alba', white; 'Bloodstone', deep red; 'Merlin', deep pink; and 'Vindictive', red. *Cultivation:* Any free-draining soil and sunny position will suit these plants well. They can be grown from seed planted in spring and can be propagated by division and from cuttings.

Opposite (top) *Justifiably popular, Aubrieta is one of the most widely-grown rock plants.*
(below) *Blechnum spicant, the native hard fern or deer fern, a plant for a shady part of the rock garden.*

Right *'Beechwood' is a lovely, colourful form of* Aster alpinus.

Below Asplenium adiantum-nigrum, *the black spleenwort, is a reliable and hardy fern.*

Artemisia

This large genus includes a number of plants with elegant, finely cut leaves that are of greater interest than the flowers. Most are too large for the rock garden but two at least are well worth a place.

A. lanata (syn. *A. pedemontana*), 30cm (6in), is an evergreen cushion-forming plant with delicately cut greyish leaves. Yellow flowers are borne from midsummer until early autumn.

A. schmidtiana 'Nana', 7.5cm (3in), makes a soft feathery clump of silvery leaves. The inconspicuous yellow flowers are borne at the end of summer.

Cultivation: Artemisias like a light soil and plenty of sun. Some protection from excessive moisture in winter is advisable. Plants are most easily increased from semi-hardwood cuttings.

Asplenium

The spleenworts are a group of more or less evergreen ferns that includes a number of hardy dwarf species particularly suitable for the rock garden.

A. adiantum-nigrum, 10cm (4in), makes black-stemmed clumps of leathery, glossy leaves.

A. ruta-muraria, 10cm (4in), the wall rue, is a remarkably tough rhizomatous plant of creeping growth.

A. trichomanes, 10cm (4in), the maiden spleenwort, is a pretty, lime-loving species with wiry stems and colourful, bright green rounded leaflets.

Cultivation: Plant in damp weather during the growing season, working plants into crevices with a gritty compost to which peat or leaf mould has been added. Propagate by the division method.

Aster

Among the asters are several dwarf species suitable for the rock garden that make a handsome show of daisy flowers.

A. alpinus, 15cm (6in), is a native of the European Alps. It forms spreading clumps of grey-green leaves and in late spring bears orange-centred flowers, which can vary in colour from pale mauve to purple. Selected forms include 'Beechwood', bluish-purple, and 'Wargrave Variety', pink with darker shading.

Cultivation: These are easy plants for well-drained sunny positions. Divide and replant every two or three years otherwise clumps become untidy and the plants less vigorous in growth.

Aubrieta

There are probably no rock garden plants more widely grown than the aubrietas. In spring they give a long and bold display of

vivid colour with little effort required of the gardener. However, they are not plants to associate with choice subjects, which they will quickly swamp.

A. deltoidea, 10cm (4in), spread 60cm (24in), is now represented in cultivation by numerous selected forms, which range in flower colour from pale pink to plum and mauve to deep blue. Choose plants when they are in flower to be certain of selecting good colour forms.

Cultivation: Any open, sunny position in the rock garden or in a wall is suitable. Cut back after flowering to keep growth neat. Although plants are easily raised from seed, selected forms must be increased by division or from individual cuttings.

Blechnum

The two species of this fern listed here are evergreen perennials that are useful in the rock garden.

B. penna-marina, 7.5cm (3in), is a creeping plant forming mats of dark green leaves.

B. spicant, 30cm (12in), an acid-loving fern, is like a larger form of *B. penna-marina*. Many of the curiously crested sports this species has produced have been maintained in cultivation.

Cultivation: Grow in well-drained soil to which peat or leaf mould has been added. Partial shade is preferable. Propagate by the division method.

of mid-green leaves during a long season that starts in mid-summer. Flowers come in many shades of blue and there is a lovely white form.

C. garganica, 10cm (4in), a good wall plant, bears masses of starry blue flowers in late summer. The form 'W. H. Paine' has dark blue flowers with white centres.

C. portenschlagiana (syn. *C. muralis*), 10cm (4in), a trailing plant that does well in a shady wall, makes a bold display of starry blue flowers in late summer. However, it is a vigorous spreader that should not be introduced mindlessly. This warning applies with greater force to the larger and more rampant *C. poscharskyana*.

C. pulla, 7.5cm (3in), is a plant with a running habit that forms loose mats and in summer produces nodding violet-blue flowers.

Cultivation: The campanulas described are plants for free-draining soil and positions in full sun or light shade. Most species are easily raised from seed and can be propagated from cuttings taken in late spring or early summer or by division.

Cassiope

The cassiopes are small evergreen shrubby members of the heather family that demand acid conditions and a moist soil. They are attractive plants for the peat bed and can be pot-grown effectively in the alpine house.

C. lycopodioides, 7.5cm (3in), is a mat-forming plant, spreading as much as 45cm (18in). The wiry stems are densely covered with tiny leaves; the dainty bell-like flowers are borne in late spring.

C. mertensiana 'Gracilis', 5cm (2in), makes a spreading mound, some 30cm (12in) across, of pale green leaves. In late spring and early summer it bears white flowers.

C. tetragona, 30–45cm (12–18in), is a plant of dark green leaves and erect growth that in late spring produces hanging white flowers, commonly tinged pink.

Cultivation: Plant in a cool position in light shade where the soil is lime-free. Propagate from cuttings or by layering.

Celmisia

These evergreen mountain daisies native to Australia and New Zealand are not all as difficult as their reputation might suggest. They are worth a place in the scree garden, for instance, not only for their flowers but also for their foliage, which in many species is strikingly silvered or white felted.

C. argentea, 7.5cm (3in), is a miniature species good for a sink garden. The woolly stemless flowers appear in early summer.

C. bellidioides, 2.5cm (1in), a low-

Campanula

The bellflowers, as they are popularly known, include some of the loveliest and most useful rock garden plants. Some of the truly alpine species are a great test of the enthusiast's skill but others are dependable rock garden plants that give a profuse display of flowers in summer.

C. arvatica, 7.5cm (3in) does best in a scree bed or planted in a crevice. The starry violet flowers are borne in mid-summer over a mat of mid-green leaves. There is also a white form, 'Alba'.

C. aucheri, 5cm (2in), makes a miniature tuft of toothed leaves. The relatively large purplish-blue flowers appear in the early summer months.

C. carpatica, 10–20cm (4–8in), is a vigorous tufted plant with trailing stems and is an excellent plant for the large rock garden. The large open bell flowers, blue or white, are borne for a long period from mid-summer. 'Ditton Blue' has deep blue flowers and 'Turbinata' is a compact blue-flowered form with greyish leaves.

C. cochlearifolia (syn. *C. pusilla*), 7.5cm (3in), is an easy plant that spreads by underground runners. The hanging flowers are borne on wiry stems over compact mats

growing species making close mats of dark green leaves above which the white flowers with bright orange centres appear in the early months of summer.

C. coriacea, 30cm (12in), forms clumps of pointed silvery leaves and produces large daisy flowers in summer borne on stout stems.

Cultivation: Celmisias need lime-free soil that although well-drained has a plentiful supply of water. They do best in lightly shaded positions. In winter those with felted leaves may need overhead protection from excessive wet. Seed germination is often not straightforward. Cuttings and division are the easiest methods of propagation.

Chaemacyparis *see* Conifers.

Chionodoxa
The common name glory-of-the-snow indicates the alpine origin of this small group of spring-flowering bulbs.

C. gigantea, 20cm (18in), the largest-flowered species and possibly merely a large form of *C. luciliae*, produces, from late winter to mid-spring, lax flower-spikes with up to three white-centred violet-blue flowers.

C. luciliae, 15cm (6in), is the most commonly grown species. In early spring the loose flower-spikes carry up to 10 bright blue flowers with white centres. Pink forms are also available.

C. sardensis, 15cm (6in), is similar to *C. luciliae* but the flowers are a deeper blue.

Cultivation: Despite their alpine origins, chionodoxas are not difficult to grow. In autumn plant in any well-drained soil in full sun. Little further attention is required. If plants become overcrowded, lift and divide as leaves die down after flowering. Seed sets freely.

Conifers
The dwarf conifers are among the most useful evergreen plants for giving the rock garden or raised bed year-round interest. In the vast range available they show great variation in habit, texture and colouring. New cultivars are constantly being introduced into commerce; the plants listed below are only a small selection of the best-known varieties.

Abies balsamae 'Hudsonia', 1m (3ft), has dark green foliage with bluish white bands on the reverse. In spring the new growth on these round-topped dwarf firs contrasts attractively with the old foliage.

Chaemacyparis lawsoniana 'Minima Aurea', 1.5m (5ft), is a dwarf false cypress of very slow growth. The twisted foliage is bright yellow.

C. obtusa 'Nana', 60cm (24in), is a very slow-growing flat-topped plant with dark green leaves.

Cryptomeria japonica 'Compressa', 1m (3ft), is a dwarf form of the Japanese cedar that makes a rounded plant with congested foliage that takes on bronze colouring in the winter months.

Juniperus communis 'Compressa', 1m (3ft), is one of the most widely planted dwarf conifers. It makes a dense column of blue-green foliage that is very slow growing.

J. squamata 'Blue Star', 1m (3ft), is a relatively new introduction of exceptional merit. The mound of silver-blue foliage is particularly bright throughout the summer.

Picea abies 'Little Gem', 60cm (24in), makes a dense, cushion-shaped bush of tiny leaves, with bright new shoots in spring.

P. mariana 'Nana', 30cm (12in), is one of the smallest of the dwarf conifers, suitable even for a sink garden. It makes a compact bun of soft blue-green leaves.

Pinus sylvestris 'Beuvronensis', 1.5m (5ft), is a blue-grey dwarf form of the Scots pine. The dense branching of the young plant generally opens out with age.

Thuja occidentalis 'Danica', 1m (3ft), a dwarf American white cedar, makes a

Opposite *(top) The campanulas, or bellflowers, include annuals, biennials and perennials for all types of rock garden.*
(below) Chionodoxa luciliae *is an attractive spring-flowering bulb.*

Above *Dwarf conifers are available in a remarkable range of colours, shapes and textures and add some height and interest to a rock garden.*

Above *The brightly-coloured brooms do best in an open, sunny position.*

Above right Crocus chrysanthus *'Blue Pearl' is an excellent named form of this popular plant.*

compact rounded bush with foliage that remains bright green throughout the year.

T. orientalis 'Aurea Nana', 1.5m (5ft), is a striking golden yellow dwarf conifer that makes a dense rounded bush of vertical sprays.

Tsuga canadensis 'Bennetts Dwarf' 1m (3ft), is a dwarf hemlock with graceful arching branches of mid-green foliage.

Cultivation: Grow dwarf conifers in reasonably moisture-retentive soil in full sun or partial shade (those with golden foliage will lose this colouring if planted in shade). At planting time ensure that trees are firmed in and well watered. Plants will benefit from an annual feed of a slow-release fertilizer.

Corydalis

The dwarf perennials of this genus are attractive for their finely divided foliage and for their quaint tubular flowers.

C. cashmeriana, 15cm (6in), a bulbous species, has bright green leaves and flowers of brilliant blue tinged green that appear in spring and early summer.

C. cheilanthifolia, 20cm (8in), is a yellow-flowered species that has pretty fern-like leaves with a slightly bronzed tinge. It flowers over a long season starting in the late spring.

Cultivation: C. cashmeriana is a rather demanding and generally short-lived plant that requires lime-free soil and a moist atmosphere. Plant the tubers in autumn. The other species are easily satisfied and are more likely to need thinning than special cultivation.

Crocus

These deservedly popular bulbous plants are among the best dwarf subjects for bringing colour into the rock garden in late winter and early spring. There are also useful and lovely species that flower in autumn. The large Dutch crocuses are more at home in the border or naturalized in grass than in the rock garden so they have not been included in this selection of species and their wonderfully varied forms.

C. chrysanthus, 7.5cm (3in), is best known for the wide range of forms of which it is a parent. Most of those mentioned flower in early spring or even late winter: 'Advance', pale yellow and bronze; 'Blue Bird', blue and cream; 'Blue Pearl', pale blue and white; 'Goldilocks', deep yellow and purple base; 'Ladykiller', purple with white interior; 'Snow Bunting', white marked with purple and having an orange base; 'Zwanenburg Bronze', bronze outside and deep yellow inside.

C. imperati, 10cm (4in), flowers in late winter. The inner petals are purple, the

outer biscuit colour streaked with purple.

C. minimus, 5cm (2in), has dull yellow flowers variously veined and feathered with deep purple, which open in the early and mid-spring.

C. speciosus, 12.5cm (5in), is an autumn-flowering species and one of the easiest to grow. The lilac-blue flowers are finely veined in dark purple. Named forms include: 'Oxonian', dark blue flowers; 'Aitchisonii', large with pale mauve flowers; and 'Albus', white.

C. tomasinianus, 7.5cm (3in), is an easy species that flowers in late winter and early spring. There is considerable variation in colour from pale mauve to deep purple. Two dark-flowered forms, 'Barr's Purple' and 'Whitewell Purple', are particularly attractive to look at.

Cultivation: In rock gardens or raised beds plant groups of corms as soon as they become available in well-drained soil in full sun. Crocuses are excellent as pan-grown plants in the alpine house. The easiest method of propagation is from the small cormlets produced by the parent corms. Plants can be raised from seed but cross-pollination may mean that seed will not come true.

Cryptomeria *see* Conifers.

Cyclamen

The hardy dwarf cyclamen are plants of strong family resemblance. They grow from corms, producing leaves that are often handsomely mottled and all have elegant flowers in white, pink or carmine with reflexed petals. There are few plants of greater quality for the rock garden and if several species are grown they provide almost year-round interest.

C. coum (syn. *C. orbiculatum*), 7.5cm (3in), makes a close little plant of rounded leaves, red underneath and sometimes prettily mottled. The flowers, about 18mm (¾in) long are borne from mid-winter till early spring.

C. hederifolium (syn. *C. neapolitanum*), 10cm (4in), is an autumn-flowering species with leaves that are frequently patterned with silvery markings. They persist into late spring, making a useful contribution themselves to the beauty of the rock garden. The flowers, which are borne over a long season, are about 2.5cm (1in) long.

C. purpurascems (syn. *C. europaeum*), 10cm (4in), has mid-green kidney-shaped leaves with light silvery patterning. The fragrant flowers are generally carmine.

Cultivation: Plant corms in late summer in well-drained soil which has had peat or leaf mould added to it. Choose sheltered positions in light shade. Corms take time to settle down – and resent disturbance. Cyclamen set seed freely (the corms do not produce offsets) and plants can be brought to flowering size in about three to four years.

Cytisus
This genus of brooms includes several free-flowering small shrubs that provide a strong splash of colour in late spring or early summer.

C. ardoinii, 15cm (6in), is a deciduous mat-forming species with downy leaves that has a spread of about 30cm (1ft). The flowers are bright yellow.

C. × beanii, 60cm (24in), a deciduous shrub with yellow flowers that forms a spreading bush up to 1m (3ft) wide.

C. × kewensis, 60cm (24in), deciduous, is a plant for the large rock garden as it can spread up to 1.2m (4ft). However, its profuse display of creamy yellow flowers makes it a worthwhile plant for those who have the room.

Cultivation: Brooms do well in almost any soil provided they have a sunny position and well-drained soil. Species can be grown from seed and propagated from cuttings. As plants transplant badly, start seeds and cuttings in single pots and when ready plant out directly in their final positions.

Daphne
The daphnes, evergreen and deciduous shrubs, include a number of dwarf species suitable for the rock garden. The individual flowers, generally sweetly scented, are quite small but they are borne in profusion.

D. arbuscula, 15cm (6in), evergreen, makes a tidy bush of dark green lustrous leaves. In mid-summer there are clusters of rosy scented flowers.

D. cneorum, 15cm (6in), the garland flower, makes an evergreen twiggy plant that bears masses of scented pink flowers in early summer. *D. c.* 'Alba' has white flowers and *D. c.* 'Eximia' is a particularly good form with flowers that are larger and deeper pink than the type.

Cultivation: Although often not long-lived, daphnes are not fussy about soil provided it is well drained. Plant in sun or partial shade, preferably where the roots are shaded by a large rock or by other plants. Daphnes transplant badly so stock raised from seed or cuttings should be grown in individual pots and planted out young in the permanent position. Layering is a slow but useful method of propagation.

Dianthus
This large genus includes not only dwarf dianthus – which are excellent plants for the rock garden, the scree bed and among paving – but also the florist's pinks and carnations. Among the large number of perennial species that are natives of rocky and alpine environments the family resemblance is very strong. The five-petalled flowers are generally borne in early summer above tufty clumps of narrow leaves.

Above Dianthus *'La Bourboulle', a low growing plant for the rock garden: the flowers grow on very short stems.*

Above Dryas octopetala, *the mountain avens, a trailing, mat-forming evergreen for the rock garden.*

Below right and opposite *The Epidmediums are hardy perennials grown for their decorative foliage and delicate flowers.*

D. alpinus, 7.5cm (3in), has large flowers in relation to the size of the clump, which is of deep green leaves. There is considerable variation in the shading of the flowers, which are not fragrant, but they are generally rose-purple with a central pale eye surrounded by a ring of dark spots.

D. deltoides, 25cm (10in), the maiden pink, is a mat-forming plant with narrow rich green leaves. The small deep pink flowers are borne over a long period in summer. Named forms include the bright pink 'Brilliant' and the striking crimson 'Flashing Light'.

D. gratianopolitanus (syn. *D. caesius*), 20cm (8in), commonly known in Britain as the Cheddar pink, forms mats of greyish leaves as much as 60cm (24in) across. The single pink flowers are fragrant. *D. g.* 'Flore Pleno' is a double form of compact growth.

D. neglectus, 10–20cm (4–8in), makes a tufty growth of mid-green leaves and bears flowers that can vary in colour from light pink to dark crimson but characteristically the underside of the petal is buff.

In addition to the species listed there are a number of dwarf hybrids, generally growing no more than 15cm (6in), that are not out of place in the rock garden. These include: 'Dubarry', deep pink; 'Fanal', bright pink; 'Fusilier', crimson; 'La Bourboulle', pink and also available in a white form; 'Little Jock', rose pink with darker eye; 'Mars', red; 'Pike's Pink', pink; and 'White Bouquet', white.

Cultivation: Many dianthus thrive in sharply drained limy soil in full sun. Most will do well in a sandy loam. Note, however, that *D. neglectus* dislikes lime and that *D. alpinus* is fairly tolerant of acid soils and does best with some light shade. Some of those described are not long-lived; it is worth taking cuttings in summer to ensure that vigorous stock is maintained. Plants of true species can be grown from seed sown in spring or early summer.

Draba

This large genus includes a number of perennial species native to harsh and mountainous regions that are well-suited to rock gardens, scree beds or, in the case of the more difficult, cultivation in the alpine house. They are characteristically cushion-forming plants with cross-shaped yellow flowers.

D. aizoides, 10cm (4in), forms a mat of inconspicuously bristled greyish leaves that can spread up to 25cm (10in) across. The pale yellow flowers, which are about 6mm (¼in) across, are borne in mid-spring.

D. bryoides (syn. *D. rigida bryoides*), 2.5cm (1in), forms a dense cushion up to 7.5cm (3in) wide. The yellow flowers are borne in early and mid-spring.

D. mollissima, 2.5cm (1in), makes downy hummocks of tightly packed rosettes, which in late spring and early summer are covered with bright yellow flowers.

D. rigida, 10cm (4in), consists of tiny rosettes of mid-green leaves over which the deep yellow flowers are borne profusely in mid-spring.

Cultivation: All the drabas listed require sharp drainage, although in spring and up

till flowering they need a plentiful supply of moisture. In the rock garden they are often best accommodated in a crevice. Those with downy leaves, such as *D. mollissima*, need protection from the wet in winter and are therefore often pot-grown in an alpine house. Plants can be propagated from seed sown in spring or from cuttings consisting of non-flowering rosettes taken in summer.

Dryas

One of the two species of this genus, an evergreen prostrate shrub native to the mountains of Europe, is a lovely rock garden plant.

D. octopetala, 10cm (4in), makes a spreading mat of glossy oak-like leaves, downy on the underside, some 60cm (24in) across. The broad eight-petalled flowers, white with an orange centre, are borne, sometimes rather sparsely, in the early to mid-summer months and followed by feathery seed heads.

Cultivation: Grow in ordinary well-drained soil in a sunny position. Plants dislike disturbance. Propagate from seed sown when ripe or from selected cuttings taken in late summer.

Epimedium

The dwarf epimediums are useful plants for shady parts of the rock garden. It is mainly for their leaves that they are grown, but their flowers have a beauty of their own.

E. alpinum, 25cm (10in), a deciduous species, has toothed leaves divided into two or three heart-shaped leaflets. In spring there are dark red flowers marked with yellow.

E. grandiflorum (syn. *E. macranthum*), 25cm (10in), a deciduous clump-forming plant with toothed triangular leaflets. Flowers, varying in colour from violet to white, are borne in early summer. The selected form 'Rose Queen' is a deep pink colour in flower.

E. × rubrum, 30cm (12in), has foliage that is handsomely tinted bronze-red when young. The flowers, which appear in late spring, are crimson.

Erica

Provided that they are planted in moderation, the dwarf forms of heather make a useful contribution to the rock garden by virtue of their attractive evergreen foliage and their winter flowering season.

E. carnea (syn. *E. herbacea*), 15–20cm (6–8in), is a very variable species with numerous dwarf named forms. The following is merely an introduction to the range available: 'Eileen Porter', deep red; 'Springwood Pink' and 'Springwood White', pink and white forms that flower particularly densely; 'Vivelii', crimson flowers and dark foliage.

Cultivation: Unlike many heathers, *E. carnea* is lime-tolerant. Grow plants in freely-draining soil in full sun. To keep growth vigorous and close shear off spent flower heads when they have faded. Propagate from cuttings with a heel, taken in late summer, or by layering.

Erinus

The single evergreen species that makes up this genus is a suitable plant for the rock or sink garden and is an attractive colonizer of wall and paving crevices.

E. alpinus, 7.5cm (3in), forms tufty mounds of toothed hairy leaves. The tubular flowers, which are borne in a long season throughout spring and summer, are rosy-purple. Named varieties include: 'Albus', white; 'Dr Hanele', carmine and the larger 'Mrs Charles Boyle', pink.

Cultivation: Grow in full sun or light shade in any sharply drained soil. Plants are generally not long-lived but are easily raised from seed.

Erodium

The scientific name derived from the Greek for 'heron' and the common name stork's bill are allusions to the beaked form of the fruit. These close relatives of the geraniums include a number of perennial and sub-shrubby plants of compact growth.

E. chrysanthum, 15cm (6in), has pretty finely cut silvery leaves and yellow flowers that are borne throughout summer.

E. corsicum, 20cm (8in), forms spreading

Above Erinus alpinus *is a tufted, hardy plant which is very suitable for most types of rock garden.*

Above Erodium corsicum, *a summer-flowering, mat-forming perennial.*

Below Erythronium tuolumnense, *a hardy bulbous plant, 3.5–4.5 centimetres (9–12 inches) in height, that flowers in March and April.*

tufts of downy grey-green leaves about 25cm (10in) wide. The flowers, pale pink veined red, are borne from mid-spring to early summer.

E. reichardii (syn. *E. chamaedryoides*), 5cm (2in), is like a more compact version of *E. corsicum.* The flowers are white with purple veining. There is a pink form, 'Roseum'.

Cultivation: Erodiums need full sun and prefer a well-drained limy soil. *E. corsicum* and *E. reichardii* should be given sheltered positions and *E. corsicum*, in particular, should be given protection from excessive wet in winter. Plants can be propagated from seed, by division, or from cuttings of roots or basal shoots.

Erythronium

The lily-like erythroniums are spring-flowering bulbs of great beauty for a cool and lightly shaded spot in the rock garden. These all have nodding flowers with reflexed petals.

E. dens-canis, 23cm (9in), the dog's-tooth violet, has mid-green foliage with darker mottling and rose-pink flowers. Named forms include: 'Pink Perfection', clear pink; 'Rose Beauty', deep pink; and 'White Splendour', white.

E. revolutum, 30cm (12in), the trout lily, has mottled foliage and flowers in shades from pink to purple with deeper markings.

E. tuolumnense, 25cm (10in), has bright green leaves and yellow flowers. Hybrids of which this plant is a parent include: 'Kondo' and 'Pagoda', both yellow.

Cultivation: Erythroniums require a moist and reasonably rich soil. Plant the corms deeply in late summer. They resent disturbances. Propagate from seed or from offsets.

Festuca

Among this genus of grasses are some relatively dwarf evergreen species that are useful in the rock garden for the contrast created by their linear foliage.

F. alpina, 10cm (4in), forms clumps of fine bright green leaves. In late summer there are green flowers tinged purple.

F. glauca, 25cm (10in), is a lovely blue-grey plant that looks attractive among paving as well as in the rock garden. It bears purple flowers in mid-summer.

Cultivation: Grow these plants in ordinary well-drained soil in full sun. When flower heads have faded remove them to avoid plants shedding seeds. Plants can be raised easily from seed or by division.

Gaultheria

Among this genus are hardy evergreen shrubs that are useful plants for lightly shaded, lime-free areas of the rock garden. The urn-like or bell-shaped flowers are followed by attractive berries.

G. cuneata, 30cm (12in), is a compact shrub with dark green leaves. The white flowers are borne in summer and followed by a striking display of rounded white berries.

G. miqueliana, 30cm (12in), may spread as much as 1m (3ft). The clusters of small white flowers, borne in early summer, are followed by white fruit that often show a pink tinge.

G. procumbens, 15cm (6in), an American species, is a creeping carpet-forming plant. In late summer there are white or pinkish flowers and in autumn red berries.

Cultivation: Plant in moisture-retentive acid soil. These dwarf species are well suited to peat beds in partial shade. Propagate from seed or from cuttings with a heel taken in summer.

Genista

Among these members of the broom family are several low-growing deciduous shrubs that in early summer give a handsome display of yellow flowers.

G. pilosa, 45cm (18in), is an almost evergreen shrub that may spread as much as 1.2m (4ft). The prostrate form, *G. p.* 'Procumbens', is ground-hugging and rarely exceeds 7.5cm (3in). In early summer the plants are covered in a mass of small yellow flowers.

G. sagittalis, 15cm (6in), is a mat-forming

plant that is rather sparsely leafed although the winged stems have a rather leaf-life appearance. The flowers are borne, in the early to mid-summer months, on very erect stems.

Cultivation: Grow in sunny positions where the soil is well-drained but moisture-retentive. Propagate straight from seed or from selected basal cuttings taken in the spring months.

Gentiana

The gentians are a large group of herbaceous plants that include some of the loveliest of all alpine perennials. The flowers are generally funnel-like or bell-shaped, and in the best known species are sumptuous blues.

G. acaulis, 7.5cm (3in), is a spring-flowering European species. It is not a difficult plant to grow in an open position with loamy soil, and its deep blue stemless flowers spotted green in the throat are of ravishing beauty. However, flowering can be erratic.

G. farreri, 10cm (4in), an Asiatic species with prostrate stems some 30cm (12in) long. The solitary flowers, borne in late summer at the end of stems, are Cambridge blue with greenish spotting and banding, and shade to white in the throat.

G. × *macaulayi,* 15cm (6in), is an autumn-flowering hybrid of Asiatic species. In growth it is similar to *G. farreri* but the flowers are deep blue.

G. septemfida, 15cm (6in), is an Asiatic species and one of the easiest gentians to grow. The flowers are borne in clusters in summer. The flower colour is variable but good forms are deep blue with lighter markings in the throat.

G. sino-ornata, 10cm (4in), another Asiatic species of prostrate growth with stems up to 30cm (12in) long. The flowers, which are borne singly in the autumn, are rich blue striped deep purple and green in colour.

G. verna, 7.5cm (3in), the spring gentian, is a native of the European Alps. This rosette-forming plant produces starry flowers of brilliant blue. *G. v.* 'Angulosa' is a robust form.

Cultivation: In general the Asiatic species, which flower in summer and autumn, are the easiest to grow, although they demand lime-free soil. The European and Asiatic species require a sunny position (*G.* × *macaulayi* will tolerate light shade) and free drainage. Some species, including *G. acaulis* and *G. sino-ornata,* can be propagated by division in spring but others resent disturbance. Seed can be sown in early spring but it can take a year to germinate.

Geranium

The common name, crane's-bill, and the scientific name are an allusion to the beaked fruit of these plants. The crane's-bills include a number of dwarf species that are excellent rock garden plants that are attractive in leaf and flower.

G. cinereum, 15cm (6in), has prettily lobed downy leaves and in spring produces pink flowers with darker veining. *G. c.* 'Ballerina' has flowers that are almost white richly veined crimson-purple.

G. dalmaticum, 10cm (4in), is a clump-forming species with glossy five-lobed leaves. These often turn red in autumn. In summer there are numerous pink flowers.

Above *The pink-flowered* Geranium dalmaticum.

Below *Between them the many different types of gentian can provide glorious blue flowers throughout the spring and summer.*

Top Hebe *'Carl Teschner', a dense spreading plant with violet flowers.*

Above Hebe pinguifolia *'Pagei' is a good form of the white flowered bush.*

Above right *Helianthemums, or rock roses, are very free flowering perennials.*

G. farreri (syn. *G. napuligerum*), 15cm (6in), forms a slow-growing mat of deeply lobed leaves. The flowers, which are pink with black anthers, are borne over a long season starting in late spring.

G. sanguineum 'Lancastriense', 7.5cm (3in), makes a spreading plant some 30cm (1ft) across. There is a long display of pink flowers throughout the summer.

G. subcaulescens, 15cm (6in), is similar to *G. cinereum* but the flowers are not veined.

Cultivation: Grow in ordinary well-drained soil in full sun. Propagate from seed sown in spring or by division.

Gypsophila

The cushion-forming habit of several dwarf alpine species is in sharp contrast to the frothy growth of the common gypsophila of borders *(G. paniculata).*

G. arietioides, 5cm (2in), makes a miniature hard grey-green cushion that is dotted with white or pale pink flowers in early summer.

G. cerastioides; 7.5cm (3in), forms spreading clumps of grey-green leaves up to 45cm (1½ft) wide. There is a long succession of white flowers with purple veins from summer to autumn.

G. repens (syn. *G. dubia*), 15cm (6in), is the most commonly grown alpine species. It makes a wide-spreading plant, to 60cm (2ft) across, with wiry stems and grey-green leaves. The small white to pink flowers are borne throughout the summer.

Cultivation: Grow in full sun in any well-drained soil. *G. repens* should be planted so that the stems can cascade down rocks or a wall. *G. arietioides* is probably best pot-grown in an alpine house. Plants can be propagated from seed, by division, and from cuttings.

Hebe

The hebes or shrubby evergreen veronicas are for the most part from New Zealand so it is not surprising that some have not proved fully hardy in European conditions. However, there are several dwarf species that are attractive shrubs for the rock garden and these are reasonably hardy.

H. buchananii 'Minor', 10cm (4in), is a really miniature little shrub with wiry stems and rounded leaves. The white flowers appear in early summer.

H. 'Carl Teschner', 30cm (12in), is a hybrid of dense habit with a spread up to 60cm (24in). The leaves are grey-green and the violet flowers are carried throughout the summer.

H. 'Pagei' (syn. *H. pinguifolia* 'Pagei'), 25cm (10in), can make a spreading bush up to 75cm (30in) broad. The blue-green leaves with a reddish margin are an attractive feature. The white flowers are borne in early summer.

Cultivation: Grow in any well-drained soil in full sun. *H. buchananii* 'Minor' makes a good subject for a sink garden. Hebe cuttings strike readily. Plants can also be

Left *Helianthemum, the rock rose, a very free flowering perennial plant.*

Below Hypericum fragile *is deep yellow in colour.*

grown from seed but as hebes hybridize freely plants may not come true.

Helianthemum
The helianthemums or rock roses are free-flowering easy evergreen shrubs for creating a broad effect in the rock garden. However, they should not be associated with quieter, less vigorous, species.

H. lunulatum, 15cm (6in), makes a neat clump of grey foliage and bears yellow flowers in summer.

H. nummularium (syn. *H. chamaecistus*), 30cm (12in), is a mat-forming European species with golden-yellow flowers in summer. From it are derived many cultivated grey-leaved forms that flower prolifically in the summer. These include: 'Ben Heckla', deep bronze; 'Ben Hope', red with orange centre; 'Mrs C. W. Earle', double scarlet; 'Sterntaler', yellow; 'The Bride', white; 'Wisley Pink', warm pink; and 'Wisley Primrose', yellow.
Cultivation: Grow in ordinary well-drained soil in full sun. Plants of named forms should be propagated form heeled cuttings in summer.

Hypericum
The common name, St John's wort, refers to the traditional belief that the plant was a protection against the devil. A less fanciful reason for growing the dwarf shrubby species is that they give a fine display of golden flowers in summer.

H. coris, 15cm (6in), is a neat little shrublet with yellow flowers borne in mid-summer.

H. fragile, 25cm (10in), a woody-based perennial, has grey-green foliage and bears yellow flowers with a slight red tinge in the late summer months.

H. olympicum, 25cm (10in), with which *H. fragile* has often been confused, makes a spreading shrub up to 30cm (1ft) wide with grey-green leaves. The bright yellow flowers are borne at the tips of stems in mid-to late summer. *H. o.* 'Citrinum' is a form with pale yellow flowers.

H. polyphyllum, 20cm (8in), is very close to *H. olympicum* except for minor botanical distinctions. The form 'Sulphureum' has pale yellow flowers.

H. reptans, 7.5cm (3in), is a deciduous species making small mats of mid-green leaves and producing a late-summer display of yellow flowers that are reddish in bud.
Cultivation: Plant in ordinary well-drained soil in sunny positions. Propagate from soft basal cuttings taken in early summer.

Iberis
Among the candytufts, probably best known for the annual species, are several perennials that are useful in the rock garden.

I. saxatilis, 10cm (4in), is a prostrate evergreen shrub that is a true alpine. The small white flowers are borne in the early summer months.

I. sempervirens, 15cm (6in), makes a

spreading bushy plant that gives a striking display of massed white flowers in late spring and early summer. 'Snowflake' is a more spreading plant with larger flowers; 'Little Gem' is a neater more erect form than the type.

Cultivation: Plant in any well-drained soil in a sunny position. *I. saxatilis* is a suitable plant for a scree bed. Propagate from softwood cuttings taken in summer.

Iris

The dwarf irises rank among the best bulbs for planting in the rock garden or for growing in pots in the alpine house. They are easy plants to grow, flower early, when the garden is still rather bare, and yet, despite their delicate appearance, withstand cold, rough weather remarkably well. They are commonly called reticulata irises, a reference to the net-like sheath around the bulb.

I. danfordiae, 10cm (4in), produces greenish-yellow flowers in late winter.

I. histrioides 'Major', 10cm (4in), flowers before the leaves appear in late winter. The flower colour, a vibrant deep blue, is set off by the bright orange crest.

I. reticulata, 15cm (6in), which flowers in late winter and early spring, has leaves first developing as the flowers come out. The

Above *The combination of different rock plants, such as iberis, saxifrage and dwarf rhododendrons will make a colourful rock garden.*

Right *The lewisias are delicate little plants with star-shaped petals, which are most commonly in shades of pink rose and salmon.*

common form has violet-blue flowers. Named forms include: 'Cantab', light blue; 'J. S. Dijt', reddish-purple; 'Clairette', bright blue and white; and 'Royal Blue', deep blue.

Cultivation: Plant the bulbs in small clumps in well-drained sunny positions, preferably in slightly alkaline soil. Most of these irises will establish themselves and maintain colonies. *I. danfordiae,* however, has a tendency to split up into numerous tiny bulblets that take a number of years to reach flowering size. The bulbous irises are most easily propagated from offsets.

Juniperus *see* Conifers.

Leontopodium
The edelweiss, a native of the European Alps, is an interesting plant that is worth a place in the rock garden.

L. alpinum, 15cm (6in), is a greyish woolly plant that in spring produces starry bracts which surround asymmetrical heads of ray-less flowers.

Cultivation: Grow in well-drained soil in sunny positions. Propagate from seed.

Leucojum
The leucojums or snowflakes, can be distinguished from snowdrops by the fact that the petals on the nodding flowers of the former are all of the same size.

L. autumnale, 25cm (10in), flowers in autumn before the leaves develop or just as they emerge. The flowers are white tinged pink at the base.

L. vernum, 20cm (8in), the spring snowflake, has strap-like green leaves and white flowers.

Cultivation: Plant in well-drained soil, *L. autumnale* in full sun, *L. vernum* in sun or light shade. Propagate from seed or offsets.

Lewisia
The lewisias are rather succulent rosette-forming perennials which are attractive in the rock garden or alpine house for their showy flowers in spring and early summer.

L. cotyledon, 30cm (12in), forms tufts of fleshy leaves that sometimes have a wavy edge. The flowers range in colour from white to coral. This species has given rise to many attractive forms and hybrids, such as: 'George Henley', brick red; 'Pinkie', pink; and 'Rose Splendour', warm pink. Some forms, such as *L. c.* 'Heckneri' (large-flowered and bright pink) and *L. c. howellii* (pink with deeper markings) have sometimes been treated as separate species.

L. tweedyi, 15cm (6in), is an evergreen species that produces a single flower per stem. The colour can vary from a lovely, soft pale pink to apricot.

Cultivation: Grow in sharply draining neutral soil in an open position. Lewisias are prone to rotting in wet weather so surround the neck of plants with a layer of chippings. Another way to avoid rotting is to plant lewisias in the crevices of walls. In the alpine house water sparingly after flowering. Plants can be grown from offsets taken in summer. Lewisias hybridize freely but seed, although it may not come true, is an easy means of propagation.

Linum
Several of the perennial and sub-shrubby flaxes make good rock garden plants that are useful for their sustained displays of bright flowers.

L. flavum, 40cm (15in), forms mounds of grey-green foliage and bears a profuse display of yellow flowers in the summer.

L. narbonense, 45cm (18in), is a rather tall species that is useful in a large rock garden for its long season of blue flowers.

L. perenne alpinum, 30cm (12in), is an alpine form of the perennial flax. The sky-blue flowers are borne over a long period in summer.

Cultivation: The flaxes are easy plants given full sun and well-drained soil. They are not long-lived but are easily grown from seed or propagated from cuttings taken in spring.

Top Leontopodium alpinum *is the well-known edelweiss, a popular plant for the rock garden.*

Above *The leucojums are hardy, bulbous plants with flowers that resemble large snowdrops.*

Right *The Oxford and Cambridge muscari,* M. tubergenianum, *has flowers of pale and dark blue in March and April.*

Below Lithospermum oleifolium, *not often grown, is an attractive rock garden plant, with deep blue flowers.*

Lithospermum

The lithospermums include a number of hardy ground-hugging plants that produce bright blue funnel-shaped flowers. Although botanists have now placed those listed here under *Lithodora*, in commerce they generally go under their old name.

L. diffusum, 10cm (4in), makes a spreading plant up to 60cm (24in) wide that flowers in summer. Two widely grown forms, 'Grace Ward' and 'Heavenly Blue', have flowers that are larger than the type and of a more intense blue.

L. oleifolium, 15cm (6in), is a smaller plant than *L. diffusum* and in bud the flowers show a pink tinge.

Cultivation: L. diffusum and its forms must have lime-free soil but otherwise these are not difficult plants given a sunny position and well-drained soil. Propagate from cuttings taken in summer.

Muscari

The common grape hyacinth, *M. neglectum*, spreads too vigorously from small offsets to make it an ideal plant for the rock garden. However, there are other choice spring-flowering species with the characteristic flowering spikes of crowded bells.

M. armeniacum, 20cm (8in), produces in mid-spring flower spikes of scented deep-blue bells with a white margin. 'Cantab' has pale clear blue flowers and 'Heavenly Blue' is a fine bright blue.

M. botryoides, 20cm (8in), is one of the best for the rock garden. Flowering mid to late spring, it produces china-blue bells with white at the mouth. The white form,

'Album', is particularly good.

M. tubergenianum (syn. *M. aucheri*), 20cm (8in), is an early-spring species with an attractive contrast between the pale blue of the upper sterile flowers and the deep blue of the lower flowers. It is sometimes listed as 'Oxford and Cambridge'.

Cultivation: Plant in full sun in ordinary well-drained soil. The more vigorous species will need to be lifted and divided every three years. Plants raised from seed can be brought to flower in about three years. Most species produce offsets freely and these provide an easy method of propagation.

Narcissus

Among the spring-flowering bulbs the daffodils and jonquils have long been considered plants of the first importance. In addition to the large-growing narcissi that are used for planting in borders and in grass, there are numerous true species and cultivated forms of dwarf habit. These are ideal for the rock garden or raised bed and are lovely when grown as pot-grown plants in the alpine house.

N. 'Baby Moon', 20cm (8in), a dwarf hybrid jonquil, has numerous fragrant yellow flowers to a stem.

N. 'Beryl', 20cm (8in), is a hybrid derived from *N. cyclamineus* that has an orange cup and yellow swept-back petals.

N. bulbocodium, 5–15cm (2–6in), is commonly known as the hoop petticoat daffodil on account of the distinctive funnel-shaped trumpet or corona, which is generally crinkled at the margin. This species, which flowers in late winter and early spring, is very variable in colour as well as size, ranging from white to deep yellow. The naming of the numerous forms is somewhat confusing but all are plants of great beauty. *N. b. romieuxii* is a lovely pale yellow form that is best suited to pot culture in the alpine house.

N. cantabricus, 10cm (4in), is very close to *N. bulbocodium* but has more open, white coronas.

N. cyclamineus, 20cm (8in), has hanging golden flowers with narrow trumpets and reflexed petals. It begins flowering in the late winter months.

N. 'February Gold', 25cm (10in), is not one of the real miniatures but is a sturdy and useful deep yellow trumpet hybrid that flowers in late winter and early spring.

N. 'February Silver', 25cm (10in), is similar to the foregoing except that the petals are creamy white.

N. 'Jack Snipe', 20cm (8in), another hybrid derived from *N. cyclamineus,* has cream petals and a yellow trumpet.

N. juncifolius, 15cm (6in), is a miniature jonquil with up to five deep yellow flowers to a stem.

N. minor, 20cm (8in), a dwarf trumpet-daffodil in which the petals are paler yellow than the trumpet.

N. 'Tête-à-Tête', 20cm (8in), is a very early-flowering hybrid that produces two or more yellow trumpets to a stem.

N. triandrus albus, to 25cm (10in), popularly known as the angel's tears daffodil, bears two or three pendent creamy-yellow flowers to a stem in early spring.

Cultivation: Plant bulbs as soon as they become available in autumn. Group them in irregular clumps in any ordinary well-drained sunny or lightly shaded position. The most vigorous miniatures can be planted to grow through creeping perennial rock garden plants. Most will naturalize readily. Clumps can be lifted and divided when the leaves die down if they become congested. Offsets provide the easiest method of propagation.

Oenothera

The evening primroses are showy plants with large funnel-shaped flowers, which, as the common name suggests, open up in the evening.

O. acaulis, 15cm (6in), makes a dandelion-like clump of leaves. The stemless flowers, white fading to pink, are borne over a long season in the summer.

O. missouriensis, 15cm (6in), is a lax plant with a spread of 45cm (18in). The large yellow flowers, produced over a long season in summer, are flushed red in the bud.

O. perennis (syn. *O. pumila*), 30cm (12in),

is a less showy plant than the others, bearing small yellow flowers in mid-summer.
Cultivation: These are easy plants for ordinary well-drained soil and sunny positions. *O. acaulis* is often treated as a biennial. Grow plants from seed or propagate by division or from cuttings.

Papaver

Although generally short-lived, the dwarf poppies self-seed readily and are therefore not difficult to maintain in the rock garden. They are worth a place for the long succession they provide of bright elegant flowers.

P. alpinum, 10cm (4in), forms mounds of prettily divided grey-green leaves. The flowers, which are borne in summer, are white, pink, yellow and orange. There are numerous similar species differing only in minor botanical features. These include: *P. a. kerneri,* yellow; *P. a. rhaeticum,* same colours as *P. a. alpinum; P. a. sendtneri,* white; and *P. a. suaveolens,* yellow to red.

P. myabeanum, 10cm (4in), is in general appearance and colour range very like the European *P. alpinum,* but it is said to be longer lived.
Cultivation: These plants are easily satisfied if given sunny well-drained positions. Sow seed in the flowering position.

Penstemon

Although sometimes short-lived, the dwarf species of this large genus of North American plants are worth a place in the rock garden for their profuse summer display of snapdragon-like flowers. Many of those in cultivation have strong similarities

Top *One of the most attractive of all the narcissus species is* N. cyclamineus, *with its sweptback petals.*

Above N. triandus albus *is often described as the 'angel's tears' daffodil.*

Above *The low growing* Phlox subulata, *with flowers in shades of lilac, purple or red, makes a showy addition to the rock garden, when it forms hummocks with a tight mat of brilliant flowers in summer.*

and this has led to confusions in their naming. For this reason it is best to read the description in the catalogue, or ask at a garden centre, before buying.

P. davidsonii (syn. *P. menziesii*), 15cm (6in), is a sub-shrubby mat-forming plant with blue-purple flowers that are borne in mid-summer. *P. d. menziesii* (syn. *P. menziesii*) is rather more erect with small toothed leaves and purplish flowers.

P. fruticosus, 30cm (12in), is a shrubby erect perennial with purplish-blue flowers.

P. f. scouleri (syn. *P. scouleri*) has finely toothed leaves. *P. f. s.* 'Alba' is another lovely white form.

P. heterophyllus, 30cm (12in), is a sub-shrubby species with grey-green leaves and flowers that are bright blue to purple. 'True Blue' is a good pure blue colour.

P. laetus roezlii (syn. *P. roezlii*), 25cm (10in), forms a loose mound of downy leaves with rich red flowers.

P. rupicola (syn. *P. newberryi rupicola*), 10cm (4in), has grey-green leaves and carmine flowers.

P. × 'Six Hills', 25cm (10in), is a vigorous hybrid with grey-green leaves and very pretty lilac flowers.

Cultivation: Penstemons require full sun and gritty well-drained soil. Propagate from seed or from cuttings of non-flowering side shoots in summer.

Phlox
The North American dwarf shrubby phloxes are prolific-flowering, mat-forming plants that do well in the rock garden or even planted in a dry wall.

P. adsurgens, 20cm (8in), is a more-or-less erect plant with a creeping root-stock. In spring the plant bears white, pink or purple flowers.

P. douglasii (syn. *P. austromontana*), 10cm (4in), a prostrate species that flowers profusely in late spring and early summer, has numerous good named forms, some of which may be hybrids with *P. subulata*. Desirable forms include: 'Boothman's Variety', mauve; 'Eva', pink; and 'Mabel', mauve-pink.

P. amoena (syn. *P.* × *procumbens*), 20cm (8in), a plant of tufty growth, bears bright purple flowers in early summer.

P. subulata, 10cm (4in), the moss or mountain phlox, flowers profusely in late spring just as the aubrietas are fading. The

Above *The small* Primula allionii *is very small and has rose pink to deep red flowers in spring. There is also a white form.*

Left and opposite *The potentillas, or cinquefoils, are a large genus of plants, some shrubby, but most of them herbaceous in habit.*

flowers are pink or purple but there is great variety of colour in the selected forms. These include: 'Alexander's Surprise', salmon pink; 'G. F. Wilson', lavender-blue; 'Temiscaming', crimson; and 'White Delight', pure white.
Cultivation: Plant *P. subulata* and *P. douglasii* in any well-drained soil in a sunny position. *P. adsurgens* needs light shade and a peaty soil, and *P. amoena* a moist soil. Propagate from selected basal cuttings taken in mid-summer.

Picea *see* Conifers.

Pinus *see* Conifers.

Potentilla
The dwarf shrubby cinquefoils are valuable rock garden plants that are easy to grow and have a long flowering season in summer.
P. alba, 10cm (4in), makes a spreading mat of dark green leaves that are silvery on the underside. The flowers, borne from late spring to autumn, are white.
P. aurea, 15cm (6in), makes a loose mat of slightly silvery toothed leaves and bears deep yellow flowers with a darker eye.

There is also a double form *P. a.* 'Plena'. *P. a. chrysocraspeda* (syn. *P. ternata*) has leaves that are less sharply toothed.
P. crantzii (P. alpestris), 20cm (8in), is an attractive yellow-flowering species of which the petals generally have a deeper orange blotch at the base.
P. nitida, 7.5cm (3in), can be shy to flower. It forms silvery mats of foliage and bears stemless flowers of an apple-blossom pink colour.
P. tabernaemontani (syn. *P. verna*), 7.5cm (3in), may have a spread of up to 60cm (24in). Although the main season for the bright yellow flowers is late spring, there are odd flowers throughout the summer.
Cultivation: Plant in light, free-draining soil and in full sun. Raise plants from seed or propagate from cuttings.

Primula
Despite being a very numerous group with a wide range of growth patterns, the primulas show strong family traits. The dwarf species are some of the most beautiful. They include several rather difficult alpine plants that are a test of the specialist's skills. However, there are also

undemanding species and cultivated forms that are excellent plants in the rock garden.

P. allionii, 5cm (2in), makes tight clumps of leaves that are downy and sticky. The flowers, up to 2.5cm (1in) across and ranging in colour from white to purple, are borne early to mid-spring.

P. amoena, 15cm (6in), is sometimes listed as *P. altaica*, although this name covers several pink-flowered primulas that are probably of garden origin. All are easy and attractive plants. The true species bears yellow-eyed violet to lavender flowers in mid to late spring.

P. auricula, 15cm (6in), the parent of the show auriculas, has grey-green leaves generally covered with farina. The deep yellow fragrant flowers are borne in spring.

P. edgeworthii, 10cm (4in), has grey-green leaves with wavy margins and bears pale mauve flowers with a yellow eye in late winter and spring. There is a fine white form.

P. farinosa, 15cm (6in), produces heads of pink flowers with yellow centres in early spring. The leaves are powdery white on the underside.

P. frondosa, 15cm (6in), is like a more solid version of *P. farinosa* with heavier powdering of the leaves.

P. marginata, 10cm (4in), a species suitable for a rock crevice, has powdered leaves and in mid-spring bears lavender-blue flowers with a white eye. 'Linda Pope' is a good named form.

P. × pruhoniciana (syn. *P. × juliana*), 10cm (4in), is the name under which are listed various cultivated hybrids between *P. juliae* and other species. These include: 'Garryarde Guinevere', with bronzed foliage and pink flowers, and 'Wanda', with claret red flowers.

P. × pubescens, 10cm (4in), covers the hybrids derived from crosses between *P. auricula* and other primulas. They are generally spring-flowering and have powdery leaves. Good examples include: 'Argus', purple with white centres; 'Harlow Car', cream; 'Mrs J. H. Wilson', large violet; and 'Rufus', brick red.

Cultivation: Most of the hardy primulas listed here should be planted in light shade in humus-rich but well-drained soil. Those with powdery leaves are susceptible to winter damp and when grown outside may need to be given the protection of a glass pane. Propagate from seed sown when ripe and by division.

Pulsatilla

The pulsatillas, of which the pasque flower *(P. vulgaris)* is the best known, show strong family resemblance to the anemones, with which they were previously classified. Their beautiful silky flowers, which are followed by plumed seed heads, are attractively set off by the softly hairy and fern-like foliage.

P. alpina, 30cm (12in), a native of the mountains of Europe, makes a tuft of slightly downy leaves and in late spring and early summer bears white flowers that are tinged blue-pink in the bud. In cultivation the fine yellow-flowered form 'Sulphurea' is more common than the type.

P. halleri, 30cm (12in), is a very similar to the common pasque flower. The leaves are woolly and the flowers deep violet-blue.

P. vernalis, 15cm (6in), makes a small tuft of deep green hairy leaves and in mid-spring produces white flowers with bluish or pinkish markings on the outside.

P. vulgaris, 30cm (12in), a plant of lovely silkiness in leaf, stem, flower bud and seed head. The colour is very variable but in the commonest form is mauve. The forms 'Alba', white and 'Rubra', maroon, are pretty.

Cultivation: Plant pulsatillas in well-drained soil in sun. *P. vernalis* may need protection from winter wet. Propagate from seed sown fresh.

Ramonda

The ramondas, a small group of evergreen rosette-forming perennials, are useful shade tolerant plants suitable for planting in rock crevices.

R. myconii, 15cm (6in), has deep green leaves. The mauve flowers with gold stamens, as many as six to a stem, are borne in mid and late spring. There are good pink and white forms.

R. serbica, 10cm (4in), is very like *R. myconii,* but the flowers are slightly different – they are more cup-shaped.

Cultivation: Plant in autumn or early spring in the crevices of shady rock walls. Water must not be allowed to collect in the rosettes but the soil should be reasonably moisture-retentive. Propagate by division, from leaf cuttings taken in summer, or from the very fine seed.

Left *A red form of* Pulsatilla vulgaris, *in which the colour is more pronounced on the inside of the petals.*

Below *In this form of* Pulsatilla vulgaris, *the pasque flower, produces outstanding purplish flowers with orange centres.*

Above and right *Rhododendrons are among the most colourful and numerous of shrubs and the dwarf varieties are suitable for both large and small rock gardens.*

Raoulia

The silvery and blue-green mats and cushions formed by these creeping perennials, mainly natives of New Zealand, make attractive ground cover in the rock garden.

R. australis, 12mm (½in), forms a tight silvery mat up to 30cm (12in) wide, which in summer is dotted with tiny yellow flowers. *Cultivation:* All of these raoulias need sharply drained soil and full sun. Propagate from rooted pieces taken from the edge of the mats.

Rhododendron

Some of the most valuable evergreen and deciduous trees and shrubs for the garden belong to this very large genus. Many are tall-growing plants of woodland but there are also several low-growing species, which associate well with other dwarf plants, and numerous medium-sized shrubs, which are ideal as the occasional larger component in the rock garden. The hybrids included in this list of evergreen rhododendrons no more than suggest the enormous range of quality plants that have been developed from crossing the species.

R. calostrotum, 60cm (24in), is a plant of grey-green foliage and bright purplish-red flowers, usually borne in pairs, that appear in late spring and early summer.

R. campylogynum, 60cm (24in), has dark glossy leaves and in late spring it bears clusters of bell-shaped purple flowers.

R. 'Carmen', 60cm (24in), forms a spreading bush up to 1m (3ft) wide and produces waxy dark red bells in late spring.

R. 'Cilpinense', 1m (3ft) and of comparable width, makes a rather large plant but is of exceptional beauty. The soft pink flowers have darker markings and are borne in early spring.

R. 'Elizabeth', 60cm (24in), forms a spreading mound about 1.2m (4ft) wide. The scarlet funnel-shaped flowers are borne in mid and late spring.

R. fastigiatum, 75cm (30in), is a twiggy, grey-green shrub that produces lavender-blue flowers in mid-spring.

R. ferrugineum, 1m (3ft), a free-flowering species with dark green leaves that are rusty on the underside, bears clusters of crimson tubular flowers in early summer.

R. forrestii repens, 25cm (10in), a prostrate shrub with leathery leaves that are purplish on the underside, bears crimson flowers, generally singly or in pairs, in mid- and late spring.

R. impeditum, 75cm (30in), is a plant very similar to *R. fastigiatum*, with purple flowers borne at the end of spring.

R. keleticum, 30cm (12in), a dark-green spreading shrub up to 1m (3ft) across,

bears purple flowers singly or in pairs in late spring and early summer.

R. pemakoense, 60cm (24in), forms a spreading mound about 1m (3ft) across. The leaves are dark and glossy above and scaly blue-green on the underside. The purplish flowers are borne in early spring.

R. radicans, 10cm (4in), a tiny prostrate plant, bears purplish flowers singly at the end of spring.

Cultivation: Rhododendrons need a fairly rich acid soil that is moisture-retentive. They tolerate light shade but do well in open positions provided they are sheltered from cold winds. Early-flowering kinds should be planted so that the sun will not strike frosted blossoms before they have had a chance to thaw. An attractive way of growing rhododendrons with dwarf woodland plants and lime-haters is to plant them in raised peat beds. Propagation is generally from cuttings or by layering.

Saxifraga

This large genus of about 350 species is an important one for the rock gardener as it consists in the main of small perennials that are native of mountainous and rocky environments. The range of plants available has been expanded by the cultivation of many hybrids and selected forms. With this genus

Above *A firm, cushion-forming plant, Saxifraga × 'Jenkinsae', growing in tufa. The flowers are the palest pink.*

Among the 370 species of saxifraga most are dwarf, tufted perennial and annual plants, ideal for the rock garden. Shown here are: **Top** S. longifolia, **Above** S. grisebachii *and* **Above right** S. cotyledon.

there is scope for the real specialist who wants the challenge of growing to perfection the difficult high alpine species. However, there are plenty of species and hybrids of great charm and beauty that can be grown in the rock garden with very little trouble. It is not intended that the following selection should provide a sampling of all fifteen sections into which the saxifrages have been divided, some of which are of negligible horticultural interest.

S. × *apiculata*, 10cm (4in), forms a cushion up to 30cm (12in) wide of deep green leaves and bears yellow flowers in early spring. This hybrid of the Kabschia section has an excellent white form, 'Alba'.

S. burserana, 5cm (2in), a mat-forming species with blue-green leaves, produces large white flowers singly on reddish stems in early spring. Named forms include 'Gloria' and 'Major', both larger in size than the type.

S. cochlearis, 20cm (8in), has dense rosettes of silvery encrusted leaves from which in mid-summer emerge stems of white flowers dotted with red. There is a pretty compact form, *S. c.* 'Minor'.

S. cotyledon (syn. *S. pyramidalis*), 60cm (24in), forms large rosettes from which emerge in summer long sprays of fragrant white flowers. *S. c.* 'Caterhamensis' is a handsome form in which the flowers are heavily dotted with red.

S. grisebachii, 20cm (8in), is generally represented in cultivation by the form 'Wisley'. The beautifully patterned rosettes are about 5cm (2in) across. In spring they produce velvety flowering stems of a rich red-purple.

S. × *'Jenkinsae'*, 5cm (2in), is a vigorous hybrid that makes a low mound of tight grey-green rosettes up to 30cm (1ft) wide. The pink flowers are borne profusely in early to mid-spring.

S. longifolia, 45cm (18in), forms solitary or small groups of lime-encrusted rosettes. It may take the plant three or so years to produce its splendid arching spray of flowers, and after the plant has flowered in summer the rosette generally dies.

S. moschata, 7.5cm (3in), is a mossy hummock-forming plant that in mid- and late spring bears yellow flowers on wiry stems. The numerous named forms include: 'Atropurpurea', with red flowers, and 'Cloth of Gold', with golden foliage and white flowers. The following are good mossy hybrids derived from *S. moschata*: 'Four Winds', deep crimson; 'Peter Pan', crimson; and 'Pixie', rose-red.

S. oppositifolia, 2.5cm (1in), makes a loose mat and bears purplish flowers in early spring. 'Ruth Draper' and 'Splendens' are vigorous forms with richer colouring than the type.

S. paniculata (syn. *S. aizoon*), 15cm (6in), is a very variable species with a wide distribution in the northern hemisphere. The lime-encrusted rosettes are beautiful in themselves. The flowers, borne in sprays, are white, pink or yellow. *S. p. baldensis* is a particularly attractive miniature that forms a tight mound and bears white flowers.

S. × 'Tumbling Waters', 60cm (24in), a hybrid, one parent of which is *S. longifolia*, has the advantage over this parent that it more consistently makes offsets before the rosette dies after flowering.

S. × 'Southside Seedling', 38cm (15in), probably has as one parent *S. cotyledon*. It is similar to this parent but the flowers are handsomely blotched dark red.

Cultivation: Many saxifrages tolerate or enjoy lime in the soil, which must be well-drained and gritty. Plant in full sun or semi-shade and, where possible, in a rocky crevice. The really dwarf species and hybrids that are rather lost in the rock garden can be seen at their best grown in pots in the alpine house. Propagate from seed, by division or by separating off individual rosettes.

Scilla

Two dwarf species of this large genus of bulbous plants are commonly grown. They are both early and full-flowering plants and, unlike some bulbs, are easily controlled in the rock garden.

S. sibirica, 10cm (4in), the Siberian squill, has glossy strap-like leaves that appear before the flowers. The nodding brilliant blue bells are borne three or four to a stem in early spring. 'Spring Beauty' is a particularly vigorous and early form.

S. tubergeniana, 12.5cm (5in), is similar to *S. sibirica*, but the flowers are paler with a dark midrib and open as the shoot emerges.

Cultivation: Plant in ordinary well-drained soil in sun or partial shade as soon as bulbs become available in early autumn. Propagation is generally from seed as offsets are not freely produced.

Sedum

The stonecrops, a large genus of succulent perennials, include several of a scale that makes them useful for sunny positions in the rock garden. The five-petalled starry flowers are borne in heads above the rather crowded fleshy leaves.

S. cauticolum, 15cm (6in), a deciduous species, has blue-green leaves, and in autumn features heads of lovely deep pink flowers.

S. ewersii, 15cm (6in), is similar to, but more vigorous than *S. cauticolum*.

S. rosea (syn. *S. rhodiola*, *Rhodiola rosea*), 30cm (1ft), roseroot, owes its common name to the fact that the dried roots are sweetly scented. This deciduous species makes a rather lax clump of stems closely covered with grey-green leaves and in summer bears compact heads of greenish-yellow flowers.

S. spathulifolium, 10cm (4in), is a hummock-forming evergreen species, the leaves of which often take on a red tinge, producing yellow flowers in early summer. Two good selected forms are 'Cappa Blanca', with leaves that are almost white when young; and 'Purpureum', with waxy purplish leaves.

Cultivation: Grow in ordinary well-drained soil in sun. Propagate from seed or from stem cuttings.

Below *S. cauticolum is a hardy plant that will grow well in the rock crevices or along the top of walls.*

Above and right *The sempervivums or houseleeks, have close rosettes of leaves, some pointed and many with fine, cobweb-like hairs from leaf tip to leaf tip. There are 25 species but many varieties and hybrids can be difficult to identify accurately.*

Sempervivum

The houseleeks are perennial succulents that form dense rosettes of fleshy leaves that are often beautifully tinted and marked. Each rosette may take several years to flower, when it elongates to produce a head of starry flowers. After flowering the rosette dies but the plant is maintained by the annual production of several offsets.

S. arachnoideum, 2.5cm (1in), the cobweb houseleek, has tight rosettes, with the leaf tips connected by a web of fine white hairs. The pink flowers are borne in the summer months.

S. × 'Commander Hay', 5cm (2in), is an outstanding hybrid forming large rosettes that are beautifully stained maroon. There are pink flowers in summer.

S. grandiflorum, 5cm (2in), has rosettes that are downy and sticky, up to 10cm (4in) across. The flowers, borne in summer on stems up to 30cm (6in) tall, are greenish-yellow in colour.

S. montanum, 2.5cm (1in), is a very variable alpine species with mid-green hairy leaves and purple flowers. It is the parent of many hybrids.

S. octopodes, 2.5cm (1in), is unusual in producing offsets on thread-like stolons growing from the hair rosettes. The flowers are yellow with red at the base.

Cultivation: Grow in full sun and well-drained soil. A clump of rosettes looks attractive wedged in a rocky crevice. These plants are good subjects for pot cultivation in the alpine house and this is probably the best way to grow *S. arachnoideum* and *S. octopodes,* which resent water on the foliage. Propagate from offsets.

Soldanella

The members of this small genus of true alpines are very much alike, all having nodding bell-shaped flowers with fringed petals hanging over the rounded leathery leaves.

S. alpina, 15cm (6in), has kidney-shaped leaves and in early spring bears lavender-blue flowers.

S. montana, 20cm (8in), has bright green leaves, sometimes purplish beneath, but in most other respects is like a sturdier version of *S. alpina.*

S. villosa, 10cm (4in), a pretty miniature, has hairy leaves and flowers, which are a deep purplish-violet.

Cultivation: Plant in well-drained soil containing plenty of humus in a lightly shaded position. To counteract winter damp cover the ground around plants with sharp grit. This will also help to discourage slugs. Propagate from cuttings or by division.

Thuja *see* Conifers.

Tsuga *see* Conifers.

Above Soldanella montana *is somewhat larger than* S. alpina *and produces attractive, violet-blue flowers in the spring.*

Left Tsuga canadensis *is a fine conifer that thrives particularly well on limestone.*

Tulipa

In addition to the many tall-growing tulips that are used with such brilliant effects in bedding schemes, there are a number of dwarf species and hybrids that are fully at home in the rock garden. Although many of them are richly coloured, they have a natural grace that to some extent has been sacrificed in the other more highly cultivated forms.

T. clusiana, 30cm (12in), the lady tulip, is a very elegant species with grey leaves and white flowers flushed pink on the outside. The flowers open in mid-spring.

T. fosteriana, 30cm (12in), a mid-spring species, has brilliant scarlet flowers which have a basal black blotch that is edged with yellow. There are numerous cultivated forms and hybrids with other dwarf tulips, including *T. greigii*. Two that are particularly desirable are 'Cantata' and 'Princeps'.

T. greigii, 25cm (10in), is conspicuous for the handsome purplish streaking of its leaves as well as for the brilliant scarlet of its flowers, which open in mid-spring. Selected forms or hybrids derived from it include: 'Cape Cod', apricot; 'Oriental Beauty' and 'Red Riding Hood', which are also scarlet in colour.

T. kaufmanniana, 20cm (8in), the waterlily tulip, is a compact and early-flowering species with creamy flowers that are flushed pink on the outside. Among those derived from it are the following: 'Heart's Delight', red and pink; 'Shakespeare', warm pink shadings; and 'The First', which is creamy white with carmine and yellow in colour.

T. tarda, 15cm (6in), is a striking plant with narrow leaves and flowers opening in mid-spring, with pointed segments that are yellow at the centre and white at the points.

Cultivation: Plant in ordinary well-drained soil in full sun. Bulbs are not likely to be long-lived if left from year to year without lifting. Lift in summer after leaves have died down and store in a warm dry place before planting again in the autumn. Propagate from offsets. From seed it may take more than five years for bulbs to reach flowering size.

The brilliant colours of the dwarf tulips enhance their delicately shaped blooms. Featured are: **Below** Tulipa fosteriana, *'Dance'*, **Bottom** Tulipa greigii, *'Plaisir'*, **Bottom right** Tulipa greigii, *'Corsage'*.

Veronica

The speedwells include a number of dwarf perennials that are easy and desirable plants in the rock garden. The shrubby veronicas are now classified under *Hebe* and *Parahebe*.

V. austriaca teucrium (syn. *V. teucrium*), 20–30cm (8–12in), is a very variable sub-species of a clump-forming perennial with a long season of bright blue flowers from mid-summer. There are numerous named forms.

V. cinerea, 10cm (4in), an evergreen forming mats of downy greyish leaves and bearing violet-blue flowers over a long period in summer.

V. gentianoides 'Nana', 15cm (6in), is a useful dwarf form of the rhizomatous border plant. It has dark green leaves and pale blue flowers in early summer.

V. prostrata, 15cm (6in), is a commonly grown prostrate plant with toothed mid-green leaves and deep-blue flowers borne over a long period in summer.

Cultivation: Plant in well-drained but reasonably rich soil in sun. Propagate by division in spring or from cuttings taken in the second half of summer.

Viola

Pansies and violas, the highly developed border plants that have been raised from species of this genus, are generally not treated as perennials and in any event are too gaudy to associate well with other rock garden plants. Some of the species are, however, charming plants well worth a place.

V. aetolica (syn. *V. saxatalis aetolica*), 10cm (4in), is a tufty plant with a long and profuse display of yellow flowers in summer.

V. biflora, 7.5cm (3in), a plant with kidney-shaped mid-green leaves. Its bright

yellow, darkly veined flowers, are borne in glorious profusion throughout the summer months.

V. cornuta 'Minor', 7.5cm (3in), is a prostrate dwarf form of a good border plant. The flowers, borne in summer, are clear blue.

V. labradorica, 10cm (4in), is generally cultivated in the form 'Purpurea', which has purplish foliage and mauve flowers borne in early summer.

Cultivation: The violas are easily satisfied in well-drained soil and positions in full sun or partial shade. Propagate from seed or from selected cuttings of non-flowering basal shoots which should be taken in the mid-summer.

Above left *The veronicas or speedwells, are generally hardy and will grow well in most soils.*

Below left and below *Violas do best in moist, well-drained soil and light shade, and although many pansies now avaiable are best as border plants, there are many attractive dwarf forms for the rock garden.*

CHAPTER FOUR
WATER GARDENING

Left: *By imaginative use of brick, granite, concrete and water, a shady town garden is transformed into a 'country' retreat.*

WATER GARDENING

Opposite *The water surrounding Scotney Castle, Kent reflects the beautiful autumnal colours of the trees and shrubs.*

Below *Over the centuries, the grace and beauty of water gardens has led to some spectacular creations. Here, the cascading waterfall and fountains of the Villa d'Este, in Tivoli – a gem of the Italian Renaissance – are enhanced by elegant balustrades and classical statuary.*

The use of water as an ornamental feature in gardens has only become popular in Britain this century. Before that it was difficult to build pools which did not leak. Some people grew water-lilies in lead or zinc tanks or old household baths, but these often proved unsatisfactory as few understood the importance of correct siting, the effect of lead and the like on fish and the interdependence of plant and animal life necessary to ensure water clarity. Nor were there enough attractive water plants available to impel many gardeners to make the effort, although it is true that there were numbers of large estates with natural lakes. Many of these were spangled with white water-lilies in summer and possibly had yellow water irises and pink flowering rushes growing in the shallows. However, few suburban gardens and virtually no townsfolk owned attractive pools.

It was otherwise abroad, where the aesthetic qualities of water have long been recognized. The Hanging Gardens of Babylon reputedly owed much of their fame to the uses made of water; the Egyptians designed pools for growing lotuses and papyrus; there are water features around the Taj Mahal in India, while the fountain gardens of Versailles have attracted millions since their construction in the 17th century. We know, too, that the Romans loved running water, while nowadays their descendants, along with Spaniards and Portuguese as well as various South American countries at one time colonized by these Europeans, build their homes around water features in a central courtyard. In hot climates, playing water instils a sense of peace and coolness.

Several factors changed the neglect of water features in Britain, first to interest and then enthusiasm. Originally it was the large-scale use of concrete, which allowed strong pools to be made to any size and shape, raised above the ground or sunken and in any garden. But these proved to be fairly expensive, and leaked if not properly made. Also their construction involved much hard work – this was before the days of pre-mixed concrete and, once built, could not easily be removed. However, in spite of these drawbacks many were made, especially between the wars, when it became almost a status symbol to have a pool in your garden.

Another event which contributed to their popularity was the arrival from France at the turn of the century of a great number of water-lilies, and the wealth of colours they displayed amazed connoisseurs. No longer was it necessary to stick to white water-lilies, for now there were various shades of pinks and reds, creams and even yellows available, also large, medium-sized and miniature varieties for pools of different depths. Then, after World War II, plastics became more readily available and suddenly everyone who wanted a water garden found it possible, sometimes in a matter of hours, to have one.

Besides bringing an indefinable quality to gardening, the presence of water has many visual attractions. As well as providing a means to grow plants which would not succeed anywhere else, it attracts life in many forms. Darting fish of various colours bring movement and animation in the pool itself, while birds, bees and butterflies wing their way to its margins in search of water, and frogs, newts and toads are all attracted to water at breeding time.

The reflective properties of water provide an important bonus, duplicating the charms of nearby plants and trees. It will also mirror the clouds on a spring day or the blue of a summer sky, while the pattern of its surface changes with the weather – rippling in miniature waves during a high wind, sparkling in sunshine, becoming dark and sombre prior to a storm, and literally jumping in staccato jerks when raindrops fall. Even in winter, water is not without charm, especially when stray shafts of sunlight cause the surface of an ice covered pool to sparkle with flashing lights or frost appears on the dead stems of nearby vegetation.

There is still another attribute to water in the garden. When it moves, it creates various musical sounds and even the reeds, grasses and sedges which thrive in the vicinity of water have a musical quality when rustled by wind or disturbed by birds. Bamboos particularly, make a whispering noise, rather like the murmur of village gossips heard at a distance. All these mixed notes create sounds which contribute to the air of liveliness and enjoyment which can be experienced by those who include water features in their garden.

CHOOSING A POOL

Before deciding on the kind of pool you want, consider the alternatives carefully. There are numerous possibilities for even the smallest space and you may find an option you had not thought of for your garden.

Whichever type of pool you decide to build certain principles have to be borne in mind when dealing with water as a garden feature. It should never be used in an unnatural place, for example perched on top of a hill where it would never occur in nature, and it must receive plenty of sunshine. This is imperative even if you only intend to use the pool to reflect light and clouds. In the case of a planted pool, lack of sunshine inhibits flowering and virtually no aquatics will bloom in shade.

The pool should also be well away from overhanging trees, although the protection of a building or trees in the background towards the east or north, could be an asset in a cold spring.

It is also advantageous to be within easy distance of a source of piped water, also electricity if lighting is contemplated or a pump is to be installed to circulate the water for a waterfall or fountain.

Finally, in order to enjoy the peace and quiet generated by water it is advisable to build all water features as far away as possible from the noise and pollution of busy main roads.

Buying or building?

To buy or to build? This is a question all who want a water garden must decide for themselves. Undoubtedly the first alternative will prove the most expensive but if time or physical strength matter it may have to be considered. Or, if you want a large concrete structure it may be the only answer.

However, it is not difficult to construct a small pool, especially if you use modern materials, nor need it be prohibitively expensive. The thing to do is consider the alternatives; first the pool site and its size, then its nature, formal or informal, next the fabric – concrete, prefabricated or plastic sheeting and finally possible extras such as fountains and waterfalls. With all this decided then make a plan, decide how much you are prepared to do yourself – excavation can be hard and heavy, also concreting – then shop around for the materials and be ready to adjust your calculations when you know the prices of each item you want.

Making the most of natural features

Very few gardeners are lucky enough to have natural water in the form of a pond or stream on their property, but where it does occur, the best way of treating it is to incorporate it into an informal landscape design. This course of action has been eminently successful with many great gardens of the past, such as the lakes of Stourhead and Blenheim, or the peaceful river setting at Wilton and the Cambridge Backs, where the misty effect of budding willows and riverside gardens is reflected in the moving waters of the Cam.

The peaceful countryside of Britain is only rarely parched with drought, unlike the warmer lands of southern Europe where the coolness engendered by playing fountains is particularly welcome. In hot climates you cannot have too much water and the sound and sight of droplets constantly falling refreshes one's spirits and cools the air around. In Britain, however, there are too many dull days for fountains – with their reminders of rain – to be continually playing, and when natural water is present you can enjoy its movement and reflective properties in quieter fashion, simply by copying nature. Thus rock and water team delightfully and, if a source of local stone is available, this could prove the happiest of marriages. Height can be obtained by building up parts of the garden with soil and rocks, particularly useful in cases where the flow of water is fast as it enables it to find its way downwards in a series of falls to lakes or ponds beyond. A partnership of rock and water also enables you to grow a varied collection of plants; alpines and aquatics, moisture lovers and kinds which appreciate sharp drainage. Small areas of grass and occasional outcrops of stone, the odd shrub or tree will also fit naturally into such schemes.

If the stream or river is wide enough to merit a bridge, this can be built to make an interesting focal point. An informal stone bridge of Japanese design, constructed of oblong blocks of stone set diagonally on a strong base would be attractive in a woodland setting, especially if the bank was

The most successful pools are often designed around natural features. Here, terraces have been cut into a sloping site to produce a series of fast-moving falls, while the rocky surrounds shelter moisture-loving plants like the Candelabra primulas in the foreground.

Instead of a single pond, this garden has two matching pools, each given height and interest by the inclusion of a fountain. The pools are linked visually by their complementary designs and, physically, by a small rustic bridge which blends with the nearby trees.

planted with bog primulas, ferns, bluebells and other moisture-loving shade plants. In a more open situation, a rustic bridge might be more appropriate, especially when draped with wisteria, after the fashion of the one in the Royal Horticultural Society's Garden at Wisley.

Again, by damming or diverting a stream it is possible not only to form small cascades through rocks but also to fill large pools. Much ingenuity, however, is necessary if water is to be diverted, so it is advisable to work out a plan on paper first. Points to consider include the nature of the surrounding soil. If it is heavy clay it may be possible to puddle it to render the diversion watertight, but more probably it will be of a porous nature in which case you either risk losing the water, or flooding adjacent land. With small diversions the new area could

probably be lined with concrete or plastic sheeting in order to retain the water.

Summer droughts can also cause problems, adversely affecting both fish and plants. A simple way of reducing the flow of a stream or river away from the garden is to install a few stepping stones. This will slow it down without stopping its movement.

The law gives the riverside gardener certain rights but also imposes a number of obligations. He may use the water for normal home or garden purposes and is permitted to build up its banks to control flooding, but he must not materially affect its flow. Granted the right to enjoy flowing water through his property, he also has the right to let it flow away without hindrance to other properties. However, these rules do not apply to artificial waters such as canals and reservoirs. If in doubt on any of these points, consult your local Regional Water Authority before undertaking any alterations.

Finally, cattle ponds are frequently found on older properties, often filled with years of debris. These should be emptied and cleaned before being planted, a laborious task, although there are firms which undertake dredging if required.

Artificial pools

In many respects, artificial pools are easier to manage and offer more scope to the gardener than existing sources of water. For one thing, natural water may not be

where you want it and, although it is possible to get rid of a small disused pond, it is not so easy in the case of streams or rivers.

An artificial pool, on the other hand, can be controlled as regards size, depth and shape, and built to fit any size of garden or planting scheme. The important thing is to ensure that it fits in with the surrounds. In other words, it should be right for the position it is to occupy. The main feature of any water garden is accumulated water, either in the shape of a pond or stream – possibly with the added attraction of a waterfall, cascade or fountain. All of these can be simulated using modern materials.

No attempt has been made to hide the artificial nature of this water garden. The strictly formal lines are emphasized by neatly grouped plants and simple jets of water are used to carry the eye towards the focal point – an exotic statue fringed by bamboos.

Below *Round paving units harmonize with the circular, raised brick pool while pot plants and flower beds provide a splash of colour.*

Formal pools

A formal pool is one that is patently artificial. The aim is to create a focal point, a place to rest or 'stop and stare'. Usually it will be constructed to some geometric design such as a circle, square, half-moon or an oblong. A formal pool can either be sunk into the ground or have its sides raised to form a curb. According to preference, this curb can be quite low or fairly high and have its upper surface left flat or sloping. Some people mould the tops into scallops or other designs, perhaps repeating a pattern similar to one found round the base of a statue or fountain standing inside the pool. Curbs were occasionally built high enough to provide a seat, so that people could sit and watch and feed the fish or view the water-lilies in comfort. Indeed, low walls with a flat stone coping are often seen around modern pools for the same reasons.

Naturally, any pool with a raised coping has to be substantially constructed or it could become dangerous. For this reason they are usually made of concrete or brick faced with concrete.

In the case of a sunken pool, a border of firm paving stones provides a neat finish, especially if the pool stands in an open position, as on a lawn. This invites people to walk up to it and also provides a steady base on which to stand containers of plants.

One idea is to make the pool in the centre of a sunken plot, building it to the same shape as the surround. Thus an oblong pool would lie in the middle of an oblong plot, a circular pool in a round area and so on. Apart from the pool, all of this would be paved, although the sides could be built up with raised beds or possibly a wall and steps. The wall could be built of bricks or treated as a dry wall with yellow alyssum, campanulas, rock phlox and aubrietas trailing down between the stones. A sunken

garden of this type would make a splendid suntrap and, by fending off strong winds, would quickly become a popular retreat for much of the year.

Basin pools

These are popular in small town gardens where the presence of water is desired but not the upkeep of a planted pool. If you do not intend to keep fish or grow plants, make or purchase a round concrete container and fill it with large pebbles. Introduce water in the form of a spring or gusher and allow the water to bubble up through the stones. A pump ensures that the same water is used over and over again.

Another idea is to install a pair of these spouting bowls, one each side of a doorway leading from the house into the garden, but far enough forward to allow people to walk freely without getting wet. If the bowls have a small area of soil left around them and the

rest is paved, it will be possible to plant pansies, forget-me-nots or dwarf bedding begonias as a foil for the water.

Wall fountains

Another method of enjoying water in a small garden is by building a small formal pool close to a boundary wall and playing water into the pool via a fountain. This is usually fixed to the wall; an animal's stone head is frequently used for the purpose. Alternatively, a spouting dolphin or similar figure can be placed inside the pool; the water kept moving and returned by means of a pump.

Informal pools

Just as a formal pool is only appropriate to a formal surround, so one designed to be informal must fit in with a natural-looking background. It must also be built at the lowest point of the garden, otherwise it

Above left *A circular pool provides interest in this town garden. Spaces in the paved area have been planted with hostas, ivy and* Impatiens sultani, *a busy Lizzie with delicate, pale blooms.*

Above *In this low-maintenance garden, the pool is the most important feature. Its delightful fountain is framed with the bright yellow and green of* Caltha palustris, *the marsh marigold.*

In this classical Japanese design, a curved wooden bridge spans still waters and peaceful vistas lie around each corner. The whole scene is cut off from the outside world by judicious planting of trees.

ceases to be natural, for water always finds its own level. The liberties sometimes taken with formal pools, which are placed at unusual heights or in curious situations for effect, are completely inappropriate for informal water gardens.

Rock and water

Although water occurs in various situations in nature, such as in fields or woods adjacent to hedgerows or among rocks, the rocky site undoubtedly creates the most impressive effects. An informal pool, surrounded by rocks, attains a touch of grandeur but natural rock is hard to come by and, not surprisingly, some local authorities are now preventing its removal from unspoiled sites. Artificial rock can never match it, although as time goes by this may improve. However, there are still some sources of stone if you shop around.

One benefit of teaming rock with water is that the soil excavated when the pool is made does not have to be removed. Instead it can be built up to give height and also

provide facilities for installing a waterfall as well as rocks.

A Japanese effect

On reasonably large sites a water feature which is becoming increasingly popular is a garden in the Japanese style. Here water, stones, plants, trees, bridges and ornaments all have a place. Free use is made of stones leading across water to a small teahouse or a stone ornament. Japanese gardens are quiet gardens, never ablaze with colour but mostly in shades of green, yet indescribably beautiful and peaceful.

Bog and water

An informal pool with connecting bog garden is another idea. This is particularly appropriate for gardens which normally lie wet, for bogs help to drain surplus water from surrounding land. It also provides a place to grow those plants which must be constantly moist at their roots.

At its simplest, a bog is merely a low lying area prone to collect water. It can be constructed artificially by excavating and lining a basin about 23cm (9in) deep with plastic sheeting. Cover the base with a layer of stones or broken bricks to trap some water, then return the soil with added rotted compost and more soil to a depth of 30cm (12in). Try to avoid very sharp stones which might puncture the sheeting. The level of the soil should then be about 7.5cm (3in) above the liner. Thus the top layer of soil can drain fairly freely so that the bog area is moist but not waterlogged.

Occasionally a bog garden may have to be subdivided into sections, simply because different conditions occur in different parts of the same garden. There could, for instance, be a spot which, although in full sunshine, is perpetually wet. Not every plant would appreciate this but it would be ideal for *Iris kaempferi,* calthas, acorus and ligularias; that is, plants which will tolerate standing in water for longish periods.

However, in order to ensure that it does not become so wet that it is constantly waterlogged, the topsoil may have to be built up above the level of standing water. The roots would then remain damp, but not the crowns of the plants.

This will be the preliminary for the main section of bog and will be similar to the conditions found along the banks of a stream. In this case, 30cm (12in) of topsoil enriched with organic matter is desirable and, if the site becomes dry, water can be added with a hose or by flooding over the pool. Many plants will thrive in this section, including astilbes, bog primulas, day lilies *(Hemerocallis),* trollius, water forget-me-nots, mimulus, and rodgersias.

The last section only applies to sites which are heavily shaded. Less spectacular effects are to be expected but among a number of plants likely to succeed are bamboos, flag irises and willows.

A highlight of any visit to Bressingham Hall in Norfolk is the informal pool and its colourful selection of bog and water plants. A thatched garden house built of local flint looks out over the scene and complements the rustic mood.

BUILDING A POOL

Whether you buy a pre-fabricated pool, use a simple liner or build a more ambitious concrete structure, there are a few basic guidelines you should follow to avoid disasters and ensure success.

There are various ways of building a pool and it is only sensible to consider all the options before rushing into action.

If, for instance, you only want a modest shallow receptacle, purely for ornament rather than for growing plants, there is no need to build a huge concrete structure. Instead, an appearance of strength and permanence can be obtained very simply, by providing an edging of paving stones to a sunken pool, made of nothing more robust than a polythene sheeting liner.

On the other hand, an elaborate water garden, destined to hold deep-water aquatics, will inevitably involve a heavy weight of water, especially if there are to be ornamental additions, such as an impressive fountain, placing an extra strain on the base. The pool in this case will have to be strong and almost certainly built of concrete.

Preliminaries

Another early consideration will be the source of the water supply. If this comes from a stream or other natural source, the flow is likely to fluctuate, especially in a drought, after snow or a heavy thunder storm. You are really safer with piped water and, in any case, the pool should be within easy reach of same. Pools do need topping up from time to time and may also have to be flooded over occasionally in order to remove floating scum, flower petals and similar debris. It may also be necessary to channel water into a bog garden.

However, once the pool is built and planted, it should not be necessary to keep changing the water. This is an impetuous reaction by gardeners when the water turns green or cloudy soon after planting. But it is a mistake, for some initial cloudiness is inevitable. Everything about a new pool is raw and immature.

The soil is fresh, the plants barely rooted and the water – maybe containing chemicals – has come straight out of a tap. It takes time for all these things to adjust but, gradually, as the plants root into the mud and the oxygenators, in particular, increase, the water clears. It may be advisable to flood the pool over once to remove scum

and loose debris but after that leave it alone to settle. The aim is to obtain still, 'matured' water similar to that found in clear lakes or undisturbed ponds.

In these early stages some thought should be given to the positioning of the water garden, especially its proximity to sources of pollution. This may be caused by a number of things, such as seepage from surface water from a busy road containing perhaps oil or petrol, even sewage or, in the case of a stream or river, the water may be affected by effluent from a factory site farther back. It is much better to find out about these things before starting to build than suffer constant aggravation later on.

Having decided on the type of pool you want, formal or informal, satisfy yourself that the surrounds are suitable and then decide on its size and shape. This is sometimes difficult to assess so it is a good idea to obtain an old clothes line or a length of rope and lay this on the ground, so that it roughly outlines the proposed shape. View the result from all angles, including an upstairs room if the pool will be in constant view from the house, and move the rope about until you are satisfied with the result. Next, secure the shape to act as a guide during excavation, either by knocking in pegs or, with a spade, notch a shallow trench in the soil to follow the outline of the rope.

What depth?

An informal pool will probably need to be made in several depths 60–75cm (24–30in) for the area where fish, oxygenators and water-lilies will be living, but a fairly shallow area 20cm (8in) for marginal water plants. Most of the latter only need to have their roots submerged, leaving the stems, flowers and leaves free to grow above the surface.

Dealing with the deeper parts first, you must consider the options. There are water-lilies which need a good depth of water, which means an excavation of 75cm (30in), allowing 15cm (6in) for the container in which they are planted and 60cm (24in) of water. The majority of lilies, however, are best in water 30–45cm (12–

When building a pool, it is worth looking at its setting and the surrounding area to see what additions you could make. Here, a rockery and waterfall combine to add a new dimension to the original plan.

18in) above their containers, which means an overall depth of 45–60cm (18–24in). At these depths a complete freeze-up in winter is rarely a problem. Ice may form but not so severely as to threaten the water-lilies or fish and in any case there are precautions one can take. Accordingly, it is rarely necessary to excavate any deeper. It makes a lot of extra work to remove a further foot or so of soil, not to mention problems arising as to its disposal. Also, when the pool is eventually filled with water, very few water-lilies are able to negotiate a depth of 1–1.1m (3–3½ft) as sometimes recommended, particularly the coloured sorts. Water in a deep pool will also be much colder than in a shallow one.

Remember, too, that water flowing into a pool from a spring or stream will be constantly changing, gaining and losing water all the time. It will accordingly be cooler than static water in a pool that was originally run in from a tap, a circumstance which will not only make flowering late but probably reduce the quantity of bloom. Since water-lilies in any case do not like running water, it is advisable to plant only vigorous kinds (regardless of depth) where there is water movement.

Clay pools
Clay or dew pools, the last name referring to the fact that dews contributed to their water content, were probably the first pools to be constructed in Britain. They were mainly built and used by country folk for watering stock, although, towards the end of the nineteenth century, a number were constructed to house ornamental plants and fish.

However, the construction of a clay pool in the past was normally messy and difficult, and involved lining an excavated cavity with a good layer of coarse straw, although sometimes heather was used, topped by a thick stratum of clay. The latter was kept damp and kneaded into the straw with the aid of heavy pressure from rollers or sometimes trampling horses. Later it was smoothed over and filled with water. Normally after that, dews condensing on the cold clay, plus leakage from land drains kept it topped up, which was important to prevent cracks and subsequent leakage. Small wonder people welcomed the arrival of concrete as an alternative to the effort of making puddled clay.

For some sixty years concrete pools held the market, until the coming of plastics changed things yet again. Nowadays, small to medium-sized pools are generally made either by using prefabricated shells or by lining a cavity with plastic sheeting. However, for building pools with raised sides or those constructed in places where seepage occurs or vandals can damage plastic, concrete is still popular.

Making a concrete pool
There are advantages and disadvantages in using concrete for pool making. On the credit side, it is strong and durable and can be made to any design, including raised structures. Disadvantages include expense,

When mixing your own concrete, it is important to get the correct consistency. The most common mistake is to add too much water, leaving puddles in the mix: the correct proportions will result in a smooth consistency, as shown here.

the labour of laying and possibly mixing concrete and the fact that, once installed, concrete is difficult to remove. Also, if, for any reason, cracks appear, it will probably leak and have to be emptied and mended.

However, if you do decide to use concrete, you will find it easier to make the deepest part – which is where the fish and water-lilies will be – to a conventional shape, such as a square or rectangle. Make the walls of this section slope inwards, to an angle of approximately 20 degrees, so that the widest part is at the top. This will lessen any pressure caused by expanding ice in winter – a common cause of cracks.

This need not remain the final shape, especially if you prefer an informal pool. After the deep part is finished, construct a marginal trough all round its extremities 30cm (12in) deep but any shape you favour. This depth allows for 10cm (4in) of concrete and 10cm (4in) each of soil and water, which is ideal for most marginal aquatics. It is important to make the outer edge of the trough 2.5cm (1in) higher than the sides of the inner pool, so that when full of water this can flow over to the outer extremities and effectively disguise the fact that there is an inside part. The final height of the inner, symmetrical walls, will be 2.5cm (1in) below the surface of the water. This method will also make the pool look larger than it really is.

When taking out soil for the deep section, it is important to remember to add 15cm (6in) to all measurements. This is the thickness of concrete necessary to counteract the effects both of heavy traffic and hard winters. Thus a pool designed to be 1.8 × 1.2 × 0.4m (6 × 4 × 1½ft) deep should be excavated to 1.95 × 1.35 × 0.6m (6½ × 4½ × 2ft).

Unless the intention is to use ready-mixed concrete you will need to make your own from best Portland cement, sharp builder's sand and clean aggregate (gravel or ballast) which is free from organic particles and grading from 5–20mm (³/₁₆ to ¾ inch in the proportions of 1:2:3 (by volume – not weight). These ingredients, after being thoroughly mixed dry, should have water added to bind them, gently – not squirted through a powerful jet – after which the heap should be turned a couple of times. It is impossible to overmix concrete but very easy to add too much water, so take care. Enough should be added so that, when tested by having a shovel thrust into the heap, then drawn in and out in a series of jerks, the resulting ridges should retain their shape without settling back in a sloppy mess. Only if the ingredients are properly mixed will the blend be strong.

For any pool larger than 1.2m (4ft) square, it is a good idea to introduce some kind of reinforcement, such as galvanized wire mesh and/or expanded metal laths obtained from a builder. This gives it added strength. Before concreting, make sure that the base is firm and level, filling in cavities with hardcore if necessary. Then lay the base, applying 15cm (6in) for a small pool or, if reinforcement is to be introduced, 7.5cm (3in). The reinforcement should be laid on this while the concrete is still moist, leaving enough all round, turned up at the edges, to cast into the walls. When this is done, apply a further 7.5cm (3in) of concrete on top. This accounts for the base but, before the concrete is quite set, scratch mark the surface to a width of 15cm (6in) all round the sides, thus leaving a rough face to facilitate the joins when the sides are made.

To hold the sides while the concrete is setting, the best plan is to introduce

Making concrete is a fairly straightforward task:
1 For successful results, use ingredients of the best possible quality. Make sure that the sand and aggregate are clean and measure them carefully to the right proportions (see this page).
2 Mix the ingredients together while they are still dry, then make a crater in the centre of the heap.
3 Pour in a measured quantity of clean water.
4 Mix thoroughly, until the right consistency is achieved.

An edging of paving stones around a pool not only provides a firm footing for passers-by, it also prevents soil from crumbling into the water. The statue of a heron serves a dual purpose, too: it makes an elegant pool-side feature and, at the same time, deters real herons from coming to steal the fish.

shuttering. This takes the form of a roofless, bottomless wooden 'box' made out of boards and just 15cm (6in) shorter on all its sides than the actual pool measurements.

When making the sides, work round and round, paying particular attention to the corners.

A few days later you should, waterproof the pool and seal off the harmful free lime (which is always present in new concrete and adversely affects fish) by painting a proprietary compound all over the walls and floor.

Prefabricated pools

Prefabricated pools came in around the 1940s and found instant appeal, especially with town and suburban gardeners. In 1940, the idea of a portable pool was conceived and several were made, of a round and oblong shape, from the only material then available – aluminium. Even aluminium was in short supply at the time, but then plastics were invented and, after the war others took up the idea, using this versatile new material.

Through the years they have been steadily improved and now are either made of semirigid plastic or of fibreglass bonded with polyester resins; the latter being the toughest and also the most expensive. Designs, too, have developed so that today it is possible to obtain circular, oblong,

square and crescent-shaped pools as well as irregular shapes which are more suitable for informal water gardens. Some of the latter may be as much as 3.5m (11½ft) long, one, at least, having two deep pools linked by shallower areas between.

Many have punched-out areas of different depths so that plants in pots can be stood on them and receive the right amount of water over their roots. This is especially useful when growing marginal aquatics.

Some have inconspicuous plain edges so that they can be set unobtrusively in the ground and look quite natural. This is ideal for pools teamed with rock gardens, or having bog surrounds. Other prefabricated pools have obviously artificial rims, simulating rocks or paving stones. One round pool, for example, 1.85m (6ft 2in) in diameter and with approximately half its area 45cm (18in) deep and the rest 23cm (9in), is finished with a broad outer rim, marked into sections to represent paving stones. This would make a suitable pool for a key position in a formal area.

Although most garden centres have stocks of prefabricated pools, the most comprehensive collections are to be found in nurseries or centres which specialize in aquatic features.

Although some centres stock the flimsier semi-rigid, pre-formed pools of weather-resistant plastic, these cannot compare for strength or durability with the heavier fibreglass kinds. Admittedly, they are cheaper but there are fewer designs available. They also tend to buckle and, being somewhat fragile, are more liable to damage from sharp instruments. Repair kits are available for both these and fibreglass pools, but there is far less likelihood of them being needed for fibreglass than for weather-resistant plastic.

Installation

To install a prefabricated pool you must first take out sufficient soil to enable it to sit inside comfortably, plus an extra 15cm (6in)

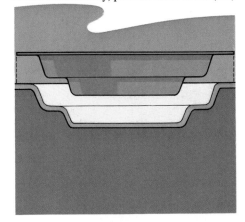

all around the sides. Next, firm the base and cover it with an inch of sand, sifted soil or ashes, then stand the pool in place and test it for levels. Use a spirit level for this, as it is important to get this point settled right at the outset, otherwise the water will run to one end when the pool is filled. Once the pool is planted, it will be impossible to alter things and its uneveness will become a recurring source of annoyance.

Now run in a little water to hold the pool steady while you backfill soil all around the edges. Ram the soil firmly at intervals as you proceed, particularly under shelves or around punched-out areas. Also test periodically that the pool edges remain absolutely level. Finally, fill the container with water. It should be ready for planting if it is a pool with an attached artificial rock or paved edge. A plain-edged pool, on the other hand, sunk to its rim in the soil, will have to be given a border of rocks, turf or paving before it is planted, otherwise debris may fall inside. In these cases it is better to delay filling until all the construction work is finished. When paving stones or rocks are used, they should project slightly over the pool edge, so that they disguise the nature of the pool and the fact that it is artificial.

The installation of an average-sized fibreglass pool is not difficult, as long as you approach the task methodically:
1 After marking out the site, dig down to the level of the first shelf of the mould. Use a spirit level to make sure that the site is level.
2 Allow about 2.5cm (1in) for the bedding sand, mark out the width of the shelf, then excavate down to the next level. Repeat this until the profile matches the mould. Try the pool form for size and fit and check that it is level.
3 When the pool fits neatly on the bedding sand, fill it with water. Check for any leaks and backfill the edges with soil. The rim of the pool should be level with the patio (or lawn).
4 An edging of concrete, with plants and shrubs completes the pool. Alternatively, it could be edged with turf or paving stones.

1

2

3

4

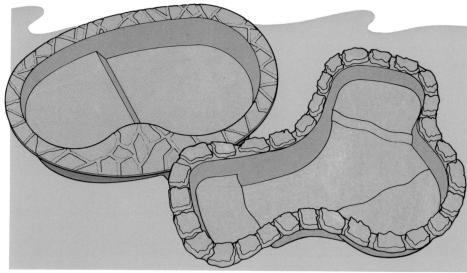

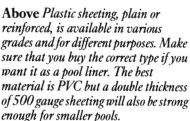

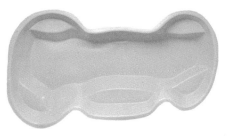

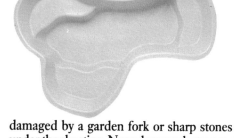

Above *Plastic sheeting, plain or reinforced, is available in various grades and for different purposes. Make sure that you buy the correct type if you want it as a pool liner. The best material is PVC but a double thickness of 500 gauge sheeting will also be strong enough for smaller pools.*

Above right *Rigid, pre-moulded liners are relatively expensive but strong and long-lasting. They have in-built ledges to accommodate plants, though this means that a hole has to be dug to match the profile.*

Fibreglass pools are available in several colours, notably pearl grey, buff, sandstone brown and sky blue. If you want the pond to look natural, choose a dark shade. Blue will remain blue in a swimming pool which is constantly being emptied and cleaned, but has little point in a garden pool open to drifting leaves and other debris, or in one containing soil that is constantly being stirred up by fish.

The advantages of fibreglass pools include their lightness, for most can be carried by a child or on the roof-rack of a car. They are quickly and easily installed, there are no problems concerning chemicals seeping from them as is the case with new concrete, so that they can be planted and stocked immediately after installation and can be taken up and moved if necessary at very short notice.

Disadvantages lie in a certain sameness about the designs and their limited size. They are also rather expensive. The flimsier vacuum-formed, semi-rigid plastic types are not worth moving, being prone to distortion and easily damaged, especially when they have been in the ground for some time.

Pool liners

At its simplest, a pool liner is a flexible sheet used to give a hole in the ground a water-proof lining. The first liners were made of thick polythene sheeting (500 or 1000 gauge) but it was soon discovered that these could be easily vandalized, as well as

damaged by a garden fork or sharp stones under the sheeting. Nowadays much stronger materials are used and most liners are either made from butyl rubber or polyvinyl chloride, commonly called PVC. When PVC in turn is reinforced with nylon it becomes exceptionally strong and stretchy, so that in spite of its flimsy appearance it is able to fit over any bumps or unevenness at the base of a pool, regardless of shape or size. Butyl is also long-lasting and strong, and for many years has been used all over the world in the construction of reservoirs. It has an estimated life in excess of 50 years and, if required, can be made larger by vulcanizing on extra sections.

A flexible liner is almost as easy to install in order to make a pool as a prefabricated fibreglass shell. Metre for metre, it is also much less expensive, and another advantage is that you are not governed by the size of a ready-made receptacle. There are no limitations in the case of liners. Construction is simple, planting can take place immediately this is completed and, if you tire of your pool, it can be emptied and the liner lifted and washed, then packed away until needed.

Calculating the size

Before purchasing a pool liner a rough guide as to the size you will require can be arrived at by calculating as follows: add the length of the pool to twice the maximum depth (disregarding any pockets or marginal shelves). Add the maximum width to twice the maximum depth.

Preparing the excavation for a pool liner is quite easy. Remember, however, that the sides should be sloped to an angle of 60° or they will cave in. This means that, for a deep pool, all other dimensions must be correspondingly large.

1 Having selected the site, mark out the shape of the pool using a length of string.

2 Remove the turves and stack them on one side. They can be used for edging the finished pool or for repairing other areas of lawn.

3 Excavate down to the depth of the first shelf. Use a spirit level and depth stick to make sure that the base is flat and even and that the slope is correctly angled.

4 On the flat base of the excavation, mark the outline of the shelf using a length of string to ensure the width is consistent.

5 Excavate down to the depth of the second shelf. Again, check that the base is level and even and that the slope is correctly angled.

6 Remove any stones or sharp objects from the hole and spread a layer of sand across the entire area to a depth of 2.5cm (1in).

Thus a pool 2.4m (8ft) long × 1.8m (6ft) wide × 45cm (18in) deep would require a liner 3.3 × 2.7m (11 × 9ft). There is no need to calculate for overlap as the material usually stretches enough to allow for this, but as a double check tell the aquatic dealer the measurement of your pool before purchase.

Installation

To install a pool liner, the soil has first to be excavated – after the outline has been marked out with a length of rope, as suggested for concrete pools. There is no need to stick to a uniform depth; instead it is desirable to have several levels. Thus the main section should be 45–60cm (18–24in) deep to take care of the fish, oxygenators and water-lilies, with a shelf, or possibly shelves, only 20cm (8in) deep to take the marginal aquatics.

If the intention is to have a paved edging,

With the excavation complete you can now fit the liner:

1 *Unfold the liner and spread it evenly across the excavation. Weight the edges down with bricks. This will keep the liner in place when it is filled with water.*

2 *Run water into the pool and allow the liner to stretch into place. Move the bricks as necessary so that the weight of the water can push the liner into the profile of the hole. When full, pleat the liner around the edges and cut off the surplus to leave at least 15cm (6in) overlap.*

3 *The finished pool can be edged with turf or with paving slabs bedded on a mortar mix. The slabs should jut out over the edge of the pool by about 5cm (2in). Set the stones level with or just below the grass surround.*

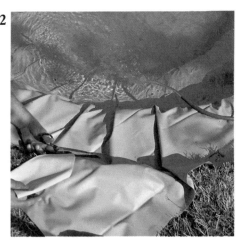

flush with a turf or soil surround, it would be a good idea to remove about 5cm (2in) of extra soil, the thickness of the paving stones, at the same time as you excavate for the pool. This saves disturbing the site once the pool is finished.

Back at the main excavation, remove any sharp stones or tree roots from the bottom and sides and tamp the soil down firmly if it is of a crumbly nature. Next spread 2.5cm (1in) of damp sand, sifted soil, ashes or even a good layer of newspapers over the base.

Drape the pool liner over the hole, leaving an even overlap of 30cm (12in) or so on all sides and secure the edges from slipping inside by anchoring them down with bricks or heavy stones. The liner can sag a little but should not be tucked down or wrinkles will form. Now run in water from a hose and, as the weight builds up, the liner will stretch and sink down to fit neatly around the shelves and bottom.

With a very large pool it is advisable to ease the strain on the material caused by a gradually increasing weight of water, by removing a few of the anchoring bricks from time to time. The liner will ease its way downwards and, when the pond is completely full of water, remove the rest of the

anchors and check for level. Adjust any faults in this direction by packing soil under the rims, then take scissors and cut away all excess liner material apart from about 15cm (6in) all round the sides. This surplus should be hidden out of sight under paving stones, rocks, turf or even soil and plants, according to whether the pool is formal or informal.

Butyl rubber or PVC sheeting can also be used to line such features as simulated streams, cascades or waterfalls, but these are difficult to make watertight. When using such accessories, it is better to install some of the fibreglass units sold by water garden specialists. Prefabricated large and small waterfalls, cascades and streamlets are all available in this material and can be linked to any type of artificial pool including concrete or flexible liners.

Ideas for small pools

Any watertight container which has nothing toxic in its makeup can usually be used for water plants and fish. Small receptacles are particularly useful where weight is a problem, as for example on balconies or roof gardens, but they can also fit in with existing garden features. There are often places in rock gardens, for instance, where small containers are useful for housing special plants, such as pygmy water-lilies or double kingcups, even by those who do not have a proper water garden. With several containers it is also possible to keep varieties of plants and fish separate; an important consideration for a keen fish breeder trying to protect timid or slow-moving ornamental kinds from attack by aggressive neighbours, such as catfish or sticklebacks.

Obvious containers include throwouts from the house like old baths, deep sinks, storage tanks and coppers. The first are fine for the purpose and when sunk to their rims in the ground and planted at the outside edges with trailing plants can be

quite attractive. Creeping Jenny *(Lysimachia nummularia)* is particularly suitable for this purpose as it will creep from soil to water and seems equally at home in both. A bath is roomy enough to take a water-lily, half a dozen oxygenators, two or three emergent shallow-water aquatics and four to six fish. After sinking the bath and testing it for levels, spread 10–12.5cm (4–5in) of heavy soil over the bottom, plant the water-lily and topdress the soil with clean, washed shingle. Fill the bath with water, add the oxygenators, also the marginal aquatics, which should be in pots, and prop the latter up on bricks so that their crowns are just covered with water. The fish can go in about five days later.

Lead containers are few and far between today and, although you can use them for aquatics, they are not suitable for fish. One must be wary, too, of copper, although this is alright for aquatic plants. Zinc tanks can be sunk into the soil and planted as for baths. If in doubt about toxicity, you can line containers with polythene sheeting, as this will form a barrier between the water and metal.

Other good containers are wooden tubs, sawn down to about 50cm (20in). Those which have held beer, wine or vinegar are best. Soap and oily substances are difficult to remove but this can be done by stuffing the tubs with dry hay or straw and setting light to it. The fire must not be allowed to burn too long, only enough to lightly char the inside. When this stage is reached, turn the tub upside down so that the flames are smothered.

All tubs should be scrubbed and well rinsed before use, also kept full of water for several days – replenished as necessary – if they leak. This will cause the staves to swell and render the tub watertight. Plant as suggested for baths, with soil at the bottom, picking a small variety of water-lily such as any of the 'Odorata' or 'Laydekeri' hybrids. Tubs can either be sunk into the ground or used free standing. One idea is to sink several close together in a depression, keeping a separate variety of water-lily and possibly a distinct kind of fish in each. Plant a few bog plants between the tubs and regularly flood these over so that the soil around becomes boggy.

Garden centres sometimes sell large concrete or plastic urns and containers for growing shrubs and trees in offices. If these have drainage holes they can be lined with polythene, otherwise there is no need, and used to make mini-pools. The lightweight plastic containers are excellent for roof gardens and all can be attractive in patios.

OPTIONAL EXTRAS

A pool will prove an attractive feature in its own right but there are various accessories to broaden its appeal: fountains, waterfalls and many lighting effects are just some of the choices open to you.

Many people are happy to settle for a simple, natural-looking pool (assuming of course that the pool was not natural in the first place) and have no wish to embellish it with fountains, waterfalls, floodlighting or underwater lighting. They are content to see the reflection of the clouds in the pool and to watch the leisurely progress of the fish. True, the pool has to be fairly large to be of much interest in the latter respect and formal pools both large and small can be made much more interesting with fountains, tumbling water and lighting. Fortunately, modern equipment has made the installation of these kind of features much easier than in the past.

Waterfalls and fountains

Waterfalls are only appropriate in water gardens of a natural kind. Similarly, fountains are inappropriate for informal pools which have simulated streams tumbling down over rocks or any with artificial plastic 'rock' courses. However, fountains can make splendid embellishments to a formal pool and have many variations as regards spray patterns. An additional attraction is provided by colourful lighting.

Waterfalls

Few people have a natural slope in their garden down which they can construct a water channel that will send water cascading into a pool. But, if soil has been excavated to make the pool and this forms part of a combined rock and water garden, then, by using the soil to build up height at the back, it is quite possible to form a gentle slope down which water can tumble.

Whatever the decision and whether you aim to make your own concrete water course or buy plastic or fibreglass units, you need to have a small 'collection area' – a shallow basin at the top into which the water is supplied to start the flow and from which it can run down via the channel and into the pool.

As with the making of pools, plastic or fibreglass water courses are easier to install than concrete and will not crack with age or split if water freezes in them in winter.

When laying a stream channel, whether it is of concrete or prefabricated units, the tricky part comes when the water falls from one level to another lower down, or finally into the pool. It should be remembered that water never falls in a perfectly straight line or even flow – instead it follows the line of least resistance through softer areas of soil or rock and so flows irregularly from one side to another. You only have to walk along a river bank for evidence of this fact.

Accordingly, you should try to emulate this natural flow pattern by providing obstacles, such as setting pieces of stone to divert the flow from a straight downward course. For such small channels prefabricated plastic fibreglass or concrete water courses are suitable and they will be waterproof and easy to install. Alternatively, anyone of a DIY bent could make a firm base to the water course by ramming broken rubble in the bottom and then laying a concrete channel – shaped to the required depth – on top of this.

In a man-made waterfall, water is normally conducted to the top of the fall through a plastic pipe. This should be hidden 2.5cm (1in) or so under soil, and will connect in turn to the outflow from an electric pump. The functions and installation of electric pumps that supply water to waterfalls and fountains are explained later in this chapter.

Fountains

There are many types and patterns available in fountains so it is worthwhile taking the trouble to examine and find out something about them before making your choice. Some will probably be more suitable than others for your particular pool. For example, there are more than a dozen jet patterns available in various types of fountain – from single jets, to two, three or even four tier jets. There is the so-called "mushroom" or water-tulip kind which throws a bell-shaped jet of water, as well as a fountain that produces three bell-shaped jets. Another kind produces a foaming jet – an effect obtained by mixing air with water.

Whether simple or ornate, a fountain will give a distinctive touch to the smallest pool and the ever-changing patterns and sounds of moving water will bring special pleasure during the long, hot days of summer.

If you want a waterfall in the garden, you can choose between a ready moulded unit or your own construction. Either way, it is important to begin by working out a design on paper: the most effective will have a collection pool at the top, with a cascade leading down to a second pool. Home-made water courses can be tricky to construct, but the pre-moulded units come in a variety of combinations and are very easy to install.

1 Mark out the site with pegs and string, then arrange the components roughly in place.

2 If starting on level ground, build up the soil base to the required height. Work from the lowest point upwards, compact the soil with the back of a spade and check that the bases are level when the components are in place.

3 Add about 12mm (½in) builder's sand to provide a smooth bedding surface. Lay the mouldings in place, again checking that the bases are level. Fill the pools with water and backfill with sand or sifted soil. Pack it in hard, especially around the shelves. These will sag and disrupt the flow of water if not properly supported.

4 Run the hose to the top of the course and cover it with rocks and soil.

1

2

3

4

One elaborate fountain displays a series of automatically changing patterns, producing 18 patterns in a set sequence with each spray pattern continuing for 12 to 16 seconds. The complete sequence lasts about 3½ minutes. Depending on the power of the pump providing the pressure, the spray height achieved with this fountain can be 2.1m (7ft) or so, covering a circle with a diameter of 1.3m (4½ft) or more.

Some fountains are illuminated from below, which provides charming rainbow effects, particularly at night. The lamp is situated immediately underneath the fountain jet and water passes over and around the coloured lens of this lamp before entering the jet.

In addition to the wide range of simple single or multiple jet fountains, which are designed to operate from the surface level of the pool, there are hosts of ornamental fountains and spouting ornaments designed to eject water. This is usually through the mouth, for example by a frog sitting on a toadstool or the ever-popular designs of statues and figurines.

Another attractive idea is to install a raised large circular stone basin with a fountain unit in its centre. Water produced by this will then splash over the sides into another basin lower down or alternatively into the pool. Some models have three tiers of basins and make attractive centre-pieces for small formal pools.

Installation of pumps

For a system of waterfalls and fountains the pump, of course, is the paramount component. Pumps come in various sizes and at widely differing prices according to the type of electric motor involved and the general quality of the materials and workmanship. You get what you pay for, as with most bits of modern equipment. Before deciding which type and pump size to buy you must determine what you want it to do. Thus, decide whether it is to provide the power to operate one or more fountains, or just one waterfall, or perhaps a waterfall and a fountain.

Another point to consider is whether you wish now or at some future date to install garden lighting, either on the surface or under the water. All these factors have to be borne in mind when deciding the size of the pump to be installed, as well as the switch gear and other items involved, if a fairly ambitious set-up is envisaged.

There are two types of electric pump: the submersible pumps which are placed under water in the pool and surface pumps which have to be installed in a waterproof building indoors – in a shed or garage or in a specially built pump-house. Then there is a further division, in that there are mains voltage pumps and also low voltage pumps which are operated from a transformer. In the event of fairly long distances occurring between the source of the mains supply and

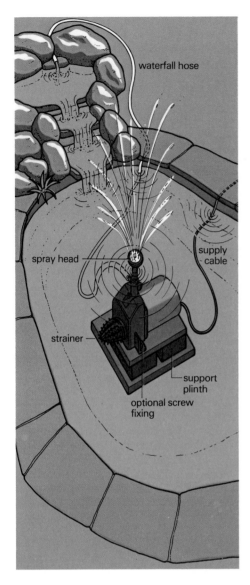

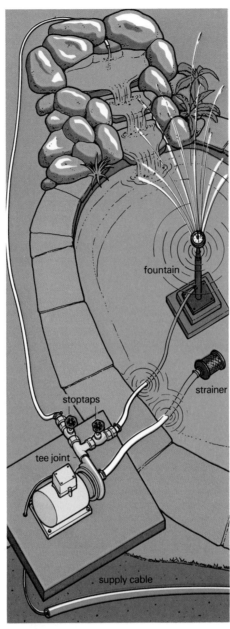

Far left *Submersible pumps are the easiest kind to install. They are fully waterproofed and need simply to be placed in the pool with the waterproof cable running to a connection with an outdoor electrical supply. Some are powerful enough to drive both a waterfall and fountain, though the pump output will determine the height and size of these. The water is sucked in through a strainer and pumped to the fountain and/or the head of the waterfall.*

Left *Surface pumps generally have a longer working life and greater output than the submersible types. They must be housed in a waterproof chamber (not shown). Hoses feed the fountain and/or waterfall in the same way as a submersible pump, but the water is sucked in through a remote strainer in the pool connected to the inlet side of the pump.*

the various installations then a mains voltage pump is essential.

The scope of low voltage transformers is limited because of the drop in voltage which occurs if there is a considerable length of cable from the transformer to the pump, fountain or lighting equipment. The range of cable length from the low voltage output side of a transformer should not be much more than about 7–9m (23–30ft). When the cable is more than about 12m (40ft) long there will usually be a voltage drop which means a reduction in the performance of the pump or fountain.

In small gardens, however, a low voltage system has much to commend it, as it is quite safe and if, as will be seen later, portable lights are to be used, a low voltage supply is really the only sensible choice.

There are also two different types of pump. The older, series-wound pumps with carbon 'brushes', wear out and require frequent renewal. These are not recommended for continuous use. Those with an induction motor are of modern design and

sophisticated materials capable of continuous running to provide water for a waterfall or fountain. The latter are the best to buy.

There is yet one more choice to be made, between the surface or the submersible pump. For all but the largest installations in gardens, the submersible pumps are the more popular choice. They usually come fitted with a strainer, a priming valve and a sufficient length of cable to connect to a waterproof plug and socket on the cable leading from the mains supply. The beauty of these submersible pumps is that there is virtually no plumbing necessary; a hose is connected to the fountain and, if desired, a waterfall, and the pump is just placed in the pool at the recommended depth below the surface, set on a base of bricks or something similar. The water is then pumped up from the pool, recirculated and sent back to the pool again. For further information on the electrical installation and safety considerations see page 245.

The range and performance of these submersible pumps is quite remarkable, from the simplest, relatively inexpensive, types, delivering an output of 910 L (200 gal) an hour with a lift of 1m (3ft), to the larger, more expensive models, delivering 1500 L (330 gal) an hour or more.

The right approach to the problem of choosing a pump for your water garden is to measure the height above ground level of the topmost water course. Then decide whether you wish to supply water only to the waterfalls, to a fountain only, or both, or, in the case of larger installations, if you wish to supply a waterfall and perhaps several fountains. Armed with this information you can go to a garden centre where, hopefully, you will be able to obtain advice on the size of pump, the choice of fountains and receive good counsel about the installation of all this equipment.

When you have to take a mains voltage supply from the source in the house it should be by means of an armoured cable if it is to be buried in the soil. This should be buried at least 60cm (24in) deep and preferably covered with concrete tiles, if there is any danger that the cable might be disturbed by somebody digging the ground above it.

All cables carrying mains voltage should be protected by what used to be called an 'earth leakage trip switch' but is now called a 'residual current device or current breaker' (RCD or RCCB). One can fit a flush fitting 13 amp socket RCD combination. Or there is a separate plug incorporating the RCD which is fitted with a test button which will show immediately if there is any fault on the line. If this unit 'trips' – if a fault develops – it must be removed from the socket. It cannot be reset until the fault is rectified. These circuit breakers should be used whenever mains voltage cables are taken outdoors for any purpose – to supply pumps, fountains, lighting, pool heaters and, of course, all kinds of electrical equipment such as lawn mowers, scarifiers, hedge trimmers, power tools such as electric drills – in fact, any appliance whose attendant cable could possibly be cut or become frayed in use.

Electricity and the water garden

Installing mains voltage wiring in the garden is no field of endeavour for the home handyman. It should always be carried out or checked by a qualified electrician – even in the home, let alone in the garden where danger of a possibly fatal electric shock is so much greater. You should make sure that the firm employed to do such work is on the roll of the National Inspection Council for Electrical Installation Contracting. Your local electricity board and any contractor on the above roll will willingly give expert help on problems of

Installing a submersible pump is a straightforward task that need only take a few minutes:

1 Assemble the components and check that none is mising. Assemble according to the manufacturer's instructions.

2 Measure the height of the spray head. You may have to build an underwater plinth to bring the spray to the required height. It should be just above the surface of the water.

3 After building the plinth, install the pump in position (you may have to secure it to the plinth by using a wooden block). If you have a waterfall, feed the hose to the top collection pool, avoiding any sharp bends or twists. Cut the hose to length and wedge the end firmly in place between two or three rocks. The pump is now ready for connection to the power source.

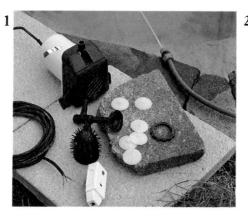

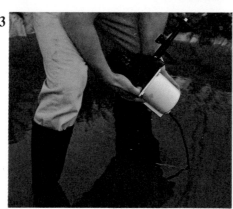

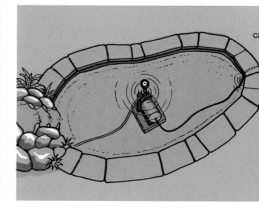

cable

outdoor electrical wiring. A leaflet 'Safety in the Garden' is available from your local electricity showroom.

There are stringent regulations governing the type of cable, switches, light sockets, as well as the junction boxes, actual laying of cable or fixing it to walls. Fixing to fences is not permitted. Such installations must be adequately earthed. It is also desirable that a residual current device – an RCD – is installed to provide additional safety.

Extensions from, say, a power socket in the house are not considered safe enough for taking cable carrying mains voltage out to the garden to operate pumps, fountains or pool lighting. All such installations should have a separate main switch and be separately fused. A much safer way of using electricity in the garden is to install a transformer, either in the house or garage, or some other waterproof building. These transformers provide low voltage current, usually 12 volts, which is safe to use in the garden.

Garden lighting equipment that can be attached to the outside wall of the house may be connected to the normal domestic installation but these types of lamp and any other equipment must be waterproof and approved for outdoor use. There are specialist firms who deal in all aspects of water gardens, pools and the like and, of course, offer a wide choice of equipment. It would pay to consult an electrician about the best type of equipment to buy and then shop around to see what it will cost.

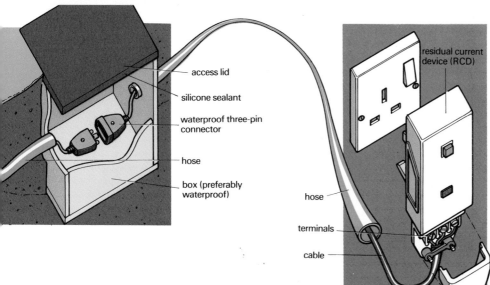

Left *Outdoor lighting will enable you to enjoy your garden long after the sun goes down and its artificial effects can be used to set a mood of mystery, adventure or light-hearted festivity.*

Below left *For a mains electrical connection, the submersible pump cable should be buried in a trench and sheathed with hose-pipe for added protection (use plastic conduit for surface mounting). House the cable connector in a waterproof box fitted with a removable lid. Make sure that the pins of the connector are on the pump side. At the supply end, fit an RCCB (residual current contact breaker) rather than an ordinary plug.*

For maximum visual effect, why not install pool lighting so that the sprays of a fountain can be seen shimmering in the night? Even more dramatic is the impact of underwater lighting, where different colours can be used singly or in groups.

Garden lighting

Garden lighting can take many forms. The simplest is probably several 500 watt lamps fixed to an outside wall which will illuminate the whole area around the house at the touch of a switch indoors. Apart from their value in lighting up the garden and for evening barbecue parties, outdoor lamps are also useful as burglar deterrents – if you hear strange sounds after dark, you can switch on the lights and few intruders would be fool enough to press on with any invasion of your property. As an added precaution, it would obviously be desirable to have another switch upstairs as well as one downstairs. Other outdoor floodlighting installations can also be connected to an indoor switch for the same deterrent purpose.

There is a wide range of lighting equipment available for use in gardens and on patios. Large weatherproof 200 watt or 100 watt lamps are available for mounting on walls or trees or on a spike which is then pushed into the ground. These are obviously ideal for spotlighting part of a building or a tree as well as the pool.

Perhaps even more interesting are the sets of portable low voltage lights which work from a transformer. You can fit up to ten 25 watt lamps, using this method. They can be stuck into the ground on short spikes. The lamps may be placed to illuminate awkward corners or hazards such as steps in the garden or to highlight some particular garden feature. You can, for example, place one of these lamps to light up a flowering cherry tree and then move it on to illuminate a playing waterfall or, in due course, some other garden feature. Certain of these sets have interchangeable clear or coloured lenses and it is remarkable how, for example, a red lens greatly enhances the beauty of a red flowered tree, shrub or group of herbaceous plants. Naturally the same effect is produced with coloured lenses directed towards blue or yellow flowered plants.

Now to perhaps the most exciting outdoor lighting of all – underwater lighting in pools or to illuminate fountains. There are both mains voltage lamps with up to 150 watt capacity, capable of producing very powerful lighting to illuminate fountains, and low voltage submersible lamps working from a transformer which can float on a pool or be set to illuminate a fountain or a waterfall.

All modern underwater lighting equipment is doubly insulated, in the case of mains voltage lamps, and with low voltage lights, they are waterproof.

As with pump installations, any lighting equipment, unless it is fixed permanently to a wall, should be protected by an RCD – a circuit breaker – which will cut off the current if a fault should develop in the outside wiring system or if a cable should be accidently cut.

Pool surrounds

Formal pools call for formal surrounds and these may be of various materials. York paving is not recommended, though it is sometimes obtainable at quite reasonable prices from local authorities, because it can become very slippery should it become coated with even a very thin layer of green algae. Nowadays there are excellent paving slabs in various sizes, easy to lay and not slippery. They are made to resemble sandstone paving but, if a bright modern look is desired, there are also coloured paving slabs available. Variety may be provided by inserting occasionally between the slabs a square filled with cobble stones set in concrete, or, if a quantity of old tiles is available, a square of these set edgeways in concrete will also break up the monotony of an area of plain paving. Again, a combination of red bricks and plain sand coloured paving can be very pleasing but try to seek out well-fired, wire-cut bricks. These, unlike ordinary bricks, are less likely to become slippery in frosty weather and do not seem to be so much affected by algae.

Whether or not the pool is built to be partly above ground, it is still possible to build a low wall around a formal pool, with or without a flat stone capping. The latter is handy to sit on or makes somewhere to set down a teacup or tumbler as you recline in a deckchair beside the pool.

For a less formal appearance, you can

The finishing touches to this pool have helped make it a favourite corner of the garden. The formal surrounds, appropriate to the formal design, are softened by low-growing plants, while a small statue, framed by flowers, creates a quiet arbour at the side.

An irregularly-shaped pool looks especially effective when edged with crazy paving.

use broken, or 'crazy', paving and there is much to be said for this type of surround if spaces are left here and there into which may be planted low-growing plants, such as thymes, thrifts, aubrietas, dwarf campanulas, helianthemums and the like. This type of surround usually looks better when built in conjunction with an irregularly shaped pool rather than a square, rectangular or circular one, although it has a place with any shape of pool if some degree of informality is desired (as when a pool is set in an area of lawn). Surrounds to pools which have a rocky finish, or with rock or simulated rock waterfalls, look best if grass is brought up to the water's edge or if a boggy area is provided.

Another effective treatment for a pool set in grass is to have a very small paved area around and approached by stepping stones set in the turf. These should be set slightly lower than the turf so that the mower can ride over them without damage to the blades. You should also try to lay the stones so that they approach the pool from several different directions, so that visitors can go and admire it, and then proceed on a tour of the garden without having to retrace their steps. Stepping stones and, indeed, all paths should always lead to somewhere interesting – or at least give promise that they will do so. Paths should never finish abruptly or at a fence with no possibility of going on.

Problem-saving accessories

Pools also bring problems. If made of concrete they will almost certainly, in time, begin to leak. A more common problem is that of algae fouling the water and making it impossible to see the fish. Even when a balance has been achieved in the relationship of fish and oxygenating plants, it can happen that further action has to be taken to keep water free from certain types of unsightly algae.

Pools freeze in winter and fish may die. Leaves may fall into the pond and lie on the bottom to rot, giving off noxious gases which may be harmful to the fish, especially if the pool freezes over and there is no provision made to keep a small area free from ice.

Leaking pools

Leaks in concrete can hopefully be prevented if the pool is well made with the sides and bottom at least 15cm (6in) thick, and later the surface is treated with a sealing primer to neutralise any free lime, and then followed by a powerful pondseal. This takes the form of a plastic paint and is available from water plant specialists in blue or natural stone colour. Such compounds may be applied to give an attractive and waterproof finish to new pools, or to repair porous, leaky or cracked pools, in spring after any danger of frost is past. There are various brands and kinds of sealants, all of which must be applied according to the manufacturers' instructions. Normally they are not applied in winter or when the air temperature is below 10°C (50°F).

Aquatic dealers also stock waterproofing powders which can be added to concrete mixes to increase the water-holding capacity of the mix.

Dealing with algae

One of the most worrying and persistent problems with pools is that caused by green algae, including the type called blanket weed. These make the water cloudy or unsightly.

In small pools, if the balance of fish and oxygenating plants is right, the water will clear after an initial greening period and remain clear. But in larger pools where perhaps the balance between fish and plants has not been achieved, the water may remain green and murky. This is more fully described on page 255. Every attempt should be made to clear the water by natural means, such as using plenty of underwater vegetation and balancing the quota of fish and plants.

Because the quantity of water in an artificial garden pool is of necessity limited, introducing chemical controls for algae can be tricky. It takes very little to overdo the dose with dire results, particularly for fish.

However, there are people who claim success from using algicides and there are several preparations on the market which have been formulated to control blanket weed and green water and which, it is claimed, will not harm plants or fish. If you use any of these do adhere strictly to the recommended quantities, but, more importantly, try to plant the pool correctly initially.

Biological filters

More recently, biological filters have come on the market. These are designed to operate outside the pool and they work continuously during spring, summer and autumn but are not necessarily active in winter. Their purpose is to break down and purify – with the aid of beneficial bacteria – solids derived from fish excreta, dead snails, algae and plants and turn them into harmless material capable of being absorbed as food by plants.

The filter is sited outside the pond, suitably camouflaged at the top of a waterfall where water is pumped through, brought up from the pool farther down and then returned to it again via the waterfall. Alternatively, the filter can be hidden somewhere near a static pool, a pump constantly sending water from the latter through the filter and back again to the pool. Quite small pumps are suitable for these filters but since they must run continuously, a submersible type is recommended. The water passes over a special gravel or foam medium on which beneficial bacteria form, converting waste materials into plant foods. It takes four to six weeks for the full effect of this biological filtration to become fully effective, after which the only servicing consists of occasional cleaning of the filter foam.

Pool heaters

Ice forming on pools in winter presents another problem, particularly for fish. Methods of dealing with this hazard in the case of small pools is described on page 256 but, if you do not want the bother of these, you can keep an area clear with an electric pond heater. These consist of a 125 watt heating element enclosed in a rod type tube, which in turn is suspended from a block of polystyrene. This keeps it floating and upright in the water and will, when in use, keep an area of about 2.8 sq m (30 sq ft) clear of ice. The heater may be connected to a mains voltage supply in the house but, as with all other appliances used outdoors should be protected by an RCD.

Nets and netting

Other accessories obtainable from aquatic specialists include fish nets of various sizes.

The small ones are useful for catching the odd fish, perhaps ill or injured, and removing it to other quarters; the larger kinds for removing floating debris or leaves as well as catching fish. There is even a net sold with an amazing 2.3m (7½ft) telescopic handle.

A number of firms sell pool nets, made of plastic with 10–20mm (⅜–¾in) mesh. Sizes vary from 3 × 2m (10 × 6½ft) up to 10.9 × 3.6m (36 × 12ft). Stretched over a pool and pegged at the edges they can be used to trap leaves or submerged below the water surface to deter herons and gulls from stealing the fish.

Herons, incidentally, do not fly or jump into a pond, but walk in from the edge and, when their feet become entangled in the net, they admit defeat and turn their attentions elsewhere.

Herons, apparently, are fiercely jealous of their particular territories and nowadays you can buy very life-like plastic models of herons which, if placed near pools, streams or even on river banks, will deter live herons from invading the garden.

Cats can also be a nuisance, snatching up fish from a pool. If there are cats around causing problems, it would pay you well to stretch a small meshed net right over the top of the pool.

For contending with cold winters and the problem of ice forming on pools, one solution is to use a pond heater.

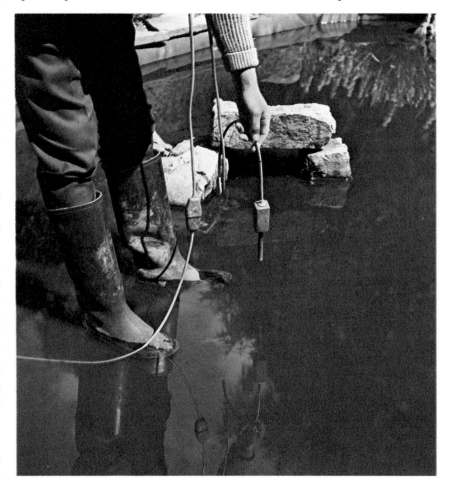

MANAGEMENT & MAINTENANCE

When your pool is complete, one of the most enjoyable tasks can be tackled – choosing from the many different water plants. There are also a number of routine checks you should make, however, to keep the pool in good order.

As soon as a pool is constructed it is natural to want to see it planted. But, before attempting to install any plants or fish, it is wise to check that the pool – or pools if there is more than one – are watertight and sit level in the soil. Since this probably represents the last opportunity to correct any unevenness or irregularities, it is worth spending a little time checking.

Also, if the pool is constructed of concrete, it will be necessary to mature the inside before plants are introduced. Most aquatics favour slightly acid rather than alkaline conditions, but the cement in new concrete releases lime into the water. This does not persist forever, but does continue to seep out for some time and, when it occurs, some plants will unaccountably fail. The effect on fish, however, will be more dramatic, because lime causes their fins to split and fray – and in some cases it kills.

For these reasons, people in the past usually made concrete pools in the autumn. They were then kept full of water all winter. Apart from giving them a good test against leakage, this period allowed most of the free lime to escape into the water. When the pool was emptied in spring, all harmful material was removed, and it was possible to plant with safety.

In the case of a late construction, however, acid was sometimes added to a filled pool in an attempt to neutralize its alkalinity. The commonest kind used was commercial syrupy phosphoric acid, added in sufficient quantity to show an acid reaction to litmus paper twice in twenty-four hours. Fortunately, today there are sealing compounds which make neither a long wait nor such chemical treatment necessary. This sealing agent is painted over the whole of the concrete interior where it blocks off any pollution. Sometimes the sealer is combined with a waterproofing agent.

Of course, none of this preliminary treatment is needed for prefabricated or polythene lined ponds. These can be planted as soon as convenient after they are constructed.

Planting water-lilies

Water-lilies, with their large, tuberous roots are the most expensive aquatic plants you are likely to buy and also those which most resent disturbance. Some kinds take a long time to get over a move, especially if they are initially put into very deep water. For this reason they should always be moved in spring, before growth is very far advanced but the sap is rising, so that new roots are quickly produced.

The roots of hardy water-lilies take two forms. Some have their tubers running horizontally through the soil like the rhizome of a bearded iris, while others are more upright and grow after the fashion of a carrot. Another interesting fact is that most of the fragrant water-lilies have horizontal tubers – the species and cultivars of *Nymphaea odorata* and *N. tuberosa*, for example.

To plant water-lilies, you must either establish them in soil already covering the base of the pool or plant them in baskets. For the first method it is usual to drain off the water, or plant them in the soil before water is added. This is certainly a practical method with very small containers, for example tubs, baths or tiny rock pools. In such cases there should be about 12.5cm (5in) of soil over the base and, after planting the lilies with a trowel, a top dressing of shingle should be spread on the surface and the water run in carefully to avoid disturbing soil or plants. If the hose is run into a flower pot lying on its side this is enough to slow the force of most jets.

This is not a suitable method for a large expanse of water, like a lake. In cases like this, the lily roots must be weighted and lowered in position, so that they can root into the muddy soil below at their own pace. This can be achieved either by planting

The choice of plants to go in and around a pool is almost infinite and, once established, they will require only occasional checks to ensure that they are healthy. In this woodland setting, interest comes as much from the surrounding foliage as the pool itself and, in the foreground, the cool colours of Hydrangea paniculata *complement the mood perfectly.*

Water-lilies are best planted in baskets placed in the appropriate depth of water for the particular variety (see page 270).
1 *Assemble the materials: a basket, compost, plastic-coated wire and sacking, plus the water-lily.*
2 *Line the basket with sacking and fill the base with compost.*
3 *Bed the crown of the water-lily well into the compost.*
4 *Pack added compost around the plant, making it as secure as possible.*
5 *Wrap sacking around to form a neat 'parcel' that will prevent compost from spilling out.*
6 *Tie the parcel firmly before the basket is sunk in water.*

1

4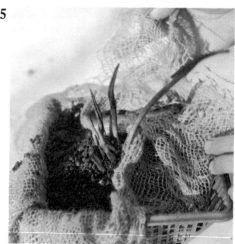

2

5

3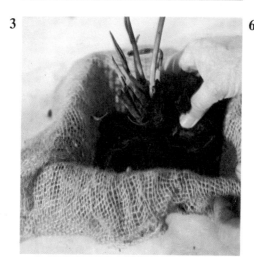

6

them in baskets first, preferably of wicker or cane as this will eventually rot away or, alternatively, sandwich each root between two turves turned grass-side inwards. The grass should be shaved very short beforehand and the packages tied together with tape, which is less likely to cut through the bundles than string. The water-lilies should then be carefully lowered, so that they settle the right way up.

Undoubtedly, however, the easiest and most satisfactory method of growing water-lilies today is to plant them in the aquatic baskets obtainable from dealers. These are made of plastic and have perforations round the sides for, curiously, the roots like to feel the influence of water and should not be forced into solid containers. Baskets are not only economical of soil but can be quickly lowered into place and, if necessary, lifted and replanted easily and without fuss.

The compost used for water-lilies should be on the heavy side, such as good garden soil or turf which has rotted down over a long period, so that there is no longer any evidence of roots or fibrous shoots. This can either be mixed with ⅙th of its bulk well-rotted cow manure or, if this is difficult to come by, with coarse bone-meal, used at the rate of a handful per basket. Because there may be a slight risk of contracting anthrax from bone-meal, always wear gloves when handling this substance.

Plant each water-lily firmly in its basket, up to the old planting mark and to within 4cm (1½in) of the top. Dampening the compost beforehand enables it to be packed down fairly easily. Next, top-dress the baskets with 2.5cm (1in) of clean washed shingle, to deter fish from rooting into the soil. Cut off any dead, damaged or broken-stemmed leaves and lower the baskets into the water. The crowns of the water-lilies should only be barely submerged at this stage, so you may have to raise the baskets on bricks for a week or two, or until new leaves can be seen coming through the soil.

If plunged under 45–60cm (18–24in) of water immediately after planting, water-lilies can be checked so badly that they may fail to flower that season, so this preliminary attention is well worthwhile.

Do not be tempted by sales talk or by well-meaning friends into adding fertilizers to water-lily compost. This applies to leafmould, compost and peat as well as chemicals. It takes very little to alter the nature of still water and the smaller the pool, the easier it is for introduced chemicals to build up to harmful proportions. You will then be faced with all the problems of decomposition and gases like methane and hydrogen sulphide occurring, plus some of the worst forms of algae. Greater liberties can be taken with a large expanse of water, such as a lake, where a wide surface area is exposed to the air.

Planting shallow-water aquatics
Most shallow-water aquatics are normally planted in pots placed on shelves or established in shallow troughs built into pools. These plants can be dealt with over a longer season than water-lilies. However, if you want to see them in flower the first season, very early bloomers like kingcups (*Caltha* spp), water forget-me-nots and giant aroids, such as lysichitons, must go in in early spring. Alternatively, wait until the flowers have gone in the case of kingcups, and deal with lysichitons when most of the foliage has died down. Most other marginal

Caltha palustris, *the marsh marigold or kingcup, is a superb plant for bog gardens and pool surrounds and its bright yellow flowers will bring a bold, attractive splash of colour to any spring-time display.*

water plants can be planted, also lifted and divided, between mid-spring and mid-summer, but even so, the earlier the better.

Plant all of these in heavy loam, without the bone-meal, as fertilizers are rarely necessary. Most aquatic plants grow rather rapidly since they do not experience the setbacks common to land plants, such as summer drought and shortage of water.

Planting oxygenators

Oxygenators rarely have many roots to worry about, but they do have to be spaced out in the pool in the first instance. To make sure that they sink to the bottom, group the slender stems together in small bunches, and either fasten these to small stones or similar weights or twist a narrow strip of lead around their bases. It is also possible to dibble a number – like cuttings – into a shallow seedtray of loam and stand this on the pool floor. Floaters present no problems as they only have to be placed on the water.

Planting bog plants

Bog plants are more individualistic, some needing richer fare than others, although the majority dislike lime. If the ground is thoroughly prepared beforehand, weeded and deeply dug with plenty of well-rotted organic material worked in, it should last a long time in fertile condition. Later, a mulch each spring of mushroom compost, leafmould, garden compost or well-rotted farmyard manure will prove beneficial for most bog plants.

Aftercare

Once your pool is filled with water, planted and occupied by fish, it should run smoothly, provided you give it reasonable maintenance and seasonal care as necessary.

Scum removal

It is not unusual for a coating of scum to appear on the water soon after planting. This is due to the newness of everything – soil, water or even something in the pool fabric. Floating debris looks unsightly and should be removed. The easiest way of doing this is to put the end of a garden hose in the pool, then turn on the water and flood it over so that the debris goes over the sides. When this is not practical, perhaps because it will swamp neighbouring land plants, pinch the end of the hose with your finger and thumb to force a strong jet and play this over the water. This breaks up any bubbles of scum and also drives the unwanted material to one end of the pool where it can be lifted out with a fish net. In the case of baths, tubs and other small containers, a quick and easy idea is to draw

a sheet of newspaper across the water surface. Any scum will adhere to the paper and can then be quickly and easily removed in that way.

Should secondary crops of scum occur, try 'beating' the water surface with a powerful jet from the hose. This usually causes it to sink, and may be repeated if necessary. Whatever happens, do not make a habit of emptying and refilling your pool, as this will check growth on the part of the underwater oxygenators and also reintroduce chemicals – such as chlorine – from the fresh tap water.

Treating green water

If the water turns green this is not necessarily harmful, indeed fish may thrive in it, but admittedly it is disfiguring. The cause is due to myriads of tiny, unicellular plants called algae. These feed on dissolved salts present in the water and derive their energy from sunlight. Once the oxygenators really get going they starve the algae of food, so it is important to do everything possible to assist them in these early stages. Competition is the key to success but, if you find the greenness more than you can bear, shade the water for a day or two by laying boards or black plastic across the surface. This will stop the algae growing by denying them light, but do not keep the shading on too long or it will also adversely affect the aquatic plants.

Autumn care

As the season advances, inevitably flowers and leaves die. These should be removed on sight; those of the water-lilies by pulling them from the rootstocks. Certain aquatics, like the water plantains *(Alisma)* are inveterate seeders and they should have their old flower heads removed as soon as the flowers fade. Bog plants, too, should be kept neat and tidy by regular weeding and the routine removal of faded or dead vegetation.

Water-lily cultivation

When water-lilies have been in their baskets for a couple of years they will probably have exhausted most of the original food supply. To keep them going a little longer, feed them with bone-meal 'pills'. These are made by mixing together equal parts of moist clay and bone-meal and moulding the resultant 'dough' into tennis-ball sized pills. Push these pills down into the sides of the baskets, giving a large and vigorous water-lily two, but a medium-sized lily only one. After five years, at the latest, the baskets should be lifted and the water-lilies divided as necessary and replanted in fresh soil.

Opposite *Many shade-loving plants are also excellent choices for a pool-side location. Here, a raised bed features the striking foliage of* Hosta fortunei *'Albopicta', astilbes and epimedium, with a large rhubarb plant* (Rheum palmatum) *beyond. Height is provided by the delicate cut leaf sumach tree (*Rhus typhina *'Laciniata') and by a tub planted with another variegated hosta, 'Thomas Hogg'.*

Dealing with leaves

Though, ideally, pools should be sited well away from trees, this is not always possible and leaves from neighbours' trees, if not your own, may well fall into the pool in autumn. They will sink to the bottom and decompose, releasing noxious gases and salts into the water which will become harmful to fish and encourages algae. It is important to keep dredging them out with a rake or, better still, prevent the leaves getting into the pool in the first place. This is achieved by trapping them as they come tumbling down in autumn gales.

It is not too difficult to construct a light cover or screen which will fit over any small to medium-sized pool, though is out of the question for large pools where dredging is best. To make the screen, knock together a light framework of 5cm (2in) laths, a couple of inches larger all round than the area of the pond. Tack small-meshed, plastic netting between the lath edges and lay the completed cover over the pool, preferably raised on bricks to keep the netting dry. However, the bricks are not essential: the main thing is to catch the leaves before they become wet and heavy. Take the screen off – this is usually a two-person job – and empty it from time to time.

The covers should be in place by the end of early autumn and only removed for storage when all leaves are down. Incidentally, such covers are sometimes useful in spring for catching tree blossoms as well as, say, the woolly catkins from poplar trees.

Winter care

When winter finally arrives and poolside reeds and sedges become withered and brown, they should be cut down to prevent them becoming cosy winter quarters for pests. But the biggest hazard will come later with the frosts, for if these are severe and ice builds up thickly there could be danger for fish, as well as more tender plants and, possibly, concrete pools.

Where there is 45cm (18in) or more water over the water-lilies, these should come to no harm and, provided they can get air, nor will the fish. Tiny rock pools and tubs may have to be emptied and the inmates housed elsewhere for the worst of the winter or, alternatively, in milder districts, they will survive if the pool is covered with boards with sacks of straw laid on top during severe frost. Such coverings must be removed when each thaw sets in, otherwise the water-lilies may start into premature growth.

The simplest method of keeping any artificial pool that holds 45cm (18ins) or more of water from freezing up completely is to float a large ball or a block of wood on top. Do this in late autumn and then, when ice forms and is about 2.5cm (1in) thick, take a kettle of boiling water outside and pour it over the ball. When the latter loosens, take it out and bale or siphon out 2.5cm (1in) of water. Now cover the hole with a sack and leave things alone until a thaw sets in. The sack should then be removed, the pool filled again with water and the ball refloated, ready for the next frost session. The purpose of all this is to keep a hole open in the ice and to let the rest of the ice act like a sheet of glass over the unfrozen water.

It is also possible to install pool heaters in order to keep a small area of water free of ice in winter.

What can go wrong?

Although you need not anticipate much going wrong in the water garden, should troubles occur it is important to recognize and deal with them at once. This particularly applies to pests.

Construction problems

These include leaks in a concrete pool and troubles caused by free lime from new concrete polluting the water. See page 250 for ways to prevent these – before they occur. If leaks appear later and are too severe to be cured by painting over the interior, line the pool with a flexible polythene liner and start again.

Damaged liners, semi-rigid vacuum-moulded pools and prefabricated glass fibre kinds can all be repaired on site with the aid of special adhesives and patching tape. Go to a specialist aquatic firm and purchase a suitable repair kit for your type of pool. There are different kits for different kinds of pools.

Weeds

Weeds are probably the greatest nuisance in a pool as they make everything look cluttered and untidy. None is more troublesome than the green tangled masses of a particular alga called blanket weed. The main causes of rapid spread with all kinds of algae are high temperatures, bright sunlight and a superabundance of mineral salts derived from the waste products of plants and animals.

Blanket weed grows in long greenish-brown tresses which feel rough to the touch. It winds itself in a smothering embrace around the underwater parts of water-lilies and submerged plants and also clings to the pool sides. If the pool is small the best way to remove it is by hand, as it can then be disentangled from brittle stems without breaking these in the process. Another method is to push a forked stick

So-called blanket weed, made up of slender threads of filamentous algae, grows on the surface of still water and can soon become unsightly. The algae thrive on sunlight and dissolved mineral salts that are often particularly plentiful in a new pool. If the growth becomes too vigorous before a natural balance is established, use a garden rake or rough stick to gather it up.

into a clump of blanket weed and, if this is rotated, the weed will be wound round the stick and can be pulled from the water.

Chemical methods of eradication are sometimes advised for bad infestation, but these can bring their own problems. If all else fails, empty the pool and, after scrubbing it out with a mild disinfectant, rinse and replant the pool including plenty of oxygenators. They are really the key to clear water and freedom from algae. You cannot have too many of them, especially during the early days when everything in the pool is settling down. Apart from absorbing dissolved mineral salts in the water, they cut down light, both of which deprive the algae of growth essentials. Natural shade will, in due course, be cast by floaters and the leaves of water-lilies, while goldfish help by consuming a small amount of algae in their diet.

Occasionally, in a large lake or pond underwater plants grow so thickly that it is impossible to see the base. However, the water will be crystal clear and the fish breed prolifically, finding food and protection in the masses of vegetation. Provided the plants remain submerged and are not annoying, they should be left alone. However one plant, a pondweed called *Potamogeton natans* will go on to produce floating leaves and brownish flowers of no great significance, both of which look unsightly *en masse*. These may have to be cut and dredged out of the water periodically, so the moral is, don't plant *Potamogeton natans* in the first place.

General problems

Water-lilies will not only fail to flower the first season, some kinds may even die if submerged too deeply directly after planting. Accordingly, lower them gradually into the water. Neither will they grow well in running water or too close to a fountain. In swift streams, use nuphars instead of nymphaeas and either keep water plants well away from fountain jets, or only play these infrequently.

If you want to safeguard your goldfish, refrain from putting pugnacious kinds like catfish and sticklebacks in the same pool. Also keep tench away from small pools if you want the water to stay clear. Overfeeding fish is another cause of cloudy water.

If cats or herons are a problem, spray a proprietary deterrent close to the pool edges (but not in the water) or adopt some of the suggestions mentioned previously (see page 249)

Pests

In late summer, blackfly often attack the aerial parts of water-lilies and other aquatics in such numbers that they completely cover the stems and leaves. This causes discoloration and decay of the affected parts. Dislodge them with a powerful jet of water from a hose so that the blackfly fall into the pool, where they can be taken by fish. Since some always crawl back, repeat as necessary. Alternatively, submerge the water-lily leaves for 24 hours.

Caddis flies and mosquitoes may visit the pool during their breeding season. Both are a nuisance. The caddis fly larvae tear pieces of plant leaves to make pupae cases while the adult mosquitoes annoy people. With fish in the pool there is no occasion for worry.

Two other possible pests are the small brown china marks moth and the water-lily beetle. Both of these lay their eggs on water-lily leaves, which later provide food for their larvae. Eventually, this reduces everything to a brown rotting mass. Again, fish will devour them after the pests have been dislodged with a strong jet of water.

When autumn comes, a time-consuming task is the collection of leaves falling from trees and shrubs. They can be kept out of the water by means of a wire-mesh 'trap' laid across the pool surface. The leaves can then be gathered up regularly, without the worry of too much debris polluting the pool.

FISH & WILDLIFE

The unique environment of a water garden will quickly attract a host of visitors both welcome and unwanted. As well as the natural wildlife, however, you will probably want to introduce a selection of fish to your pool.

Although it is not essential to have fish in a pool, there are various reasons for including them. For one thing they are delightful to watch as they dart from side to side, sometimes in schools on a 'follow my leader' basis, as is usual with golden orfe, or hovering near the surface in the case of goldfish. Fish bring life to the water garden, extending your reasons for wishing to visit it frequently and, if you feed them regularly in one place, they soon become tame enough to take food from your fingers.

They also help to provide a balanced environment, both for themselves and the pool plants. Their bodily waste fertilizes and feeds the latter, but in return fish need underwater vegetation on which to deposit their eggs and to hide the young fry which would otherwise be eaten after hatching. Most fish are cannibals.

When breathing, fish take in oxygen and exhale carbon dioxide, whereas plants use carbon dioxide in the process of manufacturing plant food but return oxygen to the water as a by-product of this process. Consequently both plants and fish utilize the waste products of the other and so form a mutually beneficial partnership.

Finally, fish protect plants from many of their enemies. They have voracious appetites and make short work of the larvae of mosquitoes and caddis flies, also snails' eggs and sundry small insects. Given the opportunity, they will even eat their own young.

The requirements of fish are few. They need a cool, shady area to retreat to in hot weather, such as that provided by the floating leaves of water-lilies, or a shelf under which they can hide. They also need sufficient water not to be overcrowded, otherwise they will be continually fighting for air.

Fish gasping at the surface are an indication of distress so it is important not to overstock the pool. Your dealer will be able to give an indication of the number you can accommodate, based on the size of your pool and its water capacity. As a rough guide, you can calculate that 2.5cm (1in) of fish needs 4.5 L (1 gal) of water. This means that a 7.5cm (3in) long fish will need 13.5 L (3 gal); a 23cm (9in) specimen 41 L (9 gal) and so on, but do make allowances for growth.

When purchased from a dealer the fish will probably be in a plastic bag. This will contain very little water, but just before it was sealed, oxygen will have been pumped inside – enough to prevent distress during travel. When you reach home, float the bag in the pool for half an hour, so that the water temperature inside this will become roughly the same as that in the pool. Now open the bag and turn it on its side so that the fish can swim out. This is better than netting, because it is less likely to frighten them or damage their scales.

Types of fish
The best kinds of fish to keep are those which have bright colours and also tend to live near the surface. They will coincidentally be the easiest to tame, as they should be constantly visible.

Goldfish
The undoubted pool favourites are goldfish, which are members of the carp family, and may be basically gold or variously patterned with red, gold, silver or black. They lay their eggs in early summer, most of the young fry appearing almost black when young and taking two or three years to assume their ultimate colouring.

Many varieties have been developed from the original species, mainly in the Orient, where they are extremely popular. One of these is the comet, which has typical goldfish colouring but a longer and slimmer body. It is a very quick mover and hardy enough to live in an outside pond.

Shubunkins are often known as calico fish because of their vivid hues and patternings. These include blues and mauves, whites and pinks or combinations of these. Those with a lot of blue colouring are the most sought after and also the most expensive. Shubunkins have few, if any, scales and are therefore more susceptible to bruising than ordinary goldfish, so treat them carefully. They will live outside in

A highly successful and popular fish for garden pools is the aptly named golden orfe. It is a lively and colourful species, typically feeding at the surface where it can be seen easily. As an added bonus, the golden orfe is a hardy fish that will survive cold weather without too much difficulty.

Golden orfe, golden carp, goldfish and golden rudd are all hardy and decorative fish for the garden pool. They bring life and movement to any water garden and will live together quite harmoniously.

sheltered places, but are best taken inside in late autumn if the pool is exposed or liable to severe freezing.

There are other goldfish variations such as elegant fantails; veiltails with long graceful tails which so slow down their speed that they appear to glide through the water; moors that are black in colour with protruding eyes; lionheads that have warty, cauliflower-like growths on their heads; and celestials, with upward poised eyes. None of these is really hardy enough for an outside pool and they are also extremely expensive. Accordingly, it is better to keep them in an indoor pool or aquarium.

Golden orfe

Golden orfe are exceptionally hardy and also very quick movers. Their slender, streamlined bodies cut through water with consummate ease. They are predominantly surface feeders and also swim in shoals, so they are visible for most of the day. Orfe are less vulnerable to disease than most pool fish, but they do need a fair sized pool, especially for breeding. If they have to be kept in a small pool, a fountain or running water should be installed during hot weather, otherwise they may die through lack of oxygen. Golden orfe are usually of a rich golden colour, sometimes with brownish flecks, but there is also a silver variety that is pale bluish-green above and silver beneath. Since orfe grow rather quickly, it is best to start with quite small specimens and watch them develop. In a large pool they will grow to 60cm (24in) in ten years.

Carp

Koi carp, also known as Nishiki Koi carp, make a handsome addition to any pool, over 6sq m (60sq ft) in size. They have been cross-bred from different types of carp, resulting in fish of fantastic colourings. Some may be mostly yellow or pale gold, while others show a rainbow mixture of blues, reds, silvers, whites, golds and black. Those with the most vivid colours command very high prices. Koi carp are quite hardy and given plenty of space reach a large size – up to 1m (3ft) in length.

Common brown carp can be kept in pools but are less attractive than goldfish; they also tend to breed with goldfish and, in time, spoil the stock. The hi-goi carp is a form of common carp and either clear yellow or red, without spots or patches of other shades. Other carp include crucian carp, leather carp which are practically devoid of scales, and mirror carp which have patches of mirror-like scales on their bodies. Although good fish for lakes and similar large expanses of water, these carp are not suitable for small ornamental pools.

Tench
The common green tench and its golden form both have slippery bodies and both make good scavengers, but since they spend most of their lives on the floor of the pool they are rarely seen and constantly stir up sediment.

Rudd
Golden rudd are quick swimmers and often feed near the surface where their brilliant gold bodies and deep red fins made a surprising contrast. They need a fairly large pool or do not thrive.

Minnows
Minnows are delightful small fish, rarely more than 9cm (3½in) in length, and usually silver grey in colour with dark green backs and darker vertical bars. At breeding times, however, the male sports a red breast and has emerald-green sides. Minnows will eat mosquito or gnat larvae, also any natural fish food in the pond. They are essentially a river fish and prefer moving water, such as a stream, but will make do with a waterfall and circulating water or even a large pool with 60cm (24in) of water. In the nineteenth century, minnows were cultivated in this country for the table and were a great delicacy at banquets.

Fish to avoid
Do not be tempted to put into a garden pool fish caught in the wild, particularly pools already containing goldfish or other domestic fish. Not only do you risk introducing spores of disease or fish parasites with them, but the introduced fish may also be pugnacious carnivores.

Fish to avoid include perch, pike, stickle-

backs and catfish, all of which will bully other fish and, in many cases, devour them. Roach, which show a tendency to contract fungus disease, should also be avoided, as well as bream and green tench. The latter two spend their lives on the floor of the pond and constantly stir up mud and organic matter which leaves water cloudy.

Dace and trout need running water, well aerated, and again are not suitable for small pools.

Feeding
Most pool fish are carnivorous, eating both vegetable and protein foods. Although they can go for a long time without artificial food, sustaining themselves on whatever occurs naturally in the pool, they will not grow much nor will they breed successfully in a restricted space unless given additional food. All fish appreciate variety in their diet,

Though pool fish that occur in the wild can be attractive, they should not be added to a pool that contains 'domestic' species such as goldfish.
1 *The common tench stirs up sediment at the bottom of pools, making the water cloudy. The fish itself is only rarely seen.*
2 *Roach are best avoided because of their vulnerability to disease.*
3 *One of the most vicious carnivores, the pike will not only bully other fish but will also feed on them.*
4 *Another bully that should never be added to a garden pool is the perch.*

By feeding fish in the same place every day, they will quickly learn to gather there, giving you the chance to admire them properly. Some will even become tame enough to feed from the hand.

but only consume small quantities at a time so, with surface feeders like goldfish particularly, it is not only wasteful to give them too much, but unwise, since the remainder will sink to the bottom and decay. The golden rule is always to feed them in one place, providing just enough food for them to clear in five minutes. This, of course, does not apply when you provide live food, such as water fleas (daphnia) which can continue swimming about until ultimately eaten.

From late spring until early autumn, pool fish can be fed daily, but as winter approaches, the diet should be high in protein so that they can build up reserves of nourishment to tide them over from late autumn to late winter. The latter will be a period of fasting when no food at all should be provided, or the fish may contract digestive troubles. Meantime, if a few sunny days in winter tempt the fish to swim around, there will be enough natural food available for their needs.

Pet stores sell a wide range of dried fish foods, such as dried daphnia, dried brine shrimps and various pelleted proprietary foods scientifically formulated to provide a balanced diet. It is also possible to obtain frozen fish foods from dealers, such as tubifex worms, daphnia and shrimps. These can be kept in a deep freeze and small portions broken off as required. They should be thawed in cold water first and then emptied into the pool.

Fish troubles

Like all living creatures, fish can contract disease, although these rarely prove troublesome if the pool is well balanced. Prevention is always better than cure, so proper feeding, enough unpolluted water for the quantity of fish stocked and good planting are the best guarantees against infection. Avoid overstocking with fish; overfeeding; allowing a build up of organic matter from manures in the planting compost, fallen leaves and similar debris; introducing wild or unhealthy specimens or the careless use of weedkillers and sprays in the garden so that they drift or seep into the water.

Danger signs to observe are fish constantly gasping or gulping air near the surface; fish rolling on their sides in the water; fish rubbing themselves against the sides of the pool in an endeavour to get rid of parasites, or the appearance of a white, cotton-wool like mucus on their skins.

When troubles do occur, act quickly. If you see a dead fish remove it at once, otherwise it may be attacked by saprophytic fungi during the process of decomposition and pollute the water. The same thing applies to dead snails or other aquatic creatures, for it only takes a few hours for the corpses to become woolly all over with a coating of saprophytic fungi. When this happens it will prove impossible to discover the real killer.

Start by eliminating possible causes. Have sprays, lawn weedkillers, laburnum seeds or flowers (both poisonous) or even walnut leaves drifted into the water? These are all harmful and, if you feel any of these may be responsible, it may be necessary to change the water.

Do the fish have white or grey, cotton-wool like tufts adhering to their fins or bodies or, if the water is green, are there green growths looking like algae? If the answer is 'yes' it is probably fungus disease caused originally by some form of injury.

Cats, fish nets, bullying larger fish, overcrowding, exhaustion after travelling or abrupt changes in temperature could all be responsible. Contrary to popular belief, fungus disease is not infectious. It only attacks weak individuals, but if a number are infected, the cause must be sought and the pool treated, first by a slow water change and then by dosing it with proprietary algicide, used according to the the manufacturer's instructions. After 10 days, dose the pool again with a preventative proprietary substance. Both of these are obtainable from fish dealers. Any badly infected fish should be removed from the pool; concentrate on protecting the rest.

Various bacteria in the water may be responsible for other visible symptoms – tail rot, fin rot, red spots and patches and ulcers. If you see any of these, the pool water is probably unhygienic and infectious, so change the water and dose it with a preventative proprietary substance.

If fish keep gulping at the surface they are probably short of oxygen. Get rid of the surplus carbon dioxide in the water, which is gradually poisoning them, by playing a fountain or pumping water through a waterfall for up to 24 hours. If you do not have either of these, splash water from a hose very vigorously on the surface or, better still, use an inexpensive aquarium pump for a few days in order to get some oxygen into the pool. Incidentally, aquarium pumps are not designed to go outdoors, so house them somewhere under cover. A plastic air line linking pool and pump will cause bubbling and agitation in the pool when the pump is turned on, bringing air into the water.

Flukes, fish lice and a creature called the anchor worm sometimes attack fish on their bodies and gills, making breathing difficult and leaving the victims pale and listless. However, if treated early, these parasites can be destroyed. Dose the pool with proprietary medicinal compound several times, at intervals of a few days. Orfe react adversely to medicinal compounds, so these should not be used when orfe are present.

Fish attacked by flukes can often be seen rubbing themselves against the sides of the pool in an endeavour to dislodge the pests. Later, as the infestation builds up, the fins may fold under, bloody patches will appear on the skin and the fish swim about slowly. Some of these parasites are too small to be seen with the naked eye, although leeches will be visible and can usually be removed with tweezers.

Other pool creatures

There was a time when water snails were looked upon as essential to the well being of a pool. This was because of their scavenging habits and the fact that they would consume small quantities of algae. However, nowadays, they are looked upon less favourably.

Many kinds will eat plants as well as algae, including the submerged oxygenators. They also breed at an alarming rate, laying their eggs in unpleasant-looking, jelly-like masses on the undersides of water lily leaves. The leaves are later nibbled by the emerging young.

Snails also use up oxygen in the water and produce carbon dioxide. They play host to various parasites and will eat fish eggs as well as fish food.

Admittedly their own eggs and very young snails are also eaten by fish, but this does not compensate for the harm they do. Consequently it is unwise to introduce them to a new pool, but if they are present and in quantities sufficient to cause problems, many can be trapped by placing a cabbage stump in the water. Leave this overnight and the next morning take it out and shake off the adhering snails. Repeat as necessary.

Frogs, toads and newts are amphibians which spend most of their lives on land but seek water at breeding time. There is no point in introducing them to the garden pool. If they are in the vicinity they will probably visit it in spring. Very rarely a male frog or toad has been known to grip a slow-moving fish so tightly that it kills the fish, but this only occurs when there are surplus males in the pool and most fish keep well out of their way.

The tadpoles are good scavengers and nibble at algae until such time as they produce legs, when they become more interested in protein foods and insects. In the meantime, frog tadpoles (toad tadpoles are rejected) make live food for fishes.

Newts can feed under water and generally return annually to the same breeding ponds, a practice repeated by their offspring with quite amazing determination. They can eat very young goldfish but are unlikely to harm adult specimens.

Various flying insects may be attracted to the pool in summer. Some, such as bees and wasps, are harmless and only come to drink. Others, such as dragonflies and water beetles, lay their eggs nearby and their larvae or nymphs can be very destructive both to plants and fish. Water boatmen, whirligig and diving beetles as well as water scorpions can sometimes be seen darting about the water, and even those which feed predominantly on other insects will sometimes attack small fish. Although they cannot be avoided and will come to a pool uninvited, if any are seen, they can be netted and destroyed.

Top *Water snails are generally thought of as being welcome inhabitants of a pool but, in fact, they can do more harm than good. Here, the great Ramshorn snail (Planorbus cornelus)* feeds underwater on the leaves of frogbit (Hydrocharis morsus-ranae).

Above left *The common frog is becoming an increasingly familiar sight in garden pools.*

Above *Though dragonfly larvae are destructive, the adults are both delicate and beautiful. Here, a Dragonfly rests with wings outstretched in the sun.*

WATER GARDEN CALENDAR

Although water gardens are relatively trouble-free, they do need regular maintenance. By following a simple time-table, you can be certain that all the necessary tasks are completed in good time.

There are some garden features that demand attention all through the year, but the water garden is not one of them. It certainly has periods of great activity, but also times when the pace slackens and it is possible to sit by the pool to enjoy the movement of water, the antics of the fish, and admire the plants.

The following calendar not only gives some reminders of the various tasks to be undertaken, but also suggests aquatics and bog plants for different seasons.

Spring

This is the most active season and an important time for planting up new pools and cleaning out old ones.

Construct new prefabricated pools in an open, sunny place, after taking out excavations slightly deeper than seems necessary. Tamp the base to make it firm, cover with 2.5cm (1in) of sand or sifted ashes and insert the pool. Test for levels and fill with water.

Prepare sites for pool liners in the same way, line excavations with the material and fill with water. Cut off surplus lining material except for 15cm (6in) all round the edges. Tuck this out of sight and conceal with paving or plants.

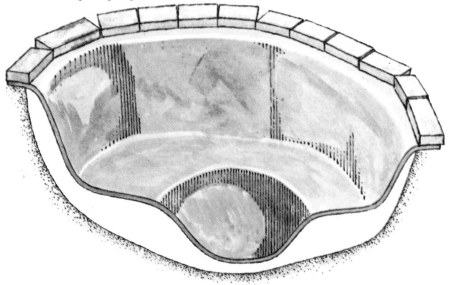
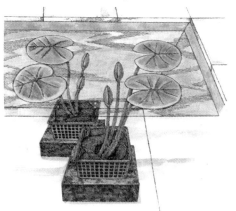

Above *When using a pool liner, make the profile an irregular shape.*
Left *Fibreglass moulds are easy to install.*
Below *Water-lilies are planted in baskets.*

Above *To divide water-lilies, cut away growing tips and plant separately.*

Plant water-lilies and other deep water aquatics in mid-spring. Top-dress their containers with shingle and sink these into the water.

Plant underwater oxygenators and marginal aquatics.

Install fish after two weeks.

If necessary, lift water-lilies in mid or late spring. It is worth doing this if they have been planted for more than four years. Wash the roots, cut away old parts of the tuber and re-plant young pieces, each with a strong shoot and about 15cm (6in) of attached tuber. Use fresh loam and bone-meal for planting compost.

Clean out old or dirty pools. Retain some of the best plants and discard the rest, along with the old soil. Scrub the pond, using either enough permanganate of potash to turn the water pink, or a mild disinfectant. Rinse, leave to dry out, then re-plant.

From early spring begin feeding fish as they become active.

Tidy and remove dead pieces of water plants killed during the winter.

Clean existing bog gardens, removing large weeds by hand. Hoe around plants and install new ones.

New bog gardens may be planted in mid-spring. Set the smaller plants in groups of three or five (more if you have the space), for maximum effect.

Plant *Calla palustris* and *Menyanthes trifoliata* roots horizontally in mud near the pool edges.

Plant bog plants from early to mid-spring.

Divide existing clumps of perennials.

Plants to enjoy in spring
Acorus (sweet flag), alnus, caltha (kingcup), *Hottonia palustris*,

lysichitum, menyanthes, metasequoia, orontium (golden club), peltiphyllum (umbrella plant), primula, ranunculus, salix, saururus (lizard's tail), scirpus (bullrushes), trollius (globe flowers).

Summer

Though not the time for any major tasks, routine checks will ensure that fish and plants stay healthy.

Remove scum from a new pool by drawing newspaper across its surface, or else flood it over with water from a hose.

To help fish in very hot or stormy weather, play a fountain or waterfall if you have them, using a pump to re-cycle the water.

Keep a sharp look-out for aphids on water-lily leaves or the foliage of marginal aquatics. Hose them into the water for the fish to take. For bad infestations, sink water-lily leaves beneath the water overnight by weighting them down with something heavy like a hoop.

If snails are chewing foliage, trap them with a cabbage stump or old lettuce plant.

Put in more oxygenating plants if water is discoloured.

Control algae if necessary (see page 255).

From time to time replace water lost by evaporation.

Left Lysichitum americanum *is a striking plant for the waterside.*
Below *The common pond snail.*

Cut off and remove old water-lily leaves and flowers.

Finish planting aquatics and bog plants before the end of early summer.

Keep the bog garden weeded, also watered if necessary.

Regularly deadhead flowers and remove dead leaves in the bog garden.

Keep inveterate self-seeders from becoming invasive by removing flowers soon after they fade.

Save seeds of primulas and sow immediately in boxes of good compost. Keep in a cold frame.

In early summer, put out water hyacinths, floating these on the surface of the pool.

Watch for cats, herons and other birds visiting the pool to catch fish.

Feed the fish regularly and in the same place.

Save seed of any special bog plants.

Thin oxygenating plants if necessary.

Plants to enjoy in summer
Acorus (sweet flag), alisma (water plantain), aponogeton (water hawthorn), astilbe, butomus (flowering rush), cimicifuga, eichhornia (water hyacinth), filipendula (meadowsweet),

Below Iris kaempferi *revels in moist soil.*
Right *and* **top** *In autumn, feed fish on high protein food such as worms. Check that the pool heater is working and install it once autumn debris is cleared (bottom right). Use the old leaves of* Gunnera manicata *to protect the plant crowns (bottom).*

Gentiana lutea, glyceria (manna grass), gunnera, hydrangea, *Hypericum elodes,* iris, juncus (corkscrew rush), lobelia, mimulus (monkey musk), myosotis (water forget-me-not), orontium (golden club), primula, ranunculus, rodgersia, sagittaria, stratiotes (water cactus), zantedeschia (arum lily).

Autumn

As the year advances, dead leaves should be gathered regularly and preparations made for the cold months ahead.

In autumn, lift a few of the smaller water hyacinths, pot these in soil fairly close together in a bowl, add a little water and store in a light, frost-free place.

Dredge fallen leaves from the pool, or better still, cover the water surface with mesh netting to trap them.

In mid-autumn feed the fish heavily with a protein food such as water fleas, worms, or proprietary foods. Cease feeding altogether at the end of late autumn.

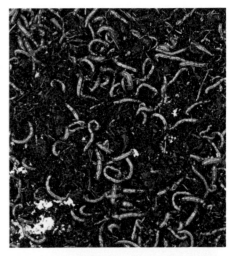

Cut down dead vegetation at the waterside.

In late autumn overhaul the pumps used for fountains and waterfalls. Remove submersible types from the water, clean and store dry.

Protect gunneras by cutting off leaves as soon as these are touched by frost and inverting them over plant crowns. Add a little hay or straw if the position is exposed.

In early autumn, gather materials for dried arrangements from bog and water plants: iris seedheads, grasses, reedmace, hydrangea flowers, and the like.

Lift a few plants of *Lobelia fulgens* and store in a cold frame all winter. They may go through satisfactorily outdoors, but this precaution safeguards the stock. Repeat with any plants you are doubtful about, or protect them with dry leaves over the crowns.

Above *Over-winter young and dwarf water-lilies by keeping in a frost-free place.*
Left Aponogeton distachys, *the water hawthorn, has white flowers.*

You can make a pool now, but avoid frosty weather. Leave the completed pool full of water all winter.

In mid-autumn plant fresh plants in the bog garden.

Lift miniature water-lilies in shallow rock pools, plant in loam in a bowl, and over-winter inside away from frost.

Plant bluebell and narcissus bulbs in the bog garden for extra colour.

Plants to enjoy in autumn or early winter
Aponogeton (water hawthorn), calla berries, cimicifuga (bugbane), decodon (for autumnal tints), eriophorum (cotton grass), *Gentiana asclepiadea*, hydrangea, kirengeshoma, lythrum, pernettya, schizostylis, sorbaria, typha (reed mace).

Winter
Some repair work can be done on warm days and steps taken to protect plants and fish against more severe weather.

Keep the pool full of water.
Float a ball or block of wood in the pool. If ice forms 2.5cm (1in) or more thick, pour boiling water over the ball and

Right *Winter tip: A rubber ball on the water of the pool.*

remove. Bale out 2.5cm (1in) of water and cover the hole with a thick sack. Top up with water after every thaw. Repeat as necessary.

Sow seeds of bog plants and aquatics early in the year, but keep under glass.

Dredge out leaves or any debris likely to rot in the pool.

Check doubtfully hardy bog plants and protect with cloches, or dry leaves and polythene.

Protect small rock plants with boards and straw matting.

Repair pools in frost-free weather.

Below *Repair concrete pools in early winter when there is no danger of frost.*

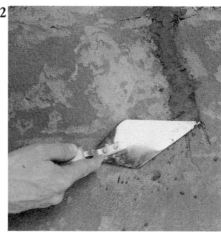

WATER PLANT GUIDE

Water plants can be both beautiful and practical: they bring colour and style to the most luxurious gardens and play an important part in ensuring that the pool itself is a healthy environment.

Having considered the various types of pool, how to make them, the fish that swim in them, and the various other creatures that breed in or are attracted to water, it is time to consider the plants.

For many gardeners, plants are the *raison d'être* of the water garden; they give it both distinction and charm. The range of plants that can be grown in and around the pool is considerable and often not fully exploited.

Mention a pool and most people immediately think of water-lilies, and it cannot be denied that these are the choicest aquatics to grow, but a well-planted pool will contain different types of plants. Besides the deep-water plants, having their roots completely submerged but the leaves and flowers floating on the surface, there should be submerged aquatics, floating plants, and the 'marginals' to grow at the edge of the pool.

Submerged aquatics

Some of these plants spend the whole of their lives submerged, and a few will even flower beneath the surface. Others may hover at or just below the surface, but at flowering time produce aerial stems carrying one or several blooms above the water. These differences are connected with their methods of pollination, for while the male spores of some reach the female flowers by water, others depend on wind or insects to achieve pollination.

Most submerged aquatics have soft foliage, usually cut or shredded into fine segments, through which water can flow without injury to the leaf blades. The plants are thus well adapted to water in all its moods, including running water and flooding. Because all submerged aquatics need carbon-dioxide for photosynthesis (the process by which plants convert light into energy), they utilize the gases breathed out by fish during respiration and therefore help to keep the water in balance. Conversely, fish must have oxygen and, since this is discharged into the pool by the plants as a by-product of photosynthesis, this also helps fish and various other types of animal life.

Because all submerged plants produce oxygen in this manner they are known as 'oxygenating plants' and will be found under that heading on page 275.

Floaters

Some aquatics spend their lives free and unanchored. During the growing season they float on the water and are carried hither and thither by its movement, a circumstance which accounts for their spread, particularly in the tropics where water hyacinths, water lettuces and salvinias (all susceptible to frost) are often a menace. Even in northern countries like Britain, duckweed can present problems.

Some floaters form 'turons' (winter buds) in autumn, a device which protects them from cold and ice. The turons then sink to the floor of the pool and overwinter in mud. When the water warms up in spring they grow again and rise to the surface.

The importance of floaters lies in the shade they cast, which is important to fish in summer, and helps to reduce algae, which need sunlight to thrive. Their tangled and dangling roots provide hiding places for myriads of small water insects and thus act as fish larders.

Marginal aquatics

As their name implies, marginal plants only need shallow water. The roots are submerged most of the time, while the leaves and flowers grow up and out of the water. Many marginal plants are highly ornamental, with attractive flowers or foliage. They break the flat outlines of a pool, relieving it of formality and, if carefully selected, provide long-term interest and a range of plant heights. Nearly all thrive in heavy loam and can be planted in spring or early summer.

Bog plants

This section includes a miscellany of plants that will survive in wet, boggy soil for some or part of the time, and plants that like to feel the influence of water without actually sitting in it. In other words they need damp but not waterlogged conditions. Many of

Well known for their large, rounded leaves and many-petalled, cup-shaped flowers, the water-lilies (Nymphaea varieties) are undoubted favourites in any garden pool.

these plants are frequently seen in borders, like *Iris sibirica*, trollius, and astilbes. Given sufficient moisture in summer they often do well in such situations, but when droughts occur the story is different. In the vicinity of a pool, which can be flooded over when necessary, or when grown in a bog garden, they never suffer privation and always make fine specimens.

Some bog plants have brilliant flowers, others have quaint practices such as catching insects in the case of sarracenias. There are even a few bulbs and trees that will live under conditions of poor drainage such as would kill most garden plants.

Deep water plants

Although it is always worth trying to find room for a range of deep water plants (see page 274), water-lilies are such attractive members of this group they will probably be the first plants pool owners will consider.

Water-lilies

The genus *Nymphaea* is widespread, with representation in most countries, particularly in the tropics although there is even one in Arctic Finland. As well as white and cream water-lilies there are pink, red, yellow and blue, most of them day bloomers but a few are night flowering. There is also a wide variation in flower sizes – from a tea plate down to miniatures small enough to slip through a wedding ring.

Water-lilies are also interesting historically, having been venerated as emblems of regeneration and purity since the times of the Pharaohs.

This symbolism was apparently linked with their annual emergence from the mud and slime of dried up pools, once they became refilled by the flood waters of the Nile. The esteem in which they were held by the Ancient Egyptians also led to their use in funeral wreaths and chaplets (this was particularly common during the 19th and 21st dynasties). Petals of *Nymphaea caerulea* were found with the mummies of both Rameses II and Amenhotep.

Many well-known symbols also have associations with water-lilies. According to Professor Goodyear (Grammar of the Lotus) the ramshorn motif of the Ionic capital owes its origin to their twisted sepals, and from that was derived the Greek fret, which doubled again became the swastika. This very early symbol, which is portrayed on many Egyptian murals and ornaments, represents light or darkness, good or evil, death or life – according to the directions assumed by the arms. Apart from such symbolical associations the starchy rhizomes of various water-lilies have been

consumed as food by Africans, North American Indians, and even Europeans in times of want. The Scots obtained a brown dye from the roots of *N. alba*, and the soft moist leaves are used in tropical countries for poultices.

The common white water-lily of Britain is *N. alba*, a vigorous plant that is able to take deeper water than most of the garden hybrids commonly sold for pools. In the 1800's a red sport of this species appeared in a lake in Sweden and became important as the first red form known to Europeans.

Credit for the wealth of colours now available is due to the tenacity and hybridizing genius of a Frenchman called Joseph Bory Latour Marliac. In 1858, reading an article in *La Revue du Jardin des Plants de Paris* about some new, brightly coloured tropical nymphaeas then growing at the Museum of Natural History, Marliac thought how marvellous it would be if the waterways of France could be planted with variously coloured, hardy water-lilies. Accordingly he started a hobby, which was to become the work of a lifetime, and set out to produce them.

The red form of *N. alba* was one of his early acquisitions, and was followed by a yellow, *N. mexicana* from Mexico, pinks from North America and various blue and red tropicals. Through the years Marliac worked on his water-lilies, crossing and recrossing the species and varieties until by the end of the century he was reaping rich rewards. Plant followed plant in quick succession until eventually the parentage of many became an enigma. Nor did he ever disclose his hybridizing methods and with his death in 1911 any prospect of discovering them vanished.

Nearly all the hardy water-lilies grown today owe their origin to Marliac's genius. Although he never achieved his ambition of producing a blue, hardy variety, he has left us a legacy of varieties which no-one will ever surpass.

Early water-lilies need heavy loam and should be planted in aquatic baskets as described on page 252.

When it comes to choosing varieties it is important to select kinds that are suitable both for the depth and available growing space. To make the choice easier, each variety described has the letter A, B or C (explained below) following the description to indicate its size and vigour:

A. *Vigorous varieties* for depths of 60-100cm (24-36in) and surface areas around 0.50-0.75sq m (5-8sq ft). For large ponds and lakes.

B. *Medium growers* for depths of 45-60cm (18-24in) and surfaces areas around 0.25–0.5 sq m (3–6 sq ft). Generally

Opposite *There is a wide range of water-lilies (*Nymphaea *spp.) to choose from, especially if you visit a specialist grower.*
1 N. lactea, *an attractive garden variety has white flowers with warm, golden centres.*
2 *'Gonnêre' is a handsome white, with double flowers. It is suitable for water up to 38cm (15in) deep.*
3 *'Sunrise', is one of the finest yellow water-lilies and is best in water up to 60cm (24in) deep.*
4 *The more tender varieties boast some of the most beautiful flowers (here, 'Director G. T. Moore') but they need special care through the winter months.*
5 *The 'Laydekeri' hybrids include many varieties listed either in their main colour groups or as named forms such as 'Laydekeri Fulgens', shown here.*
6 N. Amabilis *a variably coloured water-lily, has pink-flushed outer petals.*
7 *The delightful, dwarf yellow flowers of* N. pygmaea *'Helvola' here contrast well with those of another charming small water lily.*

suitable for small and medium pools.

C. *Small and miniature* varieties for 23-38cm (9-15in) depths. Suitable for tubs, rock pools and small prefabricated pools, but may need some protection in winter for the shallower depths.

Selecting water-lilies

There are many water-lily varieties, some rare, some common, some prolific bloomers, some shy flowering. The following varieties, graded according to colour, are normally available from specialist growers. The letters at the end of the descriptions refer to the planting depths mentioned in the previous code. When two numbers are quoted it indicates that the variety is adaptable to both sets of conditions. The letter N before the name denotes the genus *Nymphaea,* and is followed by the species name.

White
N. alba. The common white water-lily, only suitable for very large areas. A.
'Albatross'. White with gold stamens, young leaves purple, turning green with age. B.
N. candida. Small flowers, very hardy, white with red stigmas. C.
'Caroliniana Nivea'. Fragrant, larger than preceding. C.
'Gladstoniana'. Possibly the best white, very large flowers, 15-20cm (6-8in) across with rich, golden stamens. A.
'Gonnêre'. Squat, double-white with prominent green sepals. A/B.
N. 'Marliacea Albida'. Popular white, very free flowering; slightly fragrant. B.
N. odorata. The fragrant white water-lily of North America. Medium-sized flowers. B.
N. pygmaea alba. Small white flowers under 5cm (2in) across. Can be raised from seed. Needs shallow water (around 15cm/6in). C.
N. tuberosa 'Richardsonii'. Globular white flowers with green sepals; vigorous. B/C.

Pink
'Amabilis'. Star-like, soft pink flowers, deepening to salmon-rose. B.
'Brakleyi Rosea'. Splendid deep rose-pink, free flowering and fragrant. B.
'Colossea'. Soft pinkish-white, very large flowers. Vigorous. A.
'Fire Crest'. Wide, deep-pink, fragrant flowers with prominent-red-tipped stamens. B/C.
N. 'Laydekeri Lilacea'. Very free flowering, soft rosy-lilac deepening with age to rose. B/C.
N. 'Marliacea Carnea'. Pale flesh-pink, very shapely; reliable and free flowering. A/B.
N. 'Marliacea Rosea'. Similar to preceding but with richer pink colouring which sometimes does not develop fully until the second season. Fragrant. A/B.
'Masaniello'. A popular variety with sweetly scented, large, cup-shaped, deep rose flowers. B/C.
'Mme Wilfron Gonnêre'. Large, double, rose-pink. Not so free flowering as some varieties. B.
'Mrs Richmond'. Large, globular, rich pink blooms, deepening in colour towards centre. B.
N. odorata 'Turicensis'. Soft rose, free flowering, sweetly scented. C.
N. odorata 'W. B. Shaw'. Flowers cup-shaped, delicate pink, deeper inside. B/C.
'Rose Arey'. An outstanding, rich rose-pink with large star-like flowers that have slightly incurved petals; fragrant and free flowering. B.
N. tuberosa 'Rosea'. Vigorous and fragrant. Soft pink. A.

Red
'Attraction'. Large, glowing, garnet-red flowers 17-20cm (7-8in) across, tipped with white. A/B.
'Charles de Meurville'. A vigorous variety with wine-red flowers produced over a long season. A/B.
'Conqueror'. Flowers blood-red with white inside the sepals; these often stay open at night. B.
'Escarboucle'. Excellent ruby-red with huge blooms as large as tea plates; reliable and consistent. B.
'Froebeli'. Deep wine-red flowers, free flowering. C.
'James Brydon'. One of the best, and extremely free flowering. Blooms rich carmine-red, sitting squat in the water. Young leaves purple. B.
N. 'Laydekeri Purpurata'. Extremely free flowering and a great favourite for tubs and small ponds. Medium-sized, wine-red flowers. B/C.
'Newton'. Star-shaped blooms held slightly above the water, rosy vermilion with orange stamens. B.
'René Gerard'. Rich rose, star-shaped flowers up to 23cm (9in) across. These are flecked and striped with red crimson. Free flowering. B.
N. pygmaea 'Rubra'. Rose-pink flowers 6cm (2½in) across, deepening to red with age; foliage green. C.
'William Falconer'. Very dark red with yellow stamens. B.

Yellow
'Colonel A. J. Welch'. Very vigorous, but a

The delicate pink, cup-shaped blooms of N. odorata 'W. B. Shaw' are set off by showy, golden stamens.

shy bloomer. Flowers canary-yellow held just above the water. A.

N. 'Marliacea Chromatella'. Soft yellow flowers of fine shape; bright yellow stamens. One of the best yellows. Foliage chocolate-blotched. B.

'Moorei'. Very similar to preceding but foliage spotted rather than blotched. B.

N. odorata 'Sulphurea'. Small, deep yellow blooms, often standing just clear of the water; blotched leaves. C.

N. pygmaea 'Helvola'. A little charmer, soft, sulphur-yellow, 5cm (2in) across; maroon-blotched leaves. Very free flowering if left undisturbed. Grow in water 10-15cm (4-6in) deep.

'Sunrise'. Deep sunshine-yellow, the richest in colour, large and slightly fragrant. Foliage green flecked brown, red beneath. B.

Variable colours

'Graziella'. Reddish-yellow flowers, becoming paler with age; foliage variegated with purple. C.

'Indiana'. Flowers open apricot-red, gradually darkening to rich copper-red; foliage suffused with purple. B/C.

'Paul Hariot'. Flowers first apricot-yellow then orange-pink and finally almost red; maroon-spotted foliage. Very free flowering. B/C.

'Sioux'. Soft yellow suffused with red, deepening to reddish-copper.

'Solfaterre'. Flowers star-shaped, yellow flushed rose; foliage green mottled with maroon. B/C.

All these hardy water-lilies can be increased by dividing the tubers in early spring. The bulk of the old roots should be discarded, retaining only the young crowns with 7.5-10cm (3-4in) of new tuber.

Very small pieces can be grown on to flower the following season. Pot these in plain loam and stand them in a deep bowl of water with the crowns barely covered. Keep in a light place under cover. Re-pot if necessary and increase the water depth but do not plant outside until the following spring.

Tropical water-lilies are only rarely available in Britain and they are not easy to grow. Our summers are not sufficiently warm for their comfort and, even when

The carmine-red flowers of 'James Brydon' float on water almost completely covered by its maroon-splashed leaves.

started in tanks of shallow water under glass, when put outside and temperatures drop lower than 21°C (70°F), the plants stop growing.

It is also necessary to lift them in autumn when they die down, and store the tubers under cover all winter.

If you want tropical nymphaeas – and they are undeniably beautiful – with blue, purple, and yellow varieties as well as reds, pinks and whites, you will need an indoor pool, with extra heating in cold weather.

In many respects they are quite different from hardy water-lilies. The flowers stand on stiff stems well above the water surface, the rootstock is smaller and almost bulb-like, the new plant growing on top and replacing the old after a period of rest. Most tropical water-lilies produce viable seed – whereas nearly all the hardy varieties are sterile; many are richly scented; others bloom at night and some species and varieties are viviparous, developing baby plantlets on their leaves, like the well-known house plant *Tolmiea menziesii.*

Other deep water plants

Nuphars, sometimes known as pond lilies, are extremely hardy and vigorous aquatics, similar to nymphaeas but inferior. The European, including British, *N. lutea* is often called brandy bottle because of the vinous scent of its small bright yellow flowers. It produces two kinds of leaves, oval to heart-shaped, leathery floating leaves and – in deep or running water – crisped, translucent leaves.

Nuphars are useful for deep water, running streams or shady ponds – all places where nymphaeas are unlikely to succeed. But they are rampant, so plant with care.

Below Nuphar lutea *is also known as the yellow water-lily or, more popularly, the brandy bottle.*

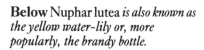

Below right *Water milfoil* (Myriophyllum spicatum), *with its feathery floating leaves, is an excellent oxygenating plant.*

The only nuphars worth growing are the less invasive *N. advena* 'Variegata' which has cream and green, variegated leaves, and *N. japonica rubrotincta* with red-tipped stamens and orange-scarlet flowers.

The water hawthorn, or caltha *Aponogeton distachyus*, is a charmer from South Africa with floating, strap-like leaves and vanilla-scented white flowers with jet-black anthers. These are grouped in forked inflorescences that float on or just above the surface of the water.

The flowering season of the water hawthorn is long, from mid or late spring until autumn; I have even picked blooms on Christmas Day and occasionally in March. The chestnut-sized tubers should be planted in loam and will adapt to 45cm (18in) of water but flower better in 15-23cm (6-9in). This is a plant for every pond, large or small.

Oxygenating plants

The importance of oxygenating plants has already been stressed but, because their ability to produce oxygen is largely linked with their rate of growth, it is important to select efficient kinds.

There is a new and growing practice by dealers of offering plants which are not submerged aquatics, but bog or even house plants. Usually these are recommended for aquaria, where they may look pretty through the glass sides for a few weeks, but they will not oxygenate the water.

Aquaria of course can have oxygen supplied by pumps, and pools by fountains, but oxygenating plants have other functions. They provide somewhere for fish to lay their eggs and are a sanctuary for the young fry. They also play a useful role in keeping down algae and other weeds.

Really efficient oxygenators are the starworts *Callitriche* spp., which remain submerged for much of the time but come to the surface to produce their insignificant flowers. They are easily recognized at such times by their small, light green, floating leaves, which form starry masses. The autumn starwort is most effective at that season and the spring starwort in spring, so it is advisable to stock both.

Elodea canadensis or Canadian pondweed, with close whorls of small leaves on branching stems and the larger, curly-leaved *Lagarosiphon major* (often sold as *Elodea crispa*) are two splendid oxygenators. They are hardy and submerged at all seasons. Milfoils (*Myriophyllum spp.*) with needle-fine leaves arranged in whorls, are also effective, as are certain pondweeds like *Potamogeton crispus* and *P. densus*.

Several oxygenators come to the surface

to flower, like the water crowfoot *(Ranunculus aquatilis)* with small white, starry buttercup flowers; the water violet *(Hottonia palustris)*, which produces whorls of pale purple flowers on 7.5-10cm (3-4in) spikes; and the bladderwort *(Utricularia vulgaris)*, a native insectivorous plant that traps water fleas and in summer produces spikes of yellow, snapdragon-like flowers.

Floaters

This is not a large group and fewer still are hardy. The smaller kinds are often eaten by fishes, which with duckweed is an advantage. There are several kinds of duckweeds, none of which should ever be introduced into ornamental ponds.

The frogbit *(Hydrocharis morsus-ranae)* has rosettes of fleshy and rounded floating leaves, each about 2.5cm (1in) across, and with trailing roots and white, three-petalled flowers.

Fairy floating mosses (*Azolla* spp.) do

Hottonia palustris, *the water violet, can be relied upon to oxygenate the water and is both attractive and practical in a garden pool.*

Despite its delightful flowers, the water hyacinth (Eichhornia crassipes) *is notorious for rampant growth that can quickly choke large stretches of water. It is not a hardy plant, however, and cold weather will check this growth naturally.*

indeed look like pale green mosses in summer, but turn red in autumn before most are killed by frost. Generally a few survive between the stems of marginal plants, however, and maintain the stock.

The water soldier or water cactus *(Stratiotes aloides)* bobs about like a pineapple top just beneath the water, but thrusts its way upwards to flower. The blooms are white and three-petalled, male and female on separate plants.

The water hyacinth *(Eichhornia crassipes)* is fortunately, perhaps, not hardy in Britain, for under congenial conditions it spreads rapidly by means of runners. It forms large mats of smooth round leaves, with sausage-like swollen leaf stalks full of spongy tissue that keep the plant afloat. Spectacular spikes of showy blue flowers with gold and dark blue peacock markings on the upper petals appear in summer. Long black roots about 30cm (12in) long, hang down in the water and keep the plants balanced. If you aim to grow this plant do not put it outside until mid-June when all danger of frost has passed, and always overwinter a few small plants in a bowl inside to retain the stock.

Two other tender floaters are sometimes grown in small pools and overwintered in the same manner. They are the water lettuce *(Pistia stratiotes)*, which does indeed resemble a velvety miniature lettuce, and the water velvets *(Salvinia* spp.), which are fern allies with distinctive ear-shaped, unwettable leaves covered with fine silky hairs.

Marginals

Marginal aquatics are mainly for decorative purposes, making an attractive setting for a pond in the same way that trees and shrubs embellish a garden. Accordingly they should be planted with a view to providing long-term interest and never allowed to become so rampant that they hide the water. You might find it useful to look at the seasonal advice on pp. 264–267 to ensure that you have marginals that will provide flowers or other features of interest spread over most of the season.

Marginal plants can be grown in pockets or troughs built into the sides of artificial pools, or in aquatic baskets (as for water-lilies) or similar containers. They can even be planted in soil at the sides of a natural pond. A depth of 5-10cm (2-4in), and a plain loam compost, is suitable for most. It is advisable to cover the soil with a dressing of washed shingle to stop fish rooting into it.

Strong and rampant growers will need lifting and dividing from time to time – approximately every third year. Nearly all the plants in this section can be increased

by division in spring; exceptions are noted in the text.

Acorus calamus, the sweet flag, is so called because its iris-like leaves and rootstock are highly aromatic when bruised. This circumstance, in Tudor times, led to its leaves being used (instead of rushes) for strewing floors in wealthy homes. The powdered root is still employed for scenting hair and tooth powders, and as an insect repellent. Calamus oil, distilled from the plant, is used to flavour various kinds of beer as well as gin and bitters.

The sweet flag, in spite of its iris appearance, is an aroid and at flowering time, short conical inflorescences (looking like miniature cattle horns), are produced near the tips of the flower stems. The species grows 60-100cm (24-36in) tall but is best represented by the white and green variegated form 'Variegata'. *A. gramineum* is dwarfer at 20-30cm (8-12in) and very slender, forming compact grassy tufts, either in wet soil or very shallow water. It, too, is most worthwhile when planted in its variegated form.

Water plantains *(Alisma* spp.) have long stemmed, plantain-like leaves and whorls of tiny, three-petalled, rosy-lilac flowers on pyramidal 30-45cm (12-18in) stems. Unfortunately they are inveterate seeders, so the old flower heads should be removed regularly before the seed is shed. The best for water gardens are *A. gramineum* with oblong leaves, or the great water plantain *A. plantago-aquatica,* for large stretches of water. Neither species will flower well except in very shallow water.

The flowering rush, *Butomus umbellatus,* is a British native occasionally found near stream edges or in wet pastures. It grows 60-100cm (24-36in) tall with narrow, smooth green leaves, which are purplish when young, and umbels of pink three-petalled flowers. It makes quite a show when grouped in water 5-15cm (2-6in) deep. The baked roots are esteemed as a vegetable in Northern Asia.

Calla palustris is the bog arum. Although unrelated, except in a broad family sense, it looks like the arum lily *(Zantedeschia),* with small white flowers and shiny, dark green, heart-shaped leaves. If pollinated, which is carried out by water snails, the flowers go on to produce globular clusters of red berries. The bog arum is a scrambling plant with creeping rhizomes. It never grows more than about 23cm (9in) high, but wends its way skilfully between shallow water and wet soil; a circumstance which makes it a useful plant for masking the edges of artificial pools.

Marsh marigold and kingcup, or 'water blob' in northern Britain, are all names for

Above left Caltha palustris, *'Flore Pleno',* is the double form of the marsh marigold (**above**): *both plants thrive in moist conditions and will flourish at the water's edge.*

Caltha palustris. It is one of our handsomest spring flowers, bearing masses of 2.5cm (1in) bright golden, buttercup-like flowers on branching stems, and entire, rounded, tooth-edged leaves. During the last century the young stems and leaves were apparently eaten by country people as spring greens and the flowers buds were pickled as a substitute for capers. But the sap has the poisonous constituents of buttercups and this is not recommended. Animals tend to avoid marsh marigolds, which is also a strong warning against the idea.

The double marigold 'Flore Pleno', or 'Monstrosa' as it is known in the United States, is particularly free flowering, usually masking the leaves and stems with dozens of golden, button-like flowers.

Most marsh marigolds bloom around mid-spring, but the taller *C. polypetala* blooms several weeks later. This is a particularly fine plant with wide spreading branches carrying the blooms. It reaches about 1m (3ft). There are also white species such as *C. leptosepala,* but these do far better in damp soil than water.

Cotula coronopifolia, a pretty little plant that associates charmingly with blue water forget-me-nots, is only recommended for wet soil or shallow water in a warm, sheltered pool. Since the round golden flowers resemble the middle disc of a daisy – with the white outer florets removed – it is commonly known as brass buttons. It grows about 15-23cm (6-9in) high and the smooth, toothed leaves smell of lemons when crushed. The plant is an annual but in a warm summer flowers freely and scatters its seed, so maintaining the stock.

The swamp loosestrife *(Decodon verticillatus)* is valued for its autumn colouring. It is a shrubby North American plant of 1-1.8m (3-6ft) with narrow, willow-like leaves in whorls along the stems. In summer these are green but become rich crimson before falling in autumn. Tiny pink flowers of a tubular shape nestle in the leaf axils.

In late summer the cotton grasses *(Eriophorum angustifolium* and *E. vaginatum)* flower and these look like blobs of snow dangling between the heathers and mosses of the native bogs. They are widespread in the arctic so naturally hardy, but never tall. They are normally between 15-45cm (6-18in) tall, with grooved, sedge-like leaves and prominent clusters of nodding spikelets, packed with silky white hairs. This down was once used in Scotland as well as northern Europe for stuffing cushions and pillows.

Glyceria maxima, the manna grass, also has some economic importance in parts of eastern Europe on account of its seeds, which are greedily taken by geese and ducks, while the grass itself is relished by horses and other domesic animals. However, the only kind attractive enough for water gardens is the variegated form, correctly *G. maxima* variegata, although frequently sold as *G. spectabilis*. This very striking plant has broad, green, yellow and white stripes and suffusions on the leaves,

as well as touches of rosy-pink on the young foliage. It grows 45-60cm (18-24in) high, with taller plumes of brown grassy flowers in late summer. To retain the variegation it must be propagated by division in spring and not by seed.

Houttuynia cordata is a strange little plant, 15-25cm (6-10in) high with bluish-green, heart shaped leaves which when bruised emit a strong, rather unpleasant smell of oranges. The little white flowers have cone-shaped centres and there is a double form 'Plena'. Both are suitable for wet soil or shallow water, but they are invasive, spreading by means of creeping root-stocks, so they need to be kept in check quite ruthlessly.

Hypericum elodes, the marsh St John's wort is a lowly aquatic relative of the rose of Sharon and useful for masking pool edges since it is equally at home in boggy soil or

Yellow flags (Iris pseudacorus) *and the spring bloom of rhododendrons make a bright contrast with the more sombre hues of distant conifers.*

shallow water. It grows 15-23cm (6-9in) high and has leafy stems with small hairy foliage and soft yellow flowers.

Irises are well known garden and bulbous plants but there are also several that are true aquatics. Our native yellow flag, *Iris pseudacorus*, with rich yellow flowers on 60-100cm (24-36in) stems is one, and has varieties with primrose-yellow blooms like 'Bastardii' and one called 'Variegata' which is magnificent early in the year because of the heavy suffusion of gold on its foliage. This gives it a real sunshine appearance, but unfortunately the display does not last for very long and by mid-summer all the leaves become a more conventional plain green.

The yellow flag is said to have been the plant chosen by Louis VII for the French royal emblem during the Crusades, when it was called after him Fleur de Louis, then fleur-de-luce or fleur-de-lis. The roasted seeds have even been used as a substitute for coffee in times of scarcity.

Iris laevigata from Japan is one of the best blue-flowered water plants available and should be included in all planting schemes. It grows about 60-75cm (24-30in) tall with long grassy leaves and rich blue flowers with golden claw markings on their falls. It has produced a number of forms including a white called 'Alba'; 'Variegata' with white stripes on the foliage; 'Colchesteri' white with deep blue patterns and fall edgings; and 'Rose Queen', a hybrid with *I. kaempferi*, which is soft rose-pink. All these irises grow well in depths of 5-12.5cm (2-5in) of water and can be increased by division after flowering.

Most rushes are weedy plants not worthy of a place in small ornamental ponds. There is just one exception: the corkscrew rush, *Juncus effusus* 'Spiralis', which is fun to grow on account of its 45cm (18in) round, pithy stems, which are twisted like corkscrews for the whole of their length.

Ludwigias are creeping plants with smooth simple leaves, purple on the undersides, soft stems, and four-petalled yellow flowers. They can be used at pool margins and are also popular for aquaria.

The bog bean *(Menyanthes trifoliata)* takes its name from the three-parted leaves which are shaped something like those of a runner bean, although much thicker. They grow about 23cm (9in) high from creeping root-stocks, which also support clusters of pink and white flowers with pretty fringed petals. Like the bog arum it makes a good marginal plant for shallow water and for rather boggy soil.

Water forget-me-nots *(Myosotis palustris)* can be raised from seed and once established renew themselves naturally.

The deep blue 'Mermaid' is one of the best.

Nymphoides peltata is the water fringe, a trailer with clusters of golden, poppy-like flowers borne just clear of the water. The 5cm (2in) round, floating leaves have crinkled edges and are heavily mottled with chocolate blotches. The plant tends to run across water rather than grow upright but looks very pretty when in flower.

Orontium aquaticum is known as the golden club on account of its aroid flowers like white pokers with golden tips. It is an adaptable plant and will either grow in deep water, when the large, oblong leaves, waxy surfaced and velvety green, will float, or in shallow water when the stems toughen and leaves and flowers thrust upwards to a height of 30-45cm (12-18in). It must have deep soil and full sun to thrive and can be propagated from seeds as well as by division.

The North American arrow arums have, as their name implies, glossy arrow-shaped leaves and arum-like flowers. In *Peltandra sagittifolia* these are white and, if pollinated by insects, go on to produce red berries; whereas *P. virginica* has green flowers and green berries. They grow 30-50cm (12-

The green arrow arum (Peltandra virginica) *is a handsome, marsh-loving perennial with deep green, arrow-shaped leaves.*

Above *The pickerel weed* (Pontederia cordata) *has flowers that resemble miniature delphiniums.*

Opposite above Sagittaria sagittifolia, *also known as arrowhead, because of the shape of its aerial leaves, has white flowers with a deep purple centre.*

Opposite below Anemone narcissiflora *has white or cream-coloured flowers, occasionally flushed with pink.*

20in) tall according to soil conditions, which, for the best results, should be deep and fertile.

The pickerel weed *(Pontederia cordata)*, is an outstanding aquatic for late summer and a plant that rarely creates problems through being rampant. Yet it is a strong and upright grower with smooth and shining, heart-shaped leaves on long 45-60cm (18-24in) stems topped with 15cm (6in) spikes of closely packed, soft blue flowers set against a white, cottonwool-like background.

The seeds of pickerel weed were once enjoyed by American Indians, but are nowadays greedily taken by duck from areas where it grows plentifully, like quiet backwaters of the River Hudson. It is quite happy in a garden pond with about 15cm (6in) of water above its crowns.

Potentilla palustris, the marsh cinquefoil, is another creeping plant for pool margins; not particularly exciting but useful to cover bare, muddy areas. It has strawberry-like leaves, purple flowers and grows to a height of about 23-30cm (9-12in).

Preslia cervina, a small plant of 30cm (12in), with tiny, lance-shaped leaves and whorls of pinkish-mauve flowers, is chiefly remarkable for its strong, minty smell. It needs wet soil or very shallow water.

Most buttercups need damp soil but the spearwort, *Ranunculus lingua* 'Grandiflora', will take standing water several inches in depth. It is a handsome aquatic 60-100cm (24-36in) high, with large 7.5cm (3in) golden buttercups borne on wide, branching stems and very large, heart-shaped leaves 60-100cm (24-36in) across. It blooms intermittently through the summer.

Sagittarias are called arrowheads because of the shape of their aerial leaves. In running water these are grass-like and completely submerged. There are many kinds, some hardy, some tender, many quite small and a few large and decorative (although usually tender in Britain). Only one is striking enough to be planted in the pool and that is a double form of our native *S. sagittifolia* called 'Flore Pleno'. This has pure white rosettes so tightly packed together that the inflorescence bears some resemblance to a white double stock. It grows around 38-45cm (15-18in) high but is not as robust as the single species, so grow it in shallow water and a sheltered corner.

The lizard's tails *(Saururus cernuus* and *S. chinensis)* are curious little plants with thick aromatic rhizomes, heart-shaped leaves and nodding 10-12.5cm (4-5in) spikes of fragrant white flowers resembling little tails. Height is 30-60cm (12-24in).

The bullrush family of *Scirpus* is a large one, widely distributed all over the world on wet moors, bogs, and in streams. In Britain, the common name is often erroneously applied to *Typha* spp. (see below) but *Scirpus lacustris* is the true bullrush. At one time it was widely used for mats and chair seats and also eaten when young as a vegetable. The round, pithy stems are common in old pools but too invasive for gardens, where the only kinds worth growing are the zebra rush *(S. tabernaemontani* 'Zebrinus') which has its stems alternately and horizontally banded like porcupine quills in green and white, and *S. tabernaemontani* 'Albescens' with cream stripes running vertically up the stems. Both are extremely ornamental and can be kept colourful by removing the odd green rush if it appears.

Typhas, the reed maces are well-known aquatics with flat, sword-shaped leaves and oblong, poker-shaped heads of velvety brown flowers. These are often cut for dried flower arrangements in winter. The larger kinds should never be planted in an ornamental pool, otherwise they will soon oust every other plant. There is really only one that can be safely introduced and that is the dwarf species *T. minima*; it grows only 30-60cm (12-24in) high and has 7.5-12.5cm (3-5in) flower spikes. It is non-invasive and quite attractive for a small pool or as a tub. It is also suitable for dried flower arrangements.

The brooklime *(Veronica beccabunga)* is a rare native with blue forget-me-not flowers and smooth, elliptical leaves on 23-30cm (9-12in) stems. It flowers all through the early summer and makes a good associate for any of the other short aquatics like bog arums and bog beans.

Bog plants

Bog plants will increase the possibilities still further, and aid the transition between the pond and the rest of the garden. Some of the plants included here are well known as border plants, others are specialized bog plants that you will probably have to search out from a specialist supplier.

The genus *Anemone* is large and varied. Most species need well-drained and sunny situations, but there are some more suited to the damp soil of a bog garden. The following may be raised from seed or propagated by division in spring.

Anemone narcissiflora, grows to about 60cm (24in) and with its branching heads of white buttercup-like flowers bears some resemblance to an early summer Japanese anemone. *A. rivularis,* also about 60cm (24in) high has branched stems bearing white flowers with blue anthers and blue outsides. *A. virginiana,* the North American thimbleweed, grows 30-45cm (12-18in) high and has deeply cut leaves and a few white or greenish flowers.

The goat's beard *(Aruncus dioicus,* also known as *A. sylvester* and *Spiraea aruncus)* is one of the most imposing and, indeed, noble plants for the boggy margin of a pond. It produces heavy trusses of creamy white flowers, up to 1.8m (6ft) with a rich scent of hay, and deeply cut leaves on stems 1.2m (4ft) long. The seed heads may be used in dried flower arrangements. The plants are happy in moist situations in sun or partial shade and may be propagated by division in spring.

Astilbes are long-lived perennials that remain in flower for many weeks and, even when over, the dried seed heads are attractive for winter arrangements. The flowers are borne in tapering plumes and there are pink, crimson, and white varieties. The compound leaves, rather like those on a strawberry plant, make excellent ground cover and show off the feathery flower spikes to perfection. Astilbes grow well in

The astilbe hybrid 'White Queen' is a first-class plant for moist soils, bog gardens or pool-sides.

any good soil in sun or light shade provided they always have plenty of water around their roots.

Named varieties of astilbe are easily propagated by division; the species may be raised from seed. Many hybrids, to which several species have contributed, are grouped under the collective name of *A x arendsii*. They vary in height from 0.6-1.2m (2-4ft) down to 30-45cm (12-18in). Among the taller varieties are 'White Gloria'; 'Erica', bright pink; 'Bremen', salmon-crimson; 'Granat', deep crimson; and 'Koblenz', salmon. Short varieties include 'Praecox Alba', white; 'Sprite', soft pink; and the very late flowering, 'Serenade', clear pink. The white-flowered species *A. thunbergii*, has a bold, erect habit and does well in light shade.

Brunnera macrophylla, often catalogued as *Anchusa myosotidiflora*, is a splendid ground cover plant for a moist situation. It has rough, heart-shaped leaves and sprays of blue flowers like large forget-me-nots. It seeds freely and can be invasive unless checked. There is a variegated form.

The bugbanes, *(Cimicifuga* spp.), have strongly scented leaves reputed to discourage bugs, but are generally grown for their white feathery plumes of late summer flowers. These are carried on leafy stems about 1.5-1.8m (5-6ft) high. The deeply cut and divided leaves are attractive all summer. *C. racemosa* and *C. simplex*, with varieties of the last such as 'Elstead Variety' or 'White Pearl', are the best choice for small gardens.

The charming meadowsweet of watery meadows is *Filipendula ulmaria.* This attractive plant with its divided leaves and 60-100cm (24-36in) branching plumes of fragant, creamy flowers is beautiful enough to bring into the garden, along with its

varieties 'Variegata' with gold-splashed leaves and the golden-foliaged 'Aurea'. There are also pink-flowered species among which the North American *F. rubra* 'Venusta', which grows to 1.2-1.5m (4-5ft), and has fragrant, rosy flowers, is a particularly fine example.

Gentians are usually associated with rock gardens but some thrive in soil that is fairly moist at all times, like the drier areas of the bog garden. The willow gentian, *Gentiana asclepiadea*, with long willow-like leaves, has arching stems 60cm (24in) long with rich blue trumpet flowers; there is also an attractive white variety.

Gentiana lutea, the great yellow gentian, is an erect leafy perennial 1.2-1.8m (4-6ft) high. It has large, broadly ovate leaves and dense clusters of 2.5cm (1in) yellow flowers towards the ends of the stems. The root is used medicinally and in the preparation of vermouth.

No plant is more impressive at the boggy margin of a large pool than *Gunnera manicata.* It is a Brazilian species with the largest entire leaves of any land plant. These bear some resemblance to a giant rhubarb and can be 1.8-2.4m (6-8ft) across on stems 1.5-3m (5-10ft) high. Greenish-brown flowers appear in early summer in spikes which bear a strong resemblance to giant bottle brush cleaners. They are usually 1-1.2m (3-4ft) long. In winter the crowns of the plants must be protected from frost by cutting the leaves and inverting these over the crowns, adding a covering of straw or leaves in very exposed situations. *G. magellanica,* from the Falkland Islands and Patagonia, is a mat-forming species a mere 7.5cm (3in) high, which makes a good ground cover plant.

Although the hostas, or plantain lilies (formerly known as funkias) will grow happily in any reasonably fertile soil in sun or shade they are happiest and look best in semi-shaded moist soil by the side of water. There they make large-leaved imposing plants. They are herbaceous perennials, easily propagated by division in spring, although it is best to clip off sections from the outside of the clumps in order to avoid disturbing the parent plants.

Plantain lilies are mainly grown for their striking foliage, which may be light or dark green or gloriously variegated, edged or striped with white or golden yellow. They also have attractive spikes of flowers. These may be white, lilac to violet or rosy purple and are often sweetly scented. There are many species and varieties available including *H. fortunei*, green, with varieties *H.f.* 'Albopicta', with yellow leaves edged with green, and *H.f.* 'Marginatoa-alba', green with white-edged leaves; *H.*

sieboldiana has huge, glaucous green leaves and there are various other varieties with white leaf margins.

Mention busy Lizzies *(Impatiens)* and most of us think of the colourful, tender species *I. sultanii* and *I. holstii* and their hybrids and varieties. While these are easily raised from seed and look charming in a moist border beside the pond, they do have to be planted out each year, after all danger of frost is past.

Quite hardy however, is the giant balsam, *I. roylei* (syn. *I. glandulifera)* from the Himalayas, which is also known – like our native *I. noli-tangere* – as touch-me-not because, at a certain stage of ripeness, if you touch the pointed tip of the seed pod it will explode and scatter its seeds over an area of several feet. At a later stage, of course, it will do this naturally, a circumstance that has allowed it to spread along many river banks and streamsides, particularly in Wales and the south of England. The plant, which is a hardy annual, grows 1.2-1.8m (4-6ft) tall with thick, succulent stems carrying oval leaves and groups of large 5cm (2in) pink, red, crimson, or white flowers in the upper leaf axils.

Irises are almost indispensable for boggy margins and among the most outstanding are the many forms of the clematis-flowered *Iris kaempferi* from Japan. These like rich, lime-free soil and plenty of water during the growing season, but drier conditions in winter. Indeed they can be grown very successfully in an ordinary garden border if they are kept moist by flooding water over them in any dry spell in summer. The flowers are unique among irises in that the falls (popularly called petals) are held horizontally and so look something like a large clematis. There are white, cream, yellow, blue, violet, crimson, and reddish-purple forms, also many bicoloured varieties, and various doubles. They grow from 60-100cm (24-36in) and are propagated by division immediately after flowering.

These irises are sometimes confused with the truly aquatic *I. laevigata* varieties, but can easily be distinguished by feeling the leaves. Those of *I. kaempferi* have a prominent mid-rib, whereas *I. laevigata* leaves are uniformly flat.

Iris sibirica is one of those adaptable plants, able to do well in moist soil or dry. No special conditions are necessary except sun, but nowhere do they look better than at the water's edge, especially when duplicated by reflection. The plants form neat, tufted clumps of 60-100cm (24-36in) with grassy leaves and small, shapely flowers in various shades of blue as well as white and purple. Good varieties are

'Ottawa', bright blue; 'Roger Perry', deep blue; 'Alba', white; 'Helen Astor', rosy-red; and 'Caesar', rich purple. *I. versicolor* needs moist soil and sun and associates well with *I. sibirica.* It grows 60cm (24in) tall and has purplish-red flowers, deep wine red in the form *I.v.* 'Kermesina'.

Kirengeshoma palmata from Japan, commonly known as yellow waxbells, flowers late in the year just when the garden is beginning to lose its floral charm. It is happy in deep, moist soil, in light or deep shade. It grows to 1-1.2m (3-4ft). The leaves are shaped like those of a maple on black stems, while the soft yellow flowers, 5cm (2in) long and shaped like shuttlecocks, hang down in loose sprays. It is propagated by seed or division but resents root disturbance, so great care is necessary with the planting.

All the ligularias favour very moist ground, otherwise the foliage quickly flags. They have daisy-like flowers of yellow or orange but are also grown for their leaves, which may be deeply cut into finger-like segments in the 1.5m (5ft) Chinese *L. przewalskii*; large and heart-shaped in the 1.2m (4ft) *L. dentata* (also known as *Senecio clivorum)*; or kidney-shaped in the small, 1m (3ft) *L. hodgsonii.*

Vivid scarlet, perennial lobelias make a spendid and long-lasting display in a boggy waterside area. Three species, with their varieties and some hybrids, are commonly grown and all reach a height of about 1m (3ft). *L. cardinalis*, the cardinal flower, has rosettes of green leaves and brilliant scarlet

Below *The clematis-flowered* Japanese Iris kaempferi *flourishes near water.*

Bottom *Valued for its large, decorative leaves, the hosta, or plantain lily, boasts a range of foliage effects, including variegated patterns of green, silver and gold.*

flowers; *L. fulgens* has crimson stems and reddish leaves as well as scarlet flowers but is not reliably hardy. Accordingly, one should lift the plants and overwinter them under cover or else root a few from cuttings and keep these in a cold frame.

The blue cardinal flower *L. syphilitica* has dense spikes of blue flowers rather smaller than the others mentioned; there is also a white variety and hybrids with violet or crimson-violet flowers.

Lysichiton, often but erroneously called skunk cabbage (the true owner of this name is *Symplocarpus foetidus)*, shares with that plant unpleasantly scented flowers. There are two species, of which the North American *L. americanum* is the most arresting. The flowers come first, huge yellow arums each about 30cm (12in) high and are followed by quite massive, rich green leaves, up to 1.2m (4ft) high and 30cm (12in) across. The plant accordingly needs plenty of room, and does equally well in shallow water or wet boggy ground in sun. *L. camtschatcense* is similar but with pure white, rather smaller flowers and has no unpleasant scent. Propagation is usually by means of self-sown seed.

The purple loosestrifes *(Lythrum salicaria* and *L. virgatum)* flower in late summer and favour damp, low-lying areas. They may be propagated by division. *L. salicaria* grows 1.2m (4ft) or more high, and has linear to oblong leaves. The flower spikes carry many reddish-purple blossoms which glow in the afternoon sunlight. There are several named varieties of rosy-red or pink. *L. virgatum* has pink flowers and there is also a variety called 'Dropmore Purple'.

Meconopsis are members of the poppy family and make beautiful associates for primulas and ferns in cool, semi-shaded, moist conditions. They need an acid soil and do not like sodden ground – moist, but never waterlogged should be the aim. They need a fairly rich soil so a generous quantity of peat, leaf soil or garden compost should be worked in before planting. Meconopsis are propagated by seed sown immediately after harvesting or, in some cases, by division.

The best-loved kind is the blue poppy, *Meconopsis betonicifolia* (syn. *M. baileyi),* which grows to about 1.2m (4ft) and carries large, cup-shaped, rich blue flowers filled with masses of golden stamens.

Below Primula pulverulenta, *one of the candelabra primulas, makes a striking display when planted in large clumps.*

Below right *Striking in both form and colour,* Lysichitum americanum *flowers in the spring.*

The Welsh poppy *(M. cambrica)* loves moist conditions, although it will grow anywhere and, if allowed to seed itself, can be a joy in spring gardens. Apart from single yellow and orange flowers, there are also double forms, all of which may be raised from seed. They grow to 30-45cm (12-18in).

Other species of meconopsis are available from seedsmen, notably the yellow-flowered *M. regia* with handsome leaves that may be silver or golden because of a heavy covering of bristly hairs; *M. napaulensis* with red, purple or blue flowers and *M. x sheldonii,* blue and longer-lived than one of its parents, *M. betonicifolia.*

Mimulus species and hybrids make charming bog plants, although they will also grow in ordinary garden soil provided they are given sun and plenty of water. Forms of the monkey musk, *M. variegatus,* with large yellow or red-spotted flowers, are not reliably hardy and are usually raised from seed each year. *M. lewisii,* 30-60cm (12-24in) has rose-pink flowers from mid-summer to early autumn, and *M. cardinalis* of similar habit produces scarlet flowers. These species may be propagated by division in early or mid-spring, or by cuttings in mid or late spring.

Monarda didyma looks rather like a large dead nettle, except that its leaves are sweetly aromatic. These are made into tea in its native North America, a circumstance which accounts for such commmon names as bee balm and Oswego tea. The variety usually grown is 'Cambridge Scarlet', a brilliant red, with square, leafy stems 60-100cm (24-36in) high. 'Croftway Pink' is rose-pink and there are white and purplish varieties. Full sun and moist soil is essential, given which the plants soon spread.

The umbrella plant *(Peltiphyllum peltatum)* has earned this name because of the shape of its large, round leaves with their central stems. The flowers come first, very early in spring, rich pink and in round heads on 1m (3ft) stems. Wet ground is essential, but the plant is indifferent to sun or shade.

Few plants create a more beautiful feature in bog gardens than the Candelabra primulas. Most dislike standing water or sour conditions and are happiest when there is plenty of water lower down so that the soil around the roots is kept moist.

All primulas like good, rich soil. So work in garden compost, or well rotted manure at planting time and mulch generously with peat, mushroom compost or well decayed leaves each spring to conserve moisture in the top few inches of soil.

Some species like the dwarf *Primula rosea* 15-23cm (6-9in), with lovely clear, rose-pink flowers, can stand being submerged for short periods and enjoy really boggy conditions. *P. florindae,* the giant cowslip with umbels of fragrant, pendent, bell-shaped yellow flowers on 1-1.5m (3-5ft) stems, will also grow in really wet ground.

The most popular kinds for boggy areas, however, are the 'Candelabra' primulas, which carry their flowers in a series of tiers up their 60-100cm (24-36in) stems. These primulas include *P. beesiana,* with fragrant rosy carmine flowers; *P. bulleyana,* buff-orange; *P. helodoxa,* golden yellow; and *P. pulverulenta,* which has produced some outstanding varieties with apricot, buff, orange-red, rose-pink and salmon forms.

Another sturdy group comprises variously coloured varieties of *P. japonica* with white, pink, or crimson flowers.

Another excellent species is *P. denticulata,* the drumstick primula, which has round balls of white, lavender, purple, or carmine flowers. It grows 30-60cm (12-24in) high and is often seen in garden borders.

All these primulas may be raised from seed or may be propagated by root division in spring.

All the buttercups *(Ranunculus* spp.) are essentially moisture-loving plants; thriving in rather heavy soil in sun or light shade. *R. aconitifolius* has dark green, divided leaves and carries masses of single white flowers on stems about 60cm (24in) high; its double form, 'Flore Pleno', the white bachelor's buttons, the most garden-worthy, but does best in light shade. *R. acris* 'Flore Pleno', the yellow bachelor's buttons, growing to about 45cm (18in), is the double form of the European buttercup, and just as much of a sun lover.

Rheums are ornamental rhubarbs which, since they grow tall and have heavy plumes of flowers, make very imposing waterside plants. They need plenty of room as they can grow up to 3m (10ft). Most popular is *R. palmatum,* which has deeply cut leaves as large as those of the cultivated rhubarb. The fluffy flower spikes are white or pink; a variety called 'Atrosanguineum' is particularly fine, with red flowers and also red leaves early in the year. Rheums may be propagated by seed or division between late autumn and early spring.

Rodgersias, commonly known as Rodger's bronze leaf, are grown as much for their large leaves, which are divided like those of a horse-chestnut (round in the case of *R. tabularis),* and either bronzed or dark olive green, as for their flowers. The last produce long, feathery, astilbe-like plumes in the summer months.

Zantedeschia aethiopica, the arum lily, can be grown outdoors in mild areas where its superb blooms will grace the outer reaches of any pool.

Rodgersias need plenty of moisture and are happy in a bog garden, in ditches, or on stream banks. The following species all grow to about 1m (3ft): *R. pinnata*, pink; *R. podophylla, R. purdomii* and *R. sambucifolia* all have creamy white flowers and all have divided foliage, as does *R. aesculifolia*, which at 1.2m (4ft) is a litle taller and has branched sprays of cream or pink flowers. *R. tabularis* also has creamy-white flowers but its large, round, green leaves resemble parasols and are individually up to 1m (3ft) across.

Insectivorous plants are nearly all denizens of bogs and, while the majority are either too small or too tender to grow outside in Britain, *Sarracenia flava*, the North American pitcher plant, will often succeed in the milder counties. It has yellow leaves converted to traps for catching insects and nodding yellow flowers shaped like parachutes on 30cm (12in) stems. The purple *S. purpurea* has become naturalized in parts of Ireland. Both plants should have sphagnum moss and peat in their compost.

The kaffir lily *(Schizostylis coccinea)* resembles a small pink gladiolus, 30cm (12in) high. It needs sun and moist rather than wet soil. It flowers very late in the year, sometimes into late autumn.

The variegated form of our common figwort, *(Scrophularia aquatica* 'Variegata') retains its cream leaf and stem splashes all summer, so is a conspicuous bog plant well worth planting. It has nettle-shaped foliage, small chocolate-red flowers and grows 60cm (24in) tall. It is best increased from cuttings.

The globe flowers, *(Trollius* spp.) are related to buttercups and like the same conditions. They must never become dry at the roots, and are easily propagated by seed or division. Their leaves are attractive, being deeply divided and act as a charming foil to the large buttercup-like, yellow, golden or orange, globe-shaped flowers. The plants grow to about 60cm (24in) and are propagated by seed or division. Popular varieties are 'Orange Princess', 'Canary Bird', 'Golden Queen' and 'Earliest of All', all of them derived from *T. europaeus* and various Chinese species.

Arum lilies, *(Zantedeschia aethiopica)* are well-known South African plants with large and glossy, dark green, arrow-shaped leaves and 12.5-15cm (5-6in) pure white flowers with a golden pencil-shaped spadix inside each. In their native Africa they are commonly found in ditches and at the sides of pools, but in Britain they are best grown above water, preferably in the drier reaches of the bog. This is due to their need for dryness in winter. If it is not possible to meet these conditions, grow the tubers in large flower pots, sinking then into the soil in spring and storing them in a shed for winter. The hardiest variety, 'Crowborough', we have grown outside for over 20 years without protection, so they will flourish in Britain. The plant is best increased from small bulblets on the old plants.

Shrubs and trees

A certain number of permanent plants are necessary in the vicinity of any water garden, in order to provide shelter from strong or cold winds. A few shrubs will possibly answer in the case of small to medium-sized gardens but, for large exposed areas, trees may prove more effective and satisfactory.

Where the ground is naturally very moist or is liable to occasional flooding, many garden trees and shrubs are unlikely to prove successful. The following, however, are reasonably tolerant of wet, some more than others – like alders and any of the willows. Most bamboos will also grow well in damp soil, as well as trees like metasequoias and taxodiums.

If room permits, *Acer rubrum*, the swamp maple, is of value for its autumn leaf colourings of scarlet and orange, but it will grow 21m (70ft) or more in height. Alders such as *Alnus glutinosa* will take very wet conditions and have attractive catkins early in the year.

Hydrangeas always do well beside water, provided the roots are not submerged; spiraeas need sun and moist soil to produce their feathery sprays of small white or crimson flowers, while the taller *Sorbaria aitchisonii* and *S. arborea*, 1.8-2.4m (6-8ft) and 3-6m (10-20ft) respectively, carry massive plumes of creamy-white florets in late summer.

Provided the soil is not limy, *Pernettya mucronata*, an evergreen shrub from Chile, will prove a real asset for acid bog gardens. The 0.6-1.5m (2-5ft) bushes have narrow leaves with spiny tips and small nodding white flowers which, when pollinated, go on to form marble-sized berries of white, pink, purple, red and near black. However, since male and female flowers are borne on separate plants it is necessary to have one male plant to every five or six female.

If more colour is wanted in the bog garden, it is a good idea to introduce a few bulbs in the drier regions, selecting kinds that will spread naturally. Examples are snowdrops, narcissi, bluebells, erythroniums; also camassias, which have slender spikes of blue flowers and grow 1m (3ft) tall in early summer. Try a few of these at first in different positions to assess their suitability.

CHAPTER FIVE
GREENHOUSE GARDENER

Left: *Even in a very limited space, a wide range of home produce can be grown in a greenhouse: French beans, tomatoes, peppers, celery.*

GREENHOUSE GARDENER

Greenhouse gardening has probably never been more popular than it is today and there have certainly never been more types and styles of greenhouse to choose from. There are greenhouses available to suit every pocket, all sizes of garden, and every type of plant, from the ever-popular tomato to decorative pot plants, orchids and cacti.

Why have a greenhouse?

There are several very good reasons why every gardener should have a greenhouse. Firstly, it enables you to carry on gardening all through the year, no matter what the weather may be doing. A far wider range of plants can be grown, but the choice does depend on the amount of artificial heat you are able to provide. Even without heat, though, a good range of tender plants, such as tomatoes, cucumbers and peppers, can still be grown in the summer. Various fruits,

like a grape vine, will succeed, and in the winter and spring the cold greenhouse can protect pots of colourful bulbs, primroses and alpines, as well as useful crops of lettuce and other vegetables.

Of course, you will be able to raise all kinds of plants from seeds, instead of buying them from garden centres, which works out much cheaper. Examples are summer bedding plants for the garden, flowering pot plants, which can also be used in the home, and tender vegetables for planting in the garden. By raising your own plants from seeds you will be able to choose cultivars (varieties) from seed catalogues which really appeal to you, instead of relying on the limited selections found in most garden centres.

Greenhouse gardening is, of course, a hobby in itself, and many thousands of gardeners gain great pleasure simply from

A very wide range of fruits and vegetables can be grown in a greenhouse, and if artificial heat is provided many of these can be enjoyed out of season. Among the easiest fruits to grow are strawberries, and fruits can be harvested several weeks ahead of plants grown in the open.

growing plants under glass. It is safe to say that this form of gardening calls for greater skills and more attention to detail and plant care than outdoor gardening. A great deal of fun is involved in learning new skills, such as sowing seeds in trays, pricking out or transplanting seedlings, raising plants from cuttings, and controlling the growing conditions by shading, ventilating, damping down and providing the right heat.

It may sound as though all this is time consuming, with plants needing constant attention, but in fact many aspects, such as ventilation, heating and even watering, can be automated, so that it is possible to leave a greenhouse unattended for several days. And these days automation in the greenhouse need not be expensive.

Florists' flowers are very expensive today, but cut flowers for the home can be produced very economically if you have a greenhouse – and with very little or no artificial heat. Among the easiest and most popular are late-flowering chrysanthemums, perpetual-flowering carnations and freesias.

Conservatories

So far we have been discussing the traditional type of greenhouse but there is great interest today in conservatories and lean-to greenhouses, which are erected against a house wall. They are used not only for growing plants but also as an extension of the home – an extra room which can be used for relaxation, entertaining and for leisure activities. What is more, these types of structure are more economical to heat, because they retain heat far better than a free-standing greenhouse.

Today there is no clear dividing line between a conservatory and lean-to greenhouse – many of the latter are often termed conservatories. The true conservatory, which was popular in Victorian times, appears as an integral part of the house – not looking as though it has been added on at a later date. It should match the style of the house – in other words, an ultra-modern design would not look right with a Victorian house, and a Victorian design (which can still be obtained today) would look out of place on a modern house.

A conservatory, or a lean-to greenhouse, ideally should have access from the house and is an ideal place to display pot plants. The walls of the structure, especially the back wall, can be clothed with climbing plants or even with a grape vine. Permanent shrubby plants, like palms and oleanders, and maybe some citrus fruits, can be grown in a soil bed or in large ornamental containers and pots. Throughout the year the conservatory could be supplied with pot plants raised in the greenhouse.

A garden feature

A free-standing greenhouse is quite a dominant feature in the average-sized garden and so it needs to be of pleasing appearance if it is to be sited in the ornamental part of the garden. Fortunately there are many attractive designs available. But there are also "utility" greenhouses intended really for growing crops like tomatoes, cucumbers and other vegetables, and included here are the polythene, walk-in tunnel houses, and other polythene-clad structures. The best place for these is in a vegetable garden, ideally screened from the ornamental part. It really pays to have a good look around greenhouse centres before buying, to see what is available. There are quite a few points to consider – not only appearance – and these are discussed overleaf.

If a greenhouse is to be sited in an ornamental part of the garden it should be of attractive design and be constructed of materials which blend in with or complement the surroundings. Utility type houses are best hidden from view in the vegetable garden.

CHOOSING A GREENHOUSE

A greenhouse is likely to be the most expensive purchase you will make for your garden, so consider the various greenhouses available, and what their strong and weak points are, before you make your choice.

A greenhouse should be chosen with care, for, like a house, it is a long-term investment. You should first decide what the greenhouse is to be used for and then choose a suitable type. For instance, if you intend growing plants mainly at ground level, such as tomatoes in the summer, chrysanthemums in autumn, and salad crops and lettuce during the winter, then choose a model which is glazed to the ground on all sides, to ensure maximum light.

However, if you intend to go in mainly for pot plants, which can also include more specialist subjects like orchids, alpines and cacti, then the ideal greenhouse would have solid sides and ends to staging height, which is approximately 1m (3ft). Generally the solid sides are formed of timber, but it is also possible to have brick sides and ends. This type of greenhouse retains heat much better than one glazed to ground level and is therefore more economical to heat. This is an important consideration, especially if your garden is in a cold area.

Or you could compromise and have a greenhouse glazed to the ground on one side, where you could have a soil border for growing tomatoes and other crops, with the other three sides being solid to bench height, where pot plants can be grown.

Consider the appearance
As mentioned previously, if the greenhouse is to be sited in the ornamental part of the garden it needs to look good and, as far as possible, blend in with the surroundings. Greenhouses with a framework of western red cedar always look attractive and aluminium houses with an anodized bronze finish blend in beautifully with the garden. White-painted timber or raw aluminium do not blend in so well, although these materials do look good when used for lean-to greenhouses and conservatories.

Where to buy
Having decided on the basic type, start looking around to see what models are available. There are many greenhouse centres throughout the country and many garden centres also have greenhouse display sites. Some of the large chain stores sell greenhouses and you can also buy direct from manufacturers. The latter often advertise in gardening magazines and national newspapers and it is a good idea to send for their catalogues and price lists.

What size?
The best advice here is to buy the largest you can afford – provided it does not completely dominate the garden. There are

Below left *This is the traditional span-roof greenhouse with solid sides to bench height. Such a house is ideal for the cultivation of pot plants, as well as more specialist plants like orchids, alpines and cacti.*

Below right *The traditionally shaped greenhouse can also be obtained with glass virtually to the ground, and is ideal if you intend growing plants, such as tomatoes, chrysanthemums and winter salad crops, mainly at ground level. Staging can also be installed on which to grow pot plants.*

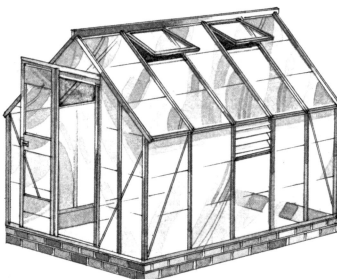

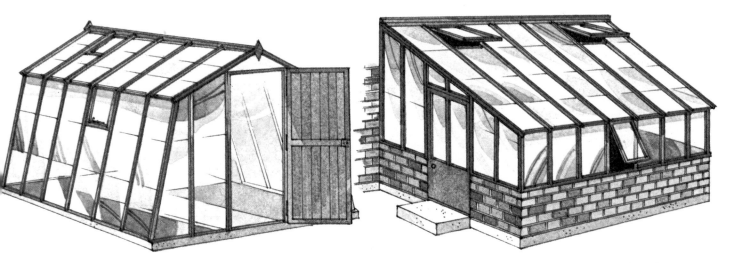

two good reasons: firstly, a very small greenhouse – such as the popular 1.8 × 2.4m (6 × 8ft) – is very quickly filled with plants so that in no time at all you find you do not have enough space. Secondly, a small greenhouse heats up very rapidly in warm weather and it is difficult to keep the temperature down to an acceptable level for plants. It is far easier to control the atmosphere and temperature in a larger house. So if space permits, think in terms of a greenhouse larger than 1.8 × 2.4m (6 × 8ft), and, if possible, buy one that can be extended at a later date.

The basic framework

Timber is the traditional framework material and these days western red cedar is very popular. Softwood framework, in pine or spruce, is also available and somewhat cheaper.

Advantages of timber framework are that the house will be slightly warmer than an aluminium framed model and condensation will be less of a problem. Also, it is easier to install equipment and, indeed, a timber framed house is much easier to erect than an aluminium one, as it is supplied in (generally) six sections, which are simply bolted together. Glazing is usually good, with no problems from draughts or leaks. There are one or two disadvantages – timber is not as strong as aluminium and therefore the framework members are thicker, which does slightly cut down on light transmission. Timber has to be treated regularly with preservative or paint to prevent splitting and decay.

Aluminium alloy is used a great deal today for the framework. There are several advantages – it needs no maintenance and the framework members are thinner than those of timber so light transmission is very good. There are some disadvantages. Erection can be very slow and sometimes rather complicated, as there are a great many parts to fit together. There could be more of a problem with condensation building up inside in cool weather. Equipment is not so easy to install, although there are special fixings for such things as insulation material, training wires, etc. Some aluminium houses have an attractive anodized or acrylic finish, but these are more expensive.

Glazing

There is no doubt that glass is the best material for cladding a greenhouse – it ensures excellent light penetration, is easy to clean, does not discolour and will last a lifetime if treated with respect.

Some greenhouses, though, are clad with flexible plastic film or PVC and these are much cheaper than those glazed with horticultural glass. However, it should be borne in mind that these materials have a short life and need replacing every two or three years. They discolour and become brittle. Furthermore, flexible plastic greenhouses lose heat very quickly and condensation can be a great problem if the greenhouse is not ventilated adequately. Plastic films with ultra-violet inhibitors should be chosen, as these have the longest life.

Rigid plastics are also being used more and more for cladding greenhouses and these have slightly better heat retention than flexible kinds and have a much longer life. They may be smooth and glass-like or corrugated.

Shapes of greenhouses

Today, there are many shapes to choose from. The span-roof house is the traditional shape with a pitched roof, each side being of equal shape and size. You can choose from models with straight sides or with slightly sloping sides for even better light penetration; and from solid sides to bench height or glass-to-ground, or a combination of the two. Span-roof houses with attractively curved eaves have been introduced in recent years.

Above left *Dutch-light style greenhouses are available in timber or aluminium. This design has good light transmission and is a useful general-purpose greenhouse, particularly recommended for vegetable cultivation.*

Above right *Lean-to versions of the traditional span-roof houses are becoming increasingly popular and are available with solid sides to bench height or glazed virtually to the ground. Erected against a wall of the dwelling house, they retain heat much better than free-standing greenhouses.*

Circular or lantern-shaped greenhouses, in timber or aluminium, make an attractive garden feature and are used mainly for displaying decorative plants, although crops like tomatoes can be grown in them. Most models are on the small side and if not equipped with plenty of ventilators will become very hot during warm weather. Circular greenhouses are available with glass virtually to the ground or, as shown here, with solid sides to bench height, and they may be six, nine or twelve sided.

The mansard, or curvilinear, greenhouse has the roof panels arranged at various angles to give a somewhat tunnel shape and excellent light transmission. It is an excellent type for displaying plants and for propagation and is available only with aluminium framework and glass-to-ground or solid walls to bench height. A mansard greenhouse is generally wide in relation to its length.

Traditionally, a Dutch light greenhouse is constructed of Dutch frame lights (or covers) bolted together to form a span-roof structure with sloping sides. A Dutch light consists of a timber frame, 1.5×0.75m ($5 \times 2\frac{1}{2}$ft) holding a single pane of glass. Such a house has good light transmission and is a useful general-purpose greenhouse, particularly recommended for vegetables. Today, you can buy Dutch-light style greenhouses in timber or aluminium.

Circular greenhouses are available with six, nine or twelve sides – they are really "lantern shaped" and make a nice feature in a garden, useful for displaying plants. Timber or aluminium versions are available, with glass-to-ground or with solid sides to bench height.

The dome-shaped or geodesic greenhouse creates a magnificent garden feature. It has excellent light transmission and plenty of space for displaying plants. It has an aluminium framework and glass almost to ground level.

The uneven-span greenhouse has one high wall, slightly sloping, which should face south. The roof slopes back from this wall. There are timber or aluminium versions and some models are clad with plastic. It is useful for vegetable crops, chrysanthemums, carnations and other plants which like high light intensity and which need plenty of headroom.

There are all kinds of mini-greenhouses available for very tiny gardens, balconies and roof gardens. You cannot get inside them, but access is easy by means of large, sliding or hinged, generally double doors. There are aluminium and timber versions and they are usually glazed to ground level. Mini-greenhouses can heat up rapidly, so ventilate well in warm weather.

Lean-to versions of traditional span-roof and mansard houses are available, for erecting against a wall. There are also mini-lean-to houses, ideal for balconies.

Conservatories are available in timber or aluminium and can be supplied in kit form or specially built by several specialist companies. Generally, they have solid brick or timber sides to bench height. It is possible these days to have virtually any size or shape and style to suit the style of your house, as well as your budget.

Polythene tunnel greenhouses are generally erected on a vegetable plot and used for growing vegetables. They consist of galvanized, tubular-steel hoops which are inserted in the ground and these are covered with flexible polythene. This is stretched tightly and the edges buried about 45cm (18in) deep in the soil. They are cheap compared with normal greenhouses, but they quickly lose heat and it is really uneconomical to use artificial heat in them. There is a door at each end, and special tunnel ventilators are also available.

Finally, you can buy a greenhouse and shed combined. It is a span-roof structure, divided down the middle, and for many people solves the problem of finding space for two separate buildings.

Siting a greenhouse

Ideally, a free-standing greenhouse should have the ridge running from east to west, but this is not essential, provided it is erected in an open, sunny part of the garden. A house which is shaded for much of the day will severely limit the range of plants that can be grown. A lean-to or conservatory is best sited on a south- or west-facing wall.

The greenhouse should be well sheltered from wind – cold winds will quickly lower the temperature inside the house and so it will be more expensive to heat. If necessary, erect a windbreak on the windward side – but some distance from the house – using windbreak netting, or plant a screen of conifers or hedging shrubs. If your garden is sloping do not erect a greenhouse at the bottom of the slope, for cold air drains down and forms a frost pocket. In this extra-cold spot, heating bills will be higher. Position the greenhouse half-way up a slope if possible.

If plants are to be grown in soil borders in the greenhouse, then choose a piece of ground that is well drained and reasonably fertile, to avoid problems later.

You may wish to run water, electricity or gas to the greenhouse, in which case it is sensible to site it as close as possible to the house, for the cost of running such services is generally very high and increases dramatically as distance increases.

Planning permission from your local council is not generally needed for a free-standing greenhouse, unless is it to be an exceptionally large structure, in which case it would be advisable to discuss the matter with the planning department first. It is advisable to get planning permission for a lean-to or conservatory and indeed it is essential if there is to be access from the house. You may find it sensible to seek the advice of an architect or local builder.

BUILDING A GREENHOUSE

Building a greenhouse can appear daunting at first, but if you follow the manufacturer's instructions carefully, and proceed in the order recommended, you shouldn't go wrong. Building your own will save you money, and you know that the job's well done.

Before ordering, let alone erecting, a lean-to greenhouse or conservatory, planning permission must be obtained. Generally there are no problems, but the structure must be erected on a substantial base. Timber-framed structures are easier and quicker to put up than those with an aluminium frame.

Free-standing greenhouse

Having decided on a greenhouse, and before it is delivered, the chosen site must be levelled. Use wooden pegs, a straight-edge board and spirit level. The first peg is inserted into the ground until the top is at the desired level. Then you work from this peg in all directions over the site, inserting pegs at about 1m (3ft) apart, and using the board and spirit level to ensure all the tops are at the same level as the original peg.

The next step is to add or take away soil as necessary so that the soil level over the entire site corresponds with the tops of all the pegs.

The greenhouse base

Most manufacturers these days supply pre-fabricated bases for their greenhouses; these can be pre-cast concrete, steel and extra-strong plastic. There is generally a post or stake of some kind bolted to each corner, and these have to be concreted into the ground. The base is simply laid on the prepared level site, ensuring the soil is really firm. The manufacturer's instructions will advise how the base should be laid. It is essential that the corners of the base are at right angles or the framework of the house will not fit. This can be assured by using a large set square. Generally, the greenhouse framework is bolted to this base and again instructions will tell you how.

To make your own base, first mark out the area of the greenhouse, using four wooden pegs and string. Then make a trench all round the outline, the depth and width of a spade. This is half filled with brick rubble and firmed.

Bricks are then placed at each corner, one on each side, and these must all be level, ensured by using a spirit level and straight-edge board. The tops of the bricks represent the final level of the concrete.

Fill up the trench to the level of the bricks with concrete – five parts ballast to one part cement. When this has set, a single row of bricks can be laid on which to stand the greenhouse, bedding them on mortar – four parts builders' sand to one part cement. They must be perfectly level, so use a spirit level while laying. Metal coach bolts should be inserted into the mortar between the bricks, about 1m (3ft) apart, in order to hold down the greenhouse framework. A damp-proof course can be provided by laying a strip of bituminized roofing felt over the bricks. If you are buying a greenhouse which requires brick walls to bench height, then continue building up with bricks to the specified height.

Assembling the framework

You can either put up the house yourself or make use of one of the erection services recommended by the manufacturer. Timber greenhouses are much easier to erect than

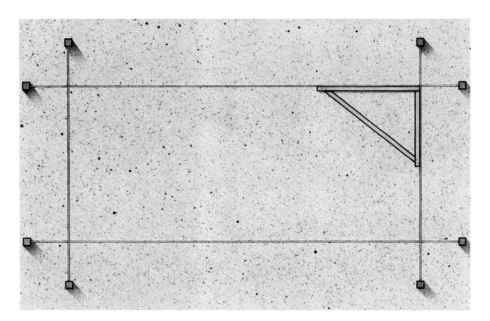

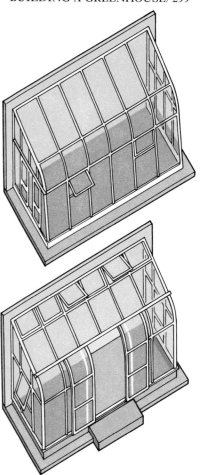

aluminium ones, as they are supplied in six sections which are simply bolted together. Some houses are even pre-glazed. Aluminium houses are supplied in many parts and you will have packages of glazing bars, vents, doors, etc. The manufacturer's instructions must be carefully studied before unpacking and making a start. Ideally, a house should be erected by two people – it makes the job easier.

The floor
Most gardeners simply have a path down the centre of the house with soil borders on either side, over which staging could be erected, of course. A path is easily made with a row of concrete paving slabs, laid on 15cm (6in) of well-rammed rubble topped with builders' sand. Bed each slab on a mix of sand and cement. If you do not wish to grow plants in the soil beds, the soil can be covered with a layer of pea shingle or horticultural aggregate. First cover the soil with a sheet of thick polythene to prevent weeds from growing through.

Lean-to greenhouse
Before placing an order for a lean-to greenhouse or conservatory, contact your local planning office and discuss the models you have short-listed. Most manufacturers supply plans for this purpose. Planning regulations for lean-to greenhouses or conservatories can be complicated but, on the other hand, most people experience few problems and the building inspector will advise you. There are certain general regulations – for instance, the concrete floor slab must be sufficiently deep around its perimeter; there must be enough opening windows; and it cannot be too near a public highway. If you intend erecting the lean-to green-

house or conservatory yourself, you will be charged 15 per cent VAT, but if you pay an extra charge for erection (about 10 per cent) you will not have to pay VAT.

Possible problems
When you have chosen a lean-to greenhouse or conservatory, but before ordering, mark out the area it will occupy. Mark with chalk the estimated level of the concrete slab and draw a line indicating where the structure would attach to the house – the ridge height and sides.

Now consider if there are any problems – do any windows or doors breach the line? If so, you may need a higher structure, or to raise the level of the slab. The level of the concrete slab must not be higher than the damp-proof course of the house. The damp-proof course of the slab can be at the same level or lower than the damp course of the house.

To save a lot of problems later, the position of the structure may have to be shifted slightly to avoid, say, rainwater pipes, inspection covers, drain covers, traps or gullies. Try to find out where underground pipes or drains are likely to run. They can be protected from the weight of the slab by encasing them in concrete.

When you have finally decided on model and site, you will need to contact your building inspector concerning planning permission and building approval. Submit the manufacturer's drawings and specifications, and a plan of your house and garden, with the proposed conservatory marked in. Do wait for approval before any work is undertaken.

Preparing the foundations
The lean-to greenhouse or conservatory is built on a concrete slab or base, which

Top left *The lean-to greenhouse or conservatory is built on a concrete slab or base, which should first be marked out with pegs and string, using the dimensions supplied by the manufacturer.*

Top *Conservatories or lean-to at the lower end of the market are supplied with a minimum of useful accessories, and often do not have enough ventilators.*

Above *Better models, though, include plenty of ventilators, a choice of door positions, guttering and various accessories.*

1. *The finished floor height should be marked on the house wall; then a second mark, 5cm (2in) below this, should be made to indicate the height of the main concrete slab.*

2. *The soil is then excavated to accommodate the concrete, but try to avoid or re-route underground pipes rather than building on top of them. However, this is not always possible.*

3. *Lay 10cm (4in) of hardcore in the excavation, but leave the foundation trench (around the edge) empty. Then add a layer of sand and rake it flat.*

4. *Before laying the concrete, a strip of polythene sheet spread against the house wall will prevent unsightly splashes and act as an extra prevention against damp.*

should first be marked out with pegs and string, using the dimensions supplied by the manufacturer. Mark the finished floor height in chalk on the house wall, then make a second mark 5cm (2in) below this for the height of the main slab.

Excavate the soil to a depth of 30cm (12in) below the level of the finished slab. A deeper trench is then dug around the inside edge of the excavation, about 15cm (6in) deeper, as the slab edges must be thicker.

Before laying hardcore, exposed drain-pipes will need encasing with concrete. Traps will need similar support. A bolt-down double seal cover plate will have to be added to any trap or inspection chamber. It must lie flush with the final floor finish.

The edges of the excavation should be lined with formwork – boarding fixed to stakes – to hold the concrete in place as it sets. Boarding should be level with the main slab height and 15cm (6in) or more below ground level. The stakes should be inserted on the outside of the perimeter line and the boards nailed to them.

Lay 10cm (4in) of hardcore in the excavation – broken bricks, etc – tamp it down level and make sure it is reasonably firm. Add a layer of sand and rake it flat. If the building inspector asks for it, now is the time to add reinforcing mesh – support it, with bits of brick, 5cm (2in) above the level of the sand.

You are now ready to lay the concrete but carry out these final checks: will the slab be large enough for the conservatory frame to overlap its edges slightly? Is there sufficient depth for 20cm (8in) of concrete below finished slab level? Is the foundation trench 30cm (12in) deep and wide?

Laying the concrete slab
You will need much more concrete than can conveniently be mixed by hand, so you will have to decide if you want to buy in ready-mixed concrete or hire a cement mixer for the job.

Whichever method you choose, you will have to work out the volume of material needed for the main slab, using the formula one part Portland cement to two parts sharp concreting sand and three parts aggregate. To help you get a sense of proportion, a standard bag of cement weighs 50kg (1cwt). Adding to this the two parts of sand, about 100kg (2cwt) and three parts of aggregate, about 150kg (3cwt) will give you 0.17 cu m (6cu ft) of concrete.

Calculating how much concrete you need requires a rough plan of the slab and the trench foundations combined. The calculation is made by multiplying the slab width by the length by the depth. Here is a sample calculation: slab – 2m wide × 2.6m long × 0.15m deep = 0.78, = slab volume 0.78cu m. To this is added the volume of the trench,

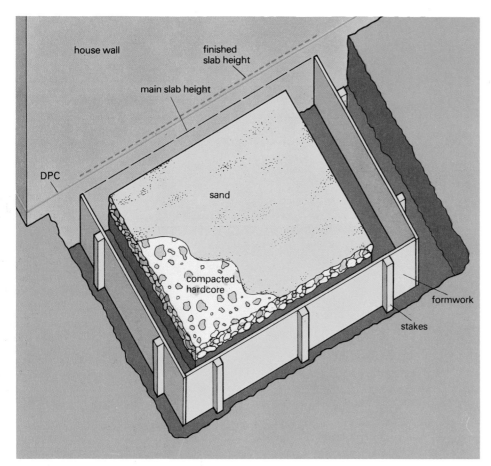

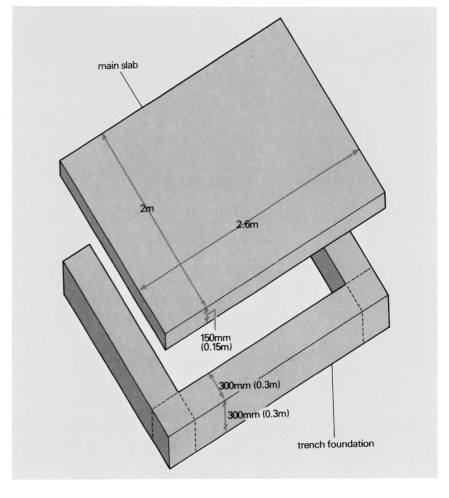

Left *This is the ideal excavation for the concrete slab: timber formwork is level with the main slab height. Extra formwork for the screed layer is added on top later.*

Below *Calculating how much concrete you need requires a rough plan of the the slab and the trench foundations combined. See sample calculation given on these pages.*

calculated in the same way as previously. Here is a sample calculation. Trench – (2m + 2m + 2.6m) = 6.6m × 0.3m × 0.3m = 0.594, = trench 0.594cu m. Total = 0.78 + 0.594 = 1.4cu m. Divide the total volume by the known yield of one bag of cement, two of sand and three of aggregate (0.17cu m) to work out the amount of each item. In this instance, four bags of cement, eight bags of sand and twelve bags of aggregate are the minimum needed.

The tools you will need are a wooden float, and for a really smooth finish a steel float, a shovel and a spirit level. You will also need a screeding board for compacting and levelling the concrete, which is easily made from a long sturdy 7.5 × 7.5cm (3 × 3in) timber with 5 × 2.5cm (2 × 1in) battens nailed to the ends for handles. The board must be long enough to stretch from one side of the slab to the other.

Before laying the concrete, a strip of polythene sheet spread against the house wall will prevent unsightly splashes and act as an extra prevention against damp. Spread this the length of the slab and from the bottom of the excavation to about 60cm (24in) above its finished height, then tack it in place. Leave it while you cast the slab.

To mix your own concrete, pour a liberal amount of water into the bowl of the concrete mixer then add the aggregate and sand and give them time to mix. Finally add

The use of a screeding board will work the concrete flat and consolidate it. A combination of scraping and chopping motions produces this result. With large areas of concrete it is best for two people to handle the screeding board. The surface will have a slight rippled effect – leave it to settle for an hour, then smooth it flat with a wooden float.

the cement and gradually more water until you have a plastic consistency. Make sure the mix is not runny. If you have put in too much water, add more of the dry ingredients in the same proportions.

A useful tip is to make an open bottomed box about 60cm (24in) square and 25cm (10in) deep so that you can measure each ingredient by volume. Each load counts as one measure.

Spread the concrete into the excavation, starting from the house side and working to the position nearest the mixing place. A garden rake or shovel can be used to spread the concrete. Tamp it down well, especially into the foundation trenches. If reinforcing mesh has been laid, take hold of it at regular intervals and give it a good shaking up and down to consolidate the concrete around it.

Continue laying, spreading and compacting the concrete until it is about 12mm (½in) above the top of the formwork. Then with the aid of a helper, work your screeding board over the surface of the concrete, using the formwork as a guide to level. With a combination of scraping and chopping motions, work the concrete flat and consolidate it by scraping away from the house wall. Add more concrete as the level goes down. Finish off with a series of light sweeps with the screeding board.

The surface will have a slight rippled effect – leave it to settle for an hour then smooth it flat with a wooden float.

Damp proofing and screed

Once the concrete slab has set, the next stage is to provide a continuous damp-proof membrane. This is tucked into the damp-proof course in the house wall. Finally a 5cm (2in) screen of finer concrete is laid to bring the slab to its final height and to give you a really smooth and pleasing finish.

The damp-proof membrane is a sheet of heavy-duty polythene which should cover the whole of the slab and be joined to the existing damp-proof course – that is, if you have one. The edges of the sheet are trimmed off after the final screed has been laid and has hardened. It is essential that the damp-proof membrane is a single sheet, and of course it must have no holes in it.

First release the strip of polythene you tacked to the wall and fold it back onto the slab. Using a bolster or an old screwdriver, remove the damp-proof course in the wall to a depth of about 4cm (1½in). If there is no damp-proof course (it looks like a layer of black tar), then rake out the course of mortar instead.

Spread out the new polythene sheet – it must overlap the edges of the slab. The edge nearest the house wall should be slipped into the groove you have raked out. It should be sealed in place with mastic – work it well into the mortar course.

Finally, you can lay the screed. First, nail a frame of 5 × 2.5cm (2 × 1in) timber to the top of the formwork, sandwiching the edges of the damp-proof membrane. The inner surface of the new frame should be in line with the edge of the concrete slab. It should be secured with strips of timber nailed to the outside.

It is easier when screeding to divide the slab area into smaller, more manageable areas, using 5 × 2.5cm (2 × 1in) wooden battens, nailed to the formwork. A screeding mix should be made up of one part cement to three parts sharp sand. Start laying it at the wall, completing one area at a time. The screeding board should be used to scrape and tamp it down. To achieve a really smooth surface, finish off with the steel float.

When the first area is dry, remove the battens and lay the second area. Use the edge of the first area as formwork and as an edge for the screeding board. Allow the screed to dry before the formwork is removed. Trim the exposed edges of the damp-proof membrane. Backfill around the edge of the slab.

Dealing with traps and gullies

If you cannot easily reposition drainage traps and gullies or inspection chambers you will have to incorporate them into the concrete slab. It means building an airtight brick box around the trap or gully and fitting a double-seal cast iron cover – obtainable from builders' merchants. The cover lies flush with the floor. Choose a cover that is bigger than the existing cover. Build up the brick box to the intended level of the top of the main slab. Cast the main slab around the box and lay the damp-proof membrane over the edges of the brick box. Place the frame of the double seal cover over the top of the box and pack up the four

Below left *Before laying the screed, cover the concrete with a damp-proof membrane and add more timber to the top of the existing formwork.*
Below right *If it is not possible to relocate traps or gullies they will have to be built into the slab. They must be airtight but accessible so a double-seal cover will be necessary. The brick 'box' is built before the slab is cast.*

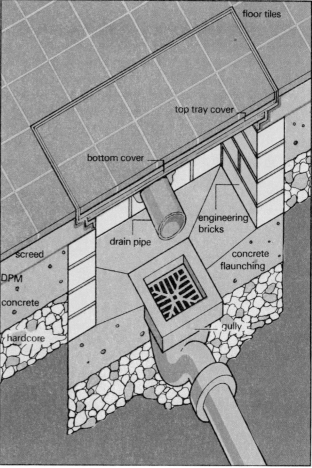

floor tiles

top tray cover

bottom cover

drain pipe

engineering bricks

screed

DPM

concrete

concrete flaunching

hardcore

gully

1. *The conservatory or lean-to is assembled in a specific sequence. Generally the main sections – walls, roof, door, etc, are assembled on a flat piece of ground.*

2. *The main framework is then bolted together: it is often easiest to up-end the frame to add roof sections, ridge, etc.*

3. *In many aluminium structures, rubber sealing strips are used and generally these are added before the framework is assembled.*

4. *If there is a gap of more than 2.5cm (1in) between framework and wall in places, a shaped wooden batten will be needed to provide a square edge. Bitumen tape forms a waterproof seal.*

5. *The glazing starts with the roof and then proceeds to the front and ends.*

6. *Door locks and window catches generally bolt on through pre-drilled holes.*

corners with cement until the frame is level. Lay the screed in the normal way. The screed must be pressed under the raised edges of the frame.

Assembling the frame

When the lean-to greenhouse or conservatory is delivered, unpack and check the contents against the list supplied, but keep all the parts in their original cartons. Then carefully read the assembly instructions, preferably several times, until you fully understand them.

The conservatory will be assembled in a specific sequence; this will vary according to make, but the instructions will, of course, advise on this. Generally the main sections – walls, roof, doors, etc, are assembled on a flat piece of ground and the main framework is then bolted together on the concrete base.

To start with, all nuts and bolts and other fixings are screwed to finger tightness. Only when the main framework is fully assembled on its base, and you are sure that it is perfectly squared up and everything fits as it should do, should you fully tighten all nuts and bolts, etc.

It is a good idea to have some trestles and planks nearby. Using them, you can work on higher parts of the greenhouse frame in relative ease, and without the distraction of worrying about losing or dropping the various components.

Position the main framework on a special prefabricated base if one has been supplied, according to instructions. Check that all is square, and that the framework butts up to the wall all round, then carry out final tightening.

Small irregularities between frame and wall will be rectified by waterproof seals. However, if there is a gap of more than 2.5cm (1in) in places, a shaped wooden batten will be needed to provide a square edge.

The base of the framework should be screwed down first: place a layer of non-setting mastic beneath it. A layer of bitumen tape is placed between the frame and the wall to form a weatherproof seal. The framework is then screwed to the wall, using masonary plugs and, ideally, rust-resistant screws.

Glazing the frame

Again, manufacturer's instructions should be followed regarding sequence and bedding the glass in the glazing bars. Usually, special sealing strips are used. Sub-frames, such as doors and ventilators, are generally glazed first, and then fitted after the main glazing has been completed. The main glazing starts with the roof and then proceeds to the front and ends.

After glazing, the structure can be tested for leaks by spraying it, including the wall,

3

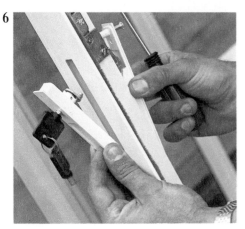

6

with a hosepipe. Any leaks can be sealed, when dry, with a clear silicone sealant, although if the conservatory is well made, and you have assembled and glazed it correctly, there really should be no leaks.

Installing a soakaway
Most conservatories and greenhouses are supplied with gutters and downpipes and if these cannot discharge into an existing drain you will have to build a soakaway. Specifications and siting can be obtained from your building inspector. However, it basically consists of a pit at least 4m (13ft) from the nearest buildings, and filled with hardcore or rubble.

The rainwater from the gutters drains along an underground pipe into the soakaway, where it gradually seeps into the subsoil.

The underground pipe at the conservatory end can be connected to a new trapped gulley where the downpipe can discharge above the grating.

Dig a trench for the underground pipe, about 25cm (10in) wide, and progressively deep enough to give the recommended fall between the trap and soakaway. The pit can be filled with rubble or hardcore. Use lengths of UPVC underground pipe between the gulley and pit. The top of the soakaway can be covered with concrete paving slabs to prevent soil washing down into it.

Finishing off
The most exciting part for most people is finishing off the interior of the greenhouse or conservatory. Consider firstly the floor. For a conservatory, the covering can be as simple as rush matting, which can look most attractive. Or you could be more ambitious and lay floor tiles, either vinyl or ceramic kinds. They will be easy to lay on the smooth level finish of the screed.

However, for a more functional greenhouse floor, you may wish to leave the screed as it is – after all, it makes a perfectly good floor. Remember, you must seal it first to prevent a dusty or powdery surface. It is possible to buy clear cement sealants for this purpose. Alternatively, paint it with flooring paint – there is a reasonably wide choice of colours available.

The rear wall can be painted a light colour to reflect the light, and to give the structure the appearance of belonging to the house rather than being merely tacked on. White or cream is a good, reflective colour for the wall.

Lighting will be needed and the best type consists of fluorescent tubes – but unless you are a competent electrician, leave this job to a qualified professional.

Equipment, such as extra ventilators, heating and automatic watering systems will need to be considered and these are discussed overleaf.

Climbing plants can be grown on the back wall, trained to trellis panels of timber or plastic-coated steel, or even to horizontal wires placed 30cm (12in) apart and fixed to the wall by means of masonary vine eyes. Leave a gap of about 4cm (1½in) between trellis or wires and the wall to ensure good air circulation. Pot plants can be grown on staging (generally supplied as an optional extra by the manufacturer of the greenhouse or conservatory) at the front and side, and larger, more permanent plants – shrubs, palms, citrus fruits, camellias, bird of paradise flowers – could be grown in large ornamental tubs and other containers. Hanging baskets could probably be secured from the roof framework.

Do not forget to landscape the outside of the building. This is a matter of personal choice: for instance, you may wish to have grass right up to the building, with a path leading from the door to the main garden path. Or you may like to have a patio alongside it, on which you could stand pots and urns of colourful spring and summer bedding plants. There is no reason why you should not have a narrow border around the building, again planted with spring and summer bedding, with winter-flowering bulbs for additional colour.

HEATING, WATERING & VENTILATION

The environment inside a greenhouse is entirely artificial, and it is up to you to provide the plants with the heat, water and fresh air that they need to thrive. Getting the balance right to start with is not difficult, and gets easier with practice.

Below *A greenhouse can today be completely automated so that it may be left unattended for varying periods. Ventilation, shading, watering and heating can all be automatic. However, if you are at home all day it really is better to keep a close eye on the greenhouse and look after plants according to weather conditions.*

Opposite *Heating pipes should ideally run underneath staging so that plants benefit from the rising warm air. Deep benches as shown here allow plants to be plunged in a moisture-retentive medium, such as sand or peat, to prevent rapid drying out.*

Controlling the environment

The greenhouse gardener must create and control the environment under glass to suit the plants being grown. This means providing the right temperature, adequate ventilation, shading from strong sunshine and water in the right amounts.

Today, much of this can be automated, so that the gardener does not have to keep a constant eye on the greenhouse, and indeed the house can be left for several days if it is well equipped.

Artificial heating increases the range of plants that can be grown and allows you to make an early start with plant raising, such as food crops and summer bedding plants. Unless you are growing tropical plants, it is not necessary to heat the house all the year round – most gardeners provide heat from early autumn to late spring.

Due to the high cost of heating, most gardeners these days maintain cool conditions in their greenhouses – a minimum temperature of 4.5C (40F). In this you can grow flowering pot plants all the year round, raise bedding and food plants, over-winter tender plants and have food crops available throughout the year. A minimum temperature of 10C (50F) enables a wider range of plants to be grown, including some of the sub-tropical kinds. A warm greenhouse has a minimum temperature of 15.5C (60F) and here tropical plants can be grown throughout the year.

A stuffy atmosphere must be avoided at all times, and therefore a greenhouse must be ventilated. You should aim for a buoyant atmosphere, which means that the right temperature is being maintained, yet there is a regular air change in the house, so that the air is always fresh. A greenhouse must, therefore, be well equipped with ventilators. Many houses do not have sufficient vents but manufacturers generally offer ventilators as optional extras, and it is always a good idea to order a few extra when placing an order for the greenhouse.

In temperate climates, plants need to be shaded from strong sunshine between mid-spring and early autumn. Shading prevents leaves from being scorched, seedlings from being "burnt up", helps to prevent the compost and soil drying out rapidly, and helps to keep the temperature down during very warm weather. It is possible to have too high a temperature for greenhouse plants, usually from 35C (95F) upwards.

Heating equipment

There are four main types of heating available – paraffin, gas, electricity and solid fuel. Among the most economical are paraffin and solid fuel, with gas and electricity being the most expensive.

Paraffin heaters

There is a wide range available – from very small to large heaters capable of keeping a 6 × 3m (20 × 10ft) greenhouse frost free. The best type of paraffin heater is one with a blue-flame burner as opposed to models with a yellow-flame burner. The former are more efficient and there is less risk of fumes being produced.

The simplest paraffin heaters are metal boxes which release their heat from holes in the top. More advanced types have pipes or ducts which distribute heat more efficiently. These are suitable for heating large houses, or for maintaining high temperatures in small structures. Paraffin heaters can be partly automated, by feeding fuel from a large drum by gravity to the heater's supply tank by means of plastic tubing. The drum can, of course, be positioned outside the greenhouse.

The advantages of paraffin heaters are that they are comparatively cheap to buy and run, they are portable and provide carbon-dioxide – beneficial to plants. There are some disadvantages. Regular attention is needed, as they must be kept clean and the wick trimmed regularly to prevent harmful fumes from being produced. The burning fuel produces water vapour which can lead to condensation, and some ventilation must be provided at all times.

Gas heaters

These are becoming quite popular now and basically they consist of a portable warm-air cabinet which emits heat from the top. Gas heaters are thermostatically controlled so they can safely be left unattended.

There are two types – natural gas and bottled gas. The former is relatively cheaper to run than bottled-gas types, but running a gas supply to a greenhouse can be costly. It is best installed and connected by a professional gas fitter. The bottled-gas heaters run off propane or butane gas, supplied in cylinders. Buy large cylinders as they work out more economical in the long run.

Gas gives off beneficial carbon-dioxide, and the heaters need the minimum of attention and maintenance. The burning fuel gives off water vapour as with paraffin, so watch out for condensation and ventilate the greenhouse accordingly.

Electric heaters

Electricity is the most efficient fuel – there is absolutely no wastage and, as heaters are thermostatically controlled, an electric heating system can be left unattended for long periods. Other advantages are that most heaters are very reliable, portable, and all give off dry heat so there are no condensation problems in winter. The disadvantages are that electricity is an expensive fuel and the cost of running a supply to the greenhouse can be high. Also, you will need an emergency heater (paraffin, for example), to use in the event of a power cut. It is advisable to have a professional electrician install the power supply, control panel and other such parts.

There are various types to choose from, the most popular being the fan heaters which blow out warm air and keep the greenhouse air circulating well.

Tubular heaters consist of hollow tubes, each containing a heating element, and these are mounted in "banks" on a wall of the greenhouse, the number depending on the amount of heat needed. They can be installed under the staging if desired.

Electric convection heaters basically consist of a cabinet; cold air is drawn in from the bottom, is heated in the cabinet,

Below left *Whether you have a large or small greenhouse it can be heated with a paraffin heater. Unfortunately, this method is not as cheap as it used to be and indeed paraffin is quite expensive, but more economical than, say, electricity.*

Below right *There are various types of electric heaters to choose from, including tubular heaters which are generally mounted beneath the staging so that warm air rises around the plants.*

and emerges, warmed, at the top. An advantage is that the greenhouse air is kept moving. Convection heaters are particularly suited to the larger greenhouse.

Electric soil-warming cables are bedded in the soil, or in sand on the greenhouse staging, and provide localized heat – that is, at soil or root level. They do very little to heat the atmosphere, but "bottom heat" is very useful for early planting (tomatoes, for example), and for propagation, like seed raising and rooting cuttings. Warming cables are cheaper to run than other electrical systems, but you will need another heater to warm the air in the greenhouse. Make sure you buy a soil-warming system with thermostatic control – not all have this facility.

Solid fuel systems
This is the traditional way of heating greenhouses, and consists of a boiler with hot-water pipes running around the walls of the greenhouse. The boiler is placed outside, but under cover. This is an ideal system if you want to maintain high temperatures in your greenhouse with economical running costs. Modern boilers need minimum attention, but of course there will be daily stoking and ash clearing. Dry heat is given off from the pipes so no condensation problems occur. A solid-fuel system is suitable for small or large greenhouses, and manufacturers will advise on the size you need and the types of fuel which can be used. Modern boilers often burn cheap-grade fuel.

Size of heater
Manufacturers will advise on the size of heater needed for your greenhouse, if you tell them the minimum temperature you wish to maintain. To conserve heat, and therefore reduce fuel bills, do insulate the inside of your greenhouse: the most popular and effective material is bubble plastic and most greenhouse manufacturers can supply special fittings to secure this to the greenhouse framework.

Watering equipment
While some gardeners prefer hand watering, with a watering can, more and more people are turning to automatic watering systems so that they can leave their greenhouse unattended for a few days. This is fine during spring and summer, but plants will need less water in autumn and winter and therefore the automatic system is best shut down during these periods and plants hand watered as they need it.

Ideally, you will need a supply of mains water to the greenhouse. There are two basic methods of automatic watering and one of these is the trickle irrigation system,

suitable for watering soil. beds and/or plants in pots. The water is distributed, via a main pipe, to small-bore flexible plastic tubes, each with a controllable nozzle to regulate the amount of water given. This system can be fully automatic, running from a header tank fitted with a ballcock valve, and connected to the mains water supply. A semi-automatic system runs from a header tank or some other kind of reservoir, which has to be filled manually. But it can be left for several days unattended. Yet other systems are connected to a tap by means of a hosepipe, and you just turn on the tap when you want plants watered. None of these is selective, and all plants are watered whether or not they need it, but this is no problem during warm weather.

Top *This is a fully automatic trickle watering system which runs from the mains water supply, via a header tank fitted with a ballcock valve. Like all automatic or semi-automatic systems it is best used only during spring and summer when plants need plenty of water.*

Above *The capillary watering system for pot plants is very popular and can be fully automatic (connected to the mains water supply via a header tank), or semi-automatic as shown here, whereby water is supplied from a reservoir bottle which needs to be filled by hand.*

Overhead sprinklers and misting systems are also available, and are either connected to a tap or to a header tank connected to the mains supply. They are useful for damping down greenhouses, especially where high humidity is needed, as when growing cucumbers.

The second type of automatic watering system is known as capillary watering, whereby potted plants are placed on some kind of water-retentive material, and they take up water when they need it. This material may be special capillary matting (something like carpet underlay) or sand. The latter will need extra-strong staging, but matting is very light in weight. Plants should be grown in plastic pots and there must be perfect contact between the bottom of the pot and the matting or sand. The matting or sand can be kept moist in several ways – via a pipe, connected to a header tank or some other kind of reservoir, or from a tank/ballcock valve connected direct to the mains water supply. You can either make up your own capillary watering system or buy a complete kit ready to assemble. In the simplest capillary system, water is supplied from a gutter running along the length of the staging, with one edge of the capillary matting dangling in it to draw up the water as needed.

Ventilating equipment

All greenhouses and conservatories are fitted with ventilators, but generally there are not enough. It's best to order a few extra when buying the greenhouse.

Every greenhouse or conservatory needs roof or ridge ventilators and side ventilators. A minimum number of each is one every 2m (6½ft) length of the structure. If you have a very long greenhouse, then continuous vents, which run the length of the greenhouse, are recommended. The area of roof ventilators must be equal to at least one-sixth of the floor area of the house. The roof vents are generally hinged at the ridge of the greenhouse, and side vents are also generally hinged, but are positioned quite near to the ground. This arrangement allows good air circulation in the building – air is drawn in at the bottom, rises through the house and escapes from the roof vents.

An alternative to the normal hinged side ventilator is the louvre vent, with adjustable glass panels so that you can regulate the air intake. They can be a bit draughty. Louvre vents replace panes of glass, so it is possible to install as many as you need. Most greenhouse manufacturers are able to supply louvre vents for their particular houses.

Automatic ventilation

Hinged ridge and side ventilators can either be opened and closed by hand or fitted with an automatic ventilator arm which will open and close them according to the temperature. If vents are fitted with these, you can completely forget about ventilation, at least in warm weather. In the autumn and winter it may be best to disconnect them and

Below left *An alternative to hinged side ventilators are the louvre vents supplied by most greenhouse manufacturers. The glass panels are adjustable so that you can regulate the air intake. They can be automatically controlled by fitting automatic ventilator arms.*

Below right *Electric fans can be used in conjunction with roof and side ventilators and they have the advantage that they keep the air moving and therefore fresh. There are two types: extractor fans which expel warm air and draw in cool air, and circulating types, as shown here, which simply keep the air moving.*

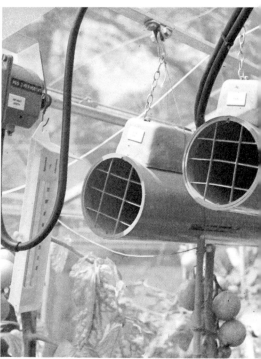

operate vents by hand, for you may need to provide some ventilation in cool or cold weather, when the automatic openers would not operate. More recently, automatic ventilator openers have become available for louvre vents.

Automatic ventilator openers are reasonably priced and so it is perfectly feasible to fit them to all ventilators. They do not need a power source as they are operated by natural heat. Most can be set to open at specific temperatures.

Electric fans can also be used for ventilation. There are simple circulating fans, which keep the greenhouse air moving, and these are mounted in the roof, ideally at the opposite end to the door. Extractor fans are placed in a similar position, and they expel warm air and draw in cool air from outside, particularly useful in hot summer weather. Both circulating fans and extractor fans should be used in conjunction with roof and side ventilators and either kind equally can be recommended for both small and large greenhouses.

Shading materials

The simplest way of providing shade is to paint the outside of the glass with a proprietary liquid shading material, the best colour being white. Modern kinds let in more light when rain makes them wet (it is generally dull when it is raining and therefore as much light as possible is needed in the greenhouse). When dry, as in warm, sunny weather, the shading is more dense.

Another way to shade greenhouse plants is to fix external roller blinds, which are pulled up and down as required. Various materials are available: wooden laths, plastic reeds, shading netting and polythene fabric. It is possible, though expensive, to have fully automatic roller blinds, operated by an electric motor.

Internal roller blinds are also available; choose white polythene film (not green) or polypropylene netting. There is also a polyester sliding system, whereby the blind is slung from a system of wires and can be pulled backwards and forwards (from one end of the house to the other).

Above left *Every greenhouse or conservatory needs ridge and side ventilators. Air is drawn in through the side vents, rises through the house and escapes via the roof vents. This ensures good air circulation which is so necessary to keep plants healthy and free from damp-loving diseases.*

Above right *Automatic ventilator arms are controlled by temperature and therefore an electricity supply is not needed. They can be fitted to roof, side and louvre vents.*

Above *Roller blinds made of wooden laths are the traditional way of shading a greenhouse and there is still nothing to beat them for durability. If you can afford it, they can be automatically controlled by means of electric winding gear.*

MANAGEMENT & MAINTENANCE

The day-to-day care in managing a greenhouse involves similar skills to managing a home. It must be kept clean, with heat, shading and fresh air according to season, the inhabitants must be fed and watered and treated against the occasional illnesses that occur.

Equipment and accessories

Relatively inexpensive compared to the initial cost of a greenhouse, equipment and accessories are worth investing in. Buy the best you can afford, to keep your repair and replacement costs down to a minimum.

Staging

Plants are raised, and pot plants are grown, on some form of benching, which in greenhouse-gardening terms is known as staging. There are two main reasons for using staging. It allows you to position plants in maximum light (there is often less light at floor level, especially in houses with partially solid sides). Staging also enables you to make maximum use of space, for some plants, particularly shade-loving kinds, can be grown underneath the staging, and dormant or resting plants and bulbs can be stored underneath, too.

Staging is often placed down one side of the house, for pot plants, and on the other side a soil border is made, for growing tall crops like tomatoes, peppers, chrysanthemums and carnations.

Many manufacturers supply staging for their greenhouses: in aluminium if you have an aluminium-framed house, or in timber if it is timber framed. Some staging comes as a single tier, but it is possible to buy it with several tiers, ideal for displaying ornamental plants.

There is a choice of staging surfaces. With slatted or openwork staging, surplus water drains rapidly, there is excellent air circulation around plants and heat is able to rise through the staging. It is specially recommended for many pot plants, including perlargoniums and orchids.

Staging can also be supplied with gravel trays which are filled with horticultural aggregate, shingle or gravel. These can also be filled with sand for capillary watering. If the trays are filled with gravel or aggregate, keep this moist in warm weather to create a humid atmosphere around suitable plants.

If you wish to use capillary matting on the staging, slatted staging must be covered with something solid, to prevent the matting from sagging through the slats – for instance, marine plywood or perhaps spare timber planks.

The main level of staging is generally about 1m (3ft) high and a maximum width is also 1m (3ft). Always leave a gap of 2.5–5cm (1–2in) between staging and the side of the greenhouse to allow warm air to rise behind it and for air circulation. Some kinds of staging can be easily dismantled and removed to make more room for summer crops such as cucumbers, tomatoes, peppers and aubergines.

Shelving

Again, many greenhouse manufacturers supply shelving, which can be put up in the roof area or fixed to the back wall. As shelving is placed in good light, it is useful for holding trays of seedlings or cuttings in the spring.

Propagating case

If you have an electricity supply to your greenhouse it is well worthwhile investing in an electrically heated propagating case for raising seeds and rooting cuttings – and also for starting off tender bulbs, corms and tubers, such as begonias. All of these techniques require high temperatures – in the region of 18–21C (65–70F) – and of course it is totally out of the question for most people to provide this temperature range in the rest of the greenhouse. An electric propagator will provide this range of temperatures and the heat will be where it is needed – at compost level. Many propagators only cost a few pence a week to run, especially if they include a built-in thermostat. There are many sizes, from very small (perhaps holding only one seed tray) to large, which can hold at least half a dozen trays of seeds. Buy the largest your greenhouse can accommodate.

Today, greenhouse staging is often very flexible, allowing you to remove or lift the decking if you want to grow tall crops like tomatoes at soil level. This saves the need to remove all the framework as well.

Top left *Plastic pots are very popular today and drip trays can be obtained for them, but these are used more for indoor pot plants than in the greenhouse.*

Top right *Clay pots were once the only type available. They went out of favour when plastic pots came in, but are now becoming popular again, possibly due to the fact that many gardeners find them easier to manage. There is not so much risk of keeping plants too wet in clay pots for the compost dries out more quickly.*

Left *There are all sorts of pieces of propagation equipment available to the greenhouse gardener. The most useful is a propagating case (shown top), ideally electrically heated. An alternative is a glass fish tank (top right). A heated propagating base (bottom right) is among the more economical pieces of equipment. Failing any of these, cuttings or seeds can be covered with glass domes or jars, with sheets of glass, or with clear polythene bags, as shown in the remainder of the photograph.*

Pots

There are many different kinds of pot to choose from, each with particular advantages. **Plastic pots** are the most widely used today and are available in a wide range of sizes. Compost does not dry out so rapidly in these as it does in clay pots, so be careful not to over-water.

Clay pots are coming back into favour after a period of neglect. Compost dries out quicker in these, so keep a close eye on water requirements, particularly in warm weather. Many people consider them to be much more attractive than their plastic counterparts. They are, however, more expensive especially the larger, decorated versions. They also tend to weigh more.

Compressed peat pots are used for raising plants – such as summer bedding plants and vegetables, which are later to be planted out in the garden. The plant is never removed from the pot, so there is no root disturbance. Bituminized-paper pots are used in the same way.

Peat pellets are bought as flat peat discs and have to be soaked in water before use to expand them into 4cm (1½in) modules. They are used for propagation – a seed can be sown in each, or a cutting inserted. When the seedlings or rooted cuttings need potting, they receive no root disturbance because the peat module is potted as well.

Soil or peat blocks have the same use as peat pellets, except that you make them up at home. They are made from special "blocking compost" and are pressed out with a special blocking tool, to form cube-shaped modules.

Seed trays

These are used for sowing seeds, for pricking out (transplanting) seedlings, and for rooting cuttings. Most are made of plastic. The standard size is 38 × 23cm (15 × 9in) and depths vary from 2.5 × 7.5cm (1 × 3in). The shallow ones are ideal for seed sowing. It's also possible to buy half-sizes trays for small quantities of seeds or seedlings. These are half the length of standard trays. Some plastic trays are rigid, while others (cheaper versions) are quite flexible.

There are trays available, in plastic or polystyrene, which are divided into compartments – one compartment for each seedling, cutting, or whatever. These are useful for growing summer bedding plants and vegetables which are later to be planted out, as the roots do not become entangled.

Growing bags

There has been something of a revolution in the growing of crops like tomatoes, peppers, aubergines, melons, cucumbers and lettuces. Instead of being grown in soil borders in the greenhouse, they are now frequently planted in growing bags. This means that the plants have good soil to grow in and are not at risk from soil-borne pests and diseases. If you grow in a soil border, you have to sterilize it each year to get rid of pests and diseases. And it has to be dug, manured and fertilized, with all the work and time that this entails.

Basically a growing bag is a long polythene bag – generally about 1.2m (4ft) long, filled with soilless compost. Holes are made in the top for planting. Place the bag on the greenhouse floor – if over a soil bed, first cover the bed with a sheet of polythene. A 1.2m (4ft) long bag will hold four tomato, pepper or aubergine plants, or two cucumber or melon plants. Growing bags are best used only once; however, a crop of winter lettuce could be planted in them when tomatoes have finished. And then the bags should definitely be discarded – the compost can be used on the garden.

Composts

Basically there are two kinds of composts. One type contains soil or loam, plus peat and sand, and is known as John Innes compost. John Innes seed compost is used for seed sowing; J.I. potting compost No. 1 is used for potting seedlings and rooted cuttings; J.I. potting compost No. 2 is used for potting plants into larger pots; and J.I. potting compost No. 3 is used for plants that need a really rich compost, as it contains a lot of fertilizer. It is used, for instance, for potting chrysanthemums into their final 20cm (8in) pots, or for large shrubs. All of these composts are available in several sizes from garden centres. Beginners are well advised to use John Innes composts, as they are easier to manage than soilless kinds (see below). They do not dry out quite so quickly, and if they are allowed to dry out they are easy to moisten again. Also, the fertilizers in the compost do not run out as quickly as they tend to do with soilless composts.

Growing bags are the modern equivalent of the greenhouse soil border. The bag should be placed on a level surface (1), and the two end flaps are normally cut off (2) to form plastic loops, which are slipped around the bag (3) to prevent it from losing its compact shape. Then most of the top of the bag is cut out (4) for planting (5). Growing bags are normally used only once, but a crop of winter lettuce, or other salad vegetable, could be planted in them when tomatoes or other summer crops have finished.

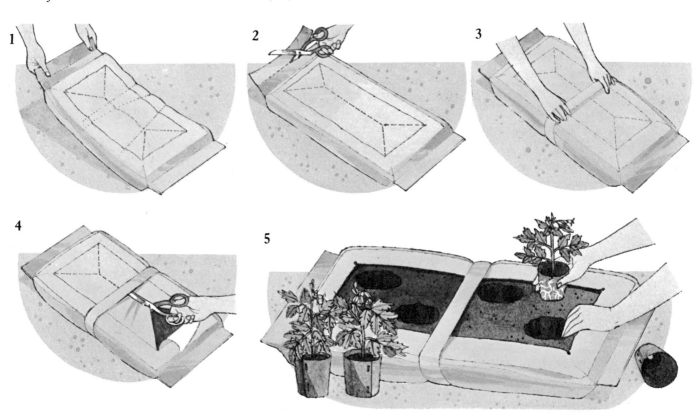

The other basic type of compost is soil-less – it may consist entirely of peat, or it may be a mixture of peat and sand, peat and perlite or peat and vermiculite, plus fertilizers, of course. These are inclined to dry out quickly in warm weather and if they are allowed to become really dry they are difficult to wet again.

There are available soilless seed composts and soilless potting composts. A trend now, though, is towards multi-purpose composts, which are used for sowing seeds, rooting cuttings and for potting. Again, soilless composts are readily available from garden centres in various-size bags.

If you are growing lime-hating plants, such as azaleas, camellias and heathers, then make sure you buy a compost which is free from lime or chalk – generally sold as ericaceous compost.

There is no doubt that the best type of compost for rooting cuttings is made at home – it consists of equal parts by volume of peat and coarse horticultural sand. Or you could use peat and perlite or peat and vermiculite. No fertilizers are necessary.

Greenhouse hygiene
Unless the greenhouse interior is kept scrupulously clean and tidy, all sorts of problems, mainly from pests and diseases, can occur.

Routine hygiene throughout the year consists of removing any dead and dying leaves and flowers from plants; and discarding dead and dying plants, seedlings and cuttings. If dead plant material is left the fungal disease grey mould, or botrytis, will grow on it and this will spread to healthy plants and infect them, too. Never leave any rubbish, such as heaps of dead leaves or plant remains, lying around in the greenhouse. And never store dirty pots or seed trays in the greenhouse – wash and sterilize them first.

Regular attention must be paid to controlling pests and diseases and further details will be found on pages 355–359.

Many people are worried by green growth on the surface of compost and soil. This may be green algae or slime, moss or liverwort. None of these primitive plants really harms cultivated plants, but if they build up

Potting and seed composts, whether soil or peat based, can be made at home as there are many suitable materials available like peats and sands, as well as base fertilizers. However, the newcomer to greenhouse gardening is advised to start off with ready-made proprietary composts.

Greenhouse smoke cones will control many pests and diseases. Some contain both insecticides and fungicides. Many gardeners use them regularly to prevent pests and diseases from gaining a foothold, but certainly light one after giving the greenhouse its annual autumn clean-up.

too much they can smother seedlings and small plants. It is therefore best to carefully scrape them off the surface and to top up with fresh compost if necessary. Regularly stirring the surface of the compost, very lightly, will help to stop this green growth.

Once a year, in the autumn, the greenhouse should be completely cleared of plants and thoroughly washed and sterilized. If you have permanent plants, such as greenhouse shrubs, climbers and perennials, growing in soil beds or borders then obviously these cannot be moved out, but during cleaning should be enclosed in polythene sheeting.

Use a solution of horticultural disinfectant and add a little detergent if the greenhouse is really dirty. Thoroughly scrub down everything – glass, framework, staging and even the path. You will find that green algae build up in the overlaps between the panes of glass. This can be removed by inserting a plastic plant label in the overlap between the panes and pushing it up and down.

Finish off by hosing down the structure and also direct the jet between the glass overlaps to clean them out.

The outside of the house should be washed down in the same way – it is essential to get the glass as clean as possible, for dirt on the glass cuts down the amount of light that enters the greenhouse.

If the glass is really dirty use one of the special greenhouse-glass cleaners. If green algae is a real problem in your greenhouse, growing on glass, staging, etc, then spray the structure after cleaning with one of the proprietary algicides.

Finally, before returning the plants, close down the house and burn one of the greenhouse smoke cones, containing fungicide and insecticide, to get rid of any remaining pests and diseases – although the washing down will dispose of many.

Sterilizing the greenhouse border

If you grow crops like tomatoes, peppers and aubergines in a soil border, then this must be sterilized each year after the crops have been cleared in autumn to kill soil-borne pests and diseases. First it should be dug and manured. Then it can be sterilized by watering it with a solution of formaldehyde. All plants must previously be removed, for the fumes from this chemical will kill them. Plants should only be returned when there is no longer any smell of fumes, and crops should not be planted in the treated border for at least six weeks.

Formaldehyde can be obtained from chemists, and it is poisonous. Dilute in water to a 2 per cent solution (follow the directions on the bottle). Drench the soil with this at a rate of 25 l per sq m (5 gal per sq yd). The soil must be soaked thoroughly to a depth of at least 15cm (6in). The ventilators and door should be fully open while applying this, because heavy fumes are given off.

On completion, cover the border with a sheet of polythene to retain the fumes and shut down the house completely. After two or three days remove the polythene, open up the greenhouse and fork over the soil to release any remaining fumes.

Repairs and preservation

It is generally most convenient to carry out any repairs and timber-preservation treatment immediately after the annual clean-up. Obviously you would replace any broken panes of glass, but also renew any that are cracked, for these can let in draughts. Any loose putty should also be replaced to prevent draughts and leaks. Rake out the putty with an old chisel and remove any pieces of broken glass at the same time. Make sure you wear gloves to protect your hands while working.

If the greenhouse or conservatory leaks in places, then fill any holes or gaps with a silicone sealant.

A cedar greenhouse should have the framework treated regularly with a horticultural timber preservative, using cedar colour. This may need doing every two years. If the framework is pine or deal, then existing paintwork should be rubbed down with glasspaper before it starts flaking, a white undercoat applied, followed by white gloss paint. Generally, paintwork should last for about three years before it needs doing again.

Cleaning containers

After use, pots and seed trays should be scrubbed clean with water to which has been added a horticultural disinfectant. This will eradicate any pests and diseases that could otherwise affect next season's planting. Dry them off and store them somewhere that is clean and dry.

Damping down

When the weather is hot and dry in the summer, you need to keep the greenhouse air humid or well charged with moisture. This is done by a technique known as

damping down. Spray the floor, staging and inside walls with plain water, once, twice, or more frequently each day, depending on weather conditions. The hotter and drier the weather, the more often you will need to damp down.

Damping down helps to prevent compost and soil drying out rapidly and to reduce the temperature, especially when done in conjunction with shading and ventilation. Do not carry out damping down during cool weather or during the autumn and winter, when the greenhouse air needs to be kept as dry as possible. The leaves of plants must also be kept dry during these periods and in cool weather.

Watering

The best time to water plants is in the morning; if it is carried out late in the day the plants and greenhouse will not dry out before nightfall and the atmosphere will be humid, favouring the development of fungal diseases. Of course, these comments do not apply when automatic watering systems are used and this is one of the disadvantages of automated watering.

If you are watering by hand, as a general rule apply water to pots or soil beds when the top 6mm (¼in) starts to dry out, ascertained by feeling the compost with your fingers. In warm weather, compost or soil will dry out more quickly than during cool or cold conditions. Indeed, in autumn and winter, plants will need very little water. Water potted plants by completely filling the space between the compost surface and the rim of the pot – the compost will then be moistened right the way through.

It is best to water soil beds with a sprinkler attached to a hosepipe. Water must penetrate to a depth of at least 15cm (6in) which means you need to apply the equivalent of 2.5cm (1in) of rain. This works out to about 27 l per sq m (4¾ gal per sq yd).

Soil-moisture indicators are available; these have a metal probe which is pushed into the soil and you read off the state of the soil on a calibrated dial – wet, moist or dry. Most are battery operated.

Shading and ventilating

Shading is needed in spring and summer to prevent the temperature rising too high, which can damage plants. It also prevents scorching of leaves and shrivelling up of seedlings. Ideally provide shading only when the sun is shining, but this is not always possible if you are out all day, in which case shading blinds should be drawn in the morning if it is likely to be a sunny day.

Ventilation also prevents the temperature rising too high in warm weather and

Below *Insulating the greenhouse with sheets of clear polythene or bubble polythene is the major method of cutting down on fuel bills, for these materials help to hold in the heat. Polythene sheeting can also be used to partition the greenhouse if you only want to heat a small section of it, or if you want to grow cucumbers in the same house as tomatoes. The former like very humid conditions while the latter prefer a drier atmosphere.*

ensures plenty of fresh air. It also helps to reduce humidity and this is especially important in the autumn and winter. Ventilation is therefore needed throughout the year, consistent with maintaining minimum temperatures. When paraffin heaters are operating a little ventilation is also necessary.

Raising plants from seeds

The majority of seeds of greenhouse and bedding plants need a temperature in the region of 18–21C (65–70F) to germinate and are, therefore, best placed in an electrically heated propagating case after sowing. Seeds can be sown in full or half-size seed trays, or in 9–10cm (3½–4in) pots, depending on the quantity you wish to sow. Always use a proprietary seed compost, according to instructions on the bag.

The surface of the compost must be very smooth and level, which can be achieved by pressing with a flat piece of wood. There are various methods of sowing seeds, but you may find the following technique helpful: estimate the quantity needed for the container and hold in the palm of one hand.

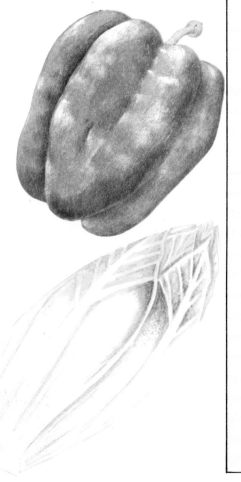

Below *Peppers will come into cropping in late spring in a warm greenhouse or in midsummer if artificial heat cannot be provided.*

Bottom *Chicory can be forced in a warm greenhouse to give 'chicons' for cutting between late winter and early spring.*

USING HEAT IN A GREENHOUSE

This table shows crops which are available in each season of the year from a greenhouse where there is gentle heat available in winter. In some cases, however, a temperature of 15.5C (60F) must be maintained, but the whole greenhouse need not be heated – a portion can be divided off with a temporary partition of plastic sheet, clear or black, depending on whether light is required or not. A large heated frame can be used instead in some cases, depending on the crop.

CROPPING SEASON	COLD GREENHOUSE *(Temperature not allowed to fall below freezing)*	WARM GREENHOUSE *(Minimum temperature of 15.5C (60F)*
Early spring	endive*, lettuce	asparagus*, beetroot, carrots, chicory*, French beans, lettuce, marrows, mushrooms, potatoes, radishes, rhubarb*, salad onions, strawberries
Mid-spring	asparagus*, lettuce, rhubarb*	beetroot, carrots, French beans, marrows, mushrooms, potatoes, strawberries, tomatoes
Late spring	French beans, lettuce	aubergines, cucumbers, grapes, marrows, peppers, tomatoes
Early summer	marrows, tomatoes	aubergines, Cape gooseberries, cucumbers, figs, grapes, melons, peaches, peppers
Mid-summer	aubergines, Cape gooseberries, cucumbers, grapes, peaches, peppers, tomatoes	figs, melons
Late summer	aubergines, Cape gooseberries, cucumbers, figs, grapes, melons, peaches, peppers, tomatoes	
Early autumn	aubergines, Cape gooseberries, cucumbers, figs, French beans, grapes, melons, peaches, peppers, tomatoes	
Mid-autumn	aubergines, Cape gooseberries, cucumbers, grapes, lettuce, melons, mushrooms, peppers, tomatoes	French beans
Late autumn	endive*, lettuce	French beans, grapes, lettuce, mushrooms
Early winter	seakale*, lettuce	chicory*, endive*, lettuce, mushrooms, rhubarb*, salad onions
Midwinter	lettuce	asparagus*, chicory*, endive*, lettuce, mushrooms, radishes, rhubarb*, salad onions, seakale
Late winter	lettuce	asparagus*, beetroot, chicory*, endive*, lettuce, mushrooms, radishes, rhubarb*, salad onions, seakale*

*indicates crops that are lifted from the soil outdoors and brought into the greenhouse for forcing in containers or under the staging, with or without light.

The common fruit and vegetables which can be grown easily out of doors during summer are not included; the table shows only those crops which grow better with protection, or can be made to crop earlier or out of season.

For the warm greenhouse crops, heat must be applied in the season during which the crop ripens, and it may also be needed for propagation as well.

Hold this hand 15cm (6in) above the surface of the compost and move it slowly from one side of the container to the other, at the same time gently tapping it with the other to allow the seeds to scatter on the surface. Seeds must be evenly spaced out and not touching each other – better to sow too thinly than too thickly. Very small seeds can be mixed with fine dry silver sand to make them easier to handle, while very large seeds can be spaced out individually. Do not cover dust-like seeds with compost, but cover the rest with a layer equal to about twice their diameter. Sift compost over them, using a fine sieve.

After sowing, stand the container in water until the surface becomes moist, then place in the propagating case.

When the seedlings are large enough to handle easily, they are pricked out, or transplanted, into other containers, such as seed trays, to give them room to grow. A standard-size seed tray will take 40 to 45 seedlings. Use John Innes potting compost No. 1 for pricking out, or an equivalent soilless type.

Feeding plants
When plants are well established in their pots or beds, they should be fed on a regular basis (say every seven to fourteen days) during the spring and summer, for the fertilizer in the compost will be used up.

Most gardeners use a liquid fertilizer, diluted according to manufacturer's instructions. Use a general-purpose kind for the majority of plants, but for tomatoes, peppers and aubergines use a tomato fertilizer, and for greenhouse chrysanthemums use a special chrysanthemum fertilizer. Alternatives to liquid feeding are fertilizer tablets and spikes, inserted in the soil or compost, or fertilizer pads placed under the pots.

Hardening off plants
Plants which are raised in a greenhouse for planting in the garden, like summer bedding plants and vegetables such as outdoor tomatoes and celery, should not be moved straight from the greenhouse to the open garden, for the change in temperature will give then a shock and check their growth. Instead, transfer them to a cold frame at least two weeks before planting-out time and subject them gradually to increased ventilation to slowly acclimatize them to outdoor conditions. This is correctly known as hardening off.

Making the most of your greenhouse
A greenhouse can be full of fruits and vegetables the year round, whether it is a cold greenhouse or heated. The accompanying tables will show you how to achieve this.

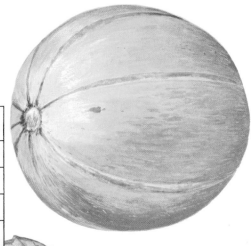

Below *Melons can be grown in a heated or unheated greenhouse and cultivars should be chosen accordingly. They are not the easiest fruits to grow but nevertheless are well worth attempting.*

Bottom *A rather unusual fruit, but one which is easily grown in an unheated greenhouse for summer cropping, is the Cape gooseberry which produces little juicy fruits with a sweet to sharp taste and which can be eaten raw or cooked.*

CROP GROWING SCHEDULES

Crop growing schedules help make your greenhouse work for you with the maximum possible efficiency. Here and on the following page are four types you might try. Planned for a typical 3 × 1.8m (10 × 6ft) house, they are obviously only a guide and can easily be adapted or simplified to suit your own requirements. For example, beginners may like to start by using just part of the SALAD CROP PLAN (see page 32), following timings given for autumn-sown lettuce, tomatoes and cucumbers.

FRUIT CROP PLAN

	ON STAGING	UNDER STAGING		BORDER	
	Strawberries	Melons	Rhubarb	Cape gooseberries	Grapes (permanent)
Early spring		sow in heat in peat pots	crops	pot into 7.5cm (3in) pots	
Mid-spring	crops	plant in grow-bags	crops	plant in border	
Late spring	crops				
Early summer		crops			
Midsummer		crops		crops	crops
Late summer	plant in 15cm (6in) pots outside	crops		crops	crops
Early autumn		crops		crops	crops
Mid-autumn		crops			crops
Late autumn					
Early winter	bring into greenhouse				
Midwinter			lift and box		
Late winter		sow in heat in peat pots	lift and box	sow in heat	

LUXURY CROP PLAN

| | ON STAGING | | UNDER STAGING | |
	Strawberries	Aubergines Peppers	Rhubarb	Mushrooms
Early spring		sow in heat	crops	
Mid-spring	crops	pot/grow-bags		
Late spring	crops			
Early summer				
Midsummer		crops		
Late summer	plant in 15cm (6in) pots outside	crops		spawn
Early autumn		crops		spawn
Mid-autumn				spawn; crops
Late autumn			lift and bring in	crops
Early winter	bring into greenhouse		lift and bring in	crops
Midwinter			lift and bring in; crops	
Late winter		sow in heat	crops	

Below *Ridge cucumbers, which have shorter fruit than the greenhouse varieties, may be started in a greenhouse, hardened off and planted out later. Unfortunately, the popular greenhouse cucumber is not a suitable companion for tomatoes (bottom) for it likes a very humid steamy atmosphere, whereas tomatoes prefer drier air. The solution is to partition off the greenhouse if you want to grow both.*

SALAD CROP PLAN

| | ON STAGING | | | |
	French beans	Lettuce	Lettuce	Lettuce
Early spring		crops		
Mid-spring	crops	crops		
Late spring	crops		crops	
Early summer			crops	
Midsummer				sow in bags/pots
Late summer				pot in 15cm (6in) pots
Early autumn				crops
Mid-autumn		sow in 5cm (2in) pots		crops
Late autumn		thin and plant		
Early winter				
Midwinter	sow in heat			
Late winter			sow in heat	

ALL YEAR ROUND PLAN

| | ON STAGING | | | |
	Lettuce	Potatoes	Melons	Cucumbers
Early spring			sow in heat in pots	pot
Mid-spring		crops	plant in grow-bags	plant
Late spring		crops	plant in grow-bags	
Early summer			crops	crops
Midsummer			crops	crops
Late summer	sow in pots		crops	crops
Early autumn	sow in pots		crops	crops
Mid-autumn			crops	crops
Late autumn				
Early winter	crops			
Midwinter	crops	plant in heat		
Late winter			sow in heat in pots	sow in heat

BORDER					
Tomatoes	Lettuce (1)	Lettuce (2)	Asparagus	Melons	Grapes *or* Peaches (permanent)
			crops		
crops			crops		
crops					
crops				sow	
crops	sow			sow	crops
	sow	sow		plant	crops
	crops	sow			crops
	crops			15.5C (60F)	crops
		crops	lift and box	crops	
sow		crops	lift and box	crops	
7.5cm (3in) pots			lift and box		
plant			crops		

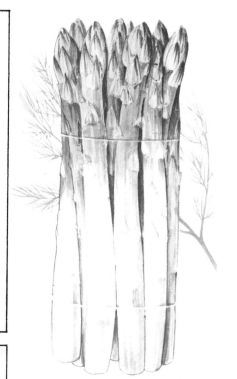

	BORDER				
Salad onions	Cucumbers	Radishes	Tomatoes	Radishes	Carrots *or* Beet
sow in heat	sow in heat		prick out	sow; crops	crops
	prick out		plant	crops	crops
crops	plant				
			crops		
	crops		crops		
	crops	sow	crops		
	crops	sow; crops	crops		
	crops	crops	crops		
			crops		
					sow in heat
			sow in heat		sow in heat

UNDER STAGING		BORDER			
Rhubarb	Mushrooms	Tomatoes	Lettuce	Carrots *or* Beet	Radishes
crops		plant			
crops					
		crops			
		crops			
		crops	sow		
	spawn	crops	sow		
	spawn				
	spawn		crops		
	spawn; crops		crops	sow in heat	
	crops				sow in heat
lift and box	crops	sow in heat		crops	sow in heat; crops
lift and box		pot		crops	crops

Top *Asparagus is a luxury crop for forcing in a cool or warm greenhouse. Roots are lifted from the garden in autumn, boxed up and forced for winter or spring harvesting.*

Above *Tasty young forcing carrots can be pulled in winter if sowings are made in the greenhouse during autumn. Heat is needed for this out of season crop.*

ORNAMENTAL PLANTS TO GROW

Keeping your greenhouse full of flowers all year round is easy to do, provided you keep it frost free. And even the smallest greenhouse should provide pot plants and cut flowers to brighten up your home, at a fraction of their store-bought cost.

Alpines

These are rock-garden plants which can be grown in special, shallow pots – or pans – and flowered in an unheated greenhouse in winter and spring. Examples are gentians, alpine primroses and saxifrages, but there are many more.

Buy young plants in autumn and plant in 15cm (6in) diameter clay or plastic pans or half-pots. Use John Innes potting compost No. 1, to which has been added one-third extra of coarse grit.

For most of the year the plants are kept in cold frames, with the covers on, but well ventilated, only in autumn and winter. Plants are transferred to a greenhouse as they are coming into flower.

Annuals, hardy

Hardy annuals, such as clarkia, cornflower, godetia and lavatera, can be flowered in the spring in pots in an unheated or cool greenhouse, if sown in late summer or early autumn. Germinate seed in a cold frame and prick off seedlings into 9cm (3½in) pots. Pot on into 12.5cm (5in) pots. Grow in a cold frame until early winter, then transfer to the greenhouse. Use a soil-based compost for sowing and growing. Keep only slightly moist in winter, provide maximum light and good ventilation. Water and feed well when plants are actively growing and flowering.

Barberton daisy

Barberton daisies *(Gerbera)* are perennial plants with large, daisy-like flowers, in many colours, in spring and summer. They need a minimum temperature of 7C (45F), and are best grown in soil-based compost. They need plenty of ventilation, good light, but shade from strong sun, and the compost should be kept only slightly moist. It is now possible to raise plants from seeds, and if these are sown in mid- or late winter they will flower the same year, as modern strains are very quick to mature.

Begonia, tuberous

The tuberous begonias have large, double flowers in many brilliant colours and flower in summer. They need a minimum temperature of 13C (55F).

In late winter or early spring, place the tubers in moist peat and start them into growth in a temperature of 18C (65F). Pot into 12.5cm (5in) pots when the shoots have formed. Use soilless or soil-based compost. Shade from strong sun and water as needed. Feed regularly when buds start to develop. After flowering, reduce watering gradually until the compost is dry and the stems have died down. Remove the tubers from pots and store in dry peat in a frost-proof place.

Bird of paradise flower

This is a large perennial plant *(Strelitzia reginae)*, with spectacular orange and blue flowers, resembling a bird's head, in summer. It is easily grown in a minimum temperature of 7C (45F), and has attractive leathery, evergreen leaves.

Pot on young plants in spring until even-

Right *The tuberous begonias are favourite summer-flowering pot plants with their double, often exceedingly large flowers. Some cultivars are pendulous in habit (as shown here) and make very fine subjects for hanging baskets or for trailing over the edge of the staging.*

Far right *The hippeastrum is a bulbous plant for a heated greenhouse, producing huge blooms in winter or spring. Red, crimson or scarlet are favourite colours, but also available are pinks, whites and bicolour cultivars.*

There are few easier and more colourful subjects for spring flowering in an unheated greenhouse than the hardy dwarf bulbs. There are many to choose from, including the popular snowdrop. Ideally this should be potted as soon as flowering is over, while the leaves are still green, as then establishment and subsequent flowering is very much better.

tually they are in a large tub or pot; or they can be grown in a soil bed in a conservatory. Plenty of sun and good ventilation are needed; keep only slightly moist in winter. Feed well in summer for steady growth. Use soilless or soil-based compost.

Brunfelsia

This easily grown evergreen shrub is suitable for an average-size greenhouse. Large, blue-purple flowers are produced in summer. The minimum temperature needed is 10C (50F).

Young plants should be potted on as required in spring, or can be grown in a soil bed in the conservatory. Use soil-based potting compost. Pinch out the growing tips of young plants to create bushy specimens. Water as required, feed in summer and shade from strong sun. Pruning is not generally needed.

Bulbs, dwarf hardy

Hardy dwarf bulbs can be grown in pots to flower in an unheated greenhouse in spring, making good companions for alpines. Examples are crocus species, glory of the snow *(Chionodoxa)*, winter aconites *(Eranthis)*, snowdrops *(Galanthus)*, grape hyacinths *(Muscari)*, miniature daffodils *(Narcissus)*, squills *(Scilla)* and dwarf tulip species.

Grow in 15cm (6in) diameter pans or half pots. Use soil-based compost. Pot in early autumn, about 2.5cm (1in) apart each way. Keep in a well-ventilated cold frame until

late autumn. After flowering return to the frame and water till leaves have died down.

Bulbs, hardy

The large-flowering daffodils, hyacinths, tulips and crocuses can be flowered in pots during winter and spring in a cold or slightly heated greenhouse.

Bulbs are planted in early autumn, generally in 15cm (6in) diameter bowls or pans. Bulb fibre can be used, or soilless compost. Keep bulbs cool and dark after planting, e.g. by plunging them 15cm (6in) deep in weathered ashes or sand in a cool shaded place outdoors. When the bulbs have produced shoots (five to eight weeks) transfer to the greenhouse. After flowering, they should be planted in the garden.

Busy Lizzies

Busy Lizzies *(Impatiens)* make good pot plants for summer flowering, after which they are discarded. Modern strains, which are raised from seeds sown in early or mid-spring, are neat, compact, free-flowering plants in a wide range of colours. A minimum temperature of 10C (50F) is needed.

They can be flowered in 12.5cm (5in) pots and soilless composts are particularly suitable. Provide light shade, high humidity and water freely. Take cuttings in summer.

Cacti

There is a wide range to choose from, but those which flower freely and regularly include the peanut cactus *(Chamaecereus)*, mammillarias and rebutias. Most will survive with a minimum temperature of 4.5C (40F).

Provide maximum light and sun – there is no need to shade them – good ventilation and a dry atmosphere. Keep the compost dry between late autumn and mid-spring and water normally for the rest of the year. Pot on as necessary, using a proprietary cactus compost. Spring is the best time for potting.

Camellias

These are evergreen shrubs with pink, red or white flowers in winter or spring. They can be flowered in an unheated or cool greenhouse or conservatory and are best grown in tubs or large pots, using lime-free or ericaceous compost.

Put the plants under glass in autumn, give good ventilation and make sure the compost remains steadily moist. After flowering, the plants can be stood outdoors in a sheltered, partially shaded spot. Never let the compost dry out, and feed regularly with a liquid fertilizer during the summer months.

Cape primrose

The Cape primroses *(Streptocarpus)* are perennials which produce tubular flowers in the summer in various colours. A minimum temperature of 7C (45F) is needed.

They can be raised from seeds sown in early spring. High humidity is appreciated in summer, together with shade from strong sun. Water regularly in spring and summer, but give the plants a rest in autumn and winter by keeping them only barely moist and cool. Plants can be propagated from leaf cuttings in summer.

Carnations

Perpetual-flowering carnations *(Dianthus)* are capable of blooming all year round, if sufficient heat is available. For flower production in winter a minimum temperature of 10C (50F) is needed. With a winter temperature of 4.5C (40F), blooms will be produced for most of the year except winter.

Provide maximum light all year round, good ventilation and a dry atmosphere in winter. Plants are bought from specialist growers, are grown in soil-based compost and eventually need a pot size of at least 15cm (6in). For large blooms, pinch out the small side buds situated around the central or main flower bud.

Chilean bellflower

This is a climber *(Lapageria rosea)* suitable for a conservatory with a minimum temperature of 4.5C (40F). Large, waxy, tubular, deep-pink blooms are produced in late summer and autumn.

It is best planted in a soil bed but can be grown in a large pot of soilless compost. In summer give good ventilation and light shading. The only pruning needed is thinning out weak stems in spring.

Although most are hardy shrubs, camellias can be flowered in an unheated or cool greenhouse. They are superb plants for the conservatory. Plants are best grown in tubs so that they can be moved outdoors after flowering. Most popular are the many cultivars of Camellia japonica.

Chrysanthemums

Late-flowering chrysanthemums bloom in the autumn and early winter, when they need the barest amount of artificial heat – just enough (coupled with ventilation) to keep the atmosphere dry. They are flowered in 20cm (8in) pots and young plants are progressively potted on to these from early spring. Use John Innes potting compost – No. 3 for final pots.

The plants are stood outdoors from early summer until early autumn, when they are returned to the greenhouse. Pinch out tips of young plants in spring to encourage branching. Allow the central flower bud on each stem to develop and remove all the surrounding small ones. Feed and water well in summer.

Cineraria

These flower in late winter and spring, producing heads of daisy-like flowers in many colours. These pot plants are raised from seeds between mid-spring and early summer and discarded after flowering. Provide a minimum temperature of 7C (45F).

Final pot size is 12.5cm (5in). Keep plants in a cold frame for the summer, well ventilated, shaded, and with steadily moist compost. Move into the greenhouse in early autumn. The greenhouse should be well ventilated, the leaves must be kept dry and the compost not allowed to become wet.

Cyclamen

These pot plants grow from tubers and bloom in autumn and winter. A minimum temperature of 10C (50F) is needed.

Seeds are sown in late summer for flowering the following year. Final-size pots are 12.5cm (5in) and soilless compost is suitable. Cool, well-ventilated conditions should be provided at all times. Plants can be kept in a shady cold frame in the second summer and re-housed in early autumn. Dry off and rest the tubers after flowering. Re-start into growth in late summer by re-potting in fresh compost and watering.

Flame nettle

The flame nettle *(Coleus)* is a short-term pot plant grown for its brightly coloured foliage. Often this is marked with various colours. Minimum temperature needed is 10C (50F).

Sow seeds in spring and pot on young plants until they are in 12.5cm (5in) pots. Use soilless or soil-based compost. Good light is needed and high humidity in warm weather. Pinch out tips of young plants to create bushy specimens. Feed and water well in summer. Discard old plants in autumn, as they become leggy.

Freesias

These are grown from corms and produce scented flowers in a wide range of colours during winter. Provide a minimum temperature of 7C (45F).

Plant corms in late summer – eight to a 15cm (6in) pot, using soil-based compost. Place in cold frame and cover with peat. Transfer to greenhouse after six weeks. Give good ventilation and water moderately. Dry off the corms after flowering and re-pot and start into growth again in late summer. Freesias can also be raised from seeds, sown in late winter or early spring.

Fuchsia

This is the most popular summer-flowering pot plant, with bell-shaped flowers in a wide range of colours. It is an ideal plant for the cool greenhouse.

Buy in young plants in spring and pot on until they are in 15cm (6in) pots. Soilless compost is particularly suitable. Provide good ventilation and shade from strong sun throughout the summer. Keep the compost steadily moist. Pinch out their growing tips to encourage branching.

Feed weekly in summer. To produce new plants, take cuttings in early summer. The resultant young plants should be over-wintered in a minimum temperature of 10C (50F). Old plants, if kept, should be rested over winter by keeping the compost dry. Plants will then drop their leaves. For old plants, a temperature of 4.5C (40F) is adequate over winter.

Gloxinia

Gloxinias *(Sinningia)* grow from tubers and produce large, bell-shaped blooms in summer in various colours. A minimum temperature of 15.5C (60F) is needed.

Pot tubers in spring, using soil-based or soilless compost: one per 12.5cm (5in) pot. Provide a temperature of 21C (70F) to start the tubers into growth. Provide shade and high humidity during summer and feed weekly. Dry off the tubers at the end of the season and store them in the pots in a frost-free greenhouse.

Hippeastrum

This bulbous plant, often called amaryllis, produces large, trumpet-shaped blooms in winter or spring. A minimum temperature of 10C (50F) is needed.

Pot one bulb per 15cm (6in) pot, using soil-based compost, and leave the upper part of the bulb exposed. Start into growth in late winter. After flowering, feed weekly; in late summer, when the leaves die down, drastically reduce watering, keeping the compost barely moist, to give the plants a rest. Start into growth again in late winter.

Below *Although cyclamen are often discarded after flowering, they can be kept for a number of years as they grow from a tuber. Eventually they make large plants with dozens of flowers.*

Far right *The late-flowering chrysanthemums are among the most popular of flowering plants for the unheated or slightly heated greenhouse. They are easily grown, in large pots, and spend the summer out of doors. Most gardeners use the blooms for cutting.*

Although it produces exotic-looking blooms, the blue passion flower is nevertheless an easily grown climber for the cool greenhouse or conservatory. It is a vigorous plant and will need regular pruning to keep it within bounds.

Hydrangeas

These produce large, mop-like blooms, pink or blue, in the spring. Provide a minimum temperature of 7C (45F).

Young plants should be potted on in spring and summer until they are in 15cm (6in) pots. Use an acid compost if blue flowers are required. Grow in a cold frame for the summer and re-house in early autumn. Keep the compost only just moist in winter. After flowering, the plants can be placed outdoors for the summer. New plants can be raised easily from cuttings taken in mid- or late spring.

Ivy

The ivies *(Hedera)* can be used as climbers or trailers. Some have plain green leaves while others are variegated. They are hardy so can be grown in an unheated greenhouse, but they are also suitable for a cool house.

The green-leaved kinds are ideal for shady parts of the greenhouse, such as under the staging, while variegated kinds need good light to maintain their colour. Shade from strong sun, though. Provide high humidity during warm weather. Feed in the growing season, and keep much drier in the winter months.

Paper flower

The paper flower *(Bougainvillea)* is a colourful climber for the heated conservatory – minimum temperature 10C (50F). Modified leaves, or bracts, around the flowers provide the colour – purple, red, magenta, crimson or orange.

The plant needs plenty of sun, good ventilation and high humidity in summer. Keep much drier in winter. Water well in summer. In early spring, cut out weak shoots and leave the strong stems. Reduce these by one-third if desired. Grow in a soil bed or large pot or tub.

Passion flower

The blue passion flower *(Passiflora caerulea)* is an easy climber for the conservatory with a minimum temperature of 10C (50F).

The passion flower needs humidity and light shade in warm weather, normal watering, but keep much drier in winter. Prune in early spring by thinning out some of the stems, if growth becomes congested. Take out the oldest and leave the younger ones. Cut back side shoots on those remaining to 15cm (6in).

Pelargonium

The regal pelargonium is a popular perennial plant for summer flowering in the heated greenhouse – a minimum winter temperature of 10C (50F) is needed. Its flowers are available in many colours.

Grow the plants in 12.5cm (5in) pots of soil-based compost. Good light is needed and adequate sun, but shade from very strong sunshine. A dry atmosphere is needed all through the year, plus good ventilation. Water as needed in summer, but keep only just moist in winter. Raise new plants from cuttings in late summer – old plants are best discarded.

Poor man's orchid

Poor man's orchid *(Schizanthus)* is a slightly tender annual and needs a minimum temperature of 7–10C (45–50F). It has orchid-like blooms in bright colour combinations and these are produced in winter or spring.

Seeds are sown in late summer and germinated in a cold frame. Grow young plants in a cold frame and pot on until final 15cm (6in) pots are reached. Take the plants into the greenhouse in early autumn and provide well-ventilated conditions. Do not allow the compost to become very wet.

Primroses

Three kinds of primroses or primula are generally grown – *Primula malacoides, P. obconica* (both in various colours), and the yellow *P. × kewensis*. They flower in winter and spring and need a minimum tempera-ture of 7C (45F). Sow seeds any time between late winter and late spring.

Pot on young plants until 12.5cm (5in) pots are reached. Grow in a cold frame from early summer to early autumn, shade from strong sun and keep moist. In the greenhouse, ensure good light, plenty of ventilation, and keep the compost steadily moist, but do not wet the foliage. Discard after flowering.

Slipperwort

The slipperwort *(Calceolaria)* is a popular pot plant for spring flowering, after which it is discarded. It has large pouched flowers in a wide range of brilliant colours. A minimum temperature of 7C (45F) is needed.

Sow seeds in early summer and pot on young plants until they are in 12.5cm (5in) pots. Grow cool at all times – they hate high temperatures. Grow young plants in a cold frame and take into the greenhouse in mid-autumn. Good light is needed and plenty of ventilation. Make sure the compost is not kept wet in autumn or winter.

Wax flower

The wax flower *(Hoya carnosa)* is an evergreen climber with clusters of white waxy flowers produced between late spring and autumn. It is ideal for the small greenhouse or conservatory, grown in a pot or in the greenhouse border. The minimum temperature needed is 7C (45F).

In summer, provide humidity and light shade from strong sun; water as required but keep barely moist in winter. Liquid feed during the summer. Pruning is not generally needed, and the long stems are often trained round circular wire frames.

Winter cherry

In autumn and winter, the winter cherry *(Solanum capsicastrum)* and Jerusalem or Christmas cherry *(S. pseudocapsicum)* produce orange or red berries. Plants are usually discarded when the display is over. A minimum temperature of 7C (45F) is needed.

Sow seeds in late winter or early spring. Young plants are potted on until they are in 12.5cm (5in) pots.

Pinch out the tips of young plants to encourage branching. Place out of doors for the summer. When the plants are in flower, spray them daily with plain water to ensure a good set of berries. Move into the greenhouse in early autumn and provide good ventilation.

Slipperworts, with their brilliant pouched flowers in spring, need to be kept as cool as possible, so are ideal short-term pot plants where minimum artificial heat is provided. They are raised from seeds sown in early summer.

VEGETABLES TO GROW

There are few aspects of greenhouse gardening more rewarding than growing your own vegetables. The range of crops you can grow is enormous, and you can also use your greenhouse to give a head start to vegetables for planting out in spring.

Below *It is possible to produce early beetroots in spring in a cold or slightly heated greenhouse, and the roots are harvested when about the size of a golf ball. Bottom: Aubergines are as easy to grow as tomatoes and indeed make ideal companion crops as they need the same conditions. Most gardeners aim to produce a summer crop.*

Far right *Although cucumbers are easy to grow if warm, very humid conditions can be provided, they are not suitable for combining with tomatoes, aubergines or peppers; however, part of the greenhouse could be screened off for cucumbers.*

Asparagus

For out-of-season asparagus, from mid-winter onwards, lift four-year-old crowns, which have not been cut from previously, in late autumn, after the foliage has died down. Leave plenty of soil around the roots. Store the crowns in a cold, dark place for about a week. Plant the crowns close together under the staging in boxes 23cm (9in) deep, covering them with 10cm (4in) sifted soil. Maintain a temperature of 15.5C (60F) and a steady supply of moisture. They should be ready for cutting three weeks later.

Aubergines

Aubergines or egg-plants are becoming quite popular with gardeners. Because they are grown in a similar way to tomatoes, and need the same conditions, these two crops can be grown successfully together.

Basic conditions needed are good light but shade from strong sunshine; plenty of ventilation; and a temperature of 15.5C–21C (60–70F), with a minimum of 13C (55F) at night. It is a summer crop, but some artificial heat will be needed in the early part of the year.

The usual time to sow seeds is in early spring. As the seeds are large, they can be spaced out 2.5cm (1in) apart on the surface of seed compost. Use a seed tray and a soil-based compost. A temperature of 15.5–18C (60–65F) is needed for germination.

Seedlings are transplanted (pricked out) individually into 7.5cm (3in) pots, and then moved on into 12.5cm (5in) pots. For both stages use a soil-based potting compost. The tips of the young plants should be pinched out when a height of 15cm (6in) has been reached as this results in bushy plants and, therefore, more fruits.

Plant in a soil border, growing-bags or large pots, when the plants are about 15cm (6in) in height. Bamboo canes or growing-bag crop supports will be needed. For details of planting see TOMATOES.

When the flowers are open, gently tap their stems to pollinate the flowers and ensure a good set of fruits. When some fruits have set, give weekly liquid feed.

Beetroots

Early beetroots are easy to produce in a cold or slightly heated greenhouse, using cultivars of round-rooted beet. They can be harvested when about the size of a golf ball.

Beetroots can be grown in a soil border but make sure it has not been freshly manured or this may result in deformed roots. Growing-bags can also be used.

Sow the seeds thinly in early spring, in seed drills 2.5cm (1in) deep, and spaced about 15cm (6in) apart. When the seedlings are large enough to handle, thin them out to 5–7.5cm (2–3in) apart. This may seem close, but the roots are gathered when small.

Keep the soil or compost steadily moist and provide good light and ventilation. You should be able to start harvesting about eight weeks after sowing.

Carrots

It is possible to obtain really early carrots by growing stump-rooted forcing cultivars in a greenhouse. For the earliest crops try to provide a temperature of about 10C (50F), although good results can also be obtained in an unheated or very cool greenhouse.

Sowings can be made in autumn or in mid-to late winter. Ideally, sow in a soil border, but growing-bags can be used. The soil must not be freshly manured or this will result in deformed roots.

Sow the seeds in drills about 15mm (½in) deep and spaced 10cm (4in) apart. Thin out the seedlings as necessary to stand about 2.5cm (1in) apart.

Carrots must have very good light and ventilation, and the soil should be kept steadily moist. Roots can be pulled as soon as they are large enough to use; pencil-thickness is fine for these delicious, out-of-season crops.

Cucumbers

This popular crop needs a very humid atmosphere, and a temperature of 18–21C (65–70F), with a minimum of 15.5C (60F) at night. It will be necessary to provide artificial heat in the early part of the year.

Cucumbers are not suitable for growing with tomatoes, aubergines or peppers,

because they need much higher humidity. However, part of the greenhouse could be screened off for the cucumbers, with a sheet of clear polythene.

Many of the cultivars listed in catalogues are F_1 hybrids: these are not as easy to grow as ordinary cultivars, so choose the latter if you do not have much experience.

The normal sowing period is early to mid-spring. Use 7.5cm (3in) pots and soilless compost. Sow one seed per pot, pushing it, on edge, into the compost. Provide a germination temperature of 18–24C (65–75F).

When young plants have produced their first true leaves, plant in a well-manured soil border, in growing-bags (two plants per bag), or in 22.5cm (9in) pots (use a rich potting compost). When planting in a soil border, set each plant on a mound of John Innes potting compost No. 3.

The top of the root-ball must be 12mm (½in) above the soil or compost to make sure water does not collect around the base of the stem, which would cause rotting. Plants are spaced 60cm (24in) apart.

The plants must be trained up horizontal wires stretched 30cm (12in) apart along one side of the greenhouse. The main stem is tied in to these, and the tip pinched out when the top wire is reached. Side shoots must be pinched out at two leaves beyond a female flower (this has a small fruit behind it) and tied to the wires. Tendrils should be removed. Some cultivars produce male and female flowers, others (mainly the F_1 hybrids) only females. Male flowers must be removed before they open (these are the ones with only a thin stalk behind them).

The greenhouse should be damped down twice a day; in warm weather spray plants with plain water twice daily. Provide light shade from hot sunshine. From six weeks after planting, feed once a week with a general-purpose liquid fertilizer. The soil must be kept constantly moist.

White roots will eventually appear on the surface of the compost – top-dress them with 2.5cm (1in) of similar compost. This must not touch the stems, though. Harvest fruits when large enough to use.

French beans

For the earliest crops of French beans, try growing them under glass. It can be unheated or just frost free. The climbing cultivars are recommended, as they produce a heavier crop than the dwarf kinds.

Seeds can be sown at various times – in early spring if you can provide heat; otherwise in mid- to late spring. For a really early crop, a sowing can be made in midwinter if you can maintain a minimum temperature of 10C (50F).

Use 9cm (3½in) pots and soil-based

compost. Sow one seed per pot. The young plants are planted in a row, 30cm (12in) apart. The stems are trained up strings fixed to a strong horizontal wire in the roof of the greenhouse. The bottom of each string can be secured at soil level with a wooden or wire peg.

The plants must be provided with good light and ventilation and the soil kept constantly moist. You should be able to start picking beans from late spring onwards.

Endive

This is a salad crop, rather like lettuce, and is grown for winter use in a cool or unheated greenhouse. The type to grow is the broad-leaved or Batavian endive.

Seeds are sown in late summer. They may be sown direct in a soil border, or in containers, and the seedlings transplanted. See LETTUCES for further details of plant raising.

Endive likes a fertile soil, so grow in a well-manured soil bed or in growing-bags. Plants should be spaced 30cm (12in) apart each way. Provide the same conditions as for lettuces.

The leaves of endive can be rather bitter unless they are blanched. To blanch, each plant is covered with a large flower pot, with the hole plugged to exclude light, several weeks before harvesting. Do not begin blanching until the endives are fully grown.

Lettuces

Lettuces can be harvested under glass from mid-autumn to mid- or late spring, depending on sowing times and cultivars grown. There are cultivars suited to unheated and heated greenhouses, and it is important to choose cultivars for your particular conditions.

Sowing time depends on the cultivars chosen, but is between late summer and midwinter. It is best to sow a small amount of seed of each cultivar in a 9cm (3½in) pot, using soil-based or soilless seed compost. The seeds should be germinated in a temperature of 10–15.5C (50–60F): no higher or the seeds may not grow. As soon as large enough to handle, transplant seedlings individually into small peat pots or soil blocks.

Lettuces can be grown in a soil border, which should have been dug and manured for a previous crop, such as tomatoes. Rake in a general-purpose fertilizer before planting. Lettuces should be planted 20cm (8in) apart each way. Do not plant too deeply; the lower leaves should be just clear of the surface. Growing-bags can also be used for lettuces, including those which previously contained a crop of tomatoes, peppers, aubergines, etc, in the summer.

Far left *Use the climbing varieties of French beans for growing in a cold or frost-free greenhouse, for they bear heavier crops than the dwarf varieties. Depending on the amount of heat available, beans can be ready for picking in spring or early summer.*

Below *There are many varieties of lettuces for growing under glass, to provide salad material between mid-autumn and late spring. Most are suitable for unheated greenhouses but a few need some artificial heat.*

Far right *Sweet peppers or capsicums are as easy to grow as tomatoes. The fruits can be picked when they are green or unripe, or when fully ripe, when they will be red or yellow, depending on variety.*

Lettuces must have maximum light and really good ventilation. The greenhouse air must be kept dry: if it is damp the fungal disease grey mould, or botrytis, will attack the plants and cause them to rot. The soil must be kept reasonably moist, but when watering try not to wet the leaves.

Lettuces can be harvested when you consider they are a suitable size, but bear in mind that most greenhouse cultivars do not produce the large solid hearts which are typical of outdoor lettuces.

Mushrooms

An easy way for the greenhouse gardener to grow mushrooms is to buy one of the proprietary mushroom kits. These can be obtained from garden centres.

These kits or packs are very often supplied in a special polythene bag or plastic tub, which contains the compost, and generally they are ready to start into growth – just follow the simple instructions supplied.

Mushrooms like a reasonably high temperature, 10–15.5C (50–60F) being ideal. If you cannot maintain this during the colder months of the year, then make a start as the weather warms up in the spring, and continue growing throughout summer and into early autumn. Contrary to popular belief, it is not necessary to grow mushrooms in completely dark conditions, but a convenient place for your mushroom kit would be under the greenhouse staging. You can expect several 'flushes' or crops of mushrooms from the proprietary kits, and they should be harvested while small. Twist them out of the compost rather than cutting the stalks.

Peppers

Sweet peppers, or capsicums, are becoming almost as popular as tomatoes and they also crop during the summer. They make good companions for tomatoes as they require the same conditions: dryish air, warmth and a good amount of sunshine. An ideal temperature range is 15.5–21C (60–70F), with a minimum at night of 13C (55F). Artificial heat will be needed in the early part of the year.

Seeds are usually sown in early spring, although you can sow from midwinter onwards if sufficient heat is available. Use a seed tray and a soil-based compost, and space out the seeds 2.5cm (1in) apart each way. The recommended germination temperature is 18C (65F). When the seedlings are large enough to handle easily, prick them out individually into 7.5cm (3in) pots, using a soil-based potting compost. Before they outgrow these, pot on into 12.5cm (5in) pots. Pinch out the tips of plants when 15cm (6in) high to ensure bushy plants and therefore more peppers.

For details of planting peppers, see TOMATOES. Set the plants 45cm (18in) apart each way. Grow in a soil border, growing-bags or in 25–30cm (10–12in) pots. Plant out when 15cm (6in) high. The plants will need supports – bamboo canes or growing-bag crop supports.

When the flowers have opened, gently tap the flower stems to pollinate the flowers and so ensure fruit setting. Keep the soil or compost steadily moist, ventilate well in warm weather and shade from strong sunshine.

When the first fruits have set, start weekly feeding, using a liquid tomato fertilizer.

The fruits can be picked and used when they are green or unripe, or they can be left until they are fully ripe, when they will be red or yellow, according to cultivar.

Potatoes

If you are maintaining a heated greenhouse, try growing some really early potatoes – to harvest in mid-spring. A temperature of 10C (50F) is needed. You can also have new potatoes in time for Christmas if you plant them in early autumn and supply sufficient heat.

To harvest in mid-spring, plant tubers or 'seed potatoes' in midwinter. First, though, you need to sprout or chit them – that is,

encourage shoots to grow. Place the tubers in a seed tray – the end where the dormant buds are situated should face upwards. Keep them in a frost-proof place with plenty of light and air. When the shoots are about 12mm (½in) long the tubers can be planted.

Potatoes can be grown in large pots. Plant three tubers per 20cm (8in) pot, or five in a 30cm (12in) pot. Growing bags can also be used and a 1.2m (4ft) long bag will hold about eight tubers.

When planting in pots, half fill each with a rich, soil-based potting compost, set the tubers an equal distance apart and cover with 5cm (2in) of compost. Water well and place on the floor of the greenhouse or on the staging. It is necessary to ensure maximum light.

More compost should be added to the pots as the shoots grow, so that the tips are only just showing. Eventually the compost level should be 2.5cm (1in) below the rim of the pot.

If planting in growing-bags, set the tubers about 7.5cm (3in) deep.

Keep the compost steadily moist and feed with a general-purpose liquid fertilizer once there is a lot of top growth.

Early cultivars of potato should be chosen for these early crops.

Radishes

In a greenhouse heated to about 10C (50F), it is possible to harvest radishes in autumn and winter. Radishes are very quick maturing and those cultivars specially bred for forcing or for early cropping should be chosen.

Sowings can be started in autumn and continued in succession throughout the winter.

Grow in a soil border, but not freshly manured, or in growing-bags. Sow the seeds thinly, as the rate of germination is usually very high. Rows should be spaced 10cm (4in) apart. If necessary, thin the seedlings to 2.5cm (1in) apart. Really good light is needed, plus generous ventilation. It is essential to keep the soil moist at all times – if allowed to dry out, growth will slow down and roots will be hard and woody.

Salad onions

These are a good crop to grow with radishes for winter supplies. Again a temperature of 10C (50F) is needed, plus good light and ventilation.

Seeds can be sown in early autumn in a soil bed, growing-bags or even large pots. In a soil bed, rows are spaced 15cm (6in) apart. Sow fairly thickly and pull as soon as large enough for use. The soil must be kept steadily moist.

Tomatoes

This is the most popular greenhouse vegetable grown for summer cropping. The recommended temperature is 15.5–21C (60–70F), with a minimum at night of 13C (55F). Do not allow the temperature to fall any lower or growth will slow down or stop. Artificial heat will be necessary in the early part of the year. Try to maintain a dryish atmosphere.

For summer crops, sow seeds in early spring, using a seed tray and soil-based seed compost. The seeds are large enough to be spaced out 2.5cm (1in) apart each way. Provide a temperature of 18C (65F) for germination. When the seedlings are large enough to handle easily, transplant them individually to 7.5cm (3in) pots, using soil-based potting compost. Before the plants outgrow these, pot on into 12.5cm (5in) pots.

When the plants are 15cm (6in) high they are planted out. If you have an unheated greenhouse, it would be advisable to buy plants, and to plant them in late spring.

Whatever method of growing is used, tomato plants should be spaced 45cm (18in) apart each way. They can be grown in a soil border, well dug and manured in the previous autumn. Apply a general-purpose fertilizer before planting.

Growing-bags are also widely used for tomatoes – if they are to be placed on a soil border, first cover the soil with a sheet of polythene. A 1.2m (4ft) long bag will hold three plants.

Tomatoes can also be grown in 25–30cm (10–12in) pots, using a rich soil-based potting compost. Again, if they are to be placed on soil, first lay a sheet of polythene.

Provide supports after planting – 1.8m (6ft) bamboo canes or growing-bag crop supports. Tie in the plants regularly as they grow. Rub out side shoots as they appear, as the tomato is trained as a single stem.

The soil or compost must be kept steadily moist – do not allow it to dry out or become very wet. Ideally, use water at greenhouse temperature. Ventilate well and shade lightly from very strong sunshine.

Flowers should be pollinated when fully open by gently tapping the flower stems. This will ensure a good set of fruit. Feed weekly, using a liquid tomato fertilizer, as soon as the first fruits have formed.

When five or six trusses of flowers have been produced, pinch out the tip of each plant to prevent further upwards growth.

A few of the lower leaves can be removed as soon as the lower fruits start to ripen to ensure good air circulation around the fruits. Do not cut off too many leaves, though, as this may prevent or retard the development of the young fruits.

Below *If a minimum temperature of 10C (50F) can be provided, salad onions can be grown for pulling in the winter. Seeds are sown quite thickly in early autumn in any suitable container or in a soil border.*

Far right *The tomato is the major crop in amateur greenhouses and most people will aim for a summer harvest, although out-of-season crops are possible if sufficient heat can be provided. Today there are many varieties available, including yellow and striped ones, and the large beef-steak kinds.*

FRUIT TO GROW

Luxury fruit – peaches, figs and grapes, for example – are expensive to buy in the shops, and their flavour can be disappointing. Use your greenhouse to grow luxury fruit to perfection, and save money, too.

Figs

The fig is a large vigorous tree and when grown under glass growth needs to be severely restricted. This is best achieved by growing the trees in 25–30cm (10–12in) pots, to restrict the root system, which gives you easily handled plants and better fruit production. The pots can be stood out of doors in the summer if desired and returned to the greenhouse in early autumn.

Buy a pot-grown fig from a garden centre in late autumn and pot it into a clay pot, with plenty of drainage material in the bottom. Figs are best potted in a limy medium loam (available from garden centres in bags) and, if available, some crushed brick rubble should be added to it. To start with, the pot should be only just big enough to hold the root system. Potting on to a larger pot in subsequent years can be carried out in midwinter, until the final size is reached, but only pot on when the existing pot is really full of roots. In the years when potting on is not carried out, top-dress with loam, first scraping away some of the old soil.

You can get two crops of fruit per year under glass – the first in early or mid-summer, the second in late summer or early autumn. To achieve an early crop, maintain a temperature of 10–15.5C (50–60F) from late winter onwards. A summer temperature of about 26C (80F) is ideal and natural warmth should be sufficient.

Damp down the greenhouse regularly in warm conditions to provide a humid atmosphere; keep the air dry, though, when fruits are ripening. Shade is unnecessary.

The trees are rested in the winter by keeping the greenhouse only frost free and the compost barely moist. Increase watering and temperature in late winter.

Pruning consists of cutting back any vigorous new shoots to five leaves from their base, in summer. Aim for a succession of new shoots which will carry the fruits.

Grapes

A grape vine grown in the traditional way – a long rod (stem) trained up into the greenhouse roof – takes up a good deal of space and is not practical in the small greenhouse. Instead, try growing a grape vine in a pot.

Buy a young plant from a garden centre and pot it in midwinter, in a 30cm (12in) clay pot, using John Innes potting compost No. 3. It can be kept out of doors and taken under glass in late winter, when a temperature of 10C (50F) should be provided. Place outdoors again after fruiting.

The main stem is trained in a spiral fashion around three 1.5–1.8m (5–6ft) bamboo canes inserted, wigwam-style, in the pot. Side shoots will be produced and will need thinning out to 30cm (12in) apart. The tips of these should then be cut out at two leaves beyond a bunch of grapes.

The main rod should be cut back annually by about half its length in winter. Cut back the side shoots, to one or two dormant buds.

The flowers must be pollinated by drawing your hand, half closed, down the truss of flowers – this distributes the pollen. Thin out the berries to give them space to grow, when they are the size of peas. Thin the centre of each bunch; further thinning may also be needed as the berries grow. Use a pair of fine-pointed scissors.

Good ventilation is needed under glass and in summer a temperature of at least 13C (55F) is needed, but this is provided by natural warmth. A humid atmosphere is needed during high temperatures, but do not damp down the greenhouse while the vines are in flower, or when the fruits are ripening, as at these stages a dry atmoshere is needed. When the vines are in full growth water heavily and feed every two weeks.

Melons

These can be grown with or without artificial heat. Choose cultivars accordingly.

In a heated greenhouse sow seeds in early spring; in an unheated greenhouse sow in mid- to late spring. Sow two seeds, on edge, in 7.5cm (3in) pots, using soil-based compost. Germinate in a temperature of 15.5C (60F). If both seeds germinate, remove the weaker. Plant out when well established in their pots. Grow in a well-manured soil border, spacing plants 45cm (18in) apart. A growing-bag can also be used: each bag will hold two plants. The top of the root-ball must be slightly above soil

Below *Although the fig is normally a large vigorous tree, it can be kept small if grown in pots. Two crops a year are possible under glass.*

Far right *Similarly, a grape vine can be kept small by growing a plant in a pot – a far better system for a small greenhouse than the traditional way of growing, which involves training stems up the side of a greenhouse and into the roof area.*

or compost level to prevent stem rot.

Tie in the main stem to horizontal wires spaced 30cm (12in) apart on one wall of the greenhouse, and even up into the roof. Pinch out the tip of the stem when the top wire is reached. Side shoots are tied in horizontally, and their tips removed just beyond the second leaf.

Keep the soil or compost moist, and try to provide a temperature of 15.5–21C (60–70F) by day, and 13C (55F) at night. In summer, aim for 21C (70F) during the day and 15.5C (60F) at night. Shade from strong sun. Ensure moderate humidity.

Female flowers must be hand pollinated (these have a small fruit behind them). A male flower is used to pollinate a female and it should be done when the flowers are fully open. Pick off a male flower (males have just a thin stalk behind them), remove the petals, and brush the centre of a female with it. Use a different male flower to pollinate each female and treat four to six females all at the same time. Only one fruit is allowed to grow on each side shoot, and when fruits start developing remove all further flowers as they appear.

Feed weekly from the time the fruits set. When the fruits start ripening in late summer or early autumn, keep the compost much drier, ventilate well and maintain a dry atmosphere. Fruits will need supporting with nets suspended from the roof from the time they are the size of a tennis ball.

Peaches

The best way to grow peaches under glass is as a pot-grown, dwarf, open-centred bush. The traditional way of fan training against a wall is generally too space consuming for the average greenhouse.

Buy and plant a one- or two-year-old tree in midwinter. Pot it into a 25cm (10in) clay pot, using John Innes potting compost No. 3, with plenty of drainage material in the bottom. Pot on in the winter until you reach a final pot size of 35cm (14in).

Initial training consists of allowing four branches to form a head. These are cut back by half in the winter after planting. All other branches, plus the main stem above them, are cut out. Routine winter pruning involves keeping the centre of the tree open, so remove any crowded, crossing, or inward-growing shoots. Old fruited shoots should be cut back to new ones, which will in turn bear fruits.

The trees can, if desired, be placed out of doors for the summer, once the fruits have formed, but select a sheltered, sunny spot.

Peaches can be grown with or without artificial heat, but they do not need heat in winter. Warmth in spring prevents the flowers being damaged by frost.

Provide good ventilation in winter, but less in spring. In spring spray the trees twice a day with plain water during warm spells, and also damp down the greenhouse. The flowers must be hand pollinated. When fully open, dab the centre of each in turn with a soft, artist's brush. Crowded new shoots must be thinned out but leave sufficient to fruit next year.

The fruitlets must be thinned out to leave only two or three per shoot.

In summer, maintain humid conditions by spraying and damping down, give plenty of ventilation, and feed with a fertilizer high in potash. Keep the atmosphere dry when fruits are ripening. In winter, keep the compost slightly moist.

Rhubarb

This can be forced in a heated greenhouse for autumn and winter use. Lift some three- or four-year-old roots in autumn once the leaves have died down. Lay them on the soil surface to become frosted for two or three weeks, then plant them in a deep box of old potting compost, with the buds level with the surface.

Water well in and put in a dark place. Cover them with an upturned box to exclude light, or put them under the greenhouse staging and black out the sides with sheets of black polythene.

The more heat you can provide, the sooner you will be able to harvest the sticks. A temperature range of 7–15.5C (45–60F) is suitable. Sticks will then be ready in five to eight weeks. Do not use the roots again.

Strawberries

Pot-grown strawberries can be forced in a heated greenhouse. To obtain a worthwhile quantity, you will need at least 12 plants.

Buy young plants in mid- or late summer and pot into 12.5cm (5in) pots, using a soil-based potting compost. Keep them out of doors until midwinter then take them into the greenhouse.

Pot on into 15cm (6in) pots. Place on staging or shelving in really good light. Once growth starts, begin providing heat – maintain 4.5C (40F) to start with. If possible, increase heat gradually so that by mid-spring, when the plants will be in bloom, a temperature of 15.5C (60F) is being maintained.

The flowers must be hand pollinated with a soft brush – when fully open dab the centre of each in turn. Feed with a liquid fertilizer every two weeks once the flowers are open, and continue until the fruits start to ripen. Keep the compost steadily moist from the time the fruits are starting to set.

After fruiting, plant the strawberries in the garden – do not force them again.

Far left *In the small greenhouse, the best way to grow a peach is as a small open-centred bush in a pot. Fruits are produced in late summer or early autumn and artificial heat is not needed.*

Below *If rhubarb is needed for autumn or winter use, force some roots in a heated greenhouse. Sticks can be ready for pulling in five to eight weeks, depending on the amount of heat provided.*

Above *Pots of strawberries placed in a heated greenhouse in midwinter will ripen their fruits several weeks earlier than plants outdoors.*

A YEAR IN YOUR GREENHOUSE

The jobs to do, the flowers to enjoy and the crops to harvest all form part of the greenhouse year. Knowing what to do and exactly when to do it comes with experience, but a greenhouse calendar will help you get it right from the start.

There are so many things going on in a greenhouse throughout the year that a checklist, even for the experienced gardener, is extremely helpful, as it ensures that you do not forget to make some vital sowing or carry out an important aspect of cultivation.

The sections on crops to harvest and flowers to enjoy will help you to decide what you want to grow and enable you to have a fully stocked and productive greenhouse throughout the year. The greenhouse need not be empty in the winter, even if you do decide you cannot afford to heat it.

The information given is very general, as the times of sowing, planting, harvesting and flowering depend on the part of the country in which you live, on weather conditions, and of course on the amount of heat you are able to provide.

Most of the plants included here need some artificial heat in the colder months, say from early autumn until late spring. Details of temperature requirements will be found under the appropriate plants in other chapters.

Plants which can be kept in a cold greenhouse (with no artificial heat whatsoever) over the winter, for flowers, foliage interest or crops, are as follows: alpines, dwarf hardy bulbs, daffodils, hyacinths, tulips, crocuses, camellias, hardy annuals for spring flowering, chrysanthemums (ideally a little heat if possible to keep the air dry while in flower), ivy, beetroots, carrots, endive, and some winter lettuces. The following popular fruits will survive quite happily without artificial heat in winter: figs, grapes and peaches.

There is no reason why a greenhouse or conservatory should not be used all the year round – indeed, too many amateur greenhouses are left to stand empty in winter. Many plants can be grown without heat in the winter.

Midwinter

Even if the temperature is low, the days are getting longer at this time and if your greenhouse is heated, there should be plenty of plants in flower now, to boost your morale. An unheated greenhouse can be colourful, too, with a display of alpine plants, heaths and camellias.

Jobs to do

Watering should be carried out very sparingly.

Ventilate whenever the weather is fine.

Sow sweet peas, Barberton daisy *(Gerbera)*, *Begonia semperflorens* and F_1 zonal pelargoniums for summer bedding.

Sow sweet peas in individual containers

Sow carrots, French beans, lettuces, onions for later planting in the garden.

Take cuttings of heliotrope and flame nettle *(Coleus)*.

Pot newly purchased peach tree, or pot on older one if required.

Pot newly purchased grape vine and stand out of doors.

Move figs into larger pots if necessary or topdress with compost.

Prune peach trees.

The centre of a peach tree is kept open

Take potted strawberry plants into the greenhouse.

Plant potato tubers in pots or growing bags.

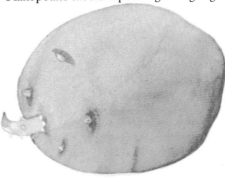

Early potatoes should be planted now

Prune grape vine.

Cut back hard old fuchsias and re-pot into fresh compost.

Bring pots and bowls of hardy bulbs into the greenhouse.

Start chrysanthemum roots into growth

Indian azaleas will be in full bloom

and take cuttings as soon as shoots are long enough.

Lilies can still be potted for flowering in the greenhouse.

Remove all dead leaves and flowers from plants to prevent an attack of botrytis, or grey mould, fungus.

Plants to enjoy

Alpines, arum or zantedeschia, azaleas, dwarf bulbs, other hardy bulbs (like daffodils, hyacinths, tulips and crocuses), camellias, carnations, cyclamen, freesias, hippeastrums, ivies throughout the winter, primroses *(Primula)*, winter cherry *(Solanum capsicastrum* and *S. pseudocapsicum)* and winter heaths *(Erica)*.

Crops to harvest

Asparagus, carrots (stump-rooted forcing cultivars), endive, lettuces, radishes, rhubarb and salad onions.

Late winter

Though the ground outdoors may be frozen hard, or even under snow, you can be busy in the cool greenhouse, sowing seeds of flowers and vegetables, and putting tuberous-rooted plants, such as begonias, to sprout. Organizing the composts, containers and seeds for the main sowing in spring, can be done now.

Jobs to do

Watering should be carried out very sparingly.

Ventilate whenever the weather is fine.

Make sowings of summer bedding plants such as lobelia, ageratum, petunias, antirrhinums, salvias.

Sow greenhouse pot plants – primroses

Sow Barberton daisy for summer blooms

Cinerarias for the cool greenhouse

(Primula), winter cherry *(Solanum capsicastrum* and *S. pseudocapsicum)*, Barberton daisy *(Gerbera)*.

Sow sweet peas for later planting out.

Sow tomatoes if you can provide plenty of heat, and broad beans and peas for later planting out in the garden.

Box up dormant dahlia tubers to provide cuttings (give gentle heat) and take

cuttings when available.

Take cuttings of fuchsias, and verbenas for summer bedding.

Pot rhizomes of achimenes and tubers of begonia and gloxinia.

Pot on young perpetual-flowering carnations.

Pot bulbs of hippeastrum.

Sow carrots for greenhouse crops.

Increase watering and temperature for figs.

Take potted grape vine into greenhouse.

Pollinate peach flowers to ensure fruit set.

Plants to enjoy

Alpines, arum or zantedeschia, azalea, dwarf bulbs, other hardy bulbs (like daffodils, hyacinths, tulips and crocuses), camellias, carnations, cinerarias, cyclamen, freesias, hippeastrum, primroses *(Primula)* and winter cherry *(Solanum capsicastrum* and *S. pseudocapsicum)*.

Crops to harvest

Asparagus, carrots, lettuces and radishes.

Pollinate peach flowers when fully open

Early spring

If your greenhouse is unheated, then the weather will very much determine what can be done at this time. Frosty weather is still a probability, so be on your guard, but whatever sunlight is about will be magnified by the greenhouse glass or plastic, making conditions more favourable for the plants inside.

Jobs to do

Ventilate more freely in favourable weather.

Watering can now be increased.

Sow half-hardy annuals or summer-bedding plants like French and African marigolds, alyssum, annual phlox, ten-

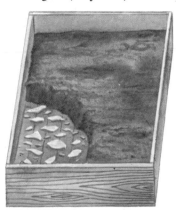

Sow seeds in well-drained trays

Large seeds can be sown in drills

Moisten compost after sowing

week stocks, zinnias, asters, busy Lizzie *(Impatiens)*, mimulus, gazanias, mesembryanthemums (or Livingstone daisies), nicotiana, verbena.

Sow aubergines, tomatoes, peppers, cucumbers, beetroots, celery for later planting out, French beans, melons.

Sow primroses *(Primula)*, freesias, Cape primrose *(Streptocarpus)*, winter cherry *(Solanum capsicastrum* and *S. Pseudo-capsicum)*.

Pinch out young fuchsias to make them branch.

Take cuttings of outdoor chrysanthemums, dahlias, heliotrope, verbena, flame nettle *(Coleus)*, perpetual-flowering carnations and many greenhouse plants.

Buy and pot up some new fuchsias.

Start old fuchsias into growth by increasing temperature and watering.

Prune the paper flower *(Bougainvillea)* and the passion flower *(Passiflora caerulea)*.

Feed autumn-sown annuals in pots.

Pot on as required young cyclamen, pelargoniums and fuchsias.

Harden off sweet peas in a cold frame ready for planting outdoors.

Pot up tubers of begonias and gloxinias.

Pot-grown daffodils make a fine spring display in a cold or cool greenhouse

Plants to enjoy

Alpines, arums or zantedeschia, azaleas, hardy annuals sown in autumn, dwarf hardy bulbs, other hardy bulbs (like daffodils, hyacinths, tulips and crocuses), camellias, carnations, cinerarias, cyclamen, freesias, hippeastrums, primroses *(Primula)*, poor man's orchid *(Schizanthus)*, slipper-wort *(Calceolaria)*, winter cherry *(Solanum capsicastrum* and *S. pseudocapsicum)*.

Crops to harvest

Asparagus, carrots, lettuces and radishes.

Mid-spring

With the increasing light levels, plant growth in the greenhouse will speed up. Be careful, though, as the light and warmth that encourage plants also encourage dormant greenhouse pests to become active again.

Jobs to do

Ventilation can now be considerably increased.

Shading should be used, especially for seedlings.

Watering will need to be increased.

Make sowings of half-hardy annuals or summer-bedding plants.

Sow vegetables – tomatoes, cucumbers, French beans.

Sow melons.

Sow pot plants – primroses *(Primulas),* busy Lizzie *(Impatiens),* cinerarias, celosia, flame nettle *(Coleus).*

Prick out seedlings sown earlier.

Prick out seedlings into trays or pots

Pollinate the flowers of strawberries when fully open.

Plant tomatoes, aubergines, cucumbers, peppers, melons in heated greenhouse.

Pot on fuchsias as necessary and give them their final stopping.

Stand camellias out of doors after flowering.

Harden off outdoor chrysanthemums in a cold frame before planting out.

Most freesias are beautifully scented

A mushroom kit can be started off now

Mushrooms can be started this month.

Take cuttings of hydrangeas.

Plant hanging baskets with suitable plants, such as trailing fuchsias, petunias, lobelia and alyssum.

Greenhouse chrysanthemums will need final potting.

Any foliage pot plants and other permanent pot plants can be potted on as necessary at this time of year.

Side shoots of grape vines will need pinching back.

Flowers of grapes will need pollinating when fully open.

Watering of cacti can be increased from now onwards.

When freesias have finished flowering, the corms can be gradually dried off.

Regular feeding of all actively growing plants can commence now and should continue throughout spring and summer.

Regular damping down can now be started.

Plants to enjoy

Alpines, arums or zantedeschia, hardy annuals, dwarf hardy bulbs, other hardy bulbs (like daffodils, hyacinths, tulips and crocuses), camellias, carnations, cinerarias, clivias, freesias, hippeastrums, hydrangeas, primroses *(Primula),* poor man's orchid *(Schizanthus)* and slipperwort *(Calceolaria).*

Crops to harvest

Asparagus, carrots, French beans, lettuces and potatoes from midwinter planting.

Late spring

With reasonable weather and a reasonably sheltered garden, you should be able to start moving some of your flower and vegetable seedlings outdoors, to harden them off before planting out. This will give you more room in the greenhouse to continue successional sowing and potting on.

Jobs to do
Water freely from now onwards.
Damp down regularly, especially in warm weather.
Give plenty of ventilation when warm.
Shade plants from strong sunshine.
Harden off in a cold frame all plants which are to be planted in the garden, including summer bedding plants.

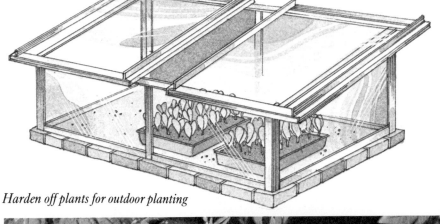

Harden off plants for outdoor planting

Pot on perpetual-flowering carnations to final pots.
Sow pot plants – cineraria, slipperwort

(Calceolaria), busy Lizzie *(Impatiens)*, primroses *(Primula)*.
Make sowings of French beans.

Plant aubergines, cucumbers, peppers, tomatoes and melons.
Mushrooms can be started, using proprietary mushroom kit.
Pollinate the flowers of grapes when fully open.
Dry off cyclamen tubers.
Cuttings can be taken of hydrangeas.

Make hydrangea cuttings from new shoots

Artificial heat can be turned off, ideally, at the end of this period.
Insulation material can be removed once the heat has been turned off.

Plants to enjoy
Hardy annuals, Barberton daisy *(Gerbera)*, bird of paradise *(Strelitzia reginae)*, carnations, clivia, fuchsias, hydrangeas, regal pelargoniums, slipperwort *(Calceolaria)* and wax flower *(Hoya carnosa)*.

Crops to harvest
Asparagus, beetroots, French beans, lettuces and strawberries.

Early summer

The days are at their longest now, and this is often one of the most attractive times of the year in the greenhouse and garden alike. With the advent of hot weather a real possibility, greenhouse watering and ventilation will become regular tasks.

Jobs to do

Provide plenty of ventilation.

Shade plants from strong sunshine.

Water plants freely.

Damp down regularly, especially in warm weather.

Greenhouse chrysanthemums can now be stood outdoors for the summer.

Stand hydrangeas outdoors when flowering is over, and fig and peach trees.

Spray open flowers of winter cherry *(Solanum capsicastrum* and *S. pseudocapsicum)* with water to encourage fruit set, and stand plants outdoors.

Place young cyclamen, cinerarias, young hydrangeas, primroses or primulas in a cold frame.

There is still time to sow primroses *(Primula)*, slipperwort *(Calceolaria)* and cinerarias.

Take cuttings of regal pelargoniums and fuchsias.

The earliest tomatoes will be ready

Pelargonium cuttings rooted now will provide next year's flowering plants

Thin bunches of grapes as soon as the berries reach the size of peas.

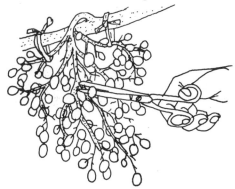

Remove male flowers of cucumbers from now onwards.

Pinch out side shoots of cucumbers and melons, and also remove side shoots of tomatoes.

Pollinate flowers of peppers, tomatoes and melons and continue pollinating for as long as necessary.

Plants to enjoy

Barberton daisy *(Gerbera)*, tuberous begonias, bird of paradise *(Strelitzia reginae)*, brunfelsia, busy Lizzie *(Impatiens)*, Cape primrose *(Strepto-*

Gloxinias need shade and high humidity

carpus), perpetual-flowering carnations, flame nettle *(Coleus)*, fuchsias, gloxinias, paper flower *(Bougainvillea)* and regal pelargoniums.

Crops to harvest

Beetroots, figs, French beans, mushrooms, peppers, strawberries and tomatoes.

Midsummer

Midsummer can be the driest, hottest time of the year and though your garden may need regular watering, it is even more crucial for plants growing in the greenhouse. Damping down, to give the greenhouse a humid atmosphere, will probably be necessary, and extra feeding, to replace the nutrients washed away by frequent watering.

Jobs to do

Ventilate freely, especially in warm weather conditions.

Shade from strong sunshine.

Water freely – twice a day may be necessary.

Damp down twice a day in warm weather.

Re-pot old cyclamen tubers into fresh compost and start into growth.

Take cuttings of fuchsias and pelargoniums.

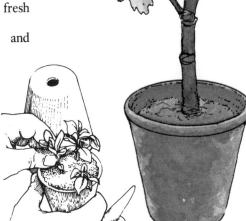

Place young perpetual-flowering carnations in cold frame for summer.

Place regal pelargoniums out of doors for a few weeks in a warm sheltered spot.

Place winter cherry *(Solanum capsicastrum* and *S. pseudocapsicum)* out of doors for the summer and spray the flowers daily with water.

Pot on any root-bound, containerized plants.

Feed greenhouse chrysanthemums and water well.

Prune fig trees – cut back new shoots.

Pot and place out of doors young strawberry plants intended for forcing.

Plants to enjoy

Achimenes, Barberton daisies *(Gerbera)*, tuberous begonias, bird of paradise *(Strelitzia reginae)*, brunfelsia, busy Lizzie *(Impatiens)*, cacti, Cape primrose *(Streptocarpus)*, carnations, celosias, fuchsias, gloxinias, paper flower *(Bougainvillea)*, passion flower *(Passiflora caerulea)* and regal pelargoniums.

Crops to harvest

Aubergines, cucumbers, figs, French beans, mushrooms, peaches, peppers and tomatoes.

Above left *Take cuttings of fuchsias. Using a dibber, plant three or four of them into each small pot.*

Above right *Figs can be pruned, cutting back any new shoots, and harvested.*

Below left *The shrub brunfelsia flowers freely throughout the summer.*

Below right *Mushrooms will be ready for gathering. Gently twist them out rather than cutting the stalks.*

Late summer

Though the days are getting shorter, they can still be very hot, and various pests and diseases, encourged by the warmth, can be a problem in the greenhouse. Whitefly, in particular, may need dealing with, and fungal infections, especially mildew.

Jobs to do

Ventilate freely, especially in warm weather conditions.

Shade from strong sunshine.

Water freely – check twice a day for requirements.

Damp down twice a day in warm conditions.

Take cuttings of regal and zonal pelargoniums.

Sow seeds of poor man's orchid *(Schizanthus)*, hardy annuals for spring flowering in pots, cyclamen.

Sow seeds of salad vegetables, including endive and lettuces.

Cyclamen seeds can be hand spaced

Pot freesia corms and place in a cold frame.

Start to reduce watering of hippeastrums to give the bulbs a rest.

Pot and place out of doors young strawberry plants intended for forcing.

Check supports for heavy-fruited plants such as melons.

Above *Cucumbers will be ready for harvesting. There is no need to wait until they become very long – small fruits are just as good.* **Right** *Cape primroses flower throughout summer and need shade and high humidity*

Plants to enjoy

Barberton daisies *(Gerbera)*, tuberous begonias, bird of paradise *(Strelitzia reginae)*, brunfelsia, busy Lizzie *(Impatiens)*, Cape primrose *(Streptocarpus)*, carnations, celosias, Chilean bellflower *(Lapageria rosea)*, fuchsias, gloxinias, paper flower *(Bougainvillea)* and passion flower *(Passiflora caerulea)*.

Crops to harvest

Aubergines, cucumbers, figs, grapes, melons, mushrooms, peaches, peppers and tomatoes.

Early autumn

With the advent of cooler weather, many greenhouse plants seem to perk up, and flower more profusely than they did in the oppressive summer heat. It is a good time to clean up the greenhouse, after all the activity of spring and summer, to make it ready for the winter season.

Jobs to do

Plants will now be requiring less water.

Shading can be dispensed with.

Give less ventilation from now onwards but continue with some ventilation throughout autumn and winter.

Stop damping down the greenhouse.

Clear out summer crops as soon as harvesting has finished (tomatoes, cucumbers, etc).

Take the opportunity of a fairly empty greenhouse to thoroughly clean it out – scrub it down and sterilize. Also sterilize the soil borders.

Soil borders can be sterilized with a solution of formaldehyde to kill pests

Carry out any repairs and preservation treatment.

Clean and sterilize all empty containers, such as pots and seed trays.

Start heating, and make sure the house is well insulated to conserve heat.

House and disbud chrysanthemums.

Return to the greenhouse any tender plants that have been out of doors or in a cold frame for the summer. These include cinerarias, cyclamen, freesias, hydrangeas, poor man's orchid *(Schizanthus),* primroses *(Primula),* winter cherries *(Solanum capsicastrum* and *S. pseudocapsicum).* Also return figs and peach trees to the greenhouse.

Place potted grape vines outdoors after fruiting.

Pot off seedlings of poor man's orchid *(Schizanthus)* and cyclamen.

Pot bulbs, such as daffodils, hyacinths, tulips, crocuses and dwarf hardy bulbs for a spring display.

Sow seeds of hardy annuals for spring flowering in pots.

Dry off tubers of begonias, gloxinias and achimenes.

Sow vegetables: carrots, lettuces, radishes in succession, and salad onions.

Buy alpine plants and pot them. Keep them in a cold frame until they are coming into flower.

Plants to enjoy

Busy Lizzie *(Impatiens),* Cape primrose *(Streptocarpus),* carnations, Chilean bellflower *(Lapageria rosea),* fuchsias, gloxinias, paper flower *(Bougainvillea)* and passion flower *(Passiflora caerulea).*

Crops to harvest

Aubergines, cucumbers, figs, grapes, melons, mushrooms, peaches, peppers, radishes and tomatoes.

Above *Aubergine or egg plant.* **Below** *Blooms of the blue passion flower*

Mid-autumn

Protection of frost-tender plants in the greenhouse is the prime responsibility this month. Heat will almost certainly be needed at night, and probably during the day as well, as the mild weather comes to an end. Watering will be much less frequent now, as plant growth slows down.

Jobs to do

Water plants very carefully and sparingly. Ventilate adequately according to weather conditions – keep air dry.

If not already done, move in all tender plants that have been out of doors or in a cold frame for the summer.

Start resting Cape primroses *(Streptocarpus)* by reducing watering.

Dry off old fuchsias to rest them over the winter.

Make sowings of carrots and lettuces.

Lift and box rhubarb crowns for forcing in heated greenhouse.

Pot lily bulbs for flowering in the greenhouse next spring/early summer.

Plants to enjoy

Busy Lizzie *(Impatiens)*, carnations, Chilean bellflower *(Lapageria rosea)*, chrysanthemums and cyclamen.

Crops to harvest

Aubergines, lettuces, peppers, radishes and tomatoes. There may be a few fruits left on the summer crops.

Below left *Whenever the weather permits, open greenhouse windows and doors to allow for plenty of ventilation. Make sure, however, that the air inside is always kept dry.*

Bottom left *Lilies can be potted up and kept out of direct light to ensure early blooms for bringing indoors or for colour in the greenhouse.*

Below *Cut chrysanthemums when full open.*

Late autumn

This is a quiet time of the year in the greenhouse, with very little sowing or potting on to be done. Though the air may be cold, as long as it is not frosty some ventilation will be needed. Fresh air helps to keep the plants healthy and to discourage the build up of fungal infections, such as damping off, associated with moist, stagnant air.

Jobs to do

Water plants very carefully and sparingly.
Ventilate adequately according to weather conditions. Keep air dry.
Start to bring in bulbs for forcing.
Cut down the stems of autumn-flowering chrysanthemums as soon as flowering is over and put plants in cold frame.

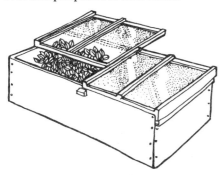

Take dwarf hardy bulbs into the greenhouse and place on the staging in good light.
Keep cacti dry from now onwards, but forest cacti (like the Christmas cactus) must not be allowed to dry out.
Take potted camellias into the greenhouse for winter and spring flowers.
Make more sowings of lettuces.
Buy a young fig tree and pot it.
Reduce watering of fig trees to rest them.
Lift and box asparagus and rhubarb crowns for forcing in a heated greenhouse.

Blanch endive for several weeks

Plants to enjoy

Carnations, chrysanthemums, cyclamen, primroses *(Primula)* winter cherry *(Solanum capsicastrum* and *S. pseudocapsicum).*

Crops to harvest

Carrots (stump-rooted forcing cultivars for autumn/winter use), endive, lettuces, radishes, rhubarb and salad onions.

Below Cacti should be kept dry from now until mid-spring but if plants shrivel excessively during the winter a little water may be given. Keep them cool and ensure they receive maximum light. **Bottom** *However, the forest cacti, like the popular Christmas cactus, should be watered all the year round, keeping the compost steadily moist*

Early winter

A cool greenhouse can be a great help in early winter, in the bringing on of flowering plants, including forced bulbs, to decorate the house for Christmas. After their stint in a centrally-heated house, the plants can be returned, together with any pot plants you may have received as gifts, to the more congenial greenhouse environment, to continue their display.

Jobs to do
Water plants very sparingly and do not splash water around.
Ventilate adequately according to weather conditions. Keep air dry.
Cut down the stems of late-flowering chrysanthemums as soon as flowering is over and put plants in cold frame.

Box up chrysanthemum roots in compost

Continue housing bulbs for forcing.
Prune grape vines and peach trees.
Hardy annuals can be transferred from the cold frame to the greenhouse.
Sow more lettuces.

Plants to enjoy
Azaleas, bulbs such as daffodils, hyacinths, tulips and crocuses, camellias, carnations, chrysanthemums, cyclamen, freesias, hippeastrum, primroses *(Primulas)*, winter cherry *(Solanum capsicastrum* and *S. pseudocapsicum)* and winter heaths *(Erica)*.

Top *Cyclamen will continue flowering for many weeks.* **Above** *One can continue forcing rhubarb roots in heat*

Crops to harvest
Carrots, endive, lettuces, radishes, rhubarb and salad onions.

PESTS & DISEASES

Even the most well-run greenhouse is occasionally vulnerable to pest and disease problems. Being able to recognize the problem, and deal with it as quickly and effectively as possible, will keep your plants healthy and happy, and cropping and flowering well.

Pests and diseases are troublesome enough in the open garden, but under glass they are even more of a nightmare. Due to the warm, favourable, greenhouse conditions, they tend to multiply very rapidly.

As far as possible, try to prevent pests and diseases building up. Maintaining clean, hygienic conditions will go a long way towards preventing troubles. Annual washing down of the greenhouse and sterilizing, using clean containers and sterilized composts, removing dead and dying plant material and generally growing plants well are all important aspects of control.

Nevertheless, pests and diseases will still appear and then you must act swiftly in an effort to eliminate them.

The most popular method is to spray plants with a liquid insecticide or fungicide. Alternatively, dusts can be used. These are particularly recommended for plants which do not like their leaves wetted, for flowers, for stored plant material and for use in autumn and winter when plants and the atmosphere should be kept dry.

Pesticides can also be applied in the form

of smoke. Smoke cannisters, rather like fireworks, are ignited in the greenhouse, which remains closed down for several hours to trap the smoke. Sometimes it is more convenient simply to pick off pests and destroy them, or to pick off the odd leaf infected with pest or disease.

Biological control of pests is being used more and more under glass. A parasitic or predatory insect or mite is introduced into the greenhouse to destroy a particular pest. The parasitic wasp *(Encarsia formosa)* is used to control whitefly, one of the most serious pests under glass. Another major pest, red spider mite, is controlled with a predatory mite *(Phytosieulus persimilis)*. These are supplied on leaves and introduced into the greenhouse at the beginning of the growing season – early to mid-spring.

Biological control should only be used when there are whitefly or red spider mites on the plants, otherwise the predators will quickly die, for they will have nothing to feed on. Pesticides must not be used in the greenhouse when biological control has been introduced.

Below left and right *Use insecticides and fungicides strictly according to the manufacturer's instructions and apply as soon as trouble is apparent.*

Common pests

1. Aphids – *greenfly or blackfly attack many plants, sucking the sap which weakens and distorts the plants. Control – pick off badly affected leaves; malathion sprays; HCH smokes.*

2. Caterpillars – *larvae of moths or butterflies, generally greenish, eat leaves of plants, including carnations. Control – pick off by hand; or spray plants with malathion, derris or HCH.*

3. Earwigs – *familiar insects with 'pincers' at the rear. Generally eat flower petals of carnations, chrysanthemums and other plants. Control – dust flowers and foliage with HCH.*

4. Eelworms – *often live inside plant tissue, microscopic. Attack many plants, including chrysanthemums and tomatoes. Severely weaken and distort growth. Control – destroy affected plants.*

5. Leaf miners – *tiny white grubs which tunnel inside leaves of chrysanthemums and cinerarias, severely weakening them. Tunnels can be clearly seen. Control – remove affected leaves; use HCH or malathion sprays.*

6. Mealy bugs – *soft bugs covered in whitish powder, which attack many plants, sucking the sap and weakening growth. Control – pick off; use malathion or HCH sprays; 'paint' with methylated spirits.*

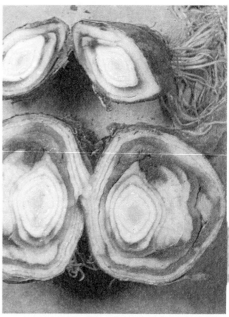

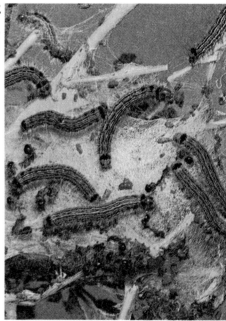

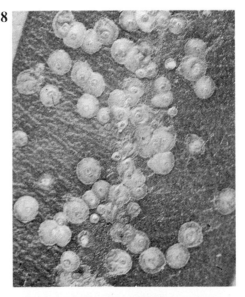

7. Red spider mites – *barely visible reddish 'spiders'. Suck sap of many plants, resulting in pale mottling on the leaves. Control – ideally biological; humid atmosphere discourages these pests.*

8. Scale insects – *scale-like creatures, brown, stationary. Suck sap of many plants, weakening them. Control – pick or scrape off; use malathion sprays if colonies are very large.*

9. Slugs – *these well-known creatures attack many soft plants, such as lettuces. They eat leaves, stems and fruits. Control – use slug pellets containing methiocarb around plants.*

10. Snails – *cause same damage as slugs and controlled in the same way.*

11. Thrips – *very small brown insects, attack many plants, sucking sap, causing speckled leaves and flowers. The photograph shows damage to gladioli flowers. Control – use sprays of malathion as soon as symptoms are noticed.*

12. Whitefly – *one of the most serious pests. Tiny white flies weaken plants by sucking sap. Found on undersides of leaves. Control – the most effective method is biological control.*

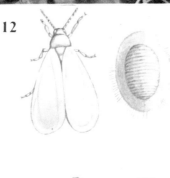

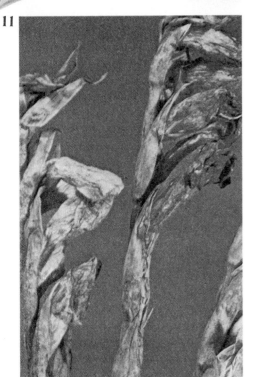

Common diseases

1. Blossom end rot – *brown or black circular patch at the 'blossom end' of tomato fruits. Caused by shortage of water when young fruits are developing. Control – make sure soil or compost never dries out completely.*

2. Botrytis – *or grey mould. Grey fungus on all parts of plants. Causes rotting. Most plants susceptible. Control – clean, hygienic conditions; ensure good ventilation; remove affected material; spray plants with benomyl fungicide.*

3. Damping off – *a seedling disease – seedlings collapse and die. Control – compost and containers must be sterilized; soak compost with Cheshunt Compound after sowing and pricking out.*

4. Mildew – *leaves and shoot tips have white powdery covering. Results in distorted growth. Many plants attacked, especially lettuces and grapes. Control – spray with benomyl; ensure good ventilation.*

5. Peach leaf curl – *leaves of peaches become curled and bright red. Also attacks nectarines. Control – in late winter spray with Bordeaux Mixture.*

6. Potato blight – *attacks potatoes and tomatoes. Brown patches on foliage; dark-brown patches on tomato fruits, followed by rotting. Control – use zineb sprays in early summer.*

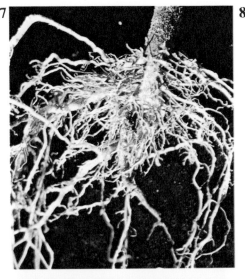

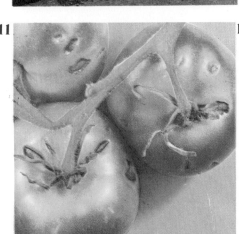

7. Root rot – *common with tomatoes. Roots rot and plant wilts. Control – generally caused by very wet soil or compost, so avoid over-watering.*

8. Rust – *several plants attacked – chrysanthemums, carnations and pelargoniums particularly. Symptoms are brown-orange spots on leaves. Control – badly affected leaves should be picked off. Use zineb or thiram sprays.*

9. Stem rot – *susceptible plants are tomatoes, melons and cucumbers. Base of stem rots, plants collapse. Control – caused by careless watering – make sure you do not wet the base of the stems.*

10. Tomato leaf-mould – *tomatoes attacked. Brown-yellow fungus on leaves, which become distorted and weakened. Control – use sprays of benomyl or thiram as soon as seen.*

11. Wilt – *another common disease of tomatoes. Plants first wilt and then collapse. Control – affected plants should be destroyed; plant only in sterilized soil or compost; maintain correct growing conditions (see TOMATOES). The photograph shows virus spotted wilt: plants with this should also be destroyed.*

12. Viruses – *many plants attacked, including tomatoes and cucumbers. Various symptoms: leaves often streaked or mottled with yellow; stunted or distorted growth; deformed fruits or flowers. Control – affected plants must be destroyed. Destroy aphids, as they spread viruses.*

CHAPTER SIX
THE GARDEN HANDYMAN

Left: *Some of the basic ingredients of garden construction: sand, cement and aggregates which can give your garden shape and structure.*

THE GARDEN HANDYMAN

Running a garden involves so much more than coaxing out beautiful blooms, grooming a lush lawn, or keeping a hedge in trim. Before you can even begin to plant out the plot or to sow your first seeds, you have to decide exactly what type of garden you want, what it will contain and how it will look.

The garden consists of many features which are reliant on each other: if one should fall by the wayside, the rest tend to follow. So it's very important to spend a lot of time on creating and maintaining an orderly plot.

Starting with the down-to-earth basics, you will need to know how to style your plot to suit your preferences – whether you want a formal courtyard-style garden with a large, paved area or a more informal effect with different-shaped flower beds and wild shrubberies and undergrowth. You may decide on a functional, neat and orderly site with a well-defined lawn, vegetable patch and planting beds or alternatively a garden that is full of colour and scent that is a joy for everybody to behold.

Identifying soil types or spotting the cause of a poorly-drained site, are some of the early gardening techniques that are easy to learn and put into practice.

Many different and versatile building materials are available for use in the garden. They can help to define the various areas of the garden: you will discover that there is so much you can do using bricks, concrete or timber, without being an expert bricklayer, builder or carpenter. Laying crazy paving or perhaps building a brick wall are tasks that can be easily undertaken and which can really enhance your garden.

Providing the garden with electric lighting, for the shed, patio and garden tools or water for nourishing your crops and blooms, should not be beyond the capabilities of the average, practical gardener. Gardening activities can then be extended beyond the daylight hours – your potting shed can become a warm, light place to work. No longer will you have to traipse through the house with watering cans or use the kitchen tap for a hosepipe – your garden can have its own tap and benefit from its own personal supply of water.

Apart from the regular weeding, pruning, mowing and watering that are very necessary for the upkeep of the garden, there will always be problems with pests, diseases and inclement weather. Pests and diseases, however, can be controlled, and often averted, by keeping a careful watch on all the plants and shrubs in the garden. Persistent pests can be kept at bay with the use of insecticides and repellents, which are easily available from garden centres and DIY shops. Plant disease is difficult to cure and once established all affected plants should be destroyed as soon as possible to protect the rest of the garden.

Once your garden is formed and maturing, and you are involved with the daily task of keeping it running smoothly, you will find that constant maintenance is of utmost importance: you should survey the site regularly to look for any danger signals. Inspect the boundaries for wind damage, for example, and beware of the onset of rot and general dilapidation caused by the passing of time and adverse weather conditions. Repairs throughout the garden should not prove to be difficult, you will soon find your self capable of fitting a new pane of glass in the greenhouse, replacing a rotten fence post, or maybe re-laying a subsided path or driveway.

Well-maintained tools and equipment should be one of the gardener's prime considerations. They should always be cleaned thoroughly after use and, where necessary, regularly sharpened and oiled. If they are neglected your garden will suffer.

When it comes to tackling more complex garden projects, you can hire equipment and machinery so that you can complete the job more quickly. A concrete mixer, for example, can be a great help when you have a large area of concrete to complete.

Choosing garden furniture can be an enjoyable pastime. You can spend some time looking at the many different styles that are available and decide what you want to buy or possibly make yourself. Basic rustic, wooden furniture has a country charm and can be easy to make. Modern, tubular furniture, alternatively, is easy to clean and comes in a variety of fabrics.

When your garden is running like clockwork, you can leave your regular chores for a while and spend some time just relaxing and enjoying your well-run garden.

Opposite *Many small building projects, using many different materials, can be undertaken in your garden to improve and enhance its features.*

DOWN-TO-EARTH BASICS

Whether you want to remodel your garden, improve poor drainage or simply bolster the soil's natural structure and resources, you'll find that basic, sound groundwork reaps the best results.

Opposite *Don't settle for a garden that's the wrong shape: careful cutting-and-filling can alter its profile to suit your requirements.*

Below *Drive a timber peg into the ground to the level you want using a club hammer.*

Bottom *Check that the pegs are at the same depth by spanning their tops with a long straightedge plank and spirit level, then carefully adjust the soil level to the peg heights.*

The secret of a successful garden lies in thorough preparation of the site. Without the initial groundwork your plot will be plagued by ailments and problems.

A steeply sloping garden, for instance, means poor access – especially with equipment such as a lawnmower or wheelbarrow; an entirely flat garden, however, may actually benefit from the introduction of changes of level. Remodelling the earth to improve unsatisfactory conditions is quite straightforward, if laborious.

Even if you don't need to alter the contours of the ground, it may be necessary to improve inadequate drainage to promote healthy plant growth. Soil care, too, is a vital part of garden maintenance, and digging techniques combined with nutritional treatments are just as important as regular weeding for a well-tended, fertile garden.

Levels and levelling

Changes in level in a garden can be visually attractive but can equally be susceptible to poor drainage, soil erosion and weak plant growth. Installing a soakaway (see p. 371) to cope with poor drainage, along with forms of soil improvement (see pp. 372–3) can aid the condition but you may find that remodelling the earth is more beneficial.

If the garden is composed of substantial differences in level, work within these contours. But remember that a slope should look as natural as possible. If it lies at an angle steeper than 30 degrees, the nourishing topsoil will be eroded by rainwater and underground water movements may cause sinking.

Cutting and filling

Improving the shape of exisiting levels can be accomplished using the cut-and-fill technique: soil is taken from one high area and used to fill in a low spot.

If a bank appears too steep, first dig out the topsoil to about 150mm (6in) and set it aside for re-use; dig out and save the same depth of topsoil from the low level.

Excavate the subsoil to the required depth and transport it by barrow to the low level. Spread it out over the exposed subsoil, then roll it or tramp over it with the heels of your boots. Replace the topsoil at the top and bottom of the bank.

Level pegging

If you want to build a patio or lay a lawn, you'll need a relatively flat, well-drained area.

Choose a suitable site that won't involve massive restructuring of the ground. Drive a 300 × 25 × 25mm (12 × 1 × 1in) timber peg into the ground with a club hammer, so that its top is set at the required level for the whole plot.

Use this 'prime datum' peg as a guide to sinking more pegs in the ground over the area you're levelling, at about 1.5m (5ft) intervals. All the pegs must be set in the ground at the same level. To check this, place one end of a 1.8m (6ft) long plank on the prime datum peg and the other end on top of the second peg. Place a spirit level on the plank edge and adjust the level of the second peg. When the second peg is level, drive in a third peg and level it with the second. Continue in this way across the site.

Adjust the level of the soil so that it's flush with the top of the pegs. Compact the area lightly to accentuate dips and fill with more soil. If there are voids that cannot be filled by cutting-and-filling, add a few extra barrowloads of soil, obtained from a garden centre. Finally rake over the site to give a flat finish.

Levelling by sight

If the ground to be levelled is very rough, you will not be able to use the peg and plank technique. Instead employ 'boning rods'.

Make up three rods, each 900 × 50 × 25mm (36 × 2 × 1in) softwood with a 300mm (12in) cross-piece nailed at the top, forming a T-shape.

Drive a 300 × 25 × 25mm (12 × 1 × 1in) softwood peg into the ground at the

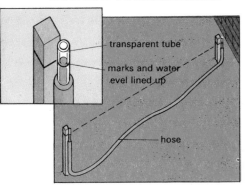

Above *Make a water level from a length of garden hose with a short piece of clear plastic tube in each end. Mark the tube with adhesive tape as a gauge. Stretch the hose between the datum peg and the one you're levelling; fill the hose with water and align the tape marks with the peg tops. Adjust the level of the second peg until the water levels are the same at each end.*

highest point, leaving about 50mm (2in) protruding. Insert a second peg about 600 mm (2ft) away and set it at the same level as the first.

Stand a boning rod upright on each peg and, crouching down, sight across the tops to the third rod held on another peg by a helper at the opposite side of the site. Adjust the third peg until the cross-pieces on all rods are level when sighted across.

Water levels

A third method is to use a water level – working on the principle that water finds its own level. Fit a short piece of clear plastic tube into each end of a long length of garden hose. Wind tape around the clear tube as a guide to levelling. Fill the hose with water and hold one end against a datum peg; get a helper to hold the other end at a second peg. Align the tape marks with the peg tops and adjust the height of the pegs until the water levels are the same at each end.

Better garden drainage

Poor garden drainage is readily identifiable: you'll notice pools of water that linger after heavy rainfall and even on dry days, drenched soil. Plant and shrub growth will be weak, and specimens may suffer attacks of mildew and rotting of the roots. Wet soils are also cold, which retards the growth of plants.

In severe cases, expansion and shrinkage in certain subsoils, as water is absorbed and lost, can actually cause subsidence in the house foundations, or can at least cause cracks to appear in the walls.

Many drainage defects can be remedied simply by improving the soil content naturally with organic additives (see pages 372–3), or by digging techniques (see page 376–7). But where the soil structure is largely impervious clay, or in area troubled

by frequent heavy rainfall, you may have to install artificial drainage.

Testing the drainage

Your priority is to identify the cause of the problem. Dig a hole about 900mm (3ft) deep by a spade's width and examine the soil you remove. Sandy or stony soil usually drains freely, and good, fertile soils composed of 100mm (4in) or more of topsoil over heavier subsoil should also be no problem. Thick, heavy clay, however, drains extremely badly.

Pour some water into the test hole; if it's still there after 48 hours, the drainage is inadequate and needs attention.

You might discover that the hole fills up with water by itself. This indicates a high water table (the level underground to which water standing on the earth's crust rises). The water table, which conforms roughly to the contours of the ground, varies in depth from area to area; it also fluctuates following wet and dry spells. If it rises in winter it can kill the roots of plants by saturation; if it falls in summer, drought can be equally fatal.

The most beneficial level for the water table is about 900mm (3ft) below ground level, serving deep-rooted and shallow-rooted plants alike.

Consult your local authority's survey or to find out if your area has a particularly high water table; if you live on low-lying ground – below sea level near the coast, or in the flood plain of a river valley – the water table may be at ground level. No drainage system will cure the problem.

In less affected areas, you can usually reduce the water table sufficiently by laying land drains. The drain can be, at its simplest, a gravel-filled trench or, more complex, a network of pipes where drainage is extremely poor.

1. Between the topsoil and rock are layers of subsoil, gravel and stones.
2. Soil types vary and you may find a clay soil, which cracks when it dries out and requires artificial drainage.
3. A sandy soil, which has a loose texture through which water and nutrients drain rapidly.
4. Loamy soil, well-balanced and the ideal growing medium for plants.

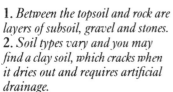

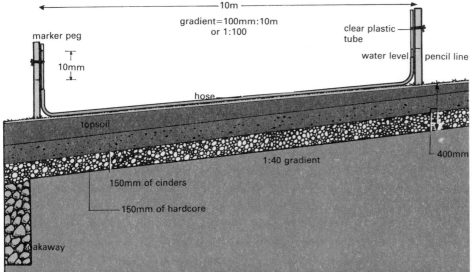

1. Dig the drainage trench about 300mm (12in) wide and 400mm (16in) deep.
2. Tip about 150mm (6in) of hardcore into the trench, add the same amount of cinders, sand or gravel then compact by tramping with your boots.

Below left *Ensure the drainage trench is set to the correct gradient towards the drainage point using a water level between marker pegs. A gradient of 1:40 is adequate.*

Whatever the type, it must lead to a suitable drainage point: this could be an existing drainage ditch or stream (but beware of draining your garden into a neighbour's!), but most probably a soak-away will need to be constructed. This is basically a rubble-filled pit, which filters the water away.

Measuring the gradient

In a garden that slopes, calculate its approximate gradient before you lay a land drain, so that you can dig your trench to the correct gradient. A gentle consistent slope of 1:40 is adequate; any steeper and water would wash along it, leaving sediment behind which would clog the drain.

You can use the 'water level' method (see page 8) to determine the gradient. Drive a peg into the ground at each end of the garden, with about 300mm (12in) protruding; draw a pencil mark 150mm (6in) from the top of each and run a hosepipe between them, with clear plastic inserts in each end. Tie the hose to the pegs and fill it with water. When the water reaches the line drawn on one end, this is the lower ground;

continue to fill the hose until the water reaches the second line.

Measure how far above the first line the water has now risen and the distance between the two pegs. If, for instance, the pegs are 10m (33ft) apart, and the height difference between the pencil marks is 100mm (4in), you have a gradient of 1:100. Where your garden slopes towards the house, you'll have to dig the drainage trench deeper to avoid the foundations.

Mark out the run of your drainage trench using string stretched between wooden pegs: if the garden slopes away from the house, run the trench towards the lowest point, where there should be a soakaway.

Digging a drainage trench

Start to dig a trench about 300mm (12in) wide along the stringline. If you're laying the drain in a lawn, carefully remove the turf in rectangles about 300 × 450mm (12 × 18in), roll them up (grass inwards) and set aside. Measure the length of the proposed trench and work out how deep it must be at the lowest end: the highest end should be a minimum of 400mm (16in) deep.

Make sure that the trench slopes gradually and consistently to the far end – place a long, straight-edged plank in the bottom of the excavation to check this.

Tip about 150mm (6in) of hardcore (broken bricks or concrete), or coarse gravel mixed with stones, into the base of the trench to act as a water filter. Don't use old gypsum plaster, however, as this will dissolve and clog up the filter. Rubble left over from other DIY building projects, or obtained from a nearby demolition site, is particularly ideal.

Add about 150mm (6in) of cinders, coarse sand or gravel to the hardcore layer then compact both layers lightly, by tramping with your boots, to discourage future subsidence. Return the topsoil to the trench so it stands proud of the surrounding ground; re-lay any turves. The trench will stand out when complete, but will sink back in due course.

Piped drainage

Where inadequate drainage affects the whole garden, you'll need to lay a system of underground pipes running into a soakaway. The most efficient set-up is to lay the pipes in a herring-bone pattern – a central spine leading to the drainage point, with branches fanning from it.

Draw a scale plan of your garden on squared paper and include on it the house, the planned pipe runs and soakaway. Note down the lengths of each section to help you work out how much pipe you'll need. Calculate the gradient of the garden and work out how deep you'll have to dig the trenches. The main spine should slope at a gradient of 1:40 to the soakaway. It's a good idea to clearly mark out the route on site with a series of stringlines.

Pipes are made in a range of materials, plastic, concrete, pitch fibre or unglazed clay. They're either perforated or unperforated in 75–100mm (3–4in) diameters. Choose the larger size for the central spine, the smaller ones for the branches.

There's little to choose between materials, although pitch fibre can be joined with snap connectors, plastic are made in long runs and can be bent (to avoid obstacles such as tree roots). Clay (known as field pipes), although inexpensive and in 400mm (16in) lengths, can't be cut without an angle grinder – a club hammer and bolster chisel would only shatter the pipe.

Prepare the trenches as previously described then line the base of each with a 50mm (2in) layer of fine gravel. Position the pipes in the trenches, starting with the spine at the lowest level.

Perforated pipes allow surplus water to filter away, so position the perforations towards the bottom. Unperforated pipes must be laid with a 12mm (½in) gap between them to allow the water to flow inside.

Some pipes – particularly pitch fibre or concrete – are porous and allow a little water to seep through their walls.

Extend the spine of the drain about 300mm (12in) into the soakaway pit so there's no danger at all of the water seeping to earth. Then you should lay the branch pipes.

Where you've left gaps between pipes, go back over the run and cover each joint with a roof tile or a small sheet of tough polythene sheeting, to stop earth and gravel clogging the pipes.

Cover the pipes with a further layer of

Below *Set land drainage pipes in the trench, the joins covered with pieces of tile, then cover with coarse gravel to within 150mm (6in) of the ground level. Top with soil or turf. The best arrangement for the system is a herringbone pattern (inset) draining towards a soakaway.*

1

2

3

4

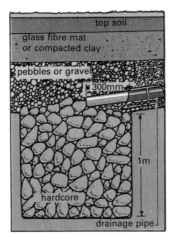

1. Lay the drain pipes in the trench on a gravel base with a 15mm (½in) gap between them.
2. Cover the joins with polythene sheet or tile then sprinkle gravel on top.
3. Continue the drain run into the centre of the soakaway.
4. Bury the pipes in gravel then add a sheet of glass fibre matting or clay to preventing silting. Fill the soakaway to ground level with topsoil then returf or plant out.

gravel, taking care not to dislodge the polythene or tile covers. Add about 150mm (6in) of topsoil to slightly over-fill the trenches and replace the turves you've previously removed.

Constructing a soakaway

The soakaway is the heart of a garden drainage system. Basically it's a large hole, filled with rubble to filter the water back to earth, and topped with a soil layer that can be cultivated.

The pit should be installed at the lowest part of the garden. Remove any turf or topsoil and set aside for re-use. Mark out the perimeter of the pit with stringlines, then dig down to the required depth: the soakaway should be 900mm (3ft) deep below the level of the incoming drainage pipe, and if you've a very large garden you could find yourself digging down this far any way, before you actually start to dig the drainage pit itself.

Fill the pit with hardcore, rubble and large stones to the level of the drainpipe. Compact the infill well using a sledge hammer (or a fence post – wear thick gloves to avoid splinters). This will reduce the likelihood of subsidence when the aggregate settles.

Now add a layer of coarse gravel or

pebbles to prevent silting, compact this well down then top with about a 150mm (6in) thick layer of clay or if you prefer, a heavy subsoil.

Roll the top layer thoroughly to produce a firm flat surface. You can substitute the clay layer for a sheet of glass fibre matting, as used in loft insulation, or even a thin screed of concrete, to prevent the topsoil filtering down and subsequently clogging the soakaway.

Add topsoil to stand proud of the hole, then re-turf the whole section if necessary, or alternatively, you can plant out the area, if you wish.

Left *The soakaway is basically a deep hole filled with hardcore, which filters water away to earth. The drain pipes should enter the hardcore section, which is then topped with gravel, a layer to stop any silting and then a layer of topsoil.*

Right *Rubbing a handful of soil between your fingers is the best way to identify its particular qualities.*

Improving your soil

Soil is your garden's natural growing medium, so it's vital for the health and successful growth of your plants and crops that you keep it well maintained.

Soil is basically rock that's been ground down by the effects of the weather over a long period of time and made fertile by decayed organic matter (derived from dead insects and leaves). There are hundreds of different soil types, but they can broadly be classified as sandy, loamy or clay, referring to their basic texture.

Texture affects the drainage, aeration and nutrient content of the soil and you may have to take steps to improve on this in certain types of soil.

Which soil type?

Take a handful of soil and run a small amount between your forefinger and thumb. Although all soils contain varying proportions of sand, silt and clay, you'll readily be able to tell the difference between the main types.

Sandy soil feels gritty when dry and even when it's wet particles will not stick together. Loams, on the other hand, can be moulded in the hand when moist, but aren't at all sticky and gritty and are fairly loose when dry. Clay soils are sticky and smooth when wet, but become polished when rubbed and baked hard when dry.

A loamy soil is a well-balanced amalgamation of sand, silt and clay, which combines excellent drainage with sufficient moisture retention to assure good growing conditions for most plants. It's fairly easy to look after, although part-loamy soils do benefit from regular applications of well-

rotted organic matter to prevent compaction.

The particle consistency of sandy soil doesn't hold water well, with the result that plant foods are often taken away by rain before they can do any good. Again well-rotted organic matter can be added to bind the soil particles together.

Clay soils are the most difficult to work, usually becoming waterlogged, when they're virtually impossible to dig. Artificial drainage (page 368–9) will probably be the first step in improving the texture of the soil and various additives will break down the structure to make use of its excellent food stocks.

Improving soil texture

There are various methods of improving your soil's texture. Essentially this requires regular applications of a well-rotted organic substance called humus, which is obtained from decayed plant and animal matter (manure, compost and seaweed each provide ample sources).

You can identify the humus content of the soil by looking at the colour: the light soils are low in organic content; whitish, sandy soils are extremely poor; the darkest, almost black soils are rich and nutritious.

Humus can be dug in to break up clay soils into a much more open texture, with the benefit of introducing nutrients essential to plant growth. Drainage will be improved also; roots able to penetrate the soil structure rather than following the cracks in the ground. Sandy soils will benefit by being bulked-up by humus-forming materials, whereas materials added to loamy soils will help to retain its existing open texture.

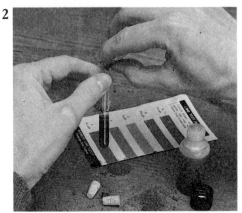

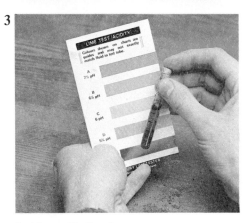

Acid or alkaline?

The presence of chalk in soil can also affect the growth of plants: some prefer slightly acid (chalk-free) soils, while others grow more successfully in alkaline, chalky soils. Most fruit and vegetables, however, grow better in neutral soil.

Although benefitting the soil in some ways, compost, manure and fertilizers (see page 372–5) can actually add to its acidity, as organisms break them down.

You can find out the degree of acidity or alkalinity in your soil by testing its pH value, using a soil-testing kit available from garden centres. A typical soil testing kit consists of two test-tubes, chemicals for estimating the acidity of the sample and a colour chart, which indicates the various pH values.

Over-acid soils can be treated with applications of lime – either hydrated (slaked) lime, or ground limestone (chalk). Of the two, ground limestone is your best choice. It may be slow acting but does permit the number of useful soil organisms to increase gradually and won't exhaust organic matter too rapidly. Hydrated lime, although quicker acting, is caustic and mustn't be allowed to blow onto crops or plants or it will burn them.

To apply lime, sprinkle on the broken topsoil and mix in lightly but don't dig in; leave to wash down by rain. Apply lime every other year if need be.

An alkaline soil can be treated with manure, garden compost or peat, well dug in.

Composts and composting

Bulky organic animal manures can be quite difficult to obtain for use in soil improvement but garden compost is an excellent substitute. You can make it yourself from waste vegetable matter from the kitchen or garden. A compost heap costs virtually nothing to make and it recycles nutrients from materials that you would otherwise burn or dispose of.

The waste material is broken down by bacteria and other micro-organisms. For them to thrive and multiply, there must be sufficient airflow through the heap to supply the oxygen they need and to remove the waste carbon dioxide they expel.

There must be enough moisture, nitrogen and non-acidic conditions present for successful composting. High temperatures within the heap, peaking at about 60°C (140°F), are also vital to produce wholesome compost – and to destroy any weed seeds present.

Above *A compost heap is an excellent way to produce your own bulky organic matter from materials you would otherwise dispose of.*

1. *Test the pH value of your soil using a soil-testing kit. Fill one tube quarter full of soil and the other half full of test solution.*
2. *Pour the solution into the tube with the soil in it, then cork and shake it.*
3. *Allow the soil to settle then compare the colour in the tube with the colours on the card.*

What to compost

For the best compost, use soft waste: lawn mowings, dead leaves, spent lettuces, stems of flowers and crops – even bonfire ashes – are ideal. Avoid woody stems, evergreen leaves and bark, which won't rot down rapidly enough.

You can add weeds to the heap, so long as you place them centrally, where the heat will destroy them and their seeds. However, don't use perennial weeds like couch grass or bindweed, or obviously diseased plants (you may spread the blight through the garden with the compost).

Some kitchen waste makes a good addition to the compost heap. Vegetable trimmings such as cabbage leaves, potato peelings, and fruit waste are all suitable. Crushed egg shells are a good source of calcium, even though they don't rot down, and tea leaves and coffee grounds are beneficial.

Never use cooked scraps, animal wastes, cheese rinds, bones or fat. Not only will they smell foul but also they'll attract vermin and flies.

Aim to make your compost heap up to its required size as quickly as is possible, between the early spring and late summer, so it will have ample time to heat up, rot and be ready for full use in about three months.

Types of compost heap

If you have space, you'll achieve rapid results from a heap measuring about 2 × 2 × 1.5m (6 × 6 × 5ft) high, but in a suburban garden where space will be limited (and materials scarce in sufficiency) it is more realistic to aim for a heap measuring a minimum of about 1.5m (5ft) square, buy a proprietary compost bin, or make an open-topped compost box.

Ready-made containers may be wire-meshed boxes with hinged access panels, or strong black polythene sacks in simple cradles.

A home-made compost bin can be a timber box, slatted for aeration or a breezeblock or corrugated iron structure.

Constructing the heap

To make a compost heap, whether it's open or enclosed, prepare the base by lightly forking the ground: this allows earthworms to gain access to the heap.

Spread a layer of woody prunings over the soil to act as an aeration layer then mix up garden and kitchen waste on the ground nearby. Moisten the mix with a little water and fork into the container (or make a 300mm/12in base layer for an open heap) then compact it lightly with the back of a spade, or tread it in carefully.

If you're making the heap in autumn or winter, pour a thin layer of a nitrogen-rich activator, such as poultry manure, blood or fish meal over the waste to feed the micro-organisms inside.

Add another layer of waste. If your soil is

1. *Make a compost container from preservative-treated planks nailed to vertical posts set in the ground.*
2. *Ensure an airflow through the heap by containing it within a circle of wire netting, plasticized to prevent rust.*
3. *One of the simplest containers is a tough black plastic sack set in a simple cradle made from old piping or timber. Puncture the sack to ensure air reaches the compost.*
4. *Breezeblocks built up without mortar, make a sturdy compost container. Support it within timber posts and raise it on bricks to ensure airflow.*
5. *Corrugated plastic sheeting held by timber posts makes a lightweight compost container, and you can allow separate sections for material in use and that in production. Lay drainpipes on the ground to introduce air to the centre of the heap.*

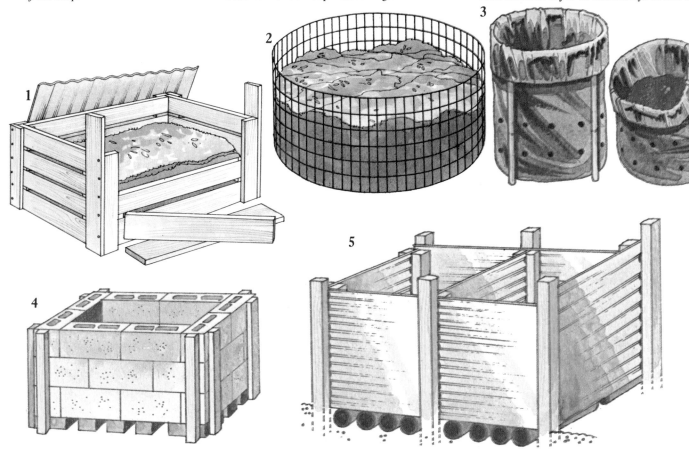

1

2

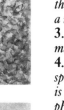

3

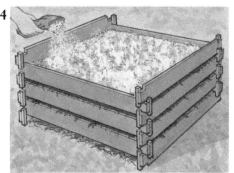

4

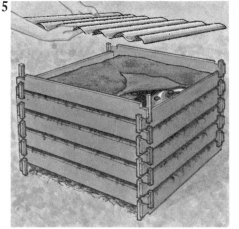

5

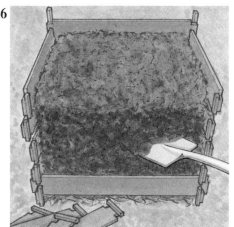

6

1. Fork the ground to allow beneficial earthworms to enter the heap.
2. Build your container (if necessary) then add an aeration layer followed by a mix of kitchen and garden waste.
3. Pour a little activator such as poultry manure on the waste.
4. Add a second layer of waste and sprinkle on ground limestone if the soil is strongly acid to maintain the correct pH.
5. Build the heap in these layers to fill the container, cover with punctured black polythylene and a piece of sacking or carpet, then add the lid.
6. Examine the material after about three months; it should be dark brown and crumbly when ready for use.

strongly acid, sprinkle ground limestone on top of the second layer to maintain the heap at the correct pH – you'll need about 120g per sq m (4oz per sq yd). Top the limestone with a layer of wood ashes or soil, about 2.4kg per sq m (5lb per sq yd), to ensure that any ammonia gas doesn't escape before the micro-organisms in the heap can use it.

Continue to build up the heap in these layers until you have filled the container (or slope an open heap up and inwards).

Spread a sheet of punctured black polythene over the heap, then cover with sacking or an old carpet, followed by the lid.

The heap should heat up to about 60°C (140°F) within seven days and after another week the material should have shrunk to about one-third of its height. Top up the heap at this stage.

Turning the heap isn't necessary if it's well insulated, although after about six weeks you should fork the cooler outsides into the warm centre.

When the heap cools you may notice red manure worms inside: these are vital to convert the compost into fine crumbs. Once the heap is cooled it will start to mature. Investigate the material after about three to four months; it should be dark brown and crumbly if it's ready for use.

Digging
Digging is an essential part of improving the quality of your soil. Not only does it enable you to incorporate organic matter, such as manure and compost, well down into the soil structure, but also it will break up hard layers of soil (called pans) lower down. These pans are often caused by cultivation of the soil to the same depth over a number of years.

Choosing and using tools
Buy the best spade and fork you can afford. Choose a spade with a stainless steel blade (which won't rust) with either a wood or alloy handle in a weight that suits you; the blade should be full-sized – 300 × 200mm (12 × 8in). A fork should have four

Single digging

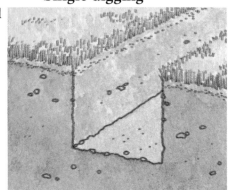

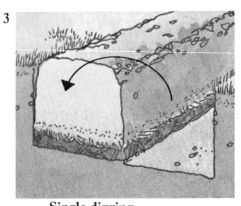

Half trenching

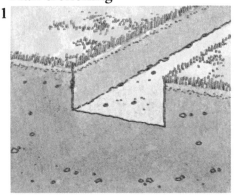

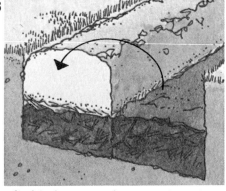

Single digging
1. *Dig a trench about 300mm (12in) deep and wide, across one end of the plot or strip.*
2. *Add some organic matter to the trench and fork it into the soil, then rake it level.*
3. *Dig a second trench parallel to the first, turning the forkful of soil into the first trench.*

Half trenching
1. *Dig a spit-deep trench 600mm (24in) wide, and transfer the soil to the other end of the plot.*
2. *Loosen the subsoil a spit deep with your fork them mix in some organic matter.*
3. *Dig a second trench, parallel to the first, and toss the earth into the first trench.*

cylindrical prongs for normal work, or square tines for breaking up hard ground.

To use a spade or fork correctly, place your right hand on the handle and your left hand on the shaft, near the handle (vice versa if you're left-handed), then insert the blade or tines perfectly upright to their full depth.

Press down with your left foot. Pull back the handle, sliding your left hand down the shaft to take the weight of the soil. Lift and tip where required.

Methods of digging
There are basically four methods of digging: single digging, half (or bastard) trenching, full trenching (double digging) and ridging.

Single digging should be carried out each autumn. Its purpose is to turn over a spadeful or forkful of soil – what's called a 'spit' or spade's depth – leaving it rough and

burying any annual weeds.

If you have a large plot, divide the area into strips with stringlines and pegs. Dig a trench about 250mm deep and 300mm wide (10 × 12in), across one end of the plot or strip. Transfer the soil by barrow to the opposite end of the plot.

If you want to add organic matter to the soil, fork it into the base of the trench and rake it.

Start to dig a second trench, about 150mm (6in) away from the first. Insert your spade or fork to its full depth, lever out a block of soil and toss it forward into the first trench, turning it completely over. Repeat this action across the strip, not forgetting to add manure or compost to each trench.

Continue down the strip, up the next and so on to the end of the plot. Shovel the soil you removed from the first trench into the last.

Half trenching is especially beneficial to heavy, or badly drained soils, and should be carried out every third year to break up a hard pan.

Divide your plot into equal strips then dig out a spit-deep trench 600mm (2ft) wide; transfer the soil to the end of the plot.

Use a fork to loosen the subsoil in the bottom of the trench a spit-deep. Incorporate organic matter with the subsoil. Step back and dig out another spade-deep trench 600mm (2ft) wide and toss (and invert) the block of earth forward into the first trench. You'll find it easier to remove these blocks in two halves, as full width ones are heavy.

Repeat this procedure to the end of the plot and fill the final trench with your barrowload of earth from the first trench.

Full trenching, or double digging, improves badly-drained soil and prepares the ground for planting permanent crops.

Divide the plot into strips, dig a trench 250 × 900mm (10 × 36in) and take the soil to the end of the plot. Divide the trench in half along its length with a stringline and dig out soil from the front half to 250mm (10in) deep. Remove this soil to the final trench position but don't mix it with the first heap.

Back at the first, deeper trench, fork the base to 250mm (10in) deep and add manure. Dig spit-deep blocks from the rear half of the original trench, and turn them over onto the broken up front half. Fork the base of the rear half of the trench to 250mm (10in) and add manure.

Mark out a 450mm (18in) wide strip and dig out the topsoil to 250mm (10in) deep. Toss this onto the 'step' in the front half of the original trench.

Dig down another 250mm (10in) and throw the blocks of soil onto the broken up soil of the rear half of the original trench.

Continue in this way across the plot. Add the smaller heap of soil taken from the low part of the first trench to the base of the last one and fill it with the larger heap of topsoil. **Ridging** exposes a large area of soil to the weather. Divide your plot into 900mm (3ft) wide strips with string and pegs.

Start at one end of the first strip and remove a trench 300mm wide × 250mm deep (12 × 10in) across it.

Work down the length of the strip, single digging in 300 × 250mm (12 × 10in) deep blocks. Throw the soil blocks from the left-hand side in towards the centre of the strip; throw the blocks from the centre spit forwards; and the blocks from the right-hand spit in towards the centre.

Repeat for the next 900mm (3ft) wide strip and so on across the plot, forming a series of steep-sided ridges.

No-digging

Some gardeners prescribe to the 'no-digging' school of thought. In this method the soil surface is permanently covered with organic matter – often compost.

The unbroken soil below has many tiny cracks and channels, caused by worms and plant roots can easily penetrate these. Ideally, the channels allow good drainage and aeration of the soil, which aids root growth. Digging, despite its benefits, destroys these channels.

The organic layer retains moisture, smothers weeds and is taken down and released at lower levels by worms. It encourages the roots of crops to grow in an undisturbed manner at the top 50mm (2in) of soil.

Full trenching

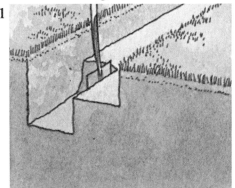
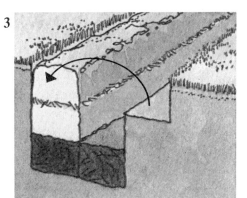
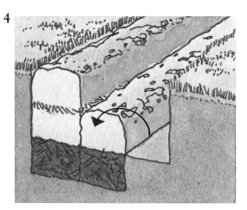

Full trenching
1. Dig a trench 250mm deep × 900mm wide (10in × 3ft), divide the trench in half, dig one half a spit deep.
2. Add organic matter to the first half, dig the second half a spit deep and turn the soil onto the first half.
3. Add organic matter to the second half, dig a second trench 250mm (10in) deep, turning it onto the first half of the first trench.
4. Dig down another 250mm (10in) and turn the earth onto the second half of the first trench.

Ridging

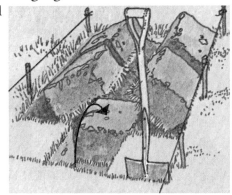

Ridging
1. Divide the plot into 900mm (3ft) wide strips; work down the strip digging 300mm (12in) wide × 250mm (10in) deep blocks. Turn the blocks from the left-hand side into the centre, those from the centre, forwards, and those from the right-hand side towards the centre.
2. Repeat this procedure for subsequent 900mm (3ft) wide strips, forming steep-sided ridges.

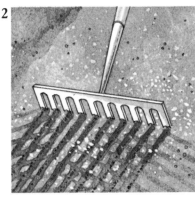

1. *Sprinkle fertilizer over the entire area you want to treat.*
2. *Rake it into the top 75mm (3in) of ground.*

Fertilizers

Plants need a plentiful supply of nutrients to remain healthy, but the natural plant foods in the soil are constantly being leached away or used up in growth. Bulky organic matter such as manure, used to condition the soil supplies some nutrients, but you will probably need to add more, in the form of fertilizer, to sustain vigorous growth.

Fertilizers are concentrated forms of chemical salts, absorbed by the plant roots to sustain growth. Whether the nutrients come from a natural organic source or from a manufactured product matters little to the plant. But it is important to realize that fertilizers are no substitute for manures and other bulky organic materials such as garden compost. Manure improves the structure and physical characteristics of the soil as well as providing some nutrients. Fertilizers and manures should be working together.

Plants require numerous chemical nutrients, notably nitrogen, phosphorus, and potassium. These elements influence the growth and development of plants but must be administered in the correct proportions.

The effects of nutrients

Nitrogen is essential to plant growth, especially leaf growth; phosphorus (absorbed in the form of phosphates) is important for root crops, seedlings, potassium is particularly useful for flower and fruit production.

A lack of nitrogen will result in spindly, weak growth with small, pale green or yellow leaves; too much will produce over-vigorous growth. Phosphorus deficiency is

similar to that of nitrogen, with scorched leaf margins; premature ripening of the plant signals an overdose of the element. Scorching of the leaf margins is indicative of low potassium reserves; plants may be bushy but any fruit will be small and woody.

It is important to realize, however, that these are very generalized symptoms and the subject is more complex than can be dealt with here. Some of these symptoms may be due to other causes.

Other essential chemicals are often present in the soil in the right quantity. 'Trace' elements, including sodium, iron, and magnesium, are needed in only tiny amounts, and you should not attempt to add these as individual elements unless you know that there is a deficiency (which may need expert diagnosis).

The amount of fertilizer needed can be affected by many things, including the type of soil, but you won't go far wrong if you follow the guidance on the packet or bottle.

Sources of fertilizer

Each of the nutrients can be obtained separately, or in various proprietary combinations. The maze of different fertilizer elements is vast. Organic sources of nitrogen, mainly derived from dead animals, include dried blood and hoof and horn meal; inorganic sources, which are less expensive, are typified by sulphate of ammonia, Nitro-chalk, nitrate of ammonia and nitrate of soda.

Phosphatic fertilizers include organic bonemeal (with calcium phosphate as its active ingredient) and inorganic super-phosphate of lime, and basic slag.

Potassium is available in the form of potash. Wood ashes and sulphate of potash are good sources of the nutrient.

This list is by no means exhaustive, the choice of fertilizers being allied strictly to your soil's particular requirements. Although single-element fertilizers such as these are the most economical to buy, combined types can enable all the necessary plant foods to be supplied in a single application. The three main types are:
● **General fertilizers** These consist of nitrogen, phosphorus, and potash.
● **Complete fertilizers** Rather like general types, they also contain trace elements as well as the three main nutrients.
● **Compound fertilizers** These are made up of two or more plant nutrients in a single chemical combination.

Mixing your own fertilizers

By purchasing single-element fertilizers, you can mix them yourself to make your own compound types. You must not combine substances that will cause an unfavourable

Right *A graphic demonstration of how nutrient deficiency affects plant growth: both tomato plants were started at the same time but the plant on the left was starved of nourishment, whereas the plant on the right was treated with force fertilizer, producing a well-proportioned, are generally much more healthy plant.*

Left *Nitrogenous fertilizer is applied in a ring around each plant.*

Below left *Apply liquid fertilizer by a watering-can fitted with a fine rose.*

reaction, however – some types will produce harmful acids if mixed and these could be harmful to the soil.

When proportioning the ingredients of your combined fertilizer, all quantities must be measured in multiples of the same basic unit of weight. To discover what the basic unit should be for your plot, muiltiply the area of the plot by the rate of application, then divide this figure by the total number of parts in the mix.

As an illustration of this, a general fertilizer (a top-dressing for vegetables or an additive prior to sowing or planting) consists of 5 parts sulphate of ammonia: 7 parts superphosphate: 2 parts sulphate of potash: 1 part steamed boneflour. It should be applied at the rate of 90g per sq m (3oz per sq yd).

If your plot measures 30sq m (30sq yd) the total amount of fertilizer is $30 \times 90g = 2700g$ ($30 \times 3oz = 90oz$). Divide this by the total number of parts in the mix (15) to arrive at $2700 \div 15 = 180g$ ($90 \div 15 = 6oz$). Your basic unit, therefore, is 180g (6oz).

Now multiply each part of the mix by the basic unit to arrive at the amounts of each ingredient you'll need:
- sulphate of ammonia = 900g (30oz)
- superphosphate = 1260g (42oz)
- sulphate of potash = 360g (12oz)
- steamed boneflour = 180g (6oz)

When mixing, make sure all the ingredients are kept perfectly dry. Use only clean tools, containers, surfaces and bags.

Ensure that all the ingredients are thoroughly blended. Place the ingredients on a large clean and flat board in layers. Shovel out a segment of the 'sandwich' and mix it thoroughly on another board. Repeat this procedure until you've used up the pile.

Liquid fertilizers

General fertilizers can also be bought in liquid form. The liquid is diluted with water and applied by watering-can (with a fine rose) or as a 'foliar' (leaf) treatment via a garden sprayer. The latter method ensures rapid absorption of the nutrients, but is more time-consuming to apply.

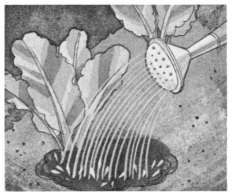

Applying dry fertilizers

Fertilizers can be applied to the soil prior to sowing or planting, or later as a top-dressing around plants. Scatter the material over the soil evenly, then rake into the top-soil and water in if necessary.

GARDEN MATERIALS

Every garden must have its basic structure to tie together the various aspects of the plot. This framework may be composed of a number of versatile materials to give the pracitcal or decorative effect you want for your style of garden.

Opposite *A selection of the bricks that can be used in the garden for a host of structures from garden boundary walls, retaining walls and decorative structures.*

Below *Cloches can be made from a variety of materials such as polythene sheeting on a wire frame, rigid PVC held together with clips, and glass, again secured in a basic wire frame.*

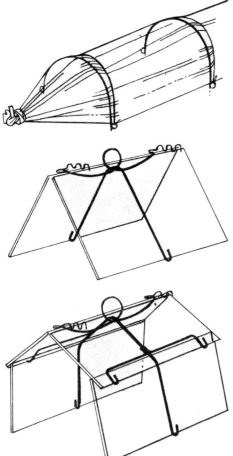

There is so much more to a garden than flower beds, a lawn and vegetable patch. Even the plainest, most compact plot is built around a framework of walls and fences, to form boundaries or to divide various areas, paths to give access through the garden, and steps in a sloping site.

Embellishing the basic skeleton, there are decorative touches such as pergolas and trellises, patterned, textured surfaces for the patio, and the functional structures – cold frames and a greenhouse for raising plants, a shed for storage and a summer-house for relaxation.

The materials used to construct all these different items range from durable concrete, versatile brick and stone, to the beauty of timber and the efficiency of glass and plastic. Each needs to be chosen with care to suit your type of garden, and needs to be regularly maintained to keep everything in prime condition and looking good.

Glass and plastic

Glass plays an important role in the garden. It is still the most widely used glazing material for greenhouses, and on a smaller scale, it is used to make cold frames and cloches to protect or force plants. Glass is better than plastic for greenhouses and cloches because it lets the sun's heat pass through, then retains it; plastic lets heat through, too, but once the sun sinks, the greenhouse cools rapidly – not ideal for healthy plants. Glass has limitations, however, because it is fragile; lightweight, durable plastics are now popular as a substitute. Plastics can also be moulded to make anything from plant labels to garden tools, equipment and accessories.

Glass and where to use it

Modern production methods produce flat, flawless sheets of glass, but such fine quality isn't necessary in the garden. So long as the glass is reasonably free from bubbles, which can concentrate the sun's burning rays onto plants, slight kinks won't have an adverse affect.

Horticultural glass is about half the price of float glass, so it is sensible to buy this if you need a replacement. You can, however, make use of any glass you have at home: an old window frame for instance, makes an exceedingly good cold frame when mounted on bricks.

Plastic and its uses

Plastic is available in numerous forms, from rigid PVC, used in sheet form for greenhouse panes and cloches (some proprietary cloches with spikes to stick into the ground are made from this material) to polythene sheeting, which is either flexible (in rolls) or rigid (in sheets). In its transparent form it can be used to clad a greenhouse with an insulating layer in winter, or in opaque black it can be used as a mulch round plants.

Where strength is needed, choose plastic sheeting reinforced with strong plastic or wire mesh, or rigid corrugated PVC sheets, which make an excellent substitute for greenhouse glass. Remember: plastic for glazing must be transparent, not coloured or tinted.

Some polythene will become brittle and can lose its transparency after about three years' exposure to the ultra-violet rays in sunlight (although a horticultural grade is made, which delays this reaction). Also, because the surface is soft, wind-blown particles can scratch it. In its favour, it is cheap to renew.

Shading for plants

On really hot days greenhouse plants need shading to prevent scorching: the cheapest method is to paint a diluted concentrate of electrostatic paint onto the outside of the greenhouse or cold frame. The paint is waterproof, but can be wiped off easily when dry. If you think this too messy, interior roller blinds with translucent PVC sheeting give adjustable shade. You can make one yourself using a roller blind kit and a sheet of tinted plastic.

Reglazing a greenhouse

Despite its flimsy nature, a greenhouse will repel most onslaughts of weather, but it will

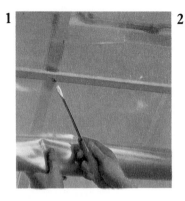  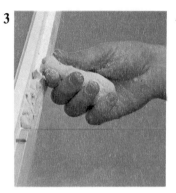 

1. *Transparent polythene sheeting acts as an effective double glazing during cold winter spells.*
2. *Carefully remove a cracked pane with thick gloves, and clean and repaint the rebate before you reglaze.*
3. *Apply putty into the clean rebates pressing it into place with your thumb. Position the new pane.*
4. *Secure the new pane with metal glazing sprigs, sliding the hammer across the glass. Trim off excess putty.*

be lucky to escape a direct hit – from a stray football or a fallen branch. But repairing a smashed pane is quite easy.

First measure the dimensions of the pane. In most greenhouses the higher panes overlap the ones below, so rainwater runs off; add an extra 9mm (³⁄₈in) to top and bottom for this. On timber-framed greenhouses the glass is usually located in rebates, bedded in a layer of putty and secured with glazing sprigs or headless brass or galvanized pins. Put on a pair of thick gloves to protect your hands and remove the broken glass.

Scrape off the old putty and prise out the pins with a pair of pincers. Sand down the rebates then repaint with white lead paint. Apply new linseed oil putty, pressing it in with your thumb. Position the replacement pane on the putty and press down evenly at the edges.

Secure by tapping new sprigs or pins into the side of the rebate under the bottom overlap (special S-shaped clips are also made). Add more pins at each side of the glass then trim off the surplus putty with a putty knife.

On aluminium-framed houses, the panes are held in the rebates on neoprene or foam rubber seal with metal clips, which can just be refixed to the new pane and carefully reinserted.

Double glazing
Although efficient greenhouse heaters are available, during a really hard winter it is wise to take steps to reduce heat loss through the glass (more so on a plastic-clad house). Here's where glass and plastic complement each other: polythene sheeting fixed firmly to the greenhouse frame, directly under the glass, makes an excellent and economical insulator.

On a timber frame, unroll some material and starting at the apex of the roof, sandwich the sheet between 25mm × 10mm (1in × ³⁄₈in) softwood battens fixed horizontally across the underside of the glazing bars. Fix the battens with 19mm (³⁄₄in) panel pins. Space the battens about 600mm (2ft) apart.

Paving
Pre-cast concrete slabs greatly simplify the job of laying a paved area, and because they're available in numerous sizes, colours, shapes and textures, there is plenty of scope for planning a decorative surface. Small-scale clay paving bricks and concrete block pavers are also available for a more intricately-patterned surface.

Hardwearing and durable, slabs and pavers are easy to lay on a sand bed over firm foundations. You can use mortar to stick the units down, although some blocks (known as 'flexible pavers') are especially made for dry-laying.

Prepare a level, flat site, incorporating the necessary drainage crossfall (pages 369–371), using pegs and a spirit-level. To prevent the paving wandering you should install edge restraints at the perimeter of the site: these can be pre-cast concrete kerbstones (in plain or wavy designs), bricks on edge, or even preservative-treated timber. If the paving abuts a wall, this can serve as the restraint.

Dig a slim trench around the proposed paved area and set the kerbstones or bricks in a 25mm (1in) thick layer of concrete; make sure they're set level or nail timber restraints to pegs. Tip loads of sand onto the foundations and rake to a consistent level about 50mm (2in) thick.

Laying concrete slabs
Concrete slabs can be laid directly on the sand bed (or bedded in fairly stiff mortar if the paved area is to be used for heavy traffic, such as a drive). Stretch a stringline across the site to align the first row of slabs, then trowel five dabs of mortar onto the sand – one at each corner of the slab; one centrally.

Lower the slab onto the mortar. Shuffle it down gently by standing on it and shifting your weight from one foot to the other, until it's well settled, or tap it gently with the handle of your club hammer. If you are laying the slabs dry, simply place them and bed them down.

Continue laying slabs to your stringline,

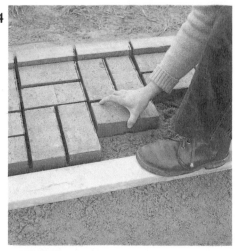

1. *Mark out the area you're going to pave with strings and pegs then dig out the base to firm, level ground.*
2. *Add a layer of hardcore (broken bricks or concrete) to the base and compact it using a fence post.*
3. *Spread a layer of sand over the hardcore and rake it to about 50mm (2in) thick.*
4. *Lay the bricks on the sand, making sure that they are evenly spaced. Tap them down and fill in between bricks.*
5. *Position the paving slabs on the sand bed on five dabs of mortar then bed them down by stamping.*
6. *Lay crazy paving in the same way but point between the joints with a fairly wet mortar mix.*

leaving 15mm (5/8in) spaces between the slabs as spacers. Place a spirit-level across the slabs to check that they're bedded evenly and gently tap them into place with the hammer handle. If a slab sinks too low, raise it, pack out underneath with more sand, then re-bed it.

Crazy paving

Crazy paving, made from broken concrete slabs, can give a random-patterned effect but does require careful planning to ensure a successful finish. Aim to fit the large, flat-edged stones at the edges or perimeter of the area, then fill in with medium-sized irregular stones and add small pieces to the spaces between.

Lay crazy paving in the same way as other paving, then point in the gaps – these shouldn't be wider than about 50mm (2in) – using a wet mortar mix. Trowel in the mortar, taking care not to smear the surface of the stones.

Laying pavers

Pavers can be laid in numerous patterns, typically herringbone and woven arrangements (see diagrams). Some can be laid on

Right *A selection of attractive patterns which can be created using brick pavers:*
1. *Herringbone*
2. *Basketweave*
3. *Parquet*
4. *Running bond*

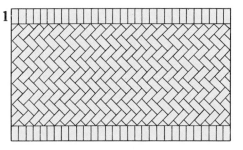

1

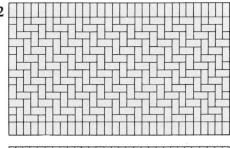

2

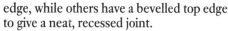

3

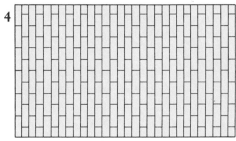

4

1. To cut a paving slab, scribe a cutting line across the face using a bolster chisel held against a straightedge length of timber.
2. Chop a groove along the line, rest it on the batten aligned with the groove, then break the slab by hitting it with a club hammer.

1

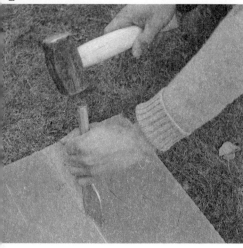

2

edge, while others have a bevelled top edge to give a neat, recessed joint.

Simply arrange the pavers in your chosen pattern on the sand bed, in a manageable area (if you have to stand on the base, spread your weight with a plank or board). Leave 2–3mm (about ⅙in) gaps between each.

Place a stout length of timber diagonally across the pavers and tap along its length with the club hammer to bed the units down evenly. Check with a spirit level that they're laid correctly, then proceed on to the next area.

Cutting slabs or pavers
You will have to cut some slabs or pavers to fit at the edges: do this by hand using a club hammer and bolster chisel, or else hire a hydraulic stone splitter which gives the cleanest cut.

To cut a slab by hand, scribe a cutting line all the way round it using a chisel, chop a groove along the line then, with the slab resting on a length of wood, aligned with the groove, tap it with a hammer handle to snap it. Do the same for cutting pavers, but after scoring, strike the chisel sharply to split it.

For very large areas of paving it is necessary to compact the units well into the sand bed, to prevent subsidence. To do this you'll need to hire a motorized plate compactor, fitted with a rubber sole plate so you don't scuff the pavers. Run over the paving with the machine to bed the units down evenly.

Filling the gaps
Once you've laid all the paving – slabs or pavers – you can fill the gaps between units. There are various ways to do this. Flexible pavers, for example, only require sand to be brushed into their joints and the surface

vibrated with a plate compactor.

Gaps between other types of paving (some slabs, and bricks for example) can be filled with dry mortar brushed in, then watered from the fine rose of a watering-can. For a really firm finish, however, point with a bricklaying mortar mix of 1 part cement to four parts soft sand, trowelled into every gap. It's a laborious, time-consuming job, but does give permanent, rigid, weed-proof joints.

Paving repairs
If the ground beneath a paved area sinks, slabs or pavers are likely to break unless they are supported evenly. Remove a broken slab or paver by levering it up. If the ground is soft, ram pieces of hardcore into the dip then top with sand to just over the level of the surrounding base. Place a new matching stone and tap it down with a club hammer over a block of wood. On a driveway it is best to fit a replacement slab on a complete bed of strong mortar mix (1 part masonry cement, three parts soft sand).

Wood in the garden
Wood is used extensively in the garden for its structural strength and decorative qualities. Whether it's for fences, sheds, greenhouses, frames for climbing plants, steps or pergolas, there's one common factor that is always a problem – the weather.

Wood in its 'manufactured' state needs regular attention to prevent deterioration. Identifying the type of wood and understanding its particular qualities will help you to care for it properly.

Types of wood
Although wood is cut from many varieties of trees, it can be divided into two main groups – softwoods and hardwoods. The

terms describe the type of tree from which the wood was cut, not its hardness (although generally hardwoods *are* harder than softwoods). Softwoods come from coniferous (cone-bearing) trees such as pine, larch and fir; hardwoods come from trees with broad leaves, such as oak and beech. Hardwoods, quite scarce and expensive, are usually reserved for jobs that require a superior finish and are rarely used in garden constructions.

Softwoods are economical and easy to saw, plane and sand, and they hold screws well, although nails can cause splitting along the grain. There are many different species of softwoods but the main ones are pine, redwood or deal.

Buying timber

Softwood is sold in a vast range of lengths and sections, either 'sawn' or 'planed'. Sawn is cheaper than planed and generally used where a smooth appearance isn't necessary: most outdoor projects fall into this category. Planed timber (commonly known by the abbreviation PAR – planed all round) is sold by its nominal planed size; the actual size is about 3mm (⅛in) less all the way round.

Timber is prepared at the sawmill in metric lengths, but many timber merchants sell it in units of 300mm (the 'metric foot'), which actually measures 11¾in. Beware when ordering: if you ask for 'six feet of timber' you may be given a piece 6 *metric* feet long – this is only 1.8m (5ft 10½in) long. If you really do want the full 6ft (1.83m) you will probably have to buy 7 metric feet (2.1m/6ft 6in) and then waste the surplus.

Consult the chart below for the full range of timber sizes that are available.

Treating wood

Most softwood used outdoors must be treated with preservative to protect it against decay and insect attack. The exception is Western red cedar, which weathers to an attractive silver-grey.

You can buy pre-treated wood from some timber merchants, which has been pressure-injected with a fluid that wards against fungal and insect attack. It is expensive, and treating the wood yourself with one of the many proprietary fluids is an appealing idea, even if the results may not be as good.

Creosote is the traditional preservative. Based on oil and tar, it stains the wood a

Above *Wood that is going to be used outside must first be treated with preservative. This is easy to do yourself and it does not take too long to apply.*

thickness mm	width mm															thickness in
	12.5	16	19	25	32	38	50	75	100	125	150	175	200	225	300	
12.5	■			■		■	■	■	■		■					½
16		■		■		■	■									⅝
19			■	■		■	■	■	■		■	■		■	■	¾
25				■		■	■	■	■	■	■	■	■	■	■	1
32					■		■	■	■		■	■		■	■	1¼
38						■	■	■	■		■			■	■	1½
50							■	■	■		■	□	□	■	□	2
75								■	■		■	□	□	■		3
100									■				□	■	■	4
width		⅝	¾	1	1¼	1½	2	3	4	5	6	7	8	9	12	

Key
■ = Available sawn or planed
□ = Available sawn only

Some of the common defects you may find when buying timber. Look out for twists and warps (1) by peering down its length; shakes (2), which are splits along the grain of the timber; knots (3), which may be loose, fall out and be difficult to cut through; Live knots may ooze resin; discoloration (4), which won't affect your choice if you're painting or creosoting the timber.

dark tone, which you may consider unattractive. Additionally, the protective effect only lasts about two years.

Solvent-based preservatives, although often more costly than creosote, offer more efficient, longer-lasting protection. There's also a selection of wood shades to choose from (and even a clear fluid, if you'd rather not alter the colour). Most preservatives, unlike creosote, can be overpainted if preferred.

The protection given by any preservative relies on thorough penetration of the wood fibres. Apply the fluid generously by brush, making sure you treat all sides equally. Apply at least two coats. The cut ends of timber, which expose the absorbent end grain, are most vulnerable, so apply more coats to these parts. Better still, stand the wood in a container of fluid and leave it to soak in for a few days, periodically brushing the fluid up the sides. Invert the wood and leave for another few days to ensure thorough soaking.

Faults in timber

Timber can suffer from a number of defects, mainly caused by too rapid or uneven drying during 'seasoning' (the process in which the moisture and sap contents are reduced for easier workability and rot resistence). Examine each piece and reject any that suffers from excessive knots (either oozing resin or dried up and loose), which make the wood difficult to saw and can fall out, warping across or along the grain; shakes, which are splits between the annular rings, or along the grain.

Using timber outdoors

Armed with a good sharp saw, a hammer and a screwdriver, there's no reason why you can't construct a variety of timber structures around the garden – anything from a basic formwork box for casting concrete, to a shed, fence or pergola. Study made-up examples and work out how they're put together, then buy your own materials and set to work.

Bear in mind the following points when erecting timber frames:

● Support the posts, for a pergola, for instance, on non-rusting metal fittings, which have a channel or socket into which the post can be bolted, and held above the ground. The metal support is bedded in concrete.
● Prevent the passage of any damp to the wood by setting posts and other components on bituminous felt. Secure the frames with metal dowels set in the concrete and driven through its end.

Types of fencing

There are numerous types of fences, and which you choose to make or erect depends on whether you want a sturdy boundary for your garden, a windbreak around a patio, or just a decorative way to define the vegetable plot, lawn and flower beds.

Closeboard fences are the most common type. Solid and durable, they make excellent garden boundaries. Vertical overlapping boards are nailed to two or three horizontal, triangular-section arris rails fixed between concrete or timber posts in slots. Boards are feathered-edged (thinner at one edge than the other) and measure about 100mm (4in) or 150mm (6in) wide; the wide edge of one overlaps the narrow edge of its neighbour. Gravel boards, which run between the posts at ground level, protect the bases of the boards from attack by rot, and can be renewed.

These fences are normally assembled on site from separate components. Versions with feather-edged boards nailed horizontally to the posts are also made.

Interwoven panels are one of the cheapest types of solid fences. Panels are made from thin larch or pine slats between 75mm (3in) and 100mm (4in) wide, which are interwoven horizontally around vertical battens to form a basketweave. This is framed with battens and the panels nailed through the frame to the posts. They're sold in 1.8m (6ft) widths, with heights between 600mm (2ft) and 1.8m (6ft).

Wavey-edged panels are made by fixing thin, irregular-edged larch or pine planks within a softwood frame. Planks overlap as in a closeboard arrangement. Panel sizes are the same as interwoven types.

Picket fencing is a boundary typically used in front gardens, and rarely exceeding 1.2 m (4ft) high. Vertical 'pales' – commonly painted, often pointed or decoratively shaped at the top – are nailed to arris rails at about 50mm (2in) intervals; the rails are fixed between posts spaced about 2m (6ft 6in) to 3m (10ft) apart. Palisade fencing is a version with pales butted together.

Post-and-rail fencing consists of posts with horizontal rails nailed or notched into them. Posts are either round and rails round or half-round, or square in section. Ranch-style fencing is similar, with thinner, planed rails for painting nailed to short posts.

Rustic fences made of wooden poles complete with bark, give a natural-looking lightweight barrier or frame for climbers.

Repairing fences

Any part of a fence that comes into contact with the damp ground is susceptible to deterioration. If a post has started to rot at the

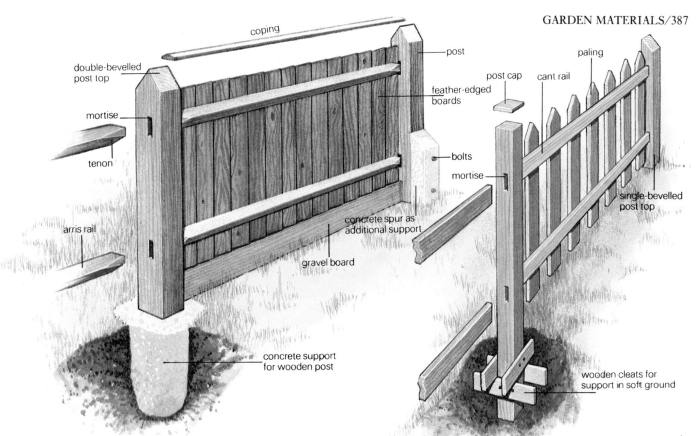

coping

double-bevelled post top

mortise

tenon

arris rail

post

feather-edged boards

bolts

mortise

concrete spur as additional support

gravel board

concrete support for wooden post

post cap

cant rail

paling

single-bevelled post top

wooden cleats for support in soft ground

base, you don't need to replace it entirely: remove the rotten section and secure the post with a pre-cast concrete spur.

Dig a hole about 600mm (2ft) deep next to the rotten post and fill the base with hardcore. Ram this down with a sledge hammer or stout post. Lower the spur in the hole, bevelled top outermost. Set it vertically, using a spirit level.

Mark the fence post through the pre-drilled holes in the spur, lift out the spur and drill holes for the coach bolts supplied for fixing. Replace the spur and hammer the coach bolts through the post into the spur from the other side of the fence. Slip on washers and secure and tighten the bolts with nuts.

Ram more hardcore around the spur then fill the hole with a coarse concrete mix.

Metal fence spikes are available for securing a rickety fence post (it's a good way to fit new posts, too). The spike, which is driven into the ground below the post, has a socket at the top into which the fence post is slotted and retained with galvanized nails in some models.

A badly rotten post should be replaced with a new one, and it's usually possible to do this without having to dismantle the entire fence. On a closeboard fence, prise off about three boards from each side of the post using a claw hammer. If it is not possible to remove the post without cutting the arris rails where they're located in the sockets; first prop the fence on both sides with wooden struts nailed to the top arris.

Saw through the arris rails flush with the

sides of the post, using a panel saw. The post will probably be set in a concrete block below ground. Dig around the base to expose the concrete. The post and fixing is likely to be very heavy, so you'll need to rig up a lever to extract it from the hole.

Drive two 100mm (4in) long nails about half-way into each side of the post, about 300mm (1ft) from the base. Bind strong rope or nylon twine around the post directly below the nails. Leave a long length of rope extra. Pile a stack of bricks about 600mm (2ft) away from the post so they're about 100mm (4in) higher than the level of the nails.

Lay a length of stout timber on the bricks and butt one end up to the original post. Drive two more nails half-way into each side about 110mm (4in) from the end. Bind the loose end of rope around the lever arm, wrapping it around the nails.

To raise the post (get a helper to support it first) lean your weight firmly down on the other end of the horizontal post to lever it out of the hole.

Fill the base of the hole with about 150mm (6in) of hardcore to give a firm, free-draining base and ram this down well with a sledge hammer or stout post. Lower the new post into the hole and set it vertically. Support it with two wooden battens temporarily nailed near the top and placed at right-angles to each other.

Add more broken bricks or concrete around the post and ram it well down. Mix up some coarse concrete and tip it into the hole. Pack the mix around the post to dispel

Above *Two popular types of fence. Closeboard fences (left) are solid, durable and the ideal garden boundaries: posts are set in the ground in concrete sleeves, connected by horizontal arris rails and clad with vertical feather-edged boards, which overlap each other. Picket fences (right) are typically used in front gardens. Horizontal cant rails are mortised into posts and are clad with vertical palings, commonly pointed or rounded at the top, usually spaced apart.*

1. *To replace a rotten closeboarded fence post, lever off the boards.*
2. *Dig out the earth around the fence post, as far down as the concrete sleeving.*
3. *Drive a nail in each side of the post and wrap strong rope around it. Pile up a stack of bricks.*
4. *Construct a lever using a stout post. Drive in nails, wrap the rope around and pull down to lift the post from its hole.*
5. *Dig out the hole, line with hardcore, then insert the new post.*
6. *Shovel in a coarse concrete mix to secure the post upright.*
7. *Refix the sawn ends of the arris rails to the new post be screwing on a galvanised metal repair bracket.*
8. *Slide the boards back under their neighbours, set vertically then secure with galvanized nails.*

air pockets, then shape the top into a bevel. Allow the concrete to harden overnight before refixing the fencing.

Refix the arris rails to the post using galvanized metal arris rail brackets: a long, angled arm fits along the rail and splayed ends fit against the post. Secure with 50mm (2in) long galvanized clout nails. (You can fix an arris rail that's snapped midway with an angled repair bracket without splayed ends; it's simply nailed across the fracture.)

Nail the feather-edged boards back on each side of the post.

Gravel boards that are rotten can be replaced. Lever off the board with a claw hammer; it will be nailed to small blocks of 38 × 25mm (1½ × 1in) softwood called 'cleats' and these may need to be replaced, too. Measure between the posts and cut a new length of 150 × 25mm (6 × 1in) softwood for the new gravel board, plus two new cleats. Treat the wood thoroughly with a good preservative treatment.

Fix the new cleats to the sides of the fence posts with 38mm (1½in) galvanized nails, set back 25mm (1in) from the face. Position the gravel board on the cleats, butted up to the bottoms of the feather-edged boards and secure with nails.

Feather-edged boards are very thin and consequently easily damaged. To replace a defective board within a section, extract its nails with a pair of pincers, then wiggle it free. If you can't grasp the nail heads with the pincers, punch them all the way through the board using a centre punch or a large blunt nail and hammer.

Cut a new board, treat it with preservative, then slot its thin edge under the thick edge of the adjacent board. Secure to the arris rail with a galvanized nail driven through its face.

You can refix a whole row of boards in the same way, but be sure to check the vertical alignment about every third board, using a spirit level.

1. *Gravel boards are usually the first to rot. Lever them off, plus their cleats, then nail on new cleats.*
2. *Nail a new length of gravel board to the cleats: the boards should be flush with the fence post and butted up to the bottoms of the boards.*

Strong winds can catch a flimsy panel fence and blow it down. Although it's easy to refix the panel; by nailing through its frame into the post as before, the frame is made of quite thin wood and it may have split. A firmer fixing is to use galvanized metal brackets.

Nail two of the U-shaped brackets to the posts about 150mm (6in) from top and bottom, using 50mm (2in) nails. Slot the panel into the channels and retain by nailing through the side flaps into the frame.

You can easily cut a panel fence to size to fit a space. Hold the panel against the gap and mark off the overlap. Scribe down the panel at this point. Prise off the end battens from both sides and refix them inside your marked line. The end battens usually extend up to the top of the top rail, but set them beneath it in the new position, leaving the excess protruding at the base of the panel. Saw off the ends of the battens then carefully saw down the surplus slats against the edge of the battens. Fit the panel in place and secure to the post.

The open-grained tops of fence posts are prone to penetration by rainwater, so it's wise to finish them off to ensure water doesn't linger. Cut the top to a steep chamfer, or a double-bevel and apply preservative liberally. Alternatively, nail on a pre-made hardwood cap, which has four bevels. Additionally, or instead, cover the top of the post with nailed sheet metal.

To discourage rot at ground level, drill a downward-sloping hole near the base and pour in preservative. Then plug the hole.

Bricks, blocks and stone

Bricks, blocks and stone can be used to create numerous structures in the garden, from practical boundary walls, planters and barbecues to decorative arches and functional flights of steps.

Choosing bricks

Bricks are made from fire-burnt clay (a process that gives them their strength and durability), concrete, or calcium silicate (sand limes). Clay bricks are graded for quality: ask for 'special quality' if you're building in exposed conditions or 'ordinary' for general use. Calcium silicate bricks come in six grades: from class two, the weakest, to class seven, the strongest.

To add to the confusion, bricks are also given names that reflect their colour, texture, and place of origin. Stocks and Flettons are common examples, but choice doesn't influence usage.

Bricks are made in a standard metric size – 225 × 112.5 × 75mm, which conforms roughly to the old Imperial size of $8^{7}/_{8}$ × $4^{3}/_{8}$ × 3in: an important point when you're matching new brickwork to old. These are 'nominal' dimensions: the actual size is 10mm ($^{3}/_{8}$in) less all round to allow for a normal mortar joint.

Of the hundreds of brick types available, there are basically three types you're likely to use in garden construction:

Facing bricks are intended to be used where an attractive appearance is needed and come in various colours and either rough or smooth textures. 'Faced' bricks have only one or two attractive sides, whereas facing bricks are good-looking all round.

Common bricks are usually used where an attractive appearance isn't necessary. They're cheaper than other bricks.

Engineering bricks are hard, dense and impervious to water. They're usually used

1. *Facing bricks, made from clay or calcium silicate, are used where an attractive appearance is wanted. They can be rough or smooth, hard or soft, and come in a range of attractive colours.*
2. *Common bricks are fairly rough in appearance and used for their practical qualities or where they're to be rendered.*
3. *Engineering bricks are the hardest and most durable bricks, ideal for use where they're likely to come into contact with damp.*

1

2

3

in damp conditions and are quite expensive. Two classes (A or B) are made, referring to strength and water resistance.

Numerous special-shaped bricks are made to give a decorative or protective finish to structures. Typical types include rounded-end 'bullheads' for completing a wall; half-round copings to neaten the top of a wall; radial stretchers for curved walls.

Some bricks have an indent in one face, called the 'frog', which forms a good bond with the mortar. The frog is normally laid uppermost. Other bricks have holes pierced through them, which serve the same purpose.

Setting out

When you're building a wall, it's vital that it runs in a straight line and is level throughout, so set up stringlines to act as a guide. For greatest accuracy, set up 'profile boards' (use the boards to mark out footings, too). Drive two 25mm sq (1in sq) wooden pegs into the ground at each end of the proposed wall, spaced slightly wider apart than the wall. Nail a length of $50 \times 25mm$ ($2 \times 1in$) softwood across the tops of the pegs.

Fix nails in the tops of the cross pieces to mark the outer edges of the wall and string lines between them.

Bricks are laid in an overlapping 'bond' to create a rigid structure and to spread the load. Single thickness (half-brick) walls are always laid in a 'running' bond; bricks are laid end to end with their long, stretcher, faces showing. Alternate rows are staggered by half a brick's length so that no

vertical joints are seen to align.

Double-thickness (single-brick) walls include courses of 'headers' – bricks laid across the width of the wall with their end faces visible.

Laying bricks

Before you start to lay bricks, check the layout of the bond by placing the first few courses dry, without mortar. Place each brick a finger-width apart to allow for the joints.

Mix up sufficient cement and soft sand mortar and trowel a very thin screed down the length of the foundation slab, between the stringlines. Use a spirit level held vertically against the stringline to transfer their positions down to the screed. Mark the mortar with your trowel at each end of the foundations and scribe along against a straight-edge.

Trowel a 10mm (⅜in) thick screed in between the scored lines. Run your trowel back over the mortar to form ridges, which aid the adhesion of the mortar through suction. Place your first brick into position on the screed (frog uppermost). Press the brick down gently with a sideways motion to bed it evenly. Tap it carefully with the handle of your trowel then scoop off any surplus mortar that's squeezed out underneath (you can use this to form the next joint).

Butter one end of another brick with mortar to form a vertical joint: scrape the mortar off the trowel onto the brick. Form it into a wedge. Place the brick on the screed,

1. *Trowel a thin screed of mortar underneath your guide strings and score a line along it, using a spirit level as a guide, to indicate the first course of bricks.*
2. *Lay the first brick on a bed of mortar then butter the end of the second brick, forming a wedge-shape for a good joint.*
3. *Place the second brick against the first, aligned with the string. Level it by tapping with your trowel handle then scoop off excess mortar.*
4. *As the courses progress, use stringlines and pins to ensure the brickwork is rising evenly. Move up the strings with each course.*

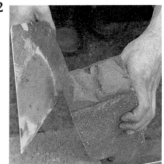

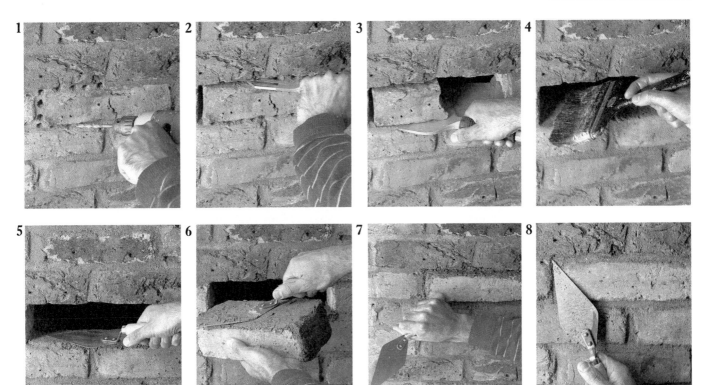

butting up the mortared end to the first brick. Tap the brick into place gently and scoop away any surplus mortar. Continue to lay bricks in this way until you complete the first course.

Check that the bricks are level across the top using a long spirit level. Adjust the thickness of the mortar bed if necessary. Check also that the row is straight, by holding your spirit level or a long straight-edge against the side.

To lay the second and subsequent course, trowel mortar onto the preceding course and bed the bricks on top. Remember, no vertical joint must align: in a stretcher-bond wall you'll have to start and finish the alternate rows with a cut brick. If you're building a corner, however, set the brick at right-angles to the other to start the new leaf.

It's usual to build up the corners or'ends of a wall first, forming a stepped structure; this 'racking back' ensures that the wall rises squarely. Fill in between the corners or racked ends in the normal way. Stretch a stringline between the ends as a guide to laying the intermediate bricks. Insert a nail in the mortar joint at each end to hold the string taut (or use special bricklayer's pins) and move the string up for subsequent courses.

Check that the courses are rising with consistently thick joints using a 'gauge rod'. Make this from a 1m (3ft 3in) length of 50 × 25mm (2 × 1in) softwood marked off in 75mm (3in) increments (brick height plus a 10mm (3/8in) mortar joint). To use the rod,

hold it against the end of the wall: the marks should align with the top of each brick if the courses are correct. Also check that the wall isn't bowing out by holding a spirit level or straightedge diagonally across the face.

You'll need to cut some bricks to size to achieve a proper bonding arrangement. Mark off the amount to be cut by scoring around the brick against another brick. Place the brick on grass or a layer of sand and tap gently around it, along the scored line, using a club hammer and bolster chisel. To break the brick cleanly, lay it frog down and tap sharply on the scored line with the chisel.

Replacing a damaged brick

Constantly exposed to the elements, it's hardly surprising that masonry can deteriorate. Common problems are crumbly mortar joints that loosen the bricks and make the structure dangerous, and cracks running through the bricks or joints.

It's possible to replace a single damaged brick (or a small area) within an area of masonry without damaging the surrounding bricks. (Don't attempt to replace more than about ten bricks without propping up the rest of the masonry.)

Drill a row of closely-spaced holes in the mortar joints surrounding the damaged brick, using a 10mm (3/8in) diameter masonry bit in an electric drill. Hack out the weakened mortar using a slim, cold chisel or a special 'plugging chisel' and a club hammer. Lever out the brick with a bolster chisel, but if it's stubborn, break it up by

1. *To replace a damaged brick, drill through the mortar joints around the brick, using a 10mm (3/8in) masonry bit.*

2. *Chop out the weakened mortar using a plugging chisel and club hammer.*

3. *Lever out the brick using a bolster chisel, breaking it into pieces if necessary.*

4. *Clean up the loose dust and debris from the hole, then dampen the masonry with clean water.*

5. *Spread a layer of mortar onto the base of the hole and one end, and furrow the surface with the trowel.*

6. *Butter the top and one end of the replacement brick with mortar and furrow it to improve the suction.*

7. *Insert the new brick into the hole and tap it into position with the handle of the trowel.*

8. *Neaten up the mortar pointing between the replacement brick and the others, following the joint profile.*

To repair spalled brickwork:
1. *Mix mortar with brick dust, apply PVA adhesive to the spalled brick, then spread on the mortar, using a batten to protect the pointing.*
2. *The repaired brick will look darker than the surrounding masonry, but will lighten as the mortar dries.*

To repair defective pointing:
1. *Rake out the loose, crumbly pointing with a plugging chisel.*
2. *Finish off the joints with new mortar, following the original pointing profile.*

drilling into it many times. If you're removing more bricks, you can easily chop into the mortar joints to release them.

Clean up all around the hole then brush out dust and debris. Dampen inside the hole with water so the bricks won't suck the water out of the repair mortar too quickly and cause it to crack. Mix up some brick-laying mortar from a small dry-mixed bag then trowel a 10mm (³⁄₈in) thick bed onto the base of the hole. Scrape some mortar up one side of the hole.

Butter the top and one end of the replacement brick (try to obtain a matching replacement: demolition sites and builders' yards are good sources) and insert it in the hole, buttered end to non-mortared end of the hole. Tap the brick gently into place with the handle of your trowel so it's flush with the surrounding masonry. Repeat the procedure for other bricks. Finally, point the joint around the brick with more mortar, matching the profile to that of the surrounding wall.

Curing spalled brickwork
Old bricks are prone to a condition called 'spalling': water penetrates the faces, freezes and breaks off the outer surface. Spalled brickwork not only looks ugly but also, if left unattended, the bricks will disintegrate.

Where a brick is badly spalled, replace it; if it's only slightly damaged, a simple, effective repair can be made. Mix up some mortar with a proprietary cement colourant powder, added according to the manufacturer's instructions. If you can't obtain a suitable match, substitute brick dust for the colourant.

Brush any loose material from the spalled brick then paint on a strong solution of PVA adhesive and water. Hold a length of thin wood over the mortar joint below the spalled brick to protect it from smears, then trowel the mortar mix over the primed surface. Carefully shape the mortar to resemble the profiles of the other bricks and leave to set. The repair will appear dark at first, but will dry lighter.

Pointing brickwork
The mortar joints are usually shaped into one of four 'pointing profiles', which deflect rainwater and prevent it from soaking between the bricks. To prepare a wall for repointing, rake out the joints to about 10mm (³⁄₈in) with a plugging chisel and brush out dust and debris. Wet the joints and refill with new mortar (pointing mortar is sold in bags dry-mixed, to which you add water). Apply the profiles with a small pointing trowel while the mortar is still wet.

● **Weathered** Starting with the horizontals, press the blade of the trowel onto the mortar and angle it inwards at the top. Slide the trowel downwards off the brick below to form a neat V-shape. Angle the vertical either way.

● **Flush** Rub a wad of sacking or hessian over the mortar when it has started to dry.

● **Rounded** Rub a length of 10mm (³/₈in) diameter tube or dowelling along the joints for a curved effect.

● **Raked** Rub the joint with a thin piece of rectangular section wood to give a recessed profile. Only suitable for sheltered sites.

Concrete walling blocks

Bricks can sometimes look too formal, especially in a 'cottagey' garden, but decorative walling blocks, which have the appearance of natural stone, offer a real alternative. They're moulded into handy units that can be laid just like bricks.

Blocks are available in various sizes, with a choice of split or pitched faces (not all faces are textured; only one long face and one end should be exposed). The blocks are concrete but some have natural stone aggregates added in manufacture to give an authentic look; numerous colours are available, such as greens, yellows, reds, greys and buff tones.

Modular blocks moulded to look like several smaller coursed stones can be used to save time in building. Treat them just like single blocks and lay them with mortar. For a double-sided wall, however, you'll need to lay two skins of blocks, as there's only one textured side.

Large-format rectangular blocks intended as single-skin, double-sided walling come with both sides textured. Matching pilasters with hollow centres to take reinforcing rods are made with some blocks to build supporting piers. Coping and cappings for the wall can be stuck on with mortar.

For a more formal but still decorative wall offering partial screening while still permitting breezes to flow through, choose screen walling blocks. Moulded from concrete with various pierced geometric patterns, they're laid in 'stack bond', one on top of the other, instead of being overlapped. Consequently, they're not structurally strong. The blocks, which usually measure 300 × 300 × 100mm (12 × 12 × 4in), slot into channelled, hollow pilasters, which are stacked to make piers. Capping and copings complete the wall.

Drystone walling gives an attractive, 'country' air to a garden, but suitable stones are not easy – or cheap – to obtain, and the construction requires quite some skill to perfect. You may, however, be able to make low walls using stones bought from a

garden centre or quarry. For a similar effect, try manufactured drystone walling blocks, which are laid in the same way without mortar.

If your requirements for a building material are purely functional, use large-format concrete blocks (breeze blocks). These moulded units measure 150–225mm (6–9in) high × 450mm (18in), 600mm (24in), and 620mm (24½in) long and 50–300mm (2–12in) thick. Various densities are made for a range of uses.

Building a rockery

Natural stone is ideal for making a rock garden. You can buy suitable rocks from a garden centre or quarry, and some hollow manufactured rocks are also made.

A rockery demands good drainage and you may have to build a soakaway beneath it (see page 391).

You'll need about 1,500kg (25cwt) of stone to build a rockery about 3m (10ft) wide and 400mm (16in) high above ground level.

Mark out the site with strings and pegs then dig out the topsoil to a depth of 150mm (6in) and retain it. Compact the soil in the hole then prepare a free-draining bedding material: mix one part grit to five parts topsoil or compost then refill the hole to a depth of 50mm (2in) below ground level.

Move the largest 'key' stone into place at the base of the rockery and pack soil under it. Add medium-sized stones, forming an L-shaped outcrop; stones should become smaller towards the back. Lean each stone back into the bank by about 15 degrees.

Fill inside the outcrop with the soil/grit mixture to just over the tops of the stones, then add a second L-shaped outcrop behind the first. Repeat the process until

Below *Reconstituted stone walling blocks come in various sizes and colours; copings are wider and pier cappings are square.*

Bottom *Used like bricks, blocks can be built up course by course to create a natural-looking wall with a rough-textured face.*

1. *When mixing concrete by hand, pour the cement right into the centre of the aggregate.*
2. *Mix the two substances together thoroughly until they are the same colour and consistency.*
3. *Form a crater in the middle of the cement mix and slowly add water. Mix well until the right consistency.*

you reach the pinnacle, which should be topped with small stones. Cover all exposed soil with a layer of grit then plant out the terraces with suitable alpine plants and dwarf shrubs and bulbs.

Concrete in the garden

Cast concrete is an extremely versatile and economical material, used typically for foundations for a garden wall, a base for a shed or coal bunker – or in its own right as a surface for a path or patio.

Concrete is a mix of Portland cement, combined aggregate, sometimes called ballast (sharp sand and stones), and water. The cement and water form a paste that bonds the particles together into a dense, strong material that can be moulded.

Garden structures such as walls must be set on a firm base to spread their load and prevent sinking. The most basic foundation is a strip of concrete, called 'footings', cast in a trench.

Larger 'rafts' are used to make bases for garden buildings and as paths and driveways. They're cast in a timber frame, called 'formwork', then compacted and levelled.

Buying concrete

There are various ways to buy concrete, largely dependent on the amount you need. For very small jobs and repairs, for example, just buy pre-packed dry-mixes with the ingredients properly proportioned for you. Dry-mix is sold in DIY stores in bags from 2.5kg (5½lb) to 50kg (1cwt). All you do is add the water.

Some minor repairs to concrete can be made using mortar, which is concrete but without the large particles of aggregate (see below).

For larger jobs, it is more economical to buy the ingredients separately in bulk from a builders' merchant and mix them yourself by hand or by hiring a mixing machine. For extensive jobs requiring over 3 cu m (4 cu yd) of concrete (making a drive, for example), buy ready-mixed. It's delivered by mixer lorry and can be deposited directly into your prepared base, so long as there's access for the vehicle. You can't dawdle over this job: be prepared to cast, compact and level the mix in just a few hours (less on a hot day) or it will harden.

Various strengths of concrete are required for certain jobs and this is determined by the ratio of ingredients (by volume) used in the mix. Most concrete work in the garden will call for one of three basic mixes, as shown in the chart below, along with its relevant usage.

If a mix is described as 1:2:3 (a general purpose mix), as in the first example, this means one volume of cement; two volumes of sand; three volumes of aggregate.

Builders' merchants often sell the sharp sand and gravel aggregate already combined as 'all-in ballast'. The size of the aggregate is important for the texture of the mix, and ranges in size from about 10mm (⅜in) to 20mm (¾in) for fine and coarse mixes respectively. The same general purpose mix, therefore, translates as 20mm 1:4 ballast; this means that there are no particles in the mix larger than 20mm (¾in) and that you'll need one part cement to four parts all-in ballast per batch. Use a bucket to proportion mixes.

How much concrete

Calculating the amount of concrete you'll need for a particular job is quite straightforward. First work out the volume of your project in cubic metres (cubic yards) by multiplying length × width × thickness in

CONCRETE MIXES	Mix-your own			Ready-mix
Use	Proportions (volume)	Amount per cu m (cu yd)	Yield per 50kg/ 1cwt bag cement	specification
General purpose (Most uses except foundations and exposed paving)	Cement 1 Sand 2 20mm (¾in) aggr. 3 or all-in ballast 4	6.4 bags 680kg (13cwt) 1175kg (23½cwt) 1855kg (36cwt)	0.15 cu m (5 cu ft)	C20P to BS 5328, medium to high workability, 20mm (¾in) max. aggregate size
Foundation (Footings, foundations and bases for precast paving)	Cement 1 Sand 2½ 20mm (¾in) aggr. 3½ or all-in ballast 5	5.6 bags 720kg (14cwt) 1165kg (23cwt) 1885kg (37cwt)	0.18 cu m (6 cu ft)	C7.5P to BS 5328, high workability, 20mm (¾in) max aggregate size
Paving (All exposed in situ paving, especially drives)	Cement 1 Sand 1½ 20mm (¾in) aggr. 2½ or all-in ballast 3½	8 bags 600kg (11cwt) 1200kg (23½cwt) 1800kg (35½cwt)	0.12 cu m (4 cu ft)	Special prescribed mix minimum cement content 33kg/m³; 4% entrained air; target slump 75mm (3in)

metres (yards). Add 10 per cent for wastage.

Study the fourth column in the chart, which gives the yield of mixed concrete per 50kg (1cwt) bag of cement, to determine the quantities of ingredients you'll need.

Ordering the correct amount and proportions of ready-mix is much simpler: you leave it up the supplier. He'll need to know the volume you require, its purpose (so he can work out a suitable mix), the delivery date, site access details, and how you propose to handle it on delivery.

The chart shows the specification for each mix, consisting of the mix number, the Standard, followed by the consistency and aggregate size.

If you're mixing your own concrete from bulk ingredients, proper storage of materials is important. Cement must be protected from moisture or it will harden: keep it in a garage or shed if posisible, or raised above the ground by about 100mm (4in) on a platform. If the bags are stored outside, cover the pile with polythene sheeting weighted down.

Mixing by hand
To mix concrete by hand, shovel the cement onto the aggregate and gradually mix the two until they're uniform in colour by heaping them into a 'volcano'.

Form a crater in the heap and add some water. Collapse the walls of the volcano and mix in the ingredients. Add more water a little at a time and mix to achieve a uniform colour and consistency. Beware of adding too much water, or you'll ruin the mix.

Turn the mix into a new pile three times to make sure the ingredients are thoroughly combined. Draw your shovel back across the heap in steps: the ridges should be firm and slump-free, without a residue of runny cement.

Mixing by machine
Small machine mixers are available for hire and take much of the toil out of mixing your own concrete. Add half the coarse aggregate and half the water to the mixer drum, then the sand. Start the motor and let the ingredients mix for a few minutes, then add all the cement and what's left of the coarse aggregate and the water. Mix until the concrete is of a consistency that it falls off the blades cleanly. Tip the mixer drum to empty the contents into a waiting barrow. Add the aggregate and water for the next batch while you're placing the first batch and leave the drum revolving to keep the blades clean.

Laying footings
Footings for a garden wall or other small brick or block structure must measure twice the width of the masonry and half as deep, and there must be a projection at each end that's half the width of the masonry. This spreads the load of the wall to firm ground. If your wall is 225mm (9in) wide (a single brick length) the margins around it will need to be about 112mm (4¾in). Deeper footings will be necessary if the structure rises above about seven courses of bricks.

To set out the footings, stretch strings between wooden stakes driven into the ground at each end of the proposed foundations; space them apart the width of the trench. If the foundation is to be built flush against a concrete path or drive, you'll only need a single stringline.

Hold a spirit level vertically against the stringlines and mark the ground directly below each line; connect the lines by scribing against a long timber straightedge with a trowel. Altérnatively, sprinkle a line of sand under the strings.

Remove the strings, but not the stakes, and dig down to the correct depth. Keep the trench sides vertical and the floor flat.

You can cast the concrete directly on a well-compacted earth base, but where the soil is soft, add a layer of hardcore (broken bricks and concrete) and ram it down well using a sledge hammer or alternatively a stout timber post.

Below: *Mix mortar by hand for small quantities. Use a spotboard to contain the mix close the job.*
1. Use strings stretched between wooden stakes fitted with cross pieces to mark the width of strip foundations.
2. Dig the trench and set timber pegs vertically in the base, level them with a spirit level and use to set the concrete to the correct depth.

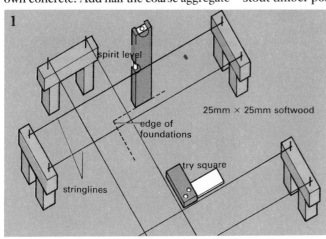

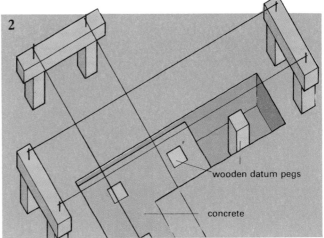

The concrete strip must be truly flat and horizontal, so timber datum pegs are used to indicate the final level. Cut enough 25mm square (1in sq) softwood pegs to be spaced at 1m (3ft) intervals along the trench; drive in the first peg so it protrudes by the depth of the concrete. Hammer in the remaining pegs. Level them with the first peg by spanning across their tops with a spirit level on a straightedge.

Mix up sufficient concrete to fill the trench, tip it in and work it around with a shovel to expel air bubbles. Add more concrete until it's just above the level of the pegs. Roughly level the surface with the back of your shovel then check with a straightedge between the peg tops to highlight voids or highspots. Add or remove concrete accordingly.

Use a length of stout timber to compact the mix and flatten the surface, in a chopping motion, moving across the strip about 50mm (2in) at a time. Leave overnight (preferably longer) to dry before starting to build on the footings.

During hot weather, cover the concrete with old sacking, kept moist to prevent too-rapid drying out of the mix, which could cause cracks. You shouldn't lay concrete during very cold weather but if a snap frost occurs, cover the slab with polythene sheeting over a layer of straw or blanket loft insulation to protect it.

Casting a large slab

A large concrete slab for a path or patio, or as a base for a a garden building, must be cast within timber formwork set at the perimeter of the site. Slab thickness depends on what the base is to be used for, but about 100–125mm (4–5in) over 75mm (3in) of hardcore is adequate for a drive; 75–100mm (3–4in) for a shed base.

Mark out the shape of your slab with strings and pegs, making sure you get the corners exactly at 90 degrees. Make a 'builder's square' from three lengths of 50 × 25mm (2 × 1in) softwood cut in the proportions 3:4:5 – 300mm; 400mm; 500mm/(12in; 16in; 20in). Nail them together with a half-lap at the right-angled

corner and with the longest side nailed on top of the other two sides. Use a straight-edge tool to check the angles.

Dig out the topsoil to the depth of the slab. Allow an extra margin all round for access. As with footings, the slab must be level over its whole area. To ensure this, drive 300mm (1ft) long 25mm square (1in sq) softwood pegs into the base at 1.5m (5ft) intervals, so the tops are level with the finished height of the concrete. Align the pegs with a spirit level on a long straight-edge, as described on pages 366–368.

Excavate the base accordingly. Add well-rammed hardcore to firm up soft ground. On long paths and drives you can level the base using sighting rods.

To make the formwork you'll need some planks of sawn softwood 25mm (1in) thick and as wide as the depth of the concrete, and some 50mm square (2in sq) softwood pegs about 300mm (1ft) long. Drive the pegs into the ground, outside the slab area, at about 1m (3ft 4in) intervals. Set the planks level and secure them to the pegs with nails.

A large slab or long path must slope to one side slightly to ensure rapid drainage of rainwater, and this must be incorporated in the setting out. Place a small offcut of timber (called a 'shim') under your spirit level when levelling the pegs and form-boards, at what will be the lower end. When the spirit level registers horizontal, the fall is correct.

Tip barrowloads of concrete into the base then compact the mix and level it with the top of the formwork. On a wide slab, you'll need assistance: use a stout tamping beam in a chopping action. Allow the concrete to harden before prising off the formwork then fill the margin around the perimeter with earth. Don't put the slab to use for about ten days.

Repairing cracks

A cracked, chipped or crumbly concrete surface looks unsightly, and paves the way for more widespread deterioration. Cracks usually appear after a hard winter, when frost penetrates crevices and expands.

To repair cracked or chipped concrete slab:
1. *Enlarge the crack to about 12–20mm (½–¾) wide using a club hammer and cold chisel, undercutting the edges to improve the grip of the filler.*
2. *Brush out dust and debris then daub on some PVA adhesive, which aids the adhesion of the mortar.*
3. *Spread some mortar into the crack, chopping with the trowel blade to force it into every crevice. Smooth it level.*
4. *Ram broken bricks into a hole in concrete using the handle of a club hammer, then apply mortar.*

1

2
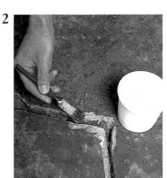

3

4

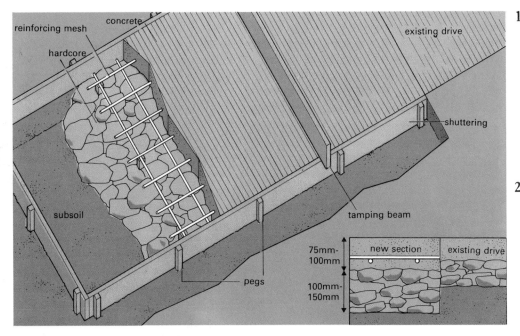

reinforcing mesh
concrete
existing drive
hardcore
shuttering
subsoil
tamping beam
75mm-100mm
new section
existing drive
100mm-150mm
pegs

Check for signs of subsidence; if the trouble is localized, simply patch the damage. If it's more extensive, renew the section.

Enlarge the crack to about 12–20mm (½–¾in) wide, using a club hammer and cold chisel. Under-cut the edges to provide a grip for the repair material. Brush out dust and debris with a stiff-bristled brush. To aid the adhesion of the patch, apply a liberal coat of PVA adhesive mixed with water (in the proportion 1:5) to the crack and allow to dry. Paint on a second coat of a stronger solution (3 parts PVA to one of water) then apply mortar while it's tacky.

Mix up some repair mortar in a bucket in a ratio of 1:3 cement/soft sand. Trowel the mortar into the crack, pressing it right into the sides. Force it into place by chopping with the trowel blade. Smooth the patch off level with the surrounding surface.

Filling holes
Holes are often caused by localised subsidence in the hardcore foundations. To repair this defect, widen the hole just enough to undercut the edges.

Ram some broken bricks deep into the hole using a stout length of wood or the shaft of your club hammer. Make up a concrete mix of 1:5 all-in ballast (see page 394), prime the hole with a PVA adhesive solution, then trowel in the mix, overfilling slightly. Compact the mix using a length of timber to give a fairly rough finish.

Renewing a section of concrete
A section of a drive or path that's seriously cracked or subsided due to a fault in the sub-base should be broken up and relaid anew. Hire a heavy-duty jack hammer and break up the affected area. Cut neatly across the sound section.

You can use the old broken-up concrete and hardcore as your sub-base, so long as it's well-rammed down. Set datum pegs in the soil to set the level of the concrete flush with the adjoining sound surface. If the ground below the subsided area is light, sandy soil, include a reinforcing mesh in the new slab. This is available in rolls from builders' merchants: you'll need 100mm square (4in sq) steel mesh made with 6mm (¼in) diameter wire.

Dig the foundations deeper than before and allow for a thicker slab. Hire a motorized plate compactor (see pages 69–71) to firm the hardcore, or use a garden roller. Rig up timber formwork nailed to pegs at the perimeter of the site and lay the mesh over the hardcore.

Mix up the concrete and pour into the formwork box. Compact the mix, making sure it's well butted up to the hard concrete edge, then tamp it level with the formboards.

Repairing crumbly edges
The edges of concrete slabs are their weakest, most vulnerable parts. Chop back the crumbly material to a sound edge and prime the edge with two coats of PVA solution. Fix a length of timber about 25mm (1in) thick and the depth of the concrete, across the front of the broken edge to mould the repair concrete. Secure it with wooden pegs driven into the ground.

Mix up some concrete and trowel it into the hole. Use a chopping action with the blade of your trowel to work the mix under the edge of the hard concrete, then compact it. Remove the formboard when the concrete has hardened fully.

Above left *If you need to renew a section of concrete, dig up the old part and lay new, deeper hardcore foundations. Set reinforcing mesh in the layer of new concrete to prevent the trouble occurring again. Undercut the edge of the old concrete to give a good key for the new concrete.*

1. *To repair a crumbly edge, chop back the material to sound concrete using a cold chisel.*
2. *Place a timber batten across the edge of the concrete, then trowel in fresh mortar. Leave to set before removing the batten.*

RUNNING THE GARDEN

Make your garden an efficient, orderly place to work by installing electric lighting, power and water on tap. You'll discover just how easy and convenient it is to tend your plants – and you'll be able to make full use of the plot, even at night.

No garden will look after itself. Left unattended, the plot will soon deteriorate into an overgrown jungle that's unkempt, unhealthy, and unworkable.

Regular grass mowing, weeding and watering are only half the battle. Plants need special care if they're to thrive and treatments with fertilizers will certainly give them the boost they may need.

The garden itself should be run with precision to keep it free from blight and the debris that has a habit of expanding – old prunings, hedge trimmings, weeds and other unwanted matter. What's useful can be committed to the compost heap; what's useless can be burned.

To speed the efficient gardener about his work (leaving time for relaxing with the fruits of his labours) the garden should be equipped with the necessary supplies: power for today's electrical gadgets (and light for the patio); water on tap for greenhouse and fish pond.

An outside tap

An outside tap offers a host of benefits. A tap fitted to your house wall, at the end of the plot (or even in both locations) makes chores such as sprinkling the lawn and watering plants so much easier and less disruptive. You can banish the trailing hose from the house, and free the kitchen tap. Additionally, you'll find an outside tap a real saviour when you're involved in messy building work such as mixing concrete, or car-washing.

Installing an outside tap into your mains water supply is a straightforward plumbing project that's made even simpler by the many DIY kits on the market.

Before you go any further, consult your local water authority: you may be limited in your choice of tap components by local restrictions – in some areas any work carried out on the rising main must be done by an authorised plumber. You will have to pay more water rates for an extra tap.

Whatever components you choose, the installation is virtually the same: the new tap and its pipework are simply connected into the house's rising main.

Choosing components

If you opt for individual components rather than a kit, you'll need a purpose-made garden bib tap (sold by garden centres and builders' or plumbers' merchants) in rustless brass. It has an inclined crutch-type handle for easy use and usually comes with a wall bracket.

You'll also need a stopvalve to isolate the supply pipe so it can be drained in winter in case of frost.

To complete the system you'll need sufficient 15mm diameter copper pipe to reach the break-in point, plus various elbow fittings (compression or capillary) and a tee fitting to connect into the mains. (If you have an old-type 22mm diameter rising main the tee must be a 22mm size reducing to 15mm.)

A tap kit is a much more convenient arrangement to fit, if your water authority allows it – most now do. It contains everything you need to make the installation, except a length of extension pipe to reach the break-in point.

A typical kit consists of: stopvalve, pipe clips, push-fit tee, brass wall elbow, pliable copper pipe (to fit through the wall), and plastic tap with hose nozzle. Most suppliers also stock lengths of 15mm polybutylene (plastic) pipe, which you can substitute for copper pipe.

Automatic supply connectors are available, which replace the standard tee. The device is clamped over the pipe and a small charge inside, when activated, will pierce the mains pipe.

Planning the installation

Before you buy the components for your new tap, consider what the installation involves. Siting the tap where it will be most convenient in use is your priority. If you need it at the front and back of the house, position it where it's accessible to both areas, using a hose. Aim to locate the tap over a drainage gully (or at least a paved area) to cope with the inevitable spillage; avoid flower beds and grass or you'll soon form a mud patch.

The tap should be connected into the

Opposite *Light the great outdoors and extend your gardening time: power the shed or outhouse worktop, or simply illuminate the garden for use in those summertime evenings.*

A garden tap makes watering the garden so much more convenient – comprehensive kits in plastic make the installation a simple, quick and satisfying job.

rising main for maximum water pressure, and the position of this pipe will influence where you run the new branch. You'll be able to identify the main: the kitchen sink's cold tap is fed directly from it, whether you've a direct system (all fixtures fed directly from the main) or an indirect one (fixtures – except the kitchen tap – fed from a cold water tank).

Once you've found where to break into the rising main, trace a route (the least conspicuous one) to your tap position.

Running a pipe through a wall
Mark the wall outside where the tap is to go: it can be any convenient height above the ground, so long as there's room for a bucket underneath and you don't have to stoop to use it. Use a reference point common to inside and outside (a window or door frame for instance) and transfer the tap position to the wall indoors, using a tape measure, try square or spirit level as a guide.

You can cut through the wall with a club hammer and long cold chisel but it's easier to use an electric hammer drill fitted with a large-diameter masonry bit. Unless you have a drill with an extension piece you'll have to form the hole from both sides: on a solid wall drill about 110mm (4¾in) then go outside and complete the hole: on a cavity wall continue until the drill bit breaks through the inner leaf, then repeat for the

outer leaf. Which ever method you use, wear stout gloves and goggles as protection against flying fragments. Test-fit a length of 15mm copper pipe in the hole.

Connecting to the rising main
So that you can work out the various lengths of pipework needed to complete the run it's best to tee into the rising main first. If you're using a conventional compression or capillary fitting, or a pushfit tee, you'll have to drain down the rising main. Turn off the main stop valve and open the kitchen cold tap to drain off the water.

Mark a cutting line on the pipe and saw through it, absolutely squarely, using a junior hacksaw (place a bowl under the pipe to catch any remaining water in the pipe). Measure from the cut the width of the tee piece. Allow for the amount that's to be slotted inside at each end (measure the depth of the internal pipe stop) then make a second cut to remove the section of pipe. File off the burrs inside and outside the cut ends and (for compression fittings) bevel the edges slightly.

To fit a compression tee, slip its capnuts onto the pipe ends, then the soft copper 'olives' (which compress to form the seal). Insert the tee fitting – you'll need to release the pipe from its brackets for fitting clearance – and tighten up the capnuts, using an adjustable spanner.

To fit a capillary tee, polish the pipe ends with wire wool then apply flux by brush. Insert the tee, then place a heat-proof board (an asbestos iron stand will do) behind the joint. Play the flame of a blowtorch over one of the joints until you see a ring of solder appear around the mouth of the fitting. Leave the joint to cool, the repeat for the other joint. Wrap a wet cloth round the first joint to prevent the solder melting again.

A plastic push-fit tee is simple to fit: just apply silicone lubricant (or washing-up liquid) to the pipe ends and inside the fitting, then slot it into the pipe run.

By far the easiest way to tap into the rising main is to use an automatic connector. Simply clamp the device to the pipe (don't even turn off the water) and leave until the rest of the pipe run is assembled and you're ready to make the connection.

Assembling the branch pipe
Fit the pipe in the exit hole: with compression or capillary fittings you'll need to fit an elbow at each end; with pliable copper just hand-bend it in the direction of the supply.

To use conventional plumbing, measure between the exit pipe and the tee fitting and cut a length of 15mm copper pipe to fit.

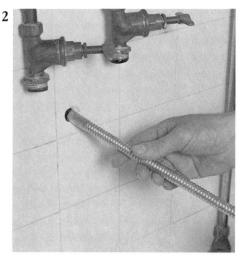

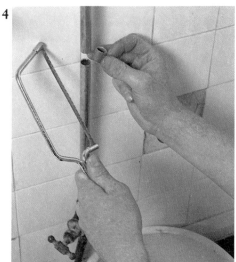

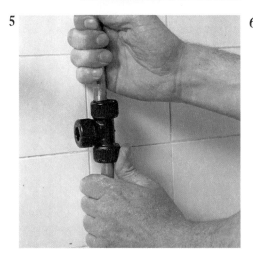

1. *Drill a hole through the outside wall to take the water supply pipe.*

2. *Use hand-bendable copper pipe as the exit pipe – it's available in convenient lengths to suit most walls.*

3. *Drain down the rising main and break into it by fitting a tee connector – a plastic push-fit fitting is the simplest to use. First mark its position on the pipe.*

4. *Cut out the section of rising main using a hacksaw, then prepare the pipe ends by deburring and lubricating ready for the connector tee.*

5. *Slot the push-fit tee onto the ends of the cut rising main – you don't have to dismantle these fittings to make a good, watertight seal, although you may need sufficient play in the pipe to enable the connection to be made.*

6. *Fit a stopcock to the end of the bendable exit pipe – it's necessary to isolate the garden supply during the winter, when bursts could occur.*

Allow for the insertion of a stop valve in this run. Assemble the run with compression or capillary fittings, as previously described, and secure the pipe to special brackets.

Outside you may need to fit a short vertical run to the tap location. Assemble this and attach an angled tap connector incorporating a wall bracket to the end. Fit an inclined bib tap with compression fittings.

To assemble a push-fit pipe run, lubricate the end of the pliable copper exit pipe and slot on the plastic stop valve. Fit a pipe clip to the wall and clip the pipe in place. Measure between the stop valve and the tee fitting on the rising main, allowing for the amount of pipe to be inserted in each end. You can use flexible polybutylene pipe for this run. It's sold in various sized reels or lengths for fitting to size: even if the run is especially long you won't need to join

7. Measure between the stopcock and the rising main tee connector, cut a length of pipe to fit, then slot it in place.
8. Outside, screw a brass wall plate and elbow to the end of the exit pipe, using the compression fittings.
9. Screw the plastic bib tap onto the elbow fitting, set it upright, then fit the optional hose nozzle. Mount the hose nearby for convenience.

7

8

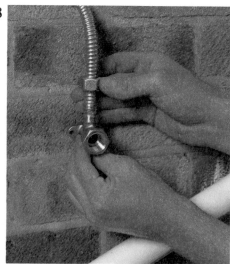

9

sections and the pipe can cope with fairly tight bends, too. Cut the pipe squarely with a hacksaw, deburr the ends and lubricate. Insert the special metal inserts supplied into each end then slot the pipe into the tee and stopvalve connections. Make sure to clip the pipe to the wall at intervals.

Outside, bend the pliable pipe downwards to the tap position and connect a compression wall elbow to its end. Screw the elbow into wall plugs, then screw the plastic bib tap into its socket. Wind some PTFE sealing tape onto the screw thread first to make a good seal and so you can fit the tap vertically. Seal the gap between wall and exit pipe with mastic.

Restore the water supply (make sure the new tap is off) and check the system for leaks. To activate an automatic connector, remove the device's plastic firing pin cap and strike the firing pin sharply with a hammer. A loud crack signals that the charge inside has pierced the rising main.

Fitting a second garden tap

A second tap is a real boon to gardening. Site it at the far end of a long plot for best effect. To make the connection, insert a tee fitting (compression or push-fit only) in the outside vertical section of the exit pipe (you'll need a special pliable pipe with an unridged mid-piece for this) and run a length of 12mm polythene or plastic pipe to the second tap position. Bury the pipe about 500mm (1ft 8in) underground in a trench, out of harm's way. At the other end, connect the pipe to a standpipe – a vertical length of pipe fixed to a stout post or to the wall of an outbuilding. Attach the second bib tap as previously described.

Watering the garden

All plants and crops demand water to survive but often nature is lax in supplying it

in sufficient quantity and it's up to the gardener to make up the balance. But knowing just how much water to administer, and when, is quite another matter.

When to water

Watering is probably most important between the months of April and September, when the plants are growing and the sun is at is strongest. Nevertheless, this depends on the rainfall in your area: some regions receive too much, others too little.

Aspect is a deciding factor (a north-facing site will dry out less quickly than one facing south), and soil type (see page 372) should also be considered (clay soil holds more water than sandy soil, yet each has its particular problems).

In short there is no simple answer, but there are priorities. Newly-planted trees, shrubs, and other plants, and of course seedlings, are high on the priority list. Among the vegetables, crops like peas and beans will give a much better yield if they don't go short of water, and radishes need plenty of moisture if they are not to go woody. Soft fruits, too, such as black currants, raspberries, and strawberries will give a much better crop if they are watered while the fruit is developing.

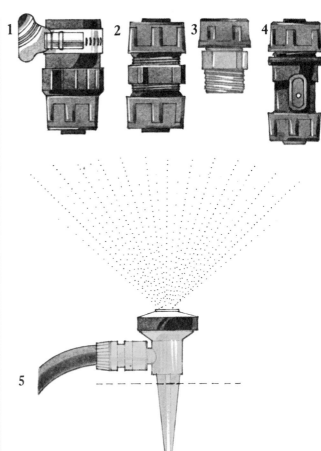

Lawns will turn brown if not watered, but they will grow again when wet weather returns. If you start to water the lawn, you will have to water heavily and frequently to keep it green.

Whatever you water, do so thoroughly even if it means less frequently. Lots of light sprinklings can encourage detrimental surface rooting.

Greenhouse watering
While a garden tap (pages 398–402) will permit hand-watering of greenhouse plants, automated systems take over the chore from you. The two principal systems depend on either capillary action from special mats or a sand base, or on a drip feed from individual nozzles. In either case they can be fed down hand-filled reservoirs, or by mains-fed cisterns.

Equipment for garden watering
A lightweight, capacious watering can is a basic need: choose one with a long spout fixed near the base in 7–9 litre (1½–2 gallon) capacity.

An adaptable hosepipe can be used on its own or in conjunction with numerous nozzles. Choose a long enough one for the job. Although some are inexpensive it is probably worth paying more for a reinforced plastic hosepipe; they are stronger and easier to handle. Unkinkable and flat-packed types are available.

As a hose attachment, a sprinkler is an ideal way to apply water over a period of time. Numerous models with oscillating, pulsating or rotating heads are made; choice will be affected by the size of the plot, the water pressure, and cost.

Above left *A selection of garden watering equipment, including perforated hose, and (clockwise from left) rotating sprinkler, watering-can hose attachment, a large rotating sprinkler, a star-shaped disc sprinkler and an oscillating sprinkler.*
1. *tap connector*
2. *hose connector*
3. *sprinkler connector*
4. *on/off connector*
5. *spiked mini sprinkler, which covers a small circular area*

Garden hygiene

A messy garden is unsightly and unhealthy. Sickly plants and decaying debris, if allowed to remain, will encourage pests and diseases. An unkempt greenhouse, too, can harbour disease. To eradicate these unsavoury elements, you need to know just what they are, where they come from, and where they lurk. Once you have identified the cause, cure is just a matter of an orderly and extremely meticulous work routine.

Pests and diseases

Trouble can come to your garden in many different ways.

Weeds can act as host to both pests and diseases, besides looking untidy and competing for nutrients. Keep your garden weed-free, then it will look nicer and the plants are likely to be healthier (the pests and diseases will still attack your plants, but they will be easier to keep under control if there is not present and flourishing infection and infestation already within the garden).

Sickly-looking plants should be viewed with suspicion, especially if they have mottled, yellowish, or crinkled leaves. These symptoms could be due to other causes, but virus diseases are likely causes. These are particularly troublesome because they cannot be controlled with sprays, but are likely to be spread to other plants of the same kind by sap-sucking insects such as aphids. If a plant looks very sickly and you just can't track the problem down to an obvious pest or disease, you must be drastic and burn it.

Diseases can also be carried on fallen leaves and rotting debris. Some fungus diseases such as botrytis may start on dead tissue but spread to healthy growth; dead leaves may also contain other harmful fungus spores (rose leaves may sometimes contain those spores that cause the black spot disease for instance).

Play safe, sweep up or pick up fallen petals and leaves, and, preferably, burn them.

Disposing of crop remains

The remains of vegetable crops are easy to dispose of, so long as they're free from disease. In the autumn, simply chop through what's left of the growth with a sharp spade, and dig into the soil. This will form a green manure that adds humus to the soil (see pages 301–3). Tough roots, or the roots of perenials that are likely to grow again, should be removed and burnt or composted. Alternatively, you can put all undiseased crop remains on your compost heap (see pages 301–3).

Sterile conditions

Soil conditioning, regular weeding, watering and feeding, coupled with general garden hygiene, is the best way to ensure a healthy plot. But the water and the compost that you use to encourage your plants to grow could actually carry pests or diseases.

The water you give to your plants and crops should be uncontaminated. And the worst source of contaminated water is the water butt. The belief that rainwater gathered in a butt from the roof is good for plants is misguided. Although it does not contain the lime that can be a problem for some plants in some areas, it is likely to have a good population of pests and diseases, as well as dead leaves and other debris.

Your safest bet is to use tap water for glass-grown plants and save the contents of the water butt for the more hardy specimens outside. Only a few greenhouse plants will resent hard tap water, but you can make special arrangements for these.

Always try to use sterilized compost for pot plants (some peat-based composts may not be sterilized but because the peat is unlikely to be contaminated, these are perfectly saftisfactory). Once the bags are opened, keep the top of the bag folded over, or transfer the compost to a clean plastic dustbin with a lid, which you can keep in the greenhouse or shed.

Most commercial methods of soil sterilization are not suitable for the amateur, but if the soil needs to be sterilized (outdoors or in the greenhouse) you could treat it with a solution of formalin (which you may be able to buy at a garden centre). Late winter or early spring is the best time for this job. First clear the soil, then dilute the formalin and use strictly according to the instructions on the container. (Avoid inhaling the fumes: they're pungent and irritating.)

Use a watering can with a rose to sprinkle the solution generously and evenly on the soil, which should be moist. Cover the area with sheets of polythene anchored with

Below *Chop through disease-free crops with a spade and turn them into the soil to form a green manure that adds beneficial humus to the soil.*

Bottom *Burn tough roots, the roots of perennials and other growths that are likely to grow again or cause obstructions.*

1. *Dig up any plants you want to save, plus crop remains, then break up large lumps in the soil. Water until moist but not sodden.*
2. *Dilute formalin with water according to the instructions on the bottle, and stir the solution well.*
3. *Sprinkle the formalin solution onto the soil from a watering can fitted with a rose; aim to drench the soil thoroughly.*
4. *Cover the treated area with sheets of black polythene held down with bricks to retain the fumes.*
5. *Two days later, uncover the soil and dig to release the fumes. Don't use the soil for three weeks.*
6. *Sterilize plant pots by immersing them in formalin solution for 48 hours, then wash thoroughly. Don't use clay pots for one week after sterilizing.*

bricks at the edges, to contain the fumes. Leave for two days. Remove the sheets and lightly dig over the soil to release all the fumes. Don't use the soil for three weeks (outdoors) or six weeks (indoors).

You can also sterilize pots, tools and other garden equipment by immersing them for two days in formalin solution, after which you should wash them thoroughly. Leave clay pots for a week before using.

Steam sterilization is the most effective method of treating your greenhouse soil, though as its unlikely that you have access to equipment to sterilize it *in situ*, it can be a tedius job to excavate it and replace it in small batches.

The soil temperature should be rapidly raised to about 82°C (180°F) and held there for about 15 minutes. Proprietary steamers are available, but it's easy to make your own – but be warned, unless the temperature and the timing are right you can actually be more harmful and leave the soil in a worse condition than before. There are complex biological and chemical reactions involved that can upset nutrient availability and even inhibit the normal germination and growth.

For very small amounts of soil, you can simply boil 300ml (½pt) water in a large saucepan and add soil to within 12mm (½in) of the rim. Put on the lid and simmer for about 15 minutes, then turn out on a clean surface for a while to completely cool down.

For larger quantities of soil, use a clean oil drum with a lid. Put the soil in the drum, inside a hessian sack, add about 50mm (2in) of water and boil rapidly to produce steam for about 20 minutes. The sack must be suspended over the water on a rod spanning the drum. A camping gas stove is the ideal medium to heat up the water in the garden.

Fumigating the greenhouse

Pests and diseases can lurk within the framework of the greenhouse, and fumigation is a good way to eradicate them. There are various chemicals sold for greenhouse fumigation, so be clear about their uses – and check which plants are likely to be damaged and therefore need removing first. In the case of sulphur fumigation, all plants must be removed.

If the greenhouse is empty, you could try the old method of burning flowers of sulphur or special sulphur candles (sometimes sold by garden centres and horticultural specialists). Position the candles or flowers of sulphur centrally, light, following the manufacturer's instructions, and vacate the greenhouse, closing the door behind you. Don't re-enter until the following day, when the fumes will have dispersed. You can safely return your plants shortly after.

You may find the various modern insecticides or fungicidal smoke cones or pellets more convenient to use. With these you actually control the pests and diseases on the plants as well as the structure, and there is no need to remove the plants (other than any that the instructions say are not suitable for treatment).

Burning garden refuse

Any garden refuse that you can't use on your compost heap should be burned. The potash that's produced can be added to the soil to improve its fertility (keep the ash dry until you are ready to use it).

A bonfire is a good way to dispose of unwanted rubbish but you must take care to build it properly and use it safely. Your aim should be to make a bonfire that burns rather than smokes – a smoky fire is a nuisance to neighbours and a health hazard. Make a cone of dry wood or crumple some wire and use this as the heart of the bonfire, to ensure the necessary updraught of air in the centre. Add only dry material to the pile. Never pour petrol or any inflammable substance on the fire – if it's slow to start, use crumpled newspaper or fire lighters.

An incinerator will contain small amounts of refuse while it's burning. Various types are made, from an expanded metal mesh box on legs to a steel-framed container with

1. A proprietary steel-framed incinerator with riddle attachment to shake out the ashes.
2. A contained dustbin incinerator with lid and chimney provides the neatest way to dispose of rubbish.
3. An expanded metal mesh incinerator in a steel, legged frame.

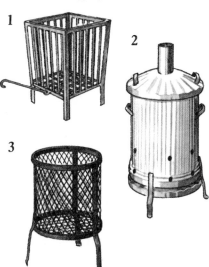

riddle base and the metal dustbin incinerator complete with chimney. When buying an incinerator, choose one with thick walls, as thin material will not withstand the intense, prolonged heat for long.

You can build your own incinerator from concrete building blocks laid without mortar. Construct a basic box shape with gaps between each block for air passage. Pile scrap piping in the base as a grate.

Electricity outdoors

Taking electricity outdoors will extend the use of your garden immensely. Whether you turn your shed into a workshop by installing sockets for power tools and appliances, bring light and heat to the greenhouse, or simply dispense with a trailing extension lead when using an electric lawnmower, you'll discover how adaptable your plot becomes. If your preferences are for far more relaxing activities, power for pool lights and pumps, illumination for the patio, complete the picture.

Before you even contemplate running a supply outside, consider what's involved. Electricity can kill, if misused. Outside, there's greater risk of fittings getting wet (electricity and water are a lethal combination) and the installation is more exposed to physical damage, from garden tools for example. In short, pay particular heed to the very stringent rules governing outdoor electricity supplies. Whatever you do must comply with the IEE (Institute of Electrical Engineers) wiring regulations, and above all *never* attempt any electrical work unless you're confident and thoroughly competent. If you're at all unsure, abandon the project and call in a qualified electrician.

Types of installation

Sensible precautions apart, an electrical supply outdoors is quite straightforward to arrange. There are basically four options open to you:
● A socket mounted externally on the house wall, which can be connected to an existing inside circuit.
● Lighting and socket outlets in a greenhouse, shed or detached garage, for which you'll need to provide a separate circuit, taken from a spare fuseway in the consumer unit (fusebox) or via a new switchfuse unit, complete with isolating switch.
● Waterproof sockets mounted on sturdy posts in the garden, using a separate circuit.
● Garden lighting and a supply for a pool pump run from a low-voltage supply, connected to a transformer, or a mains supply.

Separate circuits can be buried underground, carried overhead or fixed to a boundary wall (but *not* a fence; it could be blown over in a high wind). Armoured PVC cable and MICC (mineral insulated copper covered) cable made specially for outdoor use are available, but call for special tools to connect them up.

You could use ordinary PVC-sheathed two-core-and-earth cable through heavy-duty conduits or pipe if it runs underground (plastic conduit is available with various push-fit, solvent-weld connectors); an overhead cable must be (unbroken) at least 3.5m (11ft 6in) above the ground (5.2m/17ft over a drive) and supported by sturdy posts. If the span is more than 3.5m (11ft 6in) a catenary wire must be used to support the cable.

It's acceptable to use ordinary plastic sockets in the greenhouse or shed but impact-resistant, or metal-clad boxes are more resilient to knocks. In a greenhouse, especially, where there is a lot of moisture, it is wise to use a special greenhouse control panel. Externally, you will need to fit a metal-clad socket that's has a special waterproof casing.

All outdoor circuits must be protected against potentially lethal faults. A normal fuse or MCB (miniature circuit breaker) isn't sufficient: not only would it be too slow to react to some faults and 'blow', but also there are some faults it wouldn't even sense. You must fit a high sensitivity residual current device (RCD), sometimes called a current operated earth-leakage circuit breaker (ELCB) *in addition to* a circuit fuse or MCB.

The RCD will 'trip' and isolate the circuit when it senses a fault current as low as 30mA – and that's well below the level of a fatal shock. For a normal 30A outdoor circuit, use an RCD rated at 30A.

Socket on a house wall

A single socket fitted on the exterior wall of your house is ideal if you have a small garden. There are two ways to connect the socket to the house wiring:
● **To an existing ring main power circuit.** Connect a length of 2.5mm² two-core-and-earth cable directly to the back of an existing socket on the circuit (the socket must be on the ring main and *not* already on a spur) and run this branch to the new socket. Alternatively, you can break into the ring main (not a spur cable), install a three-terminal junction box and run your new branch from here to the new socket. The ring main and its spurs cannot serve an area greater than 100m².
● **To a radial circuit.** Connect a cable to any socket on the radial circuit and run it to the new socket. A circuit wired in 2.5mm² cable and fused at 20A can serve only

A well-lit garden patio enables you to sit out on warm summer evenings and makes the most of your garden.

1. *To fit a socket on a house wall, drill through the masonry using a large-diameter bit. Drill from both sides.*
2. *Fit plastic conduit from the break out point to the socket location, then fit a special outside socket.*
3. *Feed the electric cable through the conduit from inside the house, then trim and strip the cable cores.*
4. *Connect the cable cores to the terminals of the faceplate, making sure they're not strained.*
5. *Fit the socket faceplate to the body then fit the weatherproof cover when you're not using the socket.*
6. *Fit an ELCB between the fuse and the consumer unit to protect the entire house from danger if a fault develops.*

20m²; one wired in 4mm² cable and fused at 30A can serve only 50mm².

Choose a suitable location on the wall for the new socket and work out the easiest route to the connection point. The socket should be about 1.2m (4ft) above the ground: you may decide to run the cable up the wall to a first floor circuit, down to a ground floor one, or directly back through the wall in order to run the cable mainly inside.

Drill a downward-sloping hole through the wall, from inside (to prevent moisture trickling in), using a masonry bit that matches the diameter of a length of plastic conduit – this is to prevent the cable from chafing.

Insert the conduit, then run a length of cable through. Attach an elbow connector to direct the conduit up or down (if necessary) and add a length of conduit to reach the socket location. Fit a conduit adaptor in the socket mounting box, attach the box to the wall with screws and plugs (fixing into the bricks, not the mortar) then feed in the cable. Strip and connect the cores of the cable to the socket's terminals (red to live; black to neutral; green/yellow to earth), then fit the faceplate.

Run the cable to the break-in point, clipping it to the sides of the joists at 500mm (20in) intervals (or run it through holes drilled halfway down the joists if the route is at right-angles to them). Where the cable runs along the wall, fit it in plastic mini-trunking for neatness. Now you can connect into the power circuit.

Before you go any further, switch off the power at the mains, or remove the relevant circuit fuse or MCB. Test a socket to ensure it's dead.

If you're taking a spur from a power socket, unscrew the socket's faceplate and pull it gently forward. Feed in the new branch cable, strip the cores and connect red to live; black to neutral; and green/yellow to earth. Sleeve the earth core with green/yellow striped PVC. Replace the faceplate and restore the power.

To connect into the ring main via a junction box, cut the power cable at the point as close to the proposed new socket as possible, ideally where it runs along a joist. Screw a 30A three-terminal junction box to the joist. Connect up the cable cores to the relevant terminals (sleeve the earth core) then run in the new branch cable from the new socket. Fit the junction box cover, then restore the power.

With this type of installation it's possible to fit a 'socket outlet RCD' on the outside wall. This is a unit the size of a double socket, but containing one outlet and its own RCD. It will protect just that socket – particularly beneficial to anyone using a power tool from it.

Adding a new circuit

If you're running a completely new circuit outdoors there are two ways you can do this:
● Connect the new circuit cable to a spare fuseway in the consumer unit. If the spare fuseway isn't of the correct rating for the circuit, buy a new fuse or MCB of the correct rating and fit this in the consumer unit in the correct position (highest rating should be nearest the unit's isolating switch).
● If there's no spare fuseway, install a new switchfuse unit (really a small consumer unit) next to the existing one, and connect the new circuit cable to it. Call in the electricity board to disconnect the meter tails and reconnect them, and those from the new unit, via a 'distribution box'. This is because only two tails can actually enter the meter.

Running cable underground

Burying the new cable run is the neatest, least conspicuous method. Plan out the route first, then mark it out with string and pegs. Choose the shortest route, but avoid paths, intervening walls, flower beds and the vegetable patch (or anywhere there's likely to be deep-digging).

Dig a trench about 500mm (20in) deep × 100mm (4in) wide and add a 25mm (1in) thick layer of sand to the bottom if the ground is particularly stony. Cut a length of cable (you'll need 6mm² two-core-and-earth cable for a 30A supply) to run from the switchgear at one end of the circuit to that at the opposite end. Thread the cable through lengths of heavy-duty plastic conduit and assemble the sections, using solvent weld adhesive. You'll need to fit

1. *Dig a trench for the new cable run, leading from the house to the outbuilding. Shovel sand in the base of the trench.*
2. *Fit the cable in conduit buried in the base of the trench, then cover with a brick or stone to prevent accidental damage when digging in the future.*

elbow connectors at each end to run the cable vertically out of the ground and into the house and outbuilding.

Drill a hole and pass the cable through the wall, as previously described.

If there's a wall connecting the house with the outbuilding, run the cable along this (encased in conduit) instead of burying it. In the trench, cover the conduit with a protective roof ridge tile or slab. Don't fill in the trench until you've tested the new circuit.

Running cable overhead

Although running your new circuit cable overhead isn't as neat as an underground installation, it could be the answer if your garden is substantially paved or the route to the outbuilding especially long.

On spans up to 3m (10ft) you can fix up ordinary 6mm² twin-and-earth PVC cable without additional support, but on longer spans it must be strung onto a catenary wire, which is tensioned between an eyebolt and straining screw. At the outbuilding you'll probably have to erect a stout post to attach the incoming supply cable to. Set a length of preservative-treated 100 × 50mm (4 × 2in) sawn timber in concrete as for fixing a fence post (pages 386–387). Attach an eye bolt to the house wall and fix the catenary wire to it.

At the outbuilding, secure the turnbuckle to a second eye bolt, attach the catenary wire (which should be cut under-length) then tighten the buckle, using a pair of screwdrivers, to strain the wire.

Attach the circuit cable (remember to cut it over-length by about 300mm/12in as it will sag in the middle). Hang the cable from the wire on cable ties at roughly 500mm (20in) intervals, with loops between each so rainwater will drip off. Make a drip loop at each end before taking the cable through the

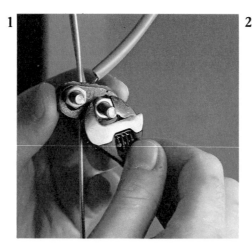

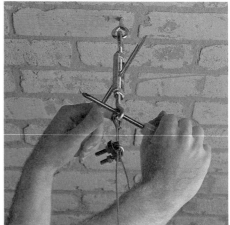

1. Overhead cable must be supported by a catenary wire. First attach the earth wire to its clamp.
2. Rig up the catenary with a turnbuckle at one end to place sufficient strain on the wire.
3. String the cable between plastic cable ties, with loops between each so rainwater will drip off.
4. The overhead set-up between house and outbuilding, showing all connections you'll need to make to ensure a safe cable run.

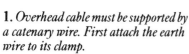

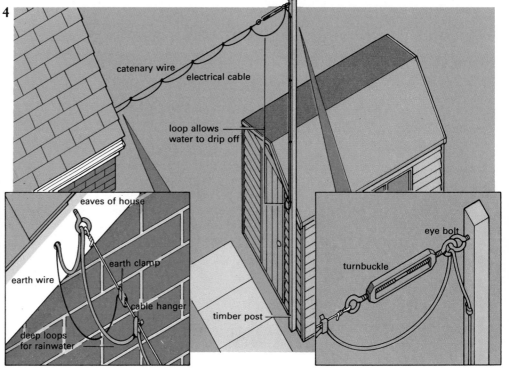

catenary wire
electrical cable
loop allows water to drip off
eaves of house
earth clamp
earth wire
cable hanger
deep loops for rainwater
timber post
eye bolt
turnbuckle

wall. The catenary wire must be earthed, using a separate green/yellow sheathed length of 6mm² single-core earth cable to run it to the connection point indoors.

Connections in the outbuilding
The connections you make in the outbuilding depend on what facilities you require.

To power just a few socket outlets and a light, connect the cores of your radial power circuit direct to a small switchfuse unit containing two fuses or MCBs. Run cables to lights and socket outlets, but be careful you don't exceed the 30A current provision or you'll have to fit larger supply cable, RCDs and main fuses of MCBs. A smaller installation only requires one 30A fuseway: you can feed a light circuit via a 5A fused connection unit.

Under recent wiring regulations, the new switchfuse unit must be fitted with an ELCB (see page 407) to provide extra protection to anyone operating a power tool outdoors run from the new socket, unless the circuit is already so protected.

Connections in the house
To provide power to your new circuit, connect the length of cable to the mains. Remember, before starting this part of the job, to switch off at the mains and don't switch back on again until you're sure everything is in working order.

Run the cable to the consumer unit. If you're connecting it direct to a spare fuseway, strip the cores and secure in the relevant terminals (remembering to sleeve the earth core). If you aren't installing an RCD to protect the entire house and outside installation as previously described, you must fit a device in the new cable run near the consumer unit.

Low-voltage power
Garden lights, underwater pool lights and pumps to power a fountain or waterfall can have either a low-voltage or direct mains supply.

With the former, a step-down transformer is used: place it inside the house or outbuilding, and run a length of special low-voltage cable to the pump or appliance. Although it's not vital to bury this cable (you wouldn't receive a fatal shock from it) it's best to insert it in conduit or a length of hosepipe for protection, and ideally to put it in a trench out of harm's way. To provide power, simply plug the transformer's flex into a spare 13A socket.

With mains supply, the pump cable is connected to a length of 0.5mm² two-core-and-earth flex run underground in conduit: the connection must be made with a heavy-duty waterproof three-pin connector, which should be firmly housed in a waterproof compartment near the pool side. The other end of the flex must be connected to a three-pin plug and inserted in a 13A socket. As an extra safety precaution, substitute the ordinary plug for a plug-in RCD (rated at 30mA and fused at 2A); it's wired up in exactly the same way as a conventional type of plug.

Ring or radial?
House power sockets are wired on a 'ring' or 'radial' circuit. You can add a spur to a ring or radial circuit socket only where no other spur has been added. So any socket with three cables entering it will already have a spur linked to it, and so cannot be used.

But telling the difference between sockets with two cables requires further investigation. In the past, spurs could have one double or two single sockets. Now only one outlet per spur is permitted. So if the socket has two cables, it could be a ring socket, the intermediate socket on an old two-outlet spur, or an intermediate socket on the old radial circuit.

To check whether a socket is on a ring circuit or not, you will need a 'continuity tester', which you can make from a 4 volt battery, a length of twin bell wire and a torch bulb. Connect the cores of the wire to the battery terminals. Then connect the bulb into just one core.

Turn off the mains current. Disconnect the live (red) cores from the socket terminals and touch the tester leads to the cores. The bulb will light if the socket is on a ring; it will stay out if it's on a radial circuit or spur. If it's a ring, you can add a spur. To discover whether the socket is a spur or on a radial circuit, trace the cables from the socket back to a ring socket and onto a socket with only one cable, then you have a spur: don't extend from the intermediate socket. If you trace the cables back to the consumer unit and looping on to more than one socket, it's a radial circuit: you can extend it (so long as the circuit doesn't serve an area greater than 20sq m/215sq ft and is wired in 2.5m² cable).

If you find these instructions complicated, or do not feel confident, call in professional advice.

FRUIT CAGES & PLANT SUPPORTS

Your garden is under threat of constant attack by birds, rodents and the unpredicatable force of the elements. Each can decimate your prize crops unless you take preventative action to protect the plot.

Unless you're wary, your garden will fall prey to numerous destructive influences. Pesticides and insecticides will cope with a large part of the problem, but there are, unfortunately, some far more determined culprits.

Birds are, in many ways, the gardener's allies: some of them consume slugs, harmful insects, and other pests that can terrorize your plot. Unfortunately our feathered friends lose favour with budding fruit growers because of their predilection for eating ripening crops. During the winter they make themselves a nuisance by pecking out the dormant blossom buds. In both cases you could find yourself sporting a fruitless fruit tree. If you've an established tree, or you're planning a mini-orchard, you should take steps to prevent birds from reaching your trees at these vulnerable times, or make provision to at least scare them off.

Vegetable gardeners can be equally frustrated by birds that eat the seeds before they germinate, or possibly seriously damage growing crops (wood pigeons are a particular problem).

Bird barriers

Repellent sprays are not really a viable proposition, because the chemicals need frequent applications when they're washed off by rain. What's needed is a physical deterrent, and there are various types you can employ.

Some bird barriers are basic in the extreme. Stringing bushes and trees with ordinary black cotton is usually an effective way to protect your fruit, but don't form a complex grid: just a few strands will suffice and eventually a bird will find it and flee. Onlooking birds will get the message, too, though some birds soon get used to cotton and are quite happy to hop around it. Don't use unbreakable nylon threads, however; the object is not to inflict any unpleasant injury on the birds.

You can buy special ultra-fine white rayon webbing in hanks from garden centres, which is ideal for draping over bushes or protecting fruit buds and ripening tree fruits, which are prone to attack. The web won't trap the hapless bird but scares it off and the material rots after a few months and disperses.

Assuming your trees have escaped attack until their fruits have formed, you have to prepare for further attacks. Safeguard individual fruits (peaches and nectarines, for instance) by wrapping them in muslin or alternatively polythene bags. If you use the latter, be sure to puncture the bags for essential ventilation. Don't make the holes too big otherwise you won't be able to ward off another flying fruit menace: the wasp. Old nylon stockings or cut up tights, also come in handy for enclosing particularly susceptible fruit.

Where you can't protect individual fruit (on a currant bush, for example) you can drape the entire bush, if it's fairly compact, with a square of 19–25mm (¾–1in) cotton or nylon mesh netting, staked to the ground all round. This treatment is ideal for protecting strawberries during their brief cropping season. Most netting – even nylon – will rot or deteriorate after exposure to

the weather and the sun, so treat this type of cover as a temporary safegard.

Cage your fruit

It's advisable to keep the netting clear of the fruit, so you can erect temporary cages over fruit bushes and plants and small trees by lashing together a framework of bamboo canes and driving the uprights into the ground. Drape netting over the framework and stake at the base. Protect the netting from snagging on the canes at the corners by extending the uprights by about 50mm (2in) and upending a jam-jar on top of each, so the net will hang smoothly on the rounded jars.

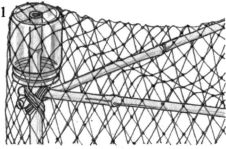

Proprietary cage systems are available; the most popular one has durable solid rubber balls pierced with six holes. Simply slot metal rods into the holes to form the frame, and attach intermediate rods with more balls, as well as at the corners.

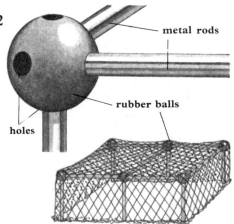

metal rods

holes

rubber balls

Aluminium rods, 12mm (½in) in diameter and in 600mm–2.4m (2–8ft) lengths are sold for the purpose of fruit cage construction.

Fruit trees grown against a wall can easily be protected. Simply hang netting like a curtain over the trees, supported on a timber frame.

For the more enthusiastic fruit-grower, you'll probably find it advantageous to grow all your fruit trees and bushes together on one large plot and to cover the entire area with a large, permanent cage. Proprietary fruit cages are available, using sturdy

aluminium alloy, galvanized steel or plasticized tubular steel as the frames. Most types are sold in a range of useful sizes and can be assembled easily by slotting the components together. Be sure to choose a size that covers all your crops and allows you to work comfortably inside.

Secure the netting to the top horizontal cross-rails using special net hooks (you'll probably be given a supply of these with the cage) and stake at the bottom with ground pins.

There may be a metal-framed door included in the cage set-up but do be sure it's sufficiently wide to admit your wheel-barrow. A doorway isn't vital, as a generous flap in the netting secured with tape or clips will serve the same purpose.

Be sure to remove the roof netting from your cage when the birds aren't likely to peck the fruit or buds, so that they can busy themselves with their more helpful task of eating all the harmful insects, grubs and eggs. You'd be wise to remove the netting in the event of a heavy fall of snow: snow can soon build up on a net, causing it to sag onto the trees and possibly tear. Far worse, the considerable weight could even demolish the entire cage and damage your crops.

If you'd rather opt for the homemade approach, there's no reason why you can't build a substantial fruit cage yourself. Choose fairly stout, perhaps 50mm square (2in sq), preservative-treated softwood for

1. Home-made cage.
2. Proprietary cage system.
3. Large, permanent cage.
4. Large, home-made cage for large fruit trees.

Below *Protect wall fruit, such as these pears, by supporting netting on wooden frames.*

Above *Protecting your shrubs and fruit trees helps to keep rodents at bay.*

Left *A sturdy prefabricated fruit cage will protect your delicate crops from the attentions of even the most persistent pests.*

Below left *You can make your cage, tailored to suit the shape, size and style of your garden, using stout timber frames with netting to keep out all the greedy pests.*

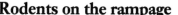

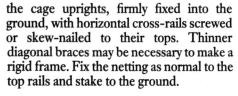

the cage uprights, firmly fixed into the ground, with horizontal cross-rails screwed or skew-nailed to their tops. Thinner diagonal braces may be necessary to make a rigid frame. Fix the netting as normal to the top rails and stake to the ground.

Rodents on the rampage

Birds aren't the only hoards with an eye on your fruit trees. Squirrels, rabbits, and hares may be frequent visitors to your orchards, and they often display cunning to bypass your defences. Squirrels have been

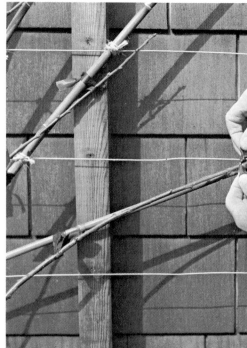

Above *Squirrels are fairly cunning when it comes to a tasty treat, and have been known to lift netting to reach ripe crops – take into account their stealth when you build your fruit cage.*

Top right *The branches of a fan-trained tree being tied to canes, which are fixed to the wires of a wall mounted support.*

Right *Espaliers, cordons and fan-trained trees can be grown on a system of horizontal wires strung between straining posts.*

Opposite *To grow wire-trained trees away from a wall, erect a frame of horizontal wires stretched between vertical wooden posts set in the ground. You'll need to add a diagonal brace to the end posts. Use straining bolts held in the end post to adjust the tension of the wires. The wires are fastened to the intermediate posts with staples, which are just hammered in.*

known to lift the netting and scramble beneath, while rabbits tend to prefer digging a tunnel to gain access.

One solution is to set 1.2m (4ft) wide, 25mm (1in) mesh wire-netting about 300mm (1ft) deep in the ground at the perimeter of the fruit-growing area, even the entire garden. Bend out the bottom of the netting to frustrate burrowing.

As a second line of defence, use perforated plastic rodent protectors or cylinder of mesh wire-netting wrapped around the base of each fruit tree (about 1m/3ft high) to fend off intruders. This also wards against the menace of cats sharpening their claws on the trunks.

Battling with the elements

Animals and birds may be deterred fairly easily from ravaging your garden but defending the plot against the elements is quite another matter. While efficient garden drainage (see page 370) will cope with the problems associated with heavy rainfall, the effects of wind and frost requires special attention.

Young trees, newly planted, for example, can be blown over even by fairly moderate winds, especially if frost combines the attack and loosens the roots before they can establish a foothold in the earth. Staking is the solution to part of the problem, and there are various methods, depending on the type of tree and its location. There is now sound evidence to suggest that trees are better *without* the traditional stake (if they can blow around a bit more, the stem becomes stronger). However, most gardeners still like to stake their trees.

Stakes are sold by garden centres, but choose pressure-treated types, where available, to ensure efficient rot protection. Alternatively, larch, spruce, or hardwoods make good stakes.

Use a proprietary horticultural preservative to treat the part of the the stake that's to be sunk in the ground, plus about 150mm (6in) above ground, making sure you thoroughly soak the wood.

Bush trees, dwarf bushes, standard and half-standard trees need what is called the 'double stake' to support them in exposed

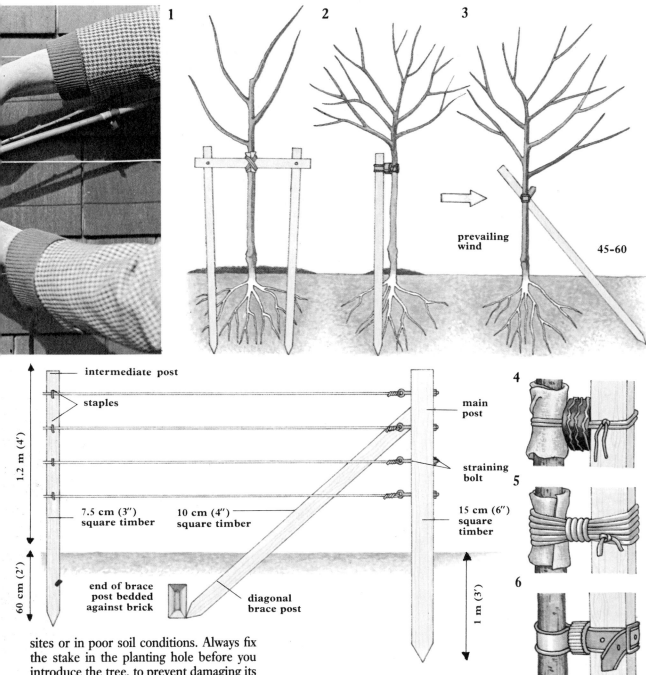

1

2

3

prevailing
wind

45–60

intermediate post

staples

1.2 m (4')

7.5 cm (3")
square timber

10 cm (4")
square timber

60 cm (2')

end of brace
post bedded
against brick

diagonal
brace post

main
post

straining
bolt

15 cm (6")
square
timber

1 m (3')

4

5

6

sites or in poor soil conditions. Always fix the stake in the planting hole before you introduce the tree, to prevent damaging its roots. To make the stake, drive two uprights into the ground about 450mm (18in), so they protrude as high as the tree's lowest branch. Screw or lash a horizontal cross-piece to each upright near the tops (you may find it easier to make up the stake before fixing it in the hole).

A single stake is suitable for supporting smaller trees. Drive the stake into the ground and secure to the stem. To support a tree that's already planted, but susceptible to damage, drive in a stake at an angle of about 45 degrees to avoid the roots, pointing towards the prevailing wind, and lash to the tree.

Exercise care in the way you tie the tree to the stake. It's important, to prevent chafing between stem and stake, to fit a buffer of some kind. Wrap a wad of hessian around the stem of the tree then wind cord around stem and stake, with the cord tied at right-angles between the two. Alternatively, tie an offcut of rubber (perhaps from an old tyre) between the tree and stake. Proprietary plastic ties are made for this purpose, if you prefer, and include a plastic buffer. These can be adjusted as the tree grows.

Wall trees also need a little extra support and this can be accomplished using horizontal wires strung across the wall between posts or threaded onto screw-in vine eyes (driven into wallplugs). If you're using wooden posts, fasten the wire using screw-in cup hooks and attach a straining bolt at one end to keep the wires taut. Use 2.50mm gauge galvanized wire.

1. *A double stake, used for standards and half-standards.*
2. *A single stake support for smaller trees.*
3. *If you need to add a stake after planting, set it at an angle to avoid the roots.*
4. *Wrap the tree with hessian and use a strip of rubber – from an old tyre – as a buffer between the stake.*
5. *Another method is to tie cord at right angles between tree and stake as a buffer.*
6. *Proprietary plastic tree ties hold the tree away from the stake and can be adjusted as it grows.*

FURNITURE IN THE GARDEN

Furnishing your garden can be great fun, and it should be treated like a room indoors – there's furniture for dining, lounging, resting or partying. You can make it yourself or buy an entire suite.

Creating a bountiful garden has its just rewards: once the hard slog is over you can take time out to admire your handywork from the vantage of a comfortable chair. Treat the garden as an outdoor living room and furnish it accordingly. Whether you fancy just lying back with a drink or a book, dining in a shady corner, or resting briefly during a stroll, taking stock of your horticultural prowess, you'll find there's numerous pieces of furniture that's sure to fit the bill.

Narrow down the field by deciding whether your furniture is to be a permanent outdoor fixture or portable, storable units. Choose a style that complements the nature of your plot: a paved courtyard suits a fairly formal approach of elegant items; a leafy, wild setting favours the rustic touch; an airy patio suggests the plush bright approach of sociable seating. Also, choose materials shrewdly: if your furniture is to remain outdoors all year round, as often happens, it

The low rattan table and stripy deckchairs are the perfect choice in a leafy courtyard plot, whether you're dining or just languishing with a drink.

must be extremely hard-wearing and durable.

Furnishing styles
The basic bench is ideal for a quiet corner or under a tree. Proprietary types are made but it's easy enough to make one from a few stout planks on a large stone or small brick columns at each end. Park benches, with backrest and armrest, are a more formal style, which look their best against a wall, or facing a pleasant view.

The deckchair is still a popular choice for sun worshippers: it's adjustable, portable, and compact when folded. Some types even have arm rests and leg rests. Still on the collapsible front, there's the lightweight metal-framed chairs with canvas or plastic covers, or the wooden-framed, canvas-covered director's side-folding chair.

If sunbathing is your aim, a simple metal-framed, stretch-covered folding lounger will be ideal.

Folding patio suites in metal or plastic frames (and with removable upholstered cushions) are the answer to complete garden furnishing. They typically consist of, at the very least, a set of four folding chairs and a table with central parasol, but some kinds feature extras such as adjustable-position loungers, wheeled sunbeds and occasionally even a swing hammock and awning.

On a practical note, the outdoor picnicker could do no worse than invest in a trestle table with integral benches, which can seat the entire family. Some have central parasols, too.

These are just a small sample of the selection of furniture you'll find in garden centres and department stores. There are many variants in both materials used and in durability, so choose wisely.

What materials?
The best all-weather furniture is plastic, which needs little maintenance and never needs to be painted. Timber, particularly

hardwood, offers better quality but requires regular attention to fend off rot. Softwoods (with the exception of cedar) must be treated with preservatives to withstand the elements.

Rust is the main enemy of metal furniture, although galvanizing, painting and plastic coatings will keep this menace at bay, so long as the surface isn't scratched or chipped. Aluminium is the saving grace as far as metal furniture is concerned; it doesn't rust, is lighter than steel and can be cast – like iron – to make ornately moulded tables and chairs reminiscent of a Victorian garden.

Regular maintenance

With a little care and attention your garden furniture will last for years. Unless it's the outdoor type, it's best to store the furniture in a well-ventilated shed or garage during the summer but to bring it indoors in the winter.

Lubricate all pivots, hinges, and screw heads with thin oil to discourage rust and ensure good working order. Smear metal-framed chairs with oil each winter and wipe off before use the next season. Treat exposed softwoods with colourless preservative each year, just before the summer season. Hardwood may need staining or varnishing.

Fitting new covers

Fabric-covered chairs are prone to splits and tears, particularly at pressure points, but in most cases it's possible to patch them up.

Pull together the torn fabric, fold over the frayed edges and stitch together using 60-gauge thread. Fit a patch of matching material over the rent and stitch it in place. Tears at seams can be stitched back together also: overstitch for strength, and carry the stitching beyond the extent of the rent.

When a fabric cover is beyond repair, you can fit a replacement. Deckchairs can be refitted with rotproof synthetic coverings (available from hardware stores in standard 445mm (17½in) widths, often in pre-cut lengths). Use the old cover as a template for the new one. Remove it by prising off its tacks with an old screwdriver.

Lay the deckchair on the floor and fold over one end of the new fabric by 25mm (1in). Fold it around the top rail and tack it to the underside of the rail. With the deckchair erected and inverted, pull the fabric around the bottom rail; this is narrower than the top rail, so fold in each side of the fabric to form a taper. Fold over the end 25mm (1in) and tack the fold to the inside edge of the rail.

Collapsible metal chairs can be recovered

similarly. Remove the damaged covering by cutting through the stitching with a sharp knife. Use the old cover to buy a new matching replacement then, with the chair open, drape the new fabric over the top bar. Fold under 12mm (½in) and backstich the fold to the cover fabric using 60-gauge thread. Make a double stitch at each end for strength. Pull the fabric behind the metal tensioning bar at the back of the seat and over the front bar. Fold the strip around with a 12mm (½in) overlap and pin it to the fabric. Test the folding action of the chair to make sure the fabric is properly tensioned then backstitch along the front fold and remove the pins.

A common problem with folding sun loungers is that the support cords, which stretch the fabric over the frame, often snap. Repair kits are available: they comprise a set of strong rubber bands and metal hooks. Remove the broken cord, which is laced between eyes in side flaps. Fit a hook at each end of a band and stretch these between the side flaps, fitting the hooks in the eyes. Work right from the centre eye outwards.

A raised sundeck with built-in bench seating and boxy armchairs made entirely from planks is one solution for an awkward plot, or if you can't spare much time to garden. The barbecue area, with comfy seating, allows the tree access, lending a natural look to the scheme.

TOOLS, MACHINERY & MAINTENANCE

No gardener can cope without a reliable set of tools. Equip yourself with the best you can afford and then tend them scrupulously so they won't let you down. And for that special job that demands a special touch, a visit to your local hire shop will suffice.

You can't tame your jungle of weeds without an adequate kit of good quality weaponry. Unless you make a point of regularly maintaining your tools, they'll soon fall foul of your neglect. But even the best-tended implements will succumb to years of hard labour, and minor repairs will be necessary to revive them.

Mechanical or electric-powered tools are an integral part of the modern gardener's equipment and they demand special care to ensure reliable working and assure safety to the user. If you prefer, most of the heavy, specialist equipment, that you will probably not use very often, is available through hire shops.

Maintaining garden tools

A few months of hard labour in the garden can leave your tools looking a little jaded, but don't just dump them in the shed for the winter without sparing them some attention.

Rust is the worst offender: it attacks anything made of iron and steel and can have a devastating effect if left unchecked. It is quite easy to inhibit the rust from forming in the first place by practising just a few simple, but extremely worthwhile preventative measures.

Regular tool care

Before you put your tools away, make sure they're clean and dry: caked-on mud, full of moisture, will soon promote an unhealthy rust to form on spade blades and fork tines. Wipe this off as soon as you've finished digging.

If you spot any signs of rust, rub them down with wire wool and daub the affected metal with oil or grease. Before you put your tools away into winter storage, spray all metal parts with a proprietary moisture-dispersing lubricant, or coat them in oil or grease. Dismantle any mechanical gadgets and give their components a thorough cleaning. Reassemble them, lubricating the working parts.

The garden shed isn't the best place to store rust-prone tools and equipment. Unless the walls are adequately lined with building paper (which discourages condensation) and the doors and windows are properly insulated against draughts, tools will quickly rust in the damp conditions. Where feasible, it's best to bring your portable tools indoors during winter. Keep them in a warm cupboard (under the stairs for instance).

This may be out of the question, of course: if you've no alternative store-room than the shed, do your best to improve the environment inside. Place small hand tools (screwdrivers, trowels, hammers) in a drawer or box (left slightly open for good air flow). Wrap the metal parts (which should be oiled or greased) in special waxed rust-inhibiting paper (available from builders' merchants) secured with elastic bands. Line the drawer or box with the paper, too. Long-handled tools can be hung up on the walls, with the metal parts wrapped in rust-inhibiting paper.

Small precision tools, tiny spanners, keys for tool adjustment, junior hacksaw blades, and drill bits can be kept in a sealed jam-jar that contains a little silica gel, a substance that drives off moisture. You can buy this from builders' merchants and chemists and is commonly used between the panes of secondary double glazing to dispel moisture.

Rot is the other enemy of garden tools: unvarnished wood such as the handles of some tools is prone to attack. Apply a light coating of linseed oil with a rag, to feed the wood and keep it supple. Leave the oil to soak in and repeat the treatment every few months.

Power tools can be dangerous if allowed to deteriorate, so check the condition of their flexes thoroughly for fraying and

Opposite Keep your lawn a cut above the rest by maintaining your lawnmower regularly. Clean the blades, oil the moving parts and adjust the height of cut to suit the length of the grass you are mowing.

splits. If there's the slightest sign of damage, renew the flex immediately. Examine the plug also: dismantle it and remake the connections so you're sure everything's sound. Re-examine at the beginning of the work season.

Curing the rust menace

When you've failed to pamper your tools and they've become the victims of an attack by rust, there's still time to make amends. Scrape off any loose, flaky rust with a wire brush then daub on a generous amount of a proprietary rust-killing chemical. These substances (either a liquid or a jelly) are usually based on phosphoric acid, which combines with the rust and makes it largerly inert. Most types prime the metal ready for repainting.

Repairing broken handles

Wooden handles on tools are fairly tough and durable but not if you misuse them. Trying to lever out too much earth when you're deep-digging in the garden is a sure way to fracture the shaft of a spade or fork, while the thinner handles of rakes and hoes will snap if left lying around and then inadvertently stepped on.

Use one of the standard-diameter handles that are available for repairing broken shafts. Long-handled tools have handles that fit in a socket formed in the top of the tool's blade; smaller tools such as

hand forks and trowels have handles that are stuck on the end of a metal tang.

New handles are usually supplied longer and thicker at the socket end than you actually need; you'll have to cut them to size and shape them to a tight fit.

The point where the shaft enters the metal socket is where the most strain is applied, and the area most likely to snap. If this happens, you have the problem of extracting the stub of the shaft from the socket. The shaft will probably be retained by a screw or rivet, and this must be removed first. Lay the tool on a flat surface, or clamp in the jaws of a vice or workbench. Withdraw the screw, applying pressure if necessary, to loosen it: if it's rusted in, soak with penetrating oil then try again. Really stubborn screws (and rivets) must be drilled out using a high speed drill bit.

If you can't get a grip on the shaft stub, drive a large 75mm (3in) No. 12 screw into the end of the stub, clamp the screw in a vice with the tool's blade hanging down, then strike the top of the blade with a mallet to pull it free.

Saw the new shaft to length then use the old stub as a template for marking the taper on the end. Place the stub end onto the new handle and draw around it. Clamp the shaft in a vice and plane down the end to the correct taper using a planer file or spokeshave. It's a good idea to leave the taper slightly oversize for a really tight fit.

Even the most basic tools need special care and attention: here a garden roller is give a dose of oil to prevent its drum from rusting.

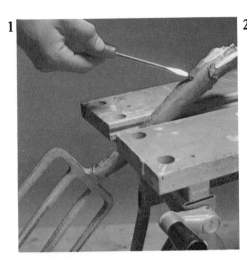

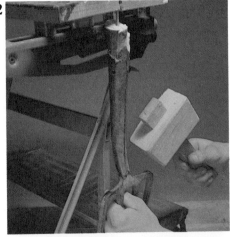

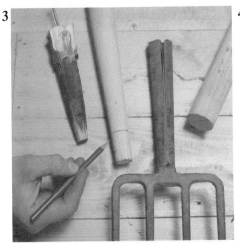

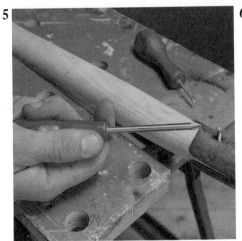

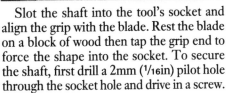

1. *Remove the broken shaft of a fork or spade by releasing its retaining screw — you may have to drill out a rivet instead.*
2. *Drive a screw into the end of the shaft stub, clamp in a vice or workbench and release the head by tapping with a mallet.*
3. *Use the old stub of the shaft to mark the length and amount of taper you'll need to cut from the replacement shaft.*
4. *Shave the end of the new shaft to the diameter you want using a small planer file, spokeshave or wood rasp, so that it fits in the head socket snugly.*
5. *Force the shaft into the socket then secure with a new galvanized screw driven in through the hole in the socket.*
6. *Before you store away metal tools, coat them liberally with mosture-dispersing lubricant to prevent rust and keep moving parts well oiled.*

Slot the shaft into the tool's socket and align the grip with the blade. Rest the blade on a block of wood then tap the grip end to force the shape into the socket. To secure the shaft, first drill a 2mm (1/16in) pilot hole through the socket hole and drive in a screw.

Sharpening blunt shears
Garden shears will become blunt with frequent use, and you can sharpen them yourself if the cutting edge isn't too badly nicked (if the blades are badly damaged, leave the job to a specialist tool sharpener).

Sharpen each blade separately for con-venient working. Remove the pivot bolt and clamp one blade in a vice. Examine the cutting edge: some blades are steeply angled, others are shallow. When you're resharpening, follow the original profile. Use a fine flat metalworking file (held at an angle of about 15 degrees for a steep angle) and file away from the edge. Work along the full length of the blade to restore its cutting edge. Repeat for the other blade, reassemble the tool and test its cutting action.

Shears cut with a scissor action and the cross-over set of the blades is important. Hold the tool upright and look at the side:

1. If garden shears don't cut properly, check the tips – they should meet. Cure the problems by filling down the back stops. Remove only a little metal, then test the cut; repeat if necessary.
2. To sharpen the shears, separate the blades, clamp in a vice and file, using a fine metalworking file, to restore the edge to its original cutting angle.

the blades should bow inwards towards the points and some only touch at the very ends. If the blades don't bow, try tightening the pivot bolt with a screwdriver to correct the fault. Hold the tool by one handle: if the blades open of their own accord, they should be correctly set. Failing this, dismantle the tool and clamp each blade upright in a vice, one at a time, and bend the tip gently. Reassemble the shears and test the cut. The blades should cross over for their entire length.

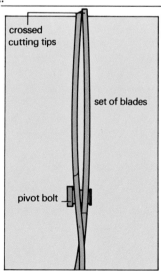

crossed cutting tips

set of blades

pivot bolt

Right *The blades of a pair of hand shears, if they're to cut properly, should cross over for their entire length. Look along the edge of the closed shears: the blades should bow and touch at the tips.*

A gap near the tips of the blades signifies that the 'stops' behind the pivot bolt are meeting too soon. Dismantle the tool and then carefully file down each stop just fractionally to correct the fault.

Lawnmowers

The lawnmower is probably one of the most frequently-used items of garden equipment during the grass-growing season: the rest of the time it stands idle, often in a damp shed, frequently caked in dried grass cuttings.

Apart from regular cleaning, basic maintenance (adjusting and sharpening the blades, lubricating the moving parts) is called for to keep your lawnmower running efficiently. Whatever type of machine you have, some procedures are common to all.

Types of lawnmower

You'll be spoilt for choice when buying a new mower – there's one to cope with every size and shape of lawn, from the tiny, flat pocket handkerchief to the undulating meadow. Initially you'll have to decide between hand-powered, electrical or petrol-engined types, then consider one of three basic cutting systems:

● **Cylinder mowers** have cutting blades fixed to a cylinder, which revolves at right-angles to the grass surface. A roller behind produces the familiar striped effect, by 'flattening' the grass in alternate directions in each row. They're either hand-operated or motor-driven, and usually have a grass-collecting box.

● **Rotary mowers** have a single bar blade, or rectangular or circular disc cutters fixed to a disc that revolves parallel to the grass. All rotary mowers are motor-driven and can tackle coarse lawns.

● **Hover mowers** are really variants of the rotary action, but float above the grass on a cushion of air. Highly maneouvrable, they're also light in weight and some models feature a grass box. Hover types can be driven electrically or by a petrol engine.

Manual models are really only viable for a small, flat lawn; lightweight electrics are good here, too, but choose a larger electric model for a medium-sized plot; petrol types deal with large areas where a trailing lead would be impractical; hover mowers can be used successfully on any size of lawn but excel on steep slopes and rough terrain.

Maintenance checklist

A simple checklist of likely trouble spots will enable you to prolong the working life of the mower. Before you start, however, make sure a powered mower is unplugged before you touch the moving parts.

● Before you start to mow, check that the height-of-cut adjusters are equal.

● Clean the blades after each mowing to remove caked-on cuttings from the deflector plate and long strands wound round the rotating parts, typically the main roller and the cylinder blade bearings.

● Lightly oil the height adjusters and clean and generously oil the cylinder blade bearings.

● On a cylinder mower, check that the cutting blades are sound. Hold a metal straightedge or ruler against the fixed bottom blade to highlight distortions; gently tap the blade with a hammer to re-align it. If it's very worn, buy and fit a new one.

● Before you put the mower away for the season, examine the drive chain compartment: remove its cover by loosening the self-tapping screws, or bolts and check the state of the nylon chain tensioner. Lubricate it and the gear teeth and chain then replace the cover.

Adjusting cylinder blades

The cylinder mower is one of the most popular models. It has two sets of blades: a fixed bottom blade, and a rotating blade that cuts against the fixed one. The height of the grass cut is determined by the height of the fixed blade from the ground. To adjust this to suit, it's usual to alter the

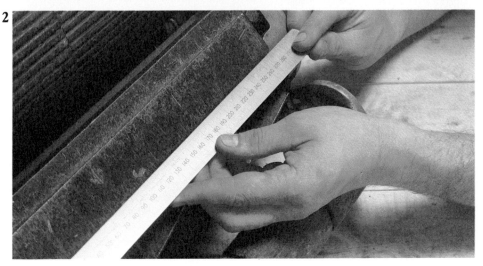

1. *Adjust the height of cut on a cylinder mower by altering the level of the roller. Slacken the side nuts and alter either end by the same amount, using a spanner.*
2. *Use a metal ruler to check that the cylinder and fixed blades of the mower are not bent.*

1. To adjust the cylinder blade in relation to the fixed blade, support the rollers off the ground with a wooden wedge, so you can turn the blades freely.
2. Gradually tighten both adjusting screws in turn until the blades will cut cleanly through a sheet of cartridge paper placed between the bottom blade and the cylinder blades.
3. To sharpen the cylinder blades using the backlapping technique, adjust the cylinder and bottom blade until they touch or until they can trap a sheet of thin paper placed between them.
4. Smear coarse grinding paste onto each blade in turn then turn the cylinder backwards to sharpen the blades. Adjust both sides as you go.

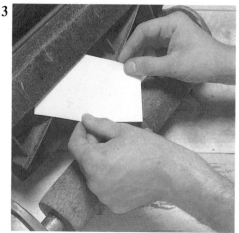

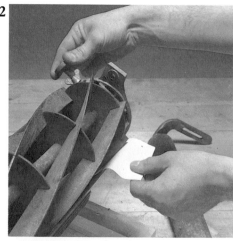

height of the front roller, which raises or lowers the mower body accordingly. This will either be accomplished on modern machines by flipping two levers into channels at each side or, on older types, by loosening a nut at each side and sliding the roller's brackets up or down.

To cut the grass properly the fixed blade and the rotary blade must be the correct distance apart: too close and they'll bind; too far apart and the grass will remain standing. Most mowers have a screw adjuster on each side of the cylinder case and by releasing these, it's possible to alter the positions of the blades. Lay the mower on its back to gain access to the fixed blade, then adjust the screws in turn to move the rotary blade. Test the cut by feeding a sheet of thickish paper between fixed and moveable blades; it should cut cleanly. Tighten the lock nuts and test the mower.

Sharpening cylinder blades

Mower blades meet all sorts of obstructions on their travels – not least of which are stones, which can ruin a cutting edge instantly. The rotary blades of a cylinder mower can be sharpened by grinding them against the fixed blade, so long as the latter is not worn unevenly. If it is, replace it first.

To be able to turn the blades you'll have

to remove the gear or chain plate at the side of the mower and disconnect the drive from the roller to the cylinder (this may be a small gear wheel or a chain). If it's a chain, find the connector link and prise off its spring clip or split pin and slide the gear off the shaft. It should now be possible to turn the cylinder with a ratchet or box spanner held on the cylinder gear locking nuts.

With some models of mower the job's much simpler: just turning the roller backwards turns the cylinder blade.

With either method, raise up the mower so the cylinder can be turned freely, and adjust the bottom blade and cylinder so they just meet. Smear a little coarse grinding paste (you can buy this from motoring accessory shops) onto the cutting edge of each blade. To sharpen, turn the cylinder backwards. As you grind you should examine the blades to make sure they're evenly in contact. Once you can see a continuous ground line on each blade, wipe off the paste and reassemble the mower.

Sharpening rotary blades

The other popular mower is the rotary-action type, in which a single, double-edged blade or series of disc-shaped or rectangular blades spin parallel to the ground. The same problem common to other mowers is the damage stones and other obstructions can do to the cutting edge. But, similarly, sharpening a blunt blade is quite straightforward.

Rotary bar blades are fixed centrally to a rotating disc by a single bolt. Grasp one end of the blade with a wad of cloths and use a hexagonal spanner to undo the bolt. Most mowers come with a suitable spanner. Remove the bolt and its spacer discs (which are used to alter the cutting height) noting which way up it goes. Take the opportunity to clean and grease the mounting and bolt.

Clamp the blade horizontally in a vice and grind the first cutting edge sharp with a fine flat metalworking file. Repeat for the cutting edge on the diagonally opposite end of the bar. The blade must be balanced to work properly: check this by fixing a large nail into a post or wall and slot the blade onto it. The end that drops is heavier and you'll have to file the back of this end until the bar balances.

Refit the bar blade with spacers (the more you add the shorter the grass will be cut), and the central bolt.

Some rotary bar blades have detachable triangular cutting edges bolted onto the ends. Blade ends aren't easy to sharpen, so it's best to replace them with new ones. Release their nuts and bolts and fit the replacements, making sure their cutting edges are facing the direction of rotation.

Some rotary mowers have bar blades with two diagonally opposite corners turned up to create a draught in rotation, which disperses the grass cuttings. Both ends must be balanced or vibration could damage the mower's engine. Remove the blade and file the heavier end, as previously described.

When a circular disc blade becomes blunt, loosen its fixing and swivel it to present a new cutting edge.

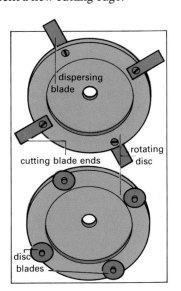

1. *To sharpen a rotary mower blade, unplug the mower, upend, then undo the bolt in the centre of the rotating disc – hold one end of the blade with a rag to stop the blade from turning.*
2. *Remove the bolt and spacer washers that secure the blade. Take note of which way up the blade is fixed. Clean the mounting and thoroughly grease the securing bolt.*
3. *Clamp the blade in a vice and use a fine engineering file to sharpen the blade to the original cutting angle – if it's badly gouged or blunted, it's easiest to buy a replacement.*

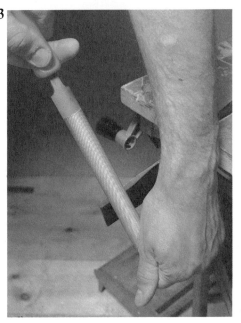

Far left *Two other types of rotary mower blades: rectangular cutting blade ends fixed to the rotating disc, and disc blades. Some can be turned to reveal new cutting edges, others must be replaced when blunt.*

INDEX